JN120912

公式 *TOEIC*®
Listening & Reading

プラクティス
リーディング編

一般財団法人 国際ビジネスコミュニケーション協会

ETS, the ETS logo, PROPELL, TOEIC and TOEIC BRIDGE are registered trademarks of Educational Testing Service, Princeton, New Jersey, U.S.A., and used in Japan under license. Copyright ©2020 Portions are copyrighted by Educational Testing Service and used with permission.

ETS TOEIC®
OFFICIAL TEST PREPARATION AND LEARNING

はじめに

『公式 *TOEIC*® Listening & Reading プラクティス　リーディング編』へようこそ。本書は、*TOEIC*® Listening & Reading Test (以下、*TOEIC*® L&R) のリーディングセクションの学習を通してリーディングの基礎力を養いながらテストの受験準備をしたいという方に、お勧めの教材です*。姉妹版の『公式 *TOEIC*® Listening & Reading プラクティス　リスニング編』と併せてご利用いただくと、総合的に *TOEIC*® L&R の受験準備ができるように設計されています。

本書の特長

● 3 ステップの段階別学習を通して、無理なく着実に、① リーディングの基礎力、② 制限時間内に問題を解く時間感覚、③ 100 問を 75 分間で一気に解く実践力を身に付けることができます。

● Step 1 のユニット学習では、リーディングセクションのパートごとに必要なスキルを身に付ける 20 の学習テーマを設定。英語を読む力の基礎固めをじっくりと行います。

● Educational Testing Service (ETS) が実際のテストと同じプロセスで作成した問題を使用しています。各ステップに掲載されている問題数は以下の通りです。また、Step 1 にはこれ以外に独自の練習問題も掲載しています。

学習ステップ	学習ステップ 名称	*TOEIC*® L&R 掲載問題数
Step 1	ユニット学習	102 問
Step 2	ミニテスト	116 問
Step 3	ファイナルテスト	100 問
	合計	318 問

● Step 3 のファイナルテストでは「参考スコア範囲の換算表」でスコア範囲を算出できます。

● 本誌の Step 1 の内容に連動した別冊付録『単語集 + 速読用英文』が付いています。ユニット学習の予習や復習に活用できます。さらに、速読用英文には特典音声（ダウンロード）が付いているため、音声を利用した学習が可能です（ダウンロード方法は次ページ参照）。

本書が、*TOEIC*® L&R の問題形式の把握と受験準備、そして皆さまの英語学習のお役に立つことを願っております。

*本書は、2014 年発行の『*TOEIC*® テスト 公式プラクティス リーディング編』を新出題形式に対応した形で全面改訂したものです。

※ 株式会社 Globee が提供するサービス abceed への会員登録（無料）が必要です。

音声ダウンロードの手順

1. パソコンまたはスマートフォンで音声ダウンロード用のサイトにアクセスします。

   右の QR コードまたはブラウザから下記にアクセスしてください。

   https://app.abceed.com/audio/iibc-officialprep

2. 表示されたページから、abceed の新規会員登録を行います。

   既に会員の場合は、ログイン情報を入力して上記 1. のサイトへアクセスします。

3. 上記 1. のサイトにアクセス後、本書の表紙画像をクリックします。

   クリックすると、教材詳細画面へ移動します。

4. スマートフォンの場合は、アプリ「abceed」の案内が出ますので、アプリからご利用ください。

   パソコンの場合は、教材詳細画面の「音声」からご利用ください。

   ※ 音声は何度でもダウンロード・再生ができます。

   ダウンロードについてのお問い合わせは下記にご連絡ください。

   E メール：support@globeejphelp.zendesk.com

   （お問い合わせ窓口の営業日：祝日を除く、月～金曜日）

STEP 1 ユニット学習

Contents

本書の使い方

本書は、3ステップの段階別学習で、じっくりとリーディングの基礎力を養いながら、テストの受験準備ができるようになっています。各ステップの目的を理解してから、学習を進めましょう。

STEP 1 ユニット学習

リーディングの基礎力を養う

Step 1 では、*TOEIC*® L&R のリーディングセクションのパート順に学習テーマが設定されたユニットの学習を通して、リーディングの基礎力を養います。ユニットの流れに従って学習を進めましょう。

テーマ解説

20 の学習テーマ別に文法事項や読解の技術について解説しています。解説をよく読んで、各ユニットのポイントを確認しましょう。

ウォームアップ

ユニットの学習事項を確認できる問題が掲載されています。テーマ解説を読んだ後に、力試しとしてトライしてみましょう。

プラクティス

チャレンジ

TOEIC® L&R の問題に挑戦します。まず、*TOEIC*® L&R の英文の一部を用いた練習問題「プラクティス」に取り組んだ後、*TOEIC*® L&R の問題がそのまま掲載された「チャレンジ」に解答してください。同じ英文を使って「プラクティス」→「チャレンジ」と解いていくことにより、英文の理解が深まり、問題を解くための道筋が分かります。なお、「チャレンジ」の「目安の解答時間」は英文をもう一度通して読んで考える時間も含んでいます。自分で時間を計りながら挑戦しましょう。

「プラクティス」と「チャレンジ」の 解答・解説

「プラクティス」と「チャレンジ」の問題文の訳、解答(例)、解説が掲載されています。各問題の解法アプローチを頭に入れましょう。

コラム

Unit 1～10、Unit 16 には学習コラムがあります。ユニットの学習テーマに関連した補足の学習事項や、リーディング力アップに効果的な学習法などを紹介しています。英語力全般の向上に役立ててください。

ミニテスト

テスト受験の時間感覚を磨く

Step 2 では、*TOEIC*® L&R のリーディングセクションの約 3 分の 1 の量（29 問）のミニテストを解いて、テスト受験の時間感覚を磨きます。全部で 4 セットあります。

TOEIC® Listening & Reading Test について

TOEIC® L&R の概要や受験申込方法を紹介しています。実際のテストの分量や内容を知っておきましょう。

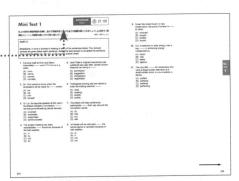

リーディングセクションの問題形式

TOEIC® L&R のリーディングセクションの問題形式を、パート別にサンプル問題とともに紹介しています。ミニテストに挑戦する前に、問題形式を把握しておきましょう。

ミニテスト

ミニテスト（各 29 問、21 分間）の問題ページです。全部で 4 セットあります。ミニテストの冒頭に、実際のテストの時間配分の目安に合わせた「目安の解答時間」を示してありますので、この時間内に解答し終えることを目標に、最後まで問題を解き、かかった時間を記録してください。

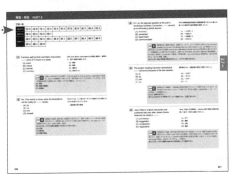

ミニテストの解答・解説

ミニテストの解答・解説ページです。冒頭の正解一覧で答え合わせをしたら、解説を確認しましょう。

※「ミニテスト 1」→「ミニテスト 1 の解答・解説」→「ミニテスト 2」→「ミニテスト 2 の解答・解説」のように、テストと解答・解説が交互に掲載されています。

結果記入シート

ミニテストの結果を記入するシートです (p.308)。各ミニテストの受験にかかった時間や正答数の記録を付け、英語力の伸びをチェックしましょう。また、各設問に関連する復習ユニットが記載されていますので、ユニット学習の該当ユニットに戻って再度学習しましょう。

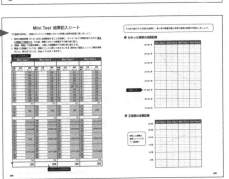

ファイナルテスト

TOEIC® L&R のリーディングセクション 1 回分に挑戦する

Step 3 では、*TOEIC*® L&R のリーディングセクション 1 回分 (100 問、75 分間) に挑戦します。

ファイナルテスト

ファイナルテストの問題ページです。本番テストを受験しているつもりで、落ち着いた環境で取り組みましょう。制限時間を守って挑戦してください。

正解一覧

ファイナルテストの正解一覧です。

参考スコア範囲の換算表

ファイナルテストの正答数から、参考スコア範囲が分かります。ご自身のスコアレベルの目安としてください。

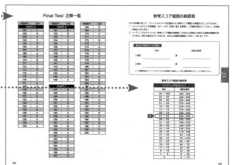

ファイナルテストの解答・解説

解説をよく読んで、間違った問題や解答に自信がなかった問題を復習し、疑問点を解消しましょう。

1 回限りの受験で終わらせず、一定の期間を置いて再度挑戦し、初回受験時と正答数を比較してみましょう。2 回続けて正解できなかった問題に着目すると、苦手分野の把握に役立ちます。

解答用紙 (マークシート)

本誌の巻末には、Step 2 のミニテスト、Step 3 のファイナルテストで使用する解答用紙 (マークシート) が付いています。

本誌から切り離して使い、テスト受験時と同じ臨場感を持って、時間を計りながら解答を塗りつぶす練習をしましょう。

※ミニテストやファイナルテストを繰り返し受験したい場合は、このマークシートをコピーしてご利用ください。

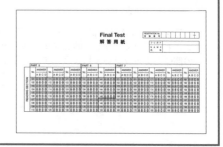

別冊付録『単語集 + 速読用英文』

ユニット学習に登場した語彙や英文を予習・復習する

別冊付録として、「Step 1：ユニット学習」の「チャレンジ」の問題で使用されている語彙や英文をまとめた『単語集 + 速読用英文』を用意しました。持ち運びしやすいサイズなので、本誌から切り離して、さまざまな場面での語彙学習や速読練習にご活用ください。

単語集

本誌の Step 1 の「チャレンジ」の問題に登場した英文の中から有用性の高い 300 の語句をピックアップ。1ユニット1ページでまとめられています。事前の予習や学習後の復習に、また本番テストに役立つ単語リストとしても活用しましょう。

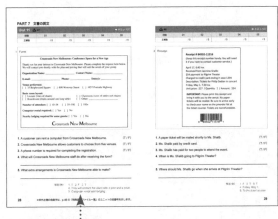

速読用英文

空所部分に正解が入った状態の Part 5 の問題文、Part 6、7 の問題文書を掲載しています。 Part 7 には独自の読解問題が付いていますので、挑戦してみましょう。
また、これらの英文には特典音声（ダウンロード）が付いていますので、音声と一緒に利用しましょう。
（ダウンロード方法は、p.3 を参照）

STEP

1

ユニット学習

Step 1 の目標は、「リーディングの基礎力を養う」です。20 の学習テーマを通して、「英語の語彙・文法」や「英語の長文を読む技術」について学んでいきましょう。

PART

5

短文穴埋め問題

Unit 1　文の要素と品詞

🗨 テーマ解説

Part 5 は一部が空所になった文を読み、空所に入る正しい語や句を選ぶ「短文穴埋め問題」です。Part 5 をスムーズに解くには、文構造の理解が欠かせません。まず Unit 1 では、英語の文の構成要素について学び、文の要素と単語の品詞との関係を理解しましょう。文の主な要素には、主語、述語動詞、目的語、補語があり、さらにこれらの要素に情報を加える修飾語があります。

主語 ▶ 文の中で「誰が／何が」「誰は／何は」を表す言葉。

文の主語になるのは名詞または代名詞です。複数の語が連なり長い句になることもありますが、その場合でも中心となる名詞や代名詞があります（**例**の色下線）。また、「（誰が／何が）～すること」という名詞的な意味を表す動名詞句や名詞節も主語になることがあります。

例　<u>Tom</u> likes curry very much.　Tom はカレーが大好きです。

　　The conference <u>hall</u> can accommodate 300 people.　会議場は 300 人の参加者を収容できます。

　　<u>Going to Bali</u> will be our vacation this year.　バリへ行くのが、今年の私たちの休暇旅行です。

述語動詞 ▶ 文の中で「どうする」という動作や「～である」という状態を表す言葉。

動詞は can や should などの助動詞を伴ったり、時制に応じて have/has や be 動詞を伴ったりして形が変化します。述語動詞とは、この動詞のまとまりを言います。副詞や前置詞を伴って 1 つの動詞のように働くものもあります（〈動詞＋前置詞〉の句動詞 → p.37）。動詞のない語の集まりは文としては不完全です。

例　There **will be** more information about this next week.
　　来週はこれについてもっと多くの情報があるでしょう。
　　Should we **wait for** the manager?
　　私たちは部長を待った方がいいですか。

目的語 ▶ 文の中で動詞の後に続いて、動作の及ぶ先や対象を示す言葉。

目的語とは、動詞の後に続いて、「～を…する」と言うときの「～を」に当たる語のまとまりを言い、中心には名詞や代名詞があります（**例**の色下線）。また、「（誰が／何が）～すること」という名詞的な意味を表す動名詞句や名詞節も目的語になります。目的語が後に続く動詞を「他動詞」と言います。

例　Please send **the new itinerary** by e-mail.　新しい旅程表を E メールで送ってください。
　　I think **(that) Susan is doing a great job.**　私は、Susan は素晴らしい仕事をしていると思います。

補語 ▶ 文の中の主語や目的語を説明する言葉。

補語とは、A is **B**. という文で主語 A を説明する B や、That news made me **happy**. という文で動詞 made の目的語 me の状態を説明する happy のような語のことを言います。補語になるのは、名詞、代名詞、名詞的な意味を表す句や節、形容詞です。特定の構文において、補語は必要不可欠な要素であり、それがないと文としては不完全になります。

例　The difference between the sales figures of the two quarters is **significant**.
　　2 つの四半期間の、その売り上げ差異は重要です。
　　Yesterday we voted Kate **chairperson**.
　　昨日、私たちは投票で Kate を議長に選出しました。

修飾語 ▶ 主語、動詞、目的語、補語に係る言葉。

修飾語とは、主語、動詞、目的語、補語にさまざまな意味や説明を加える言葉を言います。以下の 1 つ目の文では big（形容詞）が problem（名詞）を修飾し、2 つ目の文では、management（名詞）が problem（名詞）を修飾し、a big problem、a management problem で補語の働きをしています。動詞を修飾する語には副詞（句）があります。3 つ目の文では、conveniently（副詞）と near the station（副詞句）が is located（述語動詞）を修飾しています。

例　This is a **big problem**.

これは、大きな問題です。

This is a **management problem**.

これは経営上の問題です。

Our **cozy** office **is conveniently located** near the station.

私たちの居心地よいオフィスは、利便性よく駅の近くに位置しています。

ウォームアップ

以下の例を参考に、1 〜 5 の文の主語、述語動詞、目的語、補語を特定しましょう。なお、全てが含まれるとは限りません。

> 例　Jeff buys new T-shirts every summer.
> 【解答】主語：Jeff　述語動詞：buys　目的語：new T-shirts
> 【訳】Jeff は毎年夏に、新しい T シャツを買います。

1. Stella likes running in the park on Sunday.

2. During the flight, passengers will have wireless Internet access.

3. Please make your reservations ahead of time.

4. The business alliance between Hassan Co. and Lakewood Ltd. will make their relationship more stable.

5. Dick is taking the minutes of the board meeting this month.

【解答・訳】

1. 主語：Stella／述語動詞：likes／目的語：running in the park on Sunday ／ Stella は日曜日に公園で走るのが好きです。
2. 主語：passengers／述語動詞：will have／目的語：wireless Internet access ／飛行中、乗客は無線インターネットへアクセスできます。
3. 主語：なし（命令文）／述語動詞：make／目的語：your reservations ／前もってご予約をお取りください。
4. 主語：The business alliance between Hassan Co. and Lakewood Ltd.／述語動詞：will make／目的語：their relationship ／補語：more stable ／ Hassan 社と Lakewood 社の業務提携は、彼らの関係をより安定的にするでしょう。
5. 主語：Dick／述語動詞：is taking／目的語：the minutes of the board meeting ／ Dick は今月、取締役会の議事録を取っています。

TOEIC® L&R の問題文を使って、練習をしましょう。

1 ～ 6 の文を読み、各文の要素について考えながら、空所に入る語の品詞を予測しましょう。

1. During yesterday's meeting, Ms. Milne offered her ------- to the sales team for their excellent results this quarter.

💡 空所の前の offered、her に注目。

品詞 _____

2. At Reyo Foods, we know that a healthy diet is ------- important to consumers.

💡 that 節の中の主述関係に注目。文として不足する要素がないときは修飾語の可能性を検討。

品詞 _____

3. The ------- of the Kawagoe factory has had a significant impact on Inagi Technology employees' productivity.

💡 空所の前の The、後ろの of に注目。

品詞 _____

4. Ms. Lai's draft of Sientech Industries' new mission statement expresses the company's goals -------.

💡 draft「草稿」、mission statement「企業理念」。

品詞 _____

5. Among her many ------- achievements, Dr. Ahn wrote sixteen books and served as editor for three major journals.

💡 空所の前の her、many、後ろの achievements に注目。

品詞 _____

6. The university's vision is to increase graduates' ------- in the global workplace.

💡 空所の前の increase、graduates'に注目。

品詞 _____

TOEIC® L&R の問題に挑戦します。

右上の目安の解答時間を目標に、自分で時間を計りながら **1 ～ 6** の問題に答えてください。

PART
5
Unit
1

1. During yesterday's meeting, Ms. Milne offered her ------- to the sales team for their excellent results this quarter.

　(A) congratulations
　(B) congratulate
　(C) congratulating
　(D) congratulatory

2. At Reyo Foods, we know that a healthy diet is ------- important to consumers.

　(A) increase
　(B) increases
　(C) increased
　(D) increasingly

3. The ------- of the Kawagoe factory has had a significant impact on Inagi Technology employees' productivity.

　(A) expansion
　(B) expanded
　(C) expanse
　(D) expand

4. Ms. Lai's draft of Sientech Industries' new mission statement expresses the company's goals -------.

　(A) precise
　(B) more precise
　(C) preciseness
　(D) precisely

5. Among her many ------- achievements, Dr. Ahn wrote sixteen books and served as editor for three major journals.

　(A) remarkable
　(B) remarkably
　(C) remarked
　(D) remarking

6. The university's vision is to increase graduates' ------- in the global workplace.

　(A) succeed
　(B) successful
　(C) successfully
　(D) success

→解答・解説は p.16

1. During yesterday's meeting, Ms. Milne offered her ------- to the sales team for their excellent results this quarter.

(A) congratulations
(B) congratulate
(C) congratulating
(D) congratulatory

Milne さんは昨日の会議中に、営業チームへ今四半期の優秀な成績に対するお祝いの言葉を述べました。

(A) お祝いの言葉
(B) お祝いの言葉を述べる
(C) お祝いの言葉を述べている
(D) お祝いの

プラクティス

正解　名詞

空所の前に代名詞の所有格 her があることに注目する。her に続く語は名詞か名詞相当の句（動名詞など）だと考えられる。また、この文の主語は Ms. Milne、述語動詞は offered で、her ------- が目的語だが、目的語に当たる名詞がない。このことからも、文が成り立つためには空所に名詞が必要だと分かる。

チャレンジ

正解　A　代名詞の所有格 her の後に続く語として、名詞を選ぶ。名詞の複数形、(A) congratulations「お祝いの言葉」が正解。during「〜の間」、offer「〜（言葉）を述べる」、result「成績」、quarter「四半期」。
(B) (C) (D) いずれも her に続く語として不適切な品詞である。
(B) 動詞 congratulate「お祝いの言葉を述べる」の原形。
(C) 現在分詞または動名詞。
(D) 形容詞。

2. At Reyo Foods, we know that a healthy diet is ------- important to consumers.

(A) increase
(B) increases
(C) increased
(D) increasingly

私たち Reyo 食品は、消費者にとって健康的な食事はますます重要であると心得ています。

(A) 増加する
(B) 増加する
(C) 増加した
(D) ますます

プラクティス

正解　副詞

空所がなくても、この文は要素的にも意味的にも成立している。このことから、空所の後ろにある形容詞の important を修飾する語が入る可能性が高い。形容詞を修飾する語で一般的なのは副詞である。例えば、very「非常に」や extremely「極めて」などのように important の意味を強める語が適していると考えられる。

チャレンジ

正解　D　空所には、後ろの形容詞 important「重要で」を修飾する語が入るだろうという推測から、副詞を選ぶ。選択肢の中で、副詞は (D) increasingly「ますます」のみ。healthy「健康的な」、diet「食事」、consumer「消費者」。
(A) (B) (C) いずれも動詞 increase が変化した形で、不適切である。
(A) 動詞 increase「増加する」の原形。
(B) 三人称単数現在形。
(C) 過去形または過去分詞。

3. The ------- of the Kawagoe factory has had a significant impact on Inagi Technology employees' productivity.

(A) expansion
(B) expanded
(C) expanse
(D) expand

川越工場の拡張は、Inagi 技術社の従業員の生産性に、かなりの影響を与えています。

(A) 拡張
(B) 拡張された
(C) 広大な広がり
(D) 拡張する

プラクティス

正解　名詞

文が The で始まり、空所の後に of the Kawagoe factory という修飾語句が続いているので、The ------- of the Kawagoe factory のまとまりが、文の主語に相当すると推測できる。主語の名詞がないことから、空所に入る語の品詞は名詞。この文の述語動詞は has had、目的語は a significant impact である。

チャレンジ

正解　A　空所に入るのは名詞が適切だと推測した上で、選択肢から名詞を探すと、(A) expansion「拡張」と(C) expanse「広大な広がり」の2つが残る。文脈から、建物やスペースの物理的な「拡張」の意味を持つ(A) expansion が適切である。expanse は抽象的で「区切りのない広がり」を表す。significant「かなりの」、impact「影響」、productivity「生産性」。
(B) (D) いずれも文の不足している要素に品詞が合わない。
(B) 形容詞。
(D) 動詞expand「拡張する」の原形。

---

4. Ms. Lai's draft of Sientech Industries' new mission statement expresses the company's goals -------.

(A) precise
(B) more precise
(C) preciseness
(D) precisely

Sientech 産業の新しい企業理念を述べた Lai さんの草稿は、会社の目標を正確に表現しています。

(A) 正確な
(B) より正確な
(C) 正確さ
(D) 正確に

プラクティス

正解　副詞

主語は Ms. Lai's draft から statement までで、述語動詞は expresses、目的語は空所の前の the company's goals である。空所がなくてもこの文が要素的に成立することに注目すると、空所に入る語は、追加情報を付加する修飾語の可能性が高いと推測できる。述語動詞 expresses を修飾する副詞が適切である。

チャレンジ

正解　D　空所には副詞が入るのが適切だという推測を踏まえて選択肢を見ると、形容詞 precise「正確な」の活用形と派生語が並んでいる。この中では (D) precisely「正確に」だけが副詞である。mission statement「企業理念」、express「～を表現する」。
(A) (B) (C) いずれも他の選択肢は品詞が合わない。
(A) 形容詞。
(B) 形容詞の比較級。
(C) 名詞。

5. Among her many ------- achievements, Dr. Ahn wrote sixteen books and served as editor for three major journals.

(A) remarkable
(B) remarkably
(C) remarked
(D) remarking

数多くの素晴らしい業績の中でも、Ahn 博士は書籍を 16 冊執筆し、3 つの主要学会誌の編集者を務めました。

(A) 素晴らしい
(B) 素晴らしく
(C) 述べられた
(D) 述べている

プラクティス

正解　形容詞

空所が many「数多くの」と achievements「業績」の間にあるので、空所には、many に続いて名詞 achievements を修飾する語が来るのが適切。名詞を修飾する語として、空所には形容詞、もしくは形容詞に相当する語が入ると推測できる。

チャレンジ

正解　A　空所には形容詞が入るのが適切だと推測した上で、選択肢から形容詞を探す。形容詞の (A) remarkable「素晴らしい」を選ぶと、many remarkable achievements「数多くの素晴らしい業績」という意味になり、文意が通る。achievement「業績」、serve「務める」、editor「編集者」、journal「(学会などの) 専門誌」。
(B) 副詞。
(C) 動詞 remark「〜を述べる」の過去分詞または過去形。分詞には形容詞的な用法があるが、文意が通らず不適切。
(D) 動詞 remark の現在分詞。文意が通らない。

---

6. The university's vision is to increase graduates' ------- in the global workplace.

(A) succeed
(B) successful
(C) successfully
(D) success

その大学の構想は、グローバルな職場における卒業生の成功を増大させることです。

(A) 成功する
(B) 成功した
(C) 成功して
(D) 成功

プラクティス

正解　名詞

空所の直前にある、名詞の複数形の所有格 (graduates') が大きな手掛かり。所有格の後に続くのは名詞か名詞相当の句 (動名詞など) なので、空所に入る語の品詞は名詞だと分かる。また、文の構造を見ると、主語は The university's vision、述語動詞は be 動詞の is、to increase から文末までの不定詞句は補語として主語 vision の内容を説明している。空所は、不定詞 to increase「〜を増大させること」の目的語に当たる。

チャレンジ

正解　D　選択肢には、共通の語幹を持つ派生語が並んでいる。所有格に続く空所に入るのは名詞が適切だという推測を踏まえると、(D) success「成功」が正解だと分かる。vision「構想、ビジョン」、increase「〜を増やす」、graduate「卒業生」。
(A) (B) (C) いずれも他の選択肢は、不足している要素の品詞に合わないので、不適切である。
(A) 動詞 succeed「成功する」の原形。
(B) 形容詞。
(C) 副詞。

Column

◀名詞を修飾する語・句・節▶

文の主要素（主語、述語動詞、目的語、補語）に情報を加える修飾語は、形、文中での位置、働きがさまざまです。単独で名詞を修飾する形容詞、同じく単独で動詞・形容詞・文全体を修飾する副詞に加え、複数の語がまとまった句や節も、形容詞や副詞と同様の働きをすることがあります。今回は、名詞を修飾する修飾語を「語・句・節」の観点から見ていきましょう。

名詞を前から修飾する語（形容詞と名詞）

 **the significant cost reductions** ［形］著しい　　［名］経費	名詞 cost が名詞 reductions を修飾し、形容詞 significant はその cost reductions 全体を修飾しています。例のように、前から名詞を修飾する語は複数の品詞の語が連なることがあります。
例　**The significant cost reductions** are his biggest achievement. 　　大幅な経費削減は彼の最大の業績です。	

名詞を後ろから修飾する句・節（前置詞句と関係詞節）

［前置詞句］

 **the audit team** from the headquarters ［名］監査　　　　　　［前置詞句］本社からの	audit という名詞が名詞 team を修飾し、from the headquarters という〈前置詞＋名詞〉の前置詞句が、the audit team 全体を修飾して「本社からの監査チーム」という意味を表します。前置詞句が名詞を修飾するときは、例のように名詞の後ろに置かれます。
例　**The audit team from the headquarters** arrived yesterday. 　　本社からの監査チームは昨日到着しました。	

［関係詞節］

 **a rooftop space** where residents can gather ［名］屋上　　　　　　［関係詞節］住民が集まることができる	名詞 space の前に rooftop という名詞があることで、「屋上スペース」という具体的な場を示し、さらに後ろの where residents can gather という関係副詞節が a rooftop space を後ろから修飾することで、どんな屋上スペースなのかを説明しています。
例　The new complex has **a rooftop space where residents can gather**. 　　その新しい集合住宅には住民が集まることのできる屋上スペースがあります。	

名詞は前後に修飾語を伴って長い名詞句を作ることがあります。Part 5 のような空所のある文を読むときは、長い名詞句を見抜き、それが文のどの要素に当たるのかが瞬時に分かるようになると、問題を解くスピードが速くなっていきます。

Unit 2　動詞

🞂 テーマ解説

Unit 2 では、動詞の時制を問う問題や、動詞の語彙の知識を問う問題において、特に押さえておきたいポイントを取り上げます。

時制の見分け方
Part 5 で、同じ動詞の時制の異なる選択肢が並んでいる問題では、文中にある特定の語句を目印にすると、適切な時制を判断できることがあります。ここでは、代表的な時制と、その時制と一緒に用いられることの多い「時」を表す副詞 (句・節) を紹介します。

- **現在形**　常にある特徴や不変の事実、繰り返し行われる習慣について述べる動詞の形です。always「いつも」、usually「たいていは」、sometimes「時々」、often「よく」、every day/week/month/year「毎日／毎週／毎月／毎年」、never「決して～ない」などの頻度を表す副詞や副詞句と一緒に、しばしば用いられます。

  例　We **always appreciate** our customers. We **never compromise** on quality.
  私たちは常にお客さまへ感謝の念を抱いております。決して品質において妥協いたしません。

- **現在進行形**　現在進行中の動作について述べる動詞の形です。now「今」、today「今日」、this week/month/year「今週／今月／今年」、currently「現在は」、at the moment「現時点では」など、「今は、今だけ」という一時的な意味を表す副詞や副詞句をしばしば伴います。

  例　Last year, we invested in new machinery, and **this year**, we **are optimizing** our logistics.
  昨年、当社は新しい機械に投資しましたが、今年は、物流を最適化しています。

- **現在完了形**〈have/has + 過去分詞〉　現在と過去を関連付けて述べる動詞の形で、完了・経験・継続を表します。just「ちょうど」、lately「最近」、already「すでに」、before「以前」などの副詞、since「～以来」、for「～の間」などの前置詞を使った〈前置詞 + 名詞〉の副詞句、since 節などをよく伴います。

  例　Kate **has been** a math teacher **for five years**.　Kate は 5 年間数学の教師をしています。

- **過去形**　現在と切り離された、過去の特定の時に発生した出来事について述べる動詞の形です。yesterday「昨日」、last week/month/year「先週／先月／昨年」、〈数字 + years ago〉「～年前」、〈in + 年〉「～年に」など、過去の特定の時を表す副詞や副詞句、when 節などと一緒に用いられます。

  例　We **moved** to Denver **in 2010**.
  私たちは 2010 年にデンバーへ引っ越しました。

- **過去完了形**〈had + 過去分詞〉　過去のある時点を想定し、それ以前に起こった出来事の完了・経験・継続を表します。already「すでに」などの副詞や、since「～以来」、for「～の間」などの前置詞を使った〈前置詞＋名詞〉の副詞句、when 節や before 節などと一緒によく使われます。

  例　**When I started** studying for the English test last year, I **had already studied** English **for 10 years**.
  昨年、その英語試験に向けて勉強を始めたとき、私はすでに 10 年間英語を勉強していました。

■ **未来形** 〈will＋動詞の原形〉 未来に起こること、主語の人物がしようと思っていることを表す動詞の形です。tomorrow「明日」、shortly「すぐに」、soon「間もなく」、next week/month/year「来週／来月／来年」、by「〜までに（期限）」などの未来の時を表す副詞や副詞句、when 節などと一緒に用いられます。

　　例　The banquet **will start at 7 P.M. tomorrow night**.
　　　　祝宴は明晩の午後 7 時に始まります。

■ **未来完了形** 〈will have＋過去分詞〉 未来のある時点までに完了・経験・継続しているであろう出来事や行為について表す動詞の形です。tomorrow「明日」、by「〜までに（期限）」、until「〜まで（継続）」、during「〜の間」などの副詞や副詞句、until 節や while 節などと一緒によく用いられます。

　　例　I **will have finished** my report **by 6 P.M.**
　　　　午後 6 時までには、私は報告書を完成させているでしょう。

動詞の語彙を増やすポイント

Part 5 では、同じ時制で意味の異なる動詞が選択肢に並ぶ問題も登場します。そのような問題では語彙の知識が問われます。動詞の意味を覚える際は、その動詞が「自動詞のみ」、「他動詞のみ」、「自動詞も他動詞もある」のどのパターンで、それぞれどんな意味を表すのかを調べ、例文とともに覚えるようにしましょう。以下は、自動詞と他動詞の両方の意味がある develop の例文です。

　　例　[他動詞]　「〜を開発する」
　　　　　　　　　The engineering team **developed** a new robot.
　　　　　　　　　工学チームが新型ロボットを開発しました。
　　　　[自動詞]　「発展する」
　　　　　　　　　In this class we will learn how markets **develop**.
　　　　　　　　　この授業では市場がどう発展するかを学びます。

ウォームアップ

太字部分の語句をヒントに、（　　）内の動詞を適切な時制にしましょう。

1. At the moment, we (not hire) any new employees.　　　　　＿＿＿＿＿＿＿＿

2. She **always** (talk) in a friendly, approachable manner.　　　＿＿＿＿＿＿＿＿

3. Our office (be) in the center of the city **since** we **moved** there **in 1995**.　＿＿＿＿＿＿

4. Last Christmas we (go) to Guam. It was fantastic.　　　　　＿＿＿＿＿＿＿＿

5. John (run) five miles **three times a week**. He is in great shape.　　＿＿＿＿＿＿

【解答・訳】
1. are not hiring ／現在、当社は新規の社員を採用していません。　▶「限定された期間」について述べている。
2. talks ／彼女はいつも気さくで親しみやすい態度で話します。　▶「常にある特徴」について述べている。
3. has been ／1995 年に移転して以来、私たちの事業所は町の中心街にあります。　▶ 1995 年から現在に至るまでの「継続した状態」について述べている。
4. went ／昨年のクリスマスに私たちはグアムへ行きました。素晴らしかったです。　▶「過去の特定の時」を表す。
5. runs ／ John は週に 3 回、5 マイルを走ります。彼はとても健康です。　▶「繰り返し行われる習慣」を表す。

TOEIC® L&R の問題文を使って、練習をしましょう。

1 1～3の（　　）に入る動詞の適切な時制を (a)、(b) から選びましょう。

1. The product development team for Herbeve Cosmetics is (consider) <u>a package redesign</u> to try to increase sales.

💡 空所の直前の is と下線部に注目。

(a) 現在進行形 　　　　　　　(b) 現在形（受動態）

2. Karl Byquist's compelling presentation (convince) the management of Parkland Press to hire his company.

💡 動詞 convince の用法と全体の文意に注目。

(a) 現在形 　　　　　　　　　(b) 過去形

3. Lundquist Electronics (have) twelve retail stores in Japan by March of next year.

💡 状態を表す have と期限を表す by に注目。

(a) 過去形 　　　　　　　　　(b) 未来形

2 4、5の空所に入る動詞の適切な意味を (a) ～ (d) から選びましょう。また、それに対応する動詞の候補として思い付くものがあれば書きましょう。

4. Former seasonal employees seeking to be rehired must ------- a new application.
(a) ～を観察する
(b) ～を提出する
(c) ～を習熟させる
(d) ～に知らせる　　　　　　　　候補の動詞 _____

5. Ding's Café in Hong Kong ------- to serve the freshest possible seafood.
(a) ～を目指す
(b) ～を捕まえる
(c) ～を供給する
(d) ～を生産する　　　　　　　　候補の動詞 _____

3 6の空所に入る語の品詞を予測しましょう。

6. Smooth Tek's newest software makes it <u>much</u> ------- for business owners to create newsletters.

💡 動詞 make の用法と下線部に注目。

品詞 _____

TOEIC® L&R の問題に挑戦します。

右上の目安の解答時間を目標に、自分で時間を計りながら **1 ～ 6** の問題に答えてください。

1. The product development team for Herbeve Cosmetics is ------- a package redesign to try to increase sales.

(A) considered
(B) considering
(C) considers
(D) consider

2. Karl Byquist's compelling presentation ------- the management of Parkland Press to hire his company.

(A) convince
(B) convincing
(C) convinced
(D) convincingly

3. Lundquist Electronics ------- twelve retail stores in Japan by March of next year.

(A) will have
(B) has
(C) is having
(D) has had

4. Former seasonal employees seeking to be rehired must ------- a new application.

(A) observe
(B) submit
(C) familiarize
(D) inform

5. Ding's Café in Hong Kong ------- to serve the freshest possible seafood.

(A) aims
(B) catches
(C) provides
(D) produces

6. Smooth Tek's newest software makes it much ------- for business owners to create newsletters.

(A) easy
(B) easily
(C) easier
(D) ease

PART
5

Unit
2

→解答・解説は p.24

1. The product development team for Herbeve Cosmetics is ------- a package redesign to try to increase sales.

(A) considered
(B) considering
(C) considers
(D) consider

Herbeve 化粧品社の商品開発チームは、売り上げを増やそうと、包装紙のデザイン変更を検討しています。

＊選択肢の訳は省略

プラクティス

正解　(a) 現在進行形

文意から、主語の The product development team「商品開発チーム」は consider「～を検討する」という動作を行う主体で、下線部の名詞句「包装紙のデザイン変更」は consider の目的語と考えられる。よって、この文は、チームの人々の現在進行中の動作や状態について述べていると推測できる。

チャレンジ

正解　B　動詞 consider「～を検討する」の適切な形を選ぶ。空所の前に be 動詞の三人称単数現在形の is があり、後ろに「売り上げを増やそうと」という目的を表す不定詞があることから、この文は商品開発チームの進行中または継続中の動作や状態について述べている。よって、現在分詞の (B) considering が正解。product development「商品開発」。
(A) 過去分詞または過去形。受動態だと考えたとしても、後半の内容とつながらない。
(C) 三人称単数現在形。
(D) 動詞の原形。

2. Karl Byquist's compelling presentation ------- the management of Parkland Press to hire his company.

(A) convince
(B) convincing
(C) convinced
(D) convincingly

Karl Byquist の説得力あるプレゼンテーションは、Parkland 通信社の経営陣に同氏の会社を雇うことを納得させました。

(A) ～を納得させる
(B) 人を納得させるような
(C) ～を納得させた
(D) 納得させるように

プラクティス

正解　(b) 過去形

動詞 convince は、convince ～ to do の語順で「～に…するよう説得する、～を納得させて…させる」という意味を表す。人に働き掛けて行動を促す際に使われる表現で、the management of Parkland Press「Parkland 通信社の経営陣」が目的語の「～」に当たり、to hire his company「彼の会社を雇う」が to do に当たるので、常にある特徴や反復される事実ではなく、過去の特定の時における事実と考えるのが自然。(b) の過去形が適切。

チャレンジ

正解　C　述語動詞がないため、空所には動詞が必要である。動詞 convince「～を納得させる」の適切な形を選ぶ。文意から過去の事実について述べた文と考えられるので、(C) が正解。convince ～ to do で「～に…するよう説得する、～を納得させて…させる」という意味。compelling「説得力のある」、management「経営陣」。
(A) 動詞の原形。
(B) 形容詞。
(D) 副詞。

3. Lundquist Electronics ------- twelve retail stores in Japan by March of next year.

- (A) will have
- (B) has
- (C) is having
- (D) has had

Lundquist 電子機器社は、来年の３月までに日本に小売店を 12 店舗所有することになるでしょう。

＊選択肢の訳は省略

プラクティス

正解 (b) 未来形

文末に by March of next year「来年の３月までに」という未来の期限を表す句がある。未来のある時点までに起きているであろうという状態について述べた文だと推測できるので、未来形の will have が適切だと考えられる。動詞 have は未来形〈will ＋動詞の原形〉で「～を持っているだろう、～を保有しているだろう」という未来の状態を表す。

チャレンジ

正解 A 選択肢は全て動詞 have「～を持っている」の変化した形。文末に具体的な期限である by March of next year「来年の３月までに」があることから、未来を表す (A) will have が正解となる。retail store「小売店」。
(B) 三人称単数現在形。
(C) 現在進行形。進行形が近い未来を表すこともあるが、have は状態動詞のため、通常は進行形にならない。
(D) 現在完了形。現在完了形は現在と過去をつなげて述べる形。ここでは不適切。

---

4. Former seasonal employees seeking to be rehired must ------- a new application.

- (A) observe
- (B) submit
- (C) familiarize
- (D) inform

再雇用されることを希望する以前の季節労働者は、新しい申込書を提出しなければなりません。

- (A) ～を観察する
- (B) ～を提出する
- (C) ～を習熟させる
- (D) ～に知らせる

プラクティス

正解 (b) ～を提出する

候補の動詞 submit、turn in など

Former seasonal employees seeking to be rehired「再雇用されることを希望する以前の季節労働者」が主語、空所の後の a new application「新しい申込書」が目的語と考えられる。「再雇用されることを希望する以前の季節労働者は、新しい申込書を ------- する」という文脈で相性が良い動詞は「～を提出する」。この意味を表す表現としては submit や turn in が適切。

チャレンジ

正解 B 選択肢は全て動詞。a new application「新しい申込書」を目的語として文意に合うのは、(B) submit「～を提出する」。seasonal「季節の」、employee「従業員」、seek to do「～することを求める」、rehire「～を再雇用する」。
(A)(C)(D) いずれも Former seasonal employees seeking to be rehired「再雇用されることを希望する以前の季節労働者」を主語とし、application「申込書」を目的語に続ける動詞として、文意が合わない。

5. Ding's Café in Hong Kong ------- to serve the freshest possible seafood.

    (A) aims
    (B) catches
    (C) provides
    (D) produces

香港にある Ding's カフェは、可能な限り新鮮なシーフードを給仕することを目指しています。

    (A) 〜を目指す
    (B) 〜を捕まえる
    (C) 〜を供給する
    (D) 〜を生産する

プラクティス

正解 (a) 〜を目指す

候補の動詞 aims、strives など

カフェの経営方針に関して述べている文。現在の店の方針または将来的な計画について述べていると考えられる。選択肢から、文意に合う動詞の意味は、「〜を目指す」が最も適切。不定詞を後ろに続けて「〜することを目指す」という意味を表す動詞の候補には、aim「目指す」、strive「努力する」などがある。

チャレンジ

正解 **A** 文意から適切な意味の動詞を選択する。空所の後に不定詞の to serve「〜を給仕すること」があることを踏まえると、最もふさわしいのは「〜を目指す」を意味する (A) aims。aim to do で「〜することを目指す」という意味を表す。freshest は fresh「新鮮な」の最上級。
(B)(C)(D) いずれも後の不定詞句とつながらない。

---

6. Smooth Tek's newest software makes it much ------- for business owners to create newsletters.

    (A) easy
    (B) easily
    (C) easier
    (D) ease

Smooth Tek 社の最新ソフトウエアは、事業主がニュースレターを作成するのを格段に楽にします。

    (A) 楽な
    (B) 気楽に
    (C) より楽な
    (D) 気楽

プラクティス

正解 形容詞（比較級）

〈make + 目的語 + 補語〉で「〜を…にする」という意味を表す。it は目的語に当たり、空所は補語に相当するため、空所の候補としては名詞か形容詞が考えられるが、前に much があることに注目する。much は形容詞や副詞の比較級を強める副詞。よって空所には、形容詞の比較級が入るのが適切だと判断できる。候補になり得る形容詞の比較級は easier、more efficient、more economical など。

チャレンジ

正解 **C** 空所の前の副詞の much は、形容詞や副詞の比較級を修飾し、「はるかに、大いに」という意味を表す。選択肢の中では形容詞の比較級の (C) easier が適切である。目的語の it は不定詞の形式目的語で、for business owners to create newsletters「事業主がニュースレターを作成すること」を指す。business owner「事業主」。
(A) 形容詞。
(B) 副詞。
(D) 名詞。

◀ 受動態 ▶

Part 5 の動詞の知識が問われる問題では、空所の動詞が受動態か能動態かを判断することがポイントになるものもあります。以下で、受動態が使われている問題を幾つか見てみましょう。

例 Staff members are not sure who made this error, but it ------- by one of the interns.

(A) made
★ (B) could have been made
(C) will be made
(D) can make

従業員は誰がこの間違いを犯したのか確信が持てずにいるが、それは研修生の 1 人によりなされた可能性がある。

＊選択肢の訳は省略

▶ 空所の後の前置詞 by「～によって」がヒントになり、この文が受動態であることが分かるため、正解の候補が (B) と (C) に絞れる。カンマの前の節の時制から、過去の出来事について述べている文だと分かるので、過去の推量を表す (B) が正解。
(A) 能動態・過去形。 (C) 受動態・未来形。 (D) 能動態・現在形。

例 Maria Vega's keynote address at next month's Entrepreneurs Symposium in Singapore ------- by a short video.

(A) was preceded
★ (B) will be preceded
(C) would precede
(D) were to precede

来月のシンガポールの起業家討論会では、Maria Vega の基調講演の前に短いビデオ上映があるでしょう。

＊選択肢の訳は省略

▶ precede は「～に先立つ、～に先行する」という意味の他動詞。空所の後の前置詞 by から、この文が受動態だと考えられるため、正解の候補が (A) と (B) に絞れる。さらに、主語の名詞句の一部 at next month's Entrepreneurs Symposium から未来の話だと分かるので、未来形の (B) が正解。
(A) 受動態・過去形。 (C) 能動態。would は可能性の低い「推量」。 (D) 能動態。were to do は if 節で用いられて実現可能性が極めて低い仮定を表す。

次の例のように、by 以降が示されず、主体が書かれていない受動態の文もあります。受動態は、他動詞の目的語を主語にして「～される」という受け身を表す文の形であるため、動詞の自動詞・他動詞の意味の違いを押さえて文意を捉え、意味内容から「この文は受動態でないと意味が通らない」などと判断できるようになりましょう。

例 The employees at Topso Lumber ------- to wear company uniforms and identification badges at all times.

(A) expecting
(B) expects
(C) to be expecting
★ (D) are expected

Topso 材木社の従業員は、会社の制服と ID バッジを常に着用するよう求められています。

＊選択肢の訳は省略

▶ 動詞 expect は「～を求める、～を期待する」という意味の他動詞で、目的語の後に不定詞を続けて、expect ～ to do「～に…することを求める、～に…することを期待する」という意味を表す。文の意味内容から、主語の The employees at Topso Lumber が主体として制服と ID バッジを着用することを求めているのではなく、「(会社によって) 求められている」と受け身の意味で捉えた方が自然。よって、受動態で現在形の (D) が正解。
(A) 現在分詞または動名詞。 (B) 能動態・三人称単数現在形。 (C) 不定詞の進行形。

Unit 3　形容詞・副詞

テーマ解説

形容詞と副詞の違い

形容詞と副詞は、文の中で修飾語として働くという共通項を持っていますが、その働き方や形には違いがあります。Unit 3 でしっかりと確認しておきましょう。

■ **形容詞の働き**　形容詞は名詞を説明する言葉です。次の例では、1 つ目の文の形容詞 new は名詞 product を前から修飾して「どんな商品なのか」を説明し、2 つ目の文の形容詞 available は名詞 seats を後ろから修飾して「どんな席なのか」を説明しています。また、3 つ目の文の形容詞 innovative は、be 動詞の後に続いて、補語として主語の名詞を説明しています。

> 例　This is a **new product**.　これは新商品です。
>
> We still have **seats available**.　ご利用可能な座席はまだございます。
>
> This method is **innovative**.　この方法は革新的です。

■ **副詞の働き**　副詞は、動詞、形容詞、副詞、または文全体を修飾します。次の例では 1 つ目の文の副詞 newly は形容詞 developed「開発された」を修飾していますが、2 つ目の文で副詞 newly は受け身の述語動詞 was developed「〜は開発された」を修飾しています。

> 例　This is a **newly developed** method.　これは新しく開発された方法です。
>
> This method **was newly developed**.　この方法は新しく開発されました。

■ **形容詞と副詞の形**　形容詞か副詞かの判別は、new、newly のように形容詞に接尾辞 -ly が付くと副詞になる語が多いため、つづりを見ればある程度の類推ができます。ただし、friendly「愛想が良い」や costly「高い」、quarterly「年 4 回の」のように、語尾が -ly でも形容詞の単語もあります。また、次の例のように、形容詞と副詞が同じつづりの語もあるので、注意が必要です。

> 例　hard　[形容詞]　David is a **hard** worker.　David は働き者です。　▶「熱心な」
>
> 　　　　[副詞]　Kate always tries **hard**.　Kate はいつも一生懸命に努力します。　▶「熱心に」
>
> 例　late　[形容詞]　None of the students were **late** for class.　▶「遅い」
> 　　　　　　　学生は 1 人も授業に遅刻しませんでした。
>
> 　　　　[副詞]　Nancy arrived **late** for the afternoon meeting.　▶「遅くに」
> 　　　　　　　Nancy は午後の会議に遅れて到着しました。

形容詞・副詞の語彙を増やすポイント

Part 5 には、意味の異なる形容詞または副詞が並んでいる問題もよく登場します。このような問題では形容詞や副詞の語彙力が問われています。以下を参考に形容詞や副詞の語彙増強を図りましょう。

■ **接頭辞・接尾辞の知識を付ける**　語彙を増やす際、接頭辞や接尾辞の知識があると役立ちます。

次の例は、形容詞を作る主な接尾辞と、否定の意味を表す接頭辞・接尾辞の例です。

例 **形容詞を作る主な接尾辞：-able、-ible、-ent、-ant、-ous、-ive、-ful**
adjust**able**「調節できる」、access**ible**「出入りできる」、compet**ent**「有能な」、
abund**ant**「豊富な」、nerv**ous**「不安な」、excess**ive**「過度の」、help**ful**「役に立つ」

例 **否定の意味を表す接頭辞・接尾辞：dis-、un-、in-、im-、il-、ir-、-less**
dishonest「不誠実な」、**un**official「非公式の」、**in**visible「見えない」、**im**mature「未熟な」、
illegal「違法な」、**ir**regular「不規則な」、care**less**「不注意な」

■ **形容詞の慣用表現に注意する**　形容詞には、It is probable that ～「～はありそうだ」や be likely to *do*「～しそうである」のように、形式主語の it や不定詞とともに使われる慣用表現が多くあります。慣用表現はできるだけ例文とともに覚えるようにしましょう。

例 Sales **are** very **likely to increase** in the third quarter.
　　売り上げは第 3 四半期に増加する可能性が非常に高いです。

■ **-ing と -ed の形容詞はセットで覚える**　形容詞の中には、現在分詞・過去分詞が形容詞化したものもあります（分詞形容詞）。それにさらに -ly が付き、interestingly「興味深いことに」などと副詞になることもあるので、-ing と -ed、そして派生語の副詞はセットで覚えるようにしましょう。-ing は能動の意味を表し、-ed は受け身の意味を表します。

例　**interest**　［-ing］　The new housing project is **interesting** for us.　▶「興味を起こさせる」
　　　　　　　　　　　　その新しい住宅計画は、私たちにとって興味深いです。
　　　　　　　　　［-ed］　We are **interested** in the new housing project.　▶「興味を呼び起こされた」
　　　　　　　　　　　　私たちは、その新しい住宅計画に興味を持っています。

ウォームアップ

1 接頭辞や接尾辞に注目し、次の単語の対義語を答えましょう。

1. harmful　＿＿＿＿＿＿＿　　4. respectful　＿＿＿＿＿＿＿

2. proper　＿＿＿＿＿＿＿　　5. told　＿＿＿＿＿＿＿

3. responsible　＿＿＿＿＿＿＿　　6. capable　＿＿＿＿＿＿＿

2 空所に入るのに適切な語を選びましょう。

1. The warm and sunny weather ------- surprised me. 　(a) pleasant　(b) pleasantly
2. Jane is a very ------- person. 　(a) nice　(b) nicely
3. The new computer is ------- fast. 　(a) extreme　(b) extremely
4. This exam was too ------- for me. 　(a) easy　(b) easily

【解答・訳】

1 1. harmless　2. improper　3. irresponsible　4. disrespectful　5. untold　6. incapable

2 1. (b) ／暖かく晴れ渡った天気は、私を気持ちよく驚かせました。　▶ 述語動詞 surprised を修飾する副詞。

　2. (a) ／Jane はとてもすてきな人です。　▶ 名詞 person を修飾する形容詞。

　3. (b) ／新しいコンピューターは極めて速いです。　▶ 形容詞 fast を修飾する副詞。

　4. (a) ／この試験は私には簡単過ぎました。　▶ 主語の名詞 exam を説明する補語の形容詞。

TOEIC® L&R の問題文を使って、練習をしましょう。

1 （　　）内の単語を、文の意味に合う派生語に変化させましょう。

1. Mr. Ashburton has been (high) recommended <u>by all three of his references</u>.

💡 下線部は「3 カ所全ての照会先によって」という意味。

_____

2 2 ～ 5 の空所に入る形容詞または副詞の適切な意味を (a)、(b) から選びましょう。また、それに対応する形容詞または副詞の候補として思い付くものがあれば書きましょう。

2. The switch to the specialized database is ------- scheduled for May 18, but it may need to be postponed.
(a) 日常的に
(b) 暫定的に　　　　　　　　　　　　候補の単語 _____

3. The planned construction of several new office buildings in Newbury has created a ------- demand for skilled workers.
(a) かなり大きな
(b) 丈夫な　　　　　　　　　　　　候補の単語 _____

4. While the closure of Park Street's southbound lane is not -------, it will not reopen this year.
(a) 見掛けの
(b) 恒久的な　　　　　　　　　　　候補の単語 _____

5. This month, Mr. Choi has excelled at ------- processing incoming orders.
(a) 典型的に
(b) 迅速に　　　　　　　　　　　　候補の単語 _____

3 6 の空所に入る形容詞の候補を挙げましょう。

6. The employee satisfaction survey results are ------- <u>to differ among departments</u>.

💡 下線部に注目し、〈be ＋形容詞＋不定詞〉の形で使われる形容詞を考える。

候補の形容詞 _____

TOEIC® L&R の問題に挑戦します。

右上の目安の解答時間を目標に、自分で時間を計りながら **1 ～ 6** の問題に答えてください。

1. Mr. Ashburton has been ------- recommended by all three of his references.

(A) high
(B) higher
(C) highly
(D) highest

2. The switch to the specialized database is ------- scheduled for May 18, but it may need to be postponed.

(A) formerly
(B) especially
(C) regularly
(D) tentatively

3. The planned construction of several new office buildings in Newbury has created a ------- demand for skilled workers.

(A) lengthy
(B) plenty
(C) sizable
(D) durable

4. While the closure of Park Street's southbound lane is not -------, it will not reopen this year.

(A) developed
(B) apparent
(C) established
(D) permanent

5. This month, Mr. Choi has excelled at ------- processing incoming orders.

(A) typically
(B) tightly
(C) quickly
(D) lately

6. The employee satisfaction survey results are ------- to differ among departments.

(A) important
(B) likely
(C) probable
(D) recent

→解答・解説は p.32

1. Mr. Ashburton has been ------- recommended by all three of his references.

(A) high
(B) higher
(C) highly
(D) highest

Ashburton さんは 3 カ所全ての照会先から、強く推薦されています。

(A) 高い
(B) より高い
(C) 高く
(D) 最も高い

プラクティス

正解 highly

Mr. Ashburton が主語、has been recommended が述語動詞で、受け身の文である。文の要素から判断して、空所には述語動詞を修飾する副詞が入ると考えられる。high には形容詞「高い」と副詞「高く」の両方の品詞があるが、-ly が語尾に付いた highly「（評価などについて）高く、強く」という副詞もある。highly recommend「強く勧める」とすると意味が通るので、high → highly とする。

チャレンジ

正解 C 選択肢は形容詞 high の変化した形または派生語。空所の位置から、前後の述語動詞 has been recommended を修飾する副詞を選ぶ。highly recommend「強く勧める」は何かを強く推薦する場面で使える定番表現。正解は (C)。recommend「～を推薦する、～を勧める」、reference「照会先、推薦状」。
(A) 形容詞または副詞。副詞の high は物理的な高度や量・質について使うので、ここでは不適切。
(B) 形容詞の比較級。
(D) 形容詞の最上級。

---

2. The switch to the specialized database is ------- scheduled for May 18, but it may need to be postponed.

(A) formerly
(B) especially
(C) regularly
(D) tentatively

専門データベースへの切り替えは、暫定的に 5 月 18 日に予定されていますが、延期せざるを得ないかもしれません。

(A) 以前は
(B) 特に
(C) 日常的に
(D) 暫定的に

プラクティス

正解 (b) 暫定的に

候補の単語 tentatively、temporarily など

カンマの前の節の主語は The switch to the specialized database「専門データベースへの切り替え」、述語動詞は空所の前後の is scheduled for ～「～（日時）に予定されている」。カンマの前で予定日が述べられ、カンマ以降で「しかし、それは延期せざるを得ないかもしれない」と対比的な内容が述べられているので、(b) の「暫定的に」という意味の副詞を入れて、「暫定的に予定されているが、しかし～」とすれば文意が通る。

チャレンジ

正解 D 選択肢は全て副詞。カンマの前の節と後ろの節の文意のつながりを考えると、空所には (D) tentatively が正解。it はカンマの前の節の主語 The switch to the specialized database「専門データベースへの切り替え」を指す。postpone「～を延期する」。
(A) 空所の前の動詞が was ならば文意が成り立つが、現在形では不適切である。
(B) (C) 文意に合わない。

3. The planned construction of several new office buildings in Newbury has created a ------- demand for skilled workers.

    (A) lengthy
    (B) plenty
    (C) sizable
    (D) durable

Newbury における何件かの新規オフィスビルの建設計画は、熟練作業員に対するかなり大きな需要を生み出しました。

    (A) 冗長な
    (B) 〈plenty of ～で〉十分な量の～
    (C) かなり大きな
    (D) 丈夫な

PART 5 Unit 3

プラクティス

正解 (a) かなり大きな

候補の単語 huge、considerable、sizable など

空所の前に a、後ろに名詞 demand「需要」があることから、空所には名詞 demand を修飾する形容詞が入ると考えられる。文意から、新規オフィスビルの建設計画によって、熟練作業員の需要が生まれたという意味だと考えられるため、demand の規模を表す (a) の「かなり大きな」が適切。

チャレンジ

正解 C 文意を踏まえた上で、「ある1つの需要 (a demand)」を修飾するのに適した意味の形容詞を選ぶ。選択肢の中では (C) sizable「かなり大きな」が適切。planned「計画した、予定した」、construction「建設」、create「～を生み出す」、skilled「熟練した」。
(A)(D) 形容詞。いずれも、demand を修飾する語としては意味が通らない。
(B) 名詞。「十分な量の～」という意味にするには、〈plenty of ＋ 名詞〉の語順になり、plenty の前に a は付かない。

---

4. While the closure of Park Street's southbound lane is not -------, it will not reopen this year.

    (A) developed
    (B) apparent
    (C) established
    (D) permanent

Park 通りの南行き車線の閉鎖は恒久的ではないものの、それは今年は再開しないでしょう。

    (A) 発展した
    (B) 見掛けの
    (C) 確立した
    (D) 恒久的な

プラクティス

正解 (b) 恒久的な

候補の単語 permanent

文頭に「～であるものの」という譲歩を表す接続詞 while があるため、カンマの前の副詞節は、後半の「それは今年は再開しないだろう」と対立する内容を表すと推測できる。副詞節の主語は the closure「閉鎖」で、否定語の not があることを考えると、文意に合うのは (b) の「恒久的な」という意味の形容詞。「閉鎖は恒久的ではないものの、それは今年は再開しないだろう」という意味になる。

チャレンジ

正解 D 選択肢は全て形容詞。カンマの前の節と後ろの節の文意のつながりから、空所には (D) を入れて、「Park 通りの南行き車線の閉鎖は恒久的ではないものの、それ (＝南行き車線) は今年は再開しないだろう」という意味にすると適切。permanent は「恒久的な、不変の」という意味を表す。southbound「南行きの」。
(A)(C) いずれも主語の the closure「閉鎖」を説明する形容詞として不適切。
(B) 後半の節と意味がつながらない。

5. This month, Mr. Choi has excelled at ------- processing incoming orders.

(A) typically
(B) tightly
(C) quickly
(D) lately

今月 Choi さんは、受注処理の迅速な処理に抜きん出ていました。

(A) 典型的に
(B) きつく
(C) 迅速に
(D) 最近

プラクティス

正解 (b) 迅速に

候補の単語 quickly、speedily など

主語は Mr. Choi、述語動詞は has excelled at ～「～に抜きん出ている」。空所の後ろから文末までは「受注を処理すること」という意味の動名詞句で、前置詞 at の目的語だと考えられる。よって空所には、動名詞の processing を修飾する副詞が入るのが適切。「迅速に処理する」という意味にすれば、文意が通る。候補の副詞としては quickly、speedily など。

チャレンジ

正解 C 選択肢は全て副詞。文の要素や空所の位置から判断して、空所には前置詞 at の目的語の processing incoming orders「受注処理をすること」を修飾する語が入るため、(C) quickly「迅速に」が適切。excel at ～「～に抜きん出る、～に秀でる」、process「～を処理する、～を加工する」、incoming「入ってくる」、order「注文」。
(A) (B) (D) いずれも文意に合わない。

---

6. The employee satisfaction survey results are ------- to differ among departments.

(A) important
(B) likely
(C) probable
(D) recent

従業員満足度調査の結果は、部署間で異なりそうです。

(A) 重要な
(B) 〈to do を続けて〉～しそうで
(C) もっともらしい
(D) 最近の

プラクティス

候補の形容詞 expected、anticipated、likely、bound、sure、certain など

空所の前は〈主語 + be 動詞〉、空所の後ろは不定詞が続いており、文全体で「従業員満足度調査の結果は、部署間で異なることが ------- である」という意味だと考えられる。後ろの不定詞とのつながりがよい形容詞の意味としては、「調査結果は、部署間で異なることが予期されて／可能性が高い／確実で」などが考えられるので、この意味に適した形容詞を挙げる。

チャレンジ

正解 B 選択肢は全て形容詞。be likely to do で「～しそうである」という可能性を表す。よって (B) が正解。satisfaction survey「満足度調査」、differ「異なる」、department「部署」。
(A) (D) いずれも文意に合わない。
(C) probable も可能性があることを表す形容詞だが、likely のように不定詞と一緒に用いられない。

Column

◀ 比較を表す表現 ▶

Part 5 の形容詞や副詞の知識が問われる問題では、比較級や最上級が登場することがあります。以下で、基本の比較表現や、日常の場面で使われるその他の比較表現を確認しましょう。

基本の比較表現

原則として、比較級は形容詞・副詞の原級に -er を付けるか、前に more を置いて表します。一方、最上級は the とともに形容詞・副詞の原級に -est を付けるか、前に the most を置いて表します。比較級も最上級も基本的に、その後に比較の対象・範囲となる語句を伴いますが、明らかな場合は省略されることもあります。

- ■ 〈形容詞・副詞の比較級（+ than …）〉「（…より）~」
    - 例 Room A is **larger than** Room B. / Room A is **more spacious than** Room B.
      A室はB室より広いです。

- ■ 〈the + 形容詞・副詞の最上級 + of/in …〉「…の中で最も~」
    - 例 Room C has **the largest space of** our options. /
      Room C is **the most spacious of** our options.
      C室は選択できるものの中で最も広いスペースです。

2つ以上を比較して、「より~でない」、「最も~でない」と否定するには less、least を使います。

- ■ 〈less + 形容詞・副詞の原級（+ than …）〉「（…ほど）~でない」
    - 例 The leader should coach **less experienced** staff.
      リーダーはより経験の浅い作業員を指導するべきです。　▶「経験が比較的豊富でない」

- ■ 〈the least + 形容詞・副詞の原級〉「最も~でない」
    - 例 This furniture is **the least expensive** in the catalog.
      この家具がカタログの中で最も安いです。　▶「最も高くない」

「…よりも、ずっと／はるかに／さらに~だ」のように、比較の差の大きさを強調したいときには、比較級の前に much、far、even などの副詞を置きます。

- ■ 〈much／far／even + 比較級〉「ずっと／はるかに／さらにいっそう~だ」
    - 例 Using this method will allow you to work **much faster**.
      この手法を用いることでずっと速く仕事ができるようになるでしょう。

その他の比較表現

- ■ 〈not as + 原級 …〉「…ほど~でない」
    - 例 Today is **not as cold as** yesterday. = Today is **less cold than** yesterday.
      今日は昨日ほど寒くありません。

- ■ 〈the + 比較級 , the + 比較級〉「~すればますます…」
    - 例 **The earlier** we start the project, **the more** sales profit we can get.
      プロジェクトを始めるのが早ければ早いほど、当社はより多くの販売利益を得ることができます。

- ■ 〈the + 序数詞 + 最上級 + …〉「X番目に~な…だ」
    - 例 This advertising agency has **the second largest market share** in Japan.
      この広告代理店は日本で2番目に大きな市場シェアを持っています。

テーマ解説

前置詞の働き

前置詞は、名詞(句)の前に置いて、その名詞(句)を文の他の要素とつなげる語です。文中で前置詞句と呼ばれる意味のまとまりを作り、形容詞のように名詞を修飾したり、副詞のように動詞を修飾したりします。次の1つ目の文では、in Boston という前置詞句が our US office(名詞句)を後ろから修飾しており、機能的には形容詞の働きをしています。一方、2つ目の文の in Boston は is located(述語動詞)を修飾しており、副詞の働きをしています。

例 Please visit **our US office in Boston**.　ボストン市内にある当社の米国事務所へ、ぜひおいでください。

Our US office **is located in Boston**.　当社の米国事務所はボストン市内に位置しています。

前置詞が持つ基本のイメージ

前置詞は複数の意味で用いられることが多いですが、それぞれの前置詞には共通した基本のイメージがあります。例えば前置詞inは「内部」が基本のイメージで、空間的および時間的な「内部」を表します。

例 Our office is located **in** Building A.　私たちの事務所は A 棟内に位置しています。

We look forward to seeing you **in** May of next year.　来年の 5 月にお会いできるのを楽しみにしています。

次の前置詞も「空間」「時間」の両方を表します。基本のイメージを確認してください。

[前置詞]　　[基本のイメージ]
- at　▶　1 点　　例 **at** the corner of the street　通りの角で　　**at** 9 o'clock　9 時に
- on　▶　接触　　例 **on** the wall　壁に(接触して)　　**on** October 11　10 月 11 日当日に*
　　　　　　　　　　　　　　　　　　　　　　　*日付を面として捉え、その日に接触しているイメージ
- to　▶　到達点・方向　　例 **to** the city　町へ
　　　　　　　　　　It's five minutes **to** seven.　7 時まであと 5 分です。／ 7 時 5 分前です。
- from　▶　出発点・起点　　例 **from** New York　ニューヨーク出身で／ニューヨークから
　　　　　　　　　　　　from April to June　4 月から 6 月まで

前置詞の使い分けは、この基本のイメージの違いが手掛かりになります。以下の2つの文の前置詞 in、at はどちらも日本語で「〜で」と訳しますが、1つ目の文は空間的な「研究所という場所」の中を意味する in が、2つ目の文は「高等教育機関としての大学」という所属先としての場や地点を意味する at が用いられます。

例 Sally was working **in** a laboratory.　Sally は研究所で働いていた。　▶「中で」

Sally was studying archaeology **at** a university.　Sally は大学で考古学を勉強していた。　▶「場で」

この他にも、for「〜へ向かって、〜のために」、before「〜(場所・時間)の前に」、after「〜(場所・時間)の後に」、past「〜(場所・時間)を過ぎて」、through「〜(場所・時間)を通り抜けて」、by「〜(場所)のそばに、〜(期限)までに」、around「〜(場所)の周りで、〜(時間)のころ」、during「〜(特定の期間)の間中ずっと」、of「〜の、〜についての」、about「〜に関する」など、さまざまな前置詞があります。たくさんの用例を通して、感覚的にイメージをつかめるようになりましょう。

群前置詞

2 語以上が組み合わさって 1 つの前置詞のように働く言葉を「群前置詞」と言います。以下の表現はよく使われるものばかりなので、覚えておきましょう。

- owing to 〜「〜のせいで」、because of 〜「〜のために」、thanks to 〜「〜のおかげで」
- in spite of 〜「〜にもかかわらず」
- according to 〜「〜によると」
- apart from 〜「〜を除いて」
- instead of 〜「〜の代わりに」

PART

5

Unit

4

〈動詞 + 前置詞〉の句動詞

前置詞に関連してもう 1 つ押さえておきたいのは「句動詞」です。句動詞とは、動詞が副詞や前置詞と結び付いて 1 つの動詞のように働くものを言います。動詞の語彙を増やす際には、句動詞にも注意を払い、よく見かける句動詞については、用例を通して覚えるようにしましょう。句動詞の語彙が増えてくると、英語での表現力の幅も広がっていきます。

例 Each employee must understand and **abide by** the work rules of our company.

従業員一人一人が当社の就業規則を理解し、順守しなくてはいけません。　▶「〜を順守する」

To **keep up with** a rapid increase of tourists, the hotel has hired additional staff.

観光客の急増に対応するために、そのホテルは追加スタッフを新規雇用してきました。　▶「〜に付いていく」

ウォームアップ

空所に入るのに適した前置詞を選び、文を完成させましょう。

1. I am not entirely sure what to do ------- this problem.

(a) of　　　　(b) about　　　(c) besides

2. We need to complete the project ------- October 15.

(a) about　　(b) in　　　　(c) by

3. On my way to work I always walk ------- the park.

(a) through　(b) on　　　　(c) of

4. She said she had never heard ------- this project before.

(a) on　　　 (b) at　　　　(c) of

5. It is difficult to ------- bad habits.

(a) look for　(b) abide by　(c) get rid of

【解答・訳】

1. (b) ／この問題の対応について私は完全に確信があるわけではありません。　▶ about は「〜に関して」という関連を表す。

2. (c) ／私たちはそのプロジェクトを 10 月 15 日までに完了する必要があります。　▶ by は「〜までに」という期限を表す。

3. (a) ／通勤の途中、私はいつも公園を通り抜けて行きます。　▶ through は「〜を通り抜けて」という意味。

4. (c) ／彼女は、このプロジェクトの話を聞いたことはこれまでないと述べました。　▶ hear of 〜「〜のことを聞く」。

5. (c) ／悪癖を取り除くのは難しいものです。　▶ get rid of 〜で「〜を取り除く」という意味。

TOEIC® L&R の問題文を使って、練習をしましょう。

1～6 の文の空所には前置詞が入ります。(a)、(b) どちらの意味の前置詞が入るのが適切かを答えましょう。

1. Our staff will accept grant proposals ------- March 3 to April 3.

💡 空所の後ろに特定の日付が 2 つ並び、一方には to があることに注目。

(a) ～から   (b) ～の中に

2. You can look at your electricity usage ------- logging on to your online service account.

💡 空所の後半の語句が表す動作と前半の動作の関連に注目。

(a) ～によって   (b) ～のために

3. Ms. Chang was promoted to section chief ------- <u>only six months</u> on the job.

💡 期間を表す語句 (下線部) があるときは、文中の他の箇所との時間的順序を考える。

(a) ～まで   (b) ～の後に

4. Research shows that, ------- <u>eating healthily</u>, <u>exercise</u> is the most important factor in determining adult health.

💡 2 つの下線部が示す内容の関連について考える。

(a) ～にもかかわらず   (b) ～と並んで

5. The Sook-Joo Gyo Library is located slightly ------- the Green Treat Market on Jacob Avenue.

💡 be located「位置している」と相性の良い前置詞は幾つかある。この文では slightly「少し、わずかに」に注目。

(a) ～を過ぎた所に   (b) ～の間に

6. The open access database can be used to search ------- job opportunities at Steinach Publishing.

💡 動詞 search「探す」と相性の良い前置詞を考える。

(a) ～を求めて   (b) ～に

TOEIC® L&R の問題に挑戦します。

右上の目安の解答時間を目標に、自分で時間を計りながら **1 ～ 6** の問題に答えてください。

PART **5**

Unit **4**

1. Our staff will accept grant proposals ------- March 3 to April 3.

   (A) past
   (B) from
   (C) sometime
   (D) in

2. You can look at your electricity usage ------- logging on to your online service account.

   (A) for
   (B) at
   (C) over
   (D) by

3. Ms. Chang was promoted to section chief ------- only six months on the job.

   (A) besides
   (B) after
   (C) until
   (D) about

4. Research shows that, ------- eating healthily, exercise is the most important factor in determining adult health.

   (A) alongside
   (B) indeed
   (C) within
   (D) primarily

5. The Sook-Joo Gyo Library is located slightly ------- the Green Treat Market on Jacob Avenue.

   (A) into
   (B) over
   (C) among
   (D) past

6. The open access database can be used to search ------- job opportunities at Steinach Publishing.

   (A) for
   (B) up
   (C) as
   (D) to

→解答・解説は p.40

1. Our staff will accept grant proposals ------- March 3 to April 3.

(A) past
(B) from
(C) sometime
(D) in

当方の職員が、助成金の申請を 3 月 3 日から 4 月 3 日まで受け付けます。

(A) 〜を過ぎて
(B) 〜から
(C) いつか
(D) 〜の中に

プラクティス

正解 (a) 〜から

空所の前までが「当方の職員が、助成金の申請を受け付ける」という意味であること、空所の後ろに特定の日付を表す語句が 2 つあることから、この文は助成金の申請の受付期間を説明していると推測できる。April 3 の前には「〜まで」という到達点を表す前置詞 to があり、申請期間の終わりの期日を示している。従って、March 3 の前の空所に「〜から」という意味の前置詞を入れて、申請期間の始まりを表すのが適切。

チャレンジ

正解 B 空所の後ろに期日を表す語句が 2 つあり、後半では to April 3「4 月 3 日まで」という終わりの期日が示されているので、------- March 3 を「3 月 3 日から」という受付期間の始まり（起点）を表す表現にする。(B) from が正解。grant「助成金」。proposal「申し出、申し込み」。
(A) (D) 前置詞。
(C) 副詞。

---

2. You can look at your electricity usage ------- logging on to your online service account.

(A) for
(B) at
(C) over
(D) by

お客さまは、オンラインのサービスアカウントにログインすることによって、ご自身の電気使用量を見ることができます。

(A) 〜のために
(B) 〜で
(C) 〜を越えて
(D) 〜によって

プラクティス

正解 (a) 〜によって

空所の前半は「あなたは、自身の電気使用量を見ることができる」、空所の後半は「オンラインのサービスアカウントにログインすること」という意味。文のつながりを考えると、オンラインにログインするという方法によって、電気使用量を見ることができるという内容だと考えられる。(a)の「〜によって」という意味の前置詞が入るのが適切である。

チャレンジ

正解 D 空所の前後の文意を考えると、空所には方法・手段を表す前置詞 (D) by を入れるのが適切である。electricity usage「電気使用量」、log on to 〜「〜にログインする」、account「（コンピューターなどの）アカウント」。
(A) (B) (C) 前置詞。

3. Ms. Chang was promoted to section chief
------- only six months on the job.

(A) besides
(B) after
(C) until
(D) about

Chang さんは、その仕事に従事してわずか 6 カ月後に、課長に昇進しました。

(A) 〜の他に
(B) 〜の後に
(C) 〜まで
(D) 〜について

プラクティス

正解 (b) 〜の後に

空所の前半は「Chang さんは課長に昇進した」、空所の後半は「その仕事に従事してわずか 6 カ月」という意味。内容の時間的順序を考えると、「6 カ月しかたっていないのに課長に昇進した」と考えると意味が通るため、空所には (b)「〜の後に」という意味の前置詞が入る。

チャレンジ

正解 **B** 空所の前後の文意を考えると、空所には (B) after が適切。only は期間の短さを強調している。promote「〜を昇進させる」、section chief「課長」、on「〜に従事して」、job「仕事」。
(A)(C)(D) 前置詞。

---

4. Research shows that, ------- eating healthily,
exercise is the most important factor in
determining adult health.

(A) alongside
(B) indeed
(C) within
(D) primarily

研究が示すところでは、健康的に食事を取ることと並んで、運動することが成人の健康を決定する最も重要な要因です。

(A) 〜と並んで
(B) 確かに
(C) 〜以内に
(D) 主として

プラクティス

正解 (b) 〜と並んで

「健康的に食事を取ること -------、運動することが成人の健康を決める最も重要な要因だ」というのが that 節の意味。健康的な食事と運動の両方ともが健康を維持する重要な要因になり得るというのが自然な文意なので、空所には「〜と並んで」という意味の前置詞が適切。

チャレンジ

正解 **A** 文意から、that 節内の空所を含むカンマで挟まれた挿入句は、「成人の健康を決める最も重要な要因」である主語の exercise「運動」と同じく重要な要因と考えられる。このことから、空所には前置詞の (A) alongside「〜と並んで」が入るのが適切。factor「要因」、determine「〜を決定する」。
(B)(D) 副詞。
(C) 前置詞。

5. The Sook-Joo Gyo Library is located slightly ------- the Green Treat Market on Jacob Avenue.

(A) into
(B) over
(C) among
(D) past

Sook-Joo Gyo 図書館は、Jacob 通りにある Green Treat 市場を少し通り過ぎた所にあります。

(A) ～の中へ
(B) ～を越えて
(C) ～の間に
(D) ～を過ぎた所に

プラクティス

正解 (a) ～を過ぎた所に

図書館の場所を説明している文。空所の直前にある slightly 「少し」と、空所の後の the Green Treat Market「Green Treat 市場」との意味上のつながりに注目すると、(a) の「～を過ぎた所に」という意味の前置詞を入れて、「図書館は、市場を少し通り過ぎた所にある」という意味の文にするのが自然。

チャレンジ

正解 D be located は「位置する」という意味を表し、直後に「どこに」を示す前置詞句が続く。(D) past「～を過ぎた所に」を空所に入れると、slightly とつながり、意味が通る。
(A) 前置詞。
(B) 「～ (空間) を越えたところに」という意味を表すため、slightly とつながらない。
(C) among「～の間に」は 3 者以上、または不特定多数の集合体に交じっていることを表す前置詞。

---

6. The open access database can be used to search ------- job opportunities at Steinach Publishing.

(A) for
(B) up
(C) as
(D) to

そのオープンアクセス・データベースは、Steinach 出版での就業の機会を探す目的で使用することができます。

(A) ～を求めて
(B) ～の上へ
(C) ～として
(D) ～に

プラクティス

正解 (a) ～を求めて

文の前半は「そのオープンアクセス・データベースは使用されることができる」という意味で、不定詞の to 以下でデータベースを使用する目的が示されている。空所の前置詞は to search ------- という不定詞の一部に当たり、job opportunities at Steinach Publishing「Steinach 出版での就業の機会」は不定詞の目的語だと考えられる。「～を求めて検索するために」といった意味になれば、文意として自然。

チャレンジ

正解 A 「そのオープンアクセス・データベースは、就業の機会を探す目的で使用することができる」という意味になるよう、search ------- で「～を探す」という意味の句動詞になるものを、選択肢から選ぶ。search for ～は「～を探し求める」という意味で使われる。(A) for が正解。job opportunity「就業機会」。

$\mathcal{C}$olumn

◀ ビジネスで使える句動詞 ▶

ビジネスの現場で使える、〈動詞 + 前置詞〉の句動詞と例文を紹介します。同義語の動詞も紹介していますので、一緒に覚えてしまいましょう。

PART
5

Unit
4

予定・約束

- **set up** ～「～（の手はず）を整える、～を設定する」

  例　I **have set up** the kick-off meeting for 3 p.m. tomorrow.
  私は、キックオフ会議を明日の午後 3 時に設定しました。
  ▶ arrange「～を手配する」、fix「～（日時）を決める」、schedule「～（日時）を予定する」などが同義語。

- **pencil in** ～「～（人）との予定を仮で入れる、～（会議など）を予定表に入れる」

  例　Call me when you know for sure, but I'll **pencil** you **in** for Monday at 10 A.M.
  はっきりしたら電話を下さい。でも、月曜午前 10 時にあなたとの予定を仮で入れておきますね。
  ▶ 変更の可能性を念頭に置いた上で予定に書き入れるというニュアンス。

- **look forward to** ～「～を楽しみにする」

  例　I **am looking forward to** your presentation.
  あなたのプレゼンテーションを楽しみにしています。
  ▶ 手紙や E メールの締めくくりの言葉としてよく使われる表現。

- **get back to** ～「～へ返信する、～へ答える」

  例　I will share with my boss about the plan and **get back to** you by Thursday.
  その計画については上司に共有し、木曜日までにあなたへご返信します。
  ▶ reply to ～「～へ返信する」、respond to ～「～へ答える」と同様の意味で使われる。

取引・人事・人間関係

- **sign off on** ～「～を許可する」

  例　All board members **signed off on** the merger details.
  役員全員が合併の詳細を承認しました。
  ▶ authorize「～を許可する」、approve「～を承認する」と同様の意味で使われる。米語表現。

- **get ahead in** ～「～で成功する、～で出世する」

  例　In addition to knowledge and motivation, you need superior interpersonal skills to **get ahead in** the advertising industry.
  広告業界で成功するには、知識や意欲に加え、優れた対人スキルが必要です。
  ▶ in は成功している分野や場を示す。

- **look up to** ～「～を尊敬する」

  例　My first supervisor taught me a lot, and I still **look up to** her.
  最初の上司は私にたくさんのことを教えてくれたので、私は今でも彼女を尊敬しています。
  ▶ respect「～を尊敬する」、admire「～を高く評価する」と同様の意味で使われる。

- **measure up to** ～「～（基準・レベル）に達する、～（期待）にかなう」

  例　I am not sure if the new programmer will **measure up to** the quality his predecessor was able to provide.
  その新人プログラマーが、前任者が提供できていた質の高さにまで達するかどうかは分かりません。
  ▶ meet「～を満たす、～にかなう」、match「～に匹敵する」と同様の意味で使われる。

Unit 5　動名詞・不定詞・分詞

テーマ解説

Part 5 で同じ動詞の変化形が選択肢に並ぶ問題の中には、時制ではなく、動名詞・不定詞・分詞のいずれかを選ぶタイプのものもあります。Unit 5 ではこれら 3 つの形と文中での働きを見ていきます。

動名詞・不定詞・分詞の形

原則として、動名詞は動詞の原形の語尾に -ing を付けて表し、不定詞は〈to + 動詞の原形〉で表します。分詞には現在分詞（-ing）と過去分詞（-ed など）があります。

例

動名詞	不定詞	現在分詞	過去分詞
open<u>ing</u>	<u>to</u> open	open<u>ing</u>	open<u>ed</u>

形の上では、動名詞と現在分詞は同じですが、文中での働きが異なります。では、動名詞・不定詞・分詞について、働きごとに分けて、それぞれの例文を見ていきましょう。

名詞（句）としての働き　▶ 動名詞・不定詞

動名詞と不定詞は名詞（句）を作り、文中で主語や動詞の目的語になります。次の 1 つ目の文の動名詞 Smoking は文の主語、2 つ目の文の不定詞 to bring は動詞 forgets の目的語の一部です。

例　**<u>Smoking</u> is one of the top causes of heart diseases.**
喫煙は心臓病の最大の原因の 1 つです。

She always forgets <u>to bring</u> her mobile phone.
彼女はいつも携帯電話を持ってくるのを忘れます。

また、動名詞は前置詞の目的語にもなります。

例　**He came up with a good plan without <u>taking</u> much time.**
彼は大して時間をかけずに良い計画を思い付きました。

形容詞（句）としての働き　▶ 不定詞・分詞

不定詞は文中で形容詞（句）として名詞（句）を修飾することもあります。分詞も同様の働きをしますが、不定詞は修飾する名詞（句）の直後に、分詞は直前あるいは直後に置かれるのが通例です。分詞が名詞（句）を修飾する場合、現在分詞は「〜している」という能動の意味を表し、過去分詞は「〜された」という受け身の意味を表します。次の 1 つ目の文の不定詞 to visit は目的語の名詞句 the opportunity を後ろから修飾し、2 つ目の文の過去分詞 created は、主語の名詞句 A TV commercial を後ろから修飾しています。

例　**I have never had the opportunity to visit Africa.**
私は、アフリカを訪れる機会がこれまでありませんでした。

A TV commercial <u>created</u> by a younger team won the award.
若手のチームによって制作されたテレビコマーシャルが、その賞を獲得しました。

不定詞は文中で副詞句としても働き、「目的」や「結果」を表します。次の文の不定詞句 to prepare for tomorrow's presentation は「明日のプレゼンに備えるために」という目的を表します。

例　She stayed late at the office **to prepare** for tomorrow's presentation.
　　彼女は明日のプレゼンに備えるために、事務所に遅くまでいました。

分詞もまた、「分詞構文」と呼ばれる特定の構文で、副詞句として文に情報を補足することがあります。次の1つ目の文の Overwhelmed by the beauty of the lake「湖の美しさに圧倒されて」、2つ目の文の Speaking in a calm voice「落ち着いた声で話しながら」の分詞句は、それぞれ、文に情報を追加しています。それぞれの分詞（Overwhelmed / Speaking）の状態や動作の主体が、各文の主語（we / she）と一致していることを確認してください。分詞構文はカンマで区切るのが通例です。

例　**Overwhelmed** by the beauty of the lake, **we** decided to stay two more nights.
　　湖の美しさに圧倒されて、私たちはもう2泊宿泊することにしました。

　　Speaking in a calm voice, **she** explained why this wasn't a good idea.
　　落ち着いた声で話しながら、彼女はなぜこれが良い案ではないのかについて説明しました。

なお、Part 5 で同じ動詞の変化形が選択肢に並ぶ問題が出題されて、時制を答えるのか動名詞・不定詞・分詞の可能性を検討するのかについて迷う場合は、まず文の主語と述語動詞を特定するようにしましょう。文の中に述語動詞があり、他の箇所が空所になっているときは、動名詞・不定詞・分詞の可能性を検討します。文中での働きとともに、どれが適切かを考えましょう。

ウォームアップ

1〜5 の文の空所に入るのに適した語または句を選びましょう。

1. We need to replace the ------- manual.

   (a) outdating　　　　(b) outdated　　　　(c) to outdate

2. If you want to go home earlier, you had better start ------- the report in the morning.

   (a) write　　　　　(b) writing　　　　　(c) written

3. All ------- complaints from customers are kept at the general affairs department.

   (a) cataloging　　　(b) cataloged　　　　(c) to catalog

4. The manager said she was looking forward to ------- the new recruits.

   (a) meet　　　　　(b) meeting　　　　　(c) met

5. The city is dealing with an ------- number of commuters every year.

   (a) increasing　　　(b) increased　　　　(c) increase

【解答・訳】

1. (b) ／当社は、古くなったマニュアルを差し替える必要があります。

2. (b) ／もし早めに帰宅したいなら、午前中に報告書を書き始めた方がいいですよ。

3. (b) ／顧客からの分類済みの苦情全てが総務部に保管されています。

4. (b) ／部長は、新入社員と会うのを楽しみにしていると述べました。

5. (a) ／市は、毎年増え続ける通勤通学者の問題に対処しています。

TOEIC® L&R の問題文を使って、練習をしましょう。

1 1、2 の（　　）に入る動詞が「動名詞・不定詞・分詞」のどれだと適切かを (a) 〜 (c) から選びましょう。

1. By (open) offices in London, Paris, and Madrid, Sedgehill Ltd. has continued its growth into markets overseas.

💡 文頭に前置詞 By があることに注目。

(a) 動名詞
(b) 不定詞
(c) 分詞

2. The inspector will ensure that all newly (construct) commercial buildings comply with applicable codes and regulations.

💡 that 節内の主語の名詞との関係を考える。

(a) 動名詞
(b) 不定詞
(c) 分詞

2 3 〜 6 の下線部の意味を自分なりに推測して書いてみましょう。なお、（　　）の動詞は変化する可能性があります。

3. When (speak) with potential clients, remember to tell them about Gansen Capital's upcoming promotional event.

推測した意味 _____

4. *Trees Across the World*, a documentary film (depict) forest diversity, won a top prize at the arts festival.

推測した意味 _____

5. The new computer security program allows users to (monitor) any suspicious activity on their account.

推測した意味 _____

6. Poland Cell Tel is beginning a multibillion-euro process to (expand) its network.

推測した意味 _____

チャレンジ

TOEIC® L&R の問題に挑戦します。

右上の目安の解答時間を目標に、自分で時間を計りながら **1 ～ 6** の問題に答えてください。

1. By ------- offices in London, Paris, and Madrid, Sedgehill Ltd. has continued its growth into markets overseas.

   (A) opening
   (B) opened
   (C) opens
   (D) open

2. The inspector will ensure that all newly ------- commercial buildings comply with applicable codes and regulations.

   (A) constructing
   (B) construct
   (C) constructed
   (D) constructive

3. When ------- with potential clients, remember to tell them about Gansen Capital's upcoming promotional event.

   (A) spoken
   (B) speaking
   (C) spoke
   (D) to speak

4. *Trees Across the World*, a documentary film ------- forest diversity, won a top prize at the arts festival.

   (A) depiction
   (B) depicts
   (C) depicting
   (D) depicted

5. The new computer security program allows users to ------- any suspicious activity on their account.

   (A) monitoring
   (B) monitors
   (C) monitored
   (D) monitor

6. Poland Cell Tel is beginning a multibillion-euro process to ------- its network.

   (A) expanding
   (B) expand
   (C) be expanded
   (D) have expanded

→解答・解説は p.48

1. By ------- offices in London, Paris, and Madrid, Sedgehill Ltd. has continued its growth into markets overseas.

(A) opening
(B) opened
(C) opens
(D) open

ロンドン、パリ、マドリードに事務所を開設することによって、Sedgehill 社は海外市場へ成長を続けています。

＊選択肢の訳は省略

プラクティス

正解 (a) 動名詞

手段を表す前置詞 By が直前にあるので、続く箇所には名詞相当語句が入ると分かる。前置詞の後に続けられるのは (a) 動名詞。

チャレンジ

正解 A 動詞 open「～を開設する」の適切な形を選ぶ。直前に手段を表す前置詞 By があることから、空所には動詞を名詞化した動名詞が入るのが適切。「ロンドン、パリ、マドリードに事務所を開設することによって」という意味にすると、後半の「Sedgehill 社は海外市場へ成長を続けている」という内容とも合う。よって、正解は (A)。growth「成長」。
(B) 過去分詞または過去形。
(C) 三人称単数現在形。
(D) 動詞の原形。

2. The inspector will ensure that all newly ------- commercial buildings comply with applicable codes and regulations.

(A) constructing
(B) construct
(C) constructed
(D) constructive

検査官は、新しく建設された全ての商業ビルが適用条令および規制を順守していることを保証します。

(A) ～を建設している
(B) ～を建設する
(C) 建設された
(D) 建設的な

プラクティス

正解 (c) 分詞

動詞 ensure「～を保証する、～を確実にする」の目的語に当たる that 節内の主語の一部である。直後に commercial buildings「商業ビル」という主語の名詞句があるので、形容詞的な働きをする分詞を入れて、どんな商業ビルなのかを示すのが適切である。

チャレンジ

正解 C 選択肢には動詞 construct「～を建設する」の変化した形や派生語が並ぶ。空所は that 節の主語に当たる名詞 commercial buildings「商業ビル」を修飾する分詞を入れるのが適切。分詞の可能性があるのは (A)、(C) だが、受け身を表す (C) constructed を空所に入れて「新しく建設された全ての商業ビル」とすると、意味が通る。inspector「検査官」、comply with ～「～を順守する」、regulation「規則」。
(A) 現在分詞または動名詞。
(B) 動詞の原形。
(D) 形容詞。

3. When ------- with potential clients, remember to tell them about Gansen Capital's upcoming promotional event.

(A) spoken
(B) speaking
(C) spoke
(D) to speak

見込み客と話すときは、Gansen Capital 社が近日行う販売促進イベントのことを忘れずに伝えてください。

＊選択肢の訳は省略

プラクティス

推測した意味 見込み客と話すときは

When (speak) with potential clients, は、remember to tell them about ... という命令文に、副詞的に情報を補足している分詞構文だと考えられる。よって、speak を speaking に変化させ、「(あなたが) 見込み客と話すときは」という意味だと考えるのが適切。

チャレンジ

正解 B 選択肢は全て動詞 speak「話す」の変化した形。when *doing* は「～するとき」という意味を表す。空所には (B) speaking を入れて、「見込み客と話すときは」という意味にすると、主節の命令文を修飾する副詞句になり、文意が通る。この形は文法上は分詞構文だが、意味をはっきりさせるために、分詞の直前に接続詞の when を置いている。potential「潜在的な」、upcoming「近づいている、今度の」。
(A) 過去分詞。
(C) 過去形。
(D) 不定詞。

---

4. *Trees Across the World*, a documentary film ------- forest diversity, won a top prize at the arts festival.

(A) depiction
(B) depicts
(C) depicting
(D) depicted

森林の多様性を描いているドキュメンタリー映画『世界の木々』は、芸術祭で最高賞を獲得しました。

(A) 描写
(B) ～を描く
(C) ～を描いている
(D) 描かれた

プラクティス

推測した意味 森林の多様性を描いている
ドキュメンタリー映画

カンマで挟まれた a documentary film (depict) forest diversity は、*Trees Across the World* の言い換え表現で、(depict) forest diversity は名詞句 a documentary film を後ろから修飾していると考えられる。よって、depict を depicting に変化させ、下線部は「森林の多様性を描いているドキュメンタリー映画」という意味を表すと考えるのが適切。

チャレンジ

正解 C 選択肢は全て動詞 depict「～を描く」の変化した形。空所を含む名詞句 a documentary film ------- forest diversity は、直前の映画名 *Trees Across the World* の補足説明なので、現在分詞の (C) depicting を入れて、後ろから a documentary film を修飾する形にするのが適切。forest diversity は depict の目的語に当たる。diversity「多様性」、win「～ (賞など) を獲得する」、prize「賞」。
(A) 名詞。
(B) 三人称単数現在形。
(D) 過去分詞または過去形。

5. The new computer security program allows users to ------- any suspicious activity on their account.

(A) monitoring
(B) monitors
(C) monitored
(D) monitor

新しいコンピューター・セキュリティープログラムは、ユーザーが自身のアカウントに関する疑わしい動きを監視できるようにします。

＊選択肢の訳は省略

プラクティス

推測した意味 疑わしい動きを監視すること

文中の動詞 allows に注目する。allow は不定詞と組み合わさって、allow 〜 to do「〜が…することを可能にする」という意味を表す。よって、monitor は変化せず、下線部の意味は「疑わしい動きを監視すること」だと考えられる。

チャレンジ

正解 D 動詞 monitor「〜を監視する」の適切な形を選ぶ。空所の前に to があることに注目する。allow 〜 to do で「〜が…することを可能にする」という意味で、to do は不定詞。よって、空所には (D) の動詞の原形が入るのが適切である。suspicious「疑わしい」。
(A) 動名詞または現在分詞。
(B) 三人称単数現在形。
(C) 過去分詞または過去形。

6. Poland Cell Tel is beginning a multibillion-euro process to ------- its network.

(A) expanding
(B) expand
(C) be expanded
(D) have expanded

Poland Cell Tel 社は、自社ネットワークを拡張するという数十億ユーロ規模の措置を開始しようとしています。

＊選択肢の訳は省略

プラクティス

推測した意味 自社ネットワークを拡張する（という）

直前に to があるので、to (expand) は不定詞だと考えられる。よって、expand は変化せず、下線部は後ろから a multibillion-euro process を形容詞的に修飾して、「ネットワークを拡張する（という）」という意味を表していると考えられる。

チャレンジ

正解 B 動詞 expand「〜を拡張する」の適切な形を選ぶ。主語は Poland Cell Tel、述語動詞は is beginning で、a multibillion-euro から文末までの長い名詞句が目的語だと考えられる。この不定詞は a multibillion-euro process「数十億ユーロ規模の措置」を後ろから修飾し、工程の内容を説明していると考えられる。
(A) 動名詞または現在分詞。
(C) 〈be 動詞＋過去分詞〉。
(D) 現在完了形。

Column

◀ その他の動名詞・不定詞・分詞の用法 ▶

目的語は動名詞と不定詞のどちら？

動名詞と不定詞は名詞（句）を作るため、どちらも動詞の目的語になります。ただ、動名詞と不定詞のどちらを目的語として取るのかは、動詞によって異なります。以下で確認しましょう。

[動名詞を目的語に取る動詞]
　admit「～を認める」、avoid「～を避ける」、consider「～を検討する」、deny「～を否定する」、enjoy「～を楽しむ」、finish「～を終了する」、imagine「～を想像する」、keep「～を続ける」、mind「～を気にする」、miss「～をし損なう」、suggest「～を提案する」、quit「～をやめる」

[不定詞を目的語に取る動詞]
　care「～したいと思う」、decide「～を決める」、demand「～を要求する」、expect「～を期待する」、hope「～を希望する」、want「～したいと思う」、manage「どうにか～する」、mean「～するつもりである」、offer「～を申し出る」、pretend「～のふりをする」

[不定詞も動名詞も目的語に取る動詞]
　like「～を好む」、start「～を始める」、begin「～を始める」、continue「～を続ける」

[不定詞と動名詞のどちらを目的語に取るかで意味が変わる動詞]
　forget *doing*「～したことを忘れる」／ forget to *do*「～するのを忘れる」
　remember *doing*「～したことを覚えている」／ remember to *do*「～することを覚えている」

動名詞・不定詞・分詞の慣用表現

以下は動名詞・不定詞・分詞を用いた慣用表現です。覚えて使ってみましょう。

■ **worth *doing*「～する価値がある」**
　例　Chinese may be hard, but it is **worth learning**.
　　　中国語は難しいかもしれませんが、学ぶ価値があります。

■ **be good at *doing*「～が得意である」、be bad at *doing*「～が苦手である」**
　例　He **is good at** creating persuasive slides.
　　　彼は説得力のあるスライドを制作することが得意です。

■ **be happy to *do*「～するのがうれしい」、be sad to *do*「～するのが悲しい」**
　例　I am **happy to announce** that this has been our best quarter this year.
　　　今年度最高の四半期となったことを発表でき、うれしいです。

■ **too ～ to *do*「…するには～過ぎる、～過ぎて…できない」**
　例　This building is **too** beautiful **to destroy**.
　　　この建物は壊すには美し過ぎます。

■ **generally speaking「一般的に言って、概して」**
　例　**Generally speaking**, our company does not work with individual clients.
　　　一般的に申し上げて、当社は個人のお客さまとはお取引いたしません。

■ **while *doing*「～しながら」**
　例　Working **while listening** to music actually increases productivity.
　　　音楽を聞きながら働くことは、実は生産性を向上させます。

PART
5
Unit
5

Unit 6　名詞・代名詞

🔊 テーマ解説

文の主要素として働く名詞

名詞は、主語・目的語・補語など文の主要素として働く重要な役割を担う品詞です。Part 5 では、適切な名詞を選ぶ問題が多く出題されるので、以下の語彙増強の例を参考に、地道に語彙を増やしていきましょう。

■ **派生語別にまとめる**　派生語とは共通の語幹を持つ単語のことで、いわば複数の単語に枝分かれした「単語の家族」のようなものです。例えば名詞 response「反応」には responsible「責任がある」と responsive「機敏に反応する」の2つの形容詞の派生語があり、そこからさらに responsibility「責任」と responsiveness「反応の機敏さ」という名詞の派生語が存在します。このように1つの語の意味を辞書で調べるときに、共通の語幹を持つ語を関連語彙として洗い出す癖をつけると、語彙力増強に役立ちます。名詞を作る接頭辞 (bi-、sub-、sur-、inter-、co-、in-、ex- など) や接尾辞 (-tion、-sion、-ty、-ity、-ence、-ance、-ness、-ent、-ant、-ry、-age、-ness など) の知識もあると、派生語を見抜きやすくなるでしょう。

■ **使用場面別にまとめる**　場面ごとに関連する名詞をまとめて整理するのも語彙増強には有効です。例えば、「求人・求職」、「観光ツアー」、「建築工事」などのトピックに関する名詞を列挙してみましょう。例文と複数の名詞を一緒にまとめておくと、状況や場面とセットで意味を思い起こしやすくなります。

　　例　トピック：求人・求職

application	応募書類	Attached please find my **application** and **résumé** highlighting my **qualifications** for the **position** of accountant.
résumé	履歴書	
qualification	適性、資格	添付の応募書類と、会計担当者の職に対する私の適性を特に詳述した履歴書を、どうぞご確認ください。
position	職	

人称代名詞・所有代名詞・再帰代名詞

Part 5 では人称代名詞の知識を問う問題も出題されます。人・物を指し示す人称代名詞は、主格・所有格・目的格など文中の働きによって形を変えます。「所有格 + 名詞」を「〜の物」の1語で表す所有代名詞や、語尾に -self (複数形は -selves) が付いて「〜自身」を表す再帰代名詞もあります。

		人称代名詞			所有代名詞	再帰代名詞
		主格	所有格	目的格		
単数	一人称	I	my	me	mine	myself
	二人称	you	your	you	yours	yourself
	三人称	he	his	him	his	himself
		she	her	her	hers	herself
		it	its	it	—	itself
複数	一人称	we	our	us	ours	ourselves
	二人称	you	your	you	yours	yourselves
	三人称	they	their	them	theirs	themselves

再帰代名詞は目的語として用いられる他、名詞や代名詞を強調する用法があります。次の例では、themselves がなくても文は成立しますが、名詞 job applicants が強調される意味合いが加わります。

例 Please review the documents **job applicants themselves** have prepared.
　求職者たち自らが用意した書類を、よく確認してください。

不定代名詞

Part 5 では、不特定の物・人・数量を表す不定代名詞の知識を問う問題が出題されることもあります。some、every、any、no の語尾に -one、-body、-thing を付けた以下の不定代名詞は、三人称単数扱いになることを覚えておきましょう。

- someone「誰か」、 anyone「誰でも」、 no one「誰も〜ない」、 everyone「全員」
- somebody「誰か」、anybody「誰でも」、nobody「誰も〜ない」、everybody「全員」
- something「何か」、anything「何でも」、nothing「何も〜ない」、everything「全ての物」

例 There are 40 people working in accounting. **Everybody is** in the conference room.
　経理部には 40 人が働いています。全員が会議室の中にいます。

other「他の物・他の人」、another「もう 1 つ・もう 1 人」、one「1 つ・1 人」、each「それぞれ」、either「どちらか一方」、neither「(否定文で) どちらも〜ない」、both「両方」なども、不特定の物・人・数量を表します。これらは形容詞として名詞を修飾することもあります (その他の不定代名詞の用法 → p.59)。

ウォームアップ

1 空所に入るのに適切な語を選びましょう。

1. Having an MBA is not ------- to apply for this job, but it would definitely be an advantage.

　(a) an assessment　　　(b) an evaluation　　　(c) a requirement

2. The new ------- of the agreement allows us more flexibility.

　(a) version　　　(b) conference　　　(c) conclusion

3. Building ------- is the responsibility of the landlord, not the tenants.

　(a) acknowledgment　　(b) maintenance　　(c) measure

2 下線部に入るのに適切な代名詞を入れ、文を完成させましょう。

Mr. Jackson asked me if Jane was off today. I told **1.**＿＿＿＿ I hadn't seen **2.**＿＿＿＿ but I was sure **3.**＿＿＿＿ was here because we both participated in a conference call earlier today.

【解答・訳】
1 **1.** (c) ／ MBA の資格を持っていることはこの仕事に応募する必須条件ではありませんが、間違いなく有利になるでしょう。
　2. (a) ／新版の同意書は私たちにもっと柔軟性を与えてくれます。
　3. (b) ／建物の保守の責任は家主にあり、賃借人にはありません。
2 **1.** him　**2.** her　**3.** she ／ Jackson さんが私に、今日 Jane は休みかと尋ねてきました。私は彼に、彼女と会ってはいないが、今朝の電話会議に私たちは 2 人ともが参加していたので、彼女がここにいるのは間違いない、と言いました。

TOEIC® L&R の問題文を使って、練習をしましょう。

1 1～3 の空所に入る名詞の適切な意味を (a)～(d) から選びましょう。

1. Please provide as many ------- as possible when leaving a message for the technical-support team.
   (a) 品目
   (b) 詳細
   (c) 計画
   (d) 個人

2. Building public awareness of environmental issues is the primary ------- of the Florida Conservancy Group.
   (a) 使命
   (b) 理由
   (c) 手配
   (d) 紹介

3. ------- of the marketing assistant include coordinating focus groups and writing detailed reports.
   (a) 宣伝
   (b) 提供
   (c) 製造
   (d) 責務

2 4 の (　　) に入る代名詞を適切な形に変化させ、文を完成させましょう。

4. Today, in place of spokesperson Hiro Ueda, President Akiko Nomura (she) will speak with reporters.

          _____

3 5、6 の空所に入る代名詞が「人」を表すか「物」を表すかを答えましょう。

5. Joanna Nugent, CEO of Freshest Face, Inc., has earned the respect of virtually ------- in the cosmetics industry.
   (a) 人　　　　　　　　　(b) 物

6. The course taught by Prof. Brennink is intended for ------- interested in medical or health-related careers.
   (a) 人　　　　　　　　　(b) 物

チャレンジ

TOEIC® L&R の問題に挑戦します。

右上の目安の解答時間を目標に、自分で時間を計りながら **1 ～ 6** の問題に答えてください。

1. Please provide as many ------- as possible when leaving a message for the technical-support team.

  (A) items
  (B) details
  (C) programs
  (D) individuals

2. Building public awareness of environmental issues is the primary ------- of the Florida Conservancy Group.

  (A) mission
  (B) reason
  (C) arrangement
  (D) reference

3. ------- of the marketing assistant include coordinating focus groups and writing detailed reports.

  (A) Promotions
  (B) Offerings
  (C) Productions
  (D) Responsibilities

4. Today, in place of spokesperson Hiro Ueda, President Akiko Nomura ------- will speak with reporters.

  (A) she
  (B) her
  (C) hers
  (D) herself

5. Joanna Nugent, CEO of Freshest Face, Inc., has earned the respect of virtually ------- in the cosmetics industry.

  (A) everyone
  (B) anything
  (C) whatever
  (D) each other

6. The course taught by Prof. Brennink is intended for ------- interested in medical or health-related careers.

  (A) either
  (B) those
  (C) which
  (D) whom

→解答・解説は p.56

1. Please provide as many ------- as possible when leaving a message for the technical-support team.

(A) items
(B) details
(C) programs
(D) individuals

技術サポートチームに伝言を残す場合は、できるだけ多くの詳細をご提供ください。

(A) 品目
(B) 詳細
(C) 計画
(D) 個人

プラクティス

正解 (b) 詳細

Please から possible までの文の前半が「できるだけ多くの ------- を提供してほしい」という意味で、後半の when 以降が「技術サポートチームに伝言を残す場合は」という条件を表している。伝言を残す場合に重要なのは、できるだけ多くの「詳細」である。

チャレンジ

正解 **B** 選択肢は全て名詞の複数形が並ぶので、文意に合う名詞を選ぶ。when 節の「技術サポートチームに伝言を残す場合は」という状況で、できるだけ多く提供してほしいものとして適切なのは、「詳細」を意味する (B) details である。provide「～を提供する」、as many ～ as possible「できるだけ多くの～」、leave a message「（電話などで）伝言を残す」、technical-support「（パソコンやソフトウエアなどの）技術サポートの」。

2. Building public awareness of environmental issues is the primary ------- of the Florida Conservancy Group.

(A) mission
(B) reason
(C) arrangement
(D) reference

環境問題に対する市民の意識を高めることが、フロリダ自然保護団体の主たる使命です。

(A) 使命
(B) 理由
(C) 手配
(D) 紹介

プラクティス

正解 (a) 使命

文の主語は Building public awareness of environmental issues「環境問題に対する市民の意識を高めること」で、空所は A is B. という文の B の補語の一部に当たる。よって、主語の内容がフロリダ自然保護団体の何であるかを考えればよい。文意から、(a) の「使命」が適切である。

チャレンジ

正解 **A** 選択肢には全て名詞が並ぶ。「環境問題に対する市民の意識を高めることが、フロリダ自然保護団体の主たる ------- だ」という文全体の意味を考えると、空所には「使命」を意味する (A) mission を入れるのが適切だと判断できる。build「～を構築する」、public awareness「市民の意識、社会の認識」、environmental「環境の」、issue「問題」、primary「主たる、最上位の」、conservancy「自然保護団体」。
(B)「主たる理由」では、文意が不適切である。
(C)(D) いずれも意味が通らない。

3. ------- of the marketing assistant include coordinating focus groups and writing detailed reports.

(A) Promotions
(B) Offerings
(C) Productions
(D) Responsibilities

マーケティング・アシスタントの責務には、フォーカスグループの取りまとめと、詳細な報告書の作成が含まれます。

(A) 宣伝
(B) 提供
(C) 製造
(D) 責務

5

Unit

6

プラクティス

正解 (d) 責務

動詞 include「～を含む」の目的語として、coordinating focus groups と writing detailed reports が述べられている。おそらく the marketing assistant の業務内容について述べた文だと推測できるので (d) の「責務」なら文意が通る。

チャレンジ

正解 D 選択肢には全て名詞が並ぶ。文意から、include 以降の「フォーカスグループを取りまとめること」と「詳細な報告書を作成すること」はマーケティング・アシスタント職の業務内容を説明していると考えられることから、空所には「責務」を意味する (D) Responsibilities が適切である。coordinate「～を取りまとめる、～を調整する」、focus group「〈マーケティング用語で〉フォーカスグループ」、detailed「詳細な」、report「報告書、レポート」。

---

4. Today, in place of spokesperson Hiro Ueda, President Akiko Nomura ------- will speak with reporters.

(A) she
(B) her
(C) hers
(D) herself

本日は、広報担当者の Hiro Ueda に代わり、社長である Akiko Nomura 自らが記者たちと話をします。

(A) 彼女は
(B) 彼女を
(C) 彼女のもの
(D) 彼女自ら

プラクティス

正解 herself

文の主語は President Akiko Nomura、述語動詞は will speak で、文の要素として欠けているものがない。強意を表す再帰代名詞の herself ならば、「Akiko Nomura 自らが話をします」という意味合いになり、適切である。

チャレンジ

正解 D 選択肢は全て she の変化した代名詞が並ぶ。空所を除いても文意が成り立つことから、空所には、直前の主語の固有名詞 (President Akiko Nomura) を強める代名詞が入ると考えられる。再帰代名詞の (D) herself が正解。in place of ～「～の代わりに」、spokesperson「〈企業などの〉広報担当」。
(A) 主格。
(B) 所有格。
(C) 所有代名詞。

5. Joanna Nugent, CEO of Freshest Face, Inc., has earned the respect of virtually ------- in the cosmetics industry.

(A) everyone
(B) anything
(C) whatever
(D) each other

Freshest Face 社の CEO である Joanna Nugent は、化粧品業界にいるほぼ全ての人の尊敬を得ています。

(A) 全ての人
(B) 何か
(C) 何でも
(D) お互い

プラクティス

正解 (a) 人

文意から、Joanna Nugent という人物評の 1 文だと分かる。2 つ目の of 以下は、述語動詞 has earned の目的語 the respect「尊敬」を後ろから修飾する句であり、「～の尊敬」という意味になるので、空所には「人」を表す代名詞が適切。

チャレンジ

正解 A

文意に合う代名詞を選択する。文の大意は、Joanna Nugent が尊敬を集めているということであり、空所は「～の尊敬」の「～」に当たる。直前に virtually という副詞があることからも、「全ての人」という意味を表す (A) everyone が正解。earn「～(評判) を博する、～を得る」、respect「尊敬」、virtually「ほとんど、事実上」、cosmetics industry「化粧品業界」。
(B) (C) (D) いずれも文意に合わない。

---

6. The course taught by Prof. Brennink is intended for ------- interested in medical or health-related careers.

(A) either
(B) those
(C) which
(D) whom

Brennink 教授が教える課程は、医療または健康関連の職業に興味がある人々を対象にしています。

(A) どちらか一方
(B) 人々
(C) どちら
(D) 誰を

プラクティス

正解 (a) 人

be intended for ～で「～を対象としている、～に向けられている」という意味を表す。この文は特定の教科課程の対象受講者について述べた文だと考えられるので、空所には「人」を表す代名詞が適切。

チャレンジ

正解 B

文意に合う代名詞を選択する。空所の後ろの interested in medical or health-related careers「医療または健康関連の職業に興味がある」は形容詞句で、空所の代名詞を後ろから修飾していると考えられる。文意から、「(複数の) 人々」を表す (B) those が正解。medical「医療の」、health-related「健康関連の」。
(A) 2 人のうちの「どちらか一方」を表すので不適切。
(C) (D) 関係代名詞と考えたとしても、直前に先行詞が必要。

Column

◀ その他の不定代名詞の用法 ▶

不定代名詞の中には、意味が似ているために使い分けに迷うものがあります。ここでは迷いやすい不定代名詞を幾つか確認しましょう。

other と another

another は「もう 1 つ、もう 1 人」という他の不特定の物・人を表します。一方、other は the other(s) という形で「(残りの) 他の物、(残りの) 他の人」を表します。

例 I've decided to spend **another** year in New York.
> 私はニューヨークでもう 1 年過ごすことに決めました。

Is there **another** way to do this?
> これを実行する別の方法はありますか。

Five employees were told to come to the office at 8 on that day; **the others** were not.
> 5 人の従業員がその日 8 時に出社するよう指示されましたが、その他の人たちは指示されませんでした。

There's no **other** option but to act according to the terms of the contract.
> 契約書の条項に従って行動する以外、他に選択肢はありません。

one、each

one は不特定の複数のうちの「1 つ、1 人」を表します。文中ですでに出ている名詞に対し、繰り返しを避けるために用いられる代名詞です。each は「それぞれ」という意味ですが、注意したいのは、every「どの〜も」との違いです。同じような意味で用いられる場合もありますが every は代名詞ではなく形容詞なので、必ず〈every ＋名詞〉の形になります。一方、each は代名詞として単独で用いることも、形容詞として〈each ＋名詞〉の形で用いることもあります。

例 If you are concerned about the **battery**, you might want to buy an extra **one**.
> バッテリーに不安があるなら、予備をもう 1 つ買った方がいいかもしれません。

Each of us has to come with some ideas.
> 私たち一人一人が、幾つか案を持ち寄らなくてはいけません。

Every employee working here must follow the same rules.
> ここで働く全ての従業員が、同じ規則に従わなくてはいけません。

either、neither、both

それぞれ、either「どちらか一方」、neither「(否定文で) どちらも〜ない」、both「両方」の意味で用いられます。

例 You can borrow **either** of these books, but not **both**.
> この書籍のどちらか 1 冊を借りることができますが、両方ともは駄目です。

また、接続詞 or や and と一緒に用いて、either 〜 or …「〜か…のどちらか一方」、neither 〜 nor …「〜も…もない」、both 〜 and …「〜と…の両方とも」の形でもよく使われます。原則として、「〜」と「…」は語と語、句と句、節と節のように同じ形式を取ることが多い、ということを知っておきましょう。これらの表現については、Unit 7 のコラムで詳しく取り上げます (並列を表すセットフレーズ → p.67)。

Unit 7　つなぐ言葉（接続詞・前置詞）

テーマ解説

Unit 7 では、文の要素と要素をつなぐ接続詞とそれに類する表現を「つなぐ言葉」として、まとめて取り上げます。

並列を表す等位接続詞

and「〜と…」、or「〜か…」、「だが、しかし」という逆接を表す but、「それでも〜」という意味の yet は、前と後ろにある言葉を対等に結び付ける接続詞で、「等位接続詞」と言います。等位接続詞は、語・句・節をつなぎます。次の 1 つ目の文では and が 2 つの動名詞句をつなげ、2 つ目の文では but が 2 つの節をつなげています。

例 **Working from home and working at the office** are not that different for a
programmer.
プログラマーにとって、在宅勤務と会社での勤務はそれほど違いがありません。

I liked the design of the T-shirt, but the price was very high.
私はそのTシャツのデザインが気に入りましたが、価格が非常に高価でした。

副詞節を導く接続詞

節を後ろに続けて、主節を副詞的に修飾する接続詞を「従属接続詞」、その接続詞に導かれる節を「従属節」と言います。

例 The clinic closed last month **because** it wasn't able to hire new doctors.
そのクリニックは、新しい医師を雇うことができなかったので、先月閉院しました。

While you are away from the desk, you should lock your computer.
離席するときは、コンピューターをロックしなくてはいけません。

従属接続詞には以下のようなものがあります。

- **条件** ▶ if「もし〜ならば」、provided (that) 〜「もし〜とすれば」、suppose (that) 〜「もし〜とすれば」、unless「〜でない限り」

  例 Employees may drive to work **provided that** they find their own parking space.
  従業員は、自身の駐車スペースが見つかれば、車で通勤してもよい。

- **譲歩** ▶ though「〜であるけれども」、even though「〜にもかかわらず」、although「〜だけれども」

- **原因・理由** ▶ because「〜であるから、〜なので」、since「〜なので」、as「〜なので」

- **目的** ▶ so that 〜「〜するように」、in order that 〜「〜であるために」

- **時** ▶ when 〜「〜するとき」、after「〜する後に」、before「〜する前に」、until「〜するまで」、once「いったん〜すると」、as soon as「〜するとすぐに」、while「〜する間」

  例 **Once a decision has been made**, we will need to work quickly to implement it.
  ひとたび決断が下されたら、私たちはそれを実行に移すために素早く動かなければいけないでしょう。

名詞節を導く接続詞

that「～であること」、whether「～かどうか」、if「～かどうか」の接続詞に導かれる節は、名詞のように文中で主語、目的語、補語の働きをするので、「名詞節」と呼ばれます。

例　I'm not sure **whether** she can leave the office with us today.

今日彼女が私たちと一緒に会社を出られるかどうかは、分かりません。

The problem is **that** not all board members agree to the program.

問題は、役員全員がその計画に賛同しているわけではないということです。

接続詞と前置詞との区別

despite「～にもかかわらず」、in spite of ～「～にもかかわらず」、because of ～「～のために」、due to ～「～のために」、apart from ～「～は別として」などの前置詞・群前置詞は、似たような意味を表す接続詞と混同しやすいので、注意が必要です。接続詞は後ろに〈主語 + 動詞〉の節が続き、前置詞は後ろに名詞（句）が続くという違いがあります。

例　[接続詞]　**Although** she had undergone extensive training, she wasn't able to respond quickly under pressure.

彼女は徹底的な研修を受けたにもかかわらず、プレッシャーのせいで即答できませんでした。

[前置詞]　**Despite** her extensive training, she wasn't able to respond quickly under pressure.

徹底的な研修にもかかわらず、彼女はプレッシャーのせいで即答できませんでした。

ウォームアップ

1 ～ 4 の文の空所に入るのに適した接続詞または前置詞を選びましょう。

1. We did not invite you to the meeting ------- we did not think that the accounting department would benefit from the discussion.

   (a) because　　　　(b) despite　　　　(c) because of

2. The store will not be able to function properly ------- we finish stocking the shelves by tomorrow.

   (a) since　　　　(b) unless　　　　(c) if

3. We failed to convince the CFO, ------- the fact that we presented a very strong case.

   (a) despite　　　　(b) although　　　　(c) but

4. You do not know about this because the project was terminated ------- you were in New York.

   (a) for　　　　(b) during　　　　(c) while

【解答・訳】

1. (a) ／経理部がその議論で有益な情報を得るとは思えなかったので、あなた方を会議へ招待しませんでした。　▶ 理由を表す接続詞。

2. (b) ／明日までに品出しを終えないと、店はきちんと機能することができないでしょう。　▶ 唯一の例外的条件を表す接続詞。

3. (a) ／非常に強固な事例を提示したという事実にもかかわらず、私たちは CFO（最高財務責任者）の説得に失敗しました。
　　　▶ 前置詞。名詞句の the fact that ... が後に続いている。that 以下は the fact を後ろから修飾している。

4. (c) ／あなたがこの件を知らないのは、そのプロジェクトがあなたのニューヨーク滞在中に終了したからです。　▶ 時を表す接続詞。

TOEIC® L&R の問題文を使って、練習をしましょう。

1 ～ 6 の文の空所には接続詞または前置詞が入ります。(a)、(b) どちらの意味が入るのが適切かを答えましょう。

1. ------- the kiln's heat is set too high, the ceramic objects inside may be ruined.

💡 前半の節と後半の節の内容の関係性に注目。

(a) もし～ならば　　　　　　(b) しかし

2. Ms. Drew <u>was able to attend the popular summer marketing seminar</u> in Lisbon ------- she <u>bought her tickets</u> early.

💡 下線部の行為の関係性に注目。

(a) ～でない限り　　　　　　(b) ～なので

3. ------- all the nominations for board members <u>have been received</u>, a complete list <u>will be posted</u>.

💡 下線部の時制に注目。

(a) いったん～すると　　　　(b) 代わりに

4. The purpose of this survey is to <u>find out</u> ------- the performance of Evonee Cosmetics meets customers' expectations.

💡 空所の後ろの節は、下線部の句動詞の目的語に当たる。

(a) ～であるけれども　　　　(b) ～かどうか

5. The lawyers report that the merger was successfully concluded ------- last-minute negotiations.

💡 last-minute negotiations「土壇場の交渉」に注目。

(a) たとえ～であるとしても　　(b) ～のおかげで

6. The proposed location for the bank branch is ------- the most convenient for our customers, <u>but also</u> the most cost effective.

💡 下線部の表現とセットで使われる表現は何かを考える。

(a) ～だけでなく　　　　　　(b) ～かどうか

TOEIC® L&R の問題に挑戦します。

右上の目安の解答時間を目標に、自分で時間を計りながら **1 ～ 6** の問題に答えてください。

1. ------- the kiln's heat is set too high, the ceramic objects inside may be ruined.

  (A) So
  (B) If
  (C) But
  (D) Why

2. Ms. Drew was able to attend the popular summer marketing seminar in Lisbon ------- she bought her tickets early.

  (A) unless
  (B) finally
  (C) because
  (D) although

3. ------- all the nominations for board members have been received, a complete list will be posted.

  (A) Daily
  (B) Afterward
  (C) Once
  (D) Instead

4. The purpose of this survey is to find out ------- the performance of Evonee Cosmetics meets customers' expectations.

  (A) neither
  (B) whereas
  (C) although
  (D) whether

5. The lawyers report that the merger was successfully concluded ------- last-minute negotiations.

  (A) as well as
  (B) overall
  (C) thanks to
  (D) even if

6. The proposed location for the bank branch is ------- the most convenient for our customers, but also the most cost effective.

  (A) even though
  (B) in case
  (C) not only
  (D) whether or not

→解答・解説は p.64

1. ------- the kiln's heat is set too high, the ceramic objects inside may be ruined.

    (A) So
    (B) If
    (C) But
    (D) Why

窯の温度をあまりに高く設定すると、中の陶器が破損することがあります。

    (A) だから
    (B) もし〜ならば
    (C) しかし
    (D) なぜ

プラクティス

正解　(a) もし〜ならば

空所を含む前半の節は「窯の温度をあまりに高く設定する」という意味で、後半の節は「中の陶器が破損することがある」という意味。前の節で陶器の破損を引き起こす条件が述べられていると推測できるので、(a) の「もし〜ならば」という意味の語が入るのが適切。

チャレンジ

正解　B　空所を含む前半の節は「もし〜ならば」という意味の条件を表し、カンマの後ろの節はその条件の結果が述べられていると考えられるので、空所には (B) If が適切。kiln「窯」、set 〜 …「〜を…に設定する」、ruin「〜を崩壊させる、〜を台無しにする」。
(A)「だから〜」という結果を表す接続詞。通常は直前に原因となる内容が述べられる。
(C)「しかし」という逆接を表す接続詞。
(D) 疑問副詞。疑問文ではないので不適切。

2. Ms. Drew was able to attend the popular summer marketing seminar in Lisbon ------- she bought her tickets early.

    (A) unless
    (B) finally
    (C) because
    (D) although

Drew さんは早めにチケットを購入したので、リスボンで人気の夏期マーケティングセミナーに参加することができました。

    (A) 〜でない限り
    (B) 最後に
    (C) 〜なので
    (D) 〜だけれども

プラクティス

正解　(b) 〜なので

空所の前の節は「Drew さんはリスボンで人気の夏期マーケティングセミナーに参加することができた」という意味で、後の節は「彼女は早めにチケットを購入した」という意味。2つとも過去の出来事について述べている。早めのチケット購入は人気セミナーに参加できた理由に当たるので、(b) の「〜なので」が適している。

チャレンジ

正解　C　空所の前と後ろの節が意味的に自然につながる接続詞を選ぶ。「チケットを早めに購入した」ことが、「人気の夏期マーケティングセミナーに参加することができた」理由だと分かるので、「原因・理由」の副詞節を導く (C) because が適切。attend「〜に参加する、〜に出席する」、marketing「マーケティング、販売促進活動」、early「早期に、早めに」。
(A)「〜でない限り」という唯一の例外的条件を表す接続詞。
(B) 副詞。節を導かない。
(D) 譲歩を表す接続詞。文脈的に不自然。

3. -------- all the nominations for board members have been received, a complete list will be posted.

(A) Daily
(B) Afterward
(C) Once
(D) Instead

全ての役員指名候補が受理された時点で、完全なリストが掲示されるでしょう。

(A) 毎日
(B) 後で
(C) いったん〜すると
(D) 代わりに

プラクティス

正解 (a) いったん〜すると

前半の節が「全ての役員指名候補が受理される」という意味で、後ろの節が「完全なリストが掲示されるだろう」という意味。文意からおそらく、完全なリストが掲示されるのは、役員候補が全て出そろった直後だと考えられるので、空所には(a)の「いったん〜すると」が適切である。

チャレンジ

正解 C 〈主語＋動詞〉の節が２つあり、１つ目の節の前が空所になっているので、節を導く従属接続詞を選ぶ。接続詞は、選択肢の中で (C) Once しかない。nomination「指名、推薦」、board「役員会、委員会」、list「名簿、リスト」、post「〜を掲示する」。
(A)(B)(D) いずれも副詞。節を導かない。

---

4. The purpose of this survey is to find out ------- the performance of Evonee Cosmetics meets customers' expectations.

(A) neither
(B) whereas
(C) although
(D) whether

この調査の目的は、Evonee 化粧品社の業績が顧客の期待に応えているかどうかを調べることです。

(A) 〈〜 nor …を続けて〉〜も…もない
(B) 〜であるのに対して
(C) 〜だけれども
(D) 〜かどうか

プラクティス

正解 (b) 〜かどうか

文の構造を見ると、主語は The purpose of this survey「この調査の目的」で、述語動詞は be 動詞の is、to find 以下が主語を説明する補語に当たる。空所は不定詞の to find out「〜を調べること」の目的語の一部なので、(b)の「〜かどうか」を入れて、「Evonee 化粧品社の業績が顧客の期待に応えているかどうかを調べること」という名詞的な意味にするのが適切。

チャレンジ

正解 D 空所の後ろの節は to find out の目的語に当たるので、「〜かどうか」という意味の名詞節を導く (D) whether が正解。purpose「目的」、survey「調査」、find out 〜「〜を明らかにする」、performance「業績、仕事ぶり」、meet *one's* expectation「〜の期待に応える」。
(A) neither 〜 nor …で「〜も…もない」。
(B) 対比・対立を表す接続詞。
(C) 譲歩を表す接続詞。

5. The lawyers report that the merger was successfully concluded ------- last-minute negotiations.

(A) as well as
(B) overall
(C) thanks to
(D) even if

弁護士たちは、土壇場の交渉のおかげで合併は首尾よく締結されたと報告している。

(A) …だけでなく〜も
(B) 全体として
(C) 〜のおかげで
(D) 〜にもかかわらず

プラクティス

正解 (b) 〜のおかげで

that 節の一部が空所になっている。that 節内を見ると、空所の後ろの名詞句 last-minute negotiations「土壇場の交渉」によって、合併の締結が首尾よくいったという文意だと考えられる。空所には (b) の「〜のおかげで」という意味の表現が入ると、文意が通る。

チャレンジ

正解 C　that 節内の、空所の手前の the merger was successfully concluded「合併は首尾よく締結された」と、直後の last-minute negotiations「土壇場の交渉」という名詞句から、この名詞句は合併締結の要因の 1 つと推測できる。空所には、「〜のおかげで」という意味を表す (C) thanks to が入るのが適切。merger「合併」、successfully「首尾よく」、conclude「〜を締結する」、last-minute「土壇場の」、negotiation「交渉」。
(A) 〜 as well as …で「…だけでなく〜も」という副詞句。
(B) 副詞。
(D)「〜にもかかわらず」という譲歩を表す接続詞。

---

6. The proposed location for the bank branch is ------- the most convenient for our customers, but also the most cost effective.

(A) even though
(B) in case
(C) not only
(D) whether or not

銀行支店向けに提案された場所は、当行のお客さまにとって最も便が良いだけでなく、費用対効果も最も高いです。

(A) 〜にもかかわらず
(B) 〜の場合には
(C) 〜だけでなく
(D) 〜かどうか

プラクティス

正解 (a) 〜だけでなく

空所の後ろを見ると、the most convenient for our customers「最も便が良い」と the most cost effective「費用対効果が最も高い」という対になった表現があり、主語について 2 つの利点が述べられていると考えられる。また、後者の表現の前に but also「しかし〜もまた」があるので、空所には (c) の「〜だけでなく」という意味の表現が入ると、「最も便が良いだけでなく、費用対効果も最も高い」という意味になり、文意として自然。

チャレンジ

正解 C　文の構造をしっかり把握した上で、後半の but also に注目する。not only 〜 but also …「〜だけでなく…も」というセットフレーズを使うと、提案された場所の立地条件について、「最も便が良いだけでなく、費用対効果も最も高い」と利点を述べる内容になり、全体の文意が通る。正解は (C)。proposed「提案された」、branch「支店」、convenient「便利な」、cost effective「費用対効果の高い」。
(A) (B) (D) いずれも接続詞の働きをするが、ここでは文意が通らない。

Column

◀ 並列を表すセットフレーズ ▶

and、or、but などの等位接続詞は、「A も B も」、「A だけでなく B も」、「A か B か」のような、二者を並べて関係を示すセットフレーズを作ります。幾つか例を見てみましょう。

and を使った表現

- **both ～ and …「～と…の両方とも」** ▶「両方とも、どちらも」を強調する表現。

  例 She is **both able and motivated**.
  彼女は有能でやる気もあります。

  I like **both vanilla ice cream and chocolate ice cream**.
  私は、バニラアイスクリームもチョコアイスクリームも両方好きです。

  She is interested in **both polishing her skills as a CPA and becoming better at handling complex projects**.
  彼女は、公認会計士としての自身の技能を磨くことと、複雑なプロジェクトをもっとうまくこなせるようになることの両方に、関心があります。

or、nor を使った表現

- **either ～ or …「～か…のどちらか」** ▶「どちらか一方」を強調する表現。

  例 We are planning to visit **either Italy or France** in August.
  私たちは 8 月にイタリアかフランスのどちらかを訪問する予定です。

  If you want to discuss this matter, you have to **either come to my office first thing in the morning or meet me after work**.
  この件を話し合いたければ、朝一番に私の事務所へ来るか、仕事の後で私と会うかしていただく必要があります。

- **neither ～ nor …「～も…もない」** ▶ both ～ and …とは逆に、両方に対する否定を表す。

  例 **Neither I nor my coworkers** think this is a good idea.
  私も同僚もこれがいい案だとは思いません。

but を使った表現

- **not only ～ but (also) …「～だけでなく…（も）」** ▶ 後者の「…（も）」に重点が置かれた表現。

  例 Our group is considering opening new offices **not only in Indonesia but also in Malaysia and Singapore**.
  当グループは、インドネシアだけでなく、マレーシアとシンガポールにも新事務所を開設することを検討しています。

  Our new advertising campaign is doing a great job **not only at bringing in record sales but also at increasing local brand recognition**.
  当社の新しい広告キャンペーンは、記録的な売り上げの獲得だけでなく、地元のブランド認知度向上にも大きな役目を果たしています。

等位接続詞がつなぐ前後の要素が長く複雑になると意味が取りづらくなってしまいがちですが、セットフレーズを中心に、文の構造をしっかりと把握し、何と何が並列されているのかを見極めるようにしましょう。

MEMO

PART

6

長文穴埋め問題

Unit 8　広告・お知らせを読む

テーマ解説

Part 6 の問題

Part 6 は 80 〜 100 語前後の穴あきの文書を読んで、空所に入る適切な語・句・文を選ぶ「長文穴埋め問題」です。1 つの文書につき「語・句を選ぶ問題」3 問と「文を選ぶ問題」1 問で構成されています。

■ **語・句を選ぶ問題（3 問）**　空所に適した語・句を選ぶ問題です。Part 5 と同様に、品詞や動詞の形などを選ぶ問題と、文章全体を読んで、前後の文脈から適切な語・句を選ぶ問題があります。

■ **文を選ぶ問題（1 問）**　空所に入れるのに最も自然な文を選ぶ問題です。「自然」とは、文法・文脈ともに自然であるということです。選択肢の文に it、this などの代名詞があれば前の部分にそれに相当する語句があるか、文を空所に入れたときに前後の文のつながりに違和感がないか、などの観点から、適切なものを選びます。

Part 6 の文書を読む際のポイント

Part 6 では「まとまった量の長文を読む」ということが重要になってきます。以下は、Part 6 のような長文を読む際のポイントです。まずこれを頭に入れておきましょう。

1　**文書形式**　文書の書式やデザインの特徴から、何の文書なのかをつかむ。
2　**発信者と受信者**　誰が誰に情報を送っているのか、発信者と受信者の関係を推測する。
3　**概要（主題や目的）**　文書の主題や書き手の情報発信の目的を捉える。
4　**詳細情報**　情報の流れや関連を考慮しながら、重要な詳細情報を中心に理解する。

Part 6 は日常生活やビジネスの場の実用文書を題材としていますが、Part 7 の文書とは異なって同一の書体でシンプルな見た目をしています。ですから、さまざまな文書の書式の特徴を知識として持っておくと、1　**文書形式**を即座に判断でき、読解の助けになるでしょう。また、実際のテストでは次のような指示文が記載されるので、最初に目を通して、文書の種類を把握するようにしましょう。

例　Questions 131-134 refer to the following advertisement.　問題 131-134 は次の広告に関するものです。

広告の書式の特徴

Part 6 によく登場する文書形式に、広告や通知があります。右は広告の書式の一例です。広告はたいていの場合、1 行目に人目を引くようなタイトル（大見出し）が付いています。読解の際は、タイトルにまず目を通し、誰が何を宣伝しているのか、宣伝文句は何かなどに注意を払いながら、続けて本文を読み進めましょう。タイトルがない場合は、1 〜 2 文目と最後の文の周辺に特に注目します。また、日付や数字が書かれている箇所は、丁寧に読むようにしましょう。

広告の文書形式例

```
┌─────────────────────────┐
│   タイトル（大見出し）      │
├─────────────────────────┤
│           本文            │
│  新商品・サービスの紹介      │
│  割引率などの数字          │
│  セール期間などの日付       │
│  http://www...（ウェブページの URL など）│
└─────────────────────────┘
```

タイトルや本文に感嘆符（！）が多いのも広告の特徴

ウォームアップ

テーマ解説を参考に次の文書を読んだ後、**1 〜 4** の設問に答えましょう。

Riverside is Reopening!

The Riverside Bookstore has served this community for over 25 years. We are excited to ------- that from June 1 we are reopening our store as the Riverside Library Café. Our
3.
customers will be able to enjoy reading our vast collection of books and magazines while having coffee, tea or craft beer. -------. The first floor will have the capacity to seat 20
4.
people, the second floor, 15, and the terrace will accommodate 35 people. Also beginning June 1, the space will be available for events. If you are interested in holding an event at our café, please talk to our staff. Looking forward to seeing you at the Riverside Library Café!

Owner and "Chief Librarian,"

Jack Moses

---

1. 何に関する文書ですか。

　(a) 会社から社員に向けた業務連絡メール

　(b) 店舗から顧客に向けたお知らせ

　(c) 企業から報道機関に向けた新製品の発表

2. 文書の目的は何ですか。

　(a) 閉店のお知らせと長年の愛顧への謝辞

　(b) 近所に姉妹店を開店するという案内

　(c) 新コンセプトでの店舗再開の案内

3. 空所 **3** に入る適切な語を選びましょう。

　(a) announcing

　(b) announce

4. 空所 **4** に入る適切な文を選びましょう。

　(a) We have also made sure you will be delighted by our selection of sandwiches, salads and soups.

　(b) Otherwise, we have to inform you that our store renovation will be delayed until June 15.

【解答】

1. (b)　**2.** (c)　**3.** (b)　**4.** (a)

▶ 文書の書式やタイトルの Riverside is Reopening!、2 文目の from June 1 we are reopening our store... から、文書は店舗から顧客に向けたお知らせで、リニューアルオープンの告知をすることが目的だと分かる。

【訳】

Riverside が再開します！／Riverside 書店は 25 年超にわたり地域の皆さまへサービスを提供してまいりました。このたび私たちは、Riverside ライブラリーカフェとして 6 月 1 日からリニューアルオープンの運びであることを発表でき、非常に喜ばしく思います。お客さまはコーヒーやお茶、クラフトビールを飲みながら、当店の膨大な書籍と雑誌の蔵書をお楽しみいただけます。*当店選りすぐりのサンドイッチ、サラダ、スープにもきっと大喜びしていただけるでしょう。1 階は 20、2 階は 15、テラスは 35 の座席がございます。また、6 月 1 日より当スペースはイベントにもご利用いただけます。当カフェでのイベント開催にもご関心がありましたら、スタッフにお声掛けください。Riverside ライブラリーカフェでお会いするのを楽しみにしています！／店主兼「図書館長」　Jack Moses

*問題 **4** の挿入文の訳

TOEIC® L&R の問題文書を使って、実際に文書を読む練習をしましょう。
1 ～ 2 の指示に従って、次の文書の内容理解に挑戦してください。

Web page

Violet Sky Rewards

The Violet Sky Rewards card has the ------- travel rewards program of any card available.
-------. ① During special events, members can earn double points for purchases made at
specially ------- locations. ② Points can be redeemed to purchase airline tickets, reserve
hotel rooms, or rent cars anywhere in the world. ③ -------, the card offers special perks,
including free checked bags and priority boarding when members book travel with Tilles
Airlines. ④ To get all this for no annual fee, apply at www.vsrewards.com.

---

1. 文書を読み、概要理解に重要と思われる語句や文を丸 (◯) で囲んでみましょう。

2. 1 を参考に、メモを完成させましょう。ア〜ウは適切な選択肢に☑を付け、エ〜キは下線部を分かる範囲で埋めましょう（英語表記可）。

- 文書形式、発信者と受信者：
  （ア．□カード会社　　□宿泊施設 ）から、（イ．□潜在顧客　　□旅行代理店 ）
  へ向けた、（ウ．□会社案内　　□サービスの宣伝 ）のウェブページ。

- 概要（主題や目的）：
  Violet Sky Rewards カードには エ.＿＿＿＿＿＿＿＿＿＿ がある。

- 詳細情報：
① 特別イベントの期間中、会員は、特別な場所での買い物に対し、

  オ.＿＿＿＿＿＿＿＿＿＿ を獲得できる。

② ポイントは次のものと引き換えができる。
  航空券の購入／ホテルの部屋の予約／世界各地での車のレンタル

③ 会員が Tilles 航空で予約をすると、次のものが提供される。
  カ.＿＿＿＿＿＿＿＿　／　キ.＿＿＿＿＿＿＿＿

④ 年会費無料でこれら全てを得るためには、サイトで申し込む。

チャレンジ

TOEIC® L&R の問題に挑戦します。

右上の目安の解答時間を目標に、自分で時間を計りながら 1 ～ 4 の問題に答えてください。

Web page

Violet Sky Rewards

The Violet Sky Rewards card has the ------- travel rewards program of any card available.
1.

-------. During special events, members can earn double points for purchases made at
2.

specially ------- locations. Points can be redeemed to purchase airline tickets, reserve
3.

hotel rooms, or rent cars anywhere in the world. -------, the card offers special perks,
4.

including free checked bags and priority boarding when members book travel with Tilles

Airlines. To get all this for no annual fee, apply at www.vsrewards.com.

---

1. (A) comprehension
   (B) most comprehensive
   (C) comprehensive
   (D) most comprehensively

2. (A) Rewards card members earn one
       point for every dollar spent.
   (B) Rewards card members can pay their
       bills easily on our Web site.
   (C) You have accrued more than 1,500
       points.
   (D) You have been approved for this
       exciting offer.

3. (A) select
   (B) selects
   (C) selected
   (D) selection

4. (A) Therefore
   (B) Regardless
   (C) In addition
   (D) For instance

→解答・解説は p.74

Violet Sky Rewards

❶ The Violet Sky Rewards card has the ------- travel rewards program of any card available.
1.
-------. During special events, members can earn double points for purchases made at
2.
specially ------- locations. Points can be redeemed to purchase airline tickets, reserve
3.
hotel rooms, or rent cars anywhere in the world. -------, the card offers special perks,
4.
including free checked bags and priority boarding when members book travel with Tilles
Airlines. To get all this for no annual fee, apply at www.vsrewards.com.

Violet Sky Rewards

Violet Sky Rewards カードには、市販のカードで最も包括的な旅行ポイントプログラムが付いています。*ポイントカードの会員は、1ドル支払うごとに1ポイントを獲得します。特別イベントの期間中、会員は、特別指定店舗でのお買い物に対し、2倍のポイントを獲得することができます。ポイントは航空券のご購入、ホテルの部屋のご予約、または世界各地での車のレンタルと引き換えることができます。さらにこのカードでは、会員が Tilles 航空で旅行をご予約いただいた場合、預入荷物の無料サービスや優先搭乗などの特典をご提供しています。これら全てを年会費無料で得るには、www.vsrewards.com でお申し込みください。

*問題2の挿入文の訳

語注

reward　報酬
❶ program　計画　★rewards program は利用金額に応じてポイントを付与するプログラム
available　利用可能な、入手できる　　during　〜の間中　　member　会員　　earn　〜を稼ぐ　　double　2倍の
purchase　〈名詞〉買い物、購買　〈動詞〉〜を購入する　　location　場所　　redeem　〜を景品に換える
reserve　〜を予約する　　rent　〜を賃借する　　perks　〈複数形で〉特典　　free　無料の　　checked bag　預入荷物
priority boarding　優先搭乗　　book　〜を予約する　　annual　年間の、年1回の　　fee　料金

プラクティス

1. 例は左図参照。

2. ア．カード会社　　イ．潜在顧客　　ウ．サービスの宣伝　　エ．旅行のポイントプログラム

オ．２倍のポイント　　カ．無料の預入荷物　　キ．優先搭乗

チャレンジ

1. (A) comprehension
(B) most comprehensive
(C) comprehensive
(D) most comprehensively

(A) 包括性
(B) 最も包括的な
(C) 包括的な
(D) 最も包括的に

正解 **B** 形容詞 comprehensive「包括的な、総合的な」の変化した形や派生語が並ぶ。空所の前に定冠詞の the があり、後ろに travel rewards program という名詞句があること、さらに of any card available「市販のあらゆるカードの中で」という同類との比較対象を示す表現があることから、空所には形容詞の最上級を表す (B) が適切。〈the most ＋形容詞〉で「最も～な」という最上級を表す。
(A) 名詞。
(C) 形容詞。
(D) 副詞の最上級。

---

2. (A) Rewards card members earn one point for every dollar spent.
(B) Rewards card members can pay their bills easily on our Web site.
(C) You have accrued more than 1,500 points.
(D) You have been approved for this exciting offer.

(A) ポイントカードの会員は、1 ドル支払うごとに 1 ポイントを獲得します。
(B) ポイントカードの会員は、当社のウェブサイト上で簡単に請求書のお支払いができます。
(C) お客さまは 1,500 ポイント超を獲得されています。
(D) お客さまはこの素晴らしい提案のご利用を認められています。

正解 **A** 空所に適切な文を選ぶ問題なので、空所の前後の文に注目する。前文の❶1 行目では「Violet Sky Rewards カードには、旅行ポイントプログラムが付いている」と紹介されている。空所に続く 2 ～ 3 行目では、特別イベントの期間中、double points「2 倍のポイント」を獲得できるとあり、ポイント付与の仕組みが案内されている。よって、空所の文にもポイントに関する説明文が入るのが、文の流れとして自然。(A) が正解。
(B) ポイントの説明が前後にあるのに、支払いに関する情報が入るのは文脈的に不自然である。
(C) ポイントに関する内容だが、特定の顧客向けの文と考えられ、入会の宣伝という文書の内容にそぐわない。accrue「～を獲得する、～を蓄積する」。
(D) this exciting offer が何を指すのか不明。また、特定の顧客向けの文と考えられるため不適切。approve「～を承認する」。

---

3. (A) select
(B) selects
(C) selected
(D) selection

(A) ～を選ぶ
(B) ～を選ぶ
(C) 選ばれた
(D) 選択

正解 **C** 選択肢には動詞 select「～を選ぶ」が変化した形と派生語が並ぶ。文の構成要素としては at specially ------- locations という前置詞句の一部を成すと考えられるので、空所の後の名詞 locations「場所」を修飾できる語を選ぶ。形容詞の selected「選ばれた」が適切。正解は (C)。
(A) 動詞の原形。
(B) 三人称単数現在形。
(D) 名詞。

4. (A) Therefore
(B) Regardless
(C) In addition
(D) For instance

(A) 従って
(B) それにもかかわらず
(C) さらに
(D) 例えば

正解 **C**　選択肢には副詞の働きをする語句が並ぶ。前後の文脈を踏まえて、適切なものを選ぶ。空所の前の文では、カードに付与されたポイントの使い道が紹介されていたのに対し、空所の後の文では、会員に提供されるその他の特典が案内されている。よって、カードの利点について補足説明をしている文だと考えられるので、「さらに」という意味を表す (C) In addition が正解。
(A) (B) (D) いずれも文の流れとして不自然。

Column

◀ 長文読解に役立つメモ要約の練習 ▶

決められた時間内に、Part 6 や Part 7 のようなまとまった量の長文を読んで内容をつかむには、文章をただ漫然と読むのではなく、読み取りたい情報を具体的にイメージし、目的意識を持って読むことが大切です。「特典の内容は？」「キャンペーンの期間は？」「適用範囲は？」と、自分自身で問い掛けながら読むことで、情報を整理しながら読む習慣が身に付きます。このような読み方を身に付けるのに有効な練習として、メモを取りながら要約をする方法を紹介します。

メモ要約の練習例

テーマ解説で紹介した 1 文書形式、2 発信者と受信者、3 概要（主題や目的）、4 詳細情報という観点から、文書の要約のメモを取ってみましょう。要約のメモの取り方に特別な決まりはありません。英語でも日本語でも自分なりに分かりやすい形でまとめてみるとよいでしょう。以下の例では、まず日本語で読み取りたい項目を列挙し、矢印や黒丸記号を用いながら、読み取った情報を英語で抜き出してメモにしています。

例

> GKG Fine Food Market is a full-service grocery and gourmet food store where shoppers can find fresh local fruits and vegetables and prepared foods. The store also features a wide selection of meats and seafood as well as organic and bulk goods. We specialize in imported and hard-to-find items. Our workers are knowledgeable about the products in each department. They can guide you in selecting just what you need and explain how to prepare it.

文書形式	お知らせ、広告？
発信者→受信者	GKG Fine Food Market → shoppers
お店の特長	・fresh local fruits, vegetables, prepared foods
	・feature → a wide selection
	・specialize in → imported and hard-to-find items
	・workers → knowledgeable about the products

【訳】
GKG 良品マーケットは、お買物客の皆さまが新鮮な地物の果物や野菜、加工食品を見つけることができる食料品雑貨と高級食材の総合店です。当店はまた、幅広い品ぞろえの肉および海産物、そして有機食品やまとめ売りの商品も目玉としています。輸入品や希少品も専門に扱います。当店の各部門の従業員は商品知識が豊富です。お客さまがまさに必要な品物を選ぶご案内をし、調理法についてご説明いたします。

問題集の長文を使い、時間を決めて時間内に要約をメモに取る練習をしてみましょう。メモ要約の練習を重ねていくうちに、やがてはメモを取らなくても頭の中で同じプロセスが踏めるようになり、英文を読むのが楽になってくるはずです。

※ *TOEIC*® L&R の実際のテストでは、問題用紙への書き込みが禁止されています。解答用紙の所定欄以外には何も書かないでください。

Unit 9　記事を読む

テーマ解説

Unit 9 では記事の書式を取り上げます。Unit 8 で紹介した「長文を読む際のポイント」（→ p.70）を踏まえると、記事は、**1 文書形式**が分かった時点で、**2 発信者と受信者**が「記事の執筆者と読者」だと特定されます。ですから、指示文で Questions xxx-xxx refer to the following article. と記載されていた場合は、迷わず **3 概要（主題や目的）** を捉えることから始めましょう。

記事の書式の特徴と読み方

一般に、英文雑誌や英字新聞の記事では、タイトルが提示された後、複数の段落に分かれた本文が続き、序論（introduction）→本論（body）→結論（conclusion）という流れで展開していきます。記事のタイトル（大見出し）は非常に重要な箇所で、記事の趣旨を端的に伝えたり読者の関心を引いたりするために表現が工夫されていますので、タイトルを読めばどんな内容の記事かをある程度推測することができます。また、本文の最初の段落は「リードパラグラフ」とも呼ばれ、記事の主題を簡潔に分かりやすく伝える役割を担っています。リードパラグラフは記事の **3 概要（主題や目的）** に深く関わっているので、最初の段落の 1 文目をしっかり押さえるようにしましょう。1 文目で意味がはっきりとくみ取れないときは 2 文目、3 文目と読み進めます。その後、**4 詳細情報**が続きます。

5W1H（Who、When、Where、What、Why、How）「誰が・いつ・どこで・何を・なぜ・どうやって」をしっかり押さえて、事実関係を的確につかんでいきましょう。記事本文には、～ because …「～なのは…であるので」、also「さらに」、however「しかしながら」、compared to ～「～と比較して」のような接続詞や副詞（句）を用いながら、主題を裏付ける詳細情報や根拠となる事例を説明したり、" ～ ," said Mr. Taylor.「『～』と Taylor 氏は語った」のように関係者の発言を引用したり、記事特有のさまざまな表現や文体が登場します。多くの記事を読んで、それら特有の表現にも慣れていきましょう。

Part 6 の記事の特徴

記事の書式例

> **タイトル（大見出し）**
>
> 場所（日付）――本文
> ・because、also、however ... などの接続詞や副詞（句）
> ・"～ ," said Mr. XXX. などの人物の発言の引用

Part 7 の長い記事は、2 段組になることもある

Part 6 に登場する記事は、80 ～ 100 語前後の語数の比較的短い文章から成ります。1 段落で構成され、全ての情報が本論にまとめられていることが多いです。Part 6 の記事を読む際はタイトルと 1 文目に注目して、まず記事の概要を把握するようにしましょう。

なお、記事の書き出しでは、London（5 June）－「ロンドン（6 月 5 日）―」のように、取材場所と日付が示されることがあります。そのような情報でも、本文の詳細情報の理解に役立つこともありますので、読み飛ばさないように注意しましょう。

ウォームアップ

テーマ解説を参考に、次の文書を読んだ後、**1 〜 4** の設問に答えましょう。

Automobile Sales on the Rise

The Commerce Board predicts that by the year's end national automobile sales will have reached 910,000 units. This figure is 15 percent higher than the -------- year's number and is just short of the all-time high of three years ago. The Board attributes these gains to several factors, including the availability of lower interest rates on car loans. In contrast to the general demand for automobiles, the market for minivans has shown little to no growth these past five years despite intensive advertising efforts. --------.

3.

4.

---

1. 記事の情報源は誰ですか。

   (a) 自動車の販売代理店

   (b) 自動車メーカー

   (c) 商工会議所

2. 記事の主題は何ですか。

   (a) 自動車ローン金利の低下

   (b) 自動車販売台数の予測

   (c) 自動車の広告費の増減

3. 空所 **3** に入る適切な語を選びましょう。

   (a) following

   (b) previous

4. 空所 **4** に入る適切な文を選びましょう。

   (a) Another factor is the changes in consumer preferences.

   (b) It is even expected that some models will not be renewed next year.

【解答】

1. (c)　　**2.** (b)　　**3.** (b)　　**4.** (b)

▶ タイトルの Automobile Sales on the Rise「自動車販売台数が増加傾向」や第 1 文の The Commerce Board predicts that by the year's end national automobile sales will have reached 910,000 units. の下線部表現から、文書は、商工会議所が情報源で、国内の自動車販売台数の予測について報じている記事だと分かる。

【訳】

自動車販売台数が増加傾向

商工会議所の委員会は、年末までに国内の自動車販売台数が 91 万台に達するだろうと予測している。この数字は前年より 15 パーセント高く、3 年前の最高記録にわずかに及ばない。同委員会は、これらの増加は、自動車ローンがより低金利で利用できるようになったことをはじめとした、幾つかの要因によるものだとしている。全般的な自動車需要とは対照的に、ミニバン市場は集中的な広告施策にもかかわらず、過去 5 年間まったく言っていいほど成長していない状態だ。*一部のモデルは、来年モデルチェンジを見送るということすら見込まれている。　　　　　　　　　　　　　　　　　　　　*問題 **4** の挿入文の訳

TOEIC® L&R の問題文書を使って、実際に文書を読む練習をしましょう。
1 ～ 2 の指示に従って、次の文書の内容理解に挑戦してください。

Article

> The Crimson Bay Regional Theater will be extending its run of *Winter in Monterrey*, a play by Edna Riley. ① Because of a sudden surge in ------- for tickets, the last performance will now occur on April 19. ② The move comes as something of a surprise, given the ------- reviews written by critics following the show's opening on March 2. -------. ③ The show, however, has suddenly become popular with younger people, many of whom get their news from online sources. ④ They are ------- interested in the play's exploration of economic issues and career choices.

1. 文書を読み、概要理解に重要と思われる語句や文を丸（◯）で囲んでみましょう。

2. 1 を参考に、メモを完成させましょう。ア～ウは適切な選択肢に☑を付け、エ～キは下線部を分かる範囲で埋めましょう（英語表記可）。

- 文書形式、発信者と受信者：
  （ア. □新聞記者　　□劇場支配人 ）が、（イ. □常連客　　□読者 ）へ向けて書いた、
  （ウ. □宣伝ちらし　　□記事 ）。

- 概要（主題や目的）：
  『モンテレイの冬』という戯曲の上演が エ. _____ 。

- 詳細情報：
  ① チケットの需要が殺到したため、千秋楽は 4 月 19 日に行われる予定。

  ② 初日の評論を考慮すると、この動きは オ. _____ だ。

  ③ 舞台は突然、カ. _____ の間で、キ. _____
  になった。

  ④ 彼らは、この戯曲が描く経済問題と職業選択の追求に関心を持っている。

チャレンジ

TOEIC® L&R の問題に挑戦します。

右上の目安の解答時間を目標に、自分で時間を計りながら **1 ～ 4** の問題に答えてください。

Article

> The Crimson Bay Regional Theater will be extending its run of *Winter in Monterrey*, a play by Edna Riley. Because of a sudden surge in ------- for tickets, the last performance
> **1.**
> will now occur on April 19. The move comes as something of a surprise, given the -------
> **2.**
> reviews written by critics following the show's opening on March 2. -------. The show,
> **3.**
> however, has suddenly become popular with younger people, many of whom get their news from online sources. They are ------- interested in the play's exploration of
> **4.**
> economic issues and career choices.

1. (A) demand
(B) demanding
(C) demanded
(D) to demand

2. (A) brilliant
(B) deep
(C) harsh
(D) prompt

3. (A) Actors from the show are local residents.
(B) The premiere was attended by local business leaders.
(C) The initial box office sales had also been weak.
(D) Moreover, the theater company has been around for several years.

4. (A) apparent
(B) more apparent
(C) apparentness
(D) apparently

→解答・解説は p.82

記事

❶The Crimson Bay Regional Theater will be extending its run of *Winter in Monterrey*, a play by Edna Riley. Because of a sudden surge in ------- for tickets, the last performance will now occur on April 19. The move comes as something of a surprise, given the ------- reviews written by critics following the show's opening on March 2. -------. The show, however, has suddenly become popular with younger people, many of whom get their news from online sources. They are ------- interested in the play's exploration of economic issues and career choices.

 1.

 2.

 3.

 4.

Crimson 湾岸地域劇場は、Edna Riley 作の『モンテレイの冬』という戯曲の上演を延長する。チケットの需要が急に殺到したことにより、千秋楽は 4 月 19 日に行われることになった。3 月 2 日の初日の上演を受けて批評家たちが書いた厳しい評論を考慮すると、この動きは驚くべきものである。*当初の興行収入も低迷していた。しかしながら、この舞台は若い世代の間で突然人気となり、彼らの多くがオンラインを情報源にしている。彼らはどうやら、この戯曲が描く経済問題と職業選択の追求に関心を持っているようだ。

*問題 3 の挿入文の訳

語 注

❶ regional 地域の　　extend 〜（期間など）を延ばす　　run （劇・映画などの）連続公演　　sudden 突然の　　surge 殺到　　performance 興行　　occur 起こる、生じる　　move 動き、（意見などの）変更　　surprise 驚き、驚嘆　　given 〜〈前置詞的に〉〜を考慮すると　　★〜には名詞（句）が入る　　review 評論　　critic 批評家　　following 〜に続いて　　popular with 〜 〜に人気のある　　online オンラインの　　sources 〈複数形で〉情報源　　exploration 探求　　economic 経済の　　issue 問題、問題点　　career 職業、職歴　　choice 選択肢

プラクティス

1. 例は左図参照。

2. ア. 新聞記者　イ. 読者　ウ. 記事　エ. 延長される

　　オ. 驚き　カ. 若者たち　キ. 人気

チャレンジ

1. (A) demand
(B) demanding
(C) demanded
(D) to demand

(A) 需要
(B) 要求の厳しい
(C) 要求された
(D) 要求すること

| 正解 | A |

選択肢には動詞 demand「要求する」が変化した形や派生語が並ぶ。空所を含む in ------- for tickets は前置詞句として、直前の名詞句 a sudden surge「急な殺到」を後ろから修飾している。前置詞 in の後で、後ろの for tickets「チケットを求めて」とつながるのは名詞。(A) demand は「需要」という意味の名詞でもあり、これだと意味が通る。
(B) 形容詞。動詞 demand の動名詞と解釈したとしても、for tickets と意味がつながらない。
(C) 過去分詞。
(D) 不定詞。

---

2. (A) brilliant
(B) deep
(C) harsh
(D) prompt

(A) 素晴らしい
(B) 深い
(C) 厳しい
(D) 即座の

| 正解 | C |

選択肢は全て形容詞なので、文意に合うものを選ぶ。カンマの前の「この動きは驚くべきものだ」という〈主語＋動詞〉の節と、カンマ以降の「3月2日の初日の上演を受けて批評家たちが書いた ------ 評論を考慮すると」という前置詞句の意味がつながるようにするには、harsh「厳しい」を用いて「厳しい評論」という意味にするのが適切。正解は (C)。
(A) (B) (D) いずれも文脈に合わない。

---

3. (A) Actors from the show are local residents.
(B) The premiere was attended by local business leaders.
(C) The initial box office sales had also been weak.
(D) Moreover, the theater company has been around for several years.

(A) 舞台の俳優たちは、地元の住民である。
(B) 初演には地元の企業家のリーダーたちが出席した。
(C) 当初の興行収入も低迷していた。
(D) さらに、その劇団は数年間にわたって活動している。

| 正解 | C |

❶4〜6行目の The show ... の文に、カンマに挟まれた副詞の however「しかしながら」があることから、前文の空所には、これと対立する内容が入ると考えられる。(C)を入れて、当初の興行収入も低迷していた、だがしかし、舞台は若者に突然人気が出たという流れにするのが適切である。initial「当初の、初期の」、box office「興行成績、チケットの売れ行き」。
(A) local「地元の」、resident「居住者」。
(B) premiere「(劇などの) 初日、初演」。
(D) 舞台に関連のある theater company「劇団」が含まれるが、文脈に合わない。around「活動して、健在で」。

4. (A) apparent
(B) more apparent
(C) apparentness
(D) apparently

(A) 見掛け上の
(B) より見掛け上の
(C) 明らかであること
(D) 見たところ

正解 **D** 選択肢には形容詞 apparent「見掛け上の」の原級と比較級、または派生語が並ぶ。空所を含む文の主語は They で、are interested in 以下で興味の対象が示されており、文の要素として不足しているものはない。空所には副詞の (D) apparently「見たところ」が入るのが適切。正解は (D)。
(A) 形容詞。
(B) 形容詞の比較級。
(C) 名詞。

Column

◀ 見出しと第1段落から主題を推測 ▶

記事のタイトルと第1段落には、記事の主題が凝縮されています。以下の2つの記事のタイトルと第1段落を読んで、何についての記事か推測する練習をしてみましょう。

1

Better Blueberries?

(May 6)—Demand for blueberries has been rising worldwide for decades. Such geographically diverse countries as Canada, Peru, South Africa, and Australia now export blueberries. Through plant-breeding techniques, farmers have succeeded in extending the harvest season to ten months while making blueberries bigger, firmer, and more shelf stable.

Q. 何に関する記事ですか。
  (a) ブルーベリーの今年の収穫量   (c) ブルーベリーの関税の引き上げ
★(b) ブルーベリーの品種改良   (d) ブルーベリーを使ったレシピ

タイトルの Better Blueberries から、ブルーベリーの品質向上に関する話だと見当を付け、それを念頭にざっと読んでいくと、1文目に「ブルーベリーの需要が数十年にわたり高まり続けている」とあります。続く2～3文目には、ブルーベリー輸出国はさまざまな地域に広がり、plant-breeding techniques「品種改良の技術」によって、「より大粒かつ丈夫で常温保存ができるように」なったとあります。

2

Winkroth Opens New Plant

BREMEN (6 July)—Winkroth Telefon, the German mobile phone maker with headquarters in our city, has just announced the opening of a manufacturing facility in Toluca, Mexico, on 3 October. The facility will operate under the name Quixera and will be managed entirely locally.

Q. 何に関する記事ですか。
  (a) 新種の植物の発見   ★(c) 海外に新設される工場
  (b) 携帯電話会社の合併   (d) 工場の改装と再開

タイトルの Plant が「植物」か「工場」か一瞬迷ったかもしれませんが、動詞 opens の目的語なので、「工場」だと分かります。企業がどこかに工場を開設した記事だと見当を付けて読むと、1文目で「ドイツの Winkroth Telefon 社が10月3日にメキシコのトルカに製造施設を開設することを発表した」とあります。

【訳】

さらに良質のブルーベリー？／（5月6日）──ブルーベリーの需要は数十年にわたり世界中で高まり続けている。今ではカナダ、ペルー、南アフリカ、そしてオーストラリアなど、地理的に多様な国々がブルーベリーを輸出している。植物の品種改良技術を通じて、農家は収穫期を10カ月間に引き延ばすことに成功するとともに、ブルーベリーをより大粒かつ丈夫で常温保存ができるようにした。

Winkroth 社が新しい工場を開設／ブレーメン（7月6日）──当市に本社を置くドイツの携帯電話メーカー Winkroth Telefon 社は、10月3日にメキシコのトルカに製造施設を開設したと先ほど発表した。この施設は Quixera の名で操業され、全面的に地元で運営される予定である。

Unit 10　Eメール・手紙を読む

テーマ解説

Unit 10 では、Eメールと手紙の書式の特徴を取り上げます。以下でそれぞれの書式を確認しましょう。

Eメールの書式例

```
From:
To:
Subject:            メールヘッダー
Date:
Attachment:


Dear Mr. Jenkins,
□□□□...
□□□      本文


□□□
□□□

Sincerely,
----
XXXXX, Customer Representative,
XXX Ltd.              フッター
```

Eメールの書式の特徴

次のような情報の構造を持っています。特に、メールヘッダーは概要理解の手掛かりになる箇所ですので、必ず目を通しましょう。

- **メールヘッダー**

  From ………… 送信者。

  To …………… 受信者。同報者 (CC) が付くこともあります。

  Subject ……… 件名。頭に Re: が付くこともあります。

  Date ………… 送信日付。

  Attachment … 添付物。ファイル名が表示されます。

- **本文**

  (Dear) Mr./Ms. 〜のように宛先から始まります。親しい間柄では Hi Tom, のように名前で始まることもあります。呼び名から送信者と受信者の親密度をある程度推測することができます。その後、用件の詳細が述べられた後、最後に結びの定型句として、(Yours) Sincerely、(Best) Regards などが入ります。親しい間柄では Thanks などで終わることもあります。

- **フッター**

  送信者の氏名、所属（会社名、部署名、役職名）が書かれます。

手紙の書式の特徴

手紙は Eメールと似た構造を持っていますが、住所やレターヘッドなどから差出人の情報をより詳しくつかむことができるので、それらの箇所も読み飛ばさないようにしましょう。

- **レターヘッド**

  差出人の会社名、住所、電話番号などが記載されています。

- **宛先の氏名・住所**

  宛先の氏名・住所が書かれます。

- **日付**

  本文の前に書かれるのが一般的です。

- **本文**

  用件などの詳細が述べられます。複数の段落に分けられ、「導入部→本論→結論」で構成されるのが一般的です。最後に Sincerely、Best Regards などの結びの定型句が入ります。

- **署名**

  差出人の署名欄です。手書きの署名が基本です。下に氏名、会社名、部署名、役職名などがタイプで印字されます。

- **同封物の有無**

  Enclosure「同封物あり」と明記されることもあります。

手紙の書式例

```
            ACE Travel
    302 W XXX Blvd, XXX CA 90056

Jason Simmons                    レターヘッド
1819 Rochester Ave.
Los Angels, CA 90024    宛先の氏名・住所


May 28                           日付


Dear Mr. Simmons,               本文
□□□□...
□□□


Sincerely,


Tina Eliott
Tina Eliott, Customer Representative,
XXX Ltd.                        署名


Enclosure            同封物の有無
```

テーマ解説を参考に、次の文書を読んだ後、**1 〜 4** の設問に答えましょう。

From: Kenneth Robertson
To: Ana Figueroa
Subject: Bringhurst office
Date: December 12

Dear Ms. Figueroa,

You applied to be transferred to our Bringhurst office last July, but we were ------- to grant
                                                                                      3.
your request because no opening was available there at the time. However, the

Bringhurst office manager called today to indicate they need a new sales representative.

They want to recruit internally, and I thought you might still be interested. Could you let

me know by tomorrow? If you no longer want to work in Bringhurst, I'll need to publish a

job opening on our message board. -------.
                                    4.

Thanks,
Kenneth Robertson

---

1. 誰に宛てた E メールですか。

  (a) 就職志願者

  (b) 従業員

  (c) 取引先の顧客

2. E メールの目的の 1 つは何ですか。

  (a) 異動希望者に新しく空いた職を知らせること。

  (b) 異動予定者に異動日の変更を伝えること。

  (c) 同僚の不在時に預かった伝言を本人に伝えること。

3. 空所 **3** に入る適切な語を選びましょう。

  (a) able

  (b) unable

4. 空所 **4** に入る適切な文を選びましょう。

  (a) I'll be awaiting your decision.

  (b) We always appreciate your patronage.

【解答】
1. (b)　**2.** (a)　**3.** (b)　**4.** (a)
【訳】
送信者：Kenneth Robertson ／受信者：Ana Figueroa ／件名：Bringhurst 事務所／日付：12 月 12 日
Figueroa 様
昨年 7 月、あなたは Bringhurst 事務所への異動を申請されましたが、その時点で同事務所には欠員がなかったためご要望にお応え
することができませんでした。しかし本日、Bringhurst 事務所長が電話で新しい営業担当が必要だと知らせてきました。彼らは社内
から募集することを望んでおり、それであなたがまだ関心があるかもしれないと思った次第です。明日までにお返事を頂けますか。
もう Bringhurst で働く意思がない場合は社内掲示板に求人を掲載する必要があります。*ご決断をお待ちしております。
敬具／ Kenneth Robertson
*問題 **4** の挿入文の訳

TOEIC® L&R の問題文書を使って、実際に文書を読む練習をしましょう。

1～2 の指示に従って、次の文書の内容理解に挑戦してください。

Letter

---

17 July

Hanna Morrison
12 Hecuba Road
St. John's
Antigua and Barbuda

Dear Ms. Morrison,

① Thank you for applying for a business loan with MUN Bank of Antigua & Barbuda.

② You were able to demonstrate your eligibility for MUN Bank's loan-assistance program. ------- was greatly in your favor as your application was being considered. We can now report our decision to ------- your loan application.

③ MUN Bank is pleased to offer you a loan of $50,000 under the terms and conditions set forth in the enclosure. Please let me know by 1 August ------- you intend to accept the offer. -------.

Feel free to contact me with any questions. I look forward to speaking with you soon.

Sincerely,

Joanne Yearwood
Loan Officer, MUN Bank of Antigua & Barbuda
Enclosure

---

1. 文書を読み、概要理解に重要と思われる語句や文を丸（◯）で囲んでみましょう。

2. 1 を参考に、メモを完成させましょう。ア～ウは適切な選択肢に☑を付け、エ～カは下線部を分かる範囲で埋めましょう（英語表記可）。

- 文書形式、発信者と受信者：
  （ア．□銀行　□慈善団体 ）から、（イ．□就職希望者　□サービスの申請者 ）へ向けた、（ウ．□新商品の DM　□申請結果の通知 ）の手紙。

- 概要（主題や目的）：
  MUN 銀行は受取人に エ.＿＿＿＿＿＿＿＿＿＿＿ を知らせている。

- 詳細情報：
  ① 融資に対する申請へのお礼。
  ② あなたは融資支援プログラムに対する オ.＿＿＿＿＿＿＿＿ を証明した。
  ③ MUN Bank は カ.＿＿＿＿＿＿＿＿ を提供する。

チャレンジ

TOEIC® L&R の問題に挑戦します。

右上の目安の解答時間を目標に、自分で時間を計りながら **1 ～ 4** の問題に答えてください。

Letter

---

17 July

Hanna Morrison
12 Hecuba Road
St. John's
Antigua and Barbuda

Dear Ms. Morrison,

Thank you for applying for a business loan with MUN Bank of Antigua & Barbuda. You were able to demonstrate your eligibility for MUN Bank's loan-assistance program. ------- **1.** was greatly in your favor as your application was being considered. We can now report our decision to ------- **2.** your loan application.

MUN Bank is pleased to offer you a loan of $50,000 under the terms and conditions set forth in the enclosure. Please let me know by 1 August ------- **3.** you intend to accept the offer. -------. **4.**

Feel free to contact me with any questions. I look forward to speaking with you soon.

Sincerely,

Joanne Yearwood
Loan Officer, MUN Bank of Antigua & Barbuda
Enclosure

---

1. (A) Whichever
   (B) This
   (C) Each
   (D) Many

2. (A) track
   (B) download
   (C) modify
   (D) approve

3. (A) before
   (B) still
   (C) whether
   (D) why

4. (A) The process for examining loan applications is very rigorous.
   (B) We have been offering loans to small businesses for 40 years.
   (C) Our rates are very competitive compared with other banks.
   (D) We cannot guarantee the same loan terms after that date.

→解答・解説は p.90

手紙

17 July

Hanna Morrison

12 Hecuba Road

St. John's

Antigua and Barbuda

Dear Ms. Morrison,

❶ Thank you for applying for a business loan with MUN Bank of Antigua & Barbuda. You were able to demonstrate your eligibility for MUN Bank's loan-assistance program. ------- **1.** was greatly in your favor as your application was being considered. We can now report our decision to ------- your loan application.
2.

❷ MUN Bank is pleased to offer you a loan of $50,000 under the terms and conditions set forth in the enclosure. Please let me know by 1 August ------- you intend to accept the
3.
offer. -------.
4.

Feel free to contact me with any questions. I look forward to speaking with you soon.

Sincerely,

Joanne Yearwood

Loan Officer, MUN Bank of Antigua & Barbuda

Enclosure

7月17日／Hanna Morrison／Hecuba 通り 12 番地／セントジョンズ／アンティグア・バーブーダ

Morrison 様

アンティグア・バーブーダ MUN 銀行の事業融資にお申し込みいただき、ありがとうございます。お客さまは MUN 銀行の融資支援プログラムに対し適格性を証明することができました。このことは、お客さまの申請を検討する際、非常に有利に働きました。当行はお客さまの融資申請を承認する決定をここに報告させていただきます。

MUN 銀行は、同封物に定められた契約条件に基づき、5 万ドルの融資を提供いたしたく存じます。本申し出に応じるご意向があるかどうかについて、8 月 1 日までに当行へお知らせください。*同期日以降は、同じ融資条件を保証することは致しかねます。

ご質問がございましたら、お気軽にご連絡ください。近日中にお客さまとお話しできますことを心待ちにしております。

敬具／ Joanne Yearwood ／融資担当、アンティグア・バーブーダ MUN 銀行

同封物あり

*問題 4 の挿入文の訳

プラクティス

1. 例は左図参照。

2. ア．銀行　　イ．サービスの申請者　　ウ．申請結果の通知　　エ．事業への融資の提供
　　オ．適格性（資格があること）　　カ．５万ドルの融資

チャレンジ

1. (A) Whichever
(B) This
(C) Each
(D) Many

(A) どちらでも
(B) これ
(C) それぞれ
(D) 多数

正解 **B** 空所を含む文と前文とのつながりに注目する。前文に当たる❶1〜2行目には「お客さまはMUN銀行の融資支援プログラムに対し適格性を証明することができた」とある。また、❷1〜2行目より、手紙は融資申請の承認を知らせるものだと考えられるので、空所を含む文は、「適格性を証明できたことが、申請を検討する際、非常に有利になった」という意味だと、文脈から判断できる。下線部の前文の内容を示す (B) This が正解。
(A) 複数の選択肢がある際に用いる。
(C)「一つ一つ」または「一人一人」を表す。
(D) 複数扱いの代名詞。

2. (A) track
(B) download
(C) modify
(D) approve

(A) 〜を追跡する
(B) 〜をダウンロードする
(C) 〜を修正する
(D) 〜を承認する

正解 **D** 選択肢は全て動詞の原形。文意に合う動詞を選ぶ。文の構造を見ると、decision「決定」の内容を to ------- your loan application の不定詞句で説明している。不定詞の動詞の目的語は your loan application「お客さまの融資申請」であること、❷1〜2行目より、手紙は融資の提供を知らせるものだと考えられることから、空所には (D) approve が適切。

3. (A) before
(B) still
(C) whether
(D) why

(A) 〜の前に
(B) まだ
(C) 〜かどうか
(D) なぜ

正解 **C** 空所を含む文が Please let me know ...で始まっているので、------- you intend to accept the offer の節が know の目的語になっていると分かる。空所に (C) whether「〜かどうか」を入れると、「あなたが申し出に応じる意向があるかどうか（ということ）」という意味の名詞節になり、文意に合う。
(A) 接続詞。何を知らせてほしいのかが不明。
(B) 副詞。後半の節とつながらない。
(D) 疑問副詞。「なぜ申し出に応じる意向なのかを知らせてほしい」という意味になり、文脈的に不適切。

語 注

❶ apply for 〜　〜を申請する　　business 事業、会社　　loan 融資、ローン　　demonstrate 〜を証明する
eligibility for 〜　〜に対する適格性　　loan-assistance 融資支援の　　program プログラム、事業
in *one's* favor 〜の有利に　　application 申請書、申込書　　consider 〜を検討する　　report 〜を報告する
decision 決定
❷ be pleased to *do* 喜んで〜する　　offer 〈動詞〉〜を提供する　　terms and conditions 契約条件
set forth 〜（規則）を規定する　　enclosure 同封物　　intend to *do* 〜するつもりである　　accept 〜を受け入れる
offer 〈名詞〉申し出　　feel free to *do* 遠慮なく〜する　　look forward to 〜　〜を楽しみにする

解答・解説

4. (A) The process for examining loan applications is very rigorous.
(B) We have been offering loans to small businesses for 40 years.
(C) Our rates are very competitive compared with other banks.
(D) We cannot guarantee the same loan terms after that date.

(A) 融資申請の審査過程は、非常に厳格です。
(B) 当行は40年にわたり、中小企業に融資を提供してきました。
(C) 当行の金利は、他行と比べても極めてお得です。
(D) 同期日以降は、同じ融資条件を保証することは致しかねます。

正解 D ❷1〜2行目で、MUN銀行は5万ドルの融資を提供すると申し出た上で、Please let me know by 1 August「8月1日までに当行へ知らせてほしい」と期限を設定してMorrisonさんに返信の依頼をしている。空所はこの後に続く、段落の最終文なので、「同期日以降は、同じ融資条件を保証することは致しかねる」という内容の(D)が空所に入ると、that date が前文の1 August を指すことになり、自然な文脈になる。guarantee「〜を保証する」。
(A)(B) 話題が変わってしまい、いずれも文脈上不自然。
(A) examine「〜を審査する」、rigorous「厳しい、厳格な」。
(B) small business「中小企業」。
(C) 融資申請承認の決定の連絡で rate「金利」の利点を伝えるのは不自然。competitive「競争力のある、他に負けない」、compare 〜 with …「〜を…と比べる」。

Column

◀社内メモ▶

Part 6 や Part 7 に登場する文書形式に社内メモがあります。「メモランダム」とも言い、従業員に通知を出したり、業務上の関係者に配布したりするときに使われます。社内メモの書式は、Eメールのものと非常に似ていますが、決定事項などを迅速に回覧・配布することが主な目的であるため、返事をもらうことを想定していないという特徴があります。以下は社内メモの書式例です。

❶
To: Box Office Staff
From: G. Anders, General Director
Date: 24 November
Subject: Policy Update

❷
I am writing to inform you of a change in the seating policy for our classical music series, effective immediately. There have been many requests on the day of the concert from patrons who prefer to sit on the aisle because there is more leg room. From now on, we will accept such requests only at the time tickets are purchased. Subsequently, audience members who need extra space may ask for a seat in the back two rows, as those are not usually filled. It is further from the stage, but it is more comfortable there. This policy should help us avoid complaints once a performance has begun.

❶ To はメモの宛先、From は差出人、Date は配布した日付、Subject は件名です。通知の内容によっては添付書類が付くときもあり、その場合はメモの下部に Attachment の欄が設けられ添付書類の名称が記載されます。

❷ 例では、I am writing to inform you ... と冒頭から用件を切り出し、通知事項を明らかにしています。手紙や Eメールのように、Hi, 〜のような書き出しで始まり、終わりに Thank you in advance などの結びの定型句で締めくくる場合もあります。社内用文書のため、カジュアルな表現もよく使われます。

読む際のポイントとしては、まず、Eメールと同じく❶のヘッダー部分で提示されている情報が概要理解の手掛かりになります。❷の本文では、今後の予定の通知や方針変更の案内など、伝達事項の詳細が明確に簡潔にまとめられています。5W1H (Who、When、Where、What、Why、How)「誰が・いつ・どこで・何を・なぜ・どうやって」をしっかり押さえるようにしましょう。

【訳】
宛先：チケット窓口スタッフ各位／差出人：G. Anders、統括部長／日付：11 月 24 日／件名：方針の改訂
即時発効となる、当劇場のクラシック音楽シリーズの座席に関する方針変更をお知らせいたします。これまで、コンサート当日に、足周りの空間に余裕があるからという理由で通路側の座席を希望される得意客のご依頼が多数ありました。今後は、そのようなご依頼にはチケットご購入時に限って応じることにします。以降は、スペースの余裕が必要な観客の方は、通常は埋まることのない後方 2 列の座席を希望することが可能です。そこは舞台から遠くなりますが、より居心地の良い場所です。この方針により、演奏が開始された後は、苦情を回避できるでしょう。

MEMO

PART

7

読解問題

Unit 11　文書の概要をつかむ

テーマ解説

Part 7 の特徴

Part 7 は、1 つの文書または複数の文書を 1 セットとして読み、文書に関する複数の設問に答える「読解問題」です。1 つの文書では 2 〜 4 問が出題され、複数の文書では 2 文書または 3 文書につき 5 問が出題されます。文書の種類は、E メール、記入用紙、ウェブページ、オンライン掲示板のやりとり、広告、新聞記事など、幅広いジャンルや形式の実用文書が登場し、後半になるにつれて次第に読む分量が増えていきます。

Part 7 の文書を読む際のポイント

Part 7 の文書を読むときも、Unit 8 で紹介した「長文を読む際のポイント」が役立ちます。以下で、もう一度確認しましょう。

> 1　**文書形式**　文書の書式やデザインの特徴から、何の文書なのかをつかむ。
> 2　**発信者と受信者**　誰が誰に情報を送っているのか、発信者と受信者の関係を推測する。
> 3　**概要（主題や目的）**　文書の主題や書き手の情報発信の目的を捉える。
> 4　**詳細情報**　情報の流れや関連を考慮しながら、重要な詳細情報を中心に理解する。

1**文書形式**は、実際のテストでは、次のような指示文がヒントになるため、必ず目を通しましょう。

例　Questions 147-148 refer to the following form.　　問題 147-148 は次の記入用紙に関するものです。

2**発信者と受信者**は、E メールならメールヘッダー欄と本文の最後にあるフッター欄を、ウェブページなら URL のバーやメニュータブの情報を確認しましょう。広告ならイラスト類もヒントになります。これらの情報を押さえたら、本文を読み進め、3**概要（主題や目的）**をつかみます。特に冒頭の 1 〜 2 文から、新聞記事なら「何を報じた記事か」、説明書なら「何についての説明書か」、E メールや社内メモなら「発信者の目的は何か」などを把握しましょう。その後、4**詳細情報**の理解に移り、事実関係を押さえていきます。

「発信者」や「概要」は設問でも問われる

Part 7 の設問には、2**発信者と受信者**や3**概要（主題や目的）**を尋ねるものが頻繁に出題されます。例えば以下の設問では、1 つ目が「発信者」を、2 つ目が「目的」を尋ねています。Part 7 の文書を読む際は、まずこれらのポイントを意識して読む習慣を付けることが大切です。

例　Who most likely posted the notice?　　お知らせを掲載したのは誰だと考えられますか。
　　What is the purpose of the article?　　記事の目的は何ですか。

Part 7 では、これらの理解に加え、文書内の情報から正しく事実を読み取れているか、文脈から情報同士を関連付けられているかといった詳細の理解を問う設問も出題されます。本書で 4 つのポイントを念頭にした読解練習を繰り返し、必要な情報を短時間で捉えられるようになることを目指していきましょう。

ウォームアップ

テーマ解説を参考に次の文書を通して読んだ後、1〜3の質問に答えましょう。

Steve's Fitness Studio   New Member Registration Form

Thank you for your interest in Steve's Fitness Studio. Your journey to a healthier body and a healthier lifestyle starts with signing up! Please fill in the form below.

1. Name (as it appears on your ID):

2. Address: _____

3. Phone number: _____   E-mail: _____

4. Tell us a bit about your health conditions, fitness and sport history. Please provide concrete answers to the following items.
   - Please list any medical conditions that you have:
   - Please list any medications you are taking:
   - Have you done any of the following in the past? (check the boxes that apply, or write in a response)

   ☐ yoga   ☐ jogging   ☐ aerobics   ☐ resistance training
   ☐ Pilates   ☐ boxercise   ☐ others   _____

---

1. 何の団体が発行した文書ですか。

(a) フィットネスジム   (b) 健康専門書の出版社   (c) 医療機関

2. この文書を読むのは誰だと考えられますか。

(a) 会員履歴のある人   (b) 新たに会員登録をしたい人   (c) フィットネス器具の営業担当

3. この文書の目的は何ですか。当てはまるものを全て選びましょう。

(a) 会員の健康状態を把握して適切な治療を行う。

(b) 会員の健康状態を把握して適切な運動を奨励する。

(c) 会員の運動能力を把握して指導者として雇う。

(d) 会員の身元確認をして連絡が取れるようにする。

【解答】

1. (a) **2.** (b) **3.** (b)、(d) ▶ タイトルと冒頭の1〜2文から、フィットネスジムの新規会員の登録用紙だと分かる。

【訳】

Steve のフィットネススタジオ　新規会員登録用紙

Steve のフィットネススタジオにご関心をお寄せくださいまして、ありがとうございます。より健康的な体と健康的な生活への道のりは、会員登録から始まります！ 下記の書式にご記入ください。

1. 氏名（身元証明書に記載の通りに）：

2. 住所：_____

3. 電話番号：_____   Eメール：_____

4. 健康状態と運動やスポーツの履歴に関して少しお聞かせください。下記の項目に具体的な答えをお書きください。

　- 持病をお持ちであれば全て列挙してください：

　- 服用中のお薬があれば全て列挙してください：

　- 過去に下記のいずれかを行ったことがありますか（当てはまるものに印を付けるか、回答欄にご記入ください）

　☐ ヨガ　☐ ジョギング　☐ エアロビクス　☐ 筋力トレーニング　☐ ピラティス　☐ ボクササイズ　☐ その他 _____

TOEIC® L&R の問題文書を使って、実際に文書を読む練習をしましょう。

1、**2**それぞれの文書に対し、**1** ～ **3** の指示に従いながら、内容理解に挑戦してください。

1 Form

> ### Crossroads New Melbourne: Conference Space for a New Age
>
> Thank you for your interest in Crossroads New Melbourne. Please complete the request form below. We will contact you shortly with the plan and pricing that will suit the needs of your group.
>
> **Organization Name:** _____ **Contact Name:** _____
>
> **E-mail:** _____ **Phone:** _____ **Date(s):** _____
>
> **Venue preference:**
> [ ] 33 Brightwood Square [ ] 608 Westway Street [ ] 1057 Portside Highway
>
> **Basic room layout:**
> [ ] Lecture (rows of chairs) [ ] Classroom (rows of tables and chairs)
> [ ] Boardroom (chairs around one long table) [ ] Other: _____
>
> **Number of attendees:** [ ] 10–34 [ ] 35–100 [ ] 100+
>
> **Computer rental required:** [ ] Yes [ ] No
>
> **Nearby lodging required for some guests:** [ ] Yes [ ] No
>
> ## Crossroads New Melbourne

1. 文書を読み、概要理解に重要と思われる語句や文を丸 (◯) で囲んでみましょう。

2. **1** を参考に、メモを完成させましょう (固有名詞を含め、英語表記可)。

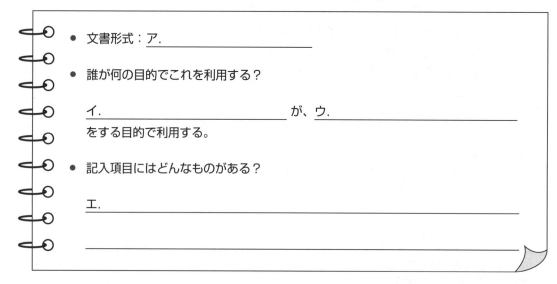

- 文書形式：ア. _____

- 誰が何の目的でこれを利用する？

  イ. _____ が、ウ. _____
  をする目的で利用する。

- 記入項目にはどんなものがある？

  エ. _____

  _____

3. <u>用紙に記入した後の流れ</u>について説明している箇所を見つけて、上の文書内に波線 (〜〜〜) を引きましょう。

2 Receipt

Receipt # 84502-11516

(Keep this receipt number handy. You will need it if you have to contact customer service.)

April 17, 6:43 P.M.
Received from Jasmine Shalib:
$54 payment to Pilgrim Theater
Charged to credit card ending in xxxx-1394
Description: Tickets for Philip Dadian in concert
Friday, May 1, 7:30 P.M.
Unit price: $27 / Quantity: 2 / Amount: $54

IMPORTANT: Please print this receipt and bring it with you to the venue. No paper tickets will be mailed. Be sure to arrive early to check your name on the preorder list at the ticket counter. Tickets are nonrefundable.

8 84502 11516 1

1. 文書を読み、概要理解に重要と思われる語句や文を丸（◯）で囲んでみましょう。

2. 1 を参考に、メモを完成させましょう（固有名詞を含め、英語表記可）。

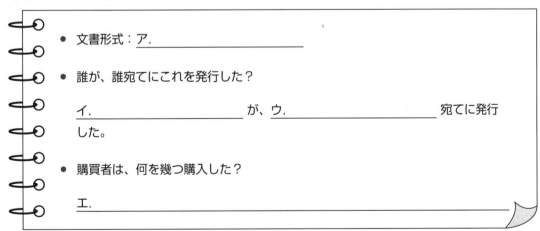

- 文書形式：ア.＿＿＿＿＿＿＿＿＿＿＿＿＿

- 誰が、誰宛てにこれを発行した？

  イ.＿＿＿＿＿＿＿＿＿＿＿ が、ウ.＿＿＿＿＿＿＿＿＿＿ 宛てに発行した。

- 購買者は、何を幾つ購入した？

  エ.＿＿＿＿＿＿＿＿＿＿＿＿＿＿＿＿＿＿＿＿＿＿＿＿＿

3. 用紙の使用方法について説明している箇所を見つけて、上の文書内に波線（〰〰）を引きましょう。

→解答・解説は p.102、104

チャレンジ

TOEIC® L&R の問題に挑戦します。

右上の目安の解答時間を目標に、自分で時間を計りながら **1 ～ 4** の問題に答えてください。

1 Form

Crossroads New Melbourne: Conference Space for a New Age

Thank you for your interest in Crossroads New Melbourne. Please complete the request form below. We will contact you shortly with the plan and pricing that will suit the needs of your group.

Organization Name: _____ **Contact Name:** _____

E-mail: _____ **Phone:** _____ **Date(s):** _____

Venue preference:
[　] 33 Brightwood Square　　[　] 608 Westway Street　　[　] 1057 Portside Highway

Basic room layout:
[　] Lecture (rows of chairs)　　　　　　　　[　] Classroom (rows of tables and chairs)
[　] Boardroom (chairs around one long table)　[　] Other: _____

Number of attendees: [　] 10–34　　[　] 35–100　　[　] 100+

Computer rental required: [　] Yes　　[　] No

Nearby lodging required for some guests: [　] Yes　　[　] No

Crossroads New Melbourne

---

1. According to the form, what will Crossroads New Melbourne staff do?

(A) Create a proposal based on the information submitted
(B) Send a brochure to conference participants
(C) Provide discounts for events with over 100 attendees
(D) Assist conference participants with registration on the day of an event

2. What is implied about Crossroads New Melbourne?

(A) It began doing business about one year ago.
(B) It has three locations.
(C) It recently began operating its own hotel.
(D) It requires presenters to bring their own laptop computers.

2 Receipt

Receipt # 84502-11516
(Keep this receipt number handy. You will need it if you have to contact customer service.)

April 17, 6:43 P.M.
Received from Jasmine Shalib:
$54 payment to Pilgrim Theater
Charged to credit card ending in xxxx-1394
Description: Tickets for Philip Dadian in concert
Friday, May 1, 7:30 P.M.
Unit price: $27 / Quantity: 2 / Amount: $54

IMPORTANT: Please print this receipt and bring it with you to the venue. No paper tickets will be mailed. Be sure to arrive early to check your name on the preorder list at the ticket counter. Tickets are nonrefundable.

8 ˮ84502ˮ11516ˮ 1

3. What does Ms. Shalib plan to do on May 1?

(A) Call the theater
(B) Request a refund
(C) Pay her credit card bill
(D) Attend a musical event

4. What must Ms. Shalib bring with her?

(A) A credit card
(B) Paper tickets
(C) A copy of a receipt
(D) A form of identification

→解答・解説は p.102、104

1

申込用紙

Crossroads New Melbourne: Conference Space for a New Age

Thank you for your interest in Crossroads New Melbourne. Please complete the request form below. We will contact you shortly with the plan and pricing that will suit the needs of your group.

Organization Name: _____   **Contact Name:** _____

E-mail: _____   **Phone:** _____   **Date(s):** _____

Venue preference:
[ ] 33 Brightwood Square   [ ] 608 Westway Street   [ ] 1057 Portside Highway

Basic room layout:
[ ] Lecture (rows of chairs)   [ ] Classroom (rows of tables and chairs)
[ ] Boardroom (chairs around one long table)   [ ] Other: _____

Number of attendees: [ ] 10–34   [ ] 35–100   [ ] 100+

Computer rental required: [ ] Yes   [ ] No

Nearby lodging required for some guests: [ ] Yes   [ ] No

Crossroads New Melbourne

Crossroads New Melbourne 社：新しい時代の会議スペース

Crossroads New Melbourne 社にご関心をお寄せくださいまして、ありがとうございます。以下の申請書の全ての項目にご記入ください。貴団体のニーズに適したプランと料金設定とともに、当社からすぐにご連絡いたします。

団体名：_____   ご担当者名：_____
Eメール：_____   電話番号：_____   利用日：_____
ご希望の会場：
[ ] Brightwood 広場 33 番地   [ ] Westway 通り 608 番地   [ ] Portside ハイウェイ 1057 番地
部屋の基本レイアウト：
[ ] 講演（椅子を列に配置）   [ ] 教室（机と椅子を列に配置）
[ ] 会議室（長机 1 台の周囲に椅子を配置）   [ ] その他：_____
出席者数：[ ] 10 ～ 34 名   [ ] 35 ～ 100 名   [ ] 100 名より多い
コンピューターの貸し出しが必要：[ ] はい   [ ] いいえ
近隣での宿泊が一部来客用に必要：[ ] はい   [ ] いいえ

語注

❶ interest 関心、興味　　complete ～に全て記入する　　request form 申請書　　contact ～に連絡する
　　shortly 間もなく、じきに　　pricing 価格設定　　needs 〈複数形で〉ニーズ、必要（なもの）
❷ organization 団体、組織　　venue 会場、開催地　　preference 好み、優先　　boardroom （重役用の）会議室
　　attendee 出席者　　require ～を必要とする、（条件として）～を要求する　　nearby 近くの　　lodging 宿

プラクティス

1. 例は左図参照。

2. ア．申込用紙。　イ．貸会場を利用したい顧客　ウ．利用の申し込みと見積もりの依頼

　エ．団体名、担当者名、連絡先、利用日、希望の会場、部屋の基本レイアウト、出席者数、コンピューターの貸し出しや宿泊手配の必要の有無。

3. 左図参照。

チャレンジ

1. According to the form, what will Crossroads New Melbourne staff do?

(A) Create a proposal based on the information submitted

(B) Send a brochure to conference participants

(C) Provide discounts for events with over 100 attendees

(D) Assist conference participants with registration on the day of an event

申込用紙によると、Crossroads New Melbourne 社のスタッフは何をしますか。

(A) 提出された情報を基に提案を作成する。

(B) 会議参加者にパンフレットを送る。

(C) 出席者が 100 人を超えるイベントに割引を提供する。

(D) イベント当日、会議の参加者の登録を手助けする。

正解 A Crossroads New Melbourne 社の申込用紙を見ると、❶2 行目に We will contact you shortly with the plan and pricing that will suit the needs of your group.「貴団体のニーズに適したプランと料金設定とともに、当社からすぐに連絡する」とある。(A) が正解。proposal「提案、提案書」。
(B) パンフレットの送付に関する言及はない。brochure「パンフレット」、participant「参加者」。
(C) 出席者数の記入項目はあるが、割引についての言及はない。
(D) コンピューターの貸し出しと宿泊施設の要望の有無以外に、サービスに関する記載はない。registration「登録」。

2. What is implied about Crossroads New Melbourne?

(A) It began doing business about one year ago.

(B) It has three locations.

(C) It recently began operating its own hotel.

(D) It requires presenters to bring their own laptop computers.

Crossroads New Melbourne 社について何が示唆されていますか。

(A) 約 1 年前に事業を始めた。

(B) 3 カ所の会場を持っている。

(C) 最近、自社ホテルの操業を始めた。

(D) 発表者に自身のノートパソコンを持ってくるよう要求している。

正解 B 申込用紙の Venue preference「希望の会場」の項目には 3 カ所の通りの名前が提示されている。このことから、Crossroads New Melbourne 社は 3 カ所の会場スペースを所有しており、それらを貸し出す事業を営んでいることが分かる。(B) が正解。
(A) 創業の年について言及はない。business「事業」。
(C) 近隣宿泊施設の要望の有無を尋ねる項目はあるが、その施設が自社ホテルであるかどうかは示されていない。operate「～を操業する」。
(D) コンピューターの貸し出しの要望の有無を尋ねる項目があり、持参は必須ではない。presenter「発表者」、laptop computer「ノートパソコン」。

2

Receipt # 84502-11516

❶ (Keep this receipt number handy. You will need it if you have to contact customer service.)

❷ April 17, 6:43 P.M.
Received from Jasmine Shalib:
$54 payment to Pilgrim Theater
Charged to credit card ending in xxxx-1394
Description: Tickets for Philip Dadian in concert
Friday, May 1, 7:30 P.M.
Unit price: $27 / Quantity: 2 / Amount: $54

❸ **IMPORTANT:** Please print this receipt and bring it with you to the venue. No paper tickets will be mailed. Be sure to arrive early to check your name on the preorder list at the ticket counter. Tickets are nonrefundable.

8 84502 11516 1

領収書番号 84502-11516

（この領収書番号はお手元に保管ください。顧客サービス部へのご連絡の際に必要になります。）

4月17日、午後6時43分
Jasmine Shalib から受領：
Pilgrim 劇場に対し 54 ドルの支払い
末尾 xxxx-1394 のクレジットカードに請求
明細：5月1日（金）、午後7時30分、Philip Dadian のコンサートチケット
単価：27 ドル／数量：2／総額：54 ドル

重要：この領収書を印刷して会場までご持参ください。紙のチケットは郵送されません。チケットカウンターで事前注文リストのお名前を確認いたしますので、お早めに到着されるようお願いします。チケットの払い戻しには応じられません。

語 注

❶ handy 手元に、すぐ近くに　　contact ～に連絡する　　customer service 顧客サービス部
❷ receive ～を受領する　　payment 支払い　　charge to ～ ～に代金を請求する　　description 明細、記載事項
　　unit price 単価　　quantity 量　　amount 総額、金額
❸ venue 会場、開催地　　mail ～を郵送する　　be sure to *do* 必ず～する　　arrive 到着する　　early 早くに
　　check ～を確認する　　preorder 事前注文、先行予約　　nonrefundable 払い戻し不可能な

プラクティス

1. 例は左図参照。

2. ア．領収書。　イ．Pilgrim 劇場　ウ．Jasmine Shalib さん

　エ．コンサートのチケットを 2 枚。

3. 左図参照。

チャレンジ

3. What does Ms. Shalib plan to do on May 1?

(A) Call the theater
(B) Request a refund
(C) Pay her credit card bill
(D) Attend a musical event

Shalib さんは 5 月 1 日に何をする予定ですか。

(A) 劇場に電話する。
(B) 払い戻しを求める。
(C) クレジットカードの請求額を支払う。
(D) 音楽イベントに参加する。

> | 正解 **D** | ❷2 行目の Received from Jasmine Shalib より、Shalib さんは領収書の受領者である。❷の 5 行目に Description「明細」があり、Tickets for Philip Dadian in concert Friday, May 1, 7:30 P.M. の記載があることから、Shalib さんは、5 月 1 日 (金) 午後 7 時 30 分のコンサートチケットを買ったことが分かる。よって、(D) の「音楽イベントに参加する」が正解。attend「～に出席する」。
>
> (A) ❶の 1 ～ 2 行目より、電話をするのは顧客サービス部に連絡する用が生じたときで、予定はされていない。
> (B) ❸の 5 行目に Tickets are nonrefundable「チケットの払い戻しには応じられない」とある。refund「払い戻し」。
> (C) ❷の 4 行目に Charged to credit card「クレジットカードに請求」とはあるが、支払日の記載はない。bill「請求額、請求書」。

4. What must Ms. Shalib bring with her?

(A) A credit card
(B) Paper tickets
(C) A copy of a receipt
(D) A form of identification

Shalib さんは何を持参しなければなりませんか。

(A) クレジットカード
(B) 紙のチケット
(C) 領収書のコピー
(D) 身元証明書

> | 正解 **C** | ❸の IMPORTANT「重要」の 1 ～ 2 行目に、Please print this receipt and bring it with you to the venue.「この領収書を印刷して会場まで持参してほしい」との注意書きがある。続く 2 ～ 5 行目に、紙のチケットは郵送されず、当日はチケットカウンターで事前注文リストの氏名確認をすると説明されていることからも、Shalib さんは、当日は領収書のコピーを持参することで入場できると推測される。よって、(C) が正解。a copy of ～「～のコピー 1 部」。
>
> (A) クレジットカード持参についての言及はない。
> (B) ❸の 2 ～ 3 行目に「紙のチケットは郵送されない」とある。
> (D) 身元証明書に関する記載はない。form「種類、書式」、identification「身元証明」。

Unit 12　詳細情報をつかむ

テーマ解説

文書の読解で、1 文書形式、2 発信者と受信者、3 概要（主題や目的）を捉えることができたら、次は事実や書き手の考えなどの4 詳細情報に目を向けます。4 詳細情報とは、例えば書き手が同一段落の冒頭で示した主題や主張などの具体例に当たる部分を言います。

情報の取捨選択が鍵

4 詳細情報を読むときは、この文は直前の文の具体例なのか、この文は結論につながる根拠を示している文なのかなど、情報の流れや情報同士の関連性に注目しながら、重要だと考える情報を中心に読み取るようにしましょう。情報のつながりや重要度を見極めることで、書き手の状況や場面をより身近にイメージすることができます。

\ 文書の内容理解に挑戦 /

では、「長文を読む際のポイント」（→ p.96）の1 ～4 を意識しながら、次ページの「ウォームアップ」の文書を読みましょう。読み方のヒントとして、以下の解説も参考にしてください。

---

1 文書形式

☑ スマートフォンのような通信機器の画面のデザインが施されています。

☑ ❶に発信者の名前と、日付と時刻が表示されています。

スマートフォンの画面に表示されたテキストメッセージと考えていいでしょう。

2 発信者と受信者

☑ ❶から発信者と送信日時が分かります。

☑ ❷1 行目 Maria, I'm ... とファーストネームで呼び掛けていることから、Maria が受信者だと考えられます。

以上から、メッセージは Rick という男性が Maria という女性に宛てたもので、2 人は比較的近しい間柄と推測できます。

3 概要（主題や目的）

☑ ❷1 ～ 3 行目で現在の状況を簡潔に伝え、this job is too big to do alone と主張しています。

メッセージの中心的な話題です。topic sentence「主題文」と呼びます。

☑ ❷9 ～ 10 行目で Can you phone Scott and ask him to come help me? と受信者に依頼しています。

Rick が Maria にメッセージを送った目的です。英語では重要な情報を最初に述べ、詳細情報を挟んだ後、最後であらためて重要な情報に言及するという構成が1 つのパターンとなっています。結びの文を concluding sentence「結論文」と呼びます。

4 詳細情報

☑ It's not what I expected. (❷3 ～ 4 行目)　　　　　　　　　▶ 感想・心理状態

☑ It's a large space that can be divided into smaller rooms, (❷4 ～ 5 行目)　▶ 主張の根拠

☑ the hotel wants a programmable system to work ... (❷5 ～ 9 行目)　▶ 主張の根拠

1 つ目の情報は Rick の感想、2 つ目と3 つ目はその前に述べた主張（主題文）の根拠を示す重要な詳細情報だと考えられます。このような主題文を説明する詳細情報の文を、supporting sentence「支持文」と言います。この直後に Rick が Maria に依頼をしており、その後依頼の直接的な理由について補足しています。

このような短いテキストメッセージでも、情報同士の関連性に注目することで、「主張→根拠→依頼」という流れが見えてきます。これらを頭に入れてから、「ウォームアップ」の質問に答えましょう。

テーマ解説を参考に次の文書を通して読んだ後、1 ～ 4 の質問に答えましょう。

1 From: Rick Barilla, Thursday, 3 October, 8:53 A.M.

2 Maria, I'm at the Baycrest Hotel, installing the new ballroom lighting system. Joe called in sick, and this job is too big to do alone. It's not what I expected. It's a large space that can be divided into smaller rooms, and the hotel wants a programmable system to work when the space is used for more than one meeting or dinner scheduled at the same time. Can you phone Scott and ask him to come help me? I don't have his mobile phone number.

1. テキストメッセージの目的は何ですか。

  (a) 番号を問い合わせる。

  (b) 手助けを求める。

  (c) 作業の完了を報告する。

2. Rick と Maria はどんな関係ですか。

  (a) 夫婦

  (b) 友人

  (c) 同僚

3. Scott とは誰ですか。

  (a) 同僚

  (b) 顧客

  (c) 家族

4. Rick はなぜ困っていますか。

  (a) 仕事の規模が大きく複雑である。

  (b) Scott が連絡をしてこない。

  (c) 間違った現場に来てしまった。

【解答】

1. (b)　2. (c)　3. (a)　4. (a)

▶ 4. ❷3行目で this job is too big to do alone と述べた後、❷4 ～ 9行目で作業規模が大きいとする具体例を説明している。

【訳】

送信者：Rick Barilla、10月3日（木）、午前8時53分

Maria、私は今 Baycrest ホテルにいて、大宴会場の新しい照明システムを設置しています。Joe から病気で休むと電話があったのですが、この仕事は1人でやるには大規模過ぎます。私が想定していたものとは違いました。ここは小部屋に分けることができる大きな空間で、ホテル側は、同一の時間に予定された2件以上の会議や夕食会にこの空間が使用される際にうまく機能するような、プログラム可能なシステムを希望しているんです。Scott に電話して、手伝いに来られるか聞いてもらえますか。私は彼の携帯電話の番号を持っていないんです。

TOEIC® L&R の問題文書を使って、実際に文書を読む練習をしましょう。

1、**2**それぞれの文書に対し、**1** 〜 **3** の指示に従いながら、内容理解に挑戦してください。

1 Information

> **Takashi Fujioka**
> *Kyoto at Twilight*
> Oil on canvas
> 114.3 cm x 99.06 cm
>
> This work is the first in Takashi Fujioka's *Kyoto Nightfall* series, which gained international recognition. Works from this series of paintings have been exhibited in museums and galleries around the world, including the Moto Contemporary Art Museum in Tokyo, the Fontaine-Shields Gallery in New York City, and the Starlit Art Gallery in London. *Kyoto at Twilight* was featured on the cover of *Modern Painting* magazine the year it was painted. It was bought four years ago by Thomas Chester Gaines for his private collection and was sold to the Clarkson-Walker Museum for our permanent collection two years ago. It has remained here with us since. Mr. Fujioka famously called this painting "my finest hour."

1. 文書を読み、概要理解に重要と思われる語句や文を丸（◯）で囲んでみましょう。

2. **1** を参考に、メモを完成させましょう（固有名詞を含め、英語表記可）。

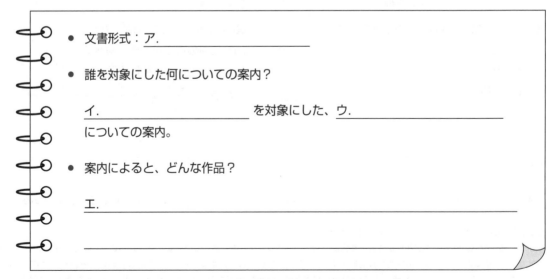

- 文書形式：ア.＿＿＿＿＿＿＿＿＿＿＿＿

- 誰を対象にした何についての案内？

  イ.＿＿＿＿＿＿＿＿＿＿ を対象にした、ウ.＿＿＿＿＿＿＿＿＿＿
  についての案内。

- 案内によると、どんな作品？

  エ.＿＿＿＿＿＿＿＿＿＿＿＿＿＿＿＿＿＿＿＿＿＿＿＿

  ＿＿＿＿＿＿＿＿＿＿＿＿＿＿＿＿＿＿＿＿＿＿＿＿＿＿

3. 所有者の変遷について説明している箇所を見つけて、上の文書内に波線（〰〰）を引きましょう。

2 Invoice

Omicron Premier Services Ltd.
83 Malet Street
London
WC1E 7HU

Invoice: 1Z67HN2
Arrival Date: 3 April

Bill to:
Dr. John Kwang
Overbrook Hospital

Ship to:
Overbrook Hospital
27 St. Stephens Green
Dublin, Ireland

Item Number	Description	Item Price
12B	5 Boxes Small Bandages	£12
12C	10 Boxes Large Bandages	£30
431Z*	2 Boxes Large Sterile Gloves	£5
10CD	5 Large Knee Braces	£25
	TOTAL	£72

Payment due upon receipt of goods.

* Item 431Z will be shipped at a later date as it is currently not in the warehouse.

---

1. 文書を読み、概要理解に重要と思われる語句や文を丸（◯）で囲んでみましょう。

2. 1 を参考に、メモを完成させましょう（固有名詞を含め、英語表記可）。

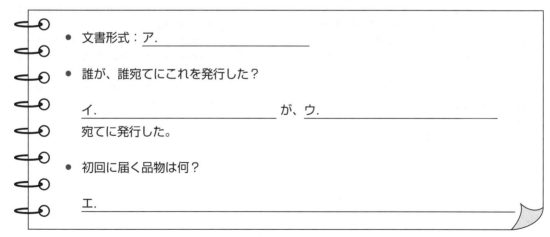

- 文書形式：ア.＿＿＿＿＿＿＿＿＿＿

- 誰が、誰宛てにこれを発行した？

  イ.＿＿＿＿＿＿＿＿＿＿＿ が、ウ.＿＿＿＿＿＿＿＿＿＿＿
  宛てに発行した。

- 初回に届く品物は何？

  エ.＿＿＿＿＿＿＿＿＿＿＿＿＿＿＿＿＿＿＿＿＿＿＿＿

3. 支払いの発生時期について説明している箇所を見つけて、上の文書内に波線（〰〰）を引きましょう。

→解答・解説は p.112、114

チャレンジ

TOEIC® L&R の問題に挑戦します。

右上の目安の解答時間を目標に、自分で時間を計りながら **1** ～ **6** の問題に答えてください。

1 Information

> **Takashi Fujioka**
> *Kyoto at Twilight*
> Oil on canvas
> 114.3 cm x 99.06 cm
>
> This work is the first in Takashi Fujioka's *Kyoto Nightfall* series, which gained international recognition. Works from this series of paintings have been exhibited in museums and galleries around the world, including the Moto Contemporary Art Museum in Tokyo, the Fontaine-Shields Gallery in New York City, and the Starlit Art Gallery in London. *Kyoto at Twilight* was featured on the cover of *Modern Painting* magazine the year it was painted. It was bought four years ago by Thomas Chester Gaines for his private collection and was sold to the Clarkson-Walker Museum for our permanent collection two years ago. It has remained here with us since. Mr. Fujioka famously called this painting "my finest hour."

1. Where is the information posted?

    (A) At the Moto Contemporary Art Museum

    (B) At the Fontaine-Shields Gallery

    (C) At the Starlit Art Gallery

    (D) At the Clarkson-Walker Museum

2. Who most likely is Mr. Gaines?

    (A) A painter

    (B) An art critic

    (C) An art collector

    (D) An exhibition director

3. What is NOT stated about *Kyoto at Twilight*?

    (A) The artist created it over a period of two years.

    (B) It has had more than one owner.

    (C) It appeared on the cover of *Modern Painting* magazine.

    (D) The artist considers it to be one of his best works.

2 Invoice

Omicron Premier Services Ltd.
83 Malet Street
London
WC1E 7HU

Invoice: 1Z67HN2
Arrival Date: 3 April

Bill to:
Dr. John Kwang
Overbrook Hospital

Ship to:
Overbrook Hospital
27 St. Stephens Green
Dublin, Ireland

Item Number	Description	Item Price
12B	5 Boxes Small Bandages	£12
12C	10 Boxes Large Bandages	£30
431Z*	2 Boxes Large Sterile Gloves	£5
10CD	5 Large Knee Braces	£25
	TOTAL	£72

Payment due upon receipt of goods.

Item 431Z will be shipped at a later date as it is currently not in the warehouse.

4. What most likely is Omicron Premier Services?

(A) A hospital
(B) A doctor's office
(C) A shipping company
(D) A medical supply company

5. According to the invoice, what will happen on April 3?

(A) An invoice will be revised.
(B) An order will be placed.
(C) A payment will be refunded.
(D) A shipment will be delivered.

6. What is indicated about the gloves?

(A) They are out of stock at the moment.
(B) They are available in one size only.
(C) They are no longer manufactured.
(D) They are the wrong brand.

→解答・解説は p.112、114

1

案内

Takashi Fujioka
Kyoto at Twilight
Oil on canvas
114.3 cm x 99.06 cm

This work is the first in Takashi Fujioka's *Kyoto Nightfall* series, which gained international recognition. Works from this series of paintings have been exhibited in museums and galleries around the world, including the Moto Contemporary Art Museum in Tokyo, the Fontaine-Shields Gallery in New York City, and the Starlit Art Gallery in London. *Kyoto at Twilight* was featured on the cover of *Modern Painting* magazine the year it was painted. It was bought four years ago by Thomas Chester Gaines for his private collection and was sold to the Clarkson-Walker Museum for our permanent collection two years ago. It has remained here with us since. Mr. Fujioka famously called this painting "my finest hour."

Takashi Fujioka
『たそがれの京都』
油絵
114.3 cm×99.06 cm

本作は、Takashi Fujioka の「京都の夕べ」シリーズの 1 作目で、国際的な注目を獲得しました。この絵画シリーズの作品は、東京の Moto 現代美術館、ニューヨーク市の Fontaine-Shields ギャラリー、ロンドンの Starlit アートギャラリーをはじめ、これまで世界中の美術館やギャラリーで展示されています。『たそがれの京都』は、同作が描かれた年に、『近現代絵画』誌の表紙を飾りました。同作は 4 年前、Thomas Chester Gaines により個人の所蔵品として購入され、2 年前に当 Clarkson-Walker 美術館の常設展示用に売却されました。それ以来、当館に所蔵されています。有名な話ですが、Fujioka 氏はこの絵を「私の最良の時期」と呼びました。

語 注

❶ twilight　たそがれ　　oil　油絵具　　canvas　カンバス

❷ work　作品　　nightfall　夕暮れ　　series　シリーズもの、一続き　　gain　～を得る　　international　国際的な　recognition　注目、(力量などを) 認めること　　exhibit　～を展示する　　museum　美術館　　gallery　ギャラリー　including　～を含めて　　contemporary　現代の　　feature　～を特集する　　cover　表紙、カバー　modern　近現代の　　private　個人的な　　collection　所蔵品　　remain　とどまる　　since　それ以来　famously　よく知られているように　　*one's* finest hour　～ (人) の最良の時期

プラクティス

1. 例は左図参照。

2. ア．絵画作品の案内。　　イ．美術館の来館者　　ウ．Takashi Fujioka の油絵

　　エ．Takashi Fujioka による「京都の夕べ」シリーズの 1 作目で、国際的な注目を獲得した。

3. 左図参照。

チャレンジ

1. Where is the information posted?

　　(A) At the Moto Contemporary Art Museum
　　(B) At the Fontaine-Shields Gallery
　　(C) At the Starlit Art Gallery
　　(D) At the Clarkson-Walker Museum

この案内はどこに掲示されていますか。

　　(A) Moto 現代美術館
　　(B) Fontaine-Shields ギャラリー
　　(C) Starlit アートギャラリー
　　(D) Clarkson-Walker 美術館

| 正解 | **D** | ❷9 行目に「それ以来、ここにある」とあるが、here「ここ」とはその前の文、同 8 ～ 9 行目の「2 年前に当 Clarkson-Walker 美術館の常設展示用に売却された」に記載の Clarkson-Walker 美術館のことを指す。 |

(A) (B) (C) いずれも、Takashi Fujioka の同シリーズの別作品が展示されてきた美術館やギャラリーの名前。

2. Who most likely is Mr. Gaines?

　　(A) A painter
　　(B) An art critic
　　(C) An art collector
　　(D) An exhibition director

Gaines さんは誰だと考えられますか。

　　(A) 画家
　　(B) 美術評論家
　　(C) 美術品収集家
　　(D) 展覧会のディレクター

| 正解 | **C** | Gaines さんについては、❷の 7 ～ 8 行目「同作は 4 年前、Thomas Chester Gaines により個人の所蔵品として購入された」より、『たそがれの京都』の過去の所有者だったことが分かる。個人の所蔵品として作品を購入しているので、Gaines さんは (C) の An art collector「美術品収集家」であると判断できる。 |

(B) critic「批評家」。
(D) exhibition「展覧会」、director「ディレクター、監督」。

3. What is NOT stated about *Kyoto at Twilight*?

　　(A) The artist created it over a period of two years.
　　(B) It has had more than one owner.
　　(C) It appeared on the cover of *Modern Painting* magazine.
　　(D) The artist considers it to be one of his best works.

『たそがれの京都』について述べられていないことは何ですか。

　　(A) 画家が 2 年間かけて制作した。

　　(B) これまで複数の所有者がいた。

　　(C) 『近現代絵画』誌の表紙に載った。

　　(D) 画家はそれを、自身の最高傑作の 1 つであると考えている。

| 正解 | **A** | 述べられていないことを選ぶことに注意。❷の 5 ～ 10 行目で、これまでの所有者は Gaines さんと Clarkson-Walker 美術館の 2 者以上であること、制作された年に『近現代絵画』誌の表紙を飾ったこと、作家の Takashi Fujioka がこの作品を「私の最良の時期」と呼んだことについては、それぞれ記載がある。作品の制作期間については言及されていないので、正解は (A)。 |

(B) more than one ～「2 つ以上の～、1 つより多くの～」。

2

```
                                                                      請求書

    Omicron Premier Services Ltd.
    83 Malet Street
    London
    WC1E 7HU

❶   Invoice: 1Z67HN2
    Arrival Date: 3 April

❷   Bill to:                        ❸   Ship to:
    Dr. John Kwang                       Overbrook Hospital
    Overbrook Hospital                   27 St. Stephens Green
                                         Dublin, Ireland
```

Item Number	Description	Item Price
12B	5 Boxes Small Bandages	£12
12C	10 Boxes Large Bandages	£30
431Z*	2 Boxes Large Sterile Gloves	£5
10CD	5 Large Knee Braces	£25
	TOTAL	£72

❹

Payment due upon receipt of goods.

❺ * Item 431Z will be shipped at a later date as it is currently not in the warehouse.

Omicron Premier Services 社

Malet 通り 83 番地／ロンドン／ WC1E 7HU

請求書：1Z67HN2 ／**到着日**：4 月 3 日

請求先：

John Kwang 医師／ Overbrook 病院

送り先：

Overbrook 病院／ St. Stephens Green 27 番地／ダブリン、アイルランド

商品番号	明細	商品の金額小計
12B	包帯（小）5 箱	12 ポンド
12C	包帯（大）10 箱	30 ポンド
431Z*	無菌手袋（大）2 箱	5 ポンド
10CD	膝の固定具（大）5 個	25 ポンド
	合計	72 ポンド

商品の受取時に支払い。

* 商品 431Z は、現在在庫がないため後日発送されます。

語 注

❶ invoice 請求書、送り状　arrival 到着　date 日付
❷ bill to ～　～宛てに請求、請求先
❸ ship to ～　～宛てに発送、送り先
❹ item 商品、品目　description 明細、記載事項　price 金額、料金　bandage 包帯　sterile 無菌の、滅菌した knee brace 膝の固定具　payment 支払い　due 当然支払われるべき　upon receipt of ～　～を受領して goods〈複数形で〉商品
❺ ship ～を発送する、～を出荷する　at a later date 後日に　as ～であるので　currently 現在は warehouse 倉庫

プラクティス

1. 例は左図参照。

2. ア．請求書（送り状）。　　イ．Omicron Premier Services 社　　ウ．Overbrook 病院の John Kwang 医師　　エ．包帯（小）5 箱、包帯（大）10 箱、膝の固定具（大）5 個。

3. 左図参照。

チャレンジ

4. What most likely is Omicron Premier Services?

(A) A hospital
(B) A doctor's office
(C) A shipping company
(D) A medical supply company

Omicron Premier Services は何だと考えられますか。

(A) 病院
(B) 診療所
(C) 配送会社
(D) 医療用品会社

> **正解 D**　❷の請求先が Dr. John Kwang という医師であり、❸の送り先が病院になっている。また、注文内容が記載された❹より、bandage「包帯」や sterile glove「無菌手袋」など医療用品を取り扱っている会社だと分かる。よって、(D) の A medical supply company「医療用品会社」が正解。medical「医療の、医学の」。
> (B) doctor's office「診療所」。

5. According to the invoice, what will happen on April 3?

(A) An invoice will be revised.
(B) An order will be placed.
(C) A payment will be refunded.
(D) A shipment will be delivered.

請求書によると、4 月 3 日に何が起きますか。

(A) 請求書が修正される。
(B) 注文がなされる。
(C) 支払額が返金される。
(D) 発送品が配達される。

> **正解 D**　請求書で 4 月 3 日と書かれているのは、❶の 2 行目の Arrival Date「到着日」と記載されている箇所。その日は、注文した医療用品が配達されて、病院に届く日である。よって、(D) が正解。shipment「発送品」、deliver「〜を配達する」。
> (A) revise「〜を修正する」。
> (B) place an order「注文をする」。
> (C) refund「〜を返金する、〜を払い戻す」。

6. What is indicated about the gloves?

(A) They are out of stock at the moment.
(B) They are available in one size only.
(C) They are no longer manufactured.
(D) They are the wrong brand.

手袋について何が示されていますか。

(A) 今のところ在庫切れである。
(B) 1 サイズでのみ購入できる。
(C) もう製造されていない。
(D) 銘柄が間違っている。

> **正解 A**　❹の注文内容の 4 行目の無菌手袋の商品番号 431Z の箇所に、アスタリスク（*）が付いていることに注目する。同じ印が、❺の注記にもあり、「商品 431Z は、現在在庫がないため後日発送される」と記載されている。よって、(A) が正解。out of stock「在庫切れで」、at the moment「今のところ」。
> (C) no longer 〜「もはや〜ない」、manufacture「〜を製造する」。
> (D) wrong「間違った、誤った」、brand「銘柄、商標」。

Unit 13　推測を交えて読む

テーマ解説

文書の背景情報や場面を推測する

長文の文書を読み進めていく過程では、主題の背景情報や書き手の立場をあれこれ推測をしながら読み進めることが助けになります。Unit 13 では推測を交えながら読む練習をしてみましょう。次の手紙の書き出しから、書き手と読み手の関係、場面（状況）、背景情報を推測してみてください。

例　Dear Mr. Johnson,

We received your returned item. According to our after-service department, the item was found to be defective as you claimed in your e-mail. We would like to explain the procedures for exchanging the product or obtaining a refund.

Johnson 様、返品を受領いたしました。アフターサービス部門によると、商品は貴殿が E メールで主張されたように欠陥品でした。商品の交換または払戻金の受領のためのお手続きをご説明差し上げたく存じます。

主語 We や文体からはフォーマルな印象を受けます。幾つかのキーワード（網掛け部分）から、手紙の受取人の Johnson さんは商品購入者、差出人はメーカーの顧客窓口という関係で、返品をした Johnson さんに対し欠陥品であることを認め、その後の手続きについて説明する手紙だと推測できます。また、下線部から以前に Johnson さんが窓口へ問い合わせていたことが伺えます。このように、特定の表現から文章にはっきりと書かれていないことも含めて推測することで、多くの情報が読み取れます。

\ 文書の内容理解に挑戦 /

では、次ページの「ウォームアップ」の文書について、その背景情報も推測しながら読んでみましょう。読み方のヒントとして、以下の解説も参考にしてください。

---

1 文書形式、2 発信者と受信者、3 概要（主題や目的）

☑ ❶1 ～ 2 行目に For the first time ever, riders ... will be permitted to use the city's main streets. とあります。
おそらくこれが、文書の中心的な話題、つまり主題です。

☑ ❶2 行目 On Tuesday, the city council engaged in a heated debate.

☑ For the first time ever（❶1 行目）、As a result（同 3 行目）、Consequently（同 7 行目）

キーワード（網掛け部分）や論理を展開する副詞(句)を使った文体の特徴と、前述の主題から、この文書は記事で、「市議会による自転車競技の新コースの決定」を報じたものだと分かります。

4 詳細情報

☑ ❶3 ～ 6 行目 Longtime opponent ... was persuaded to change his mind. As a result, the council finally voted ... to run right through the center of Cloverville ...
新コースが決定された経緯について説明しています。また、文書には書かれていない、幾つかの背景情報も伺えます。

☑ ❶6 行目 In recent years, some riders have complained that the course was too short.
新コースについて、近年不満の声が上がっていたという新しい話題を持ち出しています。

☑ ❶7 ～ 8 行目 Consequently, this year's course has been lengthened slightly by including ...
新コースの決定が前文の新しい話題に与えた効果について言及しています。

推測しながら読むことが自然にできるようになってくると、文書の全体像の把握が早くなり、読むスピードも上がってくるはずです。これらを理解した上で、「ウォームアップ」の質問に答えましょう。

ウォームアップ

テーマ解説を参考に次の文書を通して読みましょう。その後、文書の内容を説明した文を読み、(a)、(b) どちらが正しいかを答えましょう。

❶ For the first time ever, riders in the Cloverville Bicycle Race will be permitted to use the city's main streets. On Tuesday, the city council engaged in a heated debate. Longtime opponent Tim Howard was persuaded to change his mind. As a result, the council finally voted in favor of allowing the race, now scheduled for September 9, to run right through the center of Cloverville before it proceeds across the Munn River Bridge. In recent years, some riders have complained that the course was too short. Consequently, this year's course has been lengthened slightly by including the Munn River Bridge crossing as part of the route.

1. Cloverville 自転車レースは、市の大通りを使用することを、[(a) 今まで許可してきた　(b) 今回初めて許可する]。

2. Tim Howard 氏は長年、自転車レースのコースが市の大通りを通ることについて、[(a) 賛成していた　(b) 反対していた]。

3. 白熱した議論の末、道路の使用許可は [(a) 投票によって市議会で可決された　(b) 市長の判断に委ねられた]。

4. レースの参加者の中には、[(a) 市街地の中を通り抜けたい　(b) コースが短過ぎる] と不満を述べる人もいた。

5. 結果的に、新しいコースは以前と比べて、[(a) 格段に短くなった　(b) 少し長くなった]。

【解答】

1. (b)　**2.** (b)　**3.** (a)　**4.** (b)　**5.** (b)

【訳】

Cloverville 自転車レースの出場選手は、史上初めて市の大通りの使用を許可されることになる。市議会は火曜日、白熱した議論を戦わせた。長年反対を唱えていた Tim Howard は説得され、考えを変えるに至った。その結果市議会はついに、現在 9 月 9 日に予定されているレースが、Munn 川橋を走り抜ける前に Cloverville 中心街をまっすぐ通過するのを認めることを、投票で可決した。近年、一部の選手からコースが短過ぎると不満の声が上がっていた。結果的に、今年のコースはルートの一部に Munn 川橋の通過が含まれることにより、わずかに長くなっている。

TOEIC® L&R の問題文書を使って、実際に文書を読む練習をしましょう。

1、**2** それぞれの文書に対し、**1** 〜 **3** の指示に従いながら、内容理解に挑戦してください。

1 Letter

Patel Dental Clinic
Block V, Rajouri Garden
New Delhi 110027

12 June

Radhika Hathi
Flat Number 1155
Navya Apartments
Tilak Nagar
New Delhi 110018

Dear Ms. Hathi:

At Patel Dental Clinic, ensuring that you have current information about your account with us is a priority. Effective 1 July, all invoices not paid at the time of service must be paid within 30 days. Please find enclosed a complete and detailed explanation of our revised billing schedule.

This necessary revision will allow us to continue to provide dental care to you and your family without increasing the cost of services this year. Should you need to make alternate payment arrangements, please contact our office manager, Jigna Gupta, at 11-2616 0002.

Sincerely,

Dr. Satish Patel
Dr. Satish Patel
Enclosure

1. 文書を読み、概要理解に重要と思われる語句や文を丸（◯）で囲んでみましょう。

2. **1** を参考に、メモを完成させましょう（固有名詞を含め、英語表記可）。

- 文書形式：ア. _____

- 誰が、誰宛てに書いた？

  イ. _____ が、ウ. _____
  宛てに書いた。

- 書き手は何を最も知らせたい？

  エ. _____

3. <u>改定に至った理由の１つ</u>について説明している箇所を見つけて、上の文書内に波線（〜〜〜）を引きましょう。

2 Survey

THE BROAD LAKE INN

Thank you for staying at the Broad Lake Inn! Customer satisfaction is very important to us, and we would appreciate your feedback. Please fill out the survey below and leave it with the receptionist at the front desk when you check out.

How satisfied were you with the Broad Lake Inn?
Please circle one selection for each category:

Service	Not satisfied	Satisfied	(Very satisfied)
Cleanliness	Not satisfied	Satisfied	(Very satisfied)
Appearance	Not satisfied	(Satisfied)	Very satisfied
Restaurant	(Not satisfied)	Satisfied	Very satisfied

Would you recommend the Broad Lake Inn to others?

No   Maybe   (Yes)

Please add any comments or suggestions you may have in the space below.

Overall, I had a wonderful experience at the inn. The employees were extremely friendly, and the inn was very clean and comfortable. Thanks to the well-equipped computer center, I was able to get a lot of work done. The restaurant, however, was quite expensive, and the food was not particularly tasty.

If you wish to be contacted regarding your feedback, please provide your name and phone number or e-mail address below:

Minna Haataja
mhaataja@feridia.fi

1. 文書を読み、概要理解に重要と思われる語句や文を丸（◯）で囲んでみましょう。

2. **1** を参考に、メモを完成させましょう（固有名詞を含め、英語表記可）。

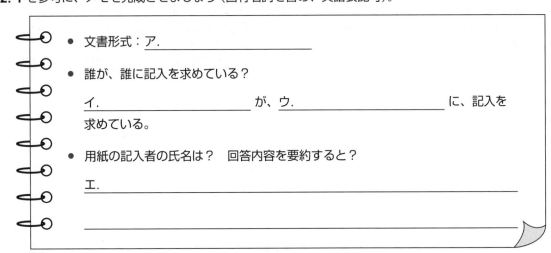

- 文書形式：ア._____

- 誰が、誰に記入を求めている？

  イ._____ が、ウ._____ に、記入を

  求めている。

- 用紙の記入者の氏名は？　回答内容を要約すると？

  エ._____

  _____

3. 最後に氏名とメールアドレスが書かれている理由が推測できる箇所を見つけて、上の文書内に波線（〜〜〜）を引きましょう。

→解答・解説は p.122、124

チャレンジ

TOEIC® L&R の問題に挑戦します。

右上の目安の解答時間を目標に、自分で時間を計りながら **1** ～ **4** の問題に答えてください。

1 Letter

Patel Dental Clinic
Block V, Rajouri Garden
New Delhi 110027

12 June

Radhika Hathi
Flat Number 1155
Navya Apartments
Tilak Nagar
New Delhi 110018

Dear Ms. Hathi:

At Patel Dental Clinic, ensuring that you have current information about your account with us is a priority. Effective 1 July, all invoices not paid at the time of service must be paid within 30 days. Please find enclosed a complete and detailed explanation of our revised billing schedule.

This necessary revision will allow us to continue to provide dental care to you and your family without increasing the cost of services this year. Should you need to make alternate payment arrangements, please contact our office manager, Jigna Gupta, at 11-2616 0002.

Sincerely,

Dr. Satish Patel

Dr. Satish Patel
Enclosure

1. Why was the letter sent to Ms. Hathi?

(A) To correct a billing mistake
(B) To publicize a newly opened clinic
(C) To announce a policy change
(D) To reschedule an appointment

2. What is indicated about Patel Dental Clinic?

(A) It has hired a new office manager.
(B) It hopes to avoid an increase in fees.
(C) It mentors dental students.
(D) It has updated its hours of operation.

2 Survey

THE BROAD LAKE INN

Thank you for staying at the Broad Lake Inn! Customer satisfaction is very important to us, and we would appreciate your feedback. Please fill out the survey below and leave it with the receptionist at the front desk when you check out.

How satisfied were you with the Broad Lake Inn?
Please circle one selection for each category:

Service	Not satisfied	Satisfied	(Very satisfied)
Cleanliness	Not satisfied	Satisfied	(Very satisfied)
Appearance	Not satisfied	(Satisfied)	Very satisfied
Restaurant	(Not satisfied)	Satisfied	Very satisfied

Would you recommend the Broad Lake Inn to others?

No   Maybe   (Yes)

Please add any comments or suggestions you may have in the space below.

Overall, I had a wonderful experience at the inn. The employees were extremely friendly, and the inn was very clean and comfortable. Thanks to the well-equipped computer center, I was able to get a lot of work done. The restaurant, however, was quite expensive, and the food was not particularly tasty.

If you wish to be contacted regarding your feedback, please provide your name and phone number or e-mail address below:

Minna Haataja
mhaataja@feridia.fi

3. What are guests asked to do?

   (A) Return a completed form
   (B) Leave their keys at the front desk
   (C) Tell their friends about the inn
   (D) Recommend staff members for
        awards

4. What is suggested about Ms. Haataja?

   (A) She is an experienced cook.
   (B) She would like a job in the hotel
        industry.
   (C) She frequently travels on business.
   (D) She would like to discuss her stay
        with hotel staff.

→解答・解説は p.122、124

1

Patel Dental Clinic
Block V, Rajouri Garden
New Delhi 110027

12 June

Radhika Hathi
Flat Number 1155
Navya Apartments
Tilak Nagar
New Delhi 110018

Dear Ms. Hathi:

❶ At Patel Dental Clinic, ensuring that you have current information about your account with us is a priority. Effective 1 July, all invoices not paid at the time of service must be paid within 30 days. Please find enclosed a complete and detailed explanation of our revised billing schedule.

❷ This necessary revision will allow us to continue to provide dental care to you and your family without increasing the cost of services this year. Should you need to make alternate payment arrangements, please contact our office manager, Jigna Gupta, at 11-2616 0002.

Sincerely,

Dr. Satish Patel
Dr. Satish Patel
Enclosure

Patel 歯科診療所
Rajouri Garden、V 地区／ニューデリー 110027

6 月 12 日

Radhika Hathi
部屋番号 1155 ／ Navya アパート／ Tilak Nagar ／ニューデリー 110018

Hathi 様

Patel 歯科診療所では、当院とのお取引に関する現在の情報を皆さまへ確実にお知らせすることを重要視しております。7 月 1 日をもって、診療時に支払われていない全ての請求書は 30 日以内に支払われなければならないものとします。当院の、改定後の請求日程の全詳細説明を同封いたしましたので、ご確認ください。

このたびの必要な改定により、当院は本年の診療費を引き上げることなく、皆さまと皆さまのご家族へ歯科治療を提供し続けることが可能になります。もし他のお支払い方法を取ることが必要な場合は、事務長の Jigna Gupta 宛てに、11-2616 0002 までご連絡ください。

敬具
Dr. Satish Patel（署名）／ Satish Patel 医師／同封物

プラクティス

1. 例は左図参照。

2. ア．手紙。　　イ．Patel 歯科診療所の Satish Patel 医師　　ウ．患者の Radhika Hathi

エ．7月1日から有効になる支払期限の改定。

3. 左図参照。

チャレンジ

1. Why was the letter sent to Ms. Hathi?

(A) To correct a billing mistake

(B) To publicize a newly opened clinic

(C) To announce a policy change

(D) To reschedule an appointment

手紙はなぜ Hathi さんに送られたのですか。

(A) 請求書作成の誤りを訂正するため。

(B) 新しく開所した診療所を宣伝するため。

(C) 方針の変更を知らせるため。

(D) 予約の日時を変更するため。

> **正解 C** 手紙の本文❶2 ～ 3 行目に、「7 月 1 日をもって、診療時に支払われていない全ての請求書は 30 日以内に支払われなければならないものとする」とあり、続けて「当院の、改定後の請求日程の全詳細説明を同封した」と記載されている。よって、手紙は支払いの方針の変更を知らせるために送られたと分かる。正解は (C)。
> (A) correct「～を訂正する」。
> (B) publicize「～を宣伝する」。
> (D) reschedule「～の日時を変更する」。

2. What is indicated about Patel Dental Clinic?

(A) It has hired a new office manager.

(B) It hopes to avoid an increase in fees.

(C) It mentors dental students.

(D) It has updated its hours of operation.

Patel 歯科診療所について何が示されていますか。

(A) 新しい事務長を雇用した。

(B) 料金の値上げを避けたいと考えている。

(C) 歯学生を指導している。

(D) 診察時間を改定した。

> **正解 B** ❷1 ～ 2 行目に「このたびの必要な改定により、当院は本年の診療費を引き上げることなく、皆と皆の家族へ歯科治療を提供し続けることが可能になる」とあり、❶の改定に至った理由が説明されている。ここから、診療所は料金の値上げを避けるために支払期限の方針の改定をしたと推測できる。正解は (B)。fee「料金」。
> (A) hire「～を雇う」。
> (C) mentor「～を指導する」。
> (D) operation「業務、営業」。

語 注

dental clinic　歯科診療所　　flat　アパート　★イギリス英語

❶ ensure (that) ～　～であることを確実にする　　current　現在の　　account　取引、(取引に使われる) 口座

priority　優先事項、重要度の高いもの　　effective ～　～以降有効で　★～には日時が入る

at the time of service　サービス提供時　　enclose　～を同封する　　complete　完全な　　detailed　詳細な

revise　～を改定する　　billing　請求書作成　　schedule　予定表

❷ revision　改定　　allow ～ to do　～が…することを許す　　dental　歯の　　care　治療　　increase　～を増大させる

need to do　～する必要がある　　alternate　代わりの　　arrangement　取り決め、計画　　contact　～に連絡する

2

調査票

THE BROAD LAKE INN

① Thank you for staying at the Broad Lake Inn! Customer satisfaction is very important to us, and we would appreciate your feedback. Please fill out the survey below and leave it with the receptionist at the front desk when you check out.

② **How satisfied were you with the Broad Lake Inn?**

Please circle one selection for each category:

Service	Not satisfied	Satisfied	(Very satisfied)
Cleanliness	Not satisfied	Satisfied	(Very satisfied)
Appearance	Not satisfied	(Satisfied)	Very satisfied
Restaurant	(Not satisfied)	Satisfied	Very satisfied

Would you recommend the Broad Lake Inn to others?

No   Maybe   (Yes)

③ **Please add any comments or suggestions you may have in the space below.**

Overall, I had a wonderful experience at the inn. The employees were extremely friendly, and the inn was very clean and comfortable. Thanks to the well-equipped computer center, I was able to get a lot of work done. The restaurant, however, was quite expensive, and the food was not particularly tasty.

④ If you wish to be contacted regarding your feedback, please provide your name and phone number or e-mail address below:

Minna Haataja
mhaataja@feridia.fi

Broad Lake ホテル

Broad Lake ホテルにご宿泊いただきありがとうございます！ お客さまの満足は私たちにとって非常に重要ですので、ご意見を頂戴できればありがたく存じます。以下の調査票にご記入いただき、チェックアウトの際にフロントの受付係にお渡しください。

Broad Lake ホテルにどの程度ご満足いただけましたか。

項目ごとに 1 つ選んで丸をしてください：

サービス	不満足	満足	(とても満足)
清潔さ	不満足	満足	(とても満足)
外観	不満足	(満足)	とても満足
レストラン	(不満足)	満足	とても満足

他の方に Broad Lake ホテルをお勧めになりますか。

いいえ   たぶん   (はい)

ご意見またはご提案がございましたら、以下の空欄にお書き加えください。

総じて、このホテルでの滞在は素晴らしかったです。従業員は非常に親切で、ホテルはとても清潔で快適でした。設備が整ったコンピューターセンターのおかげで、多くの仕事を済ませることができました。しかし、レストランはかなり値段が高く、料理も特別においしくはありませんでした。

ご意見に関して連絡を希望される場合は、以下に氏名と電話番号または E メールアドレスをご記入ください：

Minna Haataja
mhaataja@feridia.fi

プラクティス

1. 例は左図参照。

2. ア．調査票（アンケート用紙）　イ．Broad Lake ホテル　ウ．宿泊客　エ．Minna Haataja。ホテルのサービス、清潔さ、外観などには満足しているが、レストランは値段が高くおいしくなかったと感じている。

3. 左図参照。

チャレンジ

3. What are guests asked to do?

　(A) Return a completed form
　(B) Leave their keys at the front desk
　(C) Tell their friends about the inn
　(D) Recommend staff members for awards

宿泊客は何をするよう求められていますか。

　(A) 記入済みの用紙を戻す。
　(B) フロントにキーを置いていく。
　(C) 友人にホテルのことを教える。
　(D) 従業員を賞に推薦する。

> **正解 A**　❶から Broad Lake ホテルという宿泊施設が用意した調査票だと分かる。❶1～2行目に「お客さまの満足は私たちにとって非常に重要なので、意見をもらえればありがたい」とあり、続けて「以下の調査票に記入し、チェックアウトの際にフロントの受付係に渡してほしい」と案内されている。よって、宿泊客は調査票の用紙に記入して、ホテルの従業員に戻すよう求められている。正解は (A)。form「用紙」。
> (B) leave「～を置いておく、～を預ける」。
> (D) award「賞」。

4. What is suggested about Ms. Haataja?

　(A) She is an experienced cook.
　(B) She would like a job in the hotel industry.
　(C) She frequently travels on business.
　(D) She would like to discuss her stay with hotel staff.

Haataja さんについて何が分かりますか。

　(A) 彼女は経験豊富な料理人である。
　(B) 彼女はホテル業界で職を得たい。

　(C) 彼女は頻繁に出張をする。
　(D) 自身の宿泊についてホテルの従業員と話したい。

> **正解 D**　❹1～2行目の「意見に関して連絡を希望する場合は、以下に氏名と電話番号またはEメールアドレスを記入してほしい」と記載されている箇所の下に、自筆で Haataja さんの氏名とEメールアドレスが書かれている。このことから、Haataja さんは自分が記入した意見について話すためにホテルからの連絡を希望していることが分かる。(D) が正解。
> (A) (B) (C) いずれについても言及はない。
> (A) experienced「経験豊富な」。
> (C) travel on business「出張する」。

語注

❶ customer satisfaction　顧客の満足　　appreciate　～を感謝する　　feedback　意見、感想　　fill out ～　～に記入する　survey　調査票　　receptionist　受付係　　check out　（ホテルを）チェックアウトする
❷ be satisfied with ～　～に満足している　　circle　～を丸で囲む　　selection　選択　　category　区分、種類　cleanliness　清潔さ　　appearance　外観、見掛け　　recommend　～を勧める
❸ add　～を追加する　　comment　意見、見解　　suggestion　提案　　overall　総じて、全体的に　　employee　従業員　extremely　極めて　　comfortable　快適で　　thanks to ～　～のおかげで　　well-equipped　設備が整った　get ～ done　～を済ませる、～を片付ける　　however　しかしながら　　particularly　特に
❹ wish to *do*　～することを望む　　contact　～に連絡する　　regarding　～に関して

Unit 14　複数人のやりとりを読む

テーマ解説

ビジネスの現場でもモバイル機器によるコミュニケーションが広がっていることから、Part 7 の文書にも複数人の間で交わされるテキストメッセージやオンラインチャットが登場します。Unit 14 では、これらの文書で使われる英語の特徴を見ていきます。

テキストメッセージやオンラインチャットの英語の特徴

- **話し言葉に近い**　テキストメッセージやオンラインチャットは、複数の人々が同時に情報交換できる即時性が最大の特徴です。そこでは、話し言葉に近い文体で、日常会話でよく見られる What?「何ですって？」、No idea.「全然分かりません」、Okay.「分かりました」のような表現が頻繁に使われます。
- **省略された情報が多い**　短く簡潔な表現が好まれるため、情報についても省略される傾向があります。職場の同僚同士のやりとりでは、当事者間で共有されている情報についての説明は省かれ、用件のみに絞られたやりとりが多くなります。
- **情報の流れが変則的である**　3 人以上が入れ替わりで次々に発言するタイプのチャットでは、会話の流れが一方向ではありません。直前の人の質問に返事をしないまま別の人が割り込んで前の話題に戻るなど、話の筋が追いにくい傾向があります。

以上のような特徴を踏まえると、読み手は、限られた情報と前後の文脈から推測して話の筋をつかむ必要があります。繰り返し出てくる語句に着目して、「登場人物は何人か」、「彼らはどんな関係か」、「話題は何か」など場面（状況）を推測しながら、概要と詳細情報を押さえていきましょう。

\ 文書の内容理解に挑戦 /

では、以下の解説を参考に、次ページの「ウォームアップ」のテキストメッセージを読んでみましょう。

---

1 文書形式、2 発信者と受信者

☑ 区切り線のブロックは一人一人の発言のまとまりを示し、1 行目に発信者の氏名と送信時刻が示されています。

ここから人数を把握します。この場合は O'Banion さんと Delaney さんという 2 人の人物によるやりとりです。

☑ ❶、❷のやりとりから、2 人は職場の同僚同士だと推測できます。

☑ ❷ We've completed the exterior, ... with the window trim.

☑ ❹ We also have to put another coat of paint on the garage door.

家屋の外装や内装に関連する語句（網掛け部分）が出てくるため、2 人は住宅の改装業者だと考えられます。

3 概要（主題や目的）

☑ ❶ Can you give me an update on the job ...?

☑ ❸ If you'll be wrapping up before 3 P.M., I was hoping you'd ...

2 つの依頼表現（下線部）から、O'Banion さんはこれらを伝えたくて、Delaney さんに連絡をしてきたと考えられます。

4 詳細情報

☑ ❹ We also have to put another coat ... The client found some smudges.

❸で O'Banion さんが控えめに依頼したところ、Delaney さんが現場で発生中の問題を報告し始めたため、依頼の件はいったん保留されています。その後の O'Banion さんの反応からも、その問題の方が重要視されていることが読み取れます。

☑ ❼ Okay. Let's check in again around 2:30 P.M.

約 1 時間後に再び連絡を入れ合おうという O'Banion さんの提案で、やりとりは終了しています。

ウォームアップ

テーマ解説を参考に次の文書を通して読んだ後、1、2の質問に答えましょう。

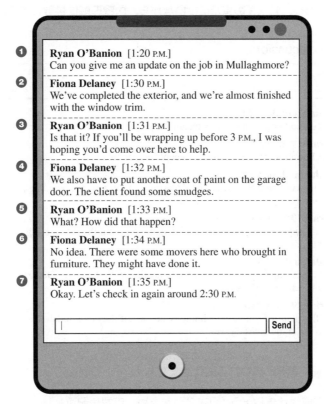

❶ Ryan O'Banion [1:20 P.M.]
Can you give me an update on the job in Mullaghmore?

❷ Fiona Delaney [1:30 P.M.]
We've completed the exterior, and we're almost finished with the window trim.

❸ Ryan O'Banion [1:31 P.M.]
Is that it? If you'll be wrapping up before 3 P.M., I was hoping you'd come over here to help.

❹ Fiona Delaney [1:32 P.M.]
We also have to put another coat of paint on the garage door. The client found some smudges.

❺ Ryan O'Banion [1:33 P.M.]
What? How did that happen?

❻ Fiona Delaney [1:34 P.M.]
No idea. There were some movers here who brought in furniture. They might have done it.

❼ Ryan O'Banion [1:35 P.M.]
Okay. Let's check in again around 2:30 P.M.

Send

1. O'Banion さんが午後 1 時 31 分に "Is that it?" と書いているのは、どういう意味だと考えられますか。
   (a) 材料に不足がないかを尋ねている。
   (b) 女性の仕事ぶりに礼を述べている。
   (c) 他の残務はないかを確認している。

2. どんな問題が起きていますか。
   (a) 窓枠用の塗料が不足している。
   (b) ガレージの扉の塗装が汚れている。
   (c) 家具を運ぶのが難しい。

【解答】

1. (c) **2.** (b)

【訳】

Ryan O'Banion ［午後 1 時 20 分］マラモア地区の仕事の状況を教えてもらえますか。

Fiona Delaney ［午後 1 時 30 分］外装が完了し、もうすぐ窓枠が終わります。

Ryan O'Banion ［午後 1 時 31 分］それで完了ですか。午後 3 時より前に終了するようなら、こっちに手伝いに来てもらえたらと思っていたんですが。

Fiona Delaney ［午後 1 時 32 分］私たちは、ガレージの扉にももう 1 層ペンキを塗らなくてはいけないんです。お客さまが幾つか汚れを見つけたので。

Ryan O'Banion ［午後 1 時 33 分］何ですって？ どうしてそんなことが起きたんですか。

Fiona Delaney ［午後 1 時 34 分］見当が付きません。家具を運び込んだ引越業者が何人かいましたからね。彼らがやったのかもしれません。

Ryan O'Banion ［午後 1 時 35 分］分かりました。午後 2 時 30 分ごろにまた連絡を入れ合いましょう。

TOEIC® L&R の問題文書を使って、実際に文書を読む練習をしましょう。

1、**2** それぞれの文書に対し、**1 ～ 3** の指示に従いながら、内容理解に挑戦してください。

1 Instant-message discussion

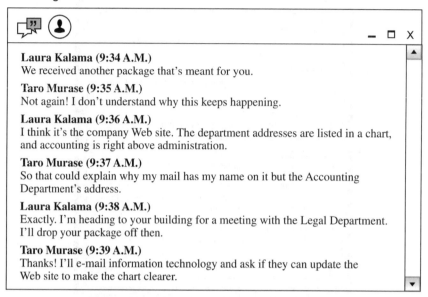

Laura Kalama (9:34 A.M.)
We received another package that's meant for you.

Taro Murase (9:35 A.M.)
Not again! I don't understand why this keeps happening.

Laura Kalama (9:36 A.M.)
I think it's the company Web site. The department addresses are listed in a chart, and accounting is right above administration.

Taro Murase (9:37 A.M.)
So that could explain why my mail has my name on it but the Accounting Department's address.

Laura Kalama (9:38 A.M.)
Exactly. I'm heading to your building for a meeting with the Legal Department. I'll drop your package off then.

Taro Murase (9:39 A.M.)
Thanks! I'll e-mail information technology and ask if they can update the Web site to make the chart clearer.

1. 文書を読み、概要理解に重要と思われる語句や文を丸 (◯) で囲んでみましょう。

2. 1 を参考に、メモを完成させましょう (固有名詞を含め、英語表記可)。

- 文書形式：ア.＿＿＿＿＿＿＿＿＿＿＿＿

- やりとりの人数と関係は？

  人数は イ.＿＿＿＿＿＿＿＿＿ 人で、ウ.＿＿＿＿＿＿＿＿＿ の
  関係。

- どんな問題が共有されている？

  エ.＿＿＿＿＿＿＿＿＿＿＿＿＿＿＿＿＿＿＿＿＿＿＿＿

  ＿＿＿＿＿＿＿＿＿＿＿＿＿＿＿＿＿＿＿＿＿＿＿＿＿＿＿

3. Kalama さん、Murase さんの所属部署は、それぞれどこだと考えられますか。

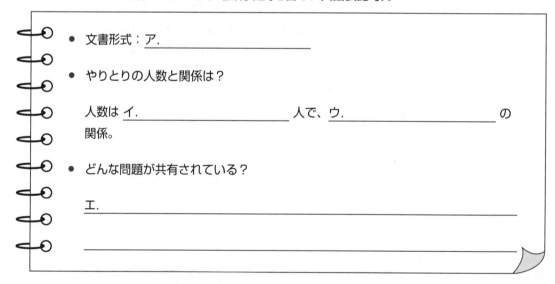

Kalama さん　☐ accounting　☐ administration　☐ legal　☐ information technology
Murase さん　☐ accounting　☐ administration　☐ legal　☐ information technology

2 Online chat discussion

Lisa Howland [11:08 A.M.]:	David, can you take a look at our Web site? I can't see the pictures of our products on my computer. Do they display on yours?
David Tanner [11:13 A.M.]:	No, same here. How long has this been going on?
Lisa Howland [11:14 A.M.]:	Probably not long. I was just contacted by someone who wanted to review an item she'd purchased but couldn't see now. No complaints earlier today or yesterday. Can you tell our IT team?
David Tanner [11:15 A.M.]:	Tim, something happened to the image files in the online store section of our Web site. Can you look into it?
Timothy Warner [11:18 A.M.]:	That's strange… Looks like they've been removed.
David Tanner [11:19 A.M.]:	I hope we've kept backup files.
Timothy Warner [11:20 A.M.]:	We always do, just in case. I'll upload them again now.
David Tanner [11:21 A.M.]:	Good. And we'll need to write a brief apology online saying that the problem has been fixed.
Lisa Howland [11:22 A.M.]:	I'll take care of that.

1. 文書を読み、概要理解に重要と思われる語句や文を丸 (◯) で囲んでみましょう。

2. 1 を参考に、メモを完成させましょう (固有名詞を含め、英語表記可)。

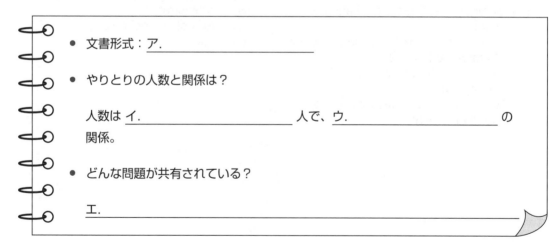

- 文書形式：ア.＿＿＿＿＿＿＿＿＿＿＿

- やりとりの人数と関係は？

  人数は イ.＿＿＿＿＿＿＿＿＿ 人で、ウ.＿＿＿＿＿＿＿＿＿ の
  関係。

- どんな問題が共有されている？

  エ.＿＿＿＿＿＿＿＿＿＿＿＿＿＿＿＿＿＿＿

3. 次の (1)、(2) について述べられている箇所をそれぞれ見つけて、上の文書内に波線 (〜〜〜) を引きましょう。

(1) 問題が発覚した経緯を説明している箇所

(2) 問題の対応策について述べている箇所

→解答・解説は p.132、134

チャレンジ

目安の解答時間（min）	実際にかかった時間
🕐 03：30	：

TOEIC® L&R の問題に挑戦します。

右上の目安の解答時間を目標に、自分で時間を計りながら **1 ～ 6** の問題に答えてください。

1 Instant-message discussion

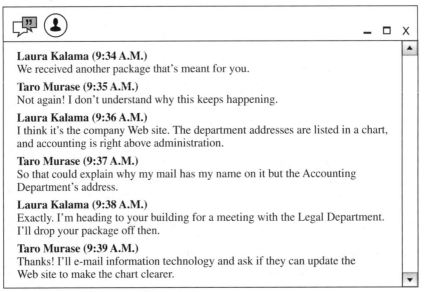

Laura Kalama (9:34 A.M.)
We received another package that's meant for you.

Taro Murase (9:35 A.M.)
Not again! I don't understand why this keeps happening.

Laura Kalama (9:36 A.M.)
I think it's the company Web site. The department addresses are listed in a chart, and accounting is right above administration.

Taro Murase (9:37 A.M.)
So that could explain why my mail has my name on it but the Accounting Department's address.

Laura Kalama (9:38 A.M.)
Exactly. I'm heading to your building for a meeting with the Legal Department. I'll drop your package off then.

Taro Murase (9:39 A.M.)
Thanks! I'll e-mail information technology and ask if they can update the Web site to make the chart clearer.

1. At 9:35 A.M., what does Mr. Murase most likely mean when he writes "Not again"?

(A) Someone returned a package he sent.

(B) He does not think Ms. Kalama needs to return to his office.

(C) His mail is often delivered to the wrong office.

(D) He does not want Ms. Kalama to send an e-mail.

2. What area does Mr. Murase work in?

(A) Accounting

(B) Administration

(C) Information Technology

(D) Legal

2 Online chat discussion

Lisa Howland [11:08 A.M.]:	David, can you take a look at our Web site? I can't see the pictures of our products on my computer. Do they display on yours?
David Tanner [11:13 A.M.]:	No, same here. How long has this been going on?
Lisa Howland [11:14 A.M.]:	Probably not long. I was just contacted by someone who wanted to review an item she'd purchased but couldn't see now. No complaints earlier today or yesterday. Can you tell our IT team?
David Tanner [11:15 A.M.]:	Tim, something happened to the image files in the online store section of our Web site. Can you look into it?
Timothy Warner [11:18 A.M.]:	That's strange… Looks like they've been removed.
David Tanner [11:19 A.M.]:	I hope we've kept backup files.
Timothy Warner [11:20 A.M.]:	We always do, just in case. I'll upload them again now.
David Tanner [11:21 A.M.]:	Good. And we'll need to write a brief apology online saying that the problem has been fixed.
Lisa Howland [11:22 A.M.]:	I'll take care of that.

3. What problem does Ms. Howland report?

(A) Payments cannot be processed in the online store.
(B) The wrong contact address is listed on the company's Web site.
(C) The company's Web site cannot be accessed.
(D) Some product information is not available online.

4. From whom did Ms. Howland learn about the problem?

(A) A customer
(B) An IT coworker
(C) A delivery company
(D) A store manager

5. At 11:19 A.M., what does Mr. Tanner most likely mean when he writes, "I hope we've kept backup files"?

(A) He is concerned about the store's customer records.
(B) He wants his coworker to explain the procedure for handling files.
(C) He is requesting access to the online store.
(D) He would like some images to be returned to the Web site.

6. What will Ms. Howland most likely do next?

(A) Update her personal profile
(B) Post a note online
(C) Contact the IT team
(D) Make an online purchase

→解答・解説は p.132、134

131

解答・解説

1

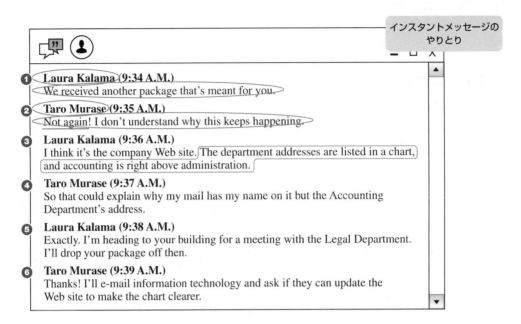

Laura Kalama（午前 9 時 34 分）
うちの部があなた宛ての荷物をまた受け取りました。

Taro Murase（午前 9 時 35 分）
またですか！ なぜこんなことが繰り返し起きるのか理解できません。

Laura Kalama（午前 9 時 36 分）
会社のウェブサイトじゃないでしょうか。部署の宛先が表内に列挙されていますが、経理部が管理部の真上にあるんです。

Taro Murase（午前 9 時 37 分）
では、郵便物に私の名前が書いてあるのに宛先が経理部なのはそういうわけなんですね。

Laura Kalama（午前 9 時 38 分）
その通りです。私はこれから法務部との会議で、あなたのいるビルへ向かいます。そのときにあなたの荷物を届けますよ。

Taro Murase（午前 9 時 39 分）
ありがとう！ 私は情報技術部に E メールを送って、ウェブサイトを更新して表をもっと分かりやすくできるかどうか尋ねてみます。

プラクティス

1. 例は左図参照。

2. ア．インスタントメッセージ。　　イ．2　　ウ．会社の同僚　　エ．Murase さん宛ての小包が Kalama さんの部署へ間違って届いてしまう。

3. Kalama さん：accounting（経理部）／ Murase さん：administration（管理部）

チャレンジ

1. At 9:35 A.M., what does Mr. Murase most likely mean when he writes "Not again"?

   (A) Someone returned a package he sent.
   (B) He does not think Ms. Kalama needs to return to his office.
   (C) His mail is often delivered to the wrong office.
   (D) He does not want Ms. Kalama to send an e-mail.

午前 9 時 35 分に、Murase さんが "Not again" と書いているのは、どういう意図だと考えられますか。

   (A) 誰かが彼が送った荷物を送り返した。
   (B) Kalama さんが自分のオフィスに戻る必要はないと考えている。
   (C) 彼宛ての郵便物がしばしば間違ったオフィスに届けられる。
   (D) Kalama さんに E メールを送ってほしくない。

正解 C Kalama さんが❶で「うちの部があなた宛ての荷物をまた受け取った」と述べたのに対して、Murase さんは❷で下線部の発言を行い、I don't understand why this keeps happening.「なぜこんなことが繰り返し起きるのか理解できない」と続けている。ここから、これまでにも、Murase さん宛ての荷物が Kalama さんの部署へ間違って届いていたことが分かる。よって、(C) が正解。wrong「間違った」。
(A) Murase さん自身は荷物を送っていない。

2. What area does Mr. Murase work in?

   (A) Accounting
   (B) Administration
   (C) Information Technology
   (D) Legal

Murase さんはどの部署で働いていますか。

   (A) 経理部
   (B) 管理部
   (C) 情報技術部
   (D) 法務部

正解 B ❶から、Murase さん宛ての郵便物を受け取っているのは Kalama さんの部署だと分かる。Kalama さんは❸で、会社のウェブサイトに載っている部署の宛先を列挙した表について、「経理部が管理部の真上にある」と述べている。それを受けて Murase さんが❹で、「では、郵便物に私の名前が書いてあるのに宛先が経理部なのはそういうわけなんだね」と述べていることから、荷物が間違って届く先は経理部で Kalama さんが所属する部署、一方の Murase さんの所属は管理部だと考えられる。正解は (B)。

語 注

❶ receive　～を受け取る　　package　荷物、小包　　be meant for ～　～に宛てられている、～に向けられている
❷ Not again.　またか。いい加減にしてくれ。　★再び起きたことに対する不満　　keep *doing*　繰り返し～する
❸ department　部署　　address　住所　　list　～を列挙する　　chart　表　　accounting　経理部
　administration　管理部
❹ explain　～を解明する、～を説明する
❺ head to ～　～へ向かう　　legal　法律の　　drop off ～　～（荷物）を届ける
❻ information technology　情報技術部　　update　～を更新する　　clear　はっきりした、明解な

2

オンラインチャットの
話し合い

Lisa Howland [11:08 A.M.]: David, can you take a look at our Web site? I can't see the pictures of our products on my computer. Do they display on yours?

David Tanner [11:13 A.M.]: No, same here. How long has this been going on?

Lisa Howland [11:14 A.M.]: Probably not long. I was just contacted by someone who wanted to review an item she'd purchased but couldn't see now. No complaints earlier today or yesterday. Can you tell our IT team?

David Tanner [11:15 A.M.]: Tim, something happened to the image files in the online store section of our Web site. Can you look into it?

Timothy Warner [11:18 A.M.]: That's strange… Looks like they've been removed.

David Tanner [11:19 A.M.]: I hope we've kept backup files.

Timothy Warner [11:20 A.M.]: We always do, just in case. I'll upload them again now.

David Tanner [11:21 A.M.]: Good. And we'll need to write a brief apology online saying that the problem has been fixed.

Lisa Howland [11:22 A.M.]: I'll take care of that.

Lisa Howland　[午前 11 時 8 分]：　David、当社のウェブサイトを見てもらえますか。私のコンピューターでは、当社の商品の写真が見えないんです。あなたのコンピューターには表示されますか。

David Tanner　[午前 11 時 13 分]：いいえ、こっちも同じです。どのくらいこの状態が続いているんですか。

Lisa Howland　[午前 11 時 14 分]：おそらく長い時間ではないです。ついさっき私は、購入品のレビューをしたかったのに現在見られないという女性から連絡を受けたんです。今日のこれまでや昨日には、苦情は来ていません。当社の IT チームに伝えてもらえますか。

David Tanner　[午前 11 時 15 分]：Tim、当社ウェブサイトのオンラインストア区画にある画像ファイルに、何かが起きました。調べてもらえますか。

Timothy Warner [午前 11 時 18 分]：おかしいな…。それらの画像ファイルが削除されてしまったようです。

David Tanner　[午前 11 時 19 分]：バックアップファイルを保存してあるといいんですが。

Timothy Warner [午前 11 時 20 分]：いつもそうしていますよ、念のためにね。今すぐ再アップロードしますね。

David Tanner　[午前 11 時 21 分]：良かった。それと、問題が解決されたことを伝える、オンライン上の短い謝罪文を書く必要があるでしょうね。

Lisa Howland　[午前 11 時 22 分]：それは私が引き受けます。

プラクティス

1. 例は左図参照。

2. ア．オンラインチャット。　　イ．3　　ウ．会社の同僚　　エ．会社のウェブサイトに商品の写真が表示されないという問題。

3. 左図参照。

チャレンジ

3. What problem does Ms. Howland report?

(A) Payments cannot be processed in the online store.

(B) The wrong contact address is listed on the company's Web site.

(C) The company's Web site cannot be accessed.

(D) Some product information is not available online.

Howland さんはどんな問題を報告していますか。

(A) オンラインストアで支払いが処理できない。

(B) 間違った連絡先が会社のウェブサイトに掲載されている。

(C) 会社のウェブサイトにアクセスできない。

(D) ある商品情報がオンライン上で利用できない。

正解 D　会社のウェブサイトについて、❶で Howland さんは「私のコンピューターでは、当社の商品の写真が見えない」と述べた後、Tanner さんへ、自身のコンピューターで確認をするように頼んでいる。それに対して❷で Tanner さんは「こっちも同じだ」と答えている。ウェブサイトの表示に問題が起きていると考えられるため、(D)「ある商品情報がオンライン上で利用できない」が正解。

(A) payment「支払い」の処理については言及がない。process「〜を処理する」。
(B) 連絡先については述べられていない。
(C) ❶より、Howland さんは会社のウェブサイトにアクセスはできている。access「〜にアクセスする」。

---

4. From whom did Ms. Howland learn about the problem?

(A) A customer

(B) An IT coworker

(C) A delivery company

(D) A store manager

Howland さんは誰から問題を知りましたか。

(A) 顧客

(B) IT 担当の同僚

(C) 配送会社

(D) 店長

正解 A　Howland さんは❸で、「ついさっき私は、購入品のレビューをしたかったのに現在見られないという女性から連絡を受けた」と説明している。購入品のレビューをする人物とは顧客だと考えられるので、(A) A customer が正解。

(B) ❹、❺より、IT 担当の同僚の Warner さんは、Tanner さんから問題を教わっている。
(C) delivery company「配送会社」。

5. At 11:19 A.M., what does Mr. Tanner most likely mean when he writes, "I hope we've kept backup files"?

(A) He is concerned about the store's customer records.

(B) He wants his coworker to explain the procedure for handling files.

(C) He is requesting access to the online store.

(D) He would like some images to be returned to the Web site.

午前 11 時 19 分に、Tanner さんが "I hope we've kept backup files" と書いているのは、どんな意図だと考えられますか。

(A) お店の顧客記録について心配している。

(B) 同僚にファイルを取り扱う手順について説明してほしいと思っている。

(C) オンラインストアへのアクセスを求めている。

(D) ウェブサイトに画像が戻されてほしいと思っている。

正解 **D** IT チームの Warner さんは、画像が表示されない原因として、❺で「それらの画像ファイルが削除されてしまったようだ」と述べている。直後の Tanner さんの下線部の発言は、Warner さんの発言を受けてのものなので、削除された画像ファイルのバックアップが保存してあって、ウェブサイトが元の状態に復元されることを願っていると分かる。正解は (D)。
(A) 顧客記録についての言及はない。
(B) Tanner さん自らがファイルを扱うつもりだとは述べられていない。
(C) ❷より、Tanner さんはすでにオンラインストアへアクセスして、画像ファイルが表示されないことを確認している。

---

6. What will Ms. Howland most likely do next?

(A) Update her personal profile
(B) Post a note online
(C) Contact the IT team
(D) Make an online purchase

Howland さんは次に何をすると考えられますか。

(A) 自身の個人プロフィールを更新する。
(B) オンライン上に注意書きを投稿する。
(C) IT チームに連絡する。
(D) オンラインショッピングをする。

正解 **B** Howland さんは❾で「それは私が引き受ける」と述べている。「それ」とは、直前の Tanner さんの❽の発言にある「問題が解決されたことを伝える、オンライン上の短い謝罪文を書く」ことを指している。よって、オンライン上に note「注意書き」を投稿するという内容の (B) が正解。
(A) 個人プロフィールについては言及がない。
(C) ❹、❺より IT チームへの連絡はすでに済んでいる。
(D) Howland さんがオンラインショッピングをするとは述べられていない。

語 注

❶ take a look at 〜 　〜を見る　　product 　商品、製品　　display 　表示される
❷ same here 　私も同じだ
❸ contact 　〜に連絡する　　review 　〜をレビューする、〜を批評する　　purchase 　〜を購入する　　complaint 　苦情　　earlier 　（時間的に）前に　　IT team 　IT チーム、情報技術部
❹ image 　画像　　look into 〜 　〜を調べる
❺ Looks like (that) 〜 　〜であるように見える　　remove 　〜を削除する、〜を取り除く
❻ backup 　（コンピューターのファイルなどの）バックアップ、コピーデータ
❼ just in case 　念のため　　upload 　〜をアップロードする
❽ brief 　短い、簡潔な　　apology 　謝罪　　fix 　〜を解決する
❾ take care of 〜 　〜を引き受ける、〜を処理する

Unit 15　段落ごとの要点をつかむ①

テーマ解説

複数段落から成る文書を読むポイント

記事のように、段落が幾つも連なって1つの文書として構成されている文章を読む際には、「段落」という情報のまとまりを認識することが、非常に大切です。一般的に、英語の文章には "one idea per paragraph"「1つの段落に1つの考え」という原則があり、段落には必ず1つの主題文があります。主題文とは、各段落の主題を紹介している文のことで、各段落の冒頭で示されることが多いです。主題文の後には、具体例などの詳細や、理由、根拠などを示す複数の支持文が続きます。また、段落の締めくくりに、主題文の内容をまとめた結論文が来ることもあります。また、これらの段落が複数集まり、文書全体で「序論→本論→結論」という基本構成を成します。

複数段落から成る長文を読む際は、このような文書の基本構成を踏まえて読んでみましょう。例えば、まず各段落の主題文だけを読んでみて概要や全体像を把握し、その後それぞれの段落の支持文を読んで細部の理解の穴を埋めていく、という読み方ができます。各段落の主題文から内容の見当を先に付け、その観点から支持文を読み進めていくことで、「これは応募条件を列挙している部分だな」とか「これは選考過程についての補足説明だな」などと、内容の予測を立てながら理解していくことができます。

\ 文書の内容理解に挑戦 /

では、「各段落の主題文を特定して概要や全体像を把握→各段落の詳細情報を理解」という流れで、以下の解説を参考に、次ページの「ウォームアップ」の記事を読んでみましょう。

---

1 文書形式、2 発信者と受信者

　タイトル（大見出し）も重要な情報の単位です。Wanted: Pottery Assistants から、この文書は求人広告だと分かります。

3 概要（主題や目的）

　☑ Potter's Lair, ... , is seeking two full-time assistants.（❶1～2行目）

　第1段落の主題文です。ここから求人元は陶器制作工房で、求人対象は2人の常勤の助手であることが分かります。第1段落の主題文は、文書全体の主題であることが多いです。

　☑ To apply, send your résumé and cover letter to yesenia@potterslair.com.（❷1行目）

　第2段落の主題文です。応募方法の話題で始まっていることから、第2段落はその説明が続くのだろうと予測できます。

　タイトル（大見出し）に加え、以上の主題文から、文書全体は陶芸の助手を募集している求人広告で、応募条件について詳述した後に応募方法を案内するという流れで書かれていると予測できます。

4 詳細情報

　☑ Qualified candidates must have ... Consistency is crucial.（❶2～4行目）

　☑ Candidates will be observed closely at first ... depending on experience.（❶4～8行目）

　第1段落の支持文です。募集職種の応募資格や要件、業務内容や時給などの条件に関する情報が述べられています。

　☑ Applicants will first be screened ... This will allow them to show off their skills in person.（❷1～4行目）

　☑ Once selected, assistants will be asked to ... as permanent employees.（❷4～7行目）

　第2段落の支持文です。応募後の選考の流れと、選ばれてから正規従業員になるまでの過程が書かれています。

ウォームアップ

テーマ解説を参考に次の文書を通して読んだ後、段落ごとの内容を説明した文を読み、内容が正しければ T、誤っていれば F を選びましょう。

Wanted: Pottery Assistants

❶ Potter's Lair, a pottery production studio based in Bradford, England, is seeking two full-time assistants. Qualified candidates must have a solid understanding of ceramic production and be comfortable learning a process and then replicating it many times throughout the day. Consistency is crucial. Candidates will be observed closely at first by the artist and must be able to handle constructive criticism so that they can improve the quality of their work. Tasks involve preparing clay for the artist, sanding final pieces, mixing and applying glazes, and cleaning the studio at the end of each work day. Payment is £8– £12 per hour, depending on experience.

❷ To apply, send your résumé and cover letter to yesenia@potterslair.com. Applicants will first be screened through a short phone conversation, then a select few will be invited to participate individually in a working interview. This will allow them to show off their skills in person. Once selected, assistants will be asked to sign a 90-day contract. During this trial period, assistants will be evaluated by the artist to determine if they have the skills necessary to be brought on as permanent employees.

[第 1 段落]

1. Potter's Lair は陶器を販売する会社で、販売員を募集している。　□ T　□ F

2. 仕事は同じ工程を何度も繰り返すことが多い。　□ T　□ F

3. 助手は作家からの批評を受け入れ、対応する姿勢が重要である。　□ T　□ F

4. 経験次第で 18 ポンドの時給をもらうことが可能である。　□ T　□ F

[第 2 段落]

5. 応募には、履歴書を直接持参する必要がある。　□ T　□ F

6. 応募者はまず、短い電話面接で審査される。　□ T　□ F

7. 対面の面接では、実技が行われる可能性がある。　□ T　□ F

8. 選考された人には 90 日間の試用期間がある。　□ T　□ F

【解答】
1. F　**2.** T　**3.** T　**4.** F　**5.** F　**6.** T　**7.** T　**8.** T
【訳】
募集：陶芸の助手
イングランドのブラッドフォード市に拠点を置く陶器制作工房の Potter's Lair 社は、常勤の助手 2 名を募集しています。適任の候補者は、陶器制作にしっかりとした知見があり、工程を身に付けて、その後一日中それを反復することをいとわない人でなければいけません。堅実さが極めて重要です。候補者は最初、作家による注意深い見守りを受けます。また、自身の仕事の質を高めるために建設的な批評に対応することができなければなりません。作業には、作家のための粘土の準備、仕上がっ

た作品の研磨、釉薬の調合や塗布、そして毎勤務日の終わりの工房清掃が含まれます。報酬は経験に応じ、時給 8 ～ 12 ポンドです。

応募するには、履歴書とカバーレターを yesenia@potterslair.com までお送りください。応募者はまず電話で短い会話による審査を受け、そこで選ばれた数名が、個々に就業面接への参加の招待を受けます。ここで候補者は自身の技能をじかに披露することができます。選ばれると、助手は 90 日間の契約を結ぶよう求められます。この試用期間中に、助手は正規従業員になるのに必要な技能を備えているかどうかを判断するために、作家による評定を受けることになります。

TOEIC® L&R の問題文書を使って、実際に文書を読む練習をしましょう。

次の文書に対し、**1 ～ 3** の指示に従いながら、内容理解に挑戦してください。

Web site

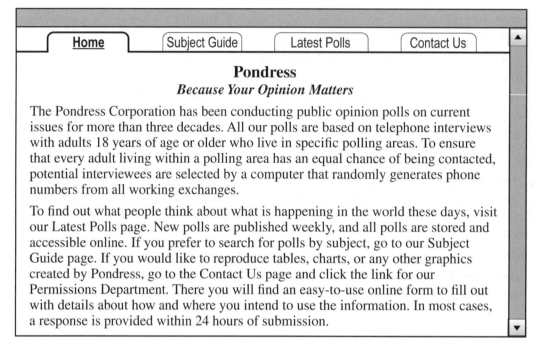

1. 文書を読み、段落ごとの主題文と、それらに関連が深いと思われる語句や文を丸（◯）で囲んでみましょう。

2. **1** を参考に、メモを完成させましょう（固有名詞を含め、英語表記可）。

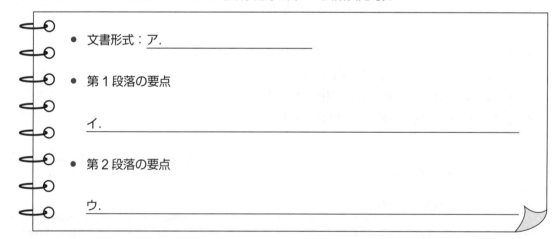

3. 次の (1)、(2) について、文書内で述べられている箇所をそれぞれ見つけて、上の文書内に波線（〰）を引きましょう。

(1) 世論調査の調査対象者を選ぶ方法

(2) Pondress 社のコンテンツを複製して利用したい場合の連絡方法

チャレンジ

TOEIC® L&R の問題に挑戦します。

右上の目安の解答時間を目標に、自分で時間を計りながら **1 ～ 4** の問題に答えてください。

Web site

| Home | Subject Guide | Latest Polls | Contact Us |

Pondress
Because Your Opinion Matters

The Pondress Corporation has been conducting public opinion polls on current issues for more than three decades. All our polls are based on telephone interviews with adults 18 years of age or older who live in specific polling areas. To ensure that every adult living within a polling area has an equal chance of being contacted, potential interviewees are selected by a computer that randomly generates phone numbers from all working exchanges.

To find out what people think about what is happening in the world these days, visit our Latest Polls page. New polls are published weekly, and all polls are stored and accessible online. If you prefer to search for polls by subject, go to our Subject Guide page. If you would like to reproduce tables, charts, or any other graphics created by Pondress, go to the Contact Us page and click the link for our Permissions Department. There you will find an easy-to-use online form to fill out with details about how and where you intend to use the information. In most cases, a response is provided within 24 hours of submission.

1. In paragraph 1, line 1, the word "current" is closest in meaning to

(A) moving
(B) customary
(C) contemporary
(D) momentary

2. What is NOT mentioned about poll participants?

(A) They are randomly selected.
(B) They are interviewed in groups.
(C) They are interviewed over the phone.
(D) They are adults.

3. What is indicated about the Pondress Corporation?

(A) It updates its Web site every week.
(B) It has offices in multiple locations.
(C) It is searching for new employees.
(D) It publishes nonfiction books.

4. How can readers get permission to reproduce graphics?

(A) By sending an e-mail
(B) By making a phone call
(C) By submitting a paper form
(D) By providing information online

→解答・解説は p.142

| Home | Subject Guide | Latest Polls | Contact Us |

Pondress
Because Your Opinion Matters

❶ The Pondress Corporation has been conducting public opinion polls on current issues for more than three decades. All our polls are based on telephone interviews with adults 18 years of age or older who live in specific polling areas. To ensure that every adult living within a polling area has an equal chance of being contacted, potential interviewees are selected by a computer that randomly generates phone numbers from all working exchanges.

❷ To find out what people think about what is happening in the world these days, visit our Latest Polls page. New polls are published weekly, and all polls are stored and accessible online. If you prefer to search for polls by subject, go to our Subject Guide page. If you would like to reproduce tables, charts, or any other graphics created by Pondress, go to the Contact Us page and click the link for our Permissions Department. There you will find an easy-to-use online form to fill out with details about how and where you intend to use the information. In most cases, a response is provided within 24 hours of submission.

ホーム　　　　　テーマガイド　　　　　最新の世論調査　　　　　連絡先

Pondress
あなたの意見は重要だから

Pondress 社は、30 年超にわたって時事問題の世論調査を行っています。当社の調査は全て、特定の調査地域に住む 18 歳以上の成人を対象にした電話インタビューに基づいています。調査地域内に居住する成人全員が連絡を受ける機会を均等に得られるように、活動中の全電話局から電話番号を無作為に生成するコンピューターによってインタビュー候補者が選ばれます。

世の中で近年起きている事象について人々がどう考えているかを知るため、当社の「最新の世論調査」のページにアクセスしてください。新しい世論調査が毎週公開されており、全世論調査がオンライン上で保存され、利用できます。テーマ別に世論調査を検索したい場合は、「テーマガイド」のページにアクセスしてください。Pondress 社が作成した表、図、その他の図版を複製利用したい場合は「連絡先」のページにアクセスし、当社の許諾部へのリンクをクリックしてください。使いやすいオンラインフォームが表示されるので、その情報をどのように、またどんな場で使用したいのか詳細をご記入ください。ほとんどの場合、回答は申請後 24 時間以内に致します。

語注

subject テーマ、題目　　matter 重要である
❶ conduct 〜を実施する　　public opinion 世論　　poll 世論調査　　current 最新の、現在の　　issue 問題
decade 10 年　　be based on 〜 〜に基づいている　　interview インタビュー、取材調査　　adult 成人
specific 特定の　　polling 世論調査　　equal 均等な　　chance 機会　　potential 可能性のある
interviewee インタビューされる人、面接を受ける人　　select 〜を選び出す　　randomly 無作為に
generate 〜を生み出す　　work 機能する　　exchange 電話局　★ここでは電話局に登録されている電話番号のこと
❷ find out 〜 〜を見つけ出す　　publish 〜を公開する　　weekly 週に 1 回　　store 〜を保管する
accessible 利用できる　　reproduce 〜を複製する、〜を再現する　　permission 許諾　　easy-to-use 使いやすい
fill out 〜 〜に記入する　　details〈複数形で〉詳細　　response 回答、返事　　submission 提出

プラクティス

1. 例は左図参照。

2. ア．企業案内のウェブサイト。　　イ．Pondress 社は、30 年超にわたって時事問題の世論調査を行っている会社である。　　ウ．Pondress 社のウェブページでは、世の中で起きている事象についての人々の考えを知ることができる。

3. 左図参照。

チャレンジ

1. In paragraph 1, line 1, the word "current" is closest in meaning to

(A) moving
(B) customary
(C) contemporary
(D) momentary

第 1 段落・1 行目にある "current" に最も意味が近いのは

(A) 感動的な
(B) 習慣的な
(C) 現代の
(D) 一瞬の

 C ❶の 1 ～ 2 行目は、この会社が 30 年超にわたって current issues「時事問題」の世論調査を行っていると説明している。この意味の current に最も近いのは「現代の、同時代の」という意味の (C) contemporary である。

2. What is NOT mentioned about poll participants?

(A) They are randomly selected.
(B) They are interviewed in groups.
(C) They are interviewed over the phone.
(D) They are adults.

世論調査の参加者について述べられていないのは何ですか。

(A) 無作為に選ばれている。
(B) 集団でインタビューされる。
(C) 電話でインタビューされる。
(D) 成人である。

 B 調査方法については、❶の 2 ～ 6 行目で述べられている。調査は全て電話インタビューで行われ、特定の調査地域に住む 18 歳以上の成人を対象にしていて、無作為に電話番号を生成するコンピューターによって選ばれていると説明されている。集団でインタビューされるとは書かれていない。よって、(B) が正解。in groups「集団で」。

3. What is indicated about the Pondress Corporation?

(A) It updates its Web site every week.
(B) It has offices in multiple locations.
(C) It is searching for new employees.
(D) It publishes nonfiction books.

Pondress 社について何が示されていますか。

(A) ウェブサイトを毎週更新している。
(B) 複数の場所にオフィスがある。
(C) 新しい従業員を探している。
(D) ノンフィクションの本を出版している。

 A ❷の 2 ～ 3 行目に、新しい世論調査が毎週公開されていると述べられている。よって、正解は (A)。(B) (C) (D) いずれについても言及されていない。

4. How can readers get permission to reproduce graphics?

(A) By sending an e-mail
(B) By making a phone call
(C) By submitting a paper form
(D) By providing information online

読者はどのようにして、図版を複製する許可を得られますか。

(A) E メールを送ることによって。
(B) 電話をすることによって。
(C) 紙の書式を提出することによって。
(D) オンライン上で情報を提供することによって。

 D ❷の 4 行目以降で、表、図、その他の図版を複製利用したい場合は「連絡先」のページにアクセスし、オンラインフォームで用途について詳細を記入して申請するよう案内されている。また、申請に対する回答はほとんどの場合 24 時間以内にされるとあり、全てオンラインでやりとりすると分かる。正解は (D)。

Unit 16　段落ごとの要点をつかむ②

テーマ解説

内容が複雑な長文は推測力や予測力を駆使

一般的に、突然の変更連絡のEメールやトラブル報告の手紙など、限定された話題に関する文書を読んで第三者が即座に内容を理解するのは、難しいものです。他にも、専門的な話題の記事や限られた読者を対象にした広告なども、話題に慣れていないと理解に時間がかかるでしょう。

そうした理由で、Part 7 の長文の各段落の主題文を読んだだけではいまひとつ文書の概要や全体像がつかめない場合は、背景情報や文書全体に散らばるキーワードに注目し、それらを段落間で関連付けて読みながら、それぞれの主題文を推測したり先の展開を予測したりしてみましょう。例えば、手紙やEメールでは、ヘッダーやフッターから得られる情報や本文中の固有名詞や日付などのキーワードから、場面や状況を推測し、その推測を基に詳細情報をつなぎ合わせて各段落の要点を理解していきます。また記事では、論理展開を頭に描き、「否定的な論調が続いているが、結論としてこれを力説したいのだろうか、それともこの後に対案として肯定的な意見が述べられるのだろうか」などと、先の流れを予測しながら読んでみます。こうした読み方が、内容に対する理解を助けます。

\ 文書の内容理解に挑戦 /

では、次ページのウォームアップのEメールを題材に、背景情報や本文中のキーワードを関連付けながら、場面や状況を具体的に推測してみましょう。

|1| **文書形式、** |2| **発信者と受信者**

　　メールヘッダーから、Rodriguez さんが Moore さんに送信した Eメールだと分かります。本文冒頭の呼び掛けが Ms. の敬称で始まっているのに対して、最後の署名欄が名前の Anthony とだけあることや、件名から、2 人は仕事上で何かの関係で、比較的近い間柄ではないかと推測できます。

|3| **概要（主題や目的）**

　　☑ Subject: Changes for 5 January / Date: 4 January

　　件名と送信日付から、「翌日の予定変更」という急を要する連絡だと分かります。

　　☑ I've had to make some changes to your list of appointments for tomorrow. (❶1 行目)

　　第 1 段落の主題文です。件名とも幾つかのキーワード（網掛け部分）が一致します。

　　☑ I printed out ... as requested. They are in a folder on your desk. (❸1 〜 2 行目)

　　第 2 段落の主題文です。件名とは別の用件が書かれています。

　　また、第 1 段落には❷の予定表があり、変更後の予定が共有されていると考えられます。まとめると、Eメールの目的は翌日の予定変更の連絡で、最後に別件が短く書き添えられています。おそらく Rodriguez さんは Moore さんの秘書でしょう。変更の内容は、第 1 段落の支持文を読めば分かるだろうと推測できます。

|4| **詳細情報**

　　☑ Your client John Seymour just phoned to cancel. He suggests rescheduling for 9 January. (❶1 〜 2 行目)

　　☑ You will notice I have replaced Mr. Seymour's time slot with the pending review of the marketing materials—I trust that that will work. (❶4 〜 5 行目)

　　☑ 11:30 A.M. / Review of marketing materials / Diana Suarez (❷5 行目)

　　キーワード（網掛け部分）から、予定変更は Seymour さんより要望があったために生じ、保留になっていた他の予定が代わりに入ったと分かります。また、表内の❷5 行目の午前 11 時 30 分の予定（下線部）は、❶5 行目にある、差し替わった予定と同一の表現（下線部）であることから、この時間帯が Seymour さんとの約束の時間だったと推測できます。

ウォームアップ

テーマ解説を参考に次の文書を通して読みましょう。その後、文書の内容を説明した文を読み、内容が正しければ T、誤っていれば F を選びましょう。

```
========================== E-Mail Message ==========================

  To:       Carol Moore

  From:     Anthony Rodriguez

  Date:     4 January

  Subject:  Changes for 5 January
```

❶
Ms. Moore,

I've had to make some changes to your list of appointments for tomorrow. Your client John Seymour just phoned to cancel. He suggests rescheduling for 9 January. You will return from the conference the day before and are free on the morning of the 9th. Shall I set up an appointment with him? You will notice I have replaced Mr. Seymour's time slot with the pending review of the marketing materials—I trust that that will work.

❷

Time	Appointment	Attendees
8:15 A.M.	New client breakfast, Green Room	Kacey Martin, Arnab Chopra
9:45 A.M.	Team meeting about Edinburgh conference (6–8 January)	Jerome Hinks, Mike Levin
11:30 A.M.	Review of marketing materials	Diana Suarez
1:45 P.M.	Payroll & budget meeting	Susan Strohl
5:38 P.M.	Leave for Edinburgh, train departs from Wellingham Station	

❸
I printed out your hotel confirmation and train tickets as requested. They are in a folder on your desk.

Regards,
Anthony

---

1. Rodriguez さんは Moore さんとの面会の約束を変更したい。　　□ T　□ F

2. Rodriguez さんが共有した予定表は、1 月 9 日のものである。　　□ T　□ F

3. 変更になったのは、午前 11 時半の約束である。　　□ T　□ F

4. Moore さんの 1 月 9 日の午前中の予定は、空いている。　　□ T　□ F

5. Rodriguez さんは、ホテルの確認書と列車の切符の印刷を依頼された。　　□ T　□ F

【解答】

1. F　**2.** F　**3.** T　**4.** T　**5.** T

→訳は p.150

TOEIC® L&R の問題文書を使って、実際に文書を読む練習をしましょう。

次の文書に対し、1～3の指示に従いながら、内容理解に挑戦してください。

Article

Construction to Add to Traffic

GREYHAVEN (12 May)—With the construction of several new office complexes under way in the downtown business district, the city's already problematic traffic is only expected to get worse. City officials are discussing a number of solutions, such as creating a new underground motorway or widening Highway 92 to accommodate more lanes of traffic. No decisions have been finalized, however.

"We simply don't have the infrastructure to support all these cars, and it is clear that something needs to be done," said Carla Radwanski, spokesperson for the highway commission. — [1] —.

"Any major construction project will take years to complete, so whatever we decide will just add to road congestion in the short term," Ms. Radwanski added. "That's the main reason we haven't committed to anything yet. The more time we spend developing a solid plan, the better managed the project will hopefully be once we begin."

While the city is considering its options, office workers are becoming increasingly agitated. — [2] —.

"My commute to work is becoming unbearable," said Paul Hodgkin, a lawyer who works downtown. "The distance from my house to the office is only about 11 kilometers, but it takes me over an hour. — [3] —."

To help alleviate traffic issues in the meantime, office managers are starting to take matters into their own hands. Some are encouraging employees to ride together or are offering incentives to employees who ride bicycles to work. — [4] —.

1. 文書を読み、段落ごとの主題文と、それらに関連が深いと思われる語句や文を丸 (◯) で囲んでみましょう。

2. 1 を参考に、メモを完成させましょう (固有名詞を含め、英語表記可)。

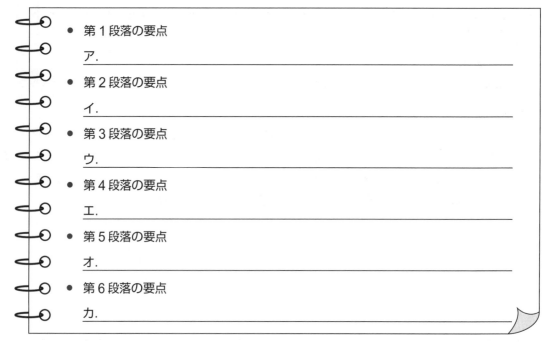

- 第 1 段落の要点
  ア.＿＿＿＿＿＿＿＿＿＿＿＿＿＿＿
- 第 2 段落の要点
  イ.＿＿＿＿＿＿＿＿＿＿＿＿＿＿＿
- 第 3 段落の要点
  ウ.＿＿＿＿＿＿＿＿＿＿＿＿＿＿＿
- 第 4 段落の要点
  エ.＿＿＿＿＿＿＿＿＿＿＿＿＿＿＿
- 第 5 段落の要点
  オ.＿＿＿＿＿＿＿＿＿＿＿＿＿＿＿
- 第 6 段落の要点
  カ.＿＿＿＿＿＿＿＿＿＿＿＿＿＿＿

3. 記事のタイトル「交通量を増す工事」に当たる全ての工事について、上の文書内に波線(〰〰)を引きましょう。

TOEIC® L&R の問題に挑戦します。

右上の目安の解答時間を目標に、自分で時間を計りながら **1 ～ 4** の問題に答えてください。

Article

Construction to Add to Traffic

GREYHAVEN (12 May)—With the construction of several new office complexes under way in the downtown business district, the city's already problematic traffic is only expected to get worse. City officials are discussing a number of solutions, such as creating a new underground motorway or widening Highway 92 to accommodate more lanes of traffic. No decisions have been finalized, however.

"We simply don't have the infrastructure to support all these cars, and it is clear that something needs to be done," said Carla Radwanski, spokesperson for the highway commission. — [1] —.

"Any major construction project will take years to complete, so whatever we decide will just add to road congestion in the short term," Ms. Radwanski added. "That's

the main reason we haven't committed to anything yet. The more time we spend developing a solid plan, the better managed the project will hopefully be once we begin."

While the city is considering its options, office workers are becoming increasingly agitated. — [2] —.

"My commute to work is becoming unbearable," said Paul Hodgkin, a lawyer who works downtown. "The distance from my house to the office is only about 11 kilometers, but it takes me over an hour. — [3] —."

To help alleviate traffic issues in the meantime, office managers are starting to take matters into their own hands. Some are encouraging employees to ride together or are offering incentives to employees who ride bicycles to work. — [4] —.

1. The word "solutions" in paragraph 1, line 6, is closest in meaning to

(A) targets
(B) answers
(C) appeals
(D) mixtures

2. According to Ms. Radwanski, why is the highway commission hesitant to begin a construction project?

(A) It is waiting for additional funding.
(B) It cannot find a qualified project manager.
(C) It does not want to intensify traffic problems.
(D) It has received many complaints from citizens.

3. What is indicated about Mr. Hodgkin?

(A) He objects to a new driving law.
(B) He disagrees with a city proposal.
(C) He is seeking a new job downtown.
(D) He is frustrated with his drive to work.

4. In which of the positions marked [1], [2], [3], and [4] does the following sentence best belong?

"Others are letting their employees work from home on certain days."

(A) [1]
(B) [2]
(C) [3]
(D) [4]

→解答・解説は p.148

Construction to Add to Traffic

❶ GREYHAVEN (12 May)—With the construction of several new office complexes under way in the downtown business district, the city's already problematic traffic is only expected to get worse. City officials are discussing a number of solutions, such as creating a new underground motorway or widening Highway 92 to accommodate more lanes of traffic. No decisions have been finalized, however.

❷ "We simply don't have the infrastructure to support all these cars, and it is clear that something needs to be done," said Carla Radwanski, spokesperson for the highway commission. — [1] —.

❸ "Any major construction project will take years to complete, so whatever we decide will just add to road congestion in the short term," Ms. Radwanski added. "That's the main reason we haven't committed to anything yet. The more time we spend developing a solid plan, the better managed the project will hopefully be once we begin."

While the city is considering its options, ❹ office workers are becoming increasingly agitated. — [2] —.

❺ "My commute to work is becoming unbearable," said Paul Hodgkin, a lawyer who works downtown. "The distance from my house to the office is only about 11 kilometers, but it takes me over an hour. — [3] —."

❻ To help alleviate traffic issues in the meantime, office managers are starting to take matters into their own hands. Some are encouraging employees to ride together or are offering incentives to employees who ride bicycles to work. — [4] —.

交通量を増す工事

GREYHAVEN (5月12日) ——中心街の商業地区で進行中の複合オフィスビル建設に伴い、市がすでに抱えている交通量の問題はさらに悪化するだけと予想されている。市の職員たちは、新しく地下に高速道路を造る、さらに車線を追加できるよう92号線を拡張するなど、多くの解決策を検討している。しかし、何の決定にも至っていない。

「これら全ての車両を支えるインフラはまったく整っておらず、何か手を打たなければならないことは明らかです」と幹線道路委員会の広報担当 Carla Radwanski さんは述べた。

「大規模な建設計画はいずれも完成するのに数年かかるため、何を決定しても、短期的にはただ道路の渋滞が増えるだけです」と Radwanski さんは付け加えた。「それこそが、私たちがまだ何もお約束できていない大きな理由です。時間をかけてしっかりした計画を練り上げればそれだけ、着手後はプロジェクトがうまく管理されることになるだろうと願っています」。

市がさまざまな選択肢を検討している一方で、オフィスで働く人々の動揺は増しつつある。

「私の通勤は耐え難いものになっています」と、中心街で働く弁護士の Paul Hodgkin は語った。「自宅からオフィスまでの距離はほんの11キロくらいなのに、1時間以上かかるんです」。

そうする間にも、経営者たちは自ら、交通量の問題を軽減しようと対処し始めている。一部には、従業員に相乗りを推奨していたり、自転車通勤をする従業員に奨励金を提供していたりする経営者もいる。*他には、特定の日に従業員に在宅勤務をさせている経営者もいる。

*問題4の挿入文の訳

語注

construction 建設　traffic 交通量
❶ complex 複合施設　under way 進行中で　downtown 中心街の　district 地区
　problematic 問題のある　be expected to *do* ～する見込みである　get worse 悪化する
　official 役人　solution 解決策　such as ～などの　underground 地下の
　motorway 高速道路　★イギリス英語。アメリカでは expressway、freeway を用いる。　widen ～を広げる
　highway 幹線道路　accommodate ～を収容できる　lane 車線　finalize ～を最終決定する
❷ infrastructure インフラ、基幹設備　support ～を支える　spokesperson 広報担当者　commission 委員会
❸ major 大きい、重要な　take ～ to *do* …するのに～（時間・金額など）を要する　congestion 混雑
　commit to ～ ～を約束する、～を決意する　solid 確かな　hopefully 願わくは　once いったん～すると
❹ increasingly 増大して　agitated 動揺して
❺ commute 通勤、通学　unbearable 耐えられない　downtown 中心街で
❻ alleviate ～を軽減する　issue 問題　in the meantime そうする間に
　take ～ into *one's* own hands ～に自分自身の手で対処する　encourage ～ to *do* ～に…するよう勧める
　incentive 奨励金、励みになるもの

プラクティス

1. 例は左図参照。

2. ア．商業地区の複合ビル建設により、すでに問題の市の交通量はさらに悪化する見込みだ。

　イ．幹線道路委員会の広報担当者は「何か手を打つべきなのは明らか」と述べている。

　ウ．何を決定しても短期間は渋滞が増えるため、委員会はまだ何も対応していない。

　エ．一方、オフィス勤務者の動揺は増している。

　オ．通勤が耐え難いものになりつつあると Paul Hodgkin は言った。

　カ．交通量の問題を軽減するため、企業の経営者は対処し始めている。

3. 左図参照。

チャレンジ

1. The word "solutions" in paragraph 1, line 6, is closest in meaning to

(A) targets

(B) answers

(C) appeals

(D) mixtures

第 1 段落・6 行目にある "solutions" に最も意味が近いのは

(A) 目標

(B) 解決策

(C) 訴え

(D) 混合物

正解 **B** ❶の 5 ～ 9 行目の文で、solutions の直後にある such as … は、solutions の具体例を示しており、直前の交通量の問題を軽減する案として挙げられている。選択肢の中で最も近いのは (B) 「解決策」。

2. According to Ms. Radwanski, why is the highway commission hesitant to begin a construction project?

(A) It is waiting for additional funding.

(B) It cannot find a qualified project manager.

(C) It does not want to intensify traffic problems.

(D) It has received many complaints from citizens.

Radwanski さんによると、幹線道路委員会はなぜ建設計画を開始することをためらっているのですか。

(A) 追加の資金提供を待っているから。

(B) 適任の事業監督者が見つからないから。

(C) 交通量の諸問題を深刻化させたくないから。

(D) 市民から多くの苦情を受け取ったから。

正解 **C** ❸の 1 ～ 4 行目に、Radwanski さんの発言として「大規模な建設計画はいずれも完成するのに数年かかるため、何を決定しても、短期的にはただ道路の渋滞が増えるだけだ」と記載されている。よって (C) が正解。hesitant to *do* 「～するのをためらって」。intensify 「～を強める、～を深刻化させる」。

(A) additional 「追加の」、funding 「資金提供」。

(B) qualified 「適任の、資格のある」。

3. What is indicated about Mr. Hodgkin?

(A) He objects to a new driving law.

(B) He disagrees with a city proposal.

(C) He is seeking a new job downtown.

(D) He is frustrated with his drive to work.

Hodgkin さんについて何が示されていますか。

(A) 運転に関する新しい法律に異議を唱えている。

(B) 市の提案に反対している。

(C) 中心街で新しい仕事を探している。

(D) 職場までの運転にいら立っている。

正解 **D** ❺1 ～ 5 行目より、Hodgkin さんは「通勤は耐え難い」と述べた後に、「自宅からオフィスまでの距離はほんの 11 キロくらいなのに、1 時間以上かかる」という理由を続けている。よって、(D) が正解。

(A) object to ～「～に反対を唱える」。

(B) disagree with ～「～に異議を唱える」。

4. In which of the positions marked [1], [2], [3], and [4] does the following sentence best belong?

"Others are letting their employees work from home on certain days."

(A) [1]
(B) [2]
(C) [3]
(D) [4]

[1]、[2]、[3] および [4] と記載された箇所のうち、次の文が入るのに最もふさわしいのはどれですか。

「他には、特定の日に従業員に在宅勤務をさせている経営者もいる」

(A) [1]
(B) [2]
(C) [3]
(D) [4]

正解 **D** 挿入文の冒頭の Others は、[4] の直前の文の Some are encouraging ... の下線部に対応しており、一部には相乗りや自転車通勤を促す経営者もいれば、他には特定の日に在宅勤務をさせている経営者もいる、という文脈になると考えられる。よって、(D) が正解。

【ウォームアップの訳】

受信者：Carol Moore
送信者：Anthony Rodriguez
日付：1 月 4 日
件名：1 月 5 日の変更

Moore さん
明日のあなたの予定表に、幾つか変更を加えなければなりませんでした。先ほど顧客の John Seymour さんより電話でキャンセルの連絡がありました。先方は 1 月 9 日に日程を変更したいそうです。あなたはその前日に協議会から戻る予定で、9 日の午前は空いています。彼との約束を設定しましょうか。ご覧の通り、Seymour さんの時間枠は、保留中のマーケティング資料の見直しに変更しました――それでうまくいくと思います。

時間	予約	出席者
午前 8 時 15 分	新規顧客と朝食、緑の間	Kacey Martin、Arnab Chopra
午前 9 時 45 分	エジンバラ協議会（1 月 6 日～ 8 日）に関するチーム会議	Jerome Hinks、Mike Levin
午前 11 時 30 分	マーケティング資料の見直し	Diana Suarez
午後 1 時 45 分	給与・予算会議	Susan Strohl
午後 5 時 38 分	エジンバラへ出発、列車はウェリンガム駅発	

ご希望通り、ホテルの確認書と列車の切符を印刷しました。デスクの上のフォルダに入れてあります。

よろしくお願いします。
Anthony

→英文は p.145

◀ 文を挿入する箇所を選ぶ問題 ▶

「文を挿入する箇所を選ぶ問題」を解く 3 つのポイント
Unit 16 の「チャレンジ」の設問 4 は、文を挿入する箇所を選ぶ問題でした。

In which of the positions marked [1], [2], [3], and [4] does the following sentence best belong?
"Others are letting their employees work from home on certain days."

PART
7
Unit
16

設問の下に挿入すべき文が示されており、その挿入文が入る適切な箇所を、文書内の [1] 〜 [4] の番号から選びます。「最もふさわしい」とは挿入文が、**①意味的に合うか**、**②話の流れ（文脈）に合うか**、**③文法・構文的に合うか**、という 3 つの観点全てにおいて合致しているかどうかということです。つまり、4 カ所全ての箇所に挿入文を当てはめて読んでみて、意味が通り、かつ文章の流れとしても自然で、さらに指示語に対応する語句の数などが一致しているものがあれば、その箇所が最も適切だと言えます。挿入文の内容がその段落の主題文に合っているか、意味・文脈・文法の面で問題ないかどうかを、一つ一つ確かめましょう。

文頭の接続詞や副詞（句）に注目
文を挿入する問題では、接続詞や副詞が大きなヒントになることがあります。ここでは文脈把握のヒントになる副詞（句）を幾つか紹介しましょう。副詞（句）の中には、文全体を修飾して、前後の文を意味的につなげる語があり、その語をヒントに、前後の文の流れを予測することができます。

- **補足・追加** ▶ 前文に続けて、追加の情報や例などを紹介する。

  furthermore「さらに」、additionally「加えて」、moreover「その上」

  例 This month's promotion is offering a 20 percent discount on shoes. **Furthermore**, accessories will be marked down 10 percent.

  今月のプロモーションでは靴を20パーセント引きでご提供します。さらにアクセサリーが10パーセント引きになります。

- **逆接** ▶ 話の流れの方向を変える。

  on the other hand「一方」、however「しかしながら」、conversely「逆に」

  例 Robert asked his supervisor for a promotion. **However**, it was declined due to budgetary reasons.

  Robert は上司に昇進を願い出ました。しかしながら、予算上の理由からそれは却下されました。

- **結果** ▶ 前文に続けて、その結果生じた内容について述べる。

  therefore「それゆえ」、thankfully「おかげで」、consequently 「結果的に」

  例 The team presented all available data and its analysis to the CEO. **Consequently**, he welcomed their initiative and promised his best support.

  チームは入手可能なあらゆるデータとその分析を CEO に提示しました。結果として、CEO は彼らの構想を歓迎し、できる限りの支援を約束しました。

- **強調** ▶ 直前の内容を強調するときなどに用いられる。

  in fact「実のところ」、indeed「実際に」

  例 The new tablet computers we ordered in March are of good quality. **In fact**, I bought another for my own use.

  3 月に注文した新しいタブレットは優れた品質です。実のところ、私は自分用にもう 1 台購入しました。

Unit 17　複数文書を関連付けて読む①

テーマ解説

Unit 17 〜 Unit 20 では、複数の文書が 1 セットになった問題を取り上げます。複数の文書が 1 セットになった問題とは、関連する 2 文書または 3 文書を読んで 5 つの設問に答える問題です。

複数文書が 1 セットになった文書の特徴

セットになった複数の文書は、特定の話題において関連し合っています。例えば、あるイベントの講演依頼の E メールと、そのイベントの開催を報じる記事が一緒に示される、といった具合です。特定の話題を軸に、文書間で出来事に時間的な前後関係があるのが特徴です。これまで以上に推測力や予測力を働かせて、全体像をつかむようにしましょう。

複数の文書を読む際のポイント

以下で、「複数の文書を読む際のポイント」を確認しましょう。

> **Step 1　文書間の大枠の場面設定をつかむ**
> 　①**文書形式、**②**発信者と受信者**を確認し、文書間に共通するキーワードを特定しながら、文書がどうつながっているか、背景にどのような場面設定があるかを推測します。
> **Step 2　各文書の概要をつかむ**
> 　文書ごとの③**概要（主題や目的）**をつかみます。
> **Step 3　詳細情報を理解する**
> 　設問を先に参照し、設問で問われていることを基に、どの文書を読むべきかを特定し、文書内の④**詳細情報**を読んで内容を理解していきます。

Step 1 では、なるべく視野を大きく取り、各文書の①**文書形式、**②**発信者と受信者**をつかむとともに、各文書に点在している共通のキーワードから、文書の背景にある大枠の場面設定をつかみます。出来事の時間的な前後関係は重要なので、日付や時刻などが出てきたら、特に注意して読み取りましょう。

Step 2 では、各文書のタイトルや冒頭の箇所に注意しながら、③**概要（主題や目的）**を把握します。

Step 3 でいったん文書から目を離し、設問に目を通します。そして、設問ごとにどの文書を読むべきかの当たりを付けて、該当する文書の④**詳細情報**を読み進めていきます。

設問は、1 つの文書だけを読めば答えられるものと、複数の文書を関連付けて初めて答えられるものの両方が登場します。また、次のように選択肢一つ一つの正誤について判断する必要があるタイプの設問では、読むべき範囲が広範囲にわたります。**Step 2** までに進めた概要理解を基に、落ち着いて各文書の内容と照合して、正誤を判断するようにしましょう。

例　What is indicated about ABC Company?　ABC 社について何が示されていますか。
　　What is NOT mentioned in the advertisement?　広告で言及されていないことは何ですか。

テーマ解説を参考に、2つの文書に共通するキーワードに注目しながら文書を読み、1〜3の問題に答えましょう。

1 Notice

Lunchtime Walking Club

On May 17, the Asher Recreation Board approved the creation of the Lunchtime Walking Club at Asher Community Park. The walking club will meet from Monday through Friday, noon–1 P.M., and the activity will run all year long. The club will meet at the trailhead by the park's north entrance at Hunter Street. Each participant should wear comfortable walking shoes and bring a bottle of drinking water. Interested residents should call or visit the park's Recreation Office to register. The club will officially meet after a minimum of seven members have joined. Please check the calendar for any updates or changes. For more information, contact club coordinator Shreya Kamdar at 215-555-0193.

2 Calendar

Weekly Activities Calendar for the Month of July		Asher Community Park
Mondays	12:00 P.M. 5:30 P.M.	**Lunchtime Walking Club** (North Trail) **Community Volleyball** (West Court)
Tuesdays	12:15 P.M.	**"Learn at Lunch"**: Butterflies (Pavilion) $7 fee, includes lunch
Wednesdays	12:00 P.M. 5:30 P.M.	**Lunchtime Walking Club** (North Trail) **Community Volleyball** (West Court)
Thursdays	12:15 P.M. 5:30 P.M.	**"Learn at Lunch"**: Fungi (Pavilion) $7 fee, includes lunch **Bird Watching** (2nd & 4th weeks) (Recreation Arena)
Fridays	12:00 P.M. 5:30 P.M.	**Lunchtime Walking Club** (North Trail) **Community Volleyball** (West Court)
Saturdays	10:00 A.M. 2:00 P.M.	**"Nature and Art"**: Painting (Recreation Building) $10 fee, includes supplies **Tour of Asher Park Lake** (Boathouse) $15 boat rental fee

For more detailed information about any of the events listed above, please contact the park's Recreation Office at 215-555-0102.

1. 1 の文書は何を案内していますか。
   (a) ウォーキングがもたらす健康上の利点
   (b) Asher 地区公園の歴史
   (c) 新しいウォーキングクラブの創設

2. 2 の文書は何ですか。
   (a) 公園のイベントカレンダー
   (b) 料理講習会の予定表
   (c) 施設管理事務所のシフト表

3. ウォーキングクラブについて当てはまるものを全て選びましょう。
   (a) 委員会の承認が下りた。
   (b) 7名の申込者がそろった。
   (c) ランチは参加費に含まれる。
   (d) 同じ曜日にバードウォッチングが行われる。

【解答】
1. (c) **2.** (a) **3.** (a)、(b)
▶ 1 のお知らせのタイトルと1文目、2 のカレンダーのタイトルから、2つとも Asher Community Park という公園についての文書で、Lunchtime Walking Club が共通する語句だと分かる。

→訳は p.163

TOEIC® L&R の問題文書を使って、実際に文書を読む練習をしましょう。

2 つの関連する文書に対し、**1 ～ 3** の指示に従いながら、内容理解に挑戦してください。

1 Advertisement

Boriken Islander

Boriken Islander is Puerto Rico's largest locally owned car rental company. We offer a range of vehicles at the lowest possible prices. If you can get a lower rate with any of our local competitors, we will match that rate and pay for a full tank of fuel! The following vehicles are available for rent:

Car Class	Description	Weekly rate
Economy	2-door vehicle suitable for 4 passengers and 2 large bags	$199.00
Compact	4-door vehicle suitable for 4 passengers and 3 large bags	$229.00
Standard	4-door vehicle suitable for 5 passengers and 4 large bags	$259.00
Premium	4-door vehicle suitable for 5 passengers and 5 large bags	$309.00

Rates listed refer to payments made in person at our customer service counter. Discounted rates and details about the features of each car type are available on our website, www.borikenislander.com. Looking for even more savings? Use our services during April and May and receive an additional 10% off the weekly rate.

2 E-mail

To:	customerservice@borikenislander.com
From:	mgutierrez@rotpa.net
Date:	April 4
Subject:	Inquiry

Hello,

I will be traveling to Puerto Rico on business during the second half of this month, so I just visited your website to make a reservation. I plan to rent a 4-door vehicle, because I will be traveling with three colleagues and want to be mindful of their comfort. At the same time, I am on a limited budget, so I intend to book the least expensive vehicle of this type.

Before finalizing the booking, though, there are two pieces of information I would like to have, both of which I was unable to locate on your site. First, if I pick up the car at your branch in San Juan and drop it off at either your Ponce or Aguadilla branch at the end of the rental period, will I be charged a drop-off fee? Second, I am unfamiliar with the roads and the traffic on the island, so I would like to add a navigation system to my order. Would that be possible? If so, how much would the weekly rate be?

Thank you for your assistance.

Magdalena Gutierrez

1. それぞれの文書にざっと目を通し、概要理解に重要と思われる語句や文を丸（◯）で囲み、次の
メモを完成させましょう。

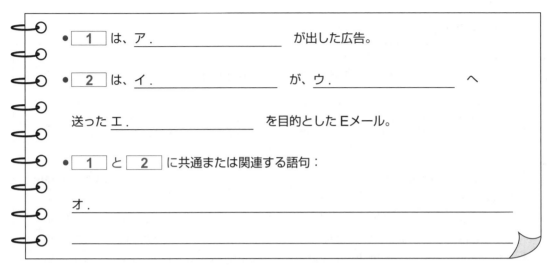

- ⬛1⬛ は、ア．_____ が出した広告。

- ⬛2⬛ は、イ．_____ が、ウ．_____ へ

  送った エ．_____ を目的とした Eメール。

- ⬛1⬛ と ⬛2⬛ に共通または関連する語句：

  オ．_____

2. それぞれの文書の内容を説明した文を読み、正しいものを全て選びましょう。

⬛1⬛ Advertisement
- (a) Boriken Islander 社はプエルトリコ最大手のレンタカー会社である。
- (b) Boriken Islander 社は地元で最安値の提供を誇っている。
- (c) 掲載された料金表は丸 1 日利用した場合のレンタル料である。
- (d) ウェブサイト経由でレンタカーを利用した人は、通常料金から 1 割引きになる。
- (e) 掲載された料金表の中で最も安い車種はエコノミーである。

⬛2⬛ E-mail
- (f) Gutierrez さんはプエルトリコの会社で営業部に所属している。
- (g) Gutierrez さんは 4 月の後半に出張の予定がある。
- (h) Gutierrez さんは出張先を 3 人の同僚とともに回る予定である。
- (i) Gutierrez さんは記事で見つけることができなかった情報について問い合わせている。
- (j) Gutierrez さんの出張の計画では、車を借りる場所と返す場所は同じである。

3. 次の (1)、(2) について、文書内で述べられている箇所をそれぞれ見つけて、左の文書内に波線（〰〰）
を引きましょう。

- (1) Gutierrez さんがプエルトリコへ行く時期とレンタルを希望する車の条件
- (2) (1) から推測される Gutierrez さんがレンタルすると思われる車種

→解答・解説は p.158

TOEIC® L&R の問題に挑戦します。

右上の目安の解答時間を目標に、自分で時間を計りながら 1 ～ 5 の問題に答えてください。

1 Advertisement

Boriken Islander

Boriken Islander is Puerto Rico's largest locally owned car rental company. We offer a range of vehicles at the lowest possible prices. If you can get a lower rate with any of our local competitors, we will match that rate and pay for a full tank of fuel! The following vehicles are available for rent:

Car Class	Description	Weekly rate
Economy	2-door vehicle suitable for 4 passengers and 2 large bags	$199.00
Compact	4-door vehicle suitable for 4 passengers and 3 large bags	$229.00
Standard	4-door vehicle suitable for 5 passengers and 4 large bags	$259.00
Premium	4-door vehicle suitable for 5 passengers and 5 large bags	$309.00

Rates listed refer to payments made in person at our customer service counter. Discounted rates and details about the features of each car type are available on our website, www.borikenislander.com. Looking for even more savings? Use our services during April and May and receive an additional 10% off the weekly rate.

2 E-mail

To:	customerservice@borikenislander.com
From:	mgutierrez@rotpa.net
Date:	April 4
Subject:	Inquiry

Hello,

I will be traveling to Puerto Rico on business during the second half of this month, so I just visited your website to make a reservation. I plan to rent a 4-door vehicle, because I will be traveling with three colleagues and want to be mindful of their comfort. At the same time, I am on a limited budget, so I intend to book the least expensive vehicle of this type.

Before finalizing the booking, though, there are two pieces of information I would like to have, both of which I was unable to locate on your site. First, if I pick up the car at your branch in San Juan and drop it off at either your Ponce or Aguadilla branch at the end of the rental period, will I be charged a drop-off fee? Second, I am unfamiliar with the roads and the traffic on the island, so I would like to add a navigation system to my order. Would that be possible? If so, how much would the weekly rate be?

Thank you for your assistance.

Magdalena Gutierrez

1. What information is NOT included in Boriken Islander's advertisement?

    (A) The rental prices for its vehicles
    (B) The number of people each kind of vehicle can accommodate
    (C) The amount of fuel each kind of vehicle typically uses
    (D) The amount of luggage space in each kind of vehicle

2. What type of car will Ms. Gutierrez most likely rent?

    (A) Economy
    (B) Compact
    (C) Standard
    (D) Premium

3. What is indicated about Boriken Islander?

    (A) It has locations in various Puerto Rican cities.
    (B) Its customers are primarily businesspeople.
    (C) It charges a cash deposit for online reservations.
    (D) It is owned by an international corporation.

4. What is suggested about Ms. Gutierrez?

    (A) She has visited Puerto Rico before.
    (B) She will be eligible for a discounted rate.
    (C) She frequently does business with Boriken Islander.
    (D) She was referred to the rental agency by another traveler.

5. According to the e-mail, what is one piece of information that Ms. Gutierrez is seeking?

    (A) The company's business hours
    (B) The company's reservation procedures
    (C) Additional details about the types of cars available
    (D) The availability of a navigation device

PART

7

Unit

17

→解答・解説は p.158

1 広告

Boriken Islander

❶ Boriken Islander is Puerto Rico's largest locally owned car rental company. We offer a range of vehicles at the lowest possible prices. If you can get a lower rate with any of our local competitors, we will match that rate and pay for a full tank of fuel! The following vehicles are available for rent:

❷

Car Class	Description	Weekly rate
Economy	2-door vehicle suitable for 4 passengers and 2 large bags	$199.00
Compact	4-door vehicle suitable for 4 passengers and 3 large bags	$229.00
Standard	4-door vehicle suitable for 5 passengers and 4 large bags	$259.00
Premium	4-door vehicle suitable for 5 passengers and 5 large bags	$309.00

❸ Rates listed refer to payments made in person at our customer service counter. Discounted rates and details about the features of each car type are available on our website, www.borikenislander.com. Looking for even more savings? Use our services during April and May and receive an additional 10% off the weekly rate.

2 Eメール

To:	customerservice@borikenislander.com
From:	mgutierrez@rotpa.net
Date:	April 4
Subject:	Inquiry

Hello,

❶ I will be traveling to Puerto Rico on business during the second half of this month, so I just visited your website to make a reservation. I plan to rent a 4-door vehicle because I will be traveling with three colleagues and want to be mindful of their comfort. At the same time, I am on a limited budget, so I intend to book the least expensive vehicle of this type.

❷ Before finalizing the booking, though, there are two pieces of information I would like to have, both of which I was unable to locate on your site. First, if I pick up the car at your branch in San Juan and drop it off at either your Ponce or Aguadilla branch at the end of the rental period, will I be charged a drop-off fee? Second, I am unfamiliar with the roads and the traffic on the island, so I would like to add a navigation system to my order. Would that be possible? If so, how much would the weekly rate be?

Thank you for your assistance.

Magdalena Gutierrez

→語注は p.162

Boriken Islander 社

Boriken Islander 社は、プエルトリコ最大の地元資本のレンタカー会社です。さまざまな車種を可能な限りの最安値でご提供いたします。地元の競合会社でもっと安価な料金が見つかりましたら、当社はその価格に合わせ、さらにガソリン満タンの費用をお支払いします！ 以下の車がレンタルいただけます。

車種	説明	週間料金
エコノミー	2 ドア車、乗客 4 名、大型荷物 2 個に適切	199 ドル
コンパクト	4 ドア車、乗客 4 名、大型荷物 3 個に適切	229 ドル
スタンダード	4 ドア車、乗客 5 名、大型荷物 4 個に適切	259 ドル
プレミアム	4 ドア車、乗客 5 名、大型荷物 5 個に適切	309 ドル

リストの料金は、当社の顧客サービスカウンターで直接お支払いいただく場合の料金です。割引料金および各車種の特徴の詳細は、当社のウェブサイト、www.borikenislander.com でご覧いただけます。さらなる割引をお求めですか。4 月および 5 月中に当社のサービスをご利用ください。そうすれば、週間料金からさらに 10 パーセントをお引きいたします。

受信者：customerservice@borikenislander.com
送信者：mgutierrez@rotpa.net
日付：4 月 4 日
件名：問い合わせ

こんにちは。

私は今月の後半、プエルトリコに出張する予定になっており、予約をするためについ先ほど貴社のウェブサイトを拝見しました。4 ドア車をレンタルする予定ですが、それは同僚 3 人と一緒の出張で彼らの居心地に気を配りたいためです。同時に、予算が限られているので、この型式の中で最も安価な車を予約するつもりです。

ただ、予約を確定する前に 2 点知りたいことがあり、そのどちらも貴社のウェブサイトで見つけることができませんでした。1 点目は、貴社のサンフアン店で車を拾って、レンタル期間終了時にポンセまたはアグアディージャのいずれかの支店で乗り捨てをする場合、乗り捨て料金を請求されますか。2 点目は、私は島の道路や交通に不案内なので、カーナビを注文に加えたいのです。それは可能でしょうか。もし可能なら、週間料金はお幾らになるでしょうか。

ご助力いただけると幸いです。

Magdalena Gutierrez

プラクティス

1. 例は p.158 の図参照。

　ア．Boriken Islander 社

　イ．Magdalena Gutierrez

　ウ．Boriken Islander 社

　エ．問い合わせ

　オ．Boriken Islander / borikenislander.com、Puerto Rico、car rental / rent、4-door vehicle、our website / your website / your site、April、weekly rate　*p.158 の文書の網掛け部分

2. (a)、(b)、(e)、(g)、(h)

3. p.158 の図参照。

チャレンジ

1. What information is NOT included in Boriken Islander's advertisement?

　(A) The rental prices for its vehicles

　(B) The number of people each kind of vehicle can accommodate

　(C) The amount of fuel each kind of vehicle typically uses

　(D) The amount of luggage space in each kind of vehicle

Boriken Islander 社の広告に含まれていない情報は何ですか。

　(A) 車のレンタル料金

　(B) それぞれの車種の乗車定員

　(C) それぞれの車種の、通常の燃料消費量

　(D) それぞれの車種の、大型荷物スペースの容量

> **正解 C**　**1**の広告に含まれていない情報が正解となるので、選択肢の中で広告に掲載されている情報を一つ一つ除外していくとよい。**1**の**2**の表は車種ごとの特徴と料金をまとめたもので、乗車定員、積載可能な大型荷物の個数、料金が記載されているが、(C) の燃料消費量は表になく、また表以外の箇所にも記載がない。よって、正解は (C)。kind「種類」、typically「普通は、典型的に」。
> (A) **1**の**2**に Weekly rate「週間料金」の欄があり、記載されている。
> (B)(D) **1**の**2**の Description「説明」の欄に掲載されている。accommodate「(乗り物が) ～ (人) を乗せる」。

2. What type of car will Ms. Gutierrez most likely rent?

　(A) Economy

　(B) Compact

　(C) Standard

　(D) Premium

Gutierrez さんは何の車種を借りると考えられますか。

　(A) エコノミー

　(B) コンパクト

　(C) スタンダード

　(D) プレミアム

> **正解 B**　Gutierrez さんがレンタルを希望する車の条件は、**2**のEメールの**1**2～3行目の I plan to rent a 4-door vehicle「4 ドア車をレンタルする予定だ」、同 3～5行目の At the same time, I am on a limited budget, so I intend to book the least expensive vehicle of this type.「同時に、予算が限られているので、この型式の中で最も安価な車を予約するつもりだ」から判断できる。4 ドア車の型式で最も料金が安価な (B) Compact が正解。
> (A) 表の中では最も安価だが、2 ドア車である。
> (C)(D) 4 ドア車だが Compact よりも高い。

3. What is indicated about Boriken Islander?

   (A) It has locations in various Puerto Rican cities.

   (B) Its customers are primarily businesspeople.

   (C) It charges a cash deposit for online reservations.

   (D) It is owned by an international corporation.

Boriken Islander 社について何が示されていますか。

   (A) プエルトリコのさまざまな都市に店舗がある。

   (B) 顧客は主にビジネス関係者である。

   (C) オンライン予約に手付金を請求する。

   (D) 国際企業により所有されている。

正解 A Gutierrez さんが❷のEメールの❷2〜4行目で、レンタル終了時の返却先として2カ所の地名を出して、レンタカーの乗り捨てに料金が請求されるかどうかを尋ねていることから、Boriken Islander 社は国内に複数の支店があると分かる。(A) が正解。location「所在地、場所」。
(B) 両文書ともに Boriken Islander 社の主な顧客層についての言及はない。
(C) online reservations「オンライン予約」や cash deposit「手付金」についての言及はない。
(D) ❶の❶1行目に Puerto Rico's largest locally owned car rental company「プエルトリコ最大の地元資本のレンタカー会社だ」とあるので内容に合わない。

4. What is suggested about Ms. Gutierrez?

   (A) She has visited Puerto Rico before.

   (B) She will be eligible for a discounted rate.

   (C) She frequently does business with Boriken Islander.

   (D) She was referred to the rental agency by another traveler.

Gutierrez さんについて何が分かりますか。

   (A) 以前にプエルトリコを訪れたことがある。

   (B) 割引料金の対象になる。

   (C) Boriken Islander社と頻繁に取引している。

   (D) 別の旅行者からそのレンタカー代理店に紹介された。

正解 B ❶の❸3〜4行目に Use our services during April and May and receive an additional 10% off the weekly rate.「4月および5月中に当社のサービスを利用してほしい。そうすれば、週間料金からさらに10パーセントを引く」とあること、❷のEメールの日付が4月4日で❶1行目に「私は今月の後半、プエルトリコに出張する予定になっている」とあることから、Gutierrez さんが車を借りるのは割引料金の対象期間内の4月後半だと分かる。正解は (B)。eligible for 〜「〜（資格など）の対象である」。
(A) ❷の❷4〜5行目に「私は島の道路や交通に不案内だ」とあり、以前訪れたとは考えにくい。
(C) ❷の❷1〜2行目より、ウェブサイトを見て不明点を問い合わせており、頻繁に利用しているとは考えにくい。
(D) 別の旅行者については言及がない。refer 〜 to …「〜を…へ紹介する」。

5. According to the e-mail, what is one piece of information that Ms. Gutierrez is seeking?

   (A) The company's business hours

   (B) The company's reservation procedures

   (C) Additional details about the types of cars available

   (D) The availability of a navigation device

Eメールによると、Gutierrez さんが求めている1つの情報は何ですか。

   (A) 会社の営業時間

   (B) 会社の予約手順

   (C) 利用できる車種のさらなる詳細

   (D) カーナビ装置の利用の可否

正解 D Gutierrez さんがレンタカー会社に問い合わせたい情報は2点で、❷の❷2〜6行目に書かれている。1つ目はレンタルした車に対し「乗り捨て料金を請求されるかどうか」、2つ目は「カーナビを注文に加えたいが可能か」である。よって、(D) が正解。availability「利用の可否」。
(A) 営業時間についての言及はない。business hours「営業時間」。
(B) 予約の手順についての言及はない。
(C) ❷の❷2〜5行目より、Gutierrez さんはすでに車種を決めている。

解答・解説

語 注

1 **広告**
❶ locally 現地で、地元で　car rental 自動車のレンタル　offer 〜を提供する　range 範囲
vehicle 車、車両　the lowest possible できる限り安い　rate 料金、価格　local 地元の
competitor 競合会社　match 〜に釣り合わせる　pay for 〜 〜の代金を支払う
full いっぱいの、ぎっしり詰まった　tank 燃料タンク　fuel 燃料　available 利用できる
for rent 貸し出して
❷ class 種類、等級　description 説明、明細　weekly 週の、週1回の　suitable for 〜 〜に適した
passenger 乗客
❸ list 〜をリストに記載する、〜を列挙する　refer to 〜 〜に適用する　payment 支払い
in person 直接に　customer service 顧客サービス　discounted 割引された
details 〈複数形で〉詳細　feature 特徴、特色　type 型式　saving 節約　additional 追加の

2 **Eメール** inquiry 問い合わせ
❶ travel 旅行する、移動する　on business 商用で　the second half of 〜 〜の後半
make a reservation 予約する　plan to *do* 〜する計画だ　colleague 同僚
mindful of 〜 〜に気を配って、〜に注意して　comfort 居心地の良さ、快適さ　at the same time 同時に
limited 限られた　budget 予算　intend to *do* 〜するつもりである　book 〜を予約する
❷ finalize 〜を成立させる　booking 予約　a piece of 〜 1つの〜
both of 〜 〜の両方　unable to *do* 〜することができない　pick up 〜を受け取る　branch 支店
drop off 〜 〜（レンタカー）を乗り捨てる　★借りた店舗と異なる店舗に返却することを示す
period 期間　charge 〜 … 〜に…を請求する　fee 料金
unfamiliar with 〜 〜に不慣れな、〜に不案内な　add 〜を加える　navigation system カーナビ
❸ assistance 助力、手助け

→英文は p.158

【ウォームアップの訳】

1 通知

ランチタイム・ウォーキングクラブ

5月17日、Asher レクリエーション委員会は、Asher 地区公園でのランチタイム・ウォーキングクラブの創設を承認しました。このウォーキングクラブは、月曜日から金曜日の、正午から午後1時に集まりを持ち、活動は年間を通して実施されます。クラブは、Hunter 通りの公園北口そばの遊歩道口に集合します。各参加者は、履き慣れた散歩靴を着用し、飲料水を1本お持ちください。興味のある居住者の方は、公園のレクリエーション事務所にお電話またはご来所にてご登録ください。クラブは、最少7名の部員の参加後、正式に集まりを持ちます。最新情報や変更事項についてはカレンダーをご確認ください。さらなる情報については、クラブのコーディネーター Shreya Kamdar へ、215-555-0193 までご連絡ください。

2 カレンダー

7月の週間活動カレンダー　　　Asher 地区公園		
月曜日	午後 0 時	ランチタイム・ウォーキングクラブ（北遊歩道）
	午後 5 時 30 分	地域バレーボール（西コート）
火曜日	午後 0 時 15 分	「ランチタイムの学び」：チョウ類（パビリオン）、料金 7 ドル（ランチ込み）
水曜日	午後 0 時	ランチタイム・ウォーキングクラブ（北遊歩道）
	午後 5 時 30 分	地域バレーボール（西コート）
木曜日	午後 0 時 15 分	「ランチタイムの学び」：菌類（パビリオン）、料金 7 ドル（ランチ込み）
	午後 5 時 30 分	バードウォッチング（第 2 週と第 4 週）（レクリエーションアリーナ）
金曜日	午後 0 時	ランチタイム・ウォーキングクラブ（北遊歩道）
	午後 5 時 30 分	地域バレーボール（西コート）
土曜日	午前 10 時	「自然とアート」：絵画（レクリエーション棟）、料金 10 ドル（用具代込み）
	午後 2 時	Asher 公園湖ツアー（ボートハウス）、レンタルボート料 15 ドル
上記記載の全てのイベントに関する詳細は、公園のレクリエーション事務所、215-555-0102 までお電話ください。		

▶ 12:00 P.M. は日本では午後 0 時（正午）に当たる。

→英文は p.153

Unit 18　複数文書を関連付けて読む②

テーマ解説

さまざまな文書の組み合わせ

複数文書が1セットになった問題では、さまざまな文書の組み合わせが想定されるため、それぞれの文書形式に合った読み方で文書ごとに ③概要（主題や目的）を素早くつかむことが大切です。中でもEメールは非常に多く登場する文書です。以下で、2文書が1セットになった問題の組み合わせパターン例を幾つか挙げてみます。「複数の文書を読む際のポイント」（p.152）のStepに沿って解説していきますので、この解説を頭に入れた上で、ウォームアップに挑戦してみましょう。

Step 1　文書間の大枠の場面設定をつかむ

■ 2文書ともEメール

2文書がどちらもEメールのときは、「仕事の依頼→依頼に対する返信」、「苦情→謝罪」、「求人の応募→結果通知」など、往復のやりとりの可能性があります。その場合、発信者と受信者の関係は、同じ会社の同僚同士、企業とその顧客、取引先同士などが考えられます。

▶ 1通目と2通目のEメールの「From:」と「To:」の氏名またはメールアドレスが、同一人物の入れ替わりになっていないか、「Subject:」に同じ件名が使われていないかを確認しましょう。同じだった場合、2通目は1通目への返信だと考えられます。また、人物間の関係を推測する手掛かりとして、フッターの署名欄だけでなく、メールアドレスのドメイン部分（xxxxx@abc.com の下線部分）が参考になります。ドメイン部分が同じ場合は会社の同僚あるいは上司と部下の可能性があり、異なる場合は取引先など別の組織に所属している者同士と推測できます。

■ 広告・予定表・お知らせとEメール

広告とそれを見た顧客や会社からの問い合わせのEメール、イベントの予定表とその主催者による作家への講演依頼のEメールなど、2文書のうちの1つがEメールでもう1つが広告・予定表・お知らせである組み合わせです。

▶ Eメールでない方の文書に目を通し、キーワードや固有名詞を確認した後、Eメールの件名や本文中に同じキーワードや固有名詞、言い換え表現などが登場していないかを確認しましょう。

■ 記事とEメール

2文書のうちの1つが記事で、もう1つがEメールである組み合わせです。場面設定としてはさまざまですが、一例を挙げると、企業の新社屋の開設を報じている記事と、経営者から従業員へ新社屋に関する通知をしているEメール、といった具合です。

▶ 記事のタイトルと本文中のキーワードや固有名詞を確認した後、Eメールの件名や本文中に同じキーワードや固有名詞、言い換え表現などが登場していないかを確認しましょう。記事とEメールの組み合わせは、記事を読むのに負担が掛かることが多いため、なるべく早い段階で共通するキーワードを特定することが大切です。

■ ウェブページとEメール

2文書のうちの1つがウェブサイトのページで、もう1つがEメールである組み合わせです。組み合わせの例としては、企業の求人広告のウェブページと就職希望者からの応募のEメール、近日予定のイベントの告知をするウェブページとその取材を依頼するEメールなどが考えられます。

▶ ウェブページに掲載される情報は、企業案内、商品広告、求人募集、問い合わせフォーム、商品レビューなど、他の文書形式よりも役割が多岐にわたる傾向があります。タイトルだけでなく、タブのメニューにある単語やURLの中の単語（schedule、formなどヒントになる語がURLの一部になっていることがある）にも注目し、何に関する情報がまとめられているのかを、まず特定するようにしましょう。

文書の組み合わせパターンに応じて読み方を素早く切り替えることができるようになると、文書間の背景にある場面設定の把握が、効率よく進むでしょう。

Step 2 各文書の概要をつかむ

文書間に共通するキーワードや文書間の関係を推測した後、各文書の概要把握に進みます。ここでも文書形式を踏まえた読み方で、効率よく読み進めていきます。広告ならタイトルと第1文から何の宣伝か、Eメールなら「Subject:」の件名と第1段落の1〜2文目から何を目的にした連絡か、段落が複数ある記事なら、タイトルと段落ごとの主題文から何に関する記事かをつかみます。

Step 3 詳細情報を理解する

Step 2でつかんだ各文書の概要理解に基づき、設問に目を通しながらどの文書を読むべきかの見当を付けます。設問には、1つの文書だけを読めば答えられるものと、複数の文書を関連付けて初めて答えられるものの2種類がありますので、それを念頭に設問を読みながら、参照すべき文書が1つなのか複数なのか、参照すべきなのはどの文書なのかを見定めましょう。

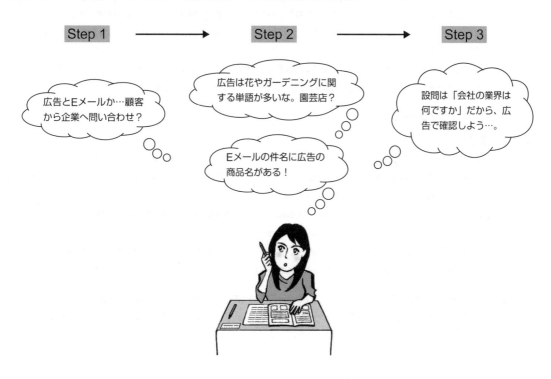

では、次ページのウォームアップを題材に、「複数の文書を読む際のポイント」の流れに沿って読んでみましょう。2文書ともEメールです。読み方のヒントとして、Step 2 の概要をつかむところまでを解説していきます。

Step 1 文書間の大枠の場面設定をつかむ

☑ 発信者と受信者の人名が Adam Petrovich、Gayan De Soysa の2人の人物名の入れ替えになっており、件名が Service request と RE: Service request で往信に対する返信になっていることから、2者によるEメールの往復のやりとりだと考えられます。

☑ 件名から、2人はサービスを提供する側とサービスを依頼する側という関係だと推測できます。

☑ 2通のEメールとも送信日付は October 11 で午前と午後という短時間のやりとりになっています。

☑ 1通目のEメール本文に、October 9、October 12 between the hours of 3 P.M. and 5 P.M.、October 13 between the hours of 9 A.M. and 11 A.M.、2通目のEメールの本文に October 12 とあり、近い日付が頻繁に登場していることから、日程の調整が話題の中心だと推測できます。

Step 2 各文書の内容をつかむ

1 [1通目のEメール]

■ 第1段落

☑ I received the service request you submitted on October 9 concerning the flickering hallway light and the broken dishwasher in your apartment.（❶1〜2行目）

1通目は Petrovich さんから De Soysa さんへのEメールで、件名と本文の冒頭の文から、おそらく Petrovich さんは建物の保守管理をする人で、De Soysa さんは入居者だと推測できます。また、Petrovich さんは De Soysa さんから、下線部の2点に関する依頼のメールを10月9日に受信していたことが伺えます。これが第1段落の主題文です。

■ 第2段落

☑ If you would like, I will have my electrician ... repair your light and dishwasher this week.（❷1〜2行目）

☑ Please let me know as soon as possible which of these times is most convenient for you.（❷3〜4行目）

1文目で、Petrovich さんは De Soysa さんから依頼されたサービスの対応策を提案しています。これが第2段落の主題文です。また、2文目で作業日の候補として、具体的な日時を挙げた後、3文目で De Soysa さんの都合を尋ねており、これがEメールの主目的だと分かります。

以上をまとめると、1通目のEメールは、入居している部屋の保守サービス依頼をした De Soysa さんに、保守管理者の Petrovich さんが依頼の受信を伝え、対応策と作業日の候補を提案しているものになります。

2 [2通目のEメール]

■ 第1段落

☑ I had heard about the plumbing issue on the third floor from another tenant, ...（❶1行目）

2通目は De Soysa さんから Petrovich さんへの返信のEメールです。下線部の「配管の問題」とは、1通目のEメールにある a broken water pipe（❶4〜5行目）を指しています。

☑ As it turns out, I managed to replace the lightbulb ..., and the light is working fine now.（❶2〜4行目）

☑ The dishwasher still needs to be repaired, however. （❶4行目）

manage to do は「何とかして〜する」という意味です。De Soysa さんは下線部で最新の状況を伝え、10月9日にサービス依頼を送ったときとは状況が変わり、「電球に関しては対応不要」であることを Petrovich さんに伝えています。

この後、De Soysa さんは、もう一方の食洗機の修理の希望日時を回答しています。また、De Soysa さんが送信したEメールの本文には、Thursday が2回出てきます。それが何日に当たるのかを、De Soysa さんの説明から読み取りましょう。

ウォームアップ

テーマ解説を参考に、2 つの文書を通して読んだ後、今が 10 月 11 日の夜だと仮定し、De Soysa さんの予定を下線部に書き入れましょう。

1 　E-mail

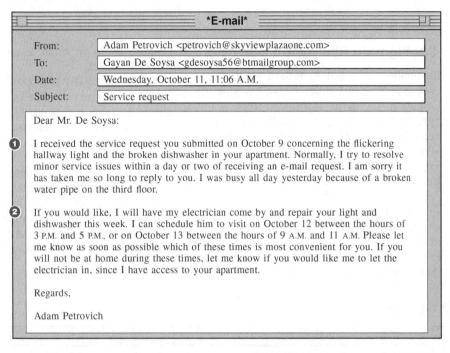

E-mail

From:	Adam Petrovich <petrovich@skyviewplazaone.com>
To:	Gayan De Soysa <gdesoysa56@btmailgroup.com>
Date:	Wednesday, October 11, 11:06 A.M.
Subject:	Service request

Dear Mr. De Soysa:

❶ I received the service request you submitted on October 9 concerning the flickering hallway light and the broken dishwasher in your apartment. Normally, I try to resolve minor service issues within a day or two of receiving an e-mail request. I am sorry it has taken me so long to reply to you. I was busy all day yesterday because of a broken water pipe on the third floor.

❷ If you would like, I will have my electrician come by and repair your light and dishwasher this week. I can schedule him to visit on October 12 between the hours of 3 P.M. and 5 P.M., or on October 13 between the hours of 9 A.M. and 11 A.M. Please let me know as soon as possible which of these times is most convenient for you. If you will not be at home during these times, let me know if you would like me to let the electrician in, since I have access to your apartment.

Regards,

Adam Petrovich

2 　E-mail

From:	Gayan De Soysa <gdesoysa56@btmailgroup.com>
To:	Adam Petrovich <petrovich@skyviewplazaone.com>
Date:	Wednesday, October 11, 4:05 P.M.
Subject:	RE: Service request

Dear Mr. Petrovich:

❶ I had heard about the plumbing issue on the third floor from another tenant, so I was not surprised that it took some time for you to respond. As it turns out, I managed to replace the lightbulb in the hallway on the same day I put in my request, and the light is working fine now. The dishwasher still needs to be repaired, however. I would prefer that the electrician come on Thursday, October 12, since I am planning to fly to Vancouver for a conference the next day and wish to be present during the repair work. Thursday is quite convenient for me, as I will be working from home that day. Please let me know if the electrician is still available that afternoon. Thank you for your attention to this matter.

Sincerely,

Gayan De Soysa
Apartment #250

10/9	： Petrovich さんへサービスの依頼の E メールを送信した。
10/11	： 作業日の希望について、Petrovich さんへ E メールで返信した。
10/12	： ア._____
10/13	： イ._____

【解答】
ア．在宅で仕事をする。　イ．バンクーバーへ出発する。　　　　　　　　　　　　　　→訳は p.177

TOEIC® L&R の問題文書を使って、実際に文書を読む練習をしましょう。

2 つの関連する文書に対し、1 ～ 3 の指示に従いながら、内容理解に挑戦してください。

1　Article

Spotlight on Real-World Business

September 15—Since retired marketing executive Warren Cralley began teaching at Ormandy Technical Institute a few years ago, he has invited guest speakers who are engaged in real-world business activities to address his classes. The speakers share their experiences with the students enrolled in introductory marketing and economics courses at Ormandy Tech.

The professor's objective is to help students to grasp how the theories they study in the classroom have practical applications in their future careers. The visitors show them that the lessons they learn in everyday life can be just as important as anything they read in a textbook.

Cralley lets students propose and invite their own classroom guests, including relatives, friends, and acquaintances. They are encouraged to approach people associated with businesses they are curious about.

Cralley's students all agree that the speakers are interesting. Although the class includes a few weeks in which students work as interns in various local companies, the guest speakers provide a very different perspective of the world of business.

2　E-mail

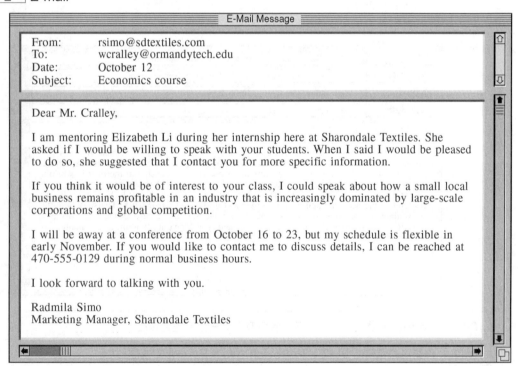

E-Mail Message

From: rsimo@sdtextiles.com
To: wcralley@ormandytech.edu
Date: October 12
Subject: Economics course

Dear Mr. Cralley,

I am mentoring Elizabeth Li during her internship here at Sharondale Textiles. She asked if I would be willing to speak with your students. When I said I would be pleased to do so, she suggested that I contact you for more specific information.

If you think it would be of interest to your class, I could speak about how a small local business remains profitable in an industry that is increasingly dominated by large-scale corporations and global competition.

I will be away at a conference from October 16 to 23, but my schedule is flexible in early November. If you would like to contact me to discuss details, I can be reached at 470-555-0129 during normal business hours.

I look forward to talking with you.

Radmila Simo
Marketing Manager, Sharondale Textiles

1. それぞれの文書にざっと目を通し、概要理解に重要と思われる語句や文を丸（◯）で囲み、次のメモを完成させましょう。

- 　1　 は、ア.＿＿＿＿＿＿＿＿＿＿＿＿＿＿＿＿ を招いて、授業で

　学生たちに話を聞かせている イ.＿＿＿＿＿＿＿＿＿＿ についての記事。

- 　2　 は、ウ.＿＿＿＿＿＿＿＿＿ から依頼されて、

　エ.＿＿＿＿＿＿＿＿＿ が Warren Cralley へ

　オ.＿＿＿＿＿＿＿＿＿＿＿＿ を申し出ている Eメール。

- 　1　 と 　2　 に共通または関連する語句：

　カ.＿＿＿＿＿＿＿＿＿＿＿＿＿＿＿＿＿＿＿＿＿

　＿＿＿＿＿＿＿＿＿＿＿＿＿＿＿＿＿＿＿＿＿＿

2. それぞれの文書の内容を説明した文を読み、正しいものを全て選びましょう。

　　1　 Article
(a) Cralley さんは学校で教える前に、民間企業で働いていた。
(b) Cralley さんの授業は実践よりもマーケティング理論を重視している。
(c) 授業に招かれるゲスト講演者は、実業界から選ばれる。
(d) 学生は自分たちでゲスト講演者を手配してもよい。
(e) 学生たちはインターンシップに参加できないため、Cralley さんの授業を歓迎している。

　　2　 E-mail
(f) Simo さんは Cralley さんの授業を扱った記事を読んで、講演を自ら申し出ている。
(g) Simo さんは Li さんとインターンシップで知り合った。
(h) Sharondale 織物社は世界的に展開する大企業である。
(i) Simo さんは中小企業が収益を維持する方法について話すつもりである。
(j) Simo さんは 10 月の最終週ならスケジュールに融通が利く。

3. Li さんが誰かについて、推測する手掛かりになる箇所をそれぞれの文書から見つけて、左の文書内に波線（〜〜〜）を引きましょう。

→解答・解説は p.172

チャレンジ

TOEIC® L&R の問題に挑戦します。

右上の目安の解答時間を目標に、自分で時間を計りながら **1 〜 5** の問題に答えてください。

---

1 Article

Spotlight on Real-World Business

September 15—Since retired marketing executive Warren Cralley began teaching at Ormandy Technical Institute a few years ago, he has invited guest speakers who are engaged in real-world business activities to address his classes. The speakers share their experiences with the students enrolled in introductory marketing and economics courses at Ormandy Tech.

The professor's objective is to help students to grasp how the theories they study in the classroom have practical applications in their future careers. The visitors show them that the lessons they learn in everyday life can be just as important as anything they read in a textbook.

Cralley lets students propose and invite their own classroom guests, including relatives, friends, and acquaintances. They are encouraged to approach people associated with businesses they are curious about.

Cralley's students all agree that the speakers are interesting. Although the class includes a few weeks in which students work as interns in various local companies, the guest speakers provide a very different perspective of the world of business.

---

2 E-mail

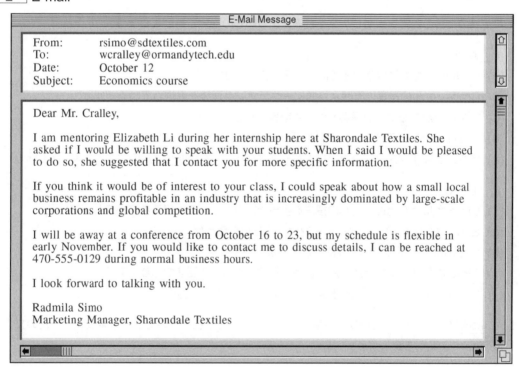

E-Mail Message

From: rsimo@sdtextiles.com
To: wcralley@ormandytech.edu
Date: October 12
Subject: Economics course

Dear Mr. Cralley,

I am mentoring Elizabeth Li during her internship here at Sharondale Textiles. She asked if I would be willing to speak with your students. When I said I would be pleased to do so, she suggested that I contact you for more specific information.

If you think it would be of interest to your class, I could speak about how a small local business remains profitable in an industry that is increasingly dominated by large-scale corporations and global competition.

I will be away at a conference from October 16 to 23, but my schedule is flexible in early November. If you would like to contact me to discuss details, I can be reached at 470-555-0129 during normal business hours.

I look forward to talking with you.

Radmila Simo
Marketing Manager, Sharondale Textiles

1. What does the article discuss?

    (A) A business leader's decision to retire
    (B) An instructor's classroom practice
    (C) A student's unusual opportunity to study abroad
    (D) An administrator's plan to change business-course requirements

2. According to the article, what is Mr. Cralley's goal?

    (A) To broaden students' understanding of business concepts
    (B) To create better business textbooks
    (C) To find ways businesses can work more efficiently
    (D) To teach workers how to become better public speakers

3. Why did Ms. Simo send the e-mail?

    (A) She would like to interview Mr. Cralley for a news article.
    (B) She has questions about marketing her business.
    (C) She is responding to an invitation.
    (D) She is recruiting interns for her company.

4. Who most likely is Ms. Li?

    (A) A student at Ormandy Technical Institute
    (B) A manager at Sharondale Textiles
    (C) A business reporter
    (D) A guest speaker in an economics course

5. What does Ms. Simo say about her schedule?

    (A) She has very little free time.
    (B) She is available only during evening hours.
    (C) She has a deadline in November.
    (D) She will soon be traveling.

PART 7

Unit 18

→解答・解説は p.172

1 記事

Spotlight on Real-World Business

❶ September 15—Since retired marketing executive Warren Cralley began teaching at Ormandy Technical Institute a few years ago, he has invited guest speakers who are engaged in real-world business activities to address his classes. The speakers share their experiences with the students enrolled in introductory marketing and economics courses at Ormandy Tech.

❷ The professor's objective is to help students to grasp how the theories they study in the classroom have practical applications in their future careers. The visitors show them that the lessons they learn in everyday life can be just as important as anything they read in a textbook.

❸ Cralley lets students propose and invite their own classroom guests, including relatives, friends, and acquaintances. They are encouraged to approach people associated with businesses they are curious about.

❹ Cralley's students all agree that the speakers are interesting. Although the class includes a few weeks in which students work as interns in various local companies, the guest speakers provide a very different perspective of the world of business.

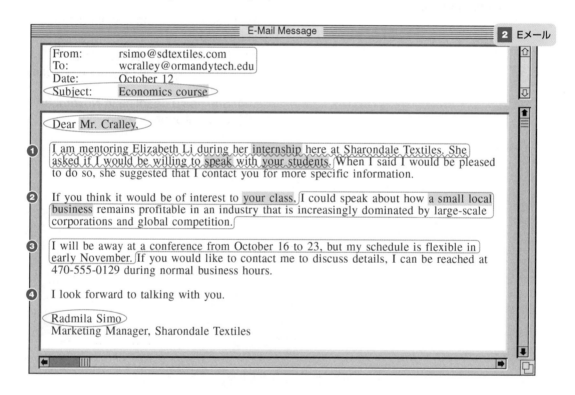

2 Eメール

```
E-Mail Message

From:      rsimo@sdtextiles.com
To:        wcralley@ormandytech.edu
Date:      October 12
Subject:   Economics course
```

Dear Mr. Cralley,

❶ I am mentoring Elizabeth Li during her internship here at Sharondale Textiles. She asked if I would be willing to speak with your students. When I said I would be pleased to do so, she suggested that I contact you for more specific information.

❷ If you think it would be of interest to your class, I could speak about how a small local business remains profitable in an industry that is increasingly dominated by large-scale corporations and global competition.

❸ I will be away at a conference from October 16 to 23, but my schedule is flexible in early November. If you would like to contact me to discuss details, I can be reached at 470-555-0129 during normal business hours.

❹ I look forward to talking with you.

Radmila Simo
Marketing Manager, Sharondale Textiles

→語注は p.176

実社会のビジネスに光を当てる

9月15日―退職したマーケティング担当役員の Warren Cralley は、数年前に Ormandy 技術学校で教壇に立つようになって以来、実社会の企業活動に従事するゲスト講演者を招き、自身のクラスに向けて話をしてもらっている。講演者は自らの経験を、Ormandy 技術学校の「マーケティング・経済学入門」を取っている学生たちに共有している。

教授の目標は、学生たちに、教室で学ぶ理論が将来の仕事でどう実地に応用できるかを理解させる手助けをすることだ。招待客たちは学生たちに、日々の生活で得る教訓も、教科書で読む内容に劣らず重要であるということを示している。

Cralley さんは学生たちに、親戚、友人、知り合いをはじめとして、自ら教室のゲストを提案させ、招待させている。学生たちは、自分が関心を持つ仕事に関わっている人々に話を持ち掛けるよう奨励されている。

Cralley さんの学生たち全員が、講演者の話は面白いという意見で一致している。授業にはさまざまな地元企業でインターンとして働く数週間が含まれてはいるが、ゲスト講演者たちの話はビジネスの世界に関する非常に異なる視点を提供してくれている。

送信者：rsimo@sdtextiles.com
受信者：wcralley@ormandytech.edu
日付：10 月 12 日
件名：経済学のコース

Cralley 様

私は、ここ Sharondale 織物社で、Elizabeth Li のインターンシップ期間中の指導をしております。私は彼女から、あなたの学生たちに話をしてほしいと依頼されました。私が喜んでそうする旨を彼女に伝えたところ、彼女は、さらに具体的な情報についてはあなたに連絡してほしいと言いました。

この件があなたのクラスにとって興味を引きそうとお考えでしたら、私は、大手企業や国際競争にますます支配されている業界で、いかに地域の中小企業が収益を維持するかということについてお話しできます。

私は 10 月 16 日から 23 日まで協議会で不在にしますが、11 月上旬のスケジュールは融通が利きます。具体的な相談でご連絡を頂ける場合は、通常の業務時間内に 470-555-0129 までお電話ください。

お話しできることを楽しみにしております。

Radmila Simo
Sharondale 織物社、マーケティング部長

プラクティス

1. 例は p.172 の図参照。

　ア．実社会で企業活動をしている人　　イ．Warren Cralley 教授　　ウ．Elizabeth Li

　エ．Radmila Simo　　オ．学生たちに自分の事業の経験を話すこと

　カ．Warren Cralley / Mr. Cralley、speakers / speak、his classes / your class、the students / your students、economics courses / Economics course、interns / internship、local companies / a small local business　　*p.172 の文書の網掛け部分

2. (a)、(c)、(d)、(g)、(i)

3. p.172 の図参照。

チャレンジ

1. What does the article discuss?　　記事は何を扱っていますか。

　(A) A business leader's decision to retire　　(A) ある実業家の退職の決意

　(B) An instructor's classroom practice　　(B) ある指導者による教室での実践

　(C) A student's unusual opportunity to study abroad　　(C) 海外留学という学生にとって類いまれな機会

　(D) An administrator's plan to change business-course requirements　　(D) 管理者によるビジネスコースの要件変更案

> **正解 B**　❶の記事のタイトルが「実社会のビジネスに光を当てる」であること、❶1〜6 行目にかつて民間企業で働いていた Cralley さんが Ormandy 技術学校の自身の授業で、「実社会の企業活動に従事するゲスト講演者を招き、自身のクラスに向けて話をしてもらっている」とあること、その他授業の目標や学生の反応について紹介していることから、記事は Cralley さんが指導する授業を扱っていると分かる。よって、(B) が正解。instructor「指導者」、practice「実践」。
> (A) retire「退職する」。
> (C) unusual「まれな、珍しい」、study abroad「海外留学をする」。
> (D) administrator「管理者」、requirement「要件、必要条件」。

2. According to the article, what is Mr. Cralley's goal?　　記事によると、Cralley さんの目標は何ですか。

　(A) To broaden students' understanding of business concepts　　(A) ビジネスの概念に関する学生の理解を広げること。

　(B) To create better business textbooks　　(B) ビジネスのより良い教科書を作ること。

　(C) To find ways businesses can work more efficiently　　(C) 企業がより効率的に活動する方法を見つけること。

　(D) To teach workers how to become better public speakers　　(D) より良い演説家になる方法を従業員に教えること。

> **正解 A**　❶の記事の❷1〜4 行目に「教授の目標は、学生たちに、教室で学ぶ理論が将来の仕事でどう実地に応用できるかを理解させる手助けをすることだ」と記載されている。「ビジネスの概念に関する学生の理解を広げること」という意味の (A) が正解。broaden「〜を広げる、〜を拡大する」、concept「概念、考え」。
> (C) work「うまくいく、機能する」、efficiently「効率的に」。
> (D) public speaker「演説家」。

3. Why did Ms. Simo send the e-mail?

    (A) She would like to interview Mr. Cralley for a news article.

    (B) She has questions about marketing her business.

    (C) She is responding to an invitation.

    (D) She is recruiting interns for her company.

SimoさんはなぜEメールを送ったのですか。

(A) ニュース記事のためにCralleyさんに取材したいと望んでいるから。

(B) 自身の事業のマーケティングについて質問があるから。

(C) 招待に応じているから。

(D) 自身の会社にインターンを募集しているから。

正解 **C** 　②のSimoさんが送ったEメールでは、「Elizabeth Liのインターンシップ期間中の指導をしている」と自己紹介した後、❶1〜2行目で「私は彼女から、あなたの学生たちに話をしてほしいと依頼された」と述べ、続けて、それに応じたいと考えており具体的な情報について尋ねるためにEメールで連絡したと説明している。つまり、Eメールを送ったきっかけは、Elizabeth Liという女性からの依頼にSimoさんが応じたからである。よって、(C) が正解。
(D) recruit「〜を募集する」。

4. Who most likely is Ms. Li?

    (A) A student at Ormandy Technical Institute

    (B) A manager at Sharondale Textiles

    (C) A business reporter

    (D) A guest speaker in an economics course

Liさんは誰だと考えられますか。

(A) Ormandy技術学校の学生

(B) Sharondale 織物社の部長

(C) 経済記者

(D) 経済学のコースのゲスト講演者

正解 **A** 　②❶の1行目で、Simoさんは自己紹介として「私は、ここSharondale 織物社で、Elizabeth Liのインターンシップ期間中の指導をしている」とLiさんの名前を挙げ、彼女からCralleyさんの学生たちに話をすることを依頼されたと説明している。一方、❶の記事の❶には、Cralleyさんが、実社会の企業活動に従事する人の話を学生たちに聞かせる授業を実践していること、❸1〜2行目には、学生自身にもゲストを提案・招待させていることが書かれている。さらに、❹2〜4行目では、授業には数週間のインターンシップが含まれていることが述べられており、これらから、LiさんはCralleyさんのクラスの学生で、現在インターンとして地元企業のSharondale 織物社で働いており、指導者のSimoさんに授業で話をしてくれるよう依頼したのだと推測できる。正解は (A)。

5. What does Ms. Simo say about her schedule?

    (A) She has very little free time.

    (B) She is available only during evening hours.

    (C) She has a deadline in November.

    (D) She will soon be traveling.

Simoさんは、自身のスケジュールについて何と言っていますか。

(A) 自由になる時間がとても少ない。

(B) 夜間にのみ都合がつく。

(C) 11月に締め切りがある。

(D) 近々出張に行く。

正解 **D** 　②の❸1〜2行目に「私は10月16日から23日まで協議会で不在にするが、11月上旬のスケジュールは融通が利く」とある。メール送信日が10月12日なので、ここから、Simoさんは数日後に出張に行くと推測できる。(D) が正解。
(A) free time「自由な時間、空き時間」。
(C) deadline「締め切り」。

解答・解説

語 注

1 記事 ❶ retired　退職した、引退した　　marketing　マーケティング、販売戦略上の　　executive　役員、重役
technical institute　技術学校　　guest speaker　ゲスト講演者、招待講演者
be engaged in ～　～に従事している　　business activity　企業活動　　address　～に向けて話をする
class　クラス、授業　　share ～ with …　～を…と共有する
enroll　～を（受講生として）登録する、～を名簿に記載する　　introductory　入門的な　　economics　経済学
course　コース、課程

❷ objective　目標、目的　　grasp　～を理解する、～を把握する　　theory　理論　　classroom　授業、教室
practical　実用的な　　application　応用　　everyday life　日常生活

❸ let ～ do　～に（自由に）…させる　　propose　～を提案する　　relative　親戚　　acquaintance　知り合い
encourage ～ to do　～に…するよう奨励する　　approach　～に話を持ち掛ける
associated with ～　～と結び付いた、～と関係を持っている　　business　仕事、企業

❹ agree (that) ～　～であると同意する　　intern　インターン　　local　地元の　　perspective　視点

2 Eメール ❶ mentor　～を指導する　　internship　インターンシップ、職業訓練　　textile　織物、繊維製品
be willing to do　～する意思がある　　suggest (that) ～　～であると言う　　specific　具体的な

❷ of interest　興味深い　　profitable　収益の多い　　industry　業界、産業　　increasingly　ますます
dominate　～を支配する　　large-scale　大規模な　　corporation　企業　　competition　競争

❸ conference　協議会、会議　　flexible　融通の利く、柔軟な　　details　〈複数形で〉詳細
reach　～に連絡する　　business hours　業務時間、営業時間

→英文は p.172

【ウォームアップの訳】

1 Eメール

送信者：Adam Petrovich <petrovich@skyviewplazaone.com>
受信者：Gayan De Soysa <gdesoysa56@btmailgroup.com>
日付：10月11日（水）、午前11時6分
件名：サービスのご依頼

De Soysa 様

お部屋の廊下の照明が点滅している件と食器洗い機が壊れている件について、10月9日にお送りくださったサービス依頼を受け取りました。通常、細かいサービス事案は、Eメールでご依頼を受けてから1、2日以内に解決するように努めています。返信が遅くなってしまい申し訳ありません。昨日は3階の水道管が壊れたため、終日手がふさがっておりました。

よろしければ、今週にも電気技師を伺わせ、照明と食器洗い機を修理させます。10月12日の午後3〜5時、または10月13日の午前9〜11時の時間帯なら、技師の訪問を予定に入れることができます。これらのうちどの日時があなたのご都合に最も合うか、できるだけ早くお知らせください。これらの時間帯にご不在の場合は、私はあなたのお部屋に入ることができますので、私が技師をお部屋に入室させることをご希望されるかどうかについて教えてください。

敬具

Adam Petrovich

---

2 Eメール

送信者：Gayan De Soysa <gdesoysa56@btmailgroup.com>
受信者：Adam Petrovich <petrovich@skyviewplazaone.com>
日付：10月11日（水）、午後4時5分
件名：RE：サービスのご依頼

Petrovich 様

他の居住者から3階の配管の問題について聞いていましたので、あなたがお返事を下さるのに少々時間がかかったことには驚いていません。結局のところ、依頼をお送りしたのと同じ日に、私は廊下の電球を何とか交換することができ、今のところ照明は問題なくついています。しかし、食器洗い機は今も修理が必要な状態です。電気技師の方には10月12日の木曜日に来ていただく方が望ましいです。というのは、私はその翌日会議のために飛行機でバンクーバーへ行く予定で、修理作業には立ち会いたいからです。その日は在宅で仕事をすることになっているので、木曜日は私にはちょうど都合がいいです。その日の午後に電気技師の方がまだ空いているかどうか教えてください。この件につきご配慮を頂き、ありがとうございます。

敬具

Gayan De Soysa
アパート250号室

→英文は p.167

Unit 19　速読法①：スキミング

■ テーマ解説

Part 7 の特徴の 1 つに、「読む分量の多さ」が挙げられます。読む速度を上げるためには、普段から類似のテーマの文書をたくさん読んで英語の文書形式や論理展開に慣れるようにしたり、語彙や構文の知識を増やしたりすることが欠かせませんが、一方で、時間内に全ての問題に解答するために、より実践的に速く読む技術を使うことが効果的な場面もあります。今回は速読法の 1 つである「スキミング」の練習をしてみましょう。

スキミング〜大意把握を目的にした読み方〜
スキミングとは、文章全体の大意をつかむことを目的として、細部の情報を深く読み込むことはせず、どんどん先を読み進める読み方を言います。論説文や長い報告書などを読む際に、文章全体を斜め読みして書き手の主張の方向性をくみ取るような場面を想像すると、分かりやすいと思います。

Part 7 の文書でスキミングをする際は、これまで「プラクティス」問題で挑戦してきた文書のメモ要約に倣い、短い要約文を頭の中で組み立てるつもりで読み取っていきましょう。組み立てる要約文は、大雑把な、短いもので構いません。5W1H（Who、When、Where、What、Why、How）「誰が・いつ・どこで・何を・なぜ・どうやって」に注目しながら、「企業が、会員カードを作った新規顧客へお礼を述べ、提供サービスを説明している（E メール）」のように、その文書の内容を簡潔に言い表す 1文を組み立てるのです。タイトルや件名がある文書では、まずそれらを中心に読み、何についての文書かを予測しながらそのまま第 1 段落へ読み進めます。主題文はたいてい最初の 1〜2 文目にあります。知らない単語があっても立ち止まらず、理解できる箇所をつなぎ合わせて、全体の内容を推測してみましょう。第 1 段落の主題文を特定したら、その内容理解を基に、続く詳細情報の部分をざっと斜め読みしていきます。次の段落がある場合は、すぐそちらへ目を移し、同様の読み方で読んでいきます。

ポイントは、① **同じ箇所を読み返さない** ということと、② **具体例や事実などの詳細情報は全てを読まなくてもいい** ということです。常に「速く読む」ことを意識しながら行うようにします。理解にあやふやな部分があると、何度も同じ箇所を読み返したくなるかもしれませんが、とにかく目線を先へと移動させ、詳細情報は必要になったら後で読み返せばいいというくらいの気持ちで、全体の大意把握に努めましょう。

実際のテストでは、詳細な事実の理解を問う設問や書き手の意図を問う設問など、大意把握だけでは答えられない設問も多く登場します。スキミングだけで素早く過不足なく Part 7 の文書を読むことができて内容理解が進むとは、一概に言えません。ですが、特に複数文書がセットになった問題で、各文書の大意・概要だけを先につかみたい際には、このスキミングという読み方が役立ちます。必要に応じてスキミングを取り入れるようにしてみましょう。

ウォームアップ

1 テーマ解説を参考に、文書のスキミングに挑戦しましょう。（制限時間：30秒）。

2 文書の内容を説明した文を読み、(a)、(b) のどちらが正しいかを答えましょう。

E-mail

To:	All Brinker Automotive employees
From:	John Throop
Subject:	Security Center Notice
Date:	July 3

To All Employees:

On Monday, Brinker Automotive will begin using enhanced security software for building access. Regular employees will not see a difference upon entering Brinker Automotive buildings. The method for documenting visitors, however, will change.

Visitors will still be required to register at the front desk. However, instead of signing a paper registration book as before, each visitor will now be entered into a new tracking Web page by the front desk attendant, who will take a photograph of the person and issue a green (temporary) ID badge to be worn at all times while in our facilities.

These rules apply to both our corporate offices and manufacturing plants. Groups taking supervised factory tours are excluded. If you have any questions, refer to section 34.1 of our updated security manual.

Sincerely,

John Throop
Security Supervisor, Brinker Automotive, Inc.

---

1. The e-mail was sent by [(a) the Security Supervisor   (b) the Chief Executive Officer].

2. A new policy will [(a) be discussed   (b) start] on Monday.

3. Visitors will still be [(a) required to register   (b) guided by a supervisor] before entering.

4. The new rules apply to [(a) offices, but not plants   (b) both offices and plants].

【解答】

2 **1.** (a)   **2.** (b)   **3.** (a)   **4.** (b)

▶ メールヘッダーの To、From、Subject と、本文の宛先と署名欄から、Eメールは自動車関連会社のセキュリティー責任者が全従業員宛てに送ったもので、セキュリティーに関する案内をしていると分かる。

→訳は p.189

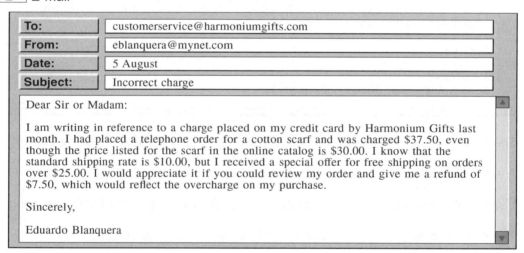

プラクティス

TOEIC® L&R の問題文書を使って、実際に文書を読む練習をしましょう。

3 つの関連する文書に対し、1 〜 3 の指示に従いながら、内容理解に挑戦してください。

1 Credit-card statement

| Eduardo Blanquera | | Page 2 |
| Account Number: XXXX XXXX XXXX 8191 | | 3 July–2 August |

Purchases		
Date	**Vendor**	**Amount**
5 July	Le Petit Bateau Café	40.05
8 July	Meyers Men's Shop	48.25
11 July	Midtown City Diner	24.11
17 July	Theta Restaurant	33.88
21 July	Harmonium Gifts	37.50
30 July	Ithaca Eatery	56.60
2 August	New Wave Office Supplies	99.87

2 E-mail

To:	customerservice@harmoniumgifts.com
From:	eblanquera@mynet.com
Date:	5 August
Subject:	Incorrect charge

Dear Sir or Madam:

I am writing in reference to a charge placed on my credit card by Harmonium Gifts last month. I had placed a telephone order for a cotton scarf and was charged $37.50, even though the price listed for the scarf in the online catalog is $30.00. I know that the standard shipping rate is $10.00, but I received a special offer for free shipping on orders over $25.00. I would appreciate it if you could review my order and give me a refund of $7.50, which would reflect the overcharge on my purchase.

Sincerely,

Eduardo Blanquera

3 E-mail

To:	eblanquera@mynet.com
From:	ftaylor@harmoniumgifts.com
Date:	8 August
Subject:	Your inquiry

Dear Mr. Blanquera:

Thank you for your e-mail of 5 August inquiring about the charge on your credit card. According to our records, you asked us to gift wrap your purchase. The additional charge reflects our standard gift wrapping rate. I sincerely apologize if there was a misunderstanding; the telephone sales representative should have made clear the total charge at the end of the call. In order to remedy our mistake, I would like to offer you a $5.00 credit on this order or a $15.00 discount on a future order (minimum purchase of $40.00). Please let me know which you would prefer and I will process it right away. As always, we appreciate your business and look forward to serving you again in the future.

Best regards,

Freda Taylor
Sales Manager
Harmonium Gifts

1. それぞれの文書をスキミングして、次のメモを完成させましょう。

- 1 は、Eduardo Blanquera の ア._____ 月上旬からの イ._____ 。

- 2 は、Eduardo Blanquera から ウ._____ へ

  エ._____ を依頼する E メール。

- 3 は、オ._____ から Eduardo Blanquera へ

  カ._____ を説明する E メール。

2. 文書間に共通または関連する語句を書き出しましょう。

1 と 2 に
共通または関連する語句：_____

2 と 3 に
共通または関連する語句：_____

3. 次の (1)、(2) について、文書内で述べられている箇所をそれぞれ見つけて、 1 ～ 3 の文書内に波線 (〜〜) を引きましょう。

(1) Blanquera さんが Harmonium ギフト社での買い物が 30 ドルであると主張する根拠。

(2) Harmonium ギフト社での買い物の代金として、37.5 ドルを請求されている理由。

→解答・解説は p.184

チャレンジ

TOEIC® L&R の問題に挑戦します。

右上の目安の解答時間を目標に、自分で時間を計りながら **1** ～ **5** の問題に答えてください。

1 Credit-card statement

Eduardo Blanquera		Page 2
Account Number: XXXX XXXX XXXX 8191		3 July–2 August
Purchases		
Date	**Vendor**	**Amount**
5 July	Le Petit Bateau Café	40.05
8 July	Meyers Men's Shop	48.25
11 July	Midtown City Diner	24.11
17 July	Theta Restaurant	33.88
21 July	Harmonium Gifts	37.50
30 July	Ithaca Eatery	56.60
2 August	New Wave Office Supplies	99.87

2 E-mail

To:	customerservice@harmoniumgifts.com
From:	eblanquera@mynet.com
Date:	5 August
Subject:	Incorrect charge

Dear Sir or Madam:

I am writing in reference to a charge placed on my credit card by Harmonium Gifts last month. I had placed a telephone order for a cotton scarf and was charged $37.50, even though the price listed for the scarf in the online catalog is $30.00. I know that the standard shipping rate is $10.00, but I received a special offer for free shipping on orders over $25.00. I would appreciate it if you could review my order and give me a refund of $7.50, which would reflect the overcharge on my purchase.

Sincerely,

Eduardo Blanquera

3   E-mail

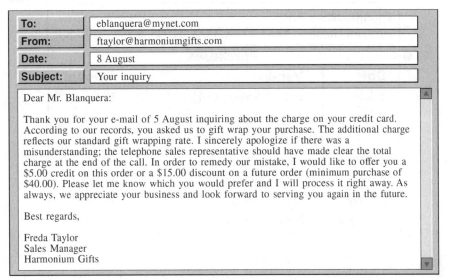

To:	eblanquera@mynet.com
From:	ftaylor@harmoniumgifts.com
Date:	8 August
Subject:	Your inquiry

Dear Mr. Blanquera:

Thank you for your e-mail of 5 August inquiring about the charge on your credit card. According to our records, you asked us to gift wrap your purchase. The additional charge reflects our standard gift wrapping rate. I sincerely apologize if there was a misunderstanding; the telephone sales representative should have made clear the total charge at the end of the call. In order to remedy our mistake, I would like to offer you a $5.00 credit on this order or a $15.00 discount on a future order (minimum purchase of $40.00). Please let me know which you would prefer and I will process it right away. As always, we appreciate your business and look forward to serving you again in the future.

Best regards,

Freda Taylor
Sales Manager
Harmonium Gifts

1. For what did Mr. Blanquera use his credit card most often in July?

(A) Office supplies
(B) Clothing
(C) Gifts
(D) Dining

2. When did Mr. Blanquera speak to Harmonium Gifts on the telephone?

(A) On July 3
(B) On July 21
(C) On August 5
(D) On August 8

3. In the first e-mail, the word "listed" in paragraph 1, line 3, is closest in meaning to

(A) ranked
(B) decided
(C) provided
(D) checked

4. How much does Harmonium Gifts charge for gift wrapping?

(A) $5.00
(B) $7.50
(C) $10.00
(D) $15.00

5. What information does Ms. Taylor want from Mr. Blanquera?

(A) Which form of compensation he prefers
(B) Which sales representative he talked to
(C) What items should be gift wrapped
(D) Where to send a refund

→解答・解説は p.184

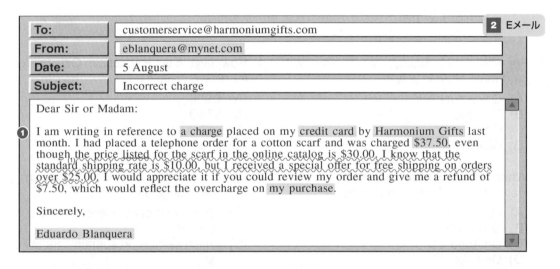

1 クレジットカードの明細

Date	Vendor	Amount
5 July	Le Petit Bateau Café	40.05
8 July	Meyers Men's Shop	48.25
11 July	Midtown City Diner	24.11
17 July	Theta Restaurant	33.88
21 July	Harmonium Gifts	37.50
30 July	Ithaca Eatery	56.60
2 August	New Wave Office Supplies	99.87

Eduardo Blanquera
Account Number: XXXX XXXX XXXX 8191   Page 2   3 July–2 August

Purchases

2 Eメール

To:	customerservice@harmoniumgifts.com
From:	eblanquera@mynet.com
Date:	5 August
Subject:	Incorrect charge

Dear Sir or Madam:

I am writing in reference to a charge placed on my credit card by Harmonium Gifts last month. I had placed a telephone order for a cotton scarf and was charged $37.50, even though the price listed for the scarf in the online catalog is $30.00. I know that the standard shipping rate is $10.00, but I received a special offer for free shipping on orders over $25.00. I would appreciate it if you could review my order and give me a refund of $7.50, which would reflect the overcharge on my purchase.

Sincerely,

Eduardo Blanquera

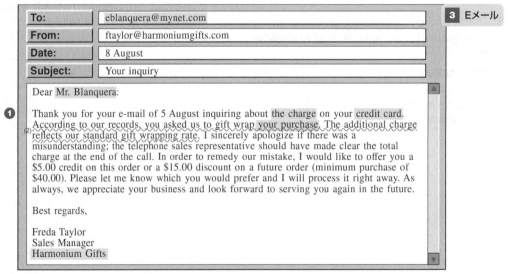

3 Eメール

To:	eblanquera@mynet.com
From:	ftaylor@harmoniumgifts.com
Date:	8 August
Subject:	Your inquiry

Dear Mr. Blanquera:

Thank you for your e-mail of 5 August inquiring about the charge on your credit card. According to our records, you asked us to gift wrap your purchase. The additional charge reflects our standard gift wrapping rate. I sincerely apologize if there was a misunderstanding; the telephone sales representative should have made clear the total charge at the end of the call. In order to remedy our mistake, I would like to offer you a $5.00 credit on this order or a $15.00 discount on a future order (minimum purchase of $40.00). Please let me know which you would prefer and I will process it right away. As always, we appreciate your business and look forward to serving you again in the future.

Best regards,

Freda Taylor
Sales Manager
Harmonium Gifts

→語注は p.188

Eduardo Blanquera		2 ページ
アカウント番号：XXXX XXXX XXXX 8191		7 月 3 日〜8 月 2 日
購入品		
日付	販売業者	金額
7 月 5 日	Le Petit Bateau カフェ	40.05
7 月 8 日	Meyers 男性用品店	48.25
7 月 11 日	Midtown City 食堂	24.11
7 月 17 日	Theta レストラン	33.88
7 月 21 日	Harmonium ギフト社	37.50
7 月 30 日	Ithaca 飲食店	56.60
8 月 2 日	New Wave 事務用品社	99.87

受信者：customerservice@harmoniumgifts.com
送信者：eblanquera@mynet.com
日付：8 月 5 日
件名：請求額の誤り

ご担当者様

Harmonium ギフト社が先月私のクレジットカードに請求した金額に関して、E メールを差し上げています。私は木綿のスカーフを電話で注文し、オンラインカタログに記載されているスカーフの価格が 30 ドルなのにもかかわらず、37 ドル 50 セント請求されました。通常配送料が 10 ドルであることは知っていますが、私は、25 ドルを超える注文に付く送料無料の特典を受けました。私の注文内容をご確認いただき、購入品に対する過剰請求分の 7 ドル 50 セントを払い戻していただければ助かります。

敬具

Eduardo Blanquera

受信者：eblanquera@mynet.com
送信者：ftaylor@harmoniumgifts.com
日付：8 月 8 日
件名：お問い合わせ

Blanquera 様

8 月 5 日付の E メールで、クレジットカードへの請求額についてお問い合わせいただきまして、ありがとうございます。当社の記録によりますと、お客さまはご購入品のギフト包装をご希望されました。追加料金は、当社のギフト包装の通常料金に当たります。誤解がございましたら、心よりおわび申し上げます。電話窓口の販売担当者が、お電話の最後に代金の総額をはっきりとお伝えすべきでした。当社の手違いの弁償といたしまして、今回の注文から 5 ドルの控除、または今後のご注文で 15 ドルの割引（最低購入金額 40 ドル）をご提供いたしたく存じます。どちらがご希望かお知らせいただければ、私が直ちにお手続きいたします。これまで同様、お客さまのご購入に感謝申し上げますとともに、今後もまた当社がお役に立てますことを願っております。

敬具

Freda Taylor ／販売部長／ Harmonium ギフト社

プラクティス

1. ア．7　イ．クレジットカードの明細　　ウ．Harmonium ギフト社の顧客サービス部

エ．請求額の誤りの確認　　オ．Harmonium ギフト社の販売部長　　カ．請求額は正しいこと

2. ┌ 1 ┐ と ┌ 2 ┐ に共通または関連する語句：

Eduardo Blanquera、Purchases / my purchase、Harmonium Gifts、($)37.50

┌ 2 ┐ と ┌ 3 ┐ に共通または関連する語句：

eblanquera@mynet.com、Eduardo Blanquera / Mr. Blanquera、a charge / the charge、credit card、my purchase / your purchase、Harmonium Gifts　　*p.184 の文書の網掛け部分

3. p.184 の図参照。

チャレンジ

1. For what did Mr. Blanquera use his credit card most often in July?

(A) Office supplies
(B) Clothing
(C) Gifts
(D) Dining

Blanquera さんが 7 月に最もよくクレジットカードを使用したのは、何に対してですか。

(A) 事務用品
(B) 衣服
(C) 土産物
(D) 食事

正解 D ❶の Blanquera さんのクレジットカードの明細で、❶に記載されている Vendor「販売業者」の欄を見ると、7 月は 5 日の Le Petit Bateau カフェ、11 日の Midtown City 食堂、17 日の Theta レストラン、30 日の Ithaca 飲食店と、全 7 回のうち合計 4 回も飲食に関する場所でクレジットカードを使用している。よって、正解は (D)。dining「食事」。
(A) ❶の❶より、8 月 2 日に 1 回だけ、New Wave 事務用品社で買い物をしている。
(B) ❶の❶より、7 月 8 日に 1 回だけ、Meyers 男性用品店で買い物をしている。
(C) ❶の❶より、7 月 21 日に 1 回だけ、Harmonium ギフト社を利用している。

2. When did Mr. Blanquera speak to Harmonium Gifts on the telephone?

(A) On July 3
(B) On July 21
(C) On August 5
(D) On August 8

Blanquera さんは Harmonium ギフト社といつ電話で話をしましたか。

(A) 7 月 3 日
(B) 7 月 21 日
(C) 8 月 5 日
(D) 8 月 8 日

正解 B ❷の 1 通目の E メールの❶2 行目で、Blanquera さんは Harmonium ギフト社の顧客サービス部へ「木綿のスカーフを電話で注文した」と書いている。一方、❶のクレジットカードの明細を見ると、Harmonium ギフト社での購入は 7 月 21 日に行われたとあるので、Blanquera さんはその日に Harmonium ギフト社に電話注文をしたと分かる。正解は (B)。
(A) ❶より、クレジットカードの 7 月の請求対象の開始日。
(C) ❷より、Blanquera さんが Harmonium ギフト社へ E メールを送信した日。
(D) ❸より、Harmonium ギフト社が Blanquera さんへ E メールを送信した日。

3. In the first e-mail, the word "listed" in paragraph 1, line 3, is closest in meaning to

(A) ranked
(B) decided
(C) provided
(D) checked

1通目のEメールの第1段落・3行目にある "listed" に最も意味が近いのは

(A) ランク付けされている
(B) 決定されている
(C) 提供されている
(D) 確認されている

正解 **C**　listed が含まれる文の従属節は、「オンラインカタログに記載されているスカーフの価格が30ドルなのにもかかわらず」という内容である。list は「~を記載する」という意味を表し、ここでは受け身の過去分詞で、「記載されて」という意味を表す。最も意味が近いのは (C)。
(A) rank「~をランク付けする、~を評価する」。
(B) decide「~を決定する」。
(D) check「~を確認する」。

---

4. How much does Harmonium Gifts charge for gift wrapping?

(A) $5.00
(B) $7.50
(C) $10.00
(D) $15.00

Harmonium ギフト社はギフト包装に幾らを請求していますか。

(A) 5ドル
(B) 7ドル50セント
(C) 10ドル
(D) 15ドル

正解 **B**　**2**の Harmonium ギフト社宛てのEメールの❶5～6行目より、Blanquera さんが過剰に請求されたと主張しているのは7ドル50セントである。Harmonium ギフト社はその金額について、**3**のEメールの❶2～3行目で、「追加料金は、当社のギフト包装の通常料金に当たる」と述べ、過剰な請求ではないことを説明している。よって、Harmonium ギフト社がギフト包装代として請求している金額は7ドル50セントである。正解は (B)。
(A) **3**の❶5～7行目より、Harmonium ギフト社が弁償として申し出ている控除額。
(C) **2**の❶3～5行目より、Harmonium ギフト社の通常の発送料。
(D) **3**の❶5～7行目より、Harmonium ギフト社が弁償として申し出ている割引額。

---

5. What information does Ms. Taylor want from Mr. Blanquera?

(A) Which form of compensation he prefers
(B) Which sales representative he talked to
(C) What items should be gift wrapped
(D) Where to send a refund

Taylor さんは Blanquera さんから何の情報を欲しいと言っていますか。

(A) どちらの種類の補償を希望するか。
(B) どの販売担当者と話をしたか。
(C) どの商品をギフト包装すべきか。
(D) 払戻金をどこに送るか。

正解 **A**　**3**の Blanquera さん宛てのEメールの❶7行目で Taylor さんは、「どちらが希望か知らせてくれれば、私が直ちに手続きする」と書いている。「どちら」とはその直前の文で Taylor さんが手違いの弁償として申し出ている「今回の注文から5ドルの控除」と「今後の注文で15ドルの割引（最低購入金額40ドル）」の2つの選択肢を指している。よって、(A) が正解。compensation「補償」。
(B) (C) (D) いずれも言及されていない。

解答・解説

語注

1 明細 credit-card クレジットカードの　statement 明細

① purchase 購入、購入品　date 日付　vendor 販売業者　amount （金）額　diner 食堂
gift ギフト、土産　eatery 飲食店　★簡易で安価な店を指すことが多い　supplies 〈複数形で〉備品

2 Eメール incorrect 誤った　charge 請求（額）

① in reference to ～　～に関して　place a charge 請求をする　place an order 注文をする
cotton 木綿　scarf スカーフ　charge ～ …　～に…を請求する　even though ～にもかかわらず
price 料金、価格　list ～を（一覧に）記載する　standard 普通の、標準の　shipping rate 送料
appreciate ～を感謝する　review ～を見直す、～を精査する　refund 払い戻し、払戻金
reflect ～を反映する　overcharge 過剰請求

3 Eメール inquiry 問い合わせ

① inquire about ～　～について問い合わせる　according to ～　～によれば　gift wrap ギフト包装する
additional 追加の　misunderstanding 誤解　representative 担当者　clear はっきりとした、明白な
at the end of ～　～の終わりに　remedy ～を賠償する　offer ～ …　～に…を提供する
credit 控除、還付金　minimum 最低限の　process ～を処理する　right away 直ちに
as always いつも通り

→英文は p.184

【ウォームアップの訳】

受信者：Brinker 自動車会社の従業員各位
送信者：John Throop
件名：セキュリティーセンターのお知らせ
日付：7月3日

従業員各位

Brinker 自動車会社は月曜日に、改良版の入退館セキュリティー・ソフトウエアの使用を開始いたします。正社員が Brinker 自動車会社の建物に入館する際の変更点は見られません。しかし、来訪者を記録する方法が変更になります。

来訪者は今後も、受付で氏名登録をする必要があります。しかしながら、これまでのように紙の台帳へ署名するのではなく、各来訪者は受付係によって新しい追跡用ウェブページに登録されます。受付係は、来訪者の写真を撮影して、当社の施設滞在中常に着用していただく緑色の（暫定使用の）ID バッジを発行します。

これらの規則は、当社のオフィスおよび製造工場の両方に適用されます。案内付きの工場見学を行う団体は除外されます。何かご質問がありましたら、最新版セキュリティーマニュアルの第 34 条第 1 項をご参照ください。

敬具

John Throop
Brinker 自動車会社、セキュリティー責任者

→英文は p.179

Unit 20　速読法②：スキャニング

テーマ解説

スキャニング〜欲しい情報だけを読む〜

Unit 20 では、スキミングと並ぶ速読法の 1 つである「スキャニング」の練習をしてみましょう。スキャニングとは、あらかじめ見つけたいキーワードや知りたい話題を特定し、それに関する情報だけを探しながら拾い読みをする読み方を言います。例えば、新聞から特定の会社の株価を見つけたり、学校の講座一覧から自分が登録している授業に関する情報を読んだりする場面を思い浮かべると、分かりやすいと思います。

Part 7 では、設問で問われている情報を文書内で見つける際に、この読み方が役立ちます。基本の手順としては、① **設問を読む** → ② **解答に必要な情報だけを文書から探す**、です。例えば、設問が Who is most likely Mr. Sumaoang?「Sumaoang さんは誰だと考えられますか」とあった場合、この名前が文書の中に出てくるのは確実なので、目線を文書へ移動させ、Sumaoang という単語を探します。箇所が特定できたら、その人物がどういう立場の人として書かれているか、周辺の情報も併せて確認し、設問に答えます。

スキミングと組み合わせた読み方

スキミングとスキャニングを組み合わせて、Part 7 の問題に取り組むことも可能です。読み方の一例として、複数文書がセットになった問題で「スキミング→スキャニング」を実践する方法を紹介します。Step 2 (p.152) で各文書の概要をつかむ場面でスキミングを取り入れます。各文書にざっと目を走らせ、それぞれの要約文を頭の中で作るつもりで読み進めます。その後 Step 3 で設問に目を通し、スキャニングに移ります。複数文書がセットになった問題では、複数の文書を関連付けないと答えられない設問もあるため、それを念頭に、どの文書のどの情報を読めば手掛かりが得られそうかを考えて、キーワードを目印に箇所を探し当てましょう。スキミングであらかじめ文章構成がある程度理解できているため、欲しい情報がさっと探せるはずです。箇所が特定できたら、周辺情報も含めて、段落やブロックのまとまりで読んでいきます。詳細情報もしっかりと読み込むようにしましょう。

スキャニング
（設問を読む→必要な情報だけを探す）

Who most likely is Mr. Sumaoang?

この名前が文書内にあるんだな。

Car Care ... Instructor: R. Sumaoang, Sumaoang Brothers Auto Repair

あった！ 自動車修理の会社の経営者？

ウォームアップ

1 下の文書を使ってスキャニングに挑戦しましょう。制限時間内に、**1**、**2** の設問に答えてください（制限時間：**30** 秒）。

1. Mary さんの質問に対し、文書から情報を探して、正しい答えを選びましょう。

Mary : I want to join the **photography** class.
I'm only free on Wednesdays.
Can I join the photography class?

You : (a) Yes, you can.
(b) No, you can't.

2. Kent さんの質問に対し、文書から情報を探して、正しい答えを選びましょう。

Kent : There's an instructor named **Mr. Nowicki**.
I think he might be my classmate from high school.
When can I see him?

You : (a) On Monday evenings.
(b) On Tuesday evenings.

Elmont Township
Continuing Education Classes–May

Continuing Education classes are open to all residents of Elmont Township aged 18 and over. Classes are held at the campus of Elmont Community College unless otherwise noted. For registration, fees, and payment information, please see page 2 of this brochure.

How to Qualify for Your Real Estate License Mondays, 6 P.M.–9 P.M., Stanton Hall, Room 114 Instructor: J. Ekua, Town and Country Real Estate Associates	**Photography for Fun and Profit** Tuesdays, 7 P.M.–9 P.M., Stanton Hall, Room 114 Instructor: B. Chao, freelance photographer
Managing a Small Business: What You Need to Know Mondays, 7 P.M.–9 P.M., Gallagher Library, Room 306 Instructor: K. Nowicki, Small Business Development Administration	**Car Care** May 22 and 24, 9 A.M.–1 P.M., Elmont Vocational High School, Auto Shop Instructor: R. Sumaoang, Sumaoang Brothers Auto Repair

---

【解答】

1 **1.** (b)   **2.** (a)

【質問の訳】

1. 写真撮影のクラスに参加したいんですが。私は水曜日だけ時間が空いています。写真撮影のクラスに参加できますか。

2. Nowicki という名前の講師がいますね。彼は私の高校時代のクラスメートかもしれません。彼にはいつ会えますか。

→訳は p.203

2 では今度は、右ページの、複数文書の、「スキミング → スキャニング」に挑戦しましょう。制限時間内に、次の**2**つの設問に答えるには、どの文書を読めばいいかを答えましょう。その後、設問に答えましょう（制限時間：**2**分**30**秒）。

1. What is Ms. Ohayon studying?

(a) Real estate

(b) Management

(c) Photography

(d) Car care

読むべき文書の番号 ＿＿＿＿＿＿＿＿＿＿＿＿＿＿

質問の解答 ＿＿＿＿＿＿＿＿＿＿＿＿＿＿

2. On what date did a rescheduled class take place?

(a) May 22

(b) May 23

(c) May 24

(d) May 27

読むべき文書の番号 ＿＿＿＿＿＿＿＿＿＿＿＿＿＿

質問の解答 ＿＿＿＿＿＿＿＿＿＿＿＿＿＿

【解答】

2 1. ⬜1⬜ と ⬜2⬜ 、(a)　2. ⬜2⬜ と ⬜3⬜ 、(d)

▶ ⬜1⬜ のパンフレットは地元のコミュニティーカレッジが開催する生涯教育の講座紹介、⬜2⬜ のEメールは Zelda Ohayon を含む 15 名の受講生に宛てた休講のお知らせ、⬜3⬜ は 1 日だけ有効な駐車許可証である。まず文書のスキミングでこれらを頭に入れ次に設問のスキャニングで、どの文書を読めばいいかをそれぞれ判断しよう。

▶ 1. Ohayon さんの名前が ⬜2⬜ のEメールの受信者にある。Eメールの本文から、Ohayon さんは Ekua さんのクラスの受講生だと分かるため、⬜1⬜ のパンフレットで Ekua さんの名前を探す。

▶ 2. ⬜2⬜ のEメールに授業の日程が変更されること、受講生には臨時の駐車許可証を送ることが書かれている。また、⬜3⬜ のTEMPORARY PASS「臨時許可証」の「有効日」の欄に 5 月 27 日とあることから、その日が変更後の授業が行われた日だと分かる。

→訳は p.203

1 Brochure

Elmont Township
Continuing Education Classes–May

Continuing Education classes are open to all residents of Elmont Township aged 18 and over. Classes are held at the campus of Elmont Community College unless otherwise noted. For registration, fees, and payment information, please see page 2 of this brochure.

How to Qualify for Your Real Estate License	**Photography for Fun and Profit**
Mondays, 6 P.M.–9 P.M., Stanton Hall, Room 114 Instructor: J. Ekua, Town and Country Real Estate Associates	Tuesdays, 7 P.M.–9 P.M., Stanton Hall, Room 114 Instructor: B. Chao, freelance photographer
Managing a Small Business: What You Need to Know	**Car Care**
Mondays, 7 P.M.–9 P.M., Gallagher Library, Room 306 Instructor: K. Nowicki, Small Business Development Administration	May 22 and 24, 9 A.M.–1 P.M., Elmont Vocational High School, Auto Shop Instructor: R. Sumaoang, Sumaoang Brothers Auto Repair

2 E-mail

E-mail	
To:	Zelda Ohayon [and fourteen others]
From:	Bill O'Toole <w.otoole@elmont.gov>
Subject:	Class canceled
Date:	May 23

Hi, all,

Ms. Ekua asked me to let everyone know that an emergency came up that she needs to attend to, so tomorrow's class has been canceled and will be rescheduled. As soon as we know the date, we'll let you know by e-mail and send you a temporary parking pass because the one you currently have will no longer be valid. Apologies for the inconvenience.

Bill

3 Pass

Elmont Community College Parking Authority
TEMPORARY PASS–GOOD FOR TODAY ONLY

LOT A
Valid: May 27
Time stamp: 6:45 P.M.

*Pass must be displayed on the dashboard of your vehicle and be visible from the outside.

TOEIC® L&R の問題文書を使って、実際に文書を読む練習をしましょう。

3 つの関連する文書に対し、1 〜 3 の指示に従いながら、内容理解に挑戦してください。

1 Web page

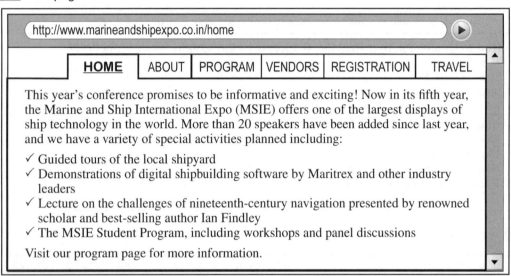

http://www.marineandshipexpo.co.in/home

| **HOME** | ABOUT | PROGRAM | VENDORS | REGISTRATION | TRAVEL |

This year's conference promises to be informative and exciting! Now in its fifth year, the Marine and Ship International Expo (MSIE) offers one of the largest displays of ship technology in the world. More than 20 speakers have been added since last year, and we have a variety of special activities planned including:

✓ Guided tours of the local shipyard
✓ Demonstrations of digital shipbuilding software by Maritrex and other industry leaders
✓ Lecture on the challenges of nineteenth-century navigation presented by renowned scholar and best-selling author Ian Findley
✓ The MSIE Student Program, including workshops and panel discussions

Visit our program page for more information.

2 E-mail

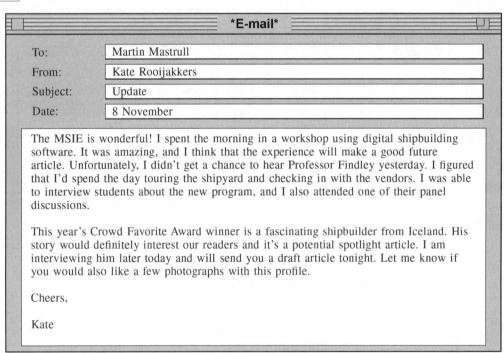

E-mail

To:	Martin Mastrull
From:	Kate Rooijakkers
Subject:	Update
Date:	8 November

The MSIE is wonderful! I spent the morning in a workshop using digital shipbuilding software. It was amazing, and I think that the experience will make a good future article. Unfortunately, I didn't get a chance to hear Professor Findley yesterday. I figured that I'd spend the day touring the shipyard and checking in with the vendors. I was able to interview students about the new program, and I also attended one of their panel discussions.

This year's Crowd Favorite Award winner is a fascinating shipbuilder from Iceland. His story would definitely interest our readers and it's a potential spotlight article. I am interviewing him later today and will send you a draft article tonight. Let me know if you would also like a few photographs with this profile.

Cheers,

Kate

3 E-mail

To:	Steinar Ericsson <sericsson418@telnordica.com>
From:	Kate Rooijakkers <krooijakkers@nordicperspectives.com>
Subject:	Photos
Date:	9 November

Dear Mr. Ericsson:

It was great talking with you yesterday. I sent the article to my editor. He loved it and made an additional request. So I wonder if I could meet with you briefly to take some photographs before you depart the expo. I want to feel confident that I have a few nice images to go with the story.

Respectfully,

Kate Rooijakkers

1. それぞれの文書をスキミングして、次のメモを完成させましょう。

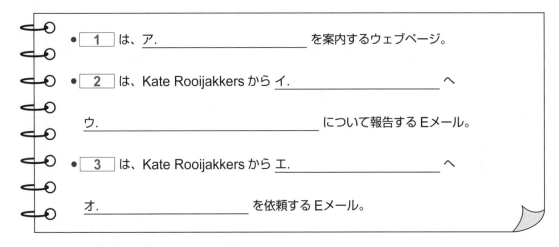

- 1 は、ア. _____ を案内するウェブページ。

- 2 は、Kate Rooijakkers から イ. _____ へ

  ウ. _____ について報告する Eメール。

- 3 は、Kate Rooijakkers から エ. _____ へ

  オ. _____ を依頼する Eメール。

2. 1 のメモを参考に、3 つの文書の内容を説明した文を読み、正しいものを全て選びましょう。

(a) MSIE は今年初めて開催される船舶の国際展示会である。

(b) 展示会で開かれる一部のイベントは、学生も参加できる。

(c) MSIE のイベントに Rooijakkers さんは満足している。

(d) Rooijakkers さんは賞の受賞者にインタビューするつもりである。

(e) Ericsson さんは Rooijakkers さんと仕事をする編集者である。

(f) Rooijakkers さんは MSIE の開催中に記事を 1 本執筆している。

3. 次の (1)、(2) について、文書内で述べられている箇所をそれぞれ見つけて、1 ～ 3 の文書内に波線 (〜〜〜) を引きましょう。

(1) Rooijakkers さんが参加したと推測される MSIE のアクティビティー

(2) Rooijakkers さんがインタビューする予定と言及した人物のプロフィール

→解答・解説は p.198

TOEIC® L&R の問題に挑戦します。

右上の目安の解答時間を目標に、自分で時間を計りながら **1 ～ 5** の問題に答えてください。

---

1 Web page

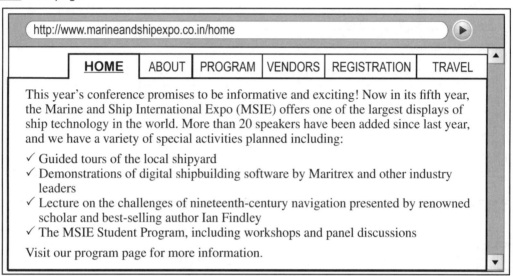

http://www.marineandshipexpo.co.in/home

HOME | ABOUT | PROGRAM | VENDORS | REGISTRATION | TRAVEL

This year's conference promises to be informative and exciting! Now in its fifth year, the Marine and Ship International Expo (MSIE) offers one of the largest displays of ship technology in the world. More than 20 speakers have been added since last year, and we have a variety of special activities planned including:

✓ Guided tours of the local shipyard
✓ Demonstrations of digital shipbuilding software by Maritrex and other industry leaders
✓ Lecture on the challenges of nineteenth-century navigation presented by renowned scholar and best-selling author Ian Findley
✓ The MSIE Student Program, including workshops and panel discussions

Visit our program page for more information.

---

2 E-mail

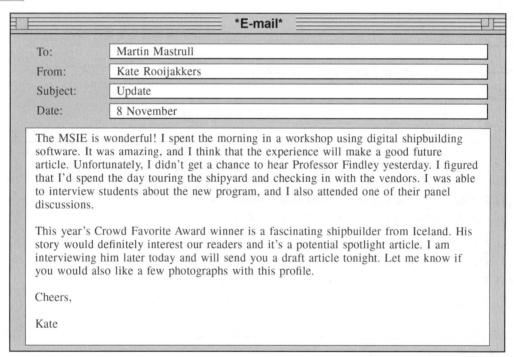

E-mail

To:	Martin Mastrull
From:	Kate Rooijakkers
Subject:	Update
Date:	8 November

The MSIE is wonderful! I spent the morning in a workshop using digital shipbuilding software. It was amazing, and I think that the experience will make a good future article. Unfortunately, I didn't get a chance to hear Professor Findley yesterday. I figured that I'd spend the day touring the shipyard and checking in with the vendors. I was able to interview students about the new program, and I also attended one of their panel discussions.

This year's Crowd Favorite Award winner is a fascinating shipbuilder from Iceland. His story would definitely interest our readers and it's a potential spotlight article. I am interviewing him later today and will send you a draft article tonight. Let me know if you would also like a few photographs with this profile.

Cheers,

Kate

3 E-mail

To:	Steinar Ericsson <sericsson418@telnordica.com>
From:	Kate Rooijakkers <krooijakkers@nordicperspectives.com>
Subject:	Photos
Date:	9 November

Dear Mr. Ericsson:

It was great talking with you yesterday. I sent the article to my editor. He loved it and made an additional request. So I wonder if I could meet with you briefly to take some photographs before you depart the expo. I want to feel confident that I have a few nice images to go with the story.

Respectfully,

Kate Rooijakkers

---

1. What is indicated about MSIE?

   (A) It is designed for newcomers to the industry.
   (B) It is held in a different country each year.
   (C) It has increased the number of its presenters.
   (D) It has increased the length of the event.

2. Who most likely is Ms. Rooijakkers?

   (A) A travel agent
   (B) A journalist
   (C) A shipbuilder
   (D) A magazine publisher

3. According to Ms. Rooijakkers, what conference activity was she unable to attend?

   (A) A lecture
   (B) A workshop
   (C) A guided tour
   (D) A student discussion

4. In the first e-mail, the word "figured" in paragraph 1, line 3, is closest in meaning to

   (A) decided
   (B) involved
   (C) represented
   (D) performed

5. What is suggested about Mr. Ericsson?

   (A) He will be speaking at next year's conference.
   (B) He met Ms. Rooijakkers in Iceland.
   (C) He is a well-known photographer.
   (D) He received an award.

→解答・解説は p.198

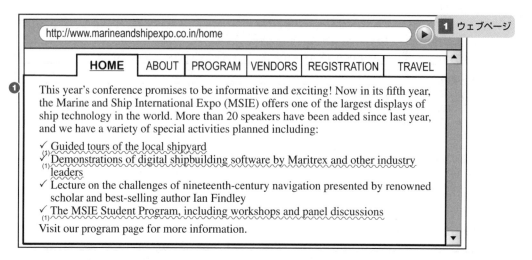

http://www.marineandshipexpo.co.in/home

| HOME | ABOUT | PROGRAM | VENDORS | REGISTRATION | TRAVEL |

This year's conference promises to be informative and exciting! Now in its fifth year, the Marine and Ship International Expo (MSIE) offers one of the largest displays of ship technology in the world. More than 20 speakers have been added since last year, and we have a variety of special activities planned including:

✓ Guided tours of the local shipyard
✓ (1)Demonstrations of digital shipbuilding software by Maritrex and other industry leaders
✓ Lecture on the challenges of nineteenth-century navigation presented by renowned scholar and best-selling author Ian Findley
✓ (1)The MSIE Student Program, including workshops and panel discussions

Visit our program page for more information.

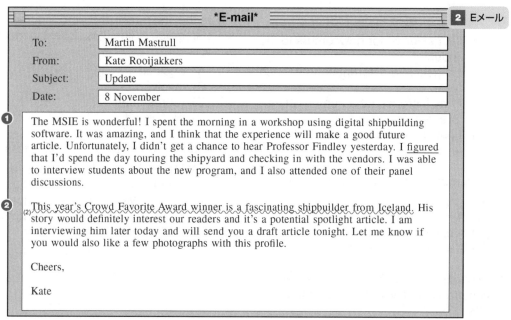

E-mail

To:	Martin Mastrull
From:	Kate Rooijakkers
Subject:	Update
Date:	8 November

The MSIE is wonderful! I spent the morning in a workshop using digital shipbuilding software. It was amazing, and I think that the experience will make a good future article. Unfortunately, I didn't get a chance to hear Professor Findley yesterday. I figured that I'd spend the day touring the shipyard and checking in with the vendors. I was able to interview students about the new program, and I also attended one of their panel discussions.

(2)This year's Crowd Favorite Award winner is a fascinating shipbuilder from Iceland. His story would definitely interest our readers and it's a potential spotlight article. I am interviewing him later today and will send you a draft article tonight. Let me know if you would also like a few photographs with this profile.

Cheers,

Kate

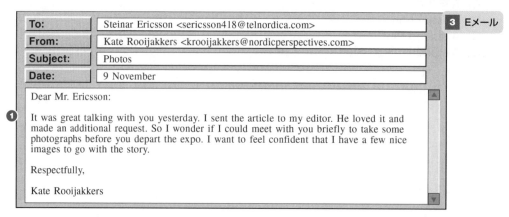

To:	Steinar Ericsson <sericsson418@telnordica.com>
From:	Kate Rooijakkers <krooijakkers@nordicperspectives.com>
Subject:	Photos
Date:	9 November

Dear Mr. Ericsson:

It was great talking with you yesterday. I sent the article to my editor. He loved it and made an additional request. So I wonder if I could meet with you briefly to take some photographs before you depart the expo. I want to feel confident that I have a few nice images to go with the story.

Respectfully,

Kate Rooijakkers

→語注は p.202

http://www.marineandshipexpo.co.in/home

ホーム　　イベントについて　　プログラム　　販売業者　　登録　　旅行

今年の会議は、役立つ情報満載で刺激的なものになる見込みです！ 5年目を迎えて、海洋船舶国際展示会（MSIE）は、世界最大級の船舶技術の展示の1つをご提供します。昨年より20名を超える講演者が加わり、次のようなさまざまな特別アクティビティーを予定しています。

☑　地元の造船所のガイド付きツアー

☑　Maritrex社および他の業界リーダーによるデジタル造船ソフトウエアのデモンストレーション

☑　高名な学者でありベストセラー作家でもあるIan Findley氏による19世紀の航海の試練に関する講演

☑　MSIE学生プログラム（ワークショップやパネルディスカッションなど）

さらなる情報については、プログラムのページをご覧ください。

受信者：Martin Mastrull
送信者：Kate Rooijakkers
件名：最新情報
日付：11月8日

MSIEは素晴らしいです！ 私は午前中、デジタル造船ソフトウエアを使ったワークショップに参加しました。それは驚くべきもので、この経験は今後いい記事になると思います。昨日は残念ながら、Findley教授の講演を聴く機会はありませんでした。造船所のツアーや販売業者との顔合わせに終日費やそうと判断したのです。新しいプログラムについて学生にインタビューができましたし、彼らのパネルディスカッションの1つにも参加しました。

今年の大衆人気賞の受賞者はとても魅力的なアイスランド人造船家です。彼の話は間違いなく私たちの読者の興味を引くでしょうし、注目記事になる可能性があります。今日、後で彼にインタビューすることになっているので、今夜あなたに記事の草稿を送ります。このプロフィールと一緒に写真も何枚かご希望でしたら、知らせてください。

ではまた。

Kate

受信者：Steinar Ericsson <sericsson418@telnordica.com>
送信者：Kate Rooijakkers <krooijakkers@nordicperspectives.com>
件名：写真
日付：11月9日

Ericsson 様

昨日はお話しさせていただき大変ありがとうございました。編集者に私の記事を送りました。彼はそれをとても気に入り、追加の依頼をしてきました。それで、展示会から出発される前に、何枚かお写真を撮るため、少しだけお目にかかれませんでしょうか。記事に合う画像が手元に何枚かあるという自信を持ちたいのです。

敬具

Kate Rooijakkers

プラクティス

1. ア. 海洋船舶国際展示会

ィ. Martin Mastrull

ウ. 展示会の様子と取材記事の送付予定

エ. Steinar Ericsson

オ. 写真撮影

2. (b)、(c)、(d)、(f)

3. p.198 の文書参照。

チャレンジ

1. What is indicated about MSIE?

(A) It is designed for newcomers to the industry.

(B) It is held in a different country each year.

(C) It has increased the number of its presenters.

(D) It has increased the length of the event.

MSIE について何が示されていますか。

(A) 業界の新規参入者向けである。

(B) 毎年違う国で開催されている。

(C) 発表者の数を増やしている。

(D) イベントの期間を延ばしている。

正解 C ❶のウェブページの❶3行目に「昨年より20名を超える講演者が加わり」とある。speakers「講演者」を presenters 「発表者」と言い換えた (C) が正解となる。

(A) ❶のウェブページのタブメニューに VENDORS「販売業者」とあるが、展示会は、同❶10行目より、学生プログラムが予定されるなど幅広い層を対象にしたイベントだと分かる。designed for ～「～のために設計された」、newcomer「新規参入者」。

(B) 開催国については記載がない。

(D) 期間の長さについては記載がない。length「(時間・行為などの) 長さ」。

2. Who most likely is Ms. Rooijakkers?

(A) A travel agent

(B) A journalist

(C) A shipbuilder

(D) A magazine publisher

Rooijakkers さんは誰だと考えられますか。

(A) 旅行代理業者

(B) ジャーナリスト

(C) 造船家

(D) 雑誌の発行者

正解 B Rooijakkers さんは❷と❸のEメールを書いた人物。❷のEメールの❶2～3行目で、参加したワークショップについて、「それは驚くべきもので、この経験は今後いい記事になると思う」と感想を述べていること、また、同❷1～2行目で賞の受賞者について、「彼の話は間違いなく私たちの読者の興味を引くだろうし、注目記事になる可能性がある」と述べていることから、Rooijakkers さんは、新聞または雑誌に関わるジャーナリストと推測できる。

(A) ❶のウェブページのタブメニューに TRAVEL「旅行」とあるが、旅行に関する言及はない。

(C) ❷の❷1～3行目より、shipbuilder「造船家」は Rooijakkers さんがインタビューをする相手。

(D) 雑誌の発行者についての言及はない。

3. According to Ms. Rooijakkers, what conference activity was she unable to attend?

(A) A lecture
(B) A workshop
(C) A guided tour
(D) A student discussion

Rooijakkers さんによると、彼女は展示会で、何のアクティビティーに出席できませんでしたか。

(A) 講演
(B) ワークショップ
(C) ガイド付きツアー
(D) 学生の討論会

PART 7 Unit 20

正解 **A** Rooijakkers さんは**2**のEメールの**①**3行目で、「昨日は残念ながら、Findley 教授の講演を聴く機会はなかった」と述べている。**1**のウェブページで案内されている特別アクティビティーを見ると、同**①**8～9行目に renowned scholar and best-selling author Ian Findley と同じ人物の名前が登場しているので、彼女が参加できなかったアクティビティーは「19 世紀の航海の試練に関する講演」だと分かる。よって、正解は (A)。attend「～に出席する」。
(B) **2**の**①**1～2行目より、午前中にワークショップに参加したと報告している。
(C) **2**の**①**3～4行目に「造船所のツアーや販売業者との顔合わせに終日費やそうと考えた」とある。
(D) **2**の**①**4～6行目より、学生のパネルディスカッションの1つに参加したと報告している。

4. In the first e-mail, the word "figured" in paragraph 1, line 3, is closest in meaning to

(A) decided
(B) involved
(C) represented
(D) performed

1 通目のEメールの第 1 段落・3 行目にある "figured" に最も意味が近いのは

(A) ～を決めた
(B) ～を伴った
(C) ～を代表した
(D) ～を実行した

正解 **A** Rooijakkers さんは、**2**の**①**3行目で「昨日は残念ながら、Findley 教授の講演を聴く機会はなかった」と報告した後、I figured that ... で他の活動に時間を費やすことにしたと説明して、Findley 教授の講演を聴かなかった理由を述べている。最も意味が近いのは (A) decided「～を決めた」。
(B) involve「～を伴う」。
(C) represent「～を代表する」。
(D) perform「～を実行する」。

5. What is suggested about Mr. Ericsson?

(A) He will be speaking at next year's conference.
(B) He met Ms. Rooijakkers in Iceland.
(C) He is a well-known photographer.
(D) He received an award.

Ericsson さんについて何が示唆されていますか。

(A) 来年の会議で講演する。
(B) Rooijakkers さんにアイスランドで会った。
(C) 有名な写真家である。
(D) 賞を受けた。

正解 **D** Ericsson さんとは、**3**で Rooijakkers さんがEメールを送信した宛先の人物。Rooijakkers さんは、**①**1行目で、前日の話に対して Ericsson さんに礼を述べた後、記事を編集者に送ったと伝えている。また、**3**のEメールの送信日付が 11 月 9 日であることから、この記事は、**2**の前日のEメールの**②**2～3行目で Rooijakkers さんが言及した a draft article と同一のものだと分かる。つまり、Ericsson さんはインタビューを受けた人物で、同**②**1行目より、「大衆人気賞の受賞者」、「とても魅力的なアイスランド人造船家」と紹介されている。(D) が正解。
(A) 来年の会議については言及されていない。
(B) **2**の**②**1行目より、アイスランドは Ericsson さんの出身国である。
(C) **2**の**②**1行目より、Ericsson さんは造船家である。well-known「有名な」、photographer「写真家、カメラマン」。

解答・解説

語 注

1 ウェブページ vendor 販売業者　registration 登録

❶ conference 会議　promise to be 〜 〜になる見込みである　informative 有益な　marine 船舶の
display 展示、展示物　a variety of 〜 さまざまな〜　guided ガイド付きの
tour 施設の見学、ツアー　shipyard 造船所　demonstration 実演、デモンストレーション
shipbuilding 造船術　challenge 試練、難題　navigation 航海　renowned 有名な、名高い
scholar 学者　best-selling ベストセラーの　author 著者
panel discussion パネルディスカッション、公開討論会

2 Eメール update 最新情報、更新

❶ amazing 驚嘆すべき、見事な　article 記事　unfortunately 残念なことに
figure 〜と判断する、〜と理解する　spend 〜 *doing* 〜（時間）を…することに費やす
check in with 〜 〜に連絡する、〜と話をする　interview 〜にインタビューする　attend 〜に出席する

❷ award 賞　winner 勝者　fascinating 魅力的な　shipbuilder 造船家
definitely きっと、絶対に　interest 〜に興味を起こさせる　potential 潜在的な
spotlight 脚光、世間の注目　later 後で　draft 草稿、下書き　photograph 写真
profile プロフィール、人物評

3 Eメール ❶ editor 編集者　additional 追加の　request 依頼、要請　briefly 簡潔に、手短に
depart 〜を出発する、〜を発つ　confident 確信して、自信に満ちた　image 画像
go with 〜 〜と調和する、〜によく似合う　story 記事

→英文は p.198

【ウォームアップの訳】

1 パンフレット

<table>
<tr><td colspan="2" align="center">Elmont 地区
生涯教育クラス－ 5 月</td></tr>
<tr><td colspan="2">生涯教育クラスは、18 歳以上の Elmont 地区の全住民が受けることができます。クラスは、特に断りのない限りは Elmont コミュニティーカレッジのキャンパスで行われます。登録、料金および支払い情報については、このパンフレットの 2 ページを参照してください。</td></tr>
<tr>
<td>**不動産免許資格を取得する方法**
月曜日、午後 6 ～ 9 時
Stanton ホール、114 教室
講師：J. Ekua。都市地方不動産協会</td>
<td>**楽しみながら稼ぐ写真術**
火曜日、午後 7 ～ 9 時
Stanton ホール、114 教室
講師：B. Chao。フリーランスの写真家</td>
</tr>
<tr>
<td>**中小企業の経営：知るべきこと**
月曜日、午後 7 ～ 9 時
Gallagher 図書館、306 教室
講師：K. Nowicki。中小企業開発局</td>
<td>**自動車の手入れ**
5 月 22 日と 24 日、午前 9 時～午後 1 時
Elmont 職業高等学校、自動車工場
講師：R. Sumaoang。Sumaoang Brothers 自動車修理</td>
</tr>
</table>

2 E メール

受信者：Zelda Ohayon［他 14 名］
送信者：Bill O'Toole <w.otoole@elmont.gov>
件名：クラスのキャンセル
日付：5 月 23 日

皆さま

Ekua 講師より、皆さんにお知らせしてほしいとの連絡がありました。緊急事態が発生し、対応しなければならないので、明日のクラスは中止になり、日程が変更されます。皆さんには、日時が分かり次第 E メールでご連絡を差し上げるとともに、現在お持ちのものが無効になるため、臨時の駐車許可証をお送りします。ご不便をお掛けすることをおわび申し上げます。

Bill

3 駐車許可証

Elmont コミュニティーカレッジ駐車局
臨時許可証－本日に限り有効
　　　　地区 A
　　　　有効日：5 月 27 日
　　　　タイムスタンプ：午後 6 時 45 分
＊許可証は車両のダッシュボードの上に置き、外から見えるようにしてください。

→英文は p.191、193

MEMO

MEMO

STEP

2

ミニテスト

Step 2 の目標は、「テスト受験の時間感覚を意識する」です。本番形式のミニテスト（29 問）4 セットに挑戦し、テストに対応する力をより実戦的なものへ仕上げていきましょう。

Mini Test

TOEIC® Listening & Reading Test について

TOEIC® Listening & Reading Test とは？

TOEIC® Listening & Reading Test（以下、*TOEIC*® L&R）は、*TOEIC*® Program のテストの 1 つで、英語の Listening（聞く）と Reading（読む）の力を測定します。結果は合格・不合格ではなく、リスニングセクション 5 ～ 495 点、リーディングセクション 5 ～ 495 点、トータル 10 ～ 990 点のスコアで評価されます。スコアの基準は常に一定であり、英語能力に変化がない限りスコアも一定に保たれます。知識・教養としての英語ではなく、オフィスや日常生活における英語によるコミュニケーション能力を幅広く測定するテストです。特定の文化を知らないと理解できない表現を排除しているので、誰もが公平に受けることができる「グローバルスタンダード」として活用されています。

問題形式

- リスニングセクション（約 45 分間・100 問）とリーディングセクション（75 分間・100 問）から成り、約 2 時間で 200 問に解答します。
- テストは英文のみで構成されており、英文和訳や和文英訳といった設問はありません。
- マークシート方式の一斉客観テストです。
- リスニングセクションにおける発音は、米国・英国・カナダ・オーストラリアが使われています。
  ※ テスト中、問題用紙への書き込みは一切禁じられています。

リスニングセクション（約 45 分間）

パート	Part Name	パート名	問題数
1	Photographs	写真描写問題	6
2	Question-Response	応答問題	25
3	Conversations	会話問題	39
4	Talks	説明文問題	30

リーディングセクション（75 分間）

パート	Part Name	パート名	問題数
5	Incomplete Sentences	短文穴埋め問題	30
6	Text Completion	長文穴埋め問題	16
7	• Single Passages	1 つの文書	29
	• Multiple Passages	複数の文書	25

TOEIC® Listening & Reading 公開テストのお申し込み

IIBC 公式サイト https://www.iibc-global.org にてテスト日程、申込方法、注意事項をご確認の上、申込受付期間内にお申し込みください。試験の実施方法などに変更があった場合には IIBC 公式サイト等でご案内いたします。

お問い合わせ

一般財団法人 国際ビジネスコミュニケーション協会　IIBC 試験運営センター
〒 100-0014　東京都千代田区永田町 2-14-2　山王グランドビル
TEL：03-5521-6033（土・日・祝日・年末年始を除く 10：00 ～ 17：00）

リーディングセクションの問題形式

リーディングセクションは次の3つのパートで構成されています。ミニテストに挑戦する前に、各パートの問題形式と指示文を確認しておきましょう。

実際のテストでは、リーディングセクションは、リスニングセクションが終わった後、そのまま続けて開始されます。

PART 5　短文穴埋め問題

空所のある不完全な文を完成させるために、4つの選択肢（語または句）の中から最も適切なものを選ぶ問題です。実際のテストでは30問出題されます。次のように、リーディングセクション全体の指示の後に続けて、指示文が示されます。

READING TEST

In the Reading test, you will read a variety of texts and answer several different types of reading comprehension questions. The entire Reading test will last 75 minutes. There are three parts, and directions are given for each part. You are encouraged to answer as many questions as possible within the time allowed.

You must mark your answers on the separate answer sheet. Do not write your answers in your test book.

PART 5
Directions: A word or phrase is missing in each of the sentences below. Four answer choices are given below each sentence. Select the best answer to complete the sentence. Then mark the letter (A), (B), (C), or (D) on your answer sheet.

リーディングテストでは、さまざまな文章を読んで、読解力を測る何種類かの問題に答えます。リーディングテストは全体で75分間です。3つのパートがあり、各パートにおいて指示が与えられます。制限時間内に、できるだけ多くの設問に答えてください。

答えは、別紙の解答用紙にマークしてください。問題用紙に答えを書き込んではいけません。

指示：以下の各文において語や句が抜けています。各文の下には選択肢が4つ与えられています。文を完成させるのに最も適切な答えを選びます。そして解答用紙の (A)、(B)、(C)、または (D) にマークしてください。

サンプル問題

1. Before ------- with the recruiter, applicants should sign in at the personnel department's reception desk.

　(A) meets
　(B) meeting
　(C) to meet
　(D) was met

【正解】1. (B)

※ 問題番号は実際のテストとは異なります。Part 5 ～ 7 のサンプル問題の訳は p.411 にあります。

PART 6 長文穴埋め問題

空所のある不完全な文書を完成させるために、4 つの選択肢（語、句、または文）の中から最も適切な ものを選ぶ問題です。1 つの文書につき、空所は 4 つあります。実際のテストでは 16 問出題されます。 Part 6 の指示文は次の通りです。

PART 6

Directions: Read the texts that follow. A word, phrase, or sentence is missing in parts of each text. Four answer choices for each question are given below the text. Select the best answer to complete the text. Then mark the letter (A), (B), (C), or (D) on your answer sheet.

指示：以下の文書を読んでください。各文書の中で語や句、または文が部分的に抜けています。文書の下には各設問の選択肢が 4 つ与えられています。文書を完成させるのに最も適切な答えを選びます。そして解答用紙の (A)、(B)、(C)、または (D) にマークしてください。

サンプル問題

Questions 1-4 refer to the following article.

SAN DIEGO (May 5)—Matino Industries has just bolstered its image with environmentally conscious customers thanks to its ------- to reduce its use of nonrenewable energy to less
1.
than 20 percent within five years. ------- . Best practices guidelines are already being
2.
revised ------- powering down and disconnecting equipment when not in use. In addition,
3.
solar-panel arrays are slated for installation on-site as early as next year. When weather
------- are clear, these panels will offset Matino's reliance on the power grid, as they
4.
already do for a growing list of companies.

---

1. (A) product
   (B) commitment
   (C) contest
   (D) workforce

2. (A) Discounts on all its products have increased Matino's customer base.
   (B) Management predicts that the takeover will result in a net financial gain.
   (C) To achieve this goal, the company will begin by improving its energy efficiency.
   (D) The initial step will involve redesigning the company's logo and slogans.

3. (A) been encouraging
   (B) have encouraged
   (C) encourages
   (D) to encourage

4. (A) conditions
   (B) instructions
   (C) views
   (D) reports

【正解】 1. (B)　2. (C)　3. (D)　4. (A)

さまざまな形式の文書（1 つまたは複数）とその内容に関する複数の設問を読んで、4 つの選択肢の中から最も適切なものを選ぶ問題です。実際のテストでは 1 つの文書に関する問題が 29 問、複数の文書に関する問題が 25 問出題されます。Part 7 の指示文は次の通りです。

PART 7

Directions: In this part you will read a selection of texts, such as magazine and newspaper articles, e-mails, and instant messages. Each text or set of texts is followed by several questions. Select the best answer for each question and mark the letter (A), (B), (C), or (D) on your answer sheet.

指示：このパートでは、雑誌や新聞記事、E メールやインスタントメッセージなどのさまざまな文書を読みます。1 つの文書または複数の文書のセットにはそれぞれ、幾つかの設問が続いています。各設問について最も適切な答えを選び、解答用紙の (A)、(B)、(C)、または (D) にマークしてください。

サンプル問題

Questions 1-2 refer to the following text-message chain.

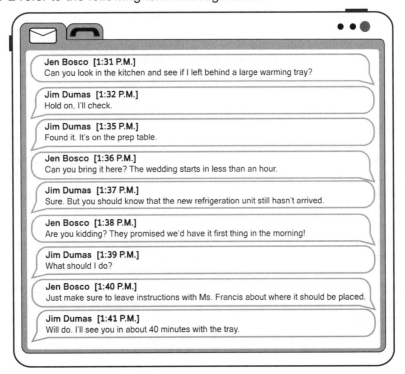

1. For whom do the writers most likely work?

(A) A catering company
(B) A home-improvement store
(C) A kitchen-design company
(D) An appliance manufacturer

2. At 1:38 P.M., what does Ms. Bosco most likely mean when she writes, "Are you kidding"?

(A) She thinks Mr. Dumas is exaggerating.
(B) She knew she would have to wait a long time.
(C) She expects the refrigeration unit to arrive soon.
(D) She is upset that a delivery has not been made.

【正解】1. (A)　2. (D)

右上の目安の解答時間を目標に、自分で時間を計りながら全ての問題を解いてみましょう。**p.308** の「結果記入シート」の説明も読んでから取り組んでください。

→解答・解説は p.220

PART 5

Directions: A word or phrase is missing in each of the sentences below. Four answer choices are given below each sentence. Select the best answer to complete the sentence. Then mark the letter (A), (B), (C), or (D) on your answer sheet.

---

1. Full-time staff at Dinh and Mann Associates ------- work 37.5 hours in a week.

(A) norm
(B) norms
(C) normal
(D) normally

2. Mr. Choi wants to know when the illustrations will be ready for ------- review.

(A) he
(B) his
(C) him
(D) himself

3. Dr. Lin, the keynote speaker at this year's Southeast Dentistry Convention, ------- several groundbreaking dental devices.

(A) invented
(B) exceeded
(C) supervised
(D) communicated

4. The project meeting has been rescheduled ------- tomorrow because of the bad weather.

(A) in
(B) by
(C) out
(D) for

5. Jane Tollen's original manuscript was published last year after Jansen Books obtained her family's -------.

(A) permission
(B) suggestion
(C) comparison
(D) registration

6. Participants arriving late are asked to enter the training seminar -------.

(A) quiet
(B) quieting
(C) quieter
(D) quietly

7. Volunteers will help conference participants ------- their way around the convention center.

(A) do
(B) find
(C) put
(D) ask

8. All tickets will be refunded ------- the soccer game is canceled because of bad weather.

(A) or
(B) if
(C) nor
(D) but

9. Given the recent boom in new construction, the price of lumber is ------- to climb.

    (A) covered
    (B) sought
    (C) limited
    (D) bound

10. Our investment in solar energy was a key ------- in achieving energy independence.

    (A) factor
    (B) role
    (C) basis
    (D) agency

11. The Voz 900, ------- for consumers who want a large-screen television at a small-screen price, is now available in stores.

    (A) perfect
    (B) perfectly
    (C) perfects
    (D) perfecting

Directions: Read the texts that follow. A word, phrase, or sentence is missing in parts of each text. Four answer choices for each question are given below the text. Select the best answer to complete the text. Then mark the letter (A), (B), (C), or (D) on your answer sheet.

Questions 12-15 refer to the following advertisement.

New Course on Inventory Management

Inventory of all types flows through supply chains. --------, it is vital for all supply chain
                                                                                  12.

professionals to understand the role, costs, and benefits of inventories. Too much inventory

can actually result in greater costs to ------- organization.
                                                              13.

This five-week course will train students in the basics of inventory management and control.

-------. Key elements of this series include the importance and use of inventory, exposure to
14.

different types of inventory, and methods ------- effectively managing inventory levels.
                                                        15.

12. (A) Anyway
    (B) Besides
    (C) Moreover
    (D) Therefore

13. (A) an
    (B) almost
    (C) once
    (D) there

14. (A) Some industries do not place high
        importance on inventory
        management.
    (B) Students who arrive late without a
        proper excuse will be dropped
        from the course.
    (C) For additional information, contact
        your instructor.
    (D) Upon completion, students will have
        greater mastery of the inventory-
        related aspects of their jobs.

15. (A) at
    (B) to
    (C) for
    (D) from

PART 7

Directions: In this part you will read a selection of texts, such as magazine and newspaper articles, e-mails, and instant messages. Each text or set of texts is followed by several questions. Select the best answer for each question and mark the letter (A), (B), (C), or (D) on your answer sheet.

Questions 16-17 refer to the following form.

Mini Test 1

WILPONT ASSOCIATES, INC.
Product Return Form

Dear Customer:

Wilpont Associates, Inc., produces our games and puzzles with the utmost care. However, if a product is damaged, or you are not satisfied for any reason, please return the item with the receipt and this completed form. A replacement will be shipped to you from the factory free of charge, or your account will be credited.

Name: _George P. Silva_

Address: _2038 Water Street, Lowry, MO 64763_

Problem description: _Parts of the item are missing._

Action requested: ☑ Replacement   ☐ Credit account

16. What product did Mr. Silva most likely buy?

(A) An accounting book
(B) A piece of clothing
(C) A bicycle
(D) A game

17. What problem is Mr. Silva reporting?

(A) Some pieces were not included.
(B) Some instructions are incorrect.
(C) The wrong product was delivered.
(D) The product was damaged during shipping.

FOR IMMEDIATE RELEASE
October 15
www.barnetinvestments.com

CHARLOTTE, NC—Barnet Investments held a ceremony today to inaugurate its new office building at 186 South Chowan Street. The company began in Cork, Ireland, ten years ago. Since then, it has expanded to offices throughout Europe, and last year, it opened its African headquarters in Johannesburg. The new headquarters in Charlotte marks the first North American location for the company.

Barnet Investments, a leading investment firm specializing in technology and electronics start-ups, includes Arno Technological Services and Karlon Electronics Superstores in its client list, along with other prominent businesses.

The headquarters will serve all clients in both North and South America. More than 500 employees have been hired to staff the location. Barnet Investments vice president Liam O'Malley will lead the new office during its first year before returning to Cork.

For further information, contact Maxine Wilton in Public Relations at 980-555-0184 or at mwilton@barnetinvestments.com.

---

18. What event took place at 186 South Chowan Street?

(A) A financial seminar
(B) An electronics show
(C) An opening celebration
(D) A hiring fair

19. What is mentioned about Barnet Investments?

(A) It serves clients on more than one continent.
(B) It is considered a leader in personal banking.
(C) Its Charlotte office was designed by a leading architectural firm.
(D) Its Charlotte office building is ten years old.

20. What is indicated about Mr. O'Malley?

(A) He was formerly the president of Arno Technological Services.
(B) He is working in Charlotte temporarily.
(C) He is one of 500 newly hired workers.
(D) He began his career at a retail store.

Questions 21-24 refer to the following online chat discussion.

 **Kathleen Vern**   ⊟ ⊠

Kathleen Vern (10:12 A.M.)
Our Australian partners have requested a video call to review the tile designs.

Mateus Ribero (10:14 A.M.)
OK. Do we have a plan yet?

Kathleen Vern (10:16 A.M.)
I'm setting it up for 7 P.M. tomorrow, our time, in room 2C. The late start is because of the time difference between Perth and Winnipeg.

Natalia Kovac (10:17 A.M.)
Could we call in to the meeting from home?

Kathleen Vern (10:19 A.M.)
I'm afraid not. The security policy states that we can't take anything out of the building, and our partners are counting on seeing the tile designs.

Natalia Kovac (10:20 A.M.)
OK. That makes sense. Now we just need approval from Ms. Feld to be here after hours.

Mateus Ribero (10:22 A.M.)
Let's check with her now. Ms. Feld, we would like to have a conference call with our partners in Perth tomorrow. Is it all right if we stay late to show them the new designs? We will be using room 2C since it has the audiovisual equipment.

Janice Feld (10:24 A.M.)
Yes, that's fine. I'll tell security so they won't lock the building until you've finished.

Kathleen Vern (10:25 A.M.)
Thanks, Mr. Ribero, for reaching out to Ms. Feld.

21. What is the online chat discussion about?

(A) Making a tile purchase
(B) Planning a business trip
(C) Arranging a meeting
(D) Extending a deadline

22. At 10:20 A.M., what does Ms. Kovac most likely mean when she writes, "That makes sense"?

(A) She knows about the time difference.
(B) She agrees that building security has improved.
(C) She realizes that she will be working late.
(D) She understands why they must work at the office.

23. What does Ms. Feld offer to do?

(A) Create a video of the tile designs
(B) Contact some colleagues in Perth
(C) Make sure that the office remains open
(D) Leave an extra set of keys in the office

24. Why does Ms. Vern thank Mr. Ribero?

(A) For obtaining approval
(B) For attending a conference
(C) For setting up some equipment
(D) For agreeing to lock the building

VILLAGE BISTRO WEEKLY SCHEDULE
June 3–9

	Head Chef	Assistant Chef	Host	Servers
Monday	Restaurant Closed			
Tuesday	Melanie	Yukiko	Luis	Enzo John
Wednesday	William	Ravi	Luis	Enzo Adam
Thursday	Melanie	Yukiko	Luis	Tania Adam
Friday	Ricardo	Ravi	Aisha	Tania Adam
Saturday	Ricardo	Yukiko	Aisha	John Meiying
Sunday	Melanie	Ravi	Aisha	Tania Meiying

From:	Melanie <melanie.villagebistro@swiftymail.com>
To:	All Staff <staff.villagebistro@swiftymail.com>
Subject:	Centerville Food Festival
Date:	May 30

Hello everyone,

The Centerville Food Festival will be held next week from June 4–9. Chef Julian Heeley from Forest Inn Restaurant is no longer able to attend and provide cooking demonstrations at the event. I have been asked to take his place. Yukiko and Adam will come along as my assistants. Ricardo has graciously volunteered to cover my shifts here at the restaurant next week, and Ravi will be filling in for Yukiko. Meiying has volunteered to work in place of Adam on Wednesday, June 5. However, Adam's shifts on Thursday and Friday are still not covered. Would someone be able to help out with this? Please let me know as soon as possible.

We are excited about participating in the festival this year. It will give us a chance to show the expected thousands of attendees what Village Bistro has to offer. It will be a busy week for all of us, but it will be well worth the effort.

Many thanks!

Melanie

25. Why was the e-mail sent?

   (A) To encourage attendance at an event
   (B) To report a change to a restaurant's business hours
   (C) To announce the retirement of a head chef
   (D) To ask employees to work extra hours

26. What is indicated about the Centerville Food Festival?

   (A) It takes place for the first time in June.
   (B) It will likely be well attended.
   (C) It takes place over two days.
   (D) It is held at Forest Inn Restaurant.

27. According to the e-mail, what benefit does participating in the festival bring to Village Bistro staff members?

   (A) They can get new menu ideas.
   (B) They will be able to promote the restaurant.
   (C) They can get a discount on restaurant supplies.
   (D) They can learn new cooking techniques.

28. Which group will NOT be affected by a change in working hours?

   (A) Head chefs
   (B) Assistant chefs
   (C) Hosts
   (D) Servers

29. Which day will Ricardo have off during the week of June 3–9?

   (A) Tuesday
   (B) Wednesday
   (C) Thursday
   (D) Friday

Mini
Test
1

Stop! This is the end of the test.

正解一覧

PART 5	1 D	2 B	3 A	4 D	5 A	6 D	7 B	8 B	9 D	10 A	11 A
PART 6	12 D	13 A	14 D	15 C							
PART 7	16 D	17 A	18 C	19 A	20 B	21 C	22 D	23 C	24 A	25 D	26 B
	27 B	28 C	29 B								

1 Full-time staff at Dinh and Mann Associates
------- work 37.5 hours in a week.

(A) norm
(B) norms
(C) normal
(D) normally

Dinh and Mann Associates社の常勤の職員は、標準的に、週37時間半勤務します。

(A) 標準
(B) 標準
(C) 標準の
(D) 標準的には

> **正解 D** 文頭から空所の前までの名詞句、Full-time staff at Dinh and Mann Associates が主語で、work が述語動詞だと考えられる。空所の語がなくても文が成立しているので、空所には動詞を修飾する副詞の (D) が適切。full-time「常勤の、フルタイムの」。
> (A) 名詞。
> (B) 名詞の複数形。
> (C) 形容詞。

2 Mr. Choi wants to know when the illustrations will be ready for ------- review.

(A) he
(B) his
(C) him
(D) himself

Choiさんは、いつ自分がイラストを検討できる状態になるのかを知りたがっています。

＊選択肢の訳は省略

> **正解 B** 選択肢は代名詞。空所の前に前置詞 for があるので、空所には続く ------- review が名詞句になるよう、所有格の (B) his を入れて名詞 review を限定する。be ready for 〜「〜の準備ができている」、review「検討、批評」。
> (A) (C) (D) いずれも空所の直後の review とつながらない。
> (A) 主格。
> (C) 目的格。
> (D) 再帰代名詞。

3 Dr. Lin, the keynote speaker at this year's Southeast Dentistry Convention, ------- several groundbreaking dental devices.

(A) invented
(B) exceeded
(C) supervised
(D) communicated

今年の南東部歯科協議会の基調演説者であるLin博士は、幾つかの革新的な歯科機器を発明しました。

(A) 〜を発明した
(B) 〜を超えた
(C) 〜を管理した
(D) 〜を伝えた

> 正解 **A** 選択肢は全て動詞の過去形。主語は Dr. Lin で、カンマで挟まれた挿入句 the keynote speaker at this year's Southeast Dentistry Convention は、Dr. Lin を説明している。
> 空所の後から文末までの名詞句 several groundbreaking dental devices は目的語だと考えられるので、述語動詞として文意に合うものを選ぶ。正解は (A) invented。keynote speaker「基調演説者」、dentistry「歯科学」、convention「協議会、代表者会議」、groundbreaking「革新的な」、dental「歯科の」、device「機器、装置」。
> (B) (C) (D) 主語と目的語の意味を考えると、いずれも文意に合わない。

Mini Test 1

4 The project meeting has been rescheduled ------- tomorrow because of the bad weather.

(A) in
(B) by
(C) out
(D) for

悪天候のため、企画会議は明日に変更されました。

(A) 〜の中で
(B) 〜までに
(C) 〜の外へ
(D) 〜に

> 正解 **D** 選択肢は全て前置詞。「企画会議は明日に変更された」という文意だと考えられるので、空所の後の tomorrow につながって文意に合う (D) for を選ぶ。reschedule 〜 for …「〜の予定を…に日時変更する」。
> (A) (C) 意味を成さない。
> (B) by tomorrow で「明日までに」という意味になり、文意に合わない。

5 Jane Tollen's original manuscript was published last year after Jansen Books obtained her family's -------.

(A) permission
(B) suggestion
(C) comparison
(D) registration

Jane Tollen の元原稿は、Jansen 出版が家族の許諾を取得した後で、昨年に出版されました。

(A) 許可
(B) 提案
(C) 比較
(D) 登録

> 正解 **A** 選択肢は全て名詞。after 節の空所を含む her family's ------- は、動詞 obtained の目的語に当たる。主節の「Jane Tollen の元原稿は、昨年に出版された」との意味のつながりを考えると、空所には (A) を入れて「Jansen 出版が家族の許諾を取得した後で」とするのが適切。manuscript「原稿」、obtain「〜を入手する、〜を得る」。
> (B) (C) (D) いずれも動詞 obtained の目的語としては適切でない。

6 Participants arriving late are asked to enter the training seminar -------.

(A) quiet
(B) quieting
(C) quieter
(D) quietly

遅れて来た参加者は、静かに研修セミナーにご参加いただくようお願い申し上げます。

(A) 静かな
(B) 静かになっている
(C) より静かな
(D) 静かに

正解 **D**　空所の語がなくても〈主語＋動詞〉の文が成立している。よって、空所には修飾語が入ると考えられる。空所には不定詞 to enter を修飾する副詞の (D) が適切。participant「参加者」、ask ～ to do「～に…するよう頼む」。
(A) 形容詞。
(B) 動詞 quiet「静かになる」の現在分詞または動名詞。
(C) 形容詞の比較級。

7 Volunteers will help conference participants ------- their way around the convention center.

(A) do
(B) find
(C) put
(D) ask

ボランティアが、会議の参加者に会議場周辺で道案内をします。

(A) ～をする
(B) ～を見つける
(C) ～を置く
(D) ～を尋ねる

正解 **B**　選択肢は全て動詞の原形。述語動詞 will help の後に名詞 conference participants があり、その後に空所が続いているので、help ～ do「～が…するのを助ける」の do に当たる動詞として、文意に合うものを選ぶ。空所の後の目的語 their way とのつながりを考えると、空所には (B) が適切。conference「会議、協議会」、participant「参加者」、find one's way「（地理に明るくて）自分で歩ける」、convention center「会議場、コンベンションセンター」。
(A) (C) (D) いずれも、their way を目的語に取っても意味が通らない。

8 All tickets will be refunded ------- the soccer game is canceled because of bad weather.

(A) or
(B) if
(C) nor
(D) but

悪天候でサッカーの試合が中止になった場合、チケットは全て払い戻しされます。

(A) あるいは
(B) もし～なら
(C) 〈neither ～ の後に続けて〉～も…もない
(D) しかし

正解 **B**　選択肢は全て接続詞。空所の前の「チケットは全て払い戻しされる予定だ」と、空所の後の「悪天候でサッカーの試合が中止になる」という2つの節の内容を適切につなぐ接続詞は (B) if。条件を表す if 節では、未来のことでも動詞は現在形で表す。refund「～を払い戻す」、cancel「～を中止する」。
(A) (C) (D) いずれも前後の内容がつながらない。

9 Given the recent boom in new construction, the price of lumber is ------- to climb.

    (A) covered
    (B) sought
    (C) limited
    (D) bound

最近の新築ブームを考えると、材木の価格はきっと上がるはずです。

    (A) 覆われて
    (B) 求められて
    (C) 限られて
    (D) 〈to do を続けて〉きっと〜するはずで

> **正解 D** 文の主語は the price of lumber である。文頭からカンマまでの副詞句「最近の新築ブームを考えると」という内容とのつながりから、空所に形容詞の (D) bound を入れて、is bound to climb「きっと上がるはずだ」という意味にすると文意が通る。given 〜「〜を考慮すると」、recent「最近の」、boom「ブーム、にわか景気」、construction「建築、建設」、lumber「材木」。
> (A) 動詞 cover「〜を覆う」の過去分詞。
> (B) 動詞 seek「〜を求める」の過去分詞。
> (C) 形容詞。

---

10 Our investment in solar energy was a key ------- in achieving energy independence.

    (A) factor
    (B) role
    (C) basis
    (D) agency

当社の太陽光エネルギーへの投資が、エネルギーの自立達成の重要な要因となりました。

    (A) 要因
    (B) 役割
    (C) 基礎
    (D) 仲介

> **正解 A** 選択肢は全て名詞。Our investment in solar energy が主語、was が述語動詞、空所が補語に当たると考えられる。後ろから修飾する語句 in achieving energy independence「エネルギーの自立達成の」との意味のつながりを考えると、空所には (A) が適切。investment「投資」、solar energy「太陽光エネルギー」、key「重要な」、achieve「〜を達成する」、independence「自立」。
> (B) (C) (D) いずれも、修飾語句の in achieving energy independence と意味がつながらない。

---

11 The Voz 900, ------- for consumers who want a large-screen television at a small-screen price, is now available in stores.

    (A) perfect
    (B) perfectly
    (C) perfects
    (D) perfecting

Voz 900 は、小型画面のテレビの価格で、大画面テレビが欲しい消費者の皆さまにぴったりで、ただ今店頭でお求めになれます。

    (A) 完璧な
    (B) 完璧に
    (C) 〜を完成する
    (D) 〜を完成している

> **正解 A** 選択肢には、形容詞 perfect「完璧な」の派生語が並ぶ。空所は、主語の The Voz 900 と述語動詞の is の間のカンマで挟まれた挿入句の一部で、主語の Voz 900 を補足説明していると考えられる。空所の後の「小型画面のテレビの価格で、大画面テレビが欲しい消費者に」という内容と自然につながるのは、形容詞の (A) perfect である。この文は分詞構文で、空所の前に現在分詞 being が省略されている。consumer「消費者」、available「入手できる」。
> (B) 副詞。
> (C) 動詞 perfect「〜を完成する」の三人称単数現在形。
> (D) 現在分詞または動名詞。

Questions 12-15 refer to the following advertisement.

New Course on Inventory Management

❶Inventory of all types flows through supply chains. -------, it is vital for all supply chain
　　　　　　　　　　　　　　　　　　　　　　　　　　　12.
professionals to understand the role, costs, and benefits of inventories. Too much inventory
can actually result in greater costs to ------- organization.
　　　　　　　　　　　　　　　　　　　13.

❷This five-week course will train students in the basics of inventory management and control.
------- . Key elements of this series include the importance and use of inventory, exposure to
14.
different types of inventory, and methods ------- effectively managing inventory levels.
　　　　　　　　　　　　　　　　　　　　15.

問題12-15は次の広告に関するものです。

在庫管理の新講座

あらゆる種類の在庫は、供給チェーンを通って流通します。従って、供給チェーンの職業従事者なら誰しも、棚卸表の役割、費用、利点を理解することは極めて重要です。過剰在庫は実際に、組織にとって経費増大につながる可能性があります。

この5週間の講座は、在庫管理・在庫調整の基礎分野で受講者を教育します。*修了時には、受講者は自身の仕事における在庫に関連する側面にもっと精通していることでしょう。このシリーズの主な学習項目には、在庫の重要性とその活用例、さまざまな種類の在庫との出合い、在庫水準を効果的に管理するための手法が含まれています。

*問題14の挿入文の訳

語 注

inventory　在庫　　management　管理
❶ flow through 〜　〜を通って流れる　　supply chain　供給チェーン、供給プロセス　　vital　極めて重要な
　professional　職業人、プロ　　role　役割　　benefit　利点　　inventories　棚卸表、在庫目録　★しばしば複数形になる
　result in 〜　〜という結果になる　　organization　組織
❷ train 〜 in …　…の分野で〜を教育する　　basics　〈複数形で〉基礎　　control　制御、管理　　key　主要な
　element　構成要素　　series　シリーズもの　　include　〜を含む　　importance　重要性
　exposure　さらされること　　method　方法　　effectively　有効に　　manage　〜を管理する　　level　水準

12
(A) Anyway
(B) Besides
(C) Moreover
(D) Therefore

(A) とにかく
(B) その上
(C) さらに
(D) 従って

正解 **D** 文意に合う副詞を選ぶ。❶の1行目の空所の前文に「あらゆる種類の在庫は、供給チェーンを通って流通する」という事実が述べられ、続けて空所を含む文で、「供給チェーンの職業従事者なら誰しも、棚卸表の役割、費用、利点を理解することは極めて重要だ」という主張が述べられている。前文はこの主張の根拠だと考えられるので、文意に合うのは (D) Therefore「従って」。
(A) (B) (C) いずれも前後の内容がつながらない。

13
(A) an
(B) almost
(C) once
(D) there

(A) 1つの
(B) ほとんど
(C) 1回
(D) そこで

正解 **A** ❶の3行目の空所を含む前置詞句 to ------- organization は「------- 組織にとって」という意味。文全体では、過剰在庫は組織にとって経費増大につながる可能性があるという一般論を述べており、この名詞 organization は任意の1つの組織を表す。単数の母音で始まる可算名詞には、冠詞の (A) an が必要。
(B) (C) (D) いずれも副詞で名詞 organization を修飾できない。

Mini Test 1

14
(A) Some industries do not place high importance on inventory management.
(B) Students who arrive late without a proper excuse will be dropped from the course.
(C) For additional information, contact your instructor.
(D) Upon completion, students will have greater mastery of the inventory-related aspects of their jobs.

(A) 在庫管理を重視しない業界もあります。
(B) 正当な理由なく遅刻する受講者は、講座から除籍されます。
(C) 追加の情報につきましては、担当の講師にご連絡ください。
(D) 修了時には、受講者は自身の仕事における在庫に関連する側面にもっと精通していることでしょう。

正解 **D** 空所の前後の文に注目する。❷1行目に、「講座は、在庫管理・在庫調整の基礎分野で受講者を教育する」とあり、2〜3行目では、講座の主な学習項目が詳しく紹介されていることから、空所は講座の概要を説明していると考えられる。(D) を入れると、受講者が在庫管理や在庫調整の基礎を学んで、どういう効果が得られるのかを説明する流れになり、適切である。completion「修了」、mastery「精通、熟練」、aspect「側面」。
(A) (B) (C) いずれも文脈に合わない。
(A) industry「業界」、place importance on 〜「〜を重視する」。
(B) proper「妥当な」、excuse「理由、言い訳」。

15
(A) at
(B) to
(C) for
(D) from

(A) 〜で
(B) 〜へ
(C) 〜のための
(D) 〜から

正解 **C** 文意に合う前置詞を選ぶ。空所を含む文の主語は Key elements of this series「このシリーズの主な学習項目」であり、述語動詞 include の後には講座で学ぶ内容が列挙されている。最後に挙げられているのが methods ------- effectively managing inventory levels で、空所以降は名詞 methods を後ろから修飾している。(C) for「〜のための」を入れると、「在庫水準を効果的に管理するための手法」となり、文意が通る。
(A) (B) (D) 文意に合わない。

Questions 16-17 refer to the following form.

WILPONT ASSOCIATES, INC.
Product Return Form

Dear Customer:

❶ Wilpont Associates, Inc., produces our games and puzzles with the utmost care. However, if a product is damaged, or you are not satisfied for any reason, please return the item with the receipt and this completed form. A replacement will be shipped to you from the factory free of charge, or your account will be credited.

❷ **Name:** _George P. Silva_

Address: _2038 Water Street, Lowry, MO 64763_

Problem description: _Parts of the item are missing._

Action requested: ☑ Replacement ☐ Credit account

問題16-17は次の用紙に関するものです。

WILPONT ASSOCIATES社
返品用紙

お客さま：

Wilpont Associates社は、細心の注意を払ってゲームやパズルを製造しております。しかしながら、商品が破損している場合や、何らかの理由でご満足いただけない場合は、領収書および記入済みの本紙とともに、商品をご返品ください。交換品を無料で工場から発送するかまたはお客さまの口座へご返金を致します。

氏名　：　George P. Silva

ご住所：　Water通り2038番地、Lowry、MO 64763

問題点の説明：　商品の部品が不足している。

ご希望の対応：　☑ 交換　　☐ 口座へ返金

16 What product did Mr. Silva most likely buy?

(A) An accounting book
(B) A piece of clothing
(C) A bicycle
(D) A game

Silvaさんはどんな商品を買ったと考えられますか。

(A) 会計帳簿
(B) 衣服
(C) 自転車
(D) ゲーム

 正解 D 見出しに「WILPONT ASSOCIATES 社　返品用紙」とあり、❷の「氏名」の欄に Silva さんの名前がある
ことから、Silva さんは WILPONT ASSOCIATES 社の商品を買い、返品用紙に記入した人物だと分かる。
また、❶の 1 行目に「Wilpont Associates 社は、細心の注意を払ってゲームやパズルを製造している」とあることから、
同社はゲーム類を作っている会社だと分かる。よって、Silva さんが買った商品は (D)「ゲーム」。
(A) accounting「会計」、book「帳簿」。
(B) clothing「衣類」。

---

17 What problem is Mr. Silva reporting?

(A) Some pieces were not included.
(B) Some instructions are incorrect.
(C) The wrong product was delivered.
(D) The product was damaged during
shipping.

Silvaさんはどんな問題を報告していますか。

(A) 幾つかの部品が入っていなかった。
(B) 説明書が間違っている。
(C) 間違った製品が届いた。
(D) 製品が配送の途中で破損した。

正解 A ❷の「問題点の説明」の欄で、「商品の部品が不足している」と Silva さんが返品の理由を書いている。「部品」
を意味する parts を pieces と言い換えている (A) が正解。piece「部品」、include「〜を同梱する」。
(B) instructions「〈複数形で〉説明書、説明」。
(C) wrong「間違った」、deliver「〜を届ける」。
(D) shipping「配送」。

語 注

product return form　返品用紙
❶ produce　〜を製造する　　utmost　最大限の　　care　注意　　damaged　破損した、傷んだ　　satisfied　満足した
for any reason　何らかの理由で　　return　〜を返す　　item　品物、品目　　receipt　領収書、レシート
completed　記入済みの　　replacement　交換品、交換　　ship　〜を発送する　　free of charge　無料で
account　（銀行の）預金口座　　credit　〜（口座など）にお金を振り込む
❷ description　説明　　part　部品、パーツ　　missing　不足している、欠けている　　action　行動、措置
request　〜を希望する、〜を依頼する

Questions 18-20 refer to the following press release.

FOR IMMEDIATE RELEASE
October 15
www.barnetinvestments.com

❶ CHARLOTTE, NC—Barnet Investments held a ceremony today to inaugurate its new office building at 186 South Chowan Street. The company began in Cork, Ireland, ten years ago. Since then, it has expanded to offices throughout Europe, and last year, it opened its African headquarters in Johannesburg. The new headquarters in Charlotte marks the first North American location for the company.

❷ Barnet Investments, a leading investment firm specializing in technology and electronics start-ups, includes Arno Technological Services and Karlon Electronics Superstores in its client list, along with other prominent businesses.

❸ The headquarters will serve all clients in both North and South America. More than 500 employees have been hired to staff the location. Barnet Investments vice president Liam O'Malley will lead the new office during its first year before returning to Cork.

❹ For further information, contact Maxine Wilton in Public Relations at 980-555-0184 or at mwilton@barnetinvestments.com.

問題18-20は次の報道発表に関するものです。

即日発表
10月15日
www.barnetinvestments.com

ノースカロライナ州シャーロット市——Barnet 投資会社は本日、南 Chowan 通り 186 番地で新オフィスビルの落成を祝う式典を開催しました。当社はアイルランドのコーク市で 10 年前に創業しました。それ以来、当社はヨーロッパの各所に事業所を展開し、昨年はヨハネスブルク市にアフリカ本部を開設しました。シャーロット市の新本部は、当社にとって北米初の拠点となります。

Barnet 投資会社は、テクノロジーおよびエレクトロニクス関連の新興企業を専門とする一流の投資会社であり、顧客リストには、Arno 技術サービス社や Karlon Electronics Superstores 社が、その他の有名企業とともに名を連ねています。

当本部は、北米・南米双方の全ての顧客に対応いたします。500 人を超える従業員が採用され、当地に配属されています。Barnet 投資会社の副社長 Liam O'Malley が、最初の 1 年間、コーク市へ戻るまでこの新事業所の指揮を執ります。

さらなる情報は、広報部の Maxine Wilton 宛てに、980-555-0184 または mwilton@barnetinvestments.com までご連絡ください。

語 注

for immediate release　即日発表
❶ NC　〈North Carolina の略で〉ノースカロライナ州　　investment　投資　　hold　〜を開催する
　　inaugurate　〜の落成を祝う、〜の落成式を行う　　expand　拡大する　　throughout 〜　〜の各所に、〜の至る所に
　　headquarters　〈複数形で〉本部、本社　　mark　〜に印を付ける、〜に商標を示す
❷ leading　一流の、トップの　　firm　会社　　specialize in 〜　〜を専門とする　　start-up　新興企業　　client　顧客
　　along with 〜　〜に加えて　　prominent　有名な、卓越した　　business　企業
❸ serve　〜に対応する　　hire　〜を雇う　　staff　〜に職員を配置する　　vice president　副社長　　lead　〜の指揮を執る
❹ further　それ以上の　　contact　〜と連絡を取る　　Public Relations　広報部

18 What event took place at 186 South Chowan Street?

- (A) A financial seminar
- (B) An electronics show
- (C) An opening celebration
- (D) A hiring fair

南Chowan通り186番地でどんなイベントが行われましたか。

- (A) 金融セミナー
- (B) エレクトロニクス展
- (C) 開所祝賀会
- (D) 採用説明会

 C 報道発表の❶1～2行目で、「Barnet投資会社は本日、南Chowan通り186番地で新オフィスビルの落成を祝う式典を開催した」と述べられている。「落成を祝う式典」をAn opening celebration「開所祝賀会」と言い換えた(C)が正解。celebration「祝賀会」。
(A) financial「金融の」。
(B) show「展示会」。
(D) fair「説明会、フェア」。

---

19 What is mentioned about Barnet Investments?

- (A) It serves clients on more than one continent.
- (B) It is considered a leader in personal banking.
- (C) Its Charlotte office was designed by a leading architectural firm.
- (D) Its Charlotte office building is ten years old.

Barnet投資会社について何が述べられていますか。

- (A) 2つ以上の大陸で顧客に対応する。
- (B) 個人向け銀行業務において主導者と見なされている。
- (C) シャーロット市の事業所は一流の建築事務所によって設計された。
- (D) シャーロット市のオフィスビルは築10年である。

 A ❶の3～4行目より、Barnet投資会社はヨーロッパとアフリカで事業所を展開していると分かる。また、❸の1行目に、「当本部は、北米・南米双方の全ての顧客に対応する」とある。これらのことから、Barnet投資会社は2つ以上の大陸の顧客に対応すると分かる。(A)が正解。more than one「1つより多くの、2つ以上の」。
(B) 個人向けの銀行業務についての言及はない。consider「～を…と見なす」。
(C) シャーロット市の事業所を設計した事務所についての言及はない。architectural「建築の」。
(D) ❶1～2行目より、落成を祝う式典をしたばかりである。

---

20 What is indicated about Mr. O'Malley?

- (A) He was formerly the president of Arno Technological Services.
- (B) He is working in Charlotte temporarily.
- (C) He is one of 500 newly hired workers.
- (D) He began his career at a retail store.

O'Malleyさんについて何が示されていますか。

- (A) 以前はArno技術サービス社の社長だった。
- (B) 一時的にシャーロット市で働いている。
- (C) 新規採用された500人の従業員の1人である。
- (D) 小売店で自身のキャリアをスタートした。

 B ❸の2～3行目に、「Barnet投資会社の副社長Liam O'Malleyが、最初の1年間、コーク市へ戻るまでこの新事業所の指揮を執る」とあるので、O'Malleyさんは1年間シャーロット市の事業所のトップを務めた後、アイルランドのコーク市へ帰国する予定だと考えられる。よって、(B)が正解。temporarily「一時的に」。
(A) O'Malleyさんの経歴についての言及はない。formerly「以前は」。
(C) ❸2～3行目より、O'MalleyさんはBarnet投資会社の副社長である。
(D) retail store「小売店」。

Questions 21-24 refer to the following online chat discussion.

👥 Kathleen Vern　　　　　　　　　　　　　　□ ⊠

❶ **Kathleen Vern (10:12 A.M.)**
Our Australian partners have requested a video call to review the tile designs.

❷ **Mateus Ribero (10:14 A.M.)**
OK. Do we have a plan yet?

❸ **Kathleen Vern (10:16 A.M.)**
I'm setting it up for 7 P.M. tomorrow, our time, in room 2C. The late start is because of the time difference between Perth and Winnipeg.

❹ **Natalia Kovac (10:17 A.M.)**
Could we call in to the meeting from home?

❺ **Kathleen Vern (10:19 A.M.)**
I'm afraid not. The security policy states that we can't take anything out of the building, and our partners are counting on seeing the tile designs.

❻ **Natalia Kovac (10:20 A.M.)**
OK. That makes sense. Now we just need approval from Ms. Feld to be here after hours.

❼ **Mateus Ribero (10:22 A.M.)**
Let's check with her now. Ms. Feld, we would like to have a conference call with our partners in Perth tomorrow. Is it all right if we stay late to show them the new designs? We will be using room 2C since it has the audiovisual equipment.

❽ **Janice Feld (10:24 A.M.)**
Yes, that's fine. I'll tell security so they won't lock the building until you've finished.

❾ **Kathleen Vern (10:25 A.M.)**
Thanks, Mr. Ribero, for reaching out to Ms. Feld.

問題21-24は次のオンラインチャットの話し合いに関するものです。

Kathleen Vern

Kathleen Vern（午前10時12分）
オーストラリアの共同事業者が、タイルのデザインを再検討するために、テレビ会議を依頼してきました。

Mateus Ribero（午前10時14分）
分かりました。もう予定は立っていますか。

Kathleen Vern（午前10時16分）
こちらの時間で明日の午後7時に、2Cの部屋で行う計画です。遅い時間の開始は、パースとウィニペグの時差のせいです。

Natalia Kovac（午前10時17分）
私たちは自宅から会議に参加できますか。

Kathleen Vern（午前10時19分）
残念ながら無理です。セキュリティーの方針では、社外へは何も持ち出せないと定められていますし、共同事業者はタイルのデザインを見るつもりでいますから。

Natalia Kovac（午前10時20分）
分かりました。それはもっともですね。では、Feldさんからの、就業時間後にここに残る許可が必要ですね。

Mateus Ribero（午前10時22分）
今すぐ彼女に確認しましょう。Feldさん、明日、パースの共同事業者とテレビ会議を行いたいのです。彼らに新しいデザインを見せるために、遅くまで残ってもいいでしょうか。AV機器があるので、2Cの部屋を使用する予定です。

Janice Feld（午前10時24分）
ええ、いいですよ。あなた方が終了するまで建物を施錠しないように、警備に伝えておきます。

Kathleen Vern（午前10時25分）
Riberoさん、Feldさんに連絡を取ってくれてありがとうございます。

語 注

❶ partner　共同事業者　　request　～を依頼する　　video call　テレビ会議、ビデオ通話　　review　～を再検討する
❸ set up ～　～を計画する　　time difference　時差　　Perth　パース　★オーストラリアの都市
　　Winnipeg　ウィニペグ　★カナダの都市
❹ call in to ～　～に参加する
❺ security policy　セキュリティーの方針　　state　～を述べる、～を明記する　　count on *doing*　～することを期待する
❻ make sense　（説明などが）理にかなっている　　approval　許可　　after hours　就業時間後に
❼ check with ～　～に確認する　　conference　会議　　audiovisual　視聴覚の、AV の　　equipment　機器
❾ reach out to ～　～に連絡を取る

21 What is the online chat discussion about?

(A) Making a tile purchase
(B) Planning a business trip
(C) Arranging a meeting
(D) Extending a deadline

オンラインチャットの話し合いは何に関するものですか。

(A) タイルを購入すること。
(B) 出張の計画をすること。
(C) 会議の手はずを整えること。
(D) 締め切りを延ばすこと。

> 正解 **C**　❶で、オーストラリアの共同事業者がテレビ会議を依頼してきたことを告げる Vern さんに対し、Ribero さんは❷で「もう予定は立っているか」と尋ねている。その後も、会議の日時や場所に関するやりとりが続いているので、(C) が正解。arrange「〜の手はずを整える、〜の準備をする」。

22 At 10:20 A.M., what does Ms. Kovac most likely mean when she writes, "That makes sense"?

(A) She knows about the time difference.
(B) She agrees that building security has improved.
(C) She realizes that she will be working late.
(D) She understands why they must work at the office.

午前 10 時 20 分に "That makes sense" と書くことで、Kovac さんは何を意図していると考えられますか。

(A) 時差について了解している。
(B) 建物のセキュリティーが改善されていることに同意している。
(C) 自分が残業することになると気付いている。
(D) 職場で働かなければいけない理由を理解している。

> 正解 **D**　下線部は、❹で「私たちは自宅から会議に参加できるか」と尋ねた Kovac さんに対し、❺で Vern さんが「残念ながら無理だ。セキュリティーの方針では、社外へは何も持ち出せないと定められているし、共同事業者はタイルのデザインを見るつもりでいる」と答えた後の応答である。Kovac さんは Vern さんの説明によって、自宅ではなく会社で会議に参加しなければならない理由を理解したと考えられるので、(D) が正解。

23 What does Ms. Feld offer to do?

(A) Create a video of the tile designs
(B) Contact some colleagues in Perth
(C) Make sure that the office remains open
(D) Leave an extra set of keys in the office

Feld さんは何をすると申し出ていますか。

(A) タイルのデザインの動画を制作する。
(B) パースにいる同僚と連絡を取る。
(C) 確実に事務所を開けたままにしておく。
(D) 事務所に予備の鍵を 1 組残しておく。

> 正解 **C**　❽で Feld さんは、「あなた方が終了するまで建物を施錠しないように、警備に伝えておく」と述べているので、(C) が正解。offer to do「〜すると申し出る」。make sure (that) 〜「確実に〜であるようにする」。
> (B) colleague「同僚」。
> (D) extra「予備の、余分の」。

24 Why does Ms. Vern thank Mr. Ribero?

(A) For obtaining approval
(B) For attending a conference
(C) For setting up some equipment
(D) For agreeing to lock the building

Vern さんはなぜ Ribero さんに感謝しているのですか。

(A) 許可を取ってくれたため。
(B) 会議に出席したため。
(C) 機器を設置したため。
(D) 建物の施錠に同意したため。

> 正解 **A**　Kovac さんの❻「Feld さんからの、就業時間後にここに残る許可が必要だ」という発言を聞いた Ribero さんは、すぐに❼で Feld さんに連絡を取って、テレビ会議のために遅くまで職場に残ってもいいかと尋ねて、❽で Feld さんから時間外に建物内に残る許可を得ている。Vern さんは、この Ribero さんの行動に感謝して❾で「ありがとう」とお礼を述べている。(A) が正解。obtain「〜を得る」。
> (C) set up「〜を設置する」。

Questions 25-29 refer to the following schedule and e-mail.

VILLAGE BISTRO WEEKLY SCHEDULE
June 3–9

スケジュール表

	Head Chef	Assistant Chef	Host	Servers
Monday	Restaurant Closed			
Tuesday	Melanie	Yukiko	Luis	Enzo John
Wednesday	William	Ravi	Luis	Enzo Adam
Thursday	Melanie	Yukiko	Luis	Tania Adam
Friday	Ricardo	Ravi	Aisha	Tania Adam
Saturday	Ricardo	Yukiko	Aisha	John Meiying
Sunday	Melanie	Ravi	Aisha	Tania Meiying

Eメール

From:	Melanie <melanie.villagebistro@swiftymail.com>
To:	All Staff <staff.villagebistro@swiftymail.com>
Subject:	Centerville Food Festival
Date:	May 30

Hello everyone,

The Centerville Food Festival will be held next week from June 4–9. Chef Julian Heeley from Forest Inn Restaurant is no longer able to attend and provide cooking demonstrations at the event. I have been asked to take his place. Yukiko and Adam will come along as my assistants. Ricardo has graciously volunteered to cover my shifts here at the restaurant next week, and Ravi will be filling in for Yukiko. Meiying has volunteered to work in place of Adam on Wednesday, June 5. However, Adam's shifts on Thursday and Friday are still not covered. Would someone be able to help out with this? Please let me know as soon as possible.

We are excited about participating in the festival this year. It will give us a chance to show the expected thousands of attendees what Village Bistro has to offer. It will be a busy week for all of us, but it will be well worth the effort.

Many thanks!

Melanie

問題25-29は次のスケジュール表とEメールに関するものです。

VILLAGEビストロ 週間スケジュール
6月3日〜9日

	料理長	料理人	給仕長	給仕係
月曜日	レストラン休業日			
火曜日	Melanie	Yukiko	Luis	Enzo John
水曜日	William	Ravi	Luis	Enzo Adam
木曜日	Melanie	Yukiko	Luis	Tania Adam
金曜日	Ricardo	Ravi	Aisha	Tania Adam
土曜日	Ricardo	Yukiko	Aisha	John Meiying
日曜日	Melanie	Ravi	Aisha	Tania Meiying

送信者：Melanie <melanie.villagebistro@swiftymail.com>
受信者：スタッフ各位 <staff.villagebistro@swiftymail.com>
件名：　Centervilleフードフェスティバル
日付：　5月30日

こんにちは、皆さん

Centerville フードフェスティバルが来週6月4日〜9日に開催されます。Forest Inn レストランの Julian Heeley シェフがイベントの参加と料理の実演をすることができなくなりました。私が彼の代役を務めるように依頼されています。Yukiko と Adam が私の補佐として同行します。Ricardo は親切にも、来週のここのレストランでの私のシフトを引き受けると申し出てくれました。そして、Ravi が Yukiko の代わりを務めます。Meiying は、6月5日の水曜日に Adam の代わりに働くと申し出てくれました。しかし、木曜日と金曜日の Adam のシフトはまだ代わりがいません。これについて誰か助けてくれる方はいませんか。できるだけ早くご連絡ください。

私たちは、今年のフェスティバルへの参加を非常に楽しみにしています。それは、何千人とも見込まれる参加者たちに対して、Village ビストロが提供できるサービスを披露する機会を与えてくれるからです。私たち全員にとって忙しい1週間になるでしょうが、頑張る価値は十分にあります。

よろしくお願いします！

Melanie

25 Why was the e-mail sent?

- (A) To encourage attendance at an event
- (B) To report a change to a restaurant's business hours
- (C) To announce the retirement of a head chef
- (D) To ask employees to work extra hours

Eメールはなぜ送られましたか。

- (A) イベントへの参加を促すため。
- (B) レストランの営業時間の変更を伝えるため。
- (C) 料理長の退職を知らせるため。
- (D) 従業員へ時間外勤務をお願いするため。

正解 D　❷のEメールの送信者である料理長のMelanieは従業員へ、❶3～6行目で、フードフェスティバルに参加することになった自分と他2名のスタッフの来週のシフト変更を伝えて、続けて同6～8行目で「しかし、木曜日と金曜日のAdamのシフトはまだ代わりがいない。これについて誰か助けてくれる人はいないか。できるだけ早く連絡してほしい」と頼んでいる。つまり、シフト外の曜日に勤務するようお願いしているので、(D)が正解。extra「余分の、追加の」。
(A) encourage「～を促す」。
(B) report「～を伝える、～を報告する」、business hours「〈複数形で〉営業時間」。
(C) announce「～を知らせる、～を発表する」、retirement「引退」。

26 What is indicated about the Centerville Food Festival?

- (A) It takes place for the first time in June.
- (B) It will likely be well attended.
- (C) It takes place over two days.
- (D) It is held at Forest Inn Restaurant.

Centervilleフードフェスティバルについて何が示されていますか。

- (A) 6月に初めて開催される。
- (B) 大勢の人が参加するだろう。
- (C) 2日間にわたって行われる。
- (D) Forest Innレストランで開催される。

正解 B　Melanieは❷の❷1～2行目でフェスティバルについて、「それは、何千人とも見込まれる参加者たちに対して、Villageビストロが提供できるサービスを披露する機会を与えてくれるからだ」と書いている。このことから、フェスティバルは多くの来場者が見込まれていると考えられる。よって、(B)が正解。be well attended「参加者が多い、出席者が多い」。
(A) フェスティバルの開催が初めてだという言及はない。take place「行われる」。
(C) ❷の❶1行目より、6月4日から9日まで6日間行われる。over「～にわたって」。
(D) Forest Innレストランは、イベントに参加できなくなったシェフの店。

27 According to the e-mail, what benefit does participating in the festival bring to Village Bistro staff members?

- (A) They can get new menu ideas.
- (B) They will be able to promote the restaurant.
- (C) They can get a discount on restaurant supplies.
- (D) They can learn new cooking techniques.

Eメールによると、フェスティバルに参加することはVillageビストロのスタッフにどんな恩恵をもたらしますか。

- (A) 新メニューのアイデアを得られる。
- (B) レストランを宣伝することができる。
- (C) レストランの備品の割引を受けられる。
- (D) 新しい調理技術を学ぶことができる。

正解 B　❷のEメールには、❷1～2行目「それは、何千人とも見込まれる参加者たちに対して、Villageビストロが提供できるサービスを披露する機会を与えてくれるからだ」と書かれており、Melanieはフェスティバルへの参加がVillageビストロの宣伝になると考えていることが分かる。よって、(B)が正解。promote「～を宣伝する」。
(C) supplies「〈複数形で〉備品、補充品」。
(D) technique「技術」。

28 Which group will NOT be affected by a change in working hours?

(A) Head chefs
(B) Assistant chefs
(C) Hosts
(D) Servers

勤務時間の変更による影響を受けないのはどのグループですか。

(A) 料理長
(B) 料理人
(C) 給仕長
(D) 給仕係

> 正解 **C** ②の❶ 3～6行目より、フェスティバルに参加するためにレストランのシフトを抜けるのは、Eメールを書いた Melanie と Yukiko、Adam の合計 3 人である。①の週間スケジュールから、3 人はそれぞれ、料理長 (Melanie)、料理人 (Yukiko)、給仕係 (Adam) だと分かるので、シフト変更の影響を受けないのはそのいずれにも該当しない職種の給仕長だと考えられる。よって、(C) が正解。affect「～に影響する」。

Mini
Test
1

29 Which day will Ricardo have off during the week of June 3–9?

(A) Tuesday
(B) Wednesday
(C) Thursday
(D) Friday

Ricardoさんは6月3日～9日の週のうち、何曜日に休みを取りますか。

(A) 火曜日
(B) 水曜日
(C) 木曜日
(D) 金曜日

> 正解 **B** ①の週間スケジュールより、Ricardo さんはもともと、金曜日と土曜日に勤務することになっている。さらに、②の❶ 4～5行目で Melanie さんが「Ricardo は親切にも、来週のここのレストランでの私のシフトを引き受けると申し出てくれた」と述べており、Ricardo さんはこの週、Melanie さんのシフトにも入ることが分かる。①の週間スケジュールから、Melanie さんのシフトは火曜日、木曜日、日曜日なので、Ricardo さんの休みは月曜日 (レストラン休業日) と水曜日ということになる。(B) の水曜日が正解。off「休み、休暇」。

語 注

① スケジュール表 head chef 料理長　assistant chef （料理長の下で働く）料理人　host 給仕長　server 給仕係
② Eメール　❶ hold ～を開催する　no longer もはや～ない　attend ～に出席する　provide ～を提供する
　　demonstration 実演　take *one's* place ～の代わりを務める　come along 一緒に来る、同行する
　　assistant 補佐、助手　graciously 親切にも　volunteer to *do* ～すると申し出る
　　cover （代理で）～を引き受ける　shift （勤務の）シフト　fill in for ～ ～の代理をする
　　in place of ～ ～の代わりに　help out with ～ ～の手助けをする
　❷ participate in ～ ～に参加する　give ～ a chance to *do* ～に…する機会を与える
　　attendee 参加者、出席者　well かなり、十分に　worth ～ ～の価値がある　effort 頑張り、努力

右上の目安の解答時間を目標に、自分で時間を計りながら全ての問題を解いてみましょう。**p.308** の「結果記入シート」の説明も読んでから取り組んでください。

→解答・解説は p.244

PART 5

Directions: A word or phrase is missing in each of the sentences below. Four answer choices are given below each sentence. Select the best answer to complete the sentence. Then mark the letter (A), (B), (C), or (D) on your answer sheet.

---

1. Randall Lee is a demanding critic, but even ------- is impressed with Schiff's Artisan Vanilla ice cream.

   (A) he
   (B) him
   (C) himself
   (D) his

2. While all her drawings are based on historical photographs, Janis Tierney relies on her ------- to fill in the details.

   (A) imagine
   (B) imaginative
   (C) imagination
   (D) imaginary

3. We would be ------- to discuss your landscaping needs in detail via e-mail or telephone.

   (A) delighting
   (B) delighted
   (C) delights
   (D) delight

4. Performing the steps in the proper sequence is ------- if the project is to succeed.

   (A) chronological
   (B) imperative
   (C) singular
   (D) orderly

5. Product ------- on the purchase order should contain the dimensions of the new office furniture.

   (A) specify
   (B) specifications
   (C) specifically
   (D) specific

6. Please ------- the enclosed instructions before attempting to install your new dishwasher.

   (A) direct
   (B) review
   (C) gather
   (D) program

7. ------- all the preliminary interviews have been completed, the top three applicants for the marketing director position will be contacted.

   (A) Compared to
   (B) As soon as
   (C) So that
   (D) Not only

8. Payments made to your account after the invoice was generated are not ------- in the balance shown.

   (A) reflected
   (B) reflects
   (C) reflecting
   (D) reflect

9. Consumers can ------- enroll online for Wozetco's current marketing study.

(A) very
(B) least
(C) easily
(D) more

10. Real estate agents claim that ------- to the landscape in the Presmont area will encourage buyers to consider homes there.

(A) continuations
(B) increments
(C) deviations
(D) enhancements

11. If the printer had been damaged during shipment, the company ------- to send Mr. Kichida a replacement.

(A) would have offered
(B) has offered
(C) is being offered
(D) would have been offered

Directions: Read the texts that follow. A word, phrase, or sentence is missing in parts of each text. Four answer choices for each question are given below the text. Select the best answer to complete the text. Then mark the letter (A), (B), (C), or (D) on your answer sheet.

Questions 12-15 refer to the following e-mail.

From: Customer Service
To: Alfred Janssen
Subject: Ridgedale Supply account
Date: 4 February

Dear Mr. Janssen,

Thank you for creating an account with Ridgedale Supply. You probably know ------- **12.** Ridgedale offers the widest selection of office supplies in the area. Your account gives you a number of extra benefits, including faster checkout, instant access to your order history, and ------- more. **13.**

Place your first order today! As an account holder, you ------- 20% off your first purchase **14.** from our Web site. -------. Our weekly e-mail newsletter will keep you informed of additional **15.** promotions like this one.

We look forward to serving all of your office supply needs.

Sincerely,

Ridgedale Supply Customer Service

12. (A) because
    (B) even
    (C) when
    (D) that

13. (A) much
    (B) any
    (C) very
    (D) all

14. (A) received
    (B) will receive
    (C) had received
    (D) to receive

15. (A) Please find your receipt for this order attached.
    (B) We no longer carry this brand.
    (C) The discount is automatically applied at checkout.
    (D) A complete list is currently available online.

Directions: In this part you will read a selection of texts, such as magazine and newspaper articles, e-mails, and instant messages. Each text or set of texts is followed by several questions. Select the best answer for each question and mark the letter (A), (B), (C), or (D) on your answer sheet.

Questions 16-17 refer to the following text message.

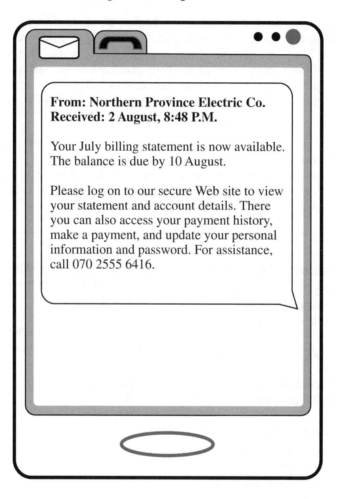

From: Northern Province Electric Co.
Received: 2 August, 8:48 P.M.

Your July billing statement is now available. The balance is due by 10 August.

Please log on to our secure Web site to view your statement and account details. There you can also access your payment history, make a payment, and update your personal information and password. For assistance, call 070 2555 6416.

Mini
Test
2

16. What is the purpose of the text message?

(A) To provide notification about a bill
(B) To give password information
(C) To correct a billing error
(D) To announce a change in the electric rate

17. What is the recipient of the text message asked to do?

(A) Place an order
(B) Access an online account
(C) Create a username
(D) Update a credit card number

Questions 18-20 refer to the following memo.

To: All Office Employees
From: Paul Sundquist
Re: Document printing
Date: Thursday, April 5

Based on the expense report from last quarter, it is clear that we must reduce our costs for office supplies. One area where we can realize savings is in printing and copying documents.

Many of us have been making color copies of basic documents, such as meeting minutes, product documentation drafts, and budget sheets. — [1] —. While multicolor documents are more attractive and attention-grabbing than black-and-white ones, color ink cartridges are very expensive. Purchasing frequent replacements ultimately leaves us with less money to spend on things like business travel and social events. — [2] —.

Rather than instituting a system wherein all jobs must first be approved by the department supervisors, I would prefer that employees make their own decisions about printing and copying. — [3] —. Please reserve the use of color for only those cases where visual appeal is a relevant factor. — [4] —. Thank you for your attention to this matter.

18. What is one purpose of the memo?

(A) To announce the release of a quarterly expense report
(B) To alert employees to a budget concern
(C) To inform staff of an error in a document
(D) To request feedback on a departmental procedure

19. What are employees advised to do?

(A) Make black-and-white copies of basic documents
(B) Tell coworkers about upcoming social events
(C) Distribute meeting notes by e-mail
(D) Report broken copy machines to their supervisors

20. In which of the positions marked [1], [2], [3], and [4] does the following sentence best belong?

"Publicity flyers intended for clients are one obvious example."

(A) [1]
(B) [2]
(C) [3]
(D) [4]

Questions 21-24 refer to the following e-mail.

To:	All staff
From:	Edna Fuentes
Date:	March 12
Subject:	Zenva Technologies

Fellow employees:

In an effort to reduce the amount of energy consumed by the company, the Environmental Steering Committee has decided to purchase for our offices a new automation system from Zenva Technologies. The system will automatically regulate thermostats and overhead lights to accommodate our usual work schedules. For example, at 7:00 P.M. each weekday, all office lights will automatically be turned off or dimmed (except for hallway and stairwell lights). Likewise, on Saturdays and Sundays, the temperature will be maintained at a steady 17° C instead of the usual 21° C during the week. This new system should help reduce our monthly utility bills by at least 15% and help us meet our environmental goal of conserving electricity.

We acknowledge that some of you will be affected by these changes more than others, particularly those whose schedules do not conform to regular working hours. If this situation applies to you, feel free to contact the personnel department to request an office change, as some sections of the building will be set to a later schedule. Bring any other concerns to your supervisor.

Sincerely,

Edna Fuentes, Vice President of Operations

Mini Test 2

21. What is the purpose of the e-mail?

 (A) To clarify the requirements of a new environmental law
 (B) To explain an upcoming change in workplace conditions
 (C) To encourage employees to develop more efficient work habits
 (D) To offer employees the opportunity to work from home

22. The word "maintained" in paragraph 1, line 6, is closest in meaning to

 (A) confirmed
 (B) repaired
 (C) taken
 (D) kept

23. What is mentioned as a benefit of the Zenva product?

 (A) It will save the company money.
 (B) It will reduce employee workloads.
 (C) It can be serviced from outside the office.
 (D) It can be used in any work environment.

24. What are employees who typically work late advised to do?

 (A) Talk to Ms. Fuentes
 (B) Consider switching offices
 (C) Change their work schedules
 (D) Take work home over the weekend

---

http://www.saltoalliance.com/membership   ▼

Current Promotions for Salto Alliance Members

From 1 July to 31 December, earn points when staying at any of the following Salto Alliance hotels.

Egidio Hotel, Florence, Italy— Earn 40 points when you reserve a single room.	**Halinski Hotel, London, England—** Earn 60 points when you reserve a double room.
Celova Inn, Siena, Italy— Opens 3 March! Earn 70 points when you reserve a single room.	**Neves Pousada, Lisbon, Portugal—** Earn 60 points when you reserve a double room.

Plus:
- Members receive free shuttle service to select local attractions and the main airport. Check with the front desk for scheduling.
- Members who rent a car from Avini Rentals receive a 10 percent discount on car rentals.

Ready to use your points?
- 500 points: Get 50 percent off a meal of up to €100 at any Salto Alliance hotel restaurant.
- 600 points: Receive a room upgrade.
- 1,000 points: Enjoy a free overnight stay at any participating Salto Alliance hotel.

For details on promotions and points, go to www.saltoalliance.com/member_rewards.

Salto Alliance

3 August

Elsa Dolanski
238 Rose Hill
BECKLEY OX3 25E
England

Dear Ms. Dolanski,

Thank you for staying at a Salto Alliance hotel. Enclosed you will find the Salto Alliance membership card that you requested during your recent stay in Florence. We have already applied the 40 points that you earned during your one-night visit, but you will need to activate your card to keep accruing points. To do so, go to our Web site at www.saltoalliance.com, click "My Account," and follow the instructions provided.

We look forward to hosting you again in the near future.

Regards,
The Guest Relations Team
Salto Alliance

http://www.saltoalliance.com/member_2378273 ▼

Ms. Dolanski, thank you for completing the survey regarding your stay at Celova Inn, 4–5 October. To show our appreciation, we have added 20 bonus points to your account!

Salto Alliance Membership Card: 2378273
Total Accrued Points: 510

To redeem your points, visit www.saltoalliance.com/member_rewards.

---

25. What is mentioned about Salto Alliance hotels?

(A) They have three room sizes to choose from.
(B) They prepare free breakfasts for guests.
(C) They provide coupons for nearby attractions.
(D) They offer members free transportation to local sites.

26. At what hotel did Ms. Dolanski request a membership card?

(A) Egidio Hotel
(B) Halinski Hotel
(C) Celova Inn
(D) Neves Pousada

27. In the letter, the word "keep" in paragraph 1, line 4, is closest in meaning to

(A) place
(B) continue
(C) delay
(D) hold

28. What is probably true about Ms. Dolanski?

(A) She stayed at a new hotel.
(B) She rented a car from Avini Rentals.
(C) She was unable to activate her card.
(D) She lost her membership card.

29. Why did Ms. Dolanski receive bonus points?

(A) For recommending a shuttle service
(B) For filling out a survey
(C) For extending her hotel stay
(D) For checking out early

Mini
Test
2

Stop! This is the end of the test.

正解一覧

PART 5	1 A	2 C	3 B	4 B	5 B	6 B	7 B	8 A	9 C	10 D	11 A
PART 6	12 D	13 A	14 B	15 C							
PART 7	16 A	17 B	18 B	19 A	20 D	21 B	22 D	23 A	24 B	25 D	26 A
	27 B	28 A	29 B								

1 Randall Lee is a demanding critic, but even ------- is impressed with Schiff's Artisan Vanilla ice cream.

(A) he
(B) him
(C) himself
(D) his

Randall Leeは要求の厳しい評論家ですが、彼でさえSchiff社の手作りバニラアイスクリームには感心しています。

＊選択肢の訳は省略

正解 A 選択肢は全て代名詞。空所の直後に述語動詞 is impressed があるので、空所に入る語は but 節内の主語だと判断できる。主格の (A) が正解。demanding「要求の厳しい」、critic「評論家、批評家」、be impressed with ～「～に感心する」。
(B) 目的格。
(C) 再帰代名詞。
(D) 所有格。

2 While all her drawings are based on historical photographs, Janis Tierney relies on her ------- to fill in the details.

(A) imagine
(B) imaginative
(C) imagination
(D) imaginary

その絵画全てが歴史上の写真を基にしているものの、Janis Tierneyは自身の想像力を頼みとして、細部を描き加え、完成させています。

(A) ～を想像する
(B) 想像力に富む
(C) 想像力
(D) 想像上の

正解 C 選択肢は全て動詞 imagine「～を想像する」の派生語。主節の主語は Janis Tierney で、述語動詞は relies on である。前置詞 on の後の her ------- は rely on「～に頼る」の目的語だと考えられるので、空所には名詞の (C) が入るのが適切。drawing「(鉛筆・ペンなどで描いた) 絵」、be based on ～「～に基づいている」、fill in ～「～を描き加えて完成する、～を埋める」、detail「細部」。
(A) 動詞の原形。
(B) (D) 形容詞。

3 We would be ------- to discuss your landscaping needs in detail via e-mail or telephone.

(A) delighting
(B) delighted
(C) delights
(D) delight

私どもは喜んで、お客さまの庭作りのご要望についてEメールまたはお電話で詳しくご相談を承ります。

(A) 〜を大いに喜ばせている
(B) 大いに喜んで
(C) 〜を大いに喜ばせる
(D) 〜を大いに喜ばせる

> **正解 B** 選択肢には動詞 delight「〜を大いに喜ばせる」の変化した形や派生語が並ぶ。We が主語で、空所の前に be 動詞があり、後には不定詞の形が続いているので、空所には過去分詞が形容詞化した (B) delighted が入るのが適切。be delighted to *do* で「大いに喜んで〜する」という意味。landscaping「庭作り」、needs「〈複数形で〉要望されるもの、必要なもの」、via「〜によって」。
> (A) 現在分詞。
> (C) 三人称単数現在形。
> (D) 動詞の原形。

---

4 Performing the steps in the proper sequence is ------- if the project is to succeed.

(A) chronological
(B) imperative
(C) singular
(D) orderly

もしプロジェクトは成功するべきだというのなら、各段階を正しい順序で遂行することが必須です。

(A) 年代順の
(B) 必須の
(C) 特異な
(D) 整然とした

> **正解 B** 選択肢は全て形容詞。Performing the steps in the proper sequence が主語で、is が述語動詞なので、空所には主語を説明する補語に適切なものを考える。if 節の「もしプロジェクトは成功するべきだというのなら」という文意を考えると、空所には (B) が適切。perform「〜を行う」、step「段階」、proper「正しい、適切な」、sequence「順序」、be to *do*「〜する必要がある」。
> (A) (C) (D) いずれも文意に合わない。

---

5 Product ------- on the purchase order should contain the dimensions of the new office furniture.

(A) specify
(B) specifications
(C) specifically
(D) specific

注文書にある製品仕様欄に、新しいオフィス家具の寸法が載っているはずです。

(A) 〜を詳述する
(B) 仕様
(C) 特に
(D) 特定の

> **正解 B** Product ------- on the purchase order が文の主語で、should contain が述語動詞だと考えられる。空所に名詞の (B) を入れると、product specifications「製品仕様」という複合名詞となり、主語の名詞として文意に合う。on the purchase order はその名詞を後ろから修飾している。purchase order「注文書」、contain「〜を含む」、dimensions「〈複数形で〉寸法」、furniture「家具」。
> (A) 動詞の原形。
> (C) 副詞。
> (D) 形容詞。Product を後ろから修飾していると考えても、後の修飾語句と意味がつながらない。

6 Please ------- the enclosed instructions before attempting to install your new dishwasher.

(A) direct
(B) review
(C) gather
(D) program

新しい食器洗い機の設置を試みる前に、同封の取扱説明書をよく読んでください。

(A) 〜を指示する
(B) 〜を吟味する
(C) 〜を集める
(D) 〜を計画する

> **正解 B** 選択肢は全て動詞の原形。文は Please から始まる命令文だと考えられるので、空所には、後の名詞句 the enclosed instructions「同封の取扱説明書」を目的語に取る動詞として文意に合うものを選ぶ。(B) が正解。動詞 review は「〜を吟味する、〜をよく調べる」という意味で、書類の確認をする際によく使われる。enclosed「同封された」、instructions「〈複数形で〉取扱説明書」、attempt to do「〜しようと試みる」、dishwasher「食器洗い機」。
> (A) (C) (D) いずれも機器の設置の前にする行為としては不適切。

7 ------- all the preliminary interviews have been completed, the top three applicants for the marketing director position will be contacted.

(A) Compared to
(B) As soon as
(C) So that
(D) Not only

全ての予備面接が終わり次第、マーケティング部長職の応募者上位3名が連絡を受けます。

(A) 〜と比較して
(B) 〜するとすぐに
(C) 〜するように
(D) 〜だけでなく

> **正解 B** カンマの前後を見るとどちらも〈主語＋動詞〉の節なので、空所には節と節をつなぐ語句として文意に合うものを選ぶ。前半の「全ての予備面接が終了する」と後半の「マーケティング部長職の応募者上位3名が連絡を受ける」という内容から、接続詞の働きをする (B) As soon as が文意として適切。preliminary「予備の」、interview「面接」、complete「〜を完了する」、applicant「応募者」、contact「〜に連絡する」。
> (A) 後ろには名詞または名詞句を伴い、節を続けることはできない。
> (C) 2つの節の内容がつながらず、意味が通らない。
> (D) 文頭で用いられるときは、倒置が起こって〈動詞＋主語〉の順になるので、不適切。

8 Payments made to your account after the invoice was generated are not ------- in the balance shown.

(A) reflected
(B) reflects
(C) reflecting
(D) reflect

請求書発行後に預金口座に振り込まれた金額は、表示されている差引残高には反映されていません。

＊選択肢の訳は省略

> **正解 A** 動詞 reflect「〜を反映する」の適切な形を選ぶ。文頭から generated までが主語の名詞句で、空所の前に be 動詞の are があるので、時制は受動態の現在形あるいは現在進行形のいずれかが考えられる。空所に (A) を入れて受動態の現在形にすると、文の意味が通る。payment「支払額」、account「預金口座」、invoice「請求書」、generate「〜を作り出す」、balance「〈預金口座の〉差引残高」。
> (B) 三人称単数現在形。
> (C) 現在分詞。現在進行形を作るが、目的語に当たる名詞がない。
> (D) 動詞の原形。

9 Consumers can ------- enroll online for Wozetco's current marketing study.

    (A) very
    (B) least
    (C) easily
    (D) more

消費者は、Wozetco社の現在行われているマーケティング調査にインターネット上で簡単に登録できます。

    (A) とても
    (B) 最も少なく
    (C) 簡単に
    (D) より多く

> 正解 **C**　選択肢は全て副詞。空所には、動詞 enroll「登録する」を修飾するのに適切なものを選ぶ。文意に合うのは (C) easily。consumer「消費者」、enroll「登録する、入会する」、online「インターネット上で、オンラインで」、current「現在行われている、現在の」。
> (A) 動詞を修飾できない。
> (B) (D) 量や程度を表す副詞。

Mini
Test
2

10 Real estate agents claim that ------- to the landscape in the Presmont area will encourage buyers to consider homes there.

    (A) continuations
    (B) increments
    (C) deviations
    (D) enhancements

不動産仲介業者たちは、プレスモント地区の景観を向上させれば、買い手が同地区の住宅を検討する気になるだろうと主張しています。

    (A) 継続
    (B) 増加
    (C) 逸脱
    (D) 改良

> 正解 **D**　選択肢は全て名詞の複数形。that 節内の主語は空所を含む ------- to the landscape in the Presmont area で、空所には後ろの前置詞句に修飾される名詞が入ると考えられる。encourage ~ to do は「~を…する気にさせる、~に…するよう促す」という意味なので、住宅を検討することを促すものとして文意に合うのは、(D) enhancements が適切。real estate「不動産」、claim「~を主張する」、landscape「景観」、consider「~を検討する」。
> (A) (B) (C) いずれも空所の後の修飾語句と意味がつながらない。

---

11 If the printer had been damaged during shipment, the company ------- to send Mr. Kichida a replacement.

    (A) would have offered
    (B) has offered
    (C) is being offered
    (D) would have been offered

もしそのプリンターが輸送中に損傷していたのであれば、会社はKichidaさんに交換品を送ると申し出ていたでしょう。

    ＊選択肢の訳は省略

> 正解 **A**　選択肢は全て動詞 offer「~を申し出る」が変化した形。if 節の述語動詞が過去完了形の had been damaged であること、主節の内容が「会社は Kichida さんに交換品を送ることを -------」という意味であることから、空所には仮定法過去完了（能動態）の (A) が入るのが適切。shipment「輸送、出荷」、offer to do「~することを申し出る」、replacement「交換品」。
> (B) 能動態・現在完了形。if 節と時制が合わない。
> (C) 受動態・現在進行形。態、時制ともに合わない。
> (D) 受動態・仮定法過去完了。受動態では意味が通らない。

Questions 12-15 refer to the following e-mail.

From: Customer Service
To: Alfred Janssen
Subject: Ridgedale Supply account
Date: 4 February

Dear Mr. Janssen,

❶ Thank you for creating an account with Ridgedale Supply. You probably know -------
12.
Ridgedale offers the widest selection of office supplies in the area. Your account gives you a

number of extra benefits, including faster checkout, instant access to your order history, and

------- more.
13.

❷ Place your first order today! As an account holder, you ------- 20% off your first purchase
14.
from our Web site. ------- . Our weekly e-mail newsletter will keep you informed of additional
15.
promotions like this one.

❸ We look forward to serving all of your office supply needs.

Sincerely,

Ridgedale Supply Customer Service

問題12-15は次のEメールに関するものです。

送信者：顧客サービス部
受信者：Alfred Janssen
件名：　Ridgedale 用品社のアカウント
日付：　2月4日

Janssen様

Ridgedale 用品社でアカウントを作成いただき、ありがとうございます。ご存じかもしれませんが、Ridgedale 社は地域最大の品ぞろえを誇る事務用品を提供しております。お客さまのアカウントは、より迅速なご精算、ご注文履歴の即時参照、さらに多くのサービスを含め、数々の特典が受けられます。

本日すぐ、初回のご注文をなさってください！ アカウントの保有者として、当ウェブサイトから初回のご購入金額より、20 パーセントの割引を受けられます。*割引はご精算時に自動的に適用されます。当社の週1回配信のEメールによるニュースレターでは、こうした追加のキャンペーンの情報をお知らせいたします。

お客さまの事務用品に関するあらゆるご要望に対応させていただくことを、心待ちにしております。

敬具

Ridgedale 用品社顧客サービス部

*問題15の挿入文の訳

12
(A) because
(B) even
(C) when
(D) that

(A) 〜だから
(B) 〜でさえ
(C) いつ〜であるか
(D) 〜ということ

正解 **D**

空所を含む文のうち、Ridgedale offers the widest selection of office supplies in the area「Ridgedale 社は地域最大の品ぞろえを誇る事務用品を提供している」という節は、述語動詞 know の目的語だと考えられる。よって、空所には「〜ということ」という意味の名詞節を導く (D) that が入るのが適切。
(A) 接続詞。名詞節を導かない。
(B) 副詞。
(C) 接続詞。文意に合わない。

13
(A) much
(B) any
(C) very
(D) all

(A) ずっと
(B) どんな〜でも
(C) 非常に
(D) 全ての

正解 **A**

空所の後ろの more は、形容詞 many の比較級が名詞化したもので、「より多くのもの」という意味。空所にはこれを修飾する語として適切なものを選ぶ。空所に (A) を入れて and much more とすると「ずっと多くのもの」という意味になり、特典の具体例の後に続く句として文意に合う。much「〈主に比較級を修飾して〉ずっと、はるかに」。
(B) any more は否定文・疑問文で「これ以上〜 (ない)」の意味。

14
(A) received
(B) will receive
(C) had received
(D) to receive

＊選択肢の訳は省略

正解 **B**

選択肢には動詞 receive「〜を受ける」が変化した形が並ぶ。空所を含む文の直前に命令文で「本日すぐ、初回の注文をしてほしい！」と初回の購入を促す内容があり、「それ (＝初回購入) をすれば〜」という条件の下に得られる割引について述べる流れになっているので、空所には推量を表す (B) が適切。
(A) 過去形。
(C) 過去完了形。
(D) 不定詞。

15
(A) Please find your receipt for this order attached.
(B) We no longer carry this brand.
(C) The discount is automatically applied at checkout.
(D) A complete list is currently available online.

(A) 添付した本注文の領収書をご確認ください。
(B) 当社ではもうこのブランドを取り扱っておりません。
(C) 割引はご精算時に自動的に適用されます。
(D) 完全なリストは現在オンライン上で入手可能です。

正解 **C**

❷ 1〜2行目の空所の前の文では、初回購入で 20 パーセントの割引が受けられると述べられている。空所に (C) を入れると、直前に言及した割引の適用方法を補足説明することになり、文脈に合う。automatically「自動的に」、apply「〜を適用する」。
(A) 初回購入を促す Eメールなので文脈に合わない。receipt「領収書」、attach「〜を添付する」。
(B) no longer 〜「もはや〜ない」、carry「〜 (商品など) を店に置く」、brand「ブランド、銘柄」。
(D) complete「完全な」、currently「現在は」。

語 注

account （サービス利用のための）アカウント
❶ selection 品ぞろえ　　office supplies 〈複数形で〉事務用品　　a number of 〜 多くの〜　　extra benefit 特典　　including 〜を含めて　　checkout 精算　　instant 即時の　　history 履歴
❷ place an order 注文する　　holder 所有者　　purchase 購入　　weekly 週に 1 回の、毎週の　　newsletter ニュースレター　　keep 〜 informed of … 〜に…の情報を連絡する　　additional 追加の　　promotion キャンペーン、販売促進

Questions 16-17 refer to the following text message.

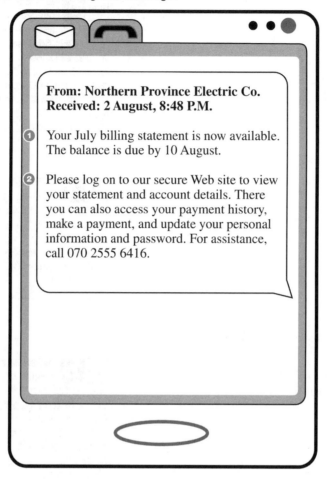

問題16-17は次のテキストメッセージに関するものです。

送信者：北部州電力会社
受信日時：8月2日、午後8時48分

7月分の請求明細書がご覧いただける状態になりました。お支払期限は8月10日です。

当社の安全なウェブサイトにログインして、明細書およびアカウントの詳細をご確認ください。そこでは、支払額の履歴にアクセスしたり、お支払いをしたり、個人情報やパスワードを更新したりすることが可能です。お手伝いをご希望の際は、070-2555-6416までお電話ください。

語 注

electric　電気の
❶ billing　請求　　statement　明細書、報告書　　available　入手できる　　balance　未払額、残額　　due　期限が来て
❷ log on to ～　　～にログインする　　secure　安全な　　view　～を見る　　account　（サービス利用のための）アカウント
details　〈複数形で〉詳細　　payment　支払い　　history　履歴　　make a payment　支払いをする
update　～を最新のものにする　　assistance　手伝い、支援

16 What is the purpose of the text message?

(A) To provide notification about a bill
(B) To give password information
(C) To correct a billing error
(D) To announce a change in the electric rate

テキストメッセージの目的は何ですか。

(A) 請求書についての通知を提供するため。
(B) パスワード情報を教えるため。
(C) 請求書の間違いを訂正するため。
(D) 電気料金の変更を告知するため。

 正解 A ❶で7月分の請求明細書の発行と支払期日を案内した後、❷1～2行目で「当社の安全なウェブサイトにログインして、明細書およびアカウントの詳細を確認してほしい」とあることから、最新の請求書の情報を伝えることがテキストメッセージの目的だと考えられる。よって、(A) が正解。provide「～を提供する」、notification「通知」、bill「請求書」。

(B) ❷2～5行目の文の最後にパスワードに関する言及があるが、ウェブサイト上で更新できると述べられているだけ。
(C) 請求書の間違いについては述べられていない。correct「～を修正する」、error「間違い」。
(D) 電気料金の変更については述べられていない。announce「～を知らせる」、rate「料金」。

---

17 What is the recipient of the text message asked to do?

(A) Place an order
(B) Access an online account
(C) Create a username
(D) Update a credit card number

テキストメッセージの受信者は何をすることを求められていますか。

(A) 注文をする。
(B) オンラインアカウントにアクセスする。
(C) ユーザー名を作成する。
(D) クレジットカード番号を更新する。

正解 B テキストメッセージの受信者は、❷の1～2行目で「当社の安全なウェブサイトにログインして、明細書およびアカウントの詳細を確認してほしい」と求められている。よって、(B) が正解。access「～にアクセスする」、online「オンラインの、インターネット上の」。

(A) 注文についての言及はない。place an order「注文をする」。
(C) ❷の2～5行目より、個人情報の更新についての言及があるだけである。create「～を作成する」、username「ユーザー名」。
(D) クレジットカード番号についての言及はない。

Questions 18-20 refer to the following memo.

To:　　All Office Employees
From: Paul Sundquist
Re:　　Document printing
Date:　Thursday, April 5

❶ Based on the expense report from last quarter, it is clear that we must reduce our costs for office supplies. One area where we can realize savings is in printing and copying documents.

❷ Many of us have been making color copies of basic documents, such as meeting minutes, product documentation drafts, and budget sheets. — [1] —. While multicolor documents are more attractive and attention-grabbing than black-and-white ones, color ink cartridges are very expensive. Purchasing frequent replacements ultimately leaves us with less money to spend on things like business travel and social events. — [2] —.

❸ Rather than instituting a system wherein all jobs must first be approved by the department supervisors, I would prefer that employees make their own decisions about printing and copying. — [3] —. Please reserve the use of color for only those cases where visual appeal is a relevant factor. — [4] —. Thank you for your attention to this matter.

問題 18-20 は次のメモに関するものです。

宛先：　　内勤職員各位
差出人：Paul Sundquist
件名：　　書類の印刷
日付：　　4月5日木曜日

前四半期の経費報告書に基づき、当社が事務用品の経費を削減しなければならないことは明らかです。節約が実現可能な1つの分野は、書類の印刷とコピーです。

私たちの多くが、会議の議事録や製品の文書の草案、予算表のような基本的な書類をカラーコピーしてきました。カラーの書類は、白黒のものより魅力的で注目を集めますが、カラーインクのカートリッジは非常に高価です。頻繁な交換品の購入により、結果として、出張や社交行事のような物事に支出できる資金があまり残らなくなってしまいます。

全ての作業が各部署長に承認されなければならないシステムを設けるよりも、むしろ、印刷やコピーに関して従業員が自分で判断する方が好ましいと私は考えています。視覚的な魅力が関係する要因である場合だけの使用に備えて、カラーコピーの使用をお控えください。*顧客向けの宣伝ちらしは、分かりやすい一例です。この件についてご配慮をよろしくお願いいたします。

*問題20の挿入文の訳

語 注

document　書類
❶ based on ～　～を基にして　　expense　経費、出費　　report　報告書　　quarter　四半期　　cost　費用　　office supplies　〈複数形で〉事務用品　　realize　～を実現する　　saving　節約
❷ minutes　〈複数形で〉議事録　　documentation　文書作成　　draft　草案、下書き　　budget　予算　　sheet　用紙　　multicolor　多色の　　attractive　魅力的な　　attention-grabbing　注意を引く　　cartridge　（印刷用インクの）カートリッジ　　purchase　～を購入する　　frequent　頻繁な　　replacement　交換品　　ultimately　最終的に、結局　　leave ～ with …　…に～を残す　　social　社交のための
❸ institute　～（制度など）を設ける　　wherein　その中で　　approve　～を承認する　　supervisor　監督者　　reserve　～を取り置く　　visual　視覚的な　　appeal　魅力　　relevant　関連した　　factor　要因

18 What is one purpose of the memo?

    (A) To announce the release of a quarterly expense report

    (B) To alert employees to a budget concern

    (C) To inform staff of an error in a document

    (D) To request feedback on a departmental procedure

メモの1つの目的は何ですか。

    (A) 四半期の経費報告書の公開を知らせるため。

    (B) 従業員に予算の懸念点への注意を喚起するため。

    (C) 従業員に書類の間違いを知らせるため。

    (D) 部署の諸手続きに関する意見を求めるため。

> 正解 **B** メモの件名は「書類の印刷」で、冒頭の❶1〜2行目で「当社が事務用品の経費を削減しなければならないことは明らかだ」と切り出して、印刷とコピーの費用削減について言及している。また、❷ではカラーコピーの多用により、他の用途に支出できる残金が少なくなるという懸念点について述べている。よって、メモの1つの目的は、印刷とコピーに関連した予算の問題を共有し、従業員の注意を喚起することだと考えられる。(B) が正解。alert 〜 to … 「〜に…への注意を喚起する」、concern「懸念」。
>
> (A) 経費報告書の公開についての言及はない。announce「〜を知らせる」、release「公開、発表」、quarterly「四半期の」。
> (C) inform 〜 of … 「〜に…を知らせる」。
> (D) 意見は求められていない。request「〜を要請する」、feedback「意見」、departmental「部署の」、procedure「手続き」。

---

19 What are employees advised to do?

    (A) Make black-and-white copies of basic documents

    (B) Tell coworkers about upcoming social events

    (C) Distribute meeting notes by e-mail

    (D) Report broken copy machines to their supervisors

従業員は何をすることを助言されていますか。

    (A) 基本的な書類は白黒でコピーを取る。

    (B) 同僚に近日中の社交行事について伝える。

    (C) 会議のメモをEメールで配布する。

    (D) 故障したコピー機について監督者に報告する。

> 正解 **A** メモでは、❷の1〜2行目で従業員が現在行っている基本的な書類のコピーの扱いについて言及し、カラーインクのカートリッジは費用がかさむと述べている。その後、❸3〜4行目で「視覚的な魅力が関係する要因である場合だけの使用に備えて、カラーコピーの使用を控えてほしい」と指示しているので、従業員は特別な場合を除き、白黒でコピーや印刷をするよう助言されていると推測できる。(A) が正解。
>
> (B) ❷の6行目で social events「社交行事」が言及されているが、予算の使途の一例として挙げられているだけである。upcoming「近づいている、今度の」。
> (C) distribute「〜を配布する」。
> (D) report「〜を報告する」。

---

20 In which of the positions marked [1], [2], [3], and [4] does the following sentence best belong?

"Publicity flyers intended for clients are one obvious example."

    (A) [1]
    (B) [2]
    (C) [3]
    (D) [4]

[1]、[2]、[3]、[4]と記載された箇所のうち、次の文が入るのに最もふさわしいのはどれですか。

「顧客向けの宣伝ちらしは、分かりやすい一例です」

    (A) [1]
    (B) [2]
    (C) [3]
    (D) [4]

> 正解 **D** ❸の3〜4行目に「視覚的な魅力が関係する要因である場合だけの使用に備えて、カラーコピーの使用を控えてほしい」とある。その直後の (D) [4] に挿入文を入れると、カラー印刷を使用してもいいと判断できる例を挙げる流れになり、文意に合う。よって、(D) が正解。publicity「宣伝、広告」、flyer「ちらし」、intend 〜 for … 「〜を…に向ける」、obvious「分かりやすい、明白な」。

Questions 21-24 refer to the following e-mail.

To:	All staff
From:	Edna Fuentes
Date:	March 12
Subject:	Zenva Technologies

Fellow employees:

① In an effort to reduce the amount of energy consumed by the company, the Environmental Steering Committee has decided to purchase for our offices a new automation system from Zenva Technologies. The system will automatically regulate thermostats and overhead lights to accommodate our usual work schedules. For example, at 7:00 P.M. each weekday, all office lights will automatically be turned off or dimmed (except for hallway and stairwell lights). Likewise, on Saturdays and Sundays, the temperature will be <u>maintained</u> at a steady 17° C instead of the usual 21° C during the week. This new system should help reduce our monthly utility bills by at least 15% and help us meet our environmental goal of conserving electricity.

② We acknowledge that some of you will be affected by these changes more than others, particularly those whose schedules do not conform to regular working hours. If this situation applies to you, feel free to contact the personnel department to request an office change, as some sections of the building will be set to a later schedule. Bring any other concerns to your supervisor.

Sincerely,

Edna Fuentes, Vice President of Operations

問題21-24は次のEメールに関するものです。

受信者： 全従業員
送信者： Edna Fuentes
日付： 3月12日
件名： Zenvaテクノロジー社

従業員の皆さま

当社のエネルギー消費量を削減するための取り組みとして、環境運営委員会は、オフィス用にZenvaテクノロジー社の新しい自動制御システムを購入することに決めました。このシステムは当社の通常の勤務スケジュールに合わせて、サーモスタットと天井の照明を自動的に調整します。例えば、平日午後7時には、全てのオフィスの照明が自動的に消灯されるか減光されます（廊下と階段吹き抜けの照明は除きます）。同様に、土曜日と日曜日には、室温が平日の通常温度の21℃ではなく、17℃に保たれます。この新システムは、当社の毎月の公共料金を少なくとも15パーセント削減することに役立ち、電気の節約という当社の環境目標を達成する一助になるはずです。

これらの変更によって、一部の方々が他の人々より影響を受けることになると認識しています。特に通常の勤務時間ではない勤務スケジュールの方たちです。この状況に当てはまる場合は、建物の幾つかの区域は遅めの時間帯に設定されることになるので、ご遠慮なく人事部に連絡して、執務室の変更を要請してください。その他、懸念点があれば何でも監督者にお伝えください。

敬具

Edna Fuentes、事業本部副部長

語 注

① effort 取り組み、努力　consume ～を消費する　environmental 環境の　steering 運営、かじ取り
committee 委員会　automation 自動制御　regulate ～を調整する、～を管理する
thermostat サーモスタット、温度自動調整器　overhead 天井から吊した　accommodate ～に対応する
turn off ～（電源など）を切る　dim ～を薄暗くする　hallway 廊下　stairwell 階段の吹き抜け　likewise 同様に
maintain ～を維持する、、～を保つ　steady 安定して　utility （電気・ガス・水道などの）公共サービス
bill 請求書　meet ～を達成する、～を満たす　goal 目標　conserve ～を節約する、～を保全する
② acknowledge ～を認める　affect ～に影響を与える　conform to ～ ～に従う　apply to ～ ～に当てはまる
feel free to do 自由に～する　contact ～に連絡を取る　personnel 人事　request ～を要請する
set ～を設定する　concern 懸念　supervisor 監督者　vice president 副部長、副社長　operation 事業

21 What is the purpose of the e-mail?

(A) To clarify the requirements of a new environmental law

(B) To explain an upcoming change in workplace conditions

(C) To encourage employees to develop more efficient work habits

(D) To offer employees the opportunity to work from home

Eメールの目的は何ですか。

(A) 新しい環境の法律の要件を明確にするため。

(B) 近々起きる職場環境の変更点を説明するため。

(C) 従業員がより効率的な勤務習慣を身に付けるよう促すため。

(D) 従業員に在宅で働く機会を提供するため。

正解 B ❶の1～3行目で、「当社のエネルギー消費量を削減するための取り組みとして、環境運営委員会は、オフィス用にZenvaテクノロジー社の新しい自動制御システムを購入することに決めた」と述べ、続けて新システムの導入による職場環境の変更点について、具体的に説明している。よって、(B) が正解。upcoming「近づいている、今度の」。
(A) clarify「～を明確にする」、requirement「要件、必要条件」。
(C) encourage ～ to do「～が…するよう促す」、develop「～ (傾向・好みなど) を持ち始める」、efficient「効率的な」。
(D) offer ～ …「～に…を提供する」、opportunity「機会」。

Mini Test 2

22 The word "maintained" in paragraph 1, line 6, is closest in meaning to

(A) confirmed

(B) repaired

(C) taken

(D) kept

第1段落・6行目にある "maintained" に最も意味が近いのは

(A) 確認された

(B) 修理された

(C) 取られた

(D) 保たれた

正解 D 下線部を含む文では、Zenva社のシステムの機能や特徴が示されていると考えられる。平日と週末の調整温度について一定の室温に維持されるという内容なので、「～を保つ」を意味する keep の過去分詞 (D) kept が最も意味が近い。
(A) (B) (C) いずれも意味が通らない。

---

23 What is mentioned as a benefit of the Zenva product?

(A) It will save the company money.

(B) It will reduce employee workloads.

(C) It can be serviced from outside the office.

(D) It can be used in any work environment.

Zenva社の製品の利点として述べられていることは何ですか。

(A) 会社の資金を節約する。

(B) 従業員の仕事量を減らす。

(C) 社外から使うことができる。

(D) どのような仕事環境でも使用できる。

正解 A Zenva社から購入する自動制御システムについて、❶の7～9行目に、「当社の毎月の公共料金を少なくとも15パーセント削減することに役立つ」とある。(A) が正解。benefit「利点」。
(B) workload「仕事量」。
(C) service「～ (機械) を使えるようにする」。

---

24 What are employees who typically work late advised to do?

(A) Talk to Ms. Fuentes

(B) Consider switching offices

(C) Change their work schedules

(D) Take work home over the weekend

通常遅い時間に働く従業員は、何をするよう助言されていますか。

(A) Fuentes さんと話す。

(B) 執務室を換えることを検討する。

(C) 勤務スケジュールを変更する。

(D) 週末に仕事を家へ持ち帰る。

正解 B 通常の勤務時間と異なる勤務スケジュールの従業員に向けて、❷2～4行目で「この状況に当てはまる場合は、建物の幾つかの区域は遅めの時間帯に設定されることになるので、遠慮なく人事部に連絡して、執務室の変更を要請してほしい」と助言している。よって、(B) が正解。typically「通常は」。consider「～を検討する」、switch「～を換える」。
(A) メールの送信者である Fuentes さんではなく、人事部に連絡を取るよう案内されている。
(C) 変更を勧められているのは執務室であって、勤務スケジュールではない。

Questions 25-29 refer to the following Web pages and letter.

1 ウェブページ

http://www.saltoalliance.com/membership

Current Promotions for Salto Alliance Members

❶ From 1 July to 31 December, earn points when staying at any of the following Salto Alliance hotels.

Egidio Hotel, Florence, Italy— Earn 40 points when you reserve a single room.	**Halinski Hotel, London, England**— Earn 60 points when you reserve a double room.
Celova Inn, Siena, Italy— Opens 3 March! Earn 70 points when you reserve a single room.	**Neves Pousada, Lisbon, Portugal**— Earn 60 points when you reserve a double room.

❷ **Plus**:
- Members receive free shuttle service to select local attractions and the main airport. Check with the front desk for scheduling.
- Members who rent a car from Avini Rentals receive a 10 percent discount on car rentals.

❸ **Ready to use your points?**
- 500 points: Get 50 percent off a meal of up to €100 at any Salto Alliance hotel restaurant.
- 600 points: Receive a room upgrade.
- 1,000 points: Enjoy a free overnight stay at any participating Salto Alliance hotel.

❹ For details on promotions and points, go to www.saltoalliance.com/member_rewards.

Salto Alliance

2 手紙

3 August

Elsa Dolanski
238 Rose Hill
BECKLEY OX3 25E
England

Dear Ms. Dolanski,

❶ Thank you for staying at a Salto Alliance hotel. Enclosed you will find the Salto Alliance membership card that you requested during your recent stay in Florence. We have already applied the 40 points that you earned during your one-night visit, but you will need to activate your card to <u>keep</u> accruing points. To do so, go to our Web site at www.saltoalliance.com, click "My Account," and follow the instructions provided.

❷ We look forward to hosting you again in the near future.

Regards,
The Guest Relations Team
Salto Alliance

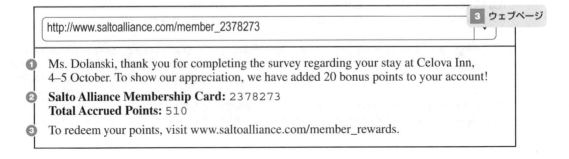

3 ウェブページ

http://www.saltoalliance.com/member_2378273

❶ Ms. Dolanski, thank you for completing the survey regarding your stay at Celova Inn, 4–5 October. To show our appreciation, we have added 20 bonus points to your account!

❷ **Salto Alliance Membership Card:** 2378273
Total Accrued Points: 510

❸ To redeem your points, visit www.saltoalliance.com/member_rewards.

問題25-29は次のウェブページと手紙に関するものです。

http://www.saltoalliance.com/membership

Salto Alliance社の会員向け現行キャンペーン

7月1日から12月31日までの期間に、以下のSalto Alliance社のホテルにご宿泊いただき、ポイントを獲得してください。

Egidio ホテル (イタリア、フィレンツェ) ― シングルのお部屋のご予約で、40 ポイント獲得。	**Halinski ホテル (イングランド、ロンドン) ―** ダブルのお部屋のご予約で、60ポイント獲得。
Celova ホテル (イタリア、シエナ) ― 3月3日オープン! シングルのお部屋のご予約で、70ポイント獲得。	**Neves ホステル (ポルトガル、リスボン) ―** ダブルのお部屋のご予約で、60ポイント獲得。

さらに:

・会員は、選り抜きの地元の名所や主要な空港へ向かう無料のシャトルバスのサービスを受けられます。ご予定を立てる際は、フロントにお問い合わせください。

・Avini レンタル社で車をレンタルされる会員の方は、車のレンタル代に10パーセントの割引を受けられます。

ポイントを使われますか。

・500ポイント:Salto Alliance社のホテルの全レストランで、100ユーロまでのお食事代が50パーセント引きになります。

・600ポイント:お部屋のグレードアップが受けられます。

・1,000ポイント:参加中のSalto Alliance社のホテルで、1泊分の無料のご滞在をお楽しみください。

キャンペーンとポイントの詳細については、www.saltoalliance.com/member_rewardsにアクセスしてください。

8月3日

Elsa Dolanski様
Rose Hill 238番地
ベックリー OX3 25E
イングランド

Dolanski様

Salto Alliance 社のホテルにご宿泊いただきありがとうございます。先日フィレンツェでご宿泊された際にお申し込みいただいた、Salto Alliance 社の会員カードを同封いたしました。1泊のご滞在でお客さまが獲得された40 ポイントは当方ですでに適用いたしましたが、ポイントを貯め続けていくためには、お客さまの方でカードを有効化していただく必要があります。そのためには、当社のウェブサイト www.saltoalliance.com へアクセスし、「私のアカウント」をクリックした後に表示される指示に従ってください。

お客さまのまたのお越しをお待ちしております。

敬具
お客さま対応チーム
Salto Alliance社

---

http://www.saltoalliance.com/member_2378273

Dolanski様、10月4日〜5日のCelovaホテルでのご滞在について、アンケートにご記入いただき、ありがとうございます。感謝の意を表して、お客さまのアカウントに20ボーナスポイントを加算いたしました!

Salto Alliance会員カード: 2378273
貯まったポイントの合計: 510

ポイントを交換するには、www.saltoalliance.com/member_rewardsにアクセスしてください。

25 What is mentioned about Salto Alliance hotels?

(A) They have three room sizes to choose from.
(B) They prepare free breakfasts for guests.
(C) They provide coupons for nearby attractions.
(D) They offer members free transportation to local sites.

Salto Alliance社のホテルについて何が述べられていますか。

(A) 3種類の部屋の広さを選べる。
(B) 宿泊客に無料の朝食を用意している。
(C) 近隣の名所のクーポンを提供している。
(D) 会員に地元の複数の場所への無料の移動手段を提供している。

> 正解 **D**　❶❷の2行目に「会員は、選り抜きの地元の名所や主要な空港へ向かう無料のシャトルバスのサービスを受けられる」とあるので、ホテルは会員向けに複数箇所への無料の移動手段を提供していると分かる。よって、(D) が正解。transportation「移動手段、交通」、site「場所」。
> (A) シングルとダブルの2種類の部屋しか言及されていない。
> (B) 無料の食事についての言及はない。
> (C) クーポンについての言及はない。nearby「近くの」。

26 At what hotel did Ms. Dolanski request a membership card?

(A) Egidio Hotel
(B) Halinski Hotel
(C) Celova Inn
(D) Neves Pousada

Dolanskiさんはどのホテルで会員カードを申し込みましたか。

(A) Egidio ホテル
(B) Halinski ホテル
(C) Celova ホテル
(D) Neves ホステル

> 正解 **A**　❷の手紙の❶1～2行目に「先日フィレンツェで宿泊された際に申し込みいただいた、Salto Alliance 社の会員カードを同封した」とあるので、Dolanski さんはフィレンツェにある Salto Alliance 社のホテルで、会員カードを申し込んだと分かる。❶のウェブページの❶の表を見ると、フィレンツェにあるのは Egidio ホテルである。(A) が正解。

27 In the letter, the word "keep" in paragraph 1, line 4, is closest in meaning to

(A) place
(B) continue
(C) delay
(D) hold

手紙の第1段落・4行目にある "keep" に最も意味が近いのは

(A) ～を置く
(B) ～を続ける
(C) ～を遅延させる
(D) ～を持つ

> 正解 **B**　接続詞 but の前後の節の内容に注目する。文頭からカンマまでの前半の節では、「1泊の滞在であなたが獲得した40ポイントは当方ですでに適用した」とホテル側の1回限りの対応を説明し、後半の keep を含む節では、「ポイントを貯め続けていくためには、あなたの方でカードを有効化してもらう必要がある」と今後のポイントの貯め方に言及している。keep *doing* で「～し続ける」という意味を表すので、それと同様の意味の (B) continue「～を続ける」が正解。
> (A) (C) (D) いずれも直後の現在分詞 accruing とつながらず、意味が通らない。

28 What is probably true about Ms. Dolanski?

(A) She stayed at a new hotel.
(B) She rented a car from Avini Rentals.
(C) She was unable to activate her card.
(D) She lost her membership card.

Dolanskiさんについて正しいと思われることは何ですか。

(A) 新しいホテルに宿泊した。
(B) Avini レンタル社から車を借りた。
(C) カードを有効化できなかった。
(D) 会員カードを紛失した。

 正解 A **3**のウェブページの**1** 1 ～ 2 行目に「10 月 4 日～ 5 日の Celova ホテルでの滞在について、アンケートに記入してくれて、ありがとう」とある。**1**のウェブページの**1**の表を見ると、Celova ホテルの箇所に「3 月 3 日オープン！」と書かれており、新しいホテルだと分かる。よって、(A) が正解。
(B) **1**の**2**より、ホテルは Avini レンタル社の割引を提供しているが、Dolanski さんが車を借りたかどうかは不明。
(C) **2**の**1**と**3**の**2**より、Dolanski さんのポイントは発行当初より増えているので、カードは有効化されている。
(D) 会員カードの紛失については言及がない。

---

29 Why did Ms. Dolanski receive bonus points?

(A) For recommending a shuttle service
(B) For filling out a survey
(C) For extending her hotel stay
(D) For checking out early

Dolanskiさんはなぜ、ボーナスポイントを受け取ったのですか。

(A) シャトルバスのサービスを勧めたから。
(B) アンケートに記入したから。
(C) ホテルの滞在を延長したから。
(D) 早くチェックアウトしたから。

正解 B **3**のウェブページの**1**に、「10 月 4 日～ 5 日の Celova ホテルでの滞在について、アンケートに記入してくれて、ありがとう。感謝の意を表して、あなたのアカウントに 20 ボーナスポイントを加算した」とある。completing を filling out と言い換えた (B) が正解。fill out「～（用紙など）に記入する」。
(A) recommend「～を勧める」。
(C) extend「～を延長する」。
(D) check out「～（ホテルなど）をチェックアウトする」。

語 注

1 ウェブページ current 現在の　　promotion （販売促進の）キャンペーン、プロモーション
1 earn ～を獲得する　　reserve ～を予約する　　inn ホテル、旅館
pousada ★ポルトガル語由来で「ホステル」のこと
2 shuttle シャトルバス　　select 選り抜きの、厳選した　　local 地元の　　attraction 名所
check with ～ ～に問い合わせる　　rent ～を賃借する、～をレンタルする
3 (be) ready to do 今にも～しようとして（いる）　　up to ～ 最大で～まで
upgrade グレードアップ、改良　　overnight 1 泊の　　participate 参加する
4 details 〈複数形で〉詳細
2 手紙 **1** Enclosed you will find ～ ～を同封しました、同封の～をご覧ください　　request ～を要請する
apply ～を適用する　　activate ～を有効化する　　accrue ～を蓄積する　　account アカウント
follow ～に従う　　instruction 指示　　provide ～を提供する
2 host ～を迎える　　relations 〈複数形で〉（人・団体との）関係、交渉
3 ウェブページ **1** complete ～（書類など）に漏れなく記入する　　survey アンケート、調査票　　regarding ～ ～に関して
3 redeem ～を（景品と）交換する

Mini Test 3

右上の目安の解答時間を目標に、自分で時間を計りながら全ての問題を解いてみましょう。**p.308 の** 「結果記入シート」 の説明も読んでから取り組んでください。

→解答・解説は p.268

PART 5

Directions: A word or phrase is missing in each of the sentences below. Four answer choices are given below each sentence. Select the best answer to complete the sentence. Then mark the letter (A), (B), (C), or (D) on your answer sheet.

---

1. The committee accepted the proposal in principle, without having examined the -------.

   (A) specifics
   (B) specify
   (C) specific
   (D) specifically

2. Students are attending the Myerson exhibition at the Wilmington Historical Museum because it ------- authentic dinosaur bones.

   (A) feature
   (B) features
   (C) featured
   (D) featuring

3. Ms. Croft began working at the Central Library five years ago and has ------- become the director.

   (A) ever
   (B) yet
   (C) so
   (D) since

4. For the past five years, Bolting Technology Ltd. has been a creative ------- in the communications industry.

   (A) motion
   (B) fashion
   (C) code
   (D) force

5. Dr. Abraham Lowery raised his national visibility with his ------- on last year's Medical Association panel.

   (A) participated
   (B) participate
   (C) participation
   (D) participatory

6. Darjing Food Company has attributed its recent popularity with consumers to changes in its recipes ------- its new packaging.

   (A) as for
   (B) even so
   (C) rather than
   (D) after all

7. Sales ------- weeks four and five will be closely monitored to determine how they will affect first-quarter profits.

   (A) opposite
   (B) beside
   (C) during
   (D) with

8. A project manager will be responsible for the information ------- to external team members.

   (A) distribute
   (B) distribution
   (C) distributes
   (D) is distributed

9. *The National Overview* is the fourth
------- distributed newspaper in the
northeastern region.

    (A) wide
    (B) widen
    (C) most widely
    (D) more widely

10. All Baxmooth appliances come with a
standard one-year warranty -------
otherwise noted.

    (A) whereas
    (B) below
    (C) neither
    (D) unless

11. We found the Staffplex payroll
management system to be the only one
------- for our needs.

    (A) cooperative
    (B) deliberate
    (C) extensive
    (D) adequate

Mini
Test
3

PART 6

Directions: Read the texts that follow. A word, phrase, or sentence is missing in parts of each text. Four answer choices for each question are given below the text. Select the best answer to complete the text. Then mark the letter (A), (B), (C), or (D) on your answer sheet.

Questions 12-15 refer to the following article.

November 30—After two years of construction, the largest hotel in Pittsburgh history is almost ready to open. The Rivertop Hotel, on the banks of the Allegheny River, will have 1,012 rooms for visitors. ------- . The first guests will arrive on December 12 as part of a
12.
medical technology conference.

The project is among four downtown-area hotels ------- . According to Kristofer Walsh,
13.
president of the Pittsburgh Hotel & Lodging Association, these new developments are a
------- . "We've had a massive influx of visitors over the past few years," said Mr. Walsh.
14.
"------- , almost all the hotels in the city are completely full. Clearly, additional hotel rooms are
15.
needed."

12. (A) It is unclear when it will be ready to accept reservations.
    (B) Building renovations will begin next month.
    (C) It will also have seven meeting rooms for groups of up to 200 people.
    (D) There are multiple companies bidding on the job.

13. (A) to construct
    (B) are constructing
    (C) were constructed
    (D) being constructed

14. (A) necessity
    (B) nuisance
    (C) risk
    (D) bargain

15. (A) On the other hand
    (B) In other words
    (C) In the first place
    (D) As a result

Directions: In this part you will read a selection of texts, such as magazine and newspaper articles, e-mails, and instant messages. Each text or set of texts is followed by several questions. Select the best answer for each question and mark the letter (A), (B), (C), or (D) on your answer sheet.

Questions 16-17 refer to the following e-mail.

Mini
Test
3

E-mail

To:	jtan@brookcent.org
From:	nicoled@wsboa.org
Date:	July 2
Re:	Request

Dear Mr. Tan,

The Westerville Small Business Owners Association (WSBOA) is exploring the possibility of booking a meeting space at the Brookhill Community Center. The event has been scheduled for August 12 from 8 to 11 a.m.

In addition to chairs and tables for 50 to 80 members, we will need a laptop, a projector, and a screen. We are also considering hiring a catering company to provide coffee, pastries, and fruit for the event. Would we be expected to contract with the Center's own catering service, or could we arrange to provide our own?

Please be so kind as to provide me with the requested information by Friday afternoon.

Thank you,

Nicole Durand
Event Manager, WSBOA

16. Why did Ms. Durand write the e-mail?
(A) To inquire about renting a facility
(B) To suggest a new date for a meeting
(C) To propose changes to a rental policy
(D) To inform members of a special event

17. What is indicated about the WSBOA meeting?
(A) It is held once a year.
(B) It includes refreshments.
(C) It requires a registration fee.
(D) It takes place in the afternoon.

Questions 18-20 refer to the following notice.

THIS OFFICE CLOSED FOR RENOVATIONS

Please be advised that the Shinjuku branch office of *Tokyo English Newspaper* (TEN) is closed for the summer as we undergo substantial improvements to our publishing offices. The Shinjuku office of TEN will re-open on 1 September.

Note that TEN's Summer Journalism Internship program is being held at our Yoyogi Park branch and runs from 1 July to 1 September. This program offers internship sessions of one week, two weeks, and four weeks for those interested in writing articles and editorials. Our Yoyogi Park branch is located across the street from the Yoyogi Park metro station on the Chiyoda line.

TEN enjoys a circulation of more than 10,000 readers, a number that continues to grow. For the past three years, *Tokyo English Newspaper* has been voted Top English Newspaper in Japan by the editors of *Global Travel Guide* magazine. For more information, visit www.tokyoenglishnewspaper.or.jp or call 03-5521-5935.

18. Where would this notice likely be seen?

(A) In a listing of job openings
(B) On a university bulletin board
(C) In the lobby of a travel center
(D) On the door of a newspaper office

19. Why has the Shinjuku branch of TEN closed?

(A) The building has been sold.
(B) The workplace is being remodeled.
(C) The branch is moving to a new location.
(D) The establishment has gone out of business.

20. What is NOT indicated about TEN?

(A) It is available only online.
(B) It has more than one office.
(C) It has been praised in a magazine.
(D) It recruits summer interns.

Questions 21-24 refer to the following e-mail.

```
╔══════════════════════ *E-mail* ══════════════════════╗
║                                                        ║
║   To:      │ Employee List                         │   ║
║   From:    │ Sophie Jang                           │   ║
║   Date:    │ 31 March                              │   ║
║   Re:      │ Second-quarter updates                │   ║
║   ┌────────────────────────────────────────────────┐  ║
║   │ First of all, I want to thank everyone for a   │  ║
║   │ successful first quarter. To help ensure       │  ║
║   │ success in the next quarter, let me give you   │  ║
║   │ some updates about adjustments to personnel    │  ║
║   │ that have been instituted recently.            │  ║
║   │                                                │  ║
║   │ I am pleased to announce that Christine Moreau │  ║
║   │ has been promoted to accounting supervisor. I  │  ║
║   │ have asked Xun Wong and his team to ensure     │  ║
║   │ that the responsibilities of Ms. Moreau's      │  ║
║   │ previous role as our budget specialist are     │  ║
║   │ covered while we work with human resources to  │  ║
║   │ recruit a permanent replacement.               │  ║
║   │                                                │  ║
║   │ As you know, Samir Abbas retired a few weeks   │  ║
║   │ ago after more than twenty years with the      │  ║
║   │ company. Taking his place as credit analyst is │  ║
║   │ Claudia Sandoval. Ms. Sandoval has more than   │  ║
║   │ seven years of experience with New Zealand     │  ║
║   │ Credit Bank and should have no trouble         │  ║
║   │ acclimating to her new position here at        │  ║
║   │ Anbaum. Please take a moment to stop by her    │  ║
║   │ office in room 128 and introduce yourself.     │  ║
║   │                                                │  ║
║   │ Sincerely,                                     │  ║
║   │                                                │  ║
║   │ Sophie Jang, Finance Manager                   │  ║
║   │ Anbaum Company                                 │  ║
║   └────────────────────────────────────────────────┘  ║
╚════════════════════════════════════════════════════════╝
```

Mini
Test
3

21. Why did Ms. Jang send the e-mail?

(A) To encourage employees to apply for a promotion
(B) To summarize recent changes in staff assignments
(C) To welcome several new employees to the company
(D) To announce changes in the company's hiring policy

22. According to the e-mail, what position is currently open?

(A) Accounting supervisor
(B) Budget specialist
(C) Credit analyst
(D) Finance manager

23. Who no longer works at Anbaum Company?

(A) Ms. Jang
(B) Ms. Moreau
(C) Mr. Wong
(D) Mr. Abbas

24. What is mentioned about Ms. Sandoval?

(A) She holds a degree in finance.
(B) She moved to New Zealand seven years ago.
(C) She was recently hired.
(D) She will supervise the accounting department.

Questions 25-29 refer to the following e-mail, meeting notes, and article.

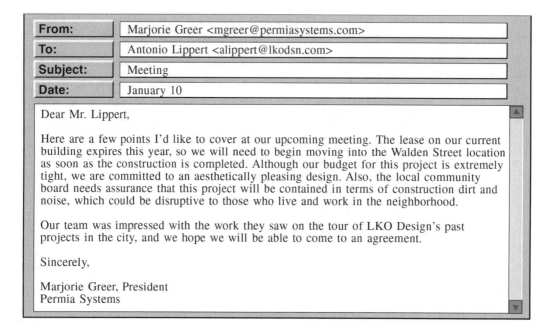

From:	Marjorie Greer <mgreer@permiasystems.com>
To:	Antonio Lippert <alippert@lkodsn.com>
Subject:	Meeting
Date:	January 10

Dear Mr. Lippert,

Here are a few points I'd like to cover at our upcoming meeting. The lease on our current building expires this year, so we will need to begin moving into the Walden Street location as soon as the construction is completed. Although our budget for this project is extremely tight, we are committed to an aesthetically pleasing design. Also, the local community board needs assurance that this project will be contained in terms of construction dirt and noise, which could be disruptive to those who live and work in the neighborhood.

Our team was impressed with the work they saw on the tour of LKO Design's past projects in the city, and we hope we will be able to come to an agreement.

Sincerely,

Marjorie Greer, President
Permia Systems

January 12

MEETING NOTES

Attending
LKO Design: Antonio Lippert, Bjarte Nielsen
Permia Systems: Marjorie Greer, Lisa Ming

Purpose
Determine next steps for Walden Street construction project

Decisions
• LKO will evaluate whether it is possible to build onto the existing structure and will draw up an initial budget.
• If the project is determined to be too expensive to undertake, Permia Systems will pay for the assessment; otherwise, it will be complimentary.
• The entire project must be finished by the first week in December to ensure adequate time for Permia Systems to move all staff into their new headquarters before the end of the year.

Amazing Transformation

(November 28)—Those who remember the vacant Quinn Office Services building on Walden Street may find it hard to believe that most of that squat, dull building still stands. That's because the old building is hidden beneath the stunning new national headquarters of Permia Systems, which is now nearly complete. LKO Design was able to use the old building's foundation and some of its existing structure.

"This was important because the client wanted to avoid disturbance to the community by minimizing the noise and dust," said Bjarte Nielsen, design engineer for LKO Design. "The first thing we did was assess the structure. Our preliminary research indicated that we would be able to save the foundation and the main support walls, which helped us attain the client's goal." — By Juno Pelletier

25. In the e-mail, the word "cover" in paragraph 1, line 1, is closest in meaning to

(A) request
(B) discuss
(C) pay for
(D) conceal

26. According to the e-mail, why is Ms. Greer interested in working with LKO Design?

(A) LKO Design is committed to environmentally friendly construction.
(B) Permia Systems has worked with LKO Design in the past.
(C) Ms. Greer would prefer to support a company from the local area.
(D) Ms. Greer's staff likes the buildings LKO Design has built for other companies.

27. What is suggested about the president of Permia Systems?

(A) She will move into a new office building in December.
(B) She serves on the community board.
(C) She lives in the Walden Street neighborhood.
(D) She has previous experience with building renovation.

28. What is implied about Permia Systems?

(A) It will not pay an evaluation fee.
(B) It is a locally owned company.
(C) It overspent its budget on the building project.
(D) It recently changed its name from Quinn Office Services.

29. According to Mr. Nielsen, why were parts of the Walden Street building's original structure retained?

(A) To preserve a historically valuable structure
(B) To comply with a safety requirement
(C) To reduce disruption to the neighborhood
(D) To achieve an aesthetically pleasing design

Stop! This is the end of the test.

正解一覧

PART 5	1 A	2 B	3 D	4 D	5 C	6 C	7 C	8 B	9 C	10 D	11 D
PART 6	12 C	13 D	14 A	15 D							
PART 7	16 A	17 B	18 D	19 B	20 A	21 B	22 B	23 D	24 C	25 B	26 D
	27 A	28 A	29 C								

1 The committee accepted the proposal in principle, without having examined the -------.

(A) specifics
(B) specify
(C) specific
(D) specifically

委員会は詳細を審査せずに、その提案を原則として受け入れました。

(A) 詳細
(B) 〜を詳述する
(C) 特定の
(D) 特に

正解 A 定冠詞 the と空所の語は、その直前の動名詞 having examined の目的語である。よって、複数形で「詳細」という意味を表す名詞の (A) が正解。committee「委員会」、proposal「提案」、in principle「原則として」、examine「〜を審査する、〜を検査する」。
(B) 動詞 specify「〜を詳述する」の原形。
(C) 形容詞。
(D) 副詞。

2 Students are attending the Myerson exhibition at the Wilmington Historical Museum because it ------- authentic dinosaur bones.

(A) feature
(B) features
(C) featured
(D) featuring

学生たちは Wilmington 歴史博物館での Myerson 展覧会を見学する予定です。というのは、その展覧会は本物の恐竜の骨を呼び物にしているためです。

＊選択肢の訳は省略

正解 B 動詞 feature「〜を呼び物にする」の適切な形を選ぶ。because 節内は、it (= the Myerson exhibition) が主語で、空所が述語動詞に当たると考えられる。主節の時制は現在進行形で、「学生たちは見学する予定だ」と近い未来の予定について述べている。空所には事実を表す現在形が適切。it は三人称単数なので (B) が正解。attend「〜に参加する」、exhibition「展覧会」、authentic「本物の」、dinosaur「恐竜」、bone「骨」。
(A) 動詞の原形。主語の it は三人称単数なので不適切。
(C) 過去形。主節は現在進行形で近い未来の予定について述べており、文意に合わない。
(D) 現在分詞。前に be 動詞が必要。

3 Ms. Croft began working at the Central Library five years ago and has ------- become the director.

(A) ever
(B) yet
(C) so
(D) since

Croftさんは5年前に中央図書館で働き始め、その後館長になりました。

(A) いつも
(B) 〈否定文で〉まだ
(C) そのように
(D) その後で

> 正解 **D**　選択肢は全て副詞。主語は Ms. Croft で、空所の前の and は2つの述語動詞 began（過去形）と has become（現在完了形）を並列している。空所に「その後で」という意味の (D) を入れると、「5年前に中央図書館で働き始めた」という過去の事実と、「館長になり、今も館長である」という過去の時点から現在まで継続している状態について述べる文になる。director「管理者」。
> (A) ever は肯定文では「いつも」という意味。現在完了形では使われない。
> (B) (C) 文意に合わない。

---

4 For the past five years, Bolting Technology Ltd. has been a creative ------- in the communications industry.

(A) motion
(B) fashion
(C) code
(D) force

この5年間、Boltingテクノロジー社は通信産業界で独創的な集団であり続けています。

(A) 動き
(B) 流行
(C) 規約
(D) 集団

> 正解 **D**　選択肢は全て名詞。主語は Bolting Technology Ltd. で、述語動詞は be 動詞の現在完了形の has been である。a creative ------- が文意に合う補語になるには、空所に (D) を入れるのが適切。force は名詞で「(勢力) 団体、一勢力」という意味。creative「独創的な、創造的な」、communications「〈複数形で〉通信技術」、industry「産業」。
> (A) (B) (C) いずれも主語の Bolting テクノロジー社を説明する名詞として意味が通らない。

---

5 Dr. Abraham Lowery raised his national visibility with his ------- on last year's Medical Association panel.

(A) participated
(B) participate
(C) participation
(D) participatory

Abraham Lowery医師は、昨年の、医師会の討論会への参加をきっかけに、全国的な知名度を上げました。

(A) 参加した
(B) 参加する
(C) 参加
(D) 参加型の

> 正解 **C**　選択肢には動詞 participate「参加する」が変化した形や派生語が並ぶ。前置詞 with があるので、his ------- は名詞句で、空所の後から文末までの前置詞句は後ろから空所を修飾していると考えられる。よって、空所には名詞の (C) が適切。前置 with は「〜が原因で、〜のために」という原因・理由を表す。visibility「知名度、認知度」、panel「公開討論会」。
> (A) 動詞の過去形または過去分詞。
> (B) 動詞の原形。
> (D) 形容詞。

6 Darjing Food Company has attributed its recent popularity with consumers to changes in its recipes ------- its new packaging.

(A) as for
(B) even so
(C) rather than
(D) after all

Darjing食品社は、最近の、同社の消費者人気は、新しいパッケージよりもむしろ、調理法の変更によるものだと見ています。

(A) 〜に関しては
(B) たとえそうでも
(C) 〜よりもむしろ
(D) 結局

> 正解 **C**　attribute 〜 to … は「〜 (結果など) を…(原因) に帰する」という意味。空所を含む to から文末までを見ると changes in its recipes と its new packaging という 2 つの名詞句を含んでいる。(C) rather than を空所に入れると、人気の要因についてこの 2 つの名詞句を比較した上で、「its new packaging よりむしろ changes in its recipes」と述べる内容になり、文意が通る。recent「最近の」、popularity「人気」。
> (A) 群前置詞。空所の前の名詞句と意味がつながらない。
> (B) (D) 副詞の働きをする句。

---

7 Sales ------- weeks four and five will be closely monitored to determine how they will affect first-quarter profits.

(A) opposite
(B) beside
(C) during
(D) with

第 4 週および第 5 週の売り上げは、第 1 四半期の利益にそれらがどんな影響を及ぼすかを見極めるために入念に監視されます。

(A) 〜の向かいに
(B) 〜のそばに
(C) 〜の間中
(D) 〜と一緒に

> 正解 **C**　選択肢は全て前置詞。Sales が主語の名詞、------- weeks four and five が Sales に係る修飾語句で、will be monitored が述語動詞だと考えられる。Sales を後ろから修飾するには、「期間」を表す (C) during「〜の間中」を空所に入れると意味が通る。closely「入念に」、monitor「〜を監視する」、determine「〜を特定する、〜を決定する」、affect「〜に影響する」、quarter「四半期」、profit「利益」。
> (A) (B) (D) いずれも、直後の weeks four and five を伴って Sales を修飾する前置詞として不適切。

---

8 A project manager will be responsible for the information ------- to external team members.

(A) distribute
(B) distribution
(C) distributes
(D) is distributed

プロジェクトマネジャーが、外部のチームメンバーへの情報伝達を担当します。

(A) 〜を配布する
(B) 配布
(C) 〜を配布する
(D) 配布される

> 正解 **B**　選択肢には動詞 distribute「〜を配布する」が変化した形や派生語が並ぶ。文頭から for までは、「プロジェクトマネジャーが〜に対して責任を負うだろう」という意味。それに続く the information ------- to external team members は前置詞 for の目的語で、責任の対象を示す名詞句だと考えられる。空所には名詞の (B) を入れて、information distribution「情報の伝達」という意味にするのが適切。be responsible for 〜「〜の責務を負っている」、external「外部の」。
> (A) 能動態・動詞の原形。
> (C) 能動態・三人称単数現在形。
> (D) 受動態・現在形。

9 *The National Overview* is the fourth ------- distributed newspaper in the northeastern region.

(A) wide
(B) widen
(C) most widely
(D) more widely

『全国概説』は、北東地域で4番目に広く配布されている新聞です。

(A) 広い
(B) 広がる
(C) 最も広く
(D) より広く

> 正解 **C**　選択肢は形容詞 wide「広い」が変化した形またはその派生語。空所の前に the fourth があること、また、fourth ------- を除くと、「『全国概説』は北東地域で配布されているその新聞だ」という文意が成立し得ることから、副詞の最上級である (C) を入れて、「4番目に最も広く」という意味にすると、より文意が明確になる。〈the + 序数詞 + 副詞の最上級〉で「X番目に最も〜」という意味を表す。region「地域」。
> (A) 形容詞。
> (B) 動詞 widen「広がる、〜を広げる」の原形。
> (D) 副詞の比較級。

---

10 All Baxmooth appliances come with a standard one-year warranty ------- otherwise noted.

(A) whereas
(B) below
(C) neither
(D) unless

Baxmooth社の電化製品には全て、別段の記載がなければ、標準の1年保証が付いています。

(A) 〜である一方で
(B) 〜の下方に
(C) 〈否定文で〉どちらも〜ない
(D) 〜でない限り

> 正解 **D**　空所の前は「Baxmooth社の電化製品には全て、標準の1年保証が付いている」という意味。空所の後と文意をつなぐには、唯一の例外的条件を表す接続詞の (D) unless を空所に入れて、unless otherwise noted「別段の記載がなければ、特に断りのない限り」という慣用表現にするとよい。appliance「電化製品」、standard「標準の」、warranty「保証」、otherwise「違って」、note「〜に特に言及する」。
> (A) 接続詞。
> (B) 前置詞または副詞。
> (C) 代名詞または副詞。

---

11 We found the Staffplex payroll management system to be the only one ------- for our needs.

(A) cooperative
(B) deliberate
(C) extensive
(D) adequate

Staffplex給与台帳管理システムが、私たちの要望に適した唯一のものであることが分かりました。

(A) 協力的な
(B) 故意の
(C) 広範な
(D) 適した

> 正解 **D**　選択肢は全て形容詞なので、文意に合うものを選ぶ。------- for our needs は直前の名詞句 the only one「唯一のもの」を後ろから修飾する修飾語句だと考えられる。空所の後の for our needs をつなげて文意に合う形容詞は、(D) adequate。(be) adequate for 〜は「〜に適して(いる)」という意味を表す。payroll「給与台帳」、management「管理」、needs「〈複数形で〉要望されるもの」。
> (A) (B) (C) いずれも意味が通らない。

Questions 12-15 refer to the following article.

❶ November 30—After two years of construction, the largest hotel in Pittsburgh history is almost ready to open. The Rivertop Hotel, on the banks of the Allegheny River, will have 1,012 rooms for visitors. ------- . The first guests will arrive on December 12 as part of a medical technology conference.

12.

❷ The project is among four downtown-area hotels ------- . According to Kristofer Walsh, president of the Pittsburgh Hotel & Lodging Association, these new developments are a ------- . "We've had a massive influx of visitors over the past few years," said Mr. Walsh. "------- , almost all the hotels in the city are completely full. Clearly, additional hotel rooms are needed."

13.

14.

15.

問題12-15は次の記事に関するものです。

11月30日──2年間の建設工事を経て、ピッツバーグ史上最大のホテルが間もなく開業しようとしている。アレゲーニー川の川岸にあるRivertopホテルは1,012の客室を有する予定だ。*また、それは最大200名までの団体が利用できる会議室を7室備えることになる。最初の宿泊客は、12月12日に医療技術会議の一環として到着する。

この事業は、中心街に建設されつつある4つのホテルのうちの1つである。ピッツバーグ・ホテル旅館協会の会長であるKristofer Walsh氏によると、これらの新規開発は必要不可欠なものだとのことだ。「ここ数年にわたり、非常に多くの観光客が押し寄せています」とWalsh氏は語った。「結果として、市内のほぼ全てのホテルが完全に満室です。明らかに、さらなるホテルの部屋が必要とされているのです」。

*問題12の挿入文の訳

語 注

❶ construction　建設工事　　be ready to *do*　今にも〜しようとして、〜する準備のできた　　bank　川岸、堤防
medical technology　医療技術　　conference　会議
❷ downtown-area　中心街の　　president　会長　　lodging　宿泊施設　　association　協会　　development　開発
massive　大量の、非常に多い　　influx　（人・物の）殺到、流入　　past　過去の、過ぎ去った
completely　すっかり、完全に　　clearly　明らかに、確かに　　additional　追加の

12
(A) It is unclear when it will be ready to accept reservations.
(B) Building renovations will begin next month.
(C) It will also have seven meeting rooms for groups of up to 200 people.
(D) There are multiple companies bidding on the job.

(A) 予約を受け付ける準備がいつ整うかは明らかでない。
(B) 建物の改修工事は来月始まる予定だ。
(C) また、それは最大200名までの団体が利用できる会議室を7室備えることになる。
(D) その仕事に入札している企業は複数ある。

正解 **C**
❶ 2〜3行目の、空所の直前にある文では、開業予定の Rivertop ホテルについて、「1,012 の客室を有する予定だ」とホテルの客室の数に言及している。よって空所には、会議室の数について言及している (C) を入れると、自然な文脈になる。up to 〜「最大で〜まで」。
(A) unclear「はっきりしない」、accept「〜を受け付ける」、reservation「予約」。
(B) renovation「改修工事」。
(D) multiple「複数の」、bid on 〜「〜に入札する」。

13
(A) to construct
(B) are constructing
(C) were constructed
(D) being constructed

＊選択肢の訳は省略

正解 **D**
選択肢には動詞 construct「〜を建設する」が変化した形が並ぶ。空所を含む文はすでに文として成立しているので、空所には four downtown-area hotels を後ろから形容詞のように修飾する、現在分詞または不定詞が入ると推測できる。(D) を入れて four downtown-area hotels being constructed「中心街に建設されつつある4つのホテル」とすると文意が通る。
(A) 不定詞。
(B) 能動態・現在進行形。
(C) 受動態・過去形。

14
(A) necessity
(B) nuisance
(C) risk
(D) bargain

(A) 必要なこと
(B) 迷惑
(C) リスク
(D) 取引

正解 **A**
選択肢は全て名詞。❷ 1〜3行目の文の主語は these new developments「これらの新規開発」で、a ------- は主語を説明する補語に当たるので、文意に適切なものを選べばよい。同4〜5行目の「明らかに、さらなるホテルの部屋が必要とされている」という Walsh 氏の発言からも、ホテルの新規建設は部屋数を増やすために必要だと考えられていることが分かるので、空所には (A) necessity が入るのが適切。
(B) Walsh 氏は新規開発が必要だと考えているので、不適切。
(C) リスクについては言及がない。

15
(A) On the other hand
(B) In other words
(C) In the first place
(D) As a result

(A) 一方では
(B) 言い換えれば
(C) まず第一に
(D) 結果として

正解 **D**
空所の前の、❷ 3行目の文で Walsh 氏は、「ここ数年にわたり、非常に多くの観光客が押し寄せている」と発言している。空所を含む文はそれに続く発言の一部で、「市内のほぼ全てのホテルが完全に満室だ」という内容である。観光客の流入という「原因」の後に「結果」が続けて書かれていると考えるのが自然な文脈の流れである。(D) As a result「結果として」が適切。
(A) (B) (C) いずれも文脈に合わない。

Questions 16-17 refer to the following e-mail.

```
╔══════════════════════════ *E-mail* ══════════════════════════╗

   To:        jtan@brookcent.org

   From:      nicoled@wsboa.org

   Date:      July 2

   Re:        Request
```

Dear Mr. Tan,

① The Westerville Small Business Owners Association (WSBOA) is exploring the possibility of booking a meeting space at the Brookhill Community Center. The event has been scheduled for August 12 from 8 to 11 a.m.

② In addition to chairs and tables for 50 to 80 members, we will need a laptop, a projector, and a screen. We are also considering hiring a catering company to provide coffee, pastries, and fruit for the event. Would we be expected to contract with the Center's own catering service, or could we arrange to provide our own?

③ Please be so kind as to provide me with the requested information by Friday afternoon.

④ Thank you,

Nicole Durand
Event Manager, WSBOA

問題16-17は次のEメールに関するものです。

受信者：jtan@brookcent.org
送信者：nicoled@wsboa.org
日付：　7月2日
件名：　ご依頼

Tan様

Westerville 中小企業家組合 (WSBOA) は、Brookhill コミュニティーセンターの、会議スペースが予約できるかどうか検討しております。イベントは、8月12日の午前8時から午前11時までの予定となっています。

50～80人の会員用の椅子とテーブルに加え、ノートパソコン、プロジェクター、そしてスクリーンが必要です。このイベントのために、コーヒーやペストリー、果物を配膳するケータリング会社の利用も検討しております。私たちは、コミュニティーセンター独自のケータリングサービスと契約することになるでしょうか、それとも私たち自身で手配することは可能でしょうか。

お伺いしている情報を金曜日の午後までに教えていただければ大変幸いです。

よろしくお願いします。

Nicole Durand
イベント管理者、WSBOA

16 Why did Ms. Durand write the e-mail?

(A) To inquire about renting a facility
(B) To suggest a new date for a meeting
(C) To propose changes to a rental policy
(D) To inform members of a special event

Durandさんはなぜ、Eメールを書いたのですか。

(A) 施設を借りることについて尋ねるため。
(B) 会議の新しい日付を提案するため。
(C) レンタルの方針変更を提案するため。
(D) 会員に、特別イベントを知らせるため。

 正解 **A** ❶の1～2行目で「Brookhillコミュニティーセンターの、会議スペースが予約できるかどうか検討している」と書かれており、その後は詳しい条件の説明が続いている。よって、(A)が正解。inquire「尋ねる」、facility「施設」。
(B) suggest「～を提案する」。
(C) propose「～を提案する」、rental「レンタルの、賃貸の」、policy「方針、規定」。
(D) ❶より、イベントで使用する会議スペースの予約に関して、コミュニティーセンターへ問い合わせているEメールである。inform ～ of …「～に…について知らせる」。

---

17 What is indicated about the WSBOA meeting?

(A) It is held once a year.
(B) It includes refreshments.
(C) It requires a registration fee.
(D) It takes place in the afternoon.

WSBOAの会議について何が示されていますか。

(A) 年に1回行われる。
(B) 軽食を含んでいる。
(C) 登録料を必要とする。
(D) 午後に行われる。

正解 **B** ❷の2～3行目で「このイベントのために、コーヒーやペストリー、果物を配膳するケータリング会社の利用も検討している」と書かれている。coffee, pastries, and fruit を refreshments「軽食」と言い換えた(B)が正解。include「～を含む」。
(A) イベント開催の頻度については記載がない。hold「～を行う」。
(C) 登録料についての記載はない。require「～を必要とする」、registration「登録」、fee「料金」。
(D) ❶2～3行目より、イベントは午前8時から午前11時まで予定されている。

語 注

❶ owner 所有者　association 組合、協会　explore the possibility of *doing* ～する可能性を検討する
book ～を予約する　be scheduled for ～（日時）に予定されている
❷ in addition to ～ ～に加えて　consider *doing* ～することを検討する　catering ケータリング、仕出し業
provide ～を提供する　pastry ペストリー ★ケーキやパイなどの焼き菓子のこと
be expected to *do* ～することが期待されている　contract with ～ ～と契約する
arrange to *do* ～するよう手配する
❸ Please be so kind as to *do* ～していただけませんか　request ～を要請する、～を依頼する
❹ manager 管理者

Questions 18-20 refer to the following notice.

THIS OFFICE CLOSED FOR RENOVATIONS

1 Please be advised that the Shinjuku branch office of *Tokyo English Newspaper* (TEN) is closed for the summer as we undergo substantial improvements to our publishing offices. The Shinjuku office of TEN will re-open on 1 September.

2 Note that TEN's Summer Journalism Internship program is being held at our Yoyogi Park branch and runs from 1 July to 1 September. This program offers internship sessions of one week, two weeks, and four weeks for those interested in writing articles and editorials. Our Yoyogi Park branch is located across the street from the Yoyogi Park metro station on the Chiyoda line.

3 TEN enjoys a circulation of more than 10,000 readers, a number that continues to grow. For the past three years, *Tokyo English Newspaper* has been voted Top English Newspaper in Japan by the editors of *Global Travel Guide* magazine. For more information, visit www.tokyoenglishnewspaper.or.jp or call 03-5521-5935.

問題18-20は次のお知らせに関するものです。

改装につき当オフィスは閉鎖中

『東京英字新聞』（TEN）の新宿支局は、当新聞事業所の大規模な改装工事を受けて、夏の期間閉鎖することをお知らせいたします。TEN の新宿ビルは、9 月 1 日に再開する予定です。

TEN の夏季ジャーナリズムインターンシッププログラムは、当社代々木公園支局で行われており、7 月 1 日から 9 月 1 日まで続くことにご留意ください。同プログラムは、記事や社説の執筆に関心のある人々のために、1 週間、2 週間、4 週間のインターンシップの活動期間を提供します。当社代々木公園支局は、地下鉄千代田線の代々木公園駅から通りを挟んだ向かい側にあります。

TEN は購読者数 10,000 を超える発行部数を誇り、部数は増え続けています。『東京英字新聞』は過去 3 年間、『世界旅行ガイド』誌の編集者によって日本一の英字新聞に選ばれています。詳細は、www.tokyoenglishnewspaper.or.jp にアクセスするか、03-5521-5935 にお電話ください。

18 Where would this notice likely be seen?

    (A) In a listing of job openings
    (B) On a university bulletin board
    (C) In the lobby of a travel center
    (D) On the door of a newspaper office

このお知らせはどこで目にされると考えられますか。

    (A) 求人一覧
    (B) 大学の掲示板
    (C) 旅行センターのロビー
    (D) 新聞社のオフィスのドア

 正解 D　タイトルに「改装につき当オフィスは閉鎖中」とあり、❶で新宿支局の閉鎖の理由や再開の予定が説明されている。よって、このお知らせは新聞社の事業所の一時的な閉鎖を知らせるもので、オフィスのドアに貼られていると考えられる。(D) が正解。
(A) インターンシップについての説明があるが、求人情報の言及はない。listing「一覧」、job opening「求人」。
(B) bulletin board「掲示板」。
(C) lobby「ロビー」。

---

19 Why has the Shinjuku branch of TEN closed?

    (A) The building has been sold.
    (B) The workplace is being remodeled.
    (C) The branch is moving to a new location.
    (D) The establishment has gone out of business.

TENの新宿支局はなぜ閉鎖されているのですか。

    (A) 建物が売却された。
    (B) 職場が改装中である。
    (C) 支局が新しい場所へ転居する予定である。
    (D) 会社が倒産した。

正解 B　❶1〜2行目に「『東京英字新聞』(TEN) の新宿支局は、当新聞事業所の大規模な改装工事を受けて、夏の期間閉鎖することを知らせる」と書かれているので、閉鎖の理由は改装工事だと分かる。よって、(B) が正解。workplace「職場」、remodel「〜を改装する」。
(A) 建物の売却については述べられていない。
(C) 支局の移転については述べられていない。
(D) establishment「会社、施設」、go out of business「倒産する」。

---

20 What is NOT indicated about TEN?

    (A) It is available only online.
    (B) It has more than one office.
    (C) It has been praised in a magazine.
    (D) It recruits summer interns.

TEN について示されていないことは何ですか。

    (A) インターネット上でだけ入手できる。
    (B) 2カ所以上のオフィスがある。
    (C) 雑誌で称賛されたことがある。
    (D) 夏季のインターンを募集している。

正解 A　❶と❷より、TENには新宿と代々木公園の2つの支局があると示されているので、(B)は当てはまる。また、❸の2〜3行目に「『東京英字新聞』は過去3年間、『世界旅行ガイド』誌の編集者によって日本一の英字新聞に選ばれている」とあることから、(C)も事実である。また、(D)の夏季のインターンシップについては、❷の1〜2行目で開催予定だと案内されている。(A)のインターネット上だけでの入手についてのみ、記載がない。available「入手できる」、online「インターネット上で、オンラインで」。
(C) praise「〜を称賛する」。
(D) recruit「〜を募集する」。

語 注

renovation　改装
❶ Please be advised (that) 〜　〜ということを通知します　　branch　支社、支店　　undergo　〜を受ける
  substantial　相当な　　improvement　改良　　publishing　出版業の　　re-open　再開する
❷ note (that) 〜　〜ということに留意する　　run　続く　　offer　〜を提供する　　session　(集団活動などの) 期間
  article　記事　　editorial　社説　　be located　位置する　　across 〜 from …　〜を挟んで…の向かい側に
❸ enjoy　〜に恵まれる　　circulation　発行部数　　vote 〜 …　〜を…に選出する　　editor　編集者

Questions 21-24 refer to the following e-mail.

```
*E-mail*

To:      Employee List
From:    Sophie Jang
Date:    31 March
Re:      Second-quarter updates
```

① First of all, I want to thank everyone for a successful first quarter. To help ensure success in the next quarter, let me give you some updates about adjustments to personnel that have been instituted recently.

② I am pleased to announce that Christine Moreau has been promoted to accounting supervisor. I have asked Xun Wong and his team to ensure that the responsibilities of Ms. Moreau's previous role as our budget specialist are covered while we work with human resources to recruit a permanent replacement.

③ As you know, Samir Abbas retired a few weeks ago after more than twenty years with the company. Taking his place as credit analyst is Claudia Sandoval. Ms. Sandoval has more than seven years of experience with New Zealand Credit Bank and should have no trouble acclimating to her new position here at Anbaum. Please take a moment to stop by her office in room 128 and introduce yourself.

Sincerely,

Sophie Jang, Finance Manager
Anbaum Company

問題21-24は次のEメールに関するものです。

受信者：従業員名簿
送信者：Sophie Jang
日付：　3月31日
件名：　第2四半期の最新情報

まず初めに、好結果だった第1四半期について、皆さんに感謝いたします。次の四半期での成功を確実にする一助とするために、最近決定した人員調整に関する最新情報をお伝えさせてください。

Christine Moreauさんが会計主任に昇進したことを喜んでお知らせいたします。私はXun Wongさんと彼のチームに、予算スペシャリストとしてのMoreauさんの以前の責務を確実に代行していただくようお願いしました。その間、私たちは人事部と協力して後任の正社員を募集します。

ご存じの通り、当社に20年超在籍したSamir Abbasさんが数週間前に退職されました。クレジットアナリストとしての彼の役職は、Claudia Sandovalさんが引き継ぎます。Sandovalさんは、ニュージーランド信用銀行で7年を超える経験があるので、ここAnbaum社での新しい役職にも問題なく慣れるでしょう。少しお時間を作って、128号室の彼女の執務室に立ち寄り、自己紹介をしてください。

敬具

Sophie Jang、財務部長
Anbaum社

┃語 注

list 名簿、一覧　　second-quarter 第2四半期の　　update 最新情報
❶ successful 好結果の、成功した　　quarter 四半期　　ensure 〜を確実にする　　adjustment 調整
　 personnel 人員　　institute 〜を制定する
❷ announce 〜を知らせる、〜を発表する　　promote 〜を昇進させる　　accounting 会計　　supervisor 主任
　 responsibility 責務　　previous 以前の　　role 役職　　budget 予算　　cover 〜を代わりにする
　 human resources 人事部　　recruit 〜を採用する、〜を募集する　　permanent 常勤の　　replacement 代わりの人
❸ retire 退職する　　take *one's* place 〜の後任になる　　credit analyst クレジットアナリスト　★証券アナリストの一種
　 have trouble *doing* 〜するのに苦労する　　acclimate to 〜 〜に慣れる　　stop by 〜 〜に立ち寄る　　finance 財務

21 Why did Ms. Jang send the e-mail?

    (A) To encourage employees to apply for a promotion

    (B) To summarize recent changes in staff assignments

    (C) To welcome several new employees to the company

    (D) To announce changes in the company's hiring policy

JangさんはなぜEメールを送ったのですか。

    (A) 従業員に昇進を求めるよう促すため。

    (B) 最近の人員配置の変更を手短に伝えるため。

    (C) 何人かの新しい従業員を会社に迎え入れるため。

    (D) 会社の雇用方針の変更を発表するため。

> 正解 **B** ❶の1～3行目に「最近決定した人員調整に関する最新情報を伝えさせてほしい」とあり、❷と❸で具体的な人事の内容が述べられている。(B) が正解。summarize「～を手短に述べる」、assignment「配属、任務」。
> (A) encourage ～ to *do*「～に…するよう促す」、apply for ～「～を求める、～に志願する」、promotion「昇進」。
> (C) 現在迎え入れる予定の新しい従業員は、❸ 2行目より Sandoval さん1名のみ。welcome「～を歓迎する」。

---

22 According to the e-mail, what position is currently open?

    (A) Accounting supervisor

    (B) Budget specialist

    (C) Credit analyst

    (D) Finance manager

Eメールによると、現在どの職に空きがありますか。

    (A) 会計主任

    (B) 予算スペシャリスト

    (C) クレジットアナリスト

    (D) 財務部長

> 正解 **B** ❷で、Moreau さんが会計主任に昇進し、後任の正社員を採用するまで Wong さんのチームが、Moreau さんの前職である予算スペシャリストの責務を代行する予定であることが述べられている。よって、現在空いている職種は (B)。currently「現在は」。
> (A) ❷ 1～2行目より、Moreau さんの昇進後の職。
> (C) ❸ 2行目より、Sandoval さんが引き継ぐ職。
> (D) 署名欄より、Eメールの送信者である Jang さんの職。

---

23 Who no longer works at Anbaum Company?

    (A) Ms. Jang

    (B) Ms. Moreau

    (C) Mr. Wong

    (D) Mr. Abbas

Anbaum社でもう働いていないのは誰ですか。

    (A) Jangさん

    (B) Moreauさん

    (C) Wongさん

    (D) Abbasさん

> 正解 **D** ❸の1～2行目で「ご存じの通り、当社に20年超在籍した Samir Abbas さんが数週間前に退職した」と述べられているので、(D) が正解。no longer「もはや～ない」。
> (A) 署名欄より、Eメールの送信者で財務部長。
> (B) ❷ 1～2行目より、会計主任に昇進した人物。
> (C) ❷ 2～4行目より、Moreau さんの後任が決まるまで、予算スペシャリストの責務を代行するチームを率いる人物。

---

24 What is mentioned about Ms. Sandoval?

    (A) She holds a degree in finance.

    (B) She moved to New Zealand seven years ago.

    (C) She was recently hired.

    (D) She will supervise the accounting department.

Sandovalさんについて述べられていることは何ですか。

    (A) 財務の学位を持っている。

    (B) 7年前にニュージーランドへ引っ越した。

    (C) 最近雇用された。

    (D) 会計部を管理する予定である。

> 正解 **C** ❸の2行目で、Sandoval さんは Abbas さんの後任者として言及されており、同2～4行目に「Sandoval さんは、ニュージーランド信用銀行で7年を超える経験がある」と述べられている。ここから、Sandoval さんは Anbaum 社に最近雇用された人物だと分かる。(C) が正解。
> (A) 学位についての言及はない。degree「学位」。
> (B) ❸ 2～4行目より、「ニュージーランド信用銀行で7年を超える経験がある」と述べられているだけである。
> (D) supervise「～を管理する」、department「部署」。

Questions 25-29 refer to the following e-mail, meeting notes, and article.

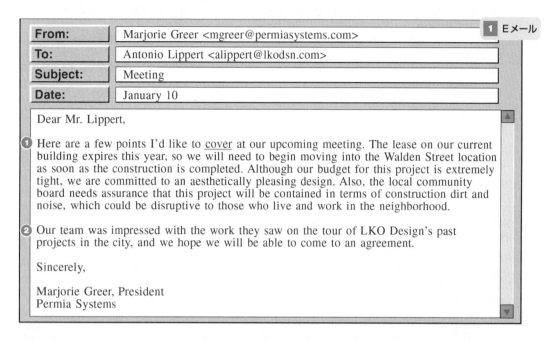

1 Eメール

From:	Marjorie Greer <mgreer@permiasystems.com>
To:	Antonio Lippert <alippert@lkodsn.com>
Subject:	Meeting
Date:	January 10

Dear Mr. Lippert,

1 Here are a few points I'd like to <u>cover</u> at our upcoming meeting. The lease on our current building expires this year, so we will need to begin moving into the Walden Street location as soon as the construction is completed. Although our budget for this project is extremely tight, we are committed to an aesthetically pleasing design. Also, the local community board needs assurance that this project will be contained in terms of construction dirt and noise, which could be disruptive to those who live and work in the neighborhood.

2 Our team was impressed with the work they saw on the tour of LKO Design's past projects in the city, and we hope we will be able to come to an agreement.

Sincerely,

Marjorie Greer, President
Permia Systems

---

2 会議の記録

January 12

MEETING NOTES

1 <u>Attending</u>
LKO Design: Antonio Lippert, Bjarte Nielsen
Permia Systems: Marjorie Greer, Lisa Ming

2 <u>Purpose</u>
Determine next steps for Walden Street construction project

3 <u>Decisions</u>
- LKO will evaluate whether it is possible to build onto the existing structure and will draw up an initial budget.
- If the project is determined to be too expensive to undertake, Permia Systems will pay for the assessment; otherwise, it will be complimentary.
- The entire project must be finished by the first week in December to ensure adequate time for Permia Systems to move all staff into their new headquarters before the end of the year.

---

3 記事

Amazing Transformation

1 (November 28)—Those who remember the vacant Quinn Office Services building on Walden Street may find it hard to believe that most of that squat, dull building still stands. That's because the old building is hidden beneath the stunning new national headquarters of Permia Systems, which is now nearly complete. LKO Design was able to use the old building's foundation and some of its existing structure.

2 "This was important because the client wanted to avoid disturbance to the community by minimizing the noise and dust," said Bjarte Nielsen, design engineer for LKO Design. "The first thing we did was assess the structure. Our preliminary research indicated that we would be able to save the foundation and the main support walls, which helped us attain the client's goal." — By Juno Pelletier

問題25-29は次のEメール、会議の記録、記事に関するものです。

送信者：Marjorie Greer <mgreer@permiasystems.com>
受信者：Antonio Lippert <alippert@lkodsn.com>
件名： 会議
日付： 1月10日

Lippert様

こちらが、近く行われる会議で扱いたい何点かの問題です。当社の現在のビルの賃貸借契約は今年で終了するので、私たちは建設工事が完了次第、Walden通りの物件への引っ越しを開始する必要があります。このプロジェクトに対する当社の予算は非常に厳しいにもかかわらず、私たちは美的観点上好ましい設計にこだわっています。また、地元の地域委員会は、このプロジェクトが、建設工場のほこりや騒音の点において抑えられるという保証を必要としています。それらは近隣に居住または勤務している人々にとって問題になり得るものだからです。

当チームは、市内におけるLKO設計事務所による過去プロジェクトの見学ツアーで拝見したお仕事に感銘を受けており、両社が契約に至ることを望んでおります。

敬具

Marjorie Greer、社長
Permia Systems社

1月12日

会議の記録

出席者
LKO設計事務所： Antonio Lippert、Bjarte Nielsen
Permia Systems社： Marjorie Greer、Lisa Ming

目的
Walden通りの建設計画について、今後の工程を決定する

決定事項
・LKO事務所は、既存の構造の上に建設することが可能かどうかを査定し、最初の予算案を作成する。
・プロジェクトが、費用がかかり過ぎるために着手できないと判断された場合、Permia Systems社は査定料金を支払う。そうでなければ、同料金は無料となる。
・Permia Systems社が年末までに全従業員を新しい本社へ移動させる十分な時間を保証するため、全てのプロジェクトは12月の第1週までに終了しなければならない。

驚くべき変容

(11月28日)——Walden通りにある空きビルのQuinnオフィスサービス社のビルを覚えている人は、そのずんぐりしたさえないビルの大部分がいまだに建っているということが信じ難いかもしれない。それは、その古いビルが、現在完成間近のPermia Systems社の目を見張るような新国内本社の下に隠れているためである。LKO設計事務所は、旧ビルの基礎と既存構造の一部を利用することができた。

「顧客は、騒音やほこりを最小限に抑えることで、地域に迷惑が掛かるのを避けたいと望んでいたので、このことは重要でした」と、LKO設計事務所の設計技師であるBjarte Nielsen氏は述べた。「私たちが最初に行ったのは、構造の査定です。当社の予備調査は基礎と主要な支え壁を残すことが可能であろうということを示しており、それは私たちが顧客の目標を達成する助けになりました」—— Juno Pelletier記

25 In the e-mail, the word "cover" in paragraph 1, line 1, is closest in meaning to

(A) request
(B) discuss
(C) pay for
(D) conceal

Eメールの第1段落・1行目にある "cover" に最も意味が近いのは

(A) 〜を要請する
(B) 〜について議論する
(C) 〜の代金を支払う
(D) 〜を隠す

> **正解 B** 　**1**のEメールの件名が「会議」であること、本文で会社の建設プロジェクトに関する説明が書かれていることから、cover を含む文では、近く行われる会議で話し合いたい問題を共有していると考えられる。最も意味が近いのは (B) discuss「〜について議論する」。

26 According to the e-mail, why is Ms. Greer interested in working with LKO Design?

(A) LKO Design is committed to environmentally friendly construction.
(B) Permia Systems has worked with LKO Design in the past.
(C) Ms. Greer would prefer to support a company from the local area.
(D) Ms. Greer's staff likes the buildings LKO Design has built for other companies.

Eメールによると、GreerさんはなぜLKO設計事務所と仕事をすることに関心を持っているのですか。

(A) LKO設計事務所は環境に優しい建設工事に取り組んでいるから。
(B) Permia Systems社は過去にLKO設計事務所と仕事をしたことがあるから。
(C) Greerさんは、地元地域の会社を支援した方がいいと考えているから。
(D) LKO設計事務所が他社のために建設した建物を、Greerさんの従業員が気に入っているから。

> **正解 D** 　Greer さんは、**1**の**①**で会議で扱いたい問題点について詳しく書いた後、**②**で「当チームは、市内におけるLKO設計事務所による過去プロジェクトの見学ツアーで見た仕事に感銘を受けている」と伝えている。その後、「両社が契約に至ることを望んでいる」とあることから、Greer さんの従業員がLKO設計事務所の過去の作品を気に入ったことが、同事務所に関心を持つ理由であったと分かる。よって、(D) が正解。

27 What is suggested about the president of Permia Systems?

(A) She will move into a new office building in December.
(B) She serves on the community board.
(C) She lives in the Walden Street neighborhood.
(D) She has previous experience with building renovation.

Permia Systems 社の社長について何が分かりますか。

(A) 12月に新しいオフィスビルに引っ越すだろう。
(B) 地域委員会で仕事をしている。
(C) Walden通りの近隣に住んでいる。
(D) 以前、建物の改装をした経験がある。

> **正解 A** 　**2**の会議の記録の**③** 6〜8行目に、年末までにPermia Systems社の全従業員を新しい本社へ移動させるために、全てのプロジェクトが12月の第1週までに終了しなければいけないとある。一方で、11月28日付の記事**3**の**①** 5〜8行目より、Permia Systems社の新国内本社は完成間近だと紹介されている。これらから、社長を含めたPermia Systems社の全員が、当初の計画通り12月に新しいビルに引っ越すと判断できる。よって、(A)が正解。
> (B) 彼女自身が委員会に所属しているとは述べられていない。serve「任務を果たす」。
> (D) previous「以前の」、renovation「改装」。

28 What is implied about Permia Systems?

    (A) It will not pay an evaluation fee.
    (B) It is a locally owned company.
    (C) It overspent its budget on the building project.
    (D) It recently changed its name from Quinn Office Services.

Permia Systems 社について何が示唆されていますか。

    (A) 査定料金は支払わないだろう。
    (B) 地元所有の企業である。
    (C) 建設プロジェクトで予算を超過した。
    (D) 最近、社名をQuinnオフィスサービス社から変えた。

> 正解 **A** ❷❸ 4 ～ 5 行目に「プロジェクトが、費用がかかり過ぎるために着手できないと判断された場合、Permia Systems 社は査定料金を支払う。そうでなければ、同料金は無料となる」とある。一方、❸の記事より、建設工事のプロジェクトは LKO 設計事務所が手掛けていることが分かる。よって、Permia Systems 社は査定の料金を払う必要がない。(A) が正解。
> (B) locally「地元で」。
> (C) overspend「～を使い過ぎる」。
> (D) ❸の❶ 1 ～ 8 行目より、Permia Systems 社は Quinn オフィスサービス社のビルを利用して新しい本社を建てたが、社名変更に関する言及はない。

29 According to Mr. Nielsen, why were parts of the Walden Street building's original structure retained?

    (A) To preserve a historically valuable structure
    (B) To comply with a safety requirement
    (C) To reduce disruption to the neighborhood
    (D) To achieve an aesthetically pleasing design

Nielsenさんによると、Walden通りにある建物の元の構造の一部は、なぜ維持されたのですか。

    (A) 歴史的に価値のある構造を保存するため。
    (B) 安全上の要件を満たすため。
    (C) 近隣への混乱を軽減するため。
    (D) 美的観点上好ましい設計を実現するため。

> 正解 **C** ❸の❷ 1 ～ 5 行目で、Nielsen さんは、古いビルの一部を利用したことについて、「顧客は、騒音やほこりを最小限に抑えることで、地域に迷惑が掛かるのを避けたいと望んでいたので、このことは重要だった」と述べている。よって、(C) が正解。retain「～を維持する」。reduce「～を減らす」、disruption「混乱、妨害」。
> (A) preserve「～を保存する」、valuable「価値のある」。
> (B) comply with ～「～に従う」、requirement「要件、必要条件」。
> (D) achieve「～を実現する」。

語 注

    notes 〈複数形で〉記録

1 Eメール ❶ cover　～（問題など）を扱う　　upcoming　近づいている、今度の　　lease　賃貸借契約、リース
current　現在の　　expire　終了する　　move　引っ越す、移動する　　location　所在地、場所
as soon as ～　～するとすぐに　　construction　建設　　complete　～を完了する　　budget　予算
extremely　非常に　　tight　厳しい、きつい　　be committed to ～　～に熱心に取り組む
aesthetically　美的に、芸術的に　　pleasing　満足できる、魅力的な　　local　地元の
community　地域社会、コミュニティー　　board　委員会　　assurance　保証、確約
contain　～を封じ込める　　in terms of ～　～の観点から　　dirt　ほこり　　disruptive　問題を引き起こす
❷ be impressed with ～　～に感銘を受ける　　tour　見学ツアー、見学会　　agreement　契約、合意

2 会議の記録 ❶ attend　出席する
❷ step　工程、手順
❸ evaluate　～を評価する　　existing　既存の、すでにある　　structure　構造、建物　　draw up　～を作成する
initial　最初の、当初の　　determine　～を判断する、～を決定する　　undertake　～に着手する
assessment　査定、評価　　otherwise　そうでなければ　　complimentary　無料の　　entire　全部の
ensure　～を保証する　　adequate　十分な、適切な　　headquarters　本社

3 記事 amazing　驚くべき　　transformation　変容、変化
❶ vacant　空いている　　squat　ずんぐりした、背の低い　　dull　さえない、つまらない　　foundation　基礎
❷ client　顧客、クライアント　　disturbance　迷惑　　minimize　～を最小限にする　　dust　ほこり
design engineer　設計技師　　preliminary　予備的な　　research　調査　　indicate　～を示す
save　～を保存する　　attain　～を達成する

右上の目安の解答時間を目標に、自分で時間を計りながら全ての問題を解いてみましょう。**p.308** の 「結果記入シート」 の説明も読んでから取り組んでください。

→解答・解説は p.292

PART 5

Directions: A word or phrase is missing in each of the sentences below. Four answer choices are given below each sentence. Select the best answer to complete the sentence. Then mark the letter (A), (B), (C), or (D) on your answer sheet.

---

1. Last year, the Fromley Company ------- an internship program for trade school students studying electrical technology.

   (A) expressed
   (B) specialized
   (C) signaled
   (D) established

2. See our media kit for facts and information ------- our line of lighting equipment.

   (A) pending
   (B) regarding
   (C) among
   (D) throughout

3. The Lafayette Townhome Community is ------- located near a train line that leads to the region's largest shopping mall.

   (A) conveniently
   (B) consistently
   (C) continually
   (D) commonly

4. With its moderate climate and well-qualified workforce, Huntsville is a very ------- location for investors.

   (A) offering
   (B) proposing
   (C) promising
   (D) identifying

5. Please review the repair estimate carefully ------- it has been received from the maintenance department.

   (A) then
   (B) while
   (C) ever since
   (D) as soon as

6. Over the last ten years, *Jamaica News* has built a ------- as one of the most reliable current-events programs in the Caribbean.

   (A) privilege
   (B) character
   (C) reputation
   (D) consequence

7. The owner of Petal Airlines announced that ------- is negotiating a deal with Airplexi to buy new airplanes.

   (A) him
   (B) he
   (C) his
   (D) himself

8. Rose's Bistro will close next month due to escalating operating -------.

   (A) expenses
   (B) functions
   (C) customers
   (D) occasions

9. Ms. Mills has correctly predicted that sales would increase ------- as the company's radio advertisement continues to air.

(A) arguably
(B) reportedly
(C) productively
(D) incrementally

10. Tsutomu Motohashi holds the company record for the highest sales figures in a ------- year.

(A) single
(B) singled
(C) singles
(D) singling

11. The last quarterly report showed that TNQ Electronics' earnings were ------- than anticipated.

(A) lowest
(B) lowering
(C) lower
(D) low

PART 6

Directions: Read the texts that follow. A word, phrase, or sentence is missing in parts of each text. Four answer choices for each question are given below the text. Select the best answer to complete the text. Then mark the letter (A), (B), (C), or (D) on your answer sheet.

Questions 12-15 refer to the following e-mail.

From: ben_zimmerman@avinmax.com
To: myrah_busby@kinweb.net
Date: May 4
Subject: Jollite bicycle tires

Dear Ms. Busby,

Thank you for your message on May 2. Our records indicate that you ordered two Jollite bicycle tires (product JBT1783) through our Web site on April 27 and that they were scheduled to arrive on May 1. I am sorry to hear that you have not yet received ------- .
12.
Deliveries usually take no more than three or four days.

------- . Based on this information, your order should arrive on May 5. If you do not receive
13.
your order by then, please ------- us.
14.

Again, I apologize for the delay. We rarely have problems with our delivery service. I want to emphasize that this situation is very ------- .
15.

Thank you,

Ben Zimmerman

Avinmax Sporting Goods

---

12. (A) it
(B) one
(C) them
(D) some

13. (A) We appreciate your feedback.
(B) Visit our Web site to view additional products.
(C) Unfortunately, this product is currently out of stock.
(D) We were able to track your order.

14. (A) contacted
(B) to contact
(C) contacting
(D) contact

15. (A) similar
(B) exciting
(C) unusual
(D) welcome

PART 7

Directions: In this part you will read a selection of texts, such as magazine and newspaper articles, e-mails, and instant messages. Each text or set of texts is followed by several questions. Select the best answer for each question and mark the letter (A), (B), (C), or (D) on your answer sheet.

Questions 16-17 refer to the following Web page.

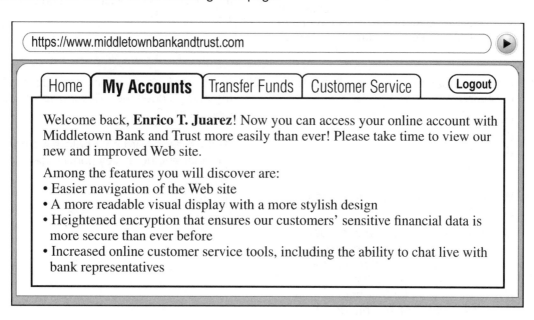

https://www.middletownbankandtrust.com

| Home | **My Accounts** | Transfer Funds | Customer Service | Logout |

Welcome back, **Enrico T. Juarez**! Now you can access your online account with Middletown Bank and Trust more easily than ever! Please take time to view our new and improved Web site.

Among the features you will discover are:
- Easier navigation of the Web site
- A more readable visual display with a more stylish design
- Heightened encryption that ensures our customers' sensitive financial data is more secure than ever before
- Increased online customer service tools, including the ability to chat live with bank representatives

16. Who most likely is Mr. Juarez?
   (A) A bank customer
   (B) A bank executive
   (C) A bank consultant
   (D) A designer of the bank Web site

17. What is NOT mentioned as a feature of the new Web site?
   (A) Enhanced visual design
   (B) A listing of all service fees
   (C) Greater security of information
   (D) The addition of customer service options

Questions 18-20 refer to the following article.

Parking Survey Awaited

Many Sumrita residents, businesses, and visitors have expressed concerns to town officials that there are not enough parking spaces. — [1] —. Some have called for construction of a second parking garage in the next two years.

With a data-collection project scheduled to begin on Tuesday, led by Paston Associates of Turnbridge, town officials will soon learn the extent of the parking problem on a typical weekday, during the evening, and at peak times when events are taking place in the center of town. — [2] —. When it is completed, the study will provide an updated inventory of all public and private parking spaces in the area and their typical rates of use. — [3] —.

"Anecdotally people say that demand has increased with the four new businesses and the residential projects we've seen in the last five years," said Planning Director Akash Singh. — [4] —.

18. How many parking garages are currently in Sumrita?

(A) One
(B) Two
(C) Four
(D) Five

19. What does the article indicate about the survey?

(A) It will study the demand for parking in three local neighborhoods.
(B) It will measure the demand for parking at various times.
(C) It will be paid for by Paston Associates of Turnbridge.
(D) It will be conducted by Sumrita's planning director.

20. In which of the positions marked [1], [2], [3], and [4] does the following sentence best belong?

"But we need hard data before we can consider another costly parking garage."

(A) [1]
(B) [2]
(C) [3]
(D) [4]

Small-Business Expert Coming to São Paulo

SÃO PAULO (May 19)—Angelo Azevedo, dubbed the "small-business expert" by *The Los Angeles Chronicle*, will be the keynote speaker at the first annual São Paulo Small Business Expo (SPSBE). The Expo will take place at the São Paulo Event Center from June 3 to June 5. More than 2,000 small-business entrepreneurs will attend workshops and showcase their businesses at booths, where visitors can collect information and ask questions.

According to an SPSBE press release, Mr. Azevedo will highlight many of the ideas from his best-selling book *Keys to Startup Success*, published just last year. Mr. Azevedo believes that there are several key decisions that must be made before launching into any new business scheme. "You can't go into it with the idea of creating a product you want to sell," Mr.

Azevedo writes in his book. "You have to create a product people want to buy. This is rule number one. And it is absolutely essential to get this right if you want your business to succeed."

Mr. Azevedo is the owner of several successful businesses in Los Angeles, where he has lived for the past ten years. "I'm originally from São Paulo," Mr. Azevedo said. "So I wanted to help the community where I got my start in any way I could, which is why I accepted the invitation to participate in the Expo. There's an outstanding opportunity there for small-business owners. Following these simple but important guidelines has worked well for me and for many other successful small-business owners."

Tickets to the Expo are R$100. They can be purchased through the Expo's Web site at www.saopauloexpo.com/br.

Mini Test 4

21. What is the article mainly about?

(A) The opening of a new business
(B) New trends in marketing
(C) A business leader's participation in an event
(D) The benefits of running a small business

22. According to the article, what has Mr. Azevedo recently done?

(A) He wrote a book.
(B) He presented an award.
(C) He led a workshop.
(D) He traveled to São Paulo.

23. What does Mr. Azevedo say is the most important consideration for new entrepreneurs?

(A) Marketing a product aggressively
(B) Developing a product that is attractive to consumers
(C) Manufacturing a product in a cost-effective way
(D) Creating a product that the business owner feels passionate about

24. Why did Mr. Azevedo decide to participate in the Expo?

(A) He is doing research for a newspaper article.
(B) He would like to recruit some employees.
(C) He is looking for ways to increase sales.
(D) He wants to support entrepreneurs in his hometown.

Questions 25-29 refer to the following e-mail, notice, and order form.

From:	Jean Moumas
To:	Khadim Nakra
Subject:	Trucking company
Date:	June 1

Hello, Mr. Nakra,

I am so glad that you have signed up for deliveries of our fresh vegetables, berries, flowers, and herbs, grown here on our twenty-acre family-owned farm. I can assure you that you and your customers will be delighted with the produce we provide.

Your store is in an area that is new to us, and we are looking forward to our quality produce entering a new market. Please let me know if you have a preferred trucking service. Our usual drivers, based in Santon, do not go out to Allentown. We would be happy to work with a company of your choice to keep the service for you as smooth as possible.

Thank you in advance for any suggestions you wish to provide.

Sincerely yours,

Jean Moumas

Shop Fresh Market

New This Week

June 26

Produce from Thomas Greens Farm

Dear customers, we'd like to draw your attention to the newest additions to our produce section. You've asked for fresh, local fruits and vegetables that have just been harvested. We're bringing these to you from Thomas Greens Farm, located just one hour from here in Carney.

✓ Tomatoes on the vine
✓ Yellow corn
✓ Fresh herbs (basil, thyme, and oregano)

✓ Baby eggplants
✓ Yellow onions (loose)

In the fall, we will be carrying fruits from Bridge Water Orchard in Eagerton. If you have any requests, please let us know.

Thomas Greens Farm

Order Form

Customer   Shop Fresh Market

Order date   June 30

Delivery date   July 3

Order Details:

Repeat last week's order with the following changes:
- No eggplants or fresh herbs needed this week.
- Instead of loose onions, please send them in burlap bags.
  (like the sample you showed us, about six to a bunch).
- Add two crates of green Brussels sprouts to the order.

P.S. You asked that we let you know if there were any problems with the delivery from Kohn Trucking. There were not. The delivery was on time, the driver was courteous, and the produce was in good condition.

Name   Khadim Nakra, Manager, Produce Department
Signature   *Khadim Nakra*

Mini Test 4

25. Why did Ms. Moumas send the e-mail?

    (A) To advertise new products
    (B) To ask for a recommendation
    (C) To request a delivery estimate
    (D) To complain about a policy change

26. Where is Shop Fresh Market probably located?

    (A) In Santon
    (B) In Allentown
    (C) In Carney
    (D) In Eagerton

27. In the notice, what is indicated about Thomas Greens Farm's produce?

    (A) It is grown relatively near the market.
    (B) It is more healthful than other products.
    (C) It will be in stock starting next month.
    (D) It will be discounted for one week.

28. What will Shop Fresh Market probably receive on July 3?

    (A) Eggplants
    (B) Herbs
    (C) Corn
    (D) Lettuce

29. What does Mr. Nakra indicate in the order form?

    (A) He has a preference for how items are packaged.
    (B) Brussels sprouts sold particularly well last week.
    (C) He was disappointed by service from Kohn Trucking.
    (D) The herbs delivered last week were not fresh.

Stop! This is the end of the test.

正解一覧

PART 5	1 D	2 B	3 A	4 C	5 D	6 C	7 B	8 A	9 D	10 A	11 C
PART 6	12 C	13 D	14 D	15 C							
PART 7	16 A	17 B	18 A	19 B	20 D	21 C	22 A	23 B	24 D	25 B	26 B
	27 A	28 C	29 A								

1 Last year, the Fromley Company ------- an internship program for trade school students studying electrical technology.

(A) expressed
(B) specialized
(C) signaled
(D) established

昨年Fromley社は、電気技術を学んでいる職業訓練校の学生のためにインターンシッププログラムを創設しました。

(A) 〜を表した
(B) 〜を特殊化した
(C) 〜を示した
(D) 〜を創設した

正解 D 選択肢は全て動詞の過去形。空所には述語動詞として文意に合うものを選ぶ。目的語のan internship program を後に続けて意味が通る動詞は (D) established。internship「インターンシップ、職業訓練」、electrical「電気の」。
(A) (B) (C) いずれも文意に合わない。

2 See our media kit for facts and information ------- our line of lighting equipment.

(A) pending
(B) regarding
(C) among
(D) throughout

当社の照明器具の商品ラインに関する事実とデータについては、報道機関向けの資料一式をご覧ください。

(A) 〜の間
(B) 〜に関して
(C) 〜の中で
(D) 〜の至る所に

正解 B 選択肢は全て前置詞。空所に入る語は、our line of lighting equipment という名詞句を伴って、空所の前の名詞句 facts and information を後ろから修飾すると考えられる。文意に合う前置詞は (B) regarding。media kit「報道機関向けの資料一式」、line「商品ライン」、lighting「照明」、equipment「器具」。
(A) (C) (D) いずれも空所の前後にある名詞句の意味がつながらない。

3 The Lafayette Townhome Community is ------- located near a train line that leads to the region's largest shopping mall.

(A) conveniently
(B) consistently
(C) continually
(D) commonly

Lafayette都市住宅コミュニティーは、地域最大のショッピングモールに通じる鉄道路線の近くに利便性よく位置しています。

(A) 便よく
(B) 一貫して
(C) 絶えず
(D) 一般に

正解 **A** 選択肢は全て副詞。述語動詞 is located「位置している」を修飾する副詞として適切なものを選ぶ。空所に (A) を入れると、「利便性よく位置している」という立地を述べる意味になり、文意が通る。lead to ～「～につながる」、region「地域」。
(B) (C) (D) いずれも文意が通らない。

4 With its moderate climate and well-qualified workforce, Huntsville is a very ------- location for investors.

(A) offering
(B) proposing
(C) promising
(D) identifying

温暖な気候と非常に有能な労働力を有するために、ハンツビル市は投資家にとって非常に有望な場所です。

(A) 提供している
(B) 提案している
(C) 見込みがある
(D) 識別している

正解 **C** 動詞の現在分詞が並ぶ。Huntsville が主語、be 動詞の is が述語動詞で、名詞句 a very ------- location が補語の働きをしている。前半の「温暖な気候と有能な労働力を有するために」という副詞句と文意が合うのは、(C) の promising。動詞 promise「見込みがある」の現在分詞 promising が名詞 location「場所」を修飾している。moderate「(気候が) 温暖な」、climate「気候」、well-qualified「とても有能な、とても適任の」、workforce「労働力」、investor「投資家」。
(A) (B) (D) いずれも名詞 location を修飾する語として不適切。

5 Please review the repair estimate carefully ------- it has been received from the maintenance department.

(A) then
(B) while
(C) ever since
(D) as soon as

保守部から受け取ったらすぐに、修繕の見積書を念入りに見直してください。

(A) その時
(B) ～する間
(C) ～して以来ずっと
(D) ～したらすぐに

正解 **D** 空所の前後にある 2 つの節をつなぐものとして文意に合う語または句を選ぶ。空所の前の「修繕の見積書を念入りに見直してほしい」という指示の内容と、後の「それを保守部から受け取っている」という内容から、空所には (D) as soon as が適切。repair「修繕」、estimate「見積書」、maintenance「保守」、department「部署」。
(A) 副詞。文意が合わない。
(B)「同時」を表す接続詞。
(C) ever since は「それ以来ずっと」という副詞句または「～して以来ずっと」という接続詞の働きをするが、いずれも文意が合わない。

6 Over the last ten years, *Jamaica News* has built a ------- as one of the most reliable current-events programs in the Caribbean.

(A) privilege
(B) character
(C) reputation
(D) consequence

過去10年にわたり、『ジャマイカニュース』は、カリブ海地域で最も信頼できる時事番組の1つとしての名声を築いてきました。

(A) 特権
(B) 特徴
(C) 評判
(D) 結果

| 正解 **C** | 選択肢は全て名詞。述語動詞 has built の目的語の名詞を選ぶ。空所の後の「カリブ海地域で最も信頼できる時事番組の1つとしての」という意味を考慮すると、空所には (C) が適切。build a reputation as ～で「～としての名声を築く」という意味。reliable「信頼できる」、current-events「時事の」、the Caribbean「カリブ海地域」。
(A) (B) (D) いずれも文意に合わない。 |

---

7 The owner of Petal Airlines announced that ------- is negotiating a deal with Airplexi to buy new airplanes.

(A) him
(B) he
(C) his
(D) himself

Petal航空会社のオーナーは、新しい航空機の購入契約をAirplexi社と交渉中だと発表しました。

＊選択肢の訳は省略

| 正解 **B** | 選択肢は全て代名詞。空所は that 節の中にあり、直後に述語動詞 is negotiating があることから、空所には主語の働きをする語が入ると考えられる。よって、主格の (B) が適切。airline「航空会社」、announce「～を発表する」、negotiate「～を交渉する」、deal「契約、取引」。
(A) 目的格。
(C) 所有格。
(D) 再帰代名詞。 |

---

8 Rose's Bistro will close next month due to escalating operating -------.

(A) expenses
(B) functions
(C) customers
(D) occasions

Rose食堂は、高騰する運営費が原因で、来月閉店します。

(A) 費用
(B) 機能
(C) 顧客
(D) 機会

| 正解 **A** | 選択肢は全て名詞の複数形。escalating operating ------- は群前置詞 due to「～の原因で」の目的語に当たる名詞句だと考えられる。「食堂は閉店する予定だ」という前半の文意から、「高騰する運営費が原因で」という意味になる (A) が適切。escalate「次第に増加する」、operating「運営の、経営の」。
(B) (C) (D) いずれも閉店の原因として文意に合わない。 |

9 Ms. Mills has correctly predicted that sales would increase ------- as the company's radio advertisement continues to air.

(A) arguably
(B) reportedly
(C) productively
(D) incrementally

会社のラジオ広告が放送され続けるに従って売り上げは徐々に増えるだろうと、Millsさんは正しく予測していました。

(A) 議論の余地はあるが
(B) 報道によれば
(C) 生産的に
(D) 徐々に増加して

正解	**D**

選択肢は全て副詞。that 節内の述語動詞 would increase を修飾する副詞として適切なものを選ぶ。as 節の「会社のラジオ広告が放送され続けるに従って」という文意とのつながりを考えると、空所には (D) を入れて、「売り上げは徐々に増えるだろう」とするのが適切。correctly「正しく」、predict (that) 〜「〜と予測する」、advertisement「広告」、continue to *do*「〜し続ける」、air「放送される」。
(A) 主節の「Mills さんは正しく予測していた」という文意とつながらない。
(B) (C) 意味が通らない。

10 Tsutomu Motohashi holds the company record for the highest sales figures in a ------- year.

(A) single
(B) singled
(C) singles
(D) singling

Tsutomu Motohashiは単年度における社内の最高売上額記録を保持しています。

(A) ただ1つの
(B) 選ばれた
(C) 〜を選ぶ
(D) 〜を選んでいる

正解	**A**

選択肢には全て動詞 single「〜を選ぶ」が変化した形またはその派生語が並ぶ。空所の前には不定冠詞 a があり、後ろには名詞 year があるので、空所には名詞を修飾する形容詞が適切である。よって、形容詞の (A) single が正解。in a ------- year は直前の the highest sales figures「最高売上額」を後ろから修飾している。figure「(数字で示された) 額」。
(B) 過去分詞。分詞は名詞を修飾する働きがあるが、文意に合わない。
(C) 三人称単数現在形。
(D) 現在分詞。year を修飾しているとしても意味が通らない。

11 The last quarterly report showed that TNQ Electronics' earnings were ------- than anticipated.

(A) lowest
(B) lowering
(C) lower
(D) low

前回の四半期報告書は、TNQ電子社の収益が予想を下回っていたことを示しました。

(A) 最も低い
(B) 下がっている
(C) より低い
(D) 低い

正解	**C**

選択肢は形容詞 low「低い」、または動詞 lower「下がる」が変化した形。空所は that 節の一部で、空所の後に than anticipated「予想されたよりも」という比較を示す表現があるので、空所には形容詞の比較級の (C) を入れて、「収益は予想されたよりも低かった」とするのが適切。quarterly「四半期ごとの」、earnings「〈複数形で〉収益」、anticipate「〜を予想する」。
(A) 形容詞の最上級。
(B) 現在分詞。
(D) 形容詞。

Questions 12-15 refer to the following e-mail.

From: ben_zimmerman@avinmax.com
To: myrah_busby@kinweb.net
Date: May 4
Subject: Jollite bicycle tires

Dear Ms. Busby,

❶ Thank you for your message on May 2. Our records indicate that you ordered two Jollite bicycle tires (product JBT1783) through our Web site on April 27 and that they were scheduled to arrive on May 1. I am sorry to hear that you have not yet received ------- .
12.
Deliveries usually take no more than three or four days.

❷ ------- . Based on this information, your order should arrive on May 5. If you do not receive
13.
your order by then, please ------- us.
14.

❸ Again, I apologize for the delay. We rarely have problems with our delivery service. I want to emphasize that this situation is very ------- .
15.

Thank you,

Ben Zimmerman

Avinmax Sporting Goods

問題 12-15 は次の E メールに関するものです。

送信者：ben_zimmerman@avinmax.com
受信者：myrah_busby@kinweb.net
日付：5 月 4 日
件名：Jollite 自転車用タイヤ

Busby 様

5 月 2 日にお問い合わせいただきまして、ありがとうございます。当社の記録によりますと、お客さまは 4 月 27 日に当社ウェブサイトから Jollite 自転車用タイヤ（製品 JBT1783）を 2 本ご注文になり、それらは 5 月 1 日に届けられる予定でございました。まだそれらをお受け取りになっていないとのこと、申し訳ございません。通常、配送は 3 日ないし 4 日以内となっております。

*当社でお客さまのご注文を追跡できました。この情報に基づきますと、ご注文品は 5 月 5 日にお手元に届くはずです。それまでにご注文品をお受け取りいただけない場合は、当社までご連絡ください。

配送の遅延につきまして重ねておわびいたします。当社の配送サービスで問題が生じることはめったにございません。今回の状況は極めて異例であることを強調させていただきたく存じます。

どうぞよろしくお願いいたします。

Ben Zimmerman
Avinmax スポーツ用品社

*問題 13 の挿入文の訳

12
(A) it
(B) one
(C) them
(D) some

(A) それ
(B) 1つ
(C) それら
(D) 幾つか

正解 **C** 選択肢は全て代名詞。❶ 1～3 行目より、Busby さんは two Jollite bicycle tires「Jollite 自転車用タイヤを2本」注文したこと、商品は 5 月 1 日に届けられる予定だったことが分かる。空所を含む文は、注文品が届いていないことを謝罪する内容である。空所には注文品の two Jollite bicycle tires を指す代名詞を入れると文意に合う。複数名詞を受ける人称代名詞の (C) them が適切。
(A) 単数名詞を指す代名詞。
(B) 不特定の「タイヤ 1 本」を指すので不適切。
(D) 不特定の「幾つか」を表すので、不適切。

13
(A) We appreciate your feedback.
(B) Visit our Web site to view additional products.
(C) Unfortunately, this product is currently out of stock.
(D) We were able to track your order.

(A) お客さまからのご意見に感謝いたします。
(B) 当社ウェブサイトにアクセスして、さらに製品をご覧ください。
(C) あいにく、現在当製品は在庫切れです。
(D) 当社でお客さまのご注文を追跡できました。

正解 **D** 空所の直後の文で、Based on this information, your order should arrive on May 5.「この情報に基づくと、注文品は 5 月 5 日に手元に届くはずだ」とあるので、this information「この情報」が指し示す内容を空所に入れる。(D)を入れると、注文品の到着予定日を確認し、それを根拠に推定する文脈になる。track「～を追跡する」。
(A) appreciate「～に感謝する」、feedback「意見」。
(B) additional「追加の、付加的な」。
(C) out of stock「在庫切れで」。

14
(A) contacted
(B) to contact
(C) contacting
(D) contact

＊選択肢の訳は省略

正解 **D** 動詞 contact「～に連絡する」の適切な形を選ぶ。空所を含む文のカンマ以降は please から始まる丁寧な命令文である。動詞の原形の (D) contact が適切。
(A) 過去形または過去分詞。
(B) 不定詞。
(C) 現在分詞または動名詞。

15
(A) similar
(B) exciting
(C) unusual
(D) welcome

(A) 類似の
(B) 刺激的な
(C) 珍しい
(D) 歓迎される

正解 **C** 選択肢は全て形容詞。that 節内の主語 this situation を説明する補語として、文意に合うものを選ぶ。空所を含む文の直前の ❸ 1 行目に、We rarely have problems with our delivery service.「当社の配送サービスで問題が生じることはめったにない」とあるので、(C) unusual「珍しい」を入れると、今回の商品の配送遅延が珍しいと強調する内容になり、文意が通る。
(A) 遅延がめったにないことを強調する文意に合わない。
(B) (D) E メールでは配送の遅延を謝罪しているので、文意に合わない。

語 注

tire　タイヤ
❶ record　記録　indicate (that) ～　～であることを示す　order　～を注文する　product　製品、商品
be scheduled to *do*　～する予定である　no more than ～　わずか～、たった～
❷ based on ～　～に基づいて　order　注文、注文品
❸ apologize for ～　～のことでわびる　delay　遅延　rarely　めったに～ない
emphasize (that) ～　～であることを強調する　situation　状況　sporting goods　スポーツ用品

Questions 16-17 refer to the following Web page.

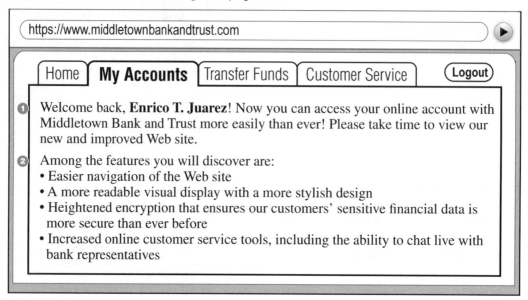

問題16-17は次のウェブページに関するものです。

https://www.middletownbankandtrust.com

ホーム　　　　**私の口座**　　　　送金　　　　お客さまサービス　　　　　　　　ログアウト

お帰りなさい、**Enrico T. Juarez**様！ お客さまのMiddletown信託銀行のオンライン口座に、これまでより簡単にアクセスできるようになりました！ どうぞお時間を取って、当行の改良された新しいウェブサイトをご覧になってください。

ご確認いただける特徴の中には、以下のものがございます：
・より分かりやすくなったウェブサイトのナビゲーション
・より洗練されたデザインで視認性が良くなった画像表示
・これまで以上にお客さまの機密財務データの安全性を保証する、強化された暗号技術
・銀行の担当者とのライブチャット機能を含め、より豊富になったオンラインの顧客サービスツール

16 Who most likely is Mr. Juarez?

    (A) A bank customer

    (B) A bank executive

    (C) A bank consultant

    (D) A designer of the bank Web site

Juarez さんは誰だと考えられますか。

    (A) 銀行の顧客

    (B) 銀行の重役

    (C) 銀行の顧問

    (D) 銀行のウェブサイトのデザイナー

正解 A ウェブページは "My Accounts" のページタブが選択されており、❶の冒頭で「お帰りなさい、Enrico T. Juarez 様！」とメッセージが始まっていて、1〜2行目で「あなたの Middletown 信託銀行のオンライン口座に、これまでより簡単にアクセスできるようになった」とある。よって、Juarez さんは銀行の自分のオンライン口座にアクセスしている顧客だと考えられる。(A) が正解。
(B) executive「重役」。
(C) consultant「顧問、コンサルタント」。
(D) ❷の3行目にデザインについての記載があるが、Juarez さんがデザインしたという記載はない。

---

17 What is NOT mentioned as a feature of the new Web site?

    (A) Enhanced visual design

    (B) A listing of all service fees

    (C) Greater security of information

    (D) The addition of customer service options

新しいウェブサイトの特徴として述べられていないことは何ですか。

    (A) 向上した視覚デザイン

    (B) 全ての手数料の一覧表

    (C) 情報のより優れた安全性

    (D) 顧客サービスの選択肢の追加

正解 B ウェブサイトの機能の詳細については❷に記載がある。(A) は3行目の「より洗練されたデザインで視認性が良くなった画像表示」に、(C) は4〜5行目の「これまで以上にあなたの機密財務データの安全性を保証する、強化された暗号技術」に、(D) は6〜7行目の「より豊富になったオンラインの顧客サービスツール」にそれぞれ記載がある。手数料についての記載はないので、(B) が正解。listing「一覧表、一覧表を作成すること」。
(A) enhance「〜を向上させる」。
(C) security「安全性」。
(D) addition「追加」、option「選択肢」。

Mini Test 4

語 注

account （銀行の）口座　　transfer　〜（金）を振り替える　　fund　資金

❶ online　オンラインの、インターネット上の　　bank and trust　信託銀行　　than ever　以前より増して
improve　〜を改良する

❷ feature　特徴　　navigation　ナビゲーション　★ウェブサイト上のメニューや主要コンテンツを記したリンク一覧のこと
readable　読みやすい、可読性の高い　　visual　視覚の　　display　表示、並べて見せること
stylish　洗練された、おしゃれな　　heighten　〜を強める、〜を高める　　encryption　暗号化　　ensure　〜を保証する
sensitive　機密の　　financial　財務の　　secure　安全な　　increase　〜を増やす　　ability　できること、能力
chat　（インターネット上で）チャットをする、おしゃべりをする　　live　ライブで、リアルタイムで
representative　担当者

Questions 18-20 refer to the following article.

Parking Survey Awaited

❶ Many Sumrita residents, businesses, and visitors have expressed concerns to town officials that there are not enough parking spaces. — [1] —. Some have called for construction of a second parking garage in the next two years.

❷ With a data-collection project scheduled to begin on Tuesday, led by Paston Associates of Turnbridge, town officials will soon learn the extent of the parking problem on a typical weekday, during the evening, and at peak times when events are taking place in the center of town. — [2] —. When it is completed, the study will provide an updated inventory of all public and private parking spaces in the area and their typical rates of use. — [3] —.

❸ "Anecdotally people say that demand has increased with the four new businesses and the residential projects we've seen in the last five years," said Planning Director Akash Singh. — [4] —.

問題18-20は次の記事に関するものです。

待たれる駐車場の調査

多くのSumrita市の住人、企業、来訪者が、十分な駐車スペースがないという懸念を、町の当局者たちへ表してきた。その中には、今後2年のうちに2棟目の駐車場ビルを建設するよう求めている人もいる。

火曜日に始まる予定のデータ収集プロジェクトは、Turnbridge地区のPaston Associates社が主導するが、当局者はそれをもって、通常の平日と夜間時、そして町の中心部でイベントが行われるピーク時の駐車場問題がどの程度のものなのかを、間もなく知ることになるだろう。それが完了する時には、その調査によって、地域の全ての官民駐車スペースとそれらの典型的な利用率に関する最新の一覧表が提供されることになるだろう。

「この5年間にあった4社の新規事業と住宅事業が原因で需要が増加した、と人々が言っていると聞きます」と、都市計画部長のAkash Singhは述べた。*「しかし、もう1カ所の高額な駐車場ビルを検討する前に、私たちには確かなデータが必要です」。

*問題20の挿入文の訳

語注

survey 調査　await ～を待つ
❶ resident 住人、居住者　business 企業、会社　express ～を表す、～を示す　concern 懸念、懸念点　official 当局者、役人　call for ～ ～を(声を上げて)求める　construction 建設　parking garage 駐車場ビル、パーキングビル
❷ collection 収集　(be) scheduled to do ～する予定で(ある)　lead ～を主導する　extent 程度、範囲　typical 典型的な　peak time ピーク時　take place 行われる　complete ～を完了する　study 調査、研究　provide ～を提供する　update ～を最新のものにする　inventory 一覧表、棚卸表　public 公共の　private 民間の　rate 比率、割合
❸ anecdotally 聞いた話に基づいて　demand 需要　residential 住宅地区の　planning 都市計画　director 部長、責任者

18 How many parking garages are currently in Sumrita?

(A) One
(B) Two
(C) Four
(D) Five

現在、Sumrita市には何棟の駐車場ビルがありますか。

(A) 1棟
(B) 2棟
(C) 4棟
(D) 5棟

<table>
<tr><td>正解</td><td>A</td><td>Sumrita 市に十分な駐車スペースがないという住民たちからの懸念について、❶の 4 〜 6 行目で「その中には、今後 2 年のうちに 2 棟目の駐車場ビルを建設するよう求めている人もいる」と書かれているので、現在は 1 棟の parking garage「駐車場ビル」しかないことが分かる。よって、(A) が正解。parking garage は建物全体が駐車場になっている専用の立体駐車場のことである。currently「現在のところ」。</td></tr>
</table>

19 What does the article indicate about the survey?

(A) It will study the demand for parking in three local neighborhoods.
(B) It will measure the demand for parking at various times.
(C) It will be paid for by Paston Associates of Turnbridge.
(D) It will be conducted by Sumrita's planning director.

記事は、調査について何を示していますか。

(A) 地元の 3 つの地区の駐車場に対する需要を調査する。
(B) さまざまな時間帯の駐車場に対する需要を測定する。
(C) Turnbridge 地区の Paston Associates 社によって、費用が支払われる。
(D) Sumrita 市の都市計画部長によって実施される。

<table>
<tr><td>正解</td><td>B</td><td>❷の 1 〜 7 行目に「火曜日に始まる予定のデータ収集プロジェクトは、Turnbridge 地区の Paston Associates 社が主導するが、当局者はそれをもって、通常の平日と夜間時、そして町の中心部でイベントが行われるピーク時の駐車場問題がどの程度のものなのかを、間もなく知ることになるだろう」とある。(B) が正解。measure「〜を測定する」。
(A) 3 つの地区については言及されていない。neighborhood「地区、地域」。
(C) Paston Associates 社は調査を主導する会社。費用負担についての言及はない。
(D) ❸ 1 〜 4 行目に都市計画部長の発言があるが、調査の実施をする人物かどうかは不明。conduct「〜を実施する」。</td></tr>
</table>

20 In which of the positions marked [1], [2], [3], and [4] does the following sentence best belong?

"But we need hard data before we can consider another costly parking garage."

(A) [1]
(B) [2]
(C) [3]
(D) [4]

[1]、[2]、[3]、[4]と記載された箇所のうち、次の文が入るのに最もふさわしいのはどれですか。

「しかし、もう 1 カ所の高額な駐車場ビルを検討する前に、私たちには確かなデータが必要です」

(A) [1]
(B) [2]
(C) [3]
(D) [4]

<table>
<tr><td>正解</td><td>D</td><td>挿入文の文頭の But「しかし」から、空所の前文と挿入文は対比的な内容を示すと考えられる。[4] に挿入文を入れると、都市計画部長 Singh さんの発言内容で、駐車スペースの需要が増加した原因について人々の噂に言及した後、「しかし、もう 1 カ所の高額な駐車場ビルを検討する前に、私たちには確かなデータが必要だ」と自身の考えを述べることになり、流れとして自然。よって、(D) が正解。hard「確かな」、consider「〜を検討する」、costly「費用のかかる」。</td></tr>
</table>

Questions 21-24 refer to the following article.

Small-Business Expert Coming to São Paulo

❶ SÃO PAULO (May 19)—Angelo Azevedo, dubbed the "small-business expert" by *The Los Angeles Chronicle*, will be the keynote speaker at the first annual São Paulo Small Business Expo (SPSBE). The Expo will take place at the São Paulo Event Center from June 3 to June 5. More than 2,000 small-business entrepreneurs will attend workshops and showcase their businesses at booths, where visitors can collect information and ask questions.

❷ According to an SPSBE press release, Mr. Azevedo will highlight many of the ideas from his best-selling book *Keys to Startup Success*, published just last year. Mr. Azevedo believes that there are several key decisions that must be made before launching into any new business scheme. "You can't go into it with the idea of creating a product you want to sell," Mr.

Azevedo writes in his book. "You have to create a product people want to buy. This is rule number one. And it is absolutely essential to get this right if you want your business to succeed."

❸ Mr. Azevedo is the owner of several successful businesses in Los Angeles, where he has lived for the past ten years. "I'm originally from São Paulo," Mr. Azevedo said. "So I wanted to help the community where I got my start in any way I could, which is why I accepted the invitation to participate in the Expo. There's an outstanding opportunity there for small-business owners. Following these simple but important guidelines has worked well for me and for many other successful small-business owners."

❹ Tickets to the Expo are R$100. They can be purchased through the Expo's Web site at www.saopauloexpo.com/br.

問題21-24は次の記事に関するものです。

中小企業の専門家がサンパウロに来訪

サンパウロ（5 月 19 日）──『ロサンゼルス・クロニクル』紙で「中小企業の専門家」との異名を取る Angelo Azevedo 氏が、第 1 回・年次サンパウロ中小企業博覧会（SPSBE）の基調講演者になる予定だ。博覧会は、サンパウロイベントセンターで、6 月 3 日から 6 月 5 日まで行われる。2,000 社を超える中小企業の起業家たちがワークショップに参加したり、自らの事業をブースで展示したりする予定で、来訪者はその場で情報収集や質問をすることができる。

　SPSBE の報道発表によると、Azevedo 氏は、昨年出版されたばかりの自身のベストセラー本『起業の成功の秘訣』から多くのアイデアを取り上げて着目させる予定だ。Azevedo 氏は、新しい事業計画を始める前には、なされるべき重要な決断が幾つかあるという信念を持っている。「自分が売りたいと思う製品を作ろうという考えで事業を始めてはいけない」と Azevedo 氏は

著書の中で書いている。「人々が買いたいと思うような製品を作る必要がある。これが、第 1 の法則である。そして、事業を成功させたいのなら、このことを正しく理解することが必要不可欠である」。

　Azevedo 氏は、ロサンゼルスに成功した企業を数社持つオーナーであり、氏はここ 10 年間その地で暮らしてきた。「私はもともとサンパウロの出身です」と Azevedo 氏は言った。「ですから、自分が世に出たその地域社会を、どのような形であれ助けたいと思いました。それが博覧会参加の招待をお受けした理由です。そこには、中小企業のオーナーにとって目覚ましい機会があります。これらの単純だが重要な指針に従うことは、私やその他多くの成功した中小企業のオーナーたちには、非常にうまくいきました」。

　博覧会のチケットは、100 レアル。同博覧会のウェブサイト www.saopauloexpo.com/br を通じて購入できる。

語 注

small-business　中小企業の　　expert　専門家

❶ dub ～ …　～を…と称する、～に…というあだ名を付ける　　chronicle　～新聞　★新聞の名前にしばしば付けられる
keynote speaker　基調講演者　　annual　年次の　　expo　博覧会　　entrepreneur　起業家
attend　～に参加する、～に出席する　　showcase　～を披露する　　booth　ブース、小部屋　　collect　～を収集する

❷ press release　報道発表　　highlight　～を強調する　　startup　立ち上げの、新進の
key　〈名詞〉秘訣　〈形容詞〉重要な　　decision　決定　　launch into ～　～を始める、～に乗り出す　　scheme　計画
product　製品　　absolutely　絶対的に　　essential　必須の　　get ～ right　～を正しく理解する

❸ successful　成功した　　originally　もともとは　　community　地域社会　　in any way I could　どのような形でも
participate in ～　～に参加する　　outstanding　目覚ましい、傑出した　　guideline　指針　　work　作用する

❹ R$　レアル　★ブラジルの通貨　　purchase　～を購入する

21 What is the article mainly about?

記事は主に何についてのものですか。

(A) The opening of a new business
(B) New trends in marketing
(C) A business leader's participation in an event
(D) The benefits of running a small business

(A) 新規事業の創業
(B) マーケティングの新たな潮流
(C) ある企業指導者のイベントへの参加
(D) 中小企業を経営することの利点

 正解 C ❶の1～5行目に「『ロサンゼルス・クロニクル』紙で『中小企業の専門家』との異名を取る Angelo Azevedo 氏が、第1回・年次サンパウロ中小企業博覧会 (SPSBE) の基調講演者になる予定だ」とあり、❷と❸では、Azevedo さんの著書や彼の発言が紹介されている。よって、(C) が正解。leader「指導者」。
(B) trend「潮流、傾向」、marketing「マーケティング」。　(D) benefit「利点」、run「～を運営する」。

---

22 According to the article, what has Mr. Azevedo recently done?

記事によると、Azevedo さんは最近何をしましたか。

(A) He wrote a book.
(B) He presented an award.
(C) He led a workshop.
(D) He traveled to São Paulo.

(A) 本を執筆した。
(B) 賞を贈呈した。
(C) ワークショップを指導した。
(D) サンパウロに旅行した。

正解 A ❷の1～4行目に昨年出版された Azevedo さんの本についての説明があるので、Azevedo さんは最近本を執筆したと分かる。(A) が正解。
(B) present「～を贈る」、award「賞」。　(C) lead「～を指導する」。

---

23 What does Mr. Azevedo say is the most important consideration for new entrepreneurs?

Azevedo さんは、新しい起業家たちが考慮すべき最も重要なことは何だと言っていますか。

(A) Marketing a product aggressively
(B) Developing a product that is attractive to consumers
(C) Manufacturing a product in a cost-effective way
(D) Creating a product that the business owner feels passionate about

(A) 製品を精力的に宣伝すること。
(B) 消費者にとって魅力的な製品を開発すること。
(C) 費用対効果の高い方法で製品を製造すること。
(D) 企業のオーナーが夢中になれる製品を作ること。

正解 B Azevedo さんは❷の 10～12 行目で「人々が買いたいと思うような製品を作る必要がある。これが、第1の法則である」と述べている。よって、a product people want to buy を a product that is attractive to consumers と表した (B) が正解。consideration「考慮すべきこと」。attractive「魅力的な」、consumer「消費者」。
(A) market「～を宣伝する」、aggressively「精力的に、積極的に」。　(C) cost-effective「費用対効果の高い」。

---

24 Why did Mr. Azevedo decide to participate in the Expo?

Azevedo さんはなぜ博覧会に参加することに決めたのですか。

(A) He is doing research for a newspaper article.
(B) He would like to recruit some employees.
(C) He is looking for ways to increase sales.
(D) He wants to support entrepreneurs in his hometown.

(A) 新聞記事のために調査をしている。
(B) 何人かの従業員を採用したい。
(C) 売り上げを増やす方法を探している。
(D) 故郷の起業家たちを支援したい。

正解 D ❸の3～5行目より、Azevedo さんはサンパウロ出身だと分かる。同5～8行目に Azevedo さんの「だから、自分が世に出たその地域社会を、どのような形であれ助けたいと思った。それが博覧会参加の招待を受けた理由だ」という発言がある。また、❸の8～10 行目に「そこには、中小企業のオーナーにとって目覚ましい機会がある」と書かれている。よって、(D) が正解。hometown「故郷、出身地」。
(A) research「調査」。　(B) recruit「～を採用する」。　(C) sales「〈複数形で〉売り上げ、売上高」。

Questions 25-29 refer to the following e-mail, notice, and order form.

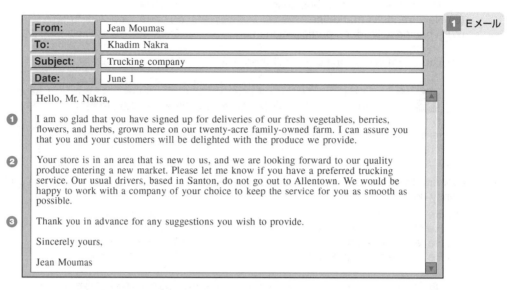

From:	Jean Moumas
To:	Khadim Nakra
Subject:	Trucking company
Date:	June 1

1 Eメール

Hello, Mr. Nakra,

I am so glad that you have signed up for deliveries of our fresh vegetables, berries, flowers, and herbs, grown here on our twenty-acre family-owned farm. I can assure you that you and your customers will be delighted with the produce we provide.

Your store is in an area that is new to us, and we are looking forward to our quality produce entering a new market. Please let me know if you have a preferred trucking service. Our usual drivers, based in Santon, do not go out to Allentown. We would be happy to work with a company of your choice to keep the service for you as smooth as possible.

Thank you in advance for any suggestions you wish to provide.

Sincerely yours,

Jean Moumas

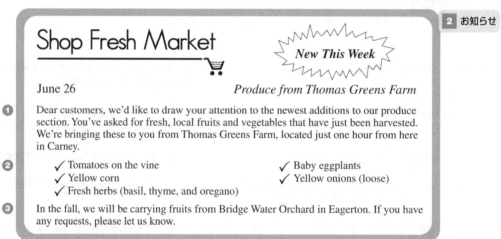

2 お知らせ

Shop Fresh Market

New This Week

June 26

Produce from Thomas Greens Farm

Dear customers, we'd like to draw your attention to the newest additions to our produce section. You've asked for fresh, local fruits and vegetables that have just been harvested. We're bringing these to you from Thomas Greens Farm, located just one hour from here in Carney.

✓ Tomatoes on the vine
✓ Yellow corn
✓ Fresh herbs (basil, thyme, and oregano)

✓ Baby eggplants
✓ Yellow onions (loose)

In the fall, we will be carrying fruits from Bridge Water Orchard in Eagerton. If you have any requests, please let us know.

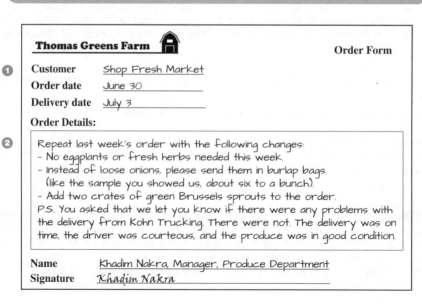

3 注文用紙

Thomas Greens Farm

Order Form

Customer — Shop Fresh Market
Order date — June 30
Delivery date — July 3

Order Details:

Repeat last week's order with the following changes:
- No eggplants or fresh herbs needed this week.
- Instead of loose onions, please send them in burlap bags.
  (like the sample you showed us, about six to a bunch).
- Add two crates of green Brussels sprouts to the order.
P.S. You asked that we let you know if there were any problems with the delivery from Kohn Trucking. There were not. The delivery was on time, the driver was courteous, and the produce was in good condition.

Name — Khadim Nakra, Manager, Produce Department
Signature — *Khadim Nakra*

問題25-29は次のEメール、お知らせ、注文用紙に関するものです。

送信者：Jean Moumas
受信者：Khadim Nakra
件名：　トラック運送会社
日付：　6月1日

こんにちは、Nakra様

ここ、20エーカーの家族経営の当農園で栽培された新鮮な野菜、ベリー類、花、ハーブの配達にご登録いただき、大変うれしく思っております。当農園が提供する農作物が、貴店や貴店のお客さまにご満足いただけることをお約束いたします。

貴店は当農園にとって新規エリアのため、当農園の良質の農作物が新たな市場に参入することを楽しみにしております。ご希望のトラック運送サービスがございましたら、お知らせください。当農園が通常依頼する運転手たちはSantonが拠点で、Allentownまでは運送いたしません。当農園は、貴店へのサービスを可能な限り円滑に保つため、貴店がお選びになる企業と喜んでお取引させていただきます。

貴店よりどんなご提案でも頂ければ幸いです。

敬具

Jean Moumas

生鮮ショップマーケット

今週新登場
Thomas Greens農園産の農作物

6月26日

お客さまへ、当店の農産物部門に加わった最新商品にぜひご注目ください。皆さまから、収穫したての新鮮な地元産の果物や野菜を求める声を頂いておりました。Carneyの、ここからわずか1時間の場所に位置するThomas Greens農園から、これらを皆さまにお届けいたします。

✓つる付きトマト	✓ベビーナス
✓黄色トウモロコシ	✓黄色タマネギ（ばら売り）
✓フレッシュハーブ（バジル、タイム、オレガノ）	

秋には、EagertonにあるBridge Water果樹園の果物をお届けする予定です。もし何かご要望があれば、当店までお知らせください。

Thomas Greens農園　　　　　　　　　　　　　　　　　　　　　　　　　　注文用紙

顧客名	生鮮ショップマーケット
注文日	6月30日
配達日	7月3日

注文詳細：
以下の変更を加えて、先週の注文と同じものをお願いします：
- 今週はナスとフレッシュハーブは不要です。
- ばらではなく、麻袋入りのタマネギを送ってください。
  （見せていただいた見本のように、1袋に6個程度のもの）
- 注文に、緑芽キャベツ2箱を追加します。

追伸　Kohnトラック運送会社の配達について何か問題があったら知らせてほしいと貴社からご依頼されていました。問題はございません。配達は時間通りで、運転手は礼儀正しく、農作物は良い状態でした。

氏名	Khadim Nakra、部長、農産物部門
署名	Khadim Nakra

25 Why did Ms. Moumas send the e-mail?

(A) To advertise new products
(B) To ask for a recommendation
(C) To request a delivery estimate
(D) To complain about a policy change

Moumas さんはなぜ E メールを送ったのですか。

(A) 新しい生産品を宣伝するため。
(B) 推薦を依頼するため。
(C) 配達の見積書を依頼するため。
(D) 方針の変更に苦情を言うため。

正解 B ❶の E メールの件名は「トラック運送会社」である。Moumas さんは Nakra さんが農作物の配達に登録したことに謝意を表した後、同❷ 2 ～ 3 行目で「希望のトラック運送サービスがあったら、知らせてほしい」、同 3 ～ 5 行目で「当農園は、貴店へのサービスを可能な限り円滑に保つため、貴店が選ぶ企業と喜んで取引する」と述べている。よって、この E メールの目的は、運送会社の推薦を求めることだと分かる。(B) が正解。ask for ～「～を求める」、recommendation「推薦」。
(A) 新しい生産品に関する言及はない。advertise「～を宣伝する」、product「生産物」。
(C) estimate「見積書」。
(D) complain about ～「～について苦情を言う」、policy「方針」。

26 Where is Shop Fresh Market probably located?

(A) In Santon
(B) In Allentown
(C) In Carney
(D) In Eagerton

生鮮ショップマーケット社はどこにあると考えられますか。

(A) Santon
(B) Allentown
(C) Carney
(D) Eagerton

正解 B 農作物のトラック運送サービスについて、Moumas さんが❶の❷ 2 ～ 3 行目で「希望のトラック運送サービスがあったら、知らせてほしい。当農園が通常依頼する運転手たちは Santon が拠点で、Allentown までは運送しない」と Nakra さんに対して述べていることから、Nakra さんの会社は Allentown にあると推測できる。一方、❸の注文用紙より、Nakra さんは生鮮ショップマーケット社の農産物部門の部長だと分かる。よって、生鮮ショップマーケット社の所在地は Allentown だと考えられる。(B) が正解。
(A) ❶の❷ 3 行目より、Thomas Greens 農園が普段使っているトラック運転手たちの拠点。
(C) ❷の❶ 3 ～ 4 行目より、Thomas Greens 農園がある場所。
(D) ❷の❸ 1 行目より、Bridge Water 果樹園がある場所。

27 In the notice, what is indicated about Thomas Greens Farm's produce?

(A) It is grown relatively near the market.
(B) It is more healthful than other products.
(C) It will be in stock starting next month.
(D) It will be discounted for one week.

お知らせの中で、Thomas Greens 農園の農作物について何が示されていますか。

(A) マーケットの比較的近くで栽培されている。
(B) 他の商品よりも衛生的である。
(C) 来月から仕入れられる。
(D) 1 週間、割引される。

正解 A 地元産の果物や野菜について、❷のお知らせの❶ 3 ～ 4 行目に「Carney の、ここからわずか 1 時間の場所に位置する Thomas Greens 農園から、これらを皆に届ける」とある。「ここ」とは生鮮ショップマーケット社を指すことから、Thomas Greens 農園は生鮮ショップマーケット社の比較的近くにあると分かる。(A) が正解。grow「～を栽培する」、relatively「比較的に」。
(B) 他の商品とは比較されていない。healthful「衛生的な」。
(C) ❷の 6 月 26 日付けのお知らせの中に「今週新登場」とあるので、少なくとも 6 月中に仕入れされている。
(D) 割引についての言及はない。discount「～を値引きする」。

28 What will Shop Fresh Market probably receive on July 3?

(A) Eggplants
(B) Herbs
(C) Corn
(D) Lettuce

生鮮ショップマーケット社は7月3日に何を受け取ると考えられますか。

(A) ナス
(B) ハーブ
(C) トウモロコシ
(D) レタス

正解 C ❷❷に生鮮ショップマーケット社が仕入れている農作物として、トウモロコシ、フレッシュハーブ、ベビーナスの記載があるが、7月3日配達予定の❸の注文用紙には、「以下の変更を加えて、先週の注文と同じものをお願いする」と言及した後、❷2行目に「今週はナスとフレッシュハーブは不要だ」とある。よって、(A) Eggplants と (B) Herbs は注文内容から除外されている。このことから、先週も注文され、かつ❸の注文用紙で除外されていない (C) Corn が7月3日に受け取る農作物だと推測できる。

Mini
Test
4

29 What does Mr. Nakra indicate in the order form?

(A) He has a preference for how items are packaged.
(B) Brussels sprouts sold particularly well last week.
(C) He was disappointed by service from Kohn Trucking.
(D) The herbs delivered last week were not fresh.

注文用紙の中でNakraさんは何を示していますか。

(A) 品物の包装の方法に好みがある。
(B) 先週は芽キャベツが特によく売れた。
(C) Kohnトラック運送会社のサービスにがっかりした。
(D) 先週配達されたハーブは新鮮ではなかった。

正解 A ❸の注文用紙の❷3〜4行目に「ばらではなく、麻袋入りのタマネギを送ってほしい。（見せてもらった見本のように、1袋に6個程度のもの）」とあるので、Nakraさんはタマネギの包装の方法について具体的な要望があると分かる。よって (A) が正解。preference「好み」、item「品物」、package「〜を包装する」。
(B) ❸の❷5行目より、芽キャベツ2箱を追加で注文しているが、先週の売れ行きに関する記載はない。particularly「特に」。
(C) ❸の❷の7行目より、運送会社には「問題はなかった」とある。disappoint「〜をがっかりさせる、〜を失望させる」。
(D) 先週届いた農作物について、❸の❷の7〜8行目に「農作物は良い状態だった」とある。

語 注

1 Eメール trucking　トラック運送
  ❶ sign up for 〜　〜に名前を登録する　　delivery　配達、配送　　berry　ベリー　　herb　ハーブ
    acre　（面積単位の）エーカー　★1エーカーは約4,000平方メートル
    assure 〜 (that) …　〜に…（であること）を保証する　　be delighted with 〜　〜に非常に満足する
    produce　農作物、農産物　　provide　〜を提供する
  ❷ look forward to 〜　〜を楽しみにする　　quality　高品質の　　enter　〜に入る　　preferred　好ましい
    usual　通常の、いつもの　　choice　選択　　smooth　円滑な、スムーズな
  ❸ in advance　前もって　　suggestion　提案
2 お知らせ ❶ attention　注意　　addition　加わったもの　　section　部門　　local　地元産の　　harvest　〜を収穫する
  ❷ vine　（植物の）つる　　loose　ばらの　　fresh　新鮮な、（乾燥ではなく）生の　　basil　バジル
    thyme　タイム　　oregano　オレガノ
  ❸ request　要望
3 注文用紙 ❷ instead of 〜　〜ではなく　　burlap　目の粗い麻布　　bunch　束、山　　crate　木箱
    Brussels sprout　芽キャベツ　　on time　時間通りに　　courteous　礼儀正しい

Mini Test 結果記入シート

下の説明を参考に、各回のミニテストの受験にかかった時間と結果を記録に残しましょう。

1. 目安の解答時間（21 分）以内に全問解答することを目標に、タイマーなどで時間を計りながら <u>最後の問題まで</u>受験する。その後、実際にかかった時間を下の表の❶に記入。
2. 「解答・解説」で正誤を確認し、正解した問題数を下の表の❷に記入する。
3. 間違った問題については、復習ユニットに戻っておさらいする（表内の「復習ユニット」の欄を参照のこと。例えば「U1」は、Step 1 の Unit 1 を示す）。

かかった時間を記入

	Mini Test 1			Mini Test 2			Mini Test 3			Mini Test 4	
❶	:			:			:			:	
問題番号	正誤(○×)	復習ユニット	問題番号	正誤(○×)	復習ユニット	問題番号	正誤(○×)	復習ユニット	問題番号	正誤(○×)	復習ユニット
1		U1	1		U6	1		U1	1		U2
2		U6	2		U1	2		U2	2		U4
3		U2	3		U2-U3	3		U2	3		U3
4		U4	4		U3	4		U6	4		U5
5		U6	5		U1	5		U1	5		U7
6		U1	6		U2	6		U3、U7	6		U6
7		U2	7		U7	7		U4	7		U6
8		U7	8		U2	8		U1	8		U6
9		U3	9		U3	9		U3	9		U3
10		U6	10		U6	10		U7	10		U1
11		U5	11		U2	11		U3	11		U3
		/11			/11			/11			/11
12			12			12			12		
13		U8	13		U10	13		U9	13		U10
14			14			14			14		
15			15			15			15		
		/4			/4			/4			/4
16		U11-U13	16		U11-U13	16		U11-U13	16		U11-U13
17			17			17			17		
18			18			18			18		
19		U15-U16	19		U15-U16	19		U15-U16	19		U15-U16
20			20			20			20		
21			21			21			21		
22		U14	22		U15-U16	22		U15-U16	22		U15-U16
23			23			23			23		
24			24			24			24		
25			25			25			25		
26			26			26			26		
27		U17-U20	27		U17-U20	27		U17-U20	27		U17-U20
28			28			28			28		
29			29			29			29		
		/14			/14			/14			/14
❷		/29			/29			/29			/29

○の付いた正答数を集計

下の折れ線グラフの見本を参考に、❶と❷の数値を基に自身の成長の記録を可視化しましょう。

❶ かかった時間の成長記録

❷ 正答数の成長記録

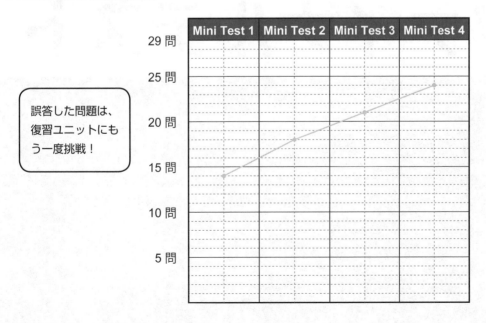

STEP

3

ファイナルテスト

STEP 3ではいよいよリーディングセクション1回分（100問、75分間）に挑戦します。落ち着いた環境を用意し、本番同様に制限時間の中で、自力でどこまで解答できるかをぜひ試してください。

Final Test

実際のテストでは問題用紙の裏側に、以下のようなテスト全体についての指示が印刷されています。
この指示を念頭に置いてテストに取り組みましょう。

General Directions

This test is designed to measure your English language ability. The test is divided into two sections: Listening and Reading.

You must mark all of your answers on the separate answer sheet. For each question, you should select the best answer from the answer choices given. Then, on your answer sheet, you should find the number of the question and fill in the space that corresponds to the letter of the answer that you have selected. If you decide to change an answer, completely erase your old answer and then mark your new answer.

全体についての指示

このテストはあなたの英語言語能力を測定するよう設計されています。テストはリスニングとリーディングという 2 つのセクションに分けられています。

答えは全て別紙の解答用紙にマークしてください。それぞれの設問について、与えられた選択肢から最も適切な答えを選びます。そして解答用紙の該当する問題番号において、選択した答えを塗りつぶしてください。修正する場合は、元の答えを完全に消してから新しい答えをマークしてください。

＊ファイナルテストは実際のテストと同じく、問題番号 101 番から始まります。

READING TEST

In the Reading test, you will read a variety of texts and answer several different types of reading comprehension questions. The entire Reading test will last 75 minutes. There are three parts, and directions are given for each part. You are encouraged to answer as many questions as possible within the time allowed.

You must mark your answers on the separate answer sheet. Do not write your answers in your test book.

PART 5

Directions: A word or phrase is missing in each of the sentences below. Four answer choices are given below each sentence. Select the best answer to complete the sentence. Then mark the letter (A), (B), (C), or (D) on your answer sheet.

101. Gelden Petrochemical exports products to customers ------- the world.

(A) all
(B) many
(C) around
(D) except

102. Mr. Daoud is expected to ------- at the conference center in Dubai at 11:00 A.M.

(A) get
(B) arrive
(C) come
(D) travel

103. The software is easy to learn and ------- increases employee productivity.

(A) great
(B) greater
(C) greatly
(D) greatness

104. The budget will be made ------- on June 9 after a final audit by the finance committee.

(A) positive
(B) ultimate
(C) official
(D) responsible

105. Eun-Yi Roh ------- to assistant deputy attorney after last week's performance review.

(A) is promoting
(B) was promoted
(C) promotes
(D) to promote

106. Mr. Ling has ------- requested funding for the airport terminal improvements.

(A) ever
(B) shortly
(C) yet
(D) already

107. The ------- course on coaching is taught by Lee Wallis of the Peyton Soccer Club.

(A) introducer
(B) introduce
(C) introducing
(D) introductory

108. Most of the morning ------- will take place on the second floor, near the conference registration desk.

(A) sessions
(B) conditions
(C) requests
(D) speakers

109. Mr. Tanaka has decided to employ a payroll service because it is becoming too difficult to manage the payroll accounts -------.

(A) him
(B) he
(C) his
(D) himself

110. Filmmakers must obtain written consent ------- use a corporate logo.

(A) in contrast to
(B) in order to
(C) as a result
(D) as well

111. To satisfy different tastes, we strive to offer a ------- assortment of brands.

(A) broad
(B) broadly
(C) broaden
(D) broadness

112. To avoid unexpected -------, ask the hotel desk clerk to explain which services are complimentary.

(A) breaks
(B) returns
(C) charges
(D) departures

113. For ------- residents who use street parking, permits are available at city hall.

(A) them
(B) those
(C) when
(D) each

114. Although they usually leave at 6:00 P.M., the employees are ------- in the store preparing for tomorrow's big event.

(A) almost
(B) less
(C) still
(D) easily

115. Renters are most excited about the ------- kitchens in the upgraded units.

(A) renovated
(B) renovation
(C) renovate
(D) renovating

116. While at Varner Bank, Ms. Uehara had the opportunity to work ------- many influential figures in finance.

(A) throughout
(B) where
(C) with
(D) despite

117. Please print your airline ticket once ------- of your credit card payment has been received.

(A) confirmation
(B) confirmed
(C) confirms
(D) confirm

118. The ------- warehouse on Front Avenue has been torn down to make room for new construction.

(A) terminated
(B) certain
(C) destructive
(D) abandoned

119. Reviewing architectural plans ------- in advance is essential in order to maintain reasonable construction costs.

(A) care
(B) careful
(C) carefully
(D) most careful

120. The cost of the final product nearly doubled ------- a rise in the price of the raw materials used to make it.

(A) but
(B) because of
(C) whereas
(D) only if

121. Most laptops are not powerful enough to run TYD's advanced gaming software, but the Inqwiri 820 is one of the ------- that can.

(A) little
(B) small
(C) any
(D) few

122. The new workstation dividers help prevent unnecessary ------- and ensure that bank tellers stay focused.

(A) distractions
(B) responsibilities
(C) clarifications
(D) deposits

GO ON TO THE NEXT PAGE

123. A student turnout of approximately 85 percent ------- at the upcoming winter concert.

(A) expects
(B) is expected
(C) will expect
(D) are expecting

124. We are proud to announce the opening of our newest restaurant, conveniently located on Beverly Road, ------- Summerdale Park.

(A) opposite
(B) between
(C) onto
(D) until

125. For all expenditures over $1,000, ------- in writing will be required.

(A) justify
(B) justification
(C) justified
(D) justifiably

126. A market analysis shows that sales of sports utility vehicles have decreased ------- over the past twelve months.

(A) considerably
(B) durably
(C) concisely
(D) expressively

127. Questions ------- reimbursement for travel expenses should be directed to the payroll office.

(A) concern
(B) concerns
(C) concerned
(D) concerning

128. Sakai Trucking hired a software specialist to ------- its delivery scheduling system.

(A) notify
(B) pronounce
(C) recruit
(D) modernize

129. Musitto, Inc., has been producing cutting-edge phones with ------- long battery-run times.

(A) has increased
(B) increases
(C) increased
(D) increasingly

130. ------- the new bylaws, all employees of Lovato Marketing are required to participate in professional development each year.

(A) Under
(B) Into
(C) Behind
(D) Toward

Directions: Read the texts that follow. A word, phrase, or sentence is missing in parts of each text. Four answer choices for each question are given below the text. Select the best answer to complete the text. Then mark the letter (A), (B), (C), or (D) on your answer sheet.

Questions 131-134 refer to the following instructions.

Periodic cleaning of the Huntington Premium Toaster Oven can greatly extend ------- useful
                                                                        131.
life. First, make sure to unplug the toaster, and let it cool off before beginning the cleaning

process. ------- . Then wipe the interior with a moist sponge. ------- , clean the exterior with
         132.   **133.**
a mild household cleaning solution. Following this process will keep your ------- looking
                                                                          134.
and working like new.

131. (A) a
   (B) its
   (C) that
   (D) another

132. (A) Afterwards, reassemble the toaster
       carefully.
   (B) Next, remove the crumb tray and
       rinse it with warm water.
   (C) Note that frozen food will take
       longer to heat.
   (D) Look for the product number on
       the underside.

133. (A) Finally
   (B) Instead
   (C) Otherwise
   (D) In the meantime

134. (A) tools
   (B) factory
   (C) fixtures
   (D) appliance

GO ON TO THE NEXT PAGE

From: customerservice@liybank.org
To: jlaurens@mailsygo.com
Subject: LIY Bank Correspondence
Date: April 2

Dear Mr. Laurens,

You requested to be notified when official mail concerning your LIY Bank account is sent to you.

------- is, therefore, to inform you that a new credit card has been issued and mailed to you. It
135.

will replace your current credit card that is ------- to expire on May 31. ------- . When it arrives,
136.   137.

please remember to activate your card through your online account on our Web site.

------- , you can go to your nearest bank branch and have it activated there by our
138.

representative.

If you have any further questions, please contact our Customer Service Center at 610-555-

0125.

Customer Service Team
LIY Bank

135. (A) Either
(B) What
(C) This
(D) He

136. (A) equal
(B) true
(C) due
(D) fair

137. (A) You may spend it as you see fit.
(B) You should receive it within a
week.
(C) However, deliveries have been on
schedule.
(D) Please confirm receipt of this
letter.

138. (A) Suddenly
(B) Specifically
(C) Accordingly
(D) Alternatively

Questions 139-142 refer to the following memo.

To: All Alanaga Corporation Employees
From: Corporate Travel Office
Subject: Travel policy update

Over the past year, the Corporate Travel Office has been working hard to save the company money ------- cost-effective travel arrangements. Yesterday we ------- an agreement with the
    139.   **140.**
Bellaria Taxi Company. From this point forward, when traveling on official Alanaga business, you are required to take a Bellaria taxi. ------- , Alanaga will receive a large discount from
             141.
Bellaria for its services. This arrangement will be used primarily for transportation between branch offices. ------- . If you have a suggestion to make your business travel easier, please
        142.
call the Corporate Travel Office at extension 523.

139. (A) it made
    (B) by making
    (C) and makes
    (D) the maker of

140. (A) finalized
    (B) canceled
    (C) highlighted
    (D) considered

141. (A) If not
    (B) However
    (C) Regardless
    (D) In turn

142. (A) However, it may also be used for travel to and from the airport.
    (B) On the other hand, taking a train may be more expensive.
    (C) Bellaria Taxi Company has been providing transportation for 25 years.
    (D) The Corporate Travel Office has an emergency phone number.

GO ON TO THE NEXT PAGE ▶

---

4 February

Liya Lim
1228 Dunlop Street
Singapore 23885

Dear Ms. Lim,

To show appreciation for your continued patronage with the Good Day Cable Company, we invite you to our annual Good Day at the Park event at Paya Park on 20 March. The evening ------- at 5:00 P.M. with a private reception at the Paya Clubhouse. While beverages and
143.
appetizers are ------- , listen to performances from local musicians. ------- . Afterward, dessert
144.   **145.**
will follow in the form of an ice cream social. ------- the social, clients are also invited to
146.
participate in a raffle and trivia games. Prizes will be awarded!

Kindly RSVP by 28 February. We hope to see you there!

Sincerely,

Jet Khoo
President of Good Day Cable Company

---

143. (A) will have commenced
 (B) will commence
 (C) commenced
 (D) has commenced

144. (A) seated
 (B) dined
 (C) served
 (D) played

145. (A) At 6:00 P.M., head to The Firepit for
   a barbecue dinner.
 (B) The Clubhouse had to be reserved
   two months ago.
 (C) Please make sure your account
   number is written on your check.
 (D) Guests may pay for their tickets at
   the door.

146. (A) During
 (B) Including
 (C) Inside
 (D) Meanwhile

Directions: In this part you will read a selection of texts, such as magazine and newspaper articles, e-mails, and instant messages. Each text or set of texts is followed by several questions. Select the best answer for each question and mark the letter (A), (B), (C), or (D) on your answer sheet.

Questions 147-148 refer to the following instructions.

How to Perform a Global Reset

Resetting your television remote-control device will delete individual settings and restore all functions to the standard manufacturer settings. To perform a global reset, follow the steps below.

Step 1
Hold the POWER button down for five seconds and release.

Step 2
Press the right ARROW button. You will hear a short beep.

Step 3
Press CLEAR. The red light at the top should turn off. If it remains lit, press the button again before proceeding to step 4.

Step 4
Enter your user code. A green light will flash, indicating that the standard settings are restored.

If desired, you can now reprogram your remote to customize the settings.

Final Test

147. What do the instructions explain?
  (A) How to turn on lights remotely
  (B) How to remove customized settings
  (C) How to order additional television channels
  (D) How to improve picture quality

148. According to the instructions, what step might need to be repeated?
  (A) Step 1
  (B) Step 2
  (C) Step 3
  (D) Step 4

GO ON TO THE NEXT PAGE

Attention All Manning & Murdoch Employees

The staff kitchen will be closed from August 15 to August 19. During this period, the kitchen will be painted and a new dishwasher and refrigerator will be installed. Please do not enter the kitchen during this time for any reason, including to make tea or coffee. A temporary beverage station will be set up for your use in the office foyer. Thank you for your cooperation.

149. What is one purpose of the notice?

(A) To advertise the opening of a company café
(B) To ask employees to keep the kitchen clean
(C) To notify employees about upcoming renovations
(D) To announce that a building will be closed temporarily

150. What will be available in the office foyer?

(A) A catered lunch
(B) A sign-up sheet
(C) Snacks for purchase
(D) Tea and coffee

> **Frances Murphy (11:25 A.M.)**
> Hi Debbie. You mentioned you were stopping at the office supply store today. Would you mind picking up some file labels for me?
>
> **Debbie Emhof (11:27 A.M.)**
> No problem. I'm at Office Check now. What exactly do you need?
>
> **Frances Murphy (11:28 A.M.)**
> I need a pack of multicolored labels.
>
> **Debbie Emhof (11:35 A.M.)**
> Well, those seem to be out of stock. Do you want me to get a different style? There are white labels available.
>
> **Frances Murphy (11:36 A.M.)**
> I can wait. Are we still on for lunch?
>
> **Debbie Emhof (11:37 A.M.)**
> Of course. I'll meet you at the cafeteria on the second floor at 12:30 P.M. Ken Mitani from the billing department is going to join us, too.

Final Test

151. At 11:36 A.M., what does Ms. Murphy most likely mean when she writes, "I can wait"?

(A) She is not very hungry.
(B) She wants only colored labels.
(C) She needs Ms. Emhof to find an item.
(D) She can meet Mr. Mitani at a later date.

152. What is probably true about the writers?

(A) They work in the same building.
(B) They commute to work together.
(C) They manage an office supply store.
(D) They are late for a business lunch.

GO ON TO THE NEXT PAGE

Excelsior Style—Your First Name in Fashion!
For a short time only, receive up to 50 percent off on all purchases!
Offer valid through May 31

Excelsiorstyle.com is your go-to Web fashion hub with thousands of items of women's and children's apparel. Browse our site for the newest styles in coats and jackets, dresses, tops, skirts, swimwear, sleepwear, shoes, and accessories.

Plus, we now offer fashions for your home through our brand-new line of interior decoration products! Visit Excelsiorstyle.com now to find the latest in home décor.

Take advantage of our long-standing policy of free delivery for purchases over $75.00.

---

153. What is being advertised?

(A) A department store's new name
(B) A recently upgraded Web site
(C) A discount on online purchases
(D) A change to a shipping policy

154. Based on the advertisement, what will happen on June 1?

(A) Customers will pay regular prices.
(B) A children's department will open.
(C) Purchases will be eligible for a free gift.
(D) All shipping costs will be discounted.

155. What is available for the first time?

(A) Footwear
(B) Home-decorating items
(C) Outerwear
(D) Children's clothing

Warm Welcome & Special Thanks

(September 7)—*Karimun Post* readers may have noticed the addition of Mei Chandra to this newspaper's masthead. We are pleased to welcome her as our first-ever intern reporter at the paper.

Ms. Chandra recently moved to Jakarta after studying English and journalism in the United States. For her first assignment, she has researched the challenges currently faced by our country's textile industry from an international perspective. Her initial article on this topic appears in this issue.

The addition of internships is just one more way we fulfill our educational mission. For the past year and a half, the *Karimun Post* has been sustained primarily by funding from local academic institutions. The paper is now focused not only on keeping the local community informed but also on serving career-development purposes.

A bonus of this new direction for the paper is the number of students who now contribute to the publication in multiple ways. The editor would like to take this opportunity to thank the many students who volunteer their time each month—including those who deliver the print version of the newspaper to the doorsteps of our subscribers on time every week.

156. What is stated about the intern position?

(A) It is new to the publication.
(B) It requires international travel.
(C) It is based in the United States.
(D) It requires a degree in journalism.

157. What is suggested about Ms. Chandra?

(A) She is an experienced translator.
(B) She is writing a series of articles.
(C) She will help recruit more interns.
(D) She used to work in the textile industry.

158. What is indicated about the *Karimun Post*?

(A) It is free to local residents.
(B) It is distributed by volunteers.
(C) It is printed in multiple languages.
(D) It is funded by advertising revenue.

Final
Test

GO ON TO THE NEXT PAGE

Questions 159-160 refer to the following memo.

MEMO

From: Harumi Ohta, Kitchen Manager
To: All Staff

It is essential that all food handlers practice good personal hygiene throughout the year, but it is especially important during the upcoming cold and flu season. Viruses can be carried on hands, linger on work surfaces such as countertops and cutting boards, and find their way onto utensils and plates. Therefore, all employees who work with food must wash their hands before handling any food or utensils used in the preparation or delivery of food. Instructions on the proper method for washing your hands are posted at the entrance to the kitchen, in the restrooms, and in the meeting room next to the lobby. Please follow them diligently.

Harumi

159. What is the memo about?

(A) Treating a common illness
(B) Following a safety practice
(C) Reviewing a sick-leave policy
(D) Using new kitchen equipment

160. What items are most likely mentioned in the posted instructions?

(A) Soap and water
(B) Milk and cheese
(C) Forks and plates
(D) Ovens and refrigerators

Questions 161-163 refer to the following e-mail.

```
*E-mail*

To:        Staff@holmana.co.uk
From:      Robin Ruiz, Facilities Manager
Date:      12 October
Subject:   New Desks

Dear staff,

We will soon be replacing all employee desks with new hybrid ones that will allow you
to work while either seated or standing. The new desks are due to arrive on 20 October.
— [1] —. I have requested that the delivery occur early in the morning before office
hours so it does not interrupt our work. — [2] —. To make the transition go faster,
please move the contents of your current desk, including personal items, into a
cardboard box on the 19th.

You can read more about the model we've ordered at wilsonofficefurniture.com/
hybrid56. — [3] —. My research showed this one to be the most user-friendly option.
The height of the desk can be changed by simply flipping a latch and pushing a button.

Many of you have been requesting hybrid desks for some time now, so I am glad we are
able to make this happen. This is only one of the changes management plans to
implement this year in our efforts to make Holmana a healthier and happier workplace.
— [4] —.

Best regards,

Robin Ruiz
```

161. How can employees help prepare for a delivery?

(A) By packing their belongings
(B) By collecting cardboard boxes
(C) By completing their work in the morning
(D) By moving furniture out of their offices

162. Why has the desk been chosen?

(A) It has a large storage area.
(B) It is easy to adjust.
(C) It can be delivered quickly.
(D) It is the cheapest option available.

163. In which of the positions marked [1], [2], [3], and [4] does the following sentence best belong?

"Any other ideas you have for us are welcome."

(A) [1]
(B) [2]
(C) [3]
(D) [4]

GO ON TO THE NEXT PAGE

Final
Test

Questions 164-167 refer to the following online chat discussion.

Ann Novak [1:31 P.M.]
Hello, everyone. Last week when we met, I asked you to come up with strategies to bring attention to the community garden program. Does anyone have progress to report?

Jay Goodwin [1:32 P.M.]
I reached out to Stuart Chan of *City Wide Now*, the local newspaper. You probably know his "City Living" column.

Mike Louden [1:33 P.M.]
The one that runs on Mondays? I never miss it!

Jay Goodwin [1:34 P.M.]
He has a large online following, too. He'd like to interview me for an upcoming issue. So that's happening next week.

Ann Novak [1:34 P.M.]
Wonderful. Will you talk about the community garden in general?

Jay Goodwin [1:35 P.M.]
I explained to Stuart that we are surveying members of the garden about issues regarding access to water. So he wants to focus on that.

Mike Louden [1:36 P.M.]
Lori and I are writing up the survey results. Ann, I'm getting ready to send you a draft. As soon as you have approved it, I can post it on our Web site.

Ann Novak [1:37 P.M.]
OK. I'll look it over this afternoon.

---

164. What is indicated about Ms. Novak?

(A) She missed last week's meeting.
(B) She has just returned from a trip.
(C) She does not like Mr. Goodwin's idea.
(D) She gave her colleagues an assignment.

165. Who is Mr. Chan?

(A) A city official
(B) A local reporter
(C) A job candidate
(D) An expert gardener

166. At 1:33 P.M., what does Mr. Louden most likely mean when he writes, "I never miss it"?

(A) He enjoys participating in community activities.
(B) He always meets project deadlines.
(C) He subscribes to *City Wide Now*.
(D) He reads a column regularly.

167. What does Mr. Louden indicate he will do?

(A) Conduct a survey
(B) Post a document online
(C) Prepare interview questions
(D) Help improve access to water

Associate Publicist Wanted
Blackhorse Publishing House

Blackhorse Publishing House produces a variety of contemporary works including fiction, nonfiction, and poetry. Some of our fiction authors include Simon Delacorte, Peter Simkin-Hall, and Katarina Sanchez. — [1] —. Our nonfiction list focuses primarily on the areas of gardening, home design, architecture, and cooking.

We are looking for an associate publicist to join our busy team. — [2] —. The successful candidate will support senior staff as well as lead publicity campaigns for authors. He or she will also organize and oversee event bookings for authors, including national and international speaking tours and other public appearances at festivals and bookstores, among other venues.

Ideal candidates will have 1–2 years of experience in trade publishing, either in a publicity or an editorial role. — [3] —. Job applicants must have wide knowledge of social media use in publishing as well as expertise with word-processing systems, excellent language and verbal skills, and commendable attention to detail. — [4]—.

If this sounds like you, please e-mail a cover letter and your résumé no later than September 21 to efine@blackhorsepublishing.com.

168. What is the purpose of the notice?

(A) To promote an upcoming job fair
(B) To notify employees about changes in senior staffing
(C) To encourage recent graduates to gain internship experience
(D) To invite qualified individuals to apply for a job

169. What do Mr. Delacorte and Ms. Sanchez have in common?

(A) They edit architecture books.
(B) They have the same publisher.
(C) They work as event planners.
(D) They have given international speaking tours.

170. What is mentioned as one of the responsibilities of an associate publicist?

(A) Arranging author appearances
(B) Updating word processing systems
(C) Interviewing prospective interns
(D) Attending professional conferences

171. In which of the positions marked [1], [2], [3], and [4] does the following sentence best belong?

"Two professional references from these positions are essential."

(A) [1]
(B) [2]
(C) [3]
(D) [4]

GO ON TO THE NEXT PAGE

To:	Isla Garrick <igarrick@gandgre.co.au>
From:	Owen Clement <oclement@congreveads.co.au>
Subject:	New service
Date:	January 7

Dear Ms. Garrick,

I noticed that you placed an order recently, and before we fill it, I wanted to tell you about an exciting opportunity. Congreve Advertising is now offering another way for you to reach your customers: automated text messages. We're combining our eye-catching lawn advertisements with the latest mobile phone technology to create a quick, easy method of increasing your customer base. We've already helped many property rental agents in your area, and we're giving free trials to new users.

Our automated text-messaging service involves just a few simple steps.

1. Go to our Web site, congreveads.co.au. Click on the Registration page and select New User. You will be guided through our quick and easy registration process, which will allow you to set up an account.

2. Once your account is set up, you can start entering the automated responses that you want interested renters to receive. Include the details about each property. You can also add images, audio, and videos, as well as links to Web sites.

3. Select a unique keyword for each property. This is what prospective renters will text in order to receive more information about a rental. The keyword shouldn't be too long or difficult to spell, and it should be easy for customers to remember.

4. Then wait. Apartment seekers will pass by the property and see the keyword. When they text it, they will instantly receive the message you programmed!

As part of your free trial, we'll print new rental signs for one of your properties so that your advertisements include the keyword. And, if you contact me by Friday, I'll add two more properties to the order. So, in addition to a month of our text-messaging service, you'll get updated signs for three rental units, all at no cost to you. After the trial period, you can choose from six reasonably priced packages, which include the option of sending daily updates to preferred customers.

I look forward to hearing from you!

Owen Clement

172. What is implied about Ms. Garrick?

(A) She is interested in finding a rental property.
(B) She works as a property rental agent.
(C) She recently bought a new mobile telephone.
(D) She sends text messages frequently.

173. What is indicated about Congreve Advertising?

(A) It is a newly created company.
(B) It fills orders quickly.
(C) It is providing a new service.
(D) It recently merged with another company.

174. What is mentioned about the automated responses?

(A) They are different for each property.
(B) They can be sent to an e-mail address.
(C) They include pictures taken by Congreve Advertising.
(D) They require apartment seekers to create a password.

175. According to the e-mail, why should Ms. Garrick contact Mr. Clement by Friday?

(A) To renew a subscription
(B) To talk about fees
(C) To schedule a property viewing
(D) To receive free services

GO ON TO THE NEXT PAGE

New This Week . . . .

After months of editing and several postponed release dates due to production delays, the documentary series *The Hidden Side of Architecture* finally hits television screens this week. The four-part program directed by Michael Moussa and Tina Erskine looks at little-known facts behind the world's most iconic buildings. Fans of actor and comedian Wesley Fleming will be happy to hear that he is the host for the series. The program was produced by Leif Bergen and will appear on the Knowledge Now channel on the dates below.

EPISODE	AIRDATE
1 **"Against All Odds"**	**April 3**

The first part takes us to Ancient Egypt, where builders managed to solve formidable engineering problems.

2 **"Building Without Modern Technology"**	**April 10**

How, without modern tools and technology, did medieval builders in Europe construct the great cathedrals that dominated cityscapes for nearly a thousand years?

3 **"Modern Cities"**	**April 17**

In this episode, we admire the beauty of modern urban structures, and we learn some gripping stories behind their planning and construction.

4 **"Road Ahead"**	**April 24**

The last part looks at ideas still in the making: new designs of ever-taller skyscrapers, bio-inspired buildings with smaller footprints, and other marvels that will one day grace our cities.

Drena Kraakevik ★ ★ ★ ★

After the first episode of *The Hidden Side of Architecture*, I can only say that I can't wait to see the remaining three parts! Fleming does a tremendous job narrating the story; he's informative yet funny. Don't miss the free downloadable booklet accompanying the series on Knowledge Now's Web site. It's a must-have if you want to learn more about the buildings featured on the program.

176. What is indicated about the making of the program?

(A) It was very expensive.
(B) It took longer than planned.
(C) It was financed by several sponsors.
(D) It involved a large team of producers.

177. Who appears in the program?

(A) Mr. Moussa
(B) Ms. Erskine
(C) Mr. Fleming
(D) Mr. Bergen

178. What episode focuses on urban planning?

(A) Episode 1
(B) Episode 2
(C) Episode 3
(D) Episode 4

179. When did Ms. Kraakevik most likely watch the program?

(A) On April 3
(B) On April 10
(C) On April 17
(D) On April 24

180. What does Ms. Kraakevik recommend doing?

(A) Purchasing movies that feature a particular actor
(B) Visiting the buildings shown in the program
(C) Obtaining additional materials online
(D) Watching other programs by the same director

GO ON TO THE NEXT PAGE

Final
Test

To:	Albert Nguyen <nguyen@wantamayolodge.com>
From:	Janna Zhukowsky <jzhukowsky@melodias.com>
Subject:	A new client
Date:	April 12

Good afternoon, Mr. Nguyen:

Once again, it has been a pleasure working with you and the entire Wantamayo Lodge staff. My clients greatly enjoyed the rain forest tour. The couple who stayed in the South Bungalow commented that the room's view of the tropical garden was breathtaking.

I would now like to place a reservation for a new client, Robert Vasquez. Please make the following arrangements for Mr. Vasquez and his guest.
Arrival: May 5 (airport shuttle service requested)
Departure: May 8 (airport shuttle service requested)
Room type: Double occupancy
Tour type: Guided rain forest tour (6-hour tour)

Flight information:
AirPars Flight 178 from Buenos Aires arriving at 2:50 P.M. May 5
AirPars Flight 152 to Buenos Aires departing at 11:00 A.M. May 8

Thank you again for the high level of attention you show to my clients.

Janna Zhukowsky
Travel Associate, Melodias Travel

To:	Janna Zhukowsky <jzhukowsky@melodias.com>
From:	Albert Nguyen <nguyen@wantamayolodge.com>
Subject:	Vasquez Reservation
Date:	April 13

Ms. Zhukowsky,

Thank you for your e-mail and for sharing the positive feedback from your clients.

Here are the details regarding the reservation for Mr. Vasquez. Please note that we had limited availability. The room we reserved for him is slightly more expensive than others, but the only other rooms available were single rooms.

Check-in date: May 5
Check-out date: May 8
Room: South Bungalow
Price: $145 USD/night   Total: $435 USD (excluding tax)
Tour type: Guided Rain Forest Tour; May 6, 8:00 A.M. to 2:00 P.M.
Tour fee: $95 USD

Note: Transportation between the airport and the lodge has been arranged. The bill must be settled in full by May 2.

We appreciate the business relationship we have with Melodias Travel. If you have any questions or concerns, please feel free to contact me.

Albert Nguyen
Guest Services, Wantamayo Lodge

181. Why did Ms. Zhukowsky write to Mr. Nguyen?

(A) To suggest a new tour destination
(B) To request flight information
(C) To assist a client
(D) To revise an itinerary

182. What is suggested about Melodias Travel?

(A) It has done business with Wantamayo Lodge in the past.
(B) It specializes in rain forest destinations.
(C) It is located near Wantamayo Lodge.
(D) It is owned by Ms. Zhukowsky.

183. What does Mr. Vasquez request?

(A) A frequent customer discount
(B) A confirmation of his reservation
(C) A meal plan
(D) A transportation service

184. What is indicated about Mr. Vasquez?

(A) He has visited Wantamayo Lodge on a previous occasion.
(B) He will stay in a room overlooking a garden.
(C) He has traveled with Mr. Nguyen.
(D) He plans to travel alone.

185. By when does Mr. Nguyen expect payment?

(A) April 13
(B) May 2
(C) May 5
(D) May 8

GO ON TO THE NEXT PAGE

---

http://www.presnellcleaning.com ▶

PRESNELL CLEANING
171 Voyager Street, Minneapolis, MN 55401

About Us	**Home**	Testimonials	Contact Us	Rates

Presnell Cleaning offers comprehensive cleaning services that cater to both domestic and commercial clientele. For more than 20 years we have provided exceptional service at competitive prices.

In addition to all regular services, we also offer a specialized cleaning service that uses all-natural, odor-free cleaning techniques as well as products designed for allergen reduction.

Clients can select weekly, twice-monthly, or monthly services. Our cleaners arrive on time and finish on time. We offer a money-back guarantee if you are not completely satisfied.

Contact us to schedule a free on-site cleaning assessment and estimate. Call 1-612-555-0108 or visit our Web site at www.presnellcleaning.com. Be sure to visit our testimonials page to read what our many satisfied customers have to say.

To:	customerservice@presnellcleaning.com
From:	dcoe@ashbachdesign.com
Re:	Cleaning service
Date:	August 13

To Whom It May Concern:

I hired Presnell Cleaning to clean my company's offices. From your advertisement and especially from your customers' recommendations on your Web site, I expected to be completely satisfied with your services. Unfortunately, that was not the case. I requested your specialized service, but your cleaners did not provide that service. Clearly something went wrong. I am considering canceling the next scheduled visit.

Deborah Coe
Ashbach Design

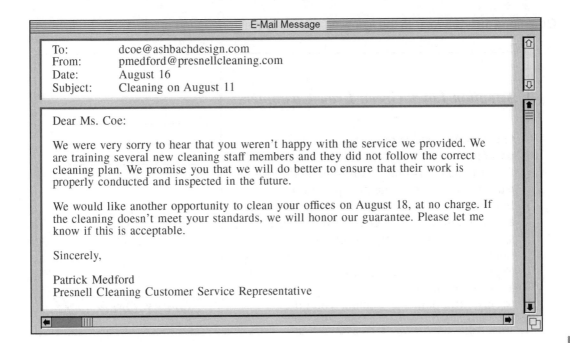

186. What is indicated about Presnell
Cleaning?

(A) It is a new business.
(B) It offers daily cleaning services.
(C) It provides complimentary
evaluations.
(D) It recently added home-cleaning
services.

187. What is suggested about Ms. Coe?

(A) She researched other cleaners
before contacting Presnell
Cleaning.
(B) She was referred to Presnell
Cleaning by a friend.
(C) She is interested in applying for a
position with Presnell Cleaning.
(D) She read online testimonials prior
to hiring Presnell Cleaning.

188. In the first e-mail, the word "case" in
paragraph 1, line 3, is closest in
meaning to

(A) project
(B) example
(C) situation
(D) container

189. Why did Ms. Coe write to complain?

(A) The office floors were not waxed.
(B) The office kitchen was not
sterilized.
(C) The cleaners did not shampoo the
carpets.
(D) The cleaners did not use natural
products.

190. What does Mr. Medford offer to do if
Ms. Coe is not satisfied after August
18?

(A) Refund her money
(B) Create a new cleaning plan
(C) Send different cleaning staff
members
(D) Provide a discount on future
cleaning services

GO ON TO THE NEXT PAGE

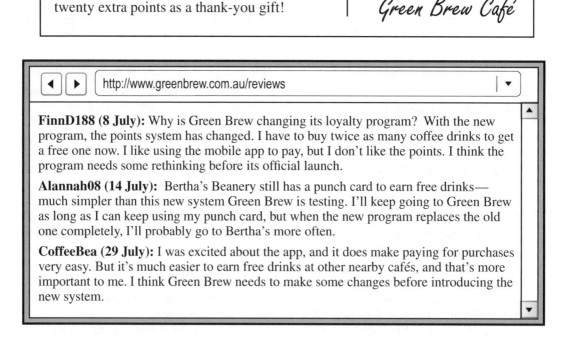

★ ★ ★ ★
Attention Loyal Green Brew Customers!
★ ★ ★ ★

Green Brew Café is redesigning our loyalty program—it's not just for coffee anymore! As a frequent customer, you're invited to participate in testing the new program. Interested? Go to greenbrew.com to read more and download the new Green Brew app. Then start accumulating points by enjoying our sandwiches, smoothies, and salads in addition to your favorite coffee drinks. When you post a review on our Web site, you will receive twenty extra points as a thank-you gift!

Green Brew Café

---

http://www.greenbrew.com.au/reviews

FinnD188 (8 July): Why is Green Brew changing its loyalty program? With the new program, the points system has changed. I have to buy twice as many coffee drinks to get a free one now. I like using the mobile app to pay, but I don't like the points. I think the program needs some rethinking before its official launch.

Alannah08 (14 July): Bertha's Beanery still has a punch card to earn free drinks— much simpler than this new system Green Brew is testing. I'll keep going to Green Brew as long as I can keep using my punch card, but when the new program replaces the old one completely, I'll probably go to Bertha's more often.

CoffeeBea (29 July): I was excited about the app, and it does make paying for purchases very easy. But it's much easier to earn free drinks at other nearby cafés, and that's more important to me. I think Green Brew needs to make some changes before introducing the new system.

A Lesson in Loyalty
By Hudson Aird
27 August
· ·

Maintaining customer loyalty can be difficult. Just ask Green Brew Café owner Taylah Carver. She recently began experimenting with a change to the café's loyalty program to reward her regular customers. Instead of the old punch-card system, which rewarded customers for coffee purchases only, the new program allows customers to earn points for buying food items as well. The points are tracked through the Green Brew app, which customers download to their mobile devices. The app can also be used to pay for orders.

The program was originally scheduled to be introduced to the general public in September, but after nearly 60 customers tried out the app for a month, Carver decided to defer the launch. Most users liked the fact that the app allows them to pay using their mobile devices, but there were many complaints about the new points system. It now takes twice as many purchases before customers accumulate enough points to be eligible for a free coffee drink, and that was too much, reviewers said. The lesson, says Ms. Carver: know your customers.

191. Why was the postcard sent?

(A) To encourage customers to place orders online
(B) To announce a change in café hours
(C) To introduce a new price list
(D) To recruit customers to test a rewards system

192. What is suggested about the people who posted reviews?

(A) They received bonus points for reviewing an app.
(B) They often meet friends at Green Brew Café.
(C) They tried some new lunch items at Green Brew Café.
(D) They are pleased about a reduction in prices.

193. What is implied about Ms. Carver?

(A) She runs a business that competes with Bertha's Beanery.
(B) She is not the original owner of Green Brew Café.
(C) She expects sales to increase in September.
(D) She decided to find a new vendor for punch cards.

194. According to the article, what is a common criticism of a new loyalty program?

(A) It is difficult to download the mobile app.
(B) Customers must spend more money to earn free items.
(C) Food purchases are not included.
(D) Points are not tracked accurately.

195. In the article, the word "takes" in paragraph 2, line 8, is closest in meaning to

(A) removes
(B) provides
(C) requires
(D) delivers

GO ON TO THE NEXT PAGE

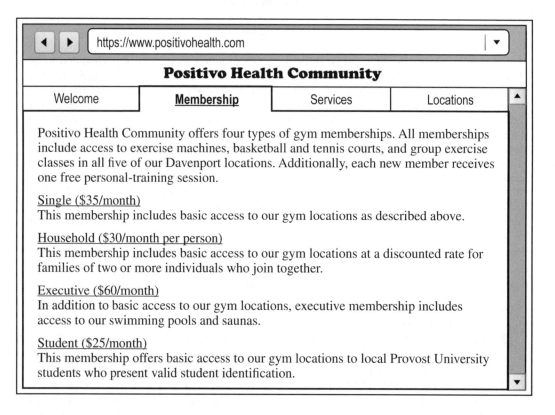

February 28

Dear Ron Mapleton,

Thank you for making Positivo Health Community a part of your total-body health program. It was so nice to meet you and your family when I showed you around our Davenport Central location in December.

We noticed that you have not yet taken advantage of your free hour of personal training. Each person on your account is entitled to one free session, but this perk expires three months after your contract is signed. Next week, the week of March 4, is the last week you will be able to use your free sessions. Please contact us today to schedule your personal-training sessions!

As a reminder, we offer one-on-one training for power yoga, Pilates, weight training, and power lifting. If you should choose to make personal training a regular part of your fitness routine, packages start at only $70 per month in addition to your monthly membership dues.

Your partner in health,

Janie Park
Janie Park, Membership Manager

Personal-Training Schedule for Next Week March 4–8 **Employee:** Kevin Pinto **Location:** Davenport Central					
	Monday	**Tuesday**	**Wednesday**	**Thursday**	**Friday**
8:00 A.M.		Stacey Lin Power Yoga	Ron Mapleton Power Yoga		Kim Dobbs Weight Training
9:00 A.M.	Pilar Hernandez Weight Training				
10:00 A.M.				Jean-Luc Curran Power Lifting	
11:00 A.M.		Jaylon Hill Power Yoga			

196. What is indicated about Positivo Health Community?

(A) It offers swimming lessons.
(B) Its members can use multiple facilities.
(C) Most of its members are students.
(D) All new members receive discounts.

197. What type of membership does Mr. Mapleton most likely have?

(A) Single
(B) Household
(C) Executive
(D) Student

198. What is indicated about Ms. Park?

(A) She is a personal trainer.
(B) She started her job in December.
(C) She creates weekly schedules for gym employees.
(D) She gave Mr. Mapleton a tour of the gym.

199. In the letter, the word "packages" in paragraph 3, line 3, is closest in meaning to

(A) gifts
(B) boxes
(C) products
(D) plans

200. What is probably true about Mr. Pinto?

(A) He does not work on Fridays.
(B) He primarily teaches power lifting.
(C) He has not trained Mr. Mapleton before.
(D) He has requested a change to his schedule.

Final Test

Stop! This is the end of the test. If you finish before time is called, you may go back to Parts 5, 6, and 7 and check your work.

Final Test
解答・解説

正解一覧

参考スコア範囲の換算表

解答・解説

Final Test 正解一覧

問題番号	正解
PART 5	
101	C
102	B
103	C
104	C
105	B
106	D
107	D
108	A
109	D
110	B
111	A
112	C
113	B
114	C
115	A
116	C
117	A
118	D
119	C
120	B
121	D
122	A
123	B
124	A
125	B
126	A
127	D
128	D
129	D
130	A

問題番号	正解
PART 6	
131	B
132	B
133	A
134	D
135	C
136	C
137	B
138	D
139	B
140	A
141	D
142	A
143	B
144	C
145	A
146	A

問題番号	正解
PART 7	
147	B
148	C
149	C
150	D
151	B
152	A
153	C
154	A
155	B
156	A
157	B
158	B
159	B
160	A
161	A
162	B
163	D
164	D
165	B
166	D
167	B

問題番号	正解
168	D
169	B
170	A
171	C
172	B
173	C
174	A
175	D
176	B
177	C
178	C
179	A
180	C
181	C
182	A
183	D
184	B
185	B
186	C
187	D
188	C
189	D
190	A
191	D
192	A
193	A
194	B
195	C
196	B
197	B
198	D
199	D
200	C

参考スコア範囲の換算表

以下の手順に従って、ファイナルテストの正答数から「参考スコア範囲」を確認することができます。

1. ファイナルテストを受験後、左ページの「正解一覧」を参照し、正答数を数えてください。正答数が素点となります。
2. リーディングセクションの「参考スコア範囲の換算表」であなたの素点に対応する換算点範囲を見つけます。例えば素点が 61 であれば、あなたの換算点範囲は「250 〜 335 点」です。

あなたの参考スコア範囲

	素点		換算点範囲
1 回目	_____	▶	_____
2 回目	_____	▶	_____

※ 一定期間を置いてファイナルテストを 2 回受験する場合は、巻末の解答用紙をコピーしてご使用ください。

参考スコア範囲の換算表

リーディングセクション	
素点	換算点範囲
96 — 100	460 — 495
91 — 95	425 — 490
86 — 90	395 — 465
81 — 85	370 — 440
76 — 80	335 — 415
71 — 75	310 — 390
66 — 70	280 — 365
例 ▶ 61 — 65	250 — 335
56 — 60	220 — 305
51 — 55	195 — 270
46 — 50	165 — 240
41 — 45	140 — 215
36 — 40	115 — 180
31 — 35	95 — 145
26 — 30	75 — 120
21 — 25	60 — 95
16 — 20	45 — 75
11 — 15	30 — 55
6 — 10	10 — 40
1 — 5	5 — 30
0	5 — 15

101 Gelden Petrochemical exports products to customers ------- the world.

(A) all
(B) many
(C) around
(D) except

Gelden石油化学社は、製品を世界中の顧客に輸出しています。

(A) 全ての
(B) 多くの
(C) ～中の
(D) ～を除いて

正解 C 文頭から products までで文の形が成立しており、to customers ------- the world は動詞 exports を修飾する句だと考えられる。名詞句 the world を後に続けて直前の名詞 customers を修飾し文意に合うのは、前置詞の (C)。export「～を輸出する」、product「製品」、around the world「世界中の」。
(A) 形容詞。all the world は「世界中の (の人・物)」を表す。
(B) 形容詞。定冠詞 the の直前には置けない。
(D) 前置詞だが、文意に合わない。

102 Mr. Daoud is expected to ------- at the conference center in Dubai at 11:00 A.M.

(A) get
(B) arrive
(C) come
(D) travel

Daoudさんは午前11時にドバイの会議センターに到着する見込みです。

(A) 至る
(B) 到着する
(C) 来る
(D) 旅行する

正解 B 選択肢は全て動詞。at the conference center という前置詞句を後に続けて文意に合うのは、(B) の arrive。arrive at ～で「～に到着する」という意味。be expected to *do*「～する見込みである」。
(A) (C) get to ～ は「～に到着する」、come to ～ は「～に来る」という意味であるため、空所の後の前置詞が to であれば get も come も意味が通るが、ここでは不適切。
(D) 文の意味が通らない。

103 The software is easy to learn and ------- increases employee productivity.

(A) great
(B) greater
(C) greatly
(D) greatness

そのソフトウエアは習得しやすく、従業員の生産性を大いに高めます。

(A) 偉大な
(B) より偉大な
(C) 大いに
(D) 偉大さ

正解 C 選択肢は形容詞 great「偉大な」の変化した形または派生語。主語の The software に対し、is easy to learn と increases employee productivity が、and で結ばれた並列関係になっており、すでに文として成立している。よって、空所には動詞 increases を修飾する副詞の (C) が適切。employee「従業員」、productivity「生産性」。
(A) 形容詞。
(B) 形容詞の比較級。
(D) 名詞。動詞 increases の主語と考えたとしても、文の意味が通らない。

104 The budget will be made ------- on June 9 after a final audit by the finance committee.

(A) positive
(B) ultimate
(C) official
(D) responsible

予算は、財務委員会による最終の会計検査の後、6月9日に公にされる予定です。

(A) 肯定的な
(B) 究極的な
(C) 公の
(D) 責任のある

正解 **C** 選択肢は全て形容詞。動詞 make 〜 … 「〜を…にする」の目的語に当たる「〜」を主語にした受動態の未来形の文で、空所は補語の「…」に当たる。文意に合うのは、(C) official。budget「予算」、audit「会計検査、監査」、finance「財務、財政」。
(A) (B) (D) いずれも文意に合わない。

---

105 Eun-Yi Roh ------- to assistant deputy attorney after last week's performance review.

(A) is promoting
(B) was promoted
(C) promotes
(D) to promote

Eun-Yi Rohさんは先週の勤務評定後に代理弁護士の補佐に昇進しました。

＊選択肢の訳は省略

正解 **B** 動詞 promote「〜を昇進させる」の適切な形を選ぶ。promote は他動詞だが、空所の直後に目的語がない。また、文頭の Eun-Yi Roh は人名で昇進させられる対象と考えられる。よって、受動態の過去形 (B) was promoted が適切。deputy attorney「代理弁護士」、performance review「勤務評定」。
(A) 能動態・現在進行形。
(C) 能動態・三人称単数現在形。
(D) 不定詞。文の述語動詞にはならないので、不適切。

---

106 Mr. Ling has ------- requested funding for the airport terminal improvements.

(A) ever
(B) shortly
(C) yet
(D) already

Lingさんはすでに空港ターミナルの改良工事に、財政的支援を要請しています。

(A) いつも
(B) 間もなく
(C) 〈否定文で〉まだ
(D) すでに

正解 **D** 選択肢は全て副詞。能動態の現在完了形 has requested「要請した」が使われているので、時制に合う副詞を選ぶ。(D) already「すでに」が正解。funding「財政的支援、資金提供」、improvement「改良工事」。
(A) ever は肯定文では「いつも」という意味なので、過去とのつながりを示す現在完了形では使われない。
(B) 文意に合わない。
(C) yet は現在完了形の否定文では「まだ〜（ない）」、疑問文で「もう」の意味で使われるが、ここでは肯定文のため、適さない。

107 The ------- course on coaching is taught by Lee Wallis of the Peyton Soccer Club.

(A) introducer
(B) introduce
(C) introducing
(D) introductory

コーチングの入門コースはペイトンサッカークラブの Lee Wallis が教えます。

(A) 紹介者
(B) 〜を紹介する
(C) 〜を紹介している
(D) 入門の

| 正解 | D |

選択肢には動詞 introduce「〜を紹介する」が変化した形や派生語が並ぶ。空所の前に定冠詞 The があり、後ろには名詞 course があるので、空所にはこれを修飾する形容詞の (D) introductory が適切。coaching「コーチング、指導」。
(A) 名詞。
(B) 動詞の原形。
(C) 現在分詞または動名詞。

108 Most of the morning ------- will take place on the second floor, near the conference registration desk.

(A) sessions
(B) conditions
(C) requests
(D) speakers

午前中の会合のほとんどは、2 階の会議登録受付所近くで行われる予定です。

(A) 会合
(B) 状態
(C) 要請
(D) 演説者

| 正解 | A |

選択肢は全て名詞の複数形。空所の後には述語動詞 will take place があるので、文頭から空所までが文の主語だと考えられる。文意に合うのは (A) sessions。take place「行われる」、conference「会議、協議会」、registration「登録」、desk「受付、フロント」。
(B) (C) (D) いずれも文意に合わない。

109 Mr. Tanaka has decided to employ a payroll service because it is becoming too difficult to manage the payroll accounts -------.

(A) him
(B) he
(C) his
(D) himself

Tanakaさんは、給与台帳簿を自ら管理するのがあまりにも難しくなってきているため、給与計算サービスを利用することに決めました。

＊選択肢の訳は省略

| 正解 | D |

選択肢は全て代名詞。空所は because 節の中にあるが、空所の語がなくても文意が成立している。よって、空所には、強調の働きをする再帰代名詞の (D) が適切。employ「〜を利用する、〜を採用する」、payroll「給与台帳、給与計算」、manage「〜を管理する」、accounts「〈複数形で〉帳簿、会計簿」。
(A) 目的格。
(B) 主格。
(C) 所有格。

110 Filmmakers must obtain written consent ------- use a corporate logo.

(A) in contrast to
(B) in order to
(C) as a result
(D) as well

映画制作者は、企業のロゴを使うためには、同意書を取得しなければなりません。

(A) ～とは対照的に
(B) ～するために
(C) 結果として
(D) その上

| 正解 | **B** |

空所の前と後ろをつなぐ、適切な表現を選ぶ。動詞 use「～を使う」の原形を後に続けて文意を成り立たせる表現として適切なのは、「～するために」という目的を表す (B) in order to *do*。filmmaker「映画制作者」、obtain「～を取得する」、consent「同意書、同意」、corporate「企業の」。
(A) 後ろには名詞(句)が続く。
(C) (D) いずれも副詞の働きを持つ句。前後の内容がつながらない。

---

111 To satisfy different tastes, we strive to offer a ------- assortment of brands.

(A) broad
(B) broadly
(C) broaden
(D) broadness

さまざまな好みに応じるために、私たちは幅広い銘柄の品ぞろえを提供できるよう努めています。

(A) 幅広い
(B) 幅広く
(C) ～を広げる
(D) 幅広さ

| 正解 | **A** |

選択肢は全て形容詞 broad「幅広い」の派生語。空所の前に不定冠詞 a があり後ろに名詞 assortment があるので、空所には名詞を修飾する形容詞の (A) broad が適切。satisfy「～(要求など)に応じる、～(欲望)を満足させる」、taste「好み、嗜好」、strive to *do*「～しようと努力する」。
(B) 副詞。
(C) 動詞の原形。
(D) 名詞。

---

112 To avoid unexpected -------, ask the hotel desk clerk to explain which services are complimentary.

(A) breaks
(B) returns
(C) charges
(D) departures

予期しない請求を避けるために、ホテルのフロント係に何のサービスが無料なのかを説明してくれるように頼みましょう。

(A) 休憩
(B) 返金
(C) 請求
(D) 出発

| 正解 | **C** |

選択肢は全て名詞の複数形。ask 以降は命令文で、何のサービスが無料かの説明をホテルに求めるよう促している。空所を含む文頭からカンマまでは目的を表す不定詞句。不定詞 (to avoid) の目的語になり文意に合う名詞は、(C) charges。avoid「～を避ける」、unexpected「予期しない」、complimentary「無料の」。
(A) (B) (D) いずれも文意に合わない。

113 For ------- residents who use street parking, permits are available at city hall.

(A) them
(B) those
(C) when
(D) each

路上駐車のスペースを利用する居住者は、市役所で許可証を入手することができます。

(A) それらを
(B) それらの
(C) 〜するとき
(D) それぞれの

> 正解 **B**　空所の直前に前置詞 For があり、直後には residents who use street parking という長い名詞句がある。よって、空所には residents を限定する (B) those が適切。street parking「路上駐車」、permit「許可証」、available「入手できる」、city hall「市役所」。
> (A) 人称代名詞 they の目的格。名詞を修飾しない。
> (C) 接続詞。後ろには節が続く。
> (D) 形容詞。each の後には単数形の名詞が続くので、不適切。

114 Although they usually leave at 6:00 P.M., the employees are ------- in the store preparing for tomorrow's big event.

(A) almost
(B) less
(C) still
(D) easily

普段は午後6時に退社しますが、従業員たちはまだ店にいて、明日の大きなイベントの準備をしています。

(A) ほとんど
(B) より少ない
(C) まだ
(D) 簡単に

> 正解 **C**　「普段は午後6時に退社するが、従業員たちは店にいて、明日の大きなイベントの準備をしている」という文意に合い、述語動詞 are「いる、存在する」を修飾する語として適切なのは、副詞の (C) still。prepare for 〜「〜の準備をする」。
> (A) (D) 副詞。いずれも文意に合わない。
> (B) 形容詞または副詞。文意に合わない。

115 Renters are most excited about the ------- kitchens in the upgraded units.

(A) renovated
(B) renovation
(C) renovate
(D) renovating

借り主たちは、グレードアップした居室の中で、リフォームされたキッチンに最も喜んでいます。

(A) リフォームされた
(B) リフォーム
(C) 〜をリフォームする
(D) 〜をリフォームしている

> 正解 **A**　選択肢には動詞 renovate「〜をリフォームする、〜を改修する」が変化した形や派生語が並ぶ。空所を含む the ------- kitchens in the upgraded units は前置詞 about の目的語の名詞句と考えられる。空所の直前に定冠詞 the があり、直後に名詞 kitchens があるので、kitchens を修飾して、文意に合うものを選ぶ。正解は過去分詞の (A)。upgrade「〜をグレードアップする、〜を改良する」、unit「(住戸の単位として)1室」。
> (B) 名詞。
> (C) 動詞の原形。
> (D) 現在分詞または動名詞。

116 While at Varner Bank, Ms. Uehara had the opportunity to work ------- many influential figures in finance.

- (A) throughout
- (B) where
- (C) with
- (D) despite

Varner銀行にいたときに、Ueharaさんは多くの財界の有力者たちと仕事をする機会がありました。

- (A) 〜の至る所に
- (B) 〜するところの
- (C) 〜と一緒に
- (D) 〜にもかかわらず

> **正解 C** 空所の直前の動詞 work「仕事をする」と、直後の名詞句 many influential figures in finance「多くの財界の有力者たち」をつなぐ語として適切なのは、前置詞の (C) with。opportunity「機会」、influential「影響力のある」、figure「人物」。
> (A) 前置詞。空間や期間を表す名詞が続く。
> (B) 関係副詞。後ろには節が必要。
> (D) 前置詞。文意に合わない。

---

117 Please print your airline ticket once ------- of your credit card payment has been received.

- (A) confirmation
- (B) confirmed
- (C) confirms
- (D) confirm

クレジットカードの支払確認書が届いたら、航空券を印刷してください。

- (A) 確認書
- (B) 確認された
- (C) 〜を確認する
- (D) 〜を確認する

> **正解 A** 選択肢は動詞 confirm「〜を確認する」が変化した形または派生語。once は「いったん〜すると」という意味の接続詞であり、once 節内の主語は空所を含む ------- of your credit card payment で、述語動詞は受動態の has been received である。once 節の主語になり、文意が通るのは、名詞の (A) confirmation。payment「支払い」。
> (B) 過去分詞または過去形。
> (C) 三人称単数現在形。
> (D) 動詞の原形。

---

118 The ------- warehouse on Front Avenue has been torn down to make room for new construction.

- (A) terminated
- (B) certain
- (C) destructive
- (D) abandoned

フロント大通りの空き倉庫は、新たな建設用地を作るために取り壊されました。

- (A) 終わらされた
- (B) 確実な
- (C) 破壊的な
- (D) 放棄された

> **正解 D** 選択肢は全て形容詞。空所の直前に定冠詞の The、直後に名詞 warehouse があるので、空所には warehouse を修飾する形容詞として文意に合うものを選ぶ。(D) が正解。abandoned は、利用されない建物について「放棄された、捨てられた」という意味を表す。warehouse「倉庫」、tear down 〜「〜を取り壊す」、room「場所、空間」、construction「建設」。
> (A) (B) (C) いずれも文意に合わない。

119 Reviewing architectural plans ------- in advance is essential in order to maintain reasonable construction costs.

(A) care
(B) careful
(C) carefully
(D) most careful

事前に建築計画を入念に精査することは、妥当な建設費を維持するために必要不可欠です。

(A) 注意
(B) 注意深い
(C) 注意深く
(D) 最も注意深い

正解 **C**　選択肢は全て名詞 care「注意」の派生語。文の主語は Reviewing architectural plans ------- in advance で述語動詞は is、補語は essential である。空所がなくても、文が成立しているので、空所には文頭の動名詞 Reviewing を修飾する副詞の (C) が適切。review「〜を精査する、〜を見直す」、architectural「建築の」、in advance「事前に、前もって」、essential「必要不可欠の」、maintain「〜を維持する」、reasonable「妥当な、手頃な」。
(A) 名詞。
(B) 形容詞。
(D) 形容詞の最上級。

120 The cost of the final product nearly doubled ------- a rise in the price of the raw materials used to make it.

(A) but
(B) because of
(C) whereas
(D) only if

完成品の原価は、その製造に使用される原料費の値上がりのために、2倍近くに増えました。

(A) しかし
(B) 〜のために
(C) 〜である一方で
(D) 〜の場合に限り

正解 **B**　空所の前に〈主語＋動詞〉の形があり、直後には文末までの長い名詞句が続いている。後ろに名詞句を伴うことができて文意に合うのは、前置詞の働きをする (B) because of のみ。nearly「ほとんど」、double「倍増する」、rise「上昇」、raw material「原料」。
(A) (C) (D) いずれも節を導く接続詞の働きをする語句。空所の後ろは名詞句なので、不適切。

121 Most laptops are not powerful enough to run TYD's advanced gaming software, but the Inqwiri 820 is one of the ------- that can.

(A) little
(B) small
(C) any
(D) few

ほとんどのノートパソコンはTYD社の先進的なゲームソフトを動かせるほどの十分な性能を備えていません。しかしInqwiri 820はそれができる少数派の1つです。

(A) 少量
(B) 小さな部分
(C) どれでも
(D) 少数

正解 **D**　空所の前に one of 〜「〜の1つ」があり、直後には関係詞節 that can があることから、空所には名詞の働きをし、かつ複数を表す語が入ると考えられる。前半の節の主語 Most laptops から、数えられる名詞を示す語が入るのが適切だと分かるため、正解は (D) few。the few で「少数派」を表す。〜 enough to do「…するほど十分に〜だ」。
(A) 数えられないものについて「少量」を表す名詞。
(B) 名詞。文意に合わない。
(C) 代名詞。定冠詞 the の後に続けることはできない。

122 The new workstation dividers help prevent unnecessary ------- and ensure that bank tellers stay focused.

(A) distractions
(B) responsibilities
(C) clarifications
(D) deposits

新しい仕事場の間仕切りは、余計な注意散漫を防ぐのに役立ち、銀行の窓口係が確実に集中力を保てるようにします。

(A) 注意散漫
(B) 責務
(C) 説明
(D) 手付金

正解 **A** 選択肢は全て名詞の複数形。間仕切りの特長を説明した文で、and 以降に「銀行の窓口係が確実に集中力を保てるようにする」とある。prevent「～を防ぐ」の目的語となり、unnecessary「余計な」に修飾される名詞として適切なのは、(A) distractions。workstation「(一人一人の) 仕事場所」、divider「間仕切り」、help do「～するのに役立つ」、prevent「～を防ぐ」、unnecessary「余計な」、ensure that ～「～であることを確実にする」、bank teller「銀行の窓口係」、focused「集中した」。
(B) (C) (D) いずれも文意に合わない。

---

123 A student turnout of approximately 85 percent ------- at the upcoming winter concert.

(A) expects
(B) is expected
(C) will expect
(D) are expecting

今度の冬のコンサートには、約 85 パーセントの学生の来場が見込まれています。

＊選択肢の訳は省略

Final Test

正解 **B** 選択肢は全て動詞 expect「～を見込む、～を予期する」が変化した形。主語が A student turnout「学生の来場」なので、空所には受動態の現在形の (B) を入れて、「～が見込まれる」という意味を表すのが適切。approximately「およそ、約」、upcoming「今度の、近づいている」。
(A) (C) (D) いずれも能動態なので、文意に合わない。
(A) 能動態・三人称単数現在形。
(C) 能動態・未来形。
(D) 能動態・現在進行形。

---

124 We are proud to announce the opening of our newest restaurant, conveniently located on Beverly Road, ------- Summerdale Park.

(A) opposite
(B) between
(C) onto
(D) until

Summerdale 公園の向かい側、Beverly 通り沿いという便利な場所に位置する、当社最新のレストランの開店をお知らせできて、光栄に思います。

(A) ～の向かい側に
(B) ～の間に
(C) ～の上へ
(D) ～まで

正解 **A** 選択肢は全て前置詞。レストランの立地について説明していることから、空所には Summerdale Park を後ろに続けて適切な位置関係を表す前置詞を選ぶ。正解は (A) opposite。be proud to do「～することを光栄に思う」、announce「～を知らせる」、conveniently「便よく」、(be) located on ～「～に位置して (いる)」。
(B) 後ろには名詞の複数形または A and B のような語句が続く。
(C) (D) いずれも文意に合わない。

125 For all expenditures over $1,000, ------- in writing will be required.

(A) justify
(B) justification
(C) justified
(D) justifiably

1,000 ドルを超える支出には全て、書面による正当な理由の説明が必要になります。

(A) 〜を正当化する
(B) 正当化の理由
(C) 正当と認められる
(D) 正当に

正解 B　選択肢は全て動詞 justify「〜を正当化する」の派生語。------- in writing が主語で、will be required が述語動詞だが、主語には中心になる名詞がない。よって、名詞 (B) justification が正解。expenditure「支出」、require「〜を必要とする」。
(A) 動詞の原形。
(C) 過去分詞または過去形。
(D) 副詞。

126 A market analysis shows that sales of sports utility vehicles have decreased ------- over the past twelve months.

(A) considerably
(B) durably
(C) concisely
(D) expressively

市場分析は、SUV車の売り上げが過去 12 カ月にわたり、著しく減少していることを示しています。

(A) 著しく
(B) 永続的に
(C) 簡潔に
(D) 表情豊かに

正解 A　選択肢は全て副詞。that節の述語動詞 have decreasedを修飾する副詞として適切なものを選ぶ。SUV車の売り上げの減少について述べられているので、文意から程度の大きさを表す (A) considerablyが適切。analysis「分析」、sports utility vehicle「SUV車、スポーツ多目的車」、decrease「減少する」。
(B) (C) (D) いずれも文意に合わない。

127 Questions ------- reimbursement for travel expenses should be directed to the payroll office.

(A) concern
(B) concerns
(C) concerned
(D) concerning

出張旅費の払い戻しに関する質問は給与課へお願いします。

(A) 関心
(B) 関心
(C) 関係している
(D) 〜に関する

正解 D　文の主語は文頭から expenses までで、述語動詞は should be directed である。空所に前置詞 (D) concerning を入れると、空所から expenses までが前置詞句として Questionsを後ろから修飾する形になる。reimbursement「払い戻し」、travel「出張」、expense「経費」、direct 〜 to …「〜を…に向ける」。
(A) 名詞または動詞 concern「〜に関係する」の原形。
(B) 名詞の複数形または動詞の三人称単数現在形。
(C) 形容詞。

128 Sakai Trucking hired a software specialist to ------- its delivery scheduling system.

(A) notify
(B) pronounce
(C) recruit
(D) modernize

Sakaiトラック運送社は配送計画システムを最新式にするために、ソフトウエアの専門家を雇いました。

(A) ～に知らせる
(B) ～を表明する
(C) ～を募集する
(D) ～を最新式にする

> **正解 D** 選択肢は全て動詞。文頭からspecialistまでで文の形が成立しており、空所の前にtoがあることから、空所には目的を表す不定詞を作るのに適切な動詞を選ぶ。正解は、(D) modernize。hire「～を雇う」、specialist「専門家、プロ」、delivery「配達」。
> (A) (B) (C) いずれも文意に合わない。

---

129 Musitto, Inc., has been producing cutting-edge phones with ------- long battery-run times.

(A) has increased
(B) increases
(C) increased
(D) increasingly

Musitto社は、より一層長時間のバッテリー駆動機能を備えた最先端の電話を製造しています。

(A) ～を増加させている
(B) 増加
(C) 増加した
(D) ますます

> **正解 D** 空所の直前に前置詞 with があるので、------- long battery-run times は名詞句である。空所には、形容詞 long を修飾する副詞の (D) increasingly が適切。cutting-edge「最先端の」、battery-run「バッテリーで動く」。
> (A) 動詞 increase「～を増加させる」の現在完了形。
> (B) 名詞の複数形または動詞の三人称単数現在形。
> (C) 形容詞または動詞の過去形。

---

130 ------- the new bylaws, all employees of Lovato Marketing are required to participate in professional development each year.

(A) Under
(B) Into
(C) Behind
(D) Toward

新しい社則に従い、Lovatoマーケティング社の全従業員は毎年、職業能力開発に参加する必要があります。

(A) ～に従って
(B) ～の中へ
(C) ～の後ろで
(D) ～に向かって

> **正解 A** 選択肢は全て前置詞。カンマの前までの the new bylaws「新しい社則」という名詞句と、カンマ以降の「Lovato マーケティング社の全従業員は毎年、職業能力開発に参加する必要がある」との内容のつながりを考える。文意に合うのは、「～（法・規則など）に従って」という意味を表す (A) Under。employee「従業員」、be required to do「～する必要がある」、participate in ～「～に参加する」、professional development「職業能力開発」。
> (B) (C) (D) いずれも文意に合わない。

Questions 131-134 refer to the following instructions.

---

❶Periodic cleaning of the Huntington Premium Toaster Oven can greatly extend ------- useful
131.
life. First, make sure to unplug the toaster, and let it cool off before beginning the cleaning
process. ------- . Then wipe the interior with a moist sponge. ------- , clean the exterior with
132.   133.
a mild household cleaning solution. Following this process will keep your ------- looking
134.
and working like new.

問題 131-134 は次の説明書に関するものです。

Huntington Premium オーブントースターは、定期的に清掃することで、その耐用年数を著しく延ばすことができます。まず、清掃の手順に取り掛かる前に、必ずトースターの電源を抜いて、トースターを冷まします。*次に、パンくずの受け皿を取り出し、ぬるま湯で洗ってください。それから、湿ったスポンジで庫内を拭きます。最後に、刺激の少ない家庭用洗剤で外側を掃除します。この手順を守ることで、ご自宅のトースターは新品のような見た目と機能を保てるでしょう。

*問題 132 の挿入文の訳

▲語 注

instructions 〈複数形で〉説明書
❶ periodic　定期的な　　 cleaning　清掃、クリーニング　　 toaster oven　オーブントースター　　 greatly　大いに
extend　～(期間)を延長する　　 useful life　耐用年数　　 make sure to do　必ず～するようにする
unplug　～の電源を抜く　　 cool off　冷める　　 process　手順、工程　　 wipe　～を拭く　　 interior　内部、内側
moist　湿った　　 sponge　スポンジ　　 exterior　外側　　 mild　刺激の少ない　　 household　家庭の
solution　溶液　　 follow　～を守る、～に従う

131
(A) a
(B) its
(C) that
(D) another

(A) 1つの
(B) その
(C) あの
(D) もう1つの

正解 **B** 　空所を含む文は、「Huntington Premium オーブントースターの定期的な清掃は ------ 耐用年数を著しく延ばすことができる」という意味で、空所には何の耐用年数なのかを示す語が入ればよいと分かる。the Huntington Premium Toaster Oven を指して、「その (耐用年数)」という意味になる (B) its が適切。
(A) (C) (D) いずれを空所に入れても、何の耐用年数を示すかあいまいで、文意に合わない。

132
(A) Afterwards, reassemble the toaster carefully.
(B) Next, remove the crumb tray and rinse it with warm water.
(C) Note that frozen food will take longer to heat.
(D) Look for the product number on the underside.

(A) その後、トースターを丁寧に組み立て直してください。
(B) 次に、パンくずの受け皿を取り出し、ぬるま湯で洗ってください。
(C) 冷凍食品は温めるのにより長い時間がかかることにご注意ください。
(D) 底面の製品番号をお探しください。

正解 **B** 　空所の前文で、オーブントースターの清掃の事前準備として、電源を抜いて本体を冷ますよう説明されている。一方、空所の後ろには、「それから、湿ったスポンジで庫内を拭く」とある。(B) の「次に、パンくずの受け皿を取り出し、ぬるま湯で洗ってほしい」という文を入れると、作業手順の流れとして自然になる。crumb「パンくず」、tray「受け皿」、rinse「～をさっと洗う」。
(A) 器具の分解は指示されていない。afterwards「その後」、reassemble「～を組み立て直す」。
(C) 食品の温めに関する注意は文脈に合わない。note that ～「～であることに注意する」、frozen food「冷凍食品」。
(D) 空所の前後の文脈に合わない。

133
(A) Finally
(B) Instead
(C) Otherwise
(D) In the meantime

(A) 最後に
(B) 代わりに
(C) そうでなければ
(D) その間に

正解 **A** 　空所を含む文の前では、清掃の手順について、First「まず」や Then「それから」を用い、順を追った説明がされている。一方、空所を含む文の直後では「この手順を守ることで新品のような見た目と機能を保てるだろう」と、直前まで説明された清掃の手順の効果に言及している。よって、空所には「最後に」を意味する (A) Finally を入れて、手順の最後を説明する文にするのが、流れとして自然。
(B) (C) (D) いずれも前後の内容とつながらない。

134
(A) tools
(B) factory
(C) fixtures
(D) appliance

(A) 道具
(B) 工場
(C) 設備
(D) 電気器具

正解 **D** 　直前まで、オーブントースターの清掃の手順が説明されており、その手順の効果に言及した文であるため、空所には toaster oven を言い換えた (D) appliance が入るのが適切。この your appliance は「あなたが購入したトースター」を示す。
(A) (B) (C) いずれも toaster oven の言い換えにならず、文意に合わない。

Questions 135-138 refer to the following e-mail.

From: customerservice@liybank.org
To: jlaurens@mailsygo.com
Subject: LIY Bank Correspondence
Date: April 2

Dear Mr. Laurens,

❶You requested to be notified when official mail concerning your LIY Bank account is sent to you.

------- is, therefore, to inform you that a new credit card has been issued and mailed to you. It
135.

will replace your current credit card that is ------- to expire on May 31. ------- . When it arrives,
136. **137.**

please remember to activate your card through your online account on our Web site.

------- , you can go to your nearest bank branch and have it activated there by our
138.

representative.

❷If you have any further questions, please contact our Customer Service Center at 610-555-

0125.

Customer Service Team
LIY Bank

問題135-138は次のEメールに関するものです。

送信者：customerservice@liybank.org
受信者：jlaurens@mailsygo.com
件名：LIY銀行からのお知らせ
日付：4月2日

Laurens様

お客さまは、LIY銀行のご自身の預金口座に関して公式の郵便物が送付された際の通知の受信を依頼されました。当Eメールは、これに従いまして、新しいクレジットカードがお客さま宛てに発行され、郵送されたことをお知らせいたします。カードは5月31日に期限切れになる予定の現在のクレジットカードと交換になります。* 1週間以内にお手元に届くでしょう。そちらが届きましたら、当行ウェブサイトのオンラインのアカウントを介して、必ずカードを有効にしていただくようお願いします。あるいは、お客さまの最寄りの当行支店へご来店になり、当行の担当者にその場でカードを有効化してもらうことも可能です。
その他にも何かご質問がございましたら当行顧客サービスセンター、610-555-0125までご連絡ください。

顧客サービスチーム
LIY銀行

*問題137の挿入文の訳

語 注

correspondence　通信、通信文
❶ request to *do*　～することを依頼する　　official　公式の　　mail　郵便物　　concerning　～に関する
account　預金口座　　therefore　従って、それゆえ　　inform ～ (that) …　～に…であることを知らせる
issue　～を発行する　　replace　～に取って代わる、～の代わりになる　　current　現時点の　　expire　期限切れになる
remember to *do*　忘れずに～する　　activate　～を有効にする　　online　オンラインの
account　（サービス利用のための）アカウント　　branch　支店　　representative　担当者
❷ further　さらなる　　customer service　顧客サービス

135
(A) Either
(B) What
(C) This
(D) He

(A) どちらか
(B) 何
(C) これ
(D) 彼は

正解 **C** ❶の１行目より、LIY 銀行は以前に、顧客の Laurens さんから公式の郵便物が送られた際に通知するよう依頼されたと分かる。空所を含む文は、この E メールがその通知であると述べたもので、主語に当たる名詞がない。よって、(C) This を空所に入れ、「これは、従って、新しいクレジットカードが発行され、郵送されたことを知らせるためのものだ」という意味にすると、前後の指示関係が明らかになる。
(A) 代名詞。
(B) 疑問代名詞または関係代名詞。
(D) 人称代名詞の三人称単数の主格。

136
(A) equal
(B) true
(C) due
(D) fair

(A) 等しい
(B) 当てはまる
(C) 予定された
(D) 公平な

正解 **C** 選択肢は全て形容詞。that 以降の関係詞節が後ろから your current credit card「あなたの現在のクレジットカード」を修飾している。to expire「期限切れになること」という不定詞があるので、不定詞を続けて適切な意味を表す形容詞を選ぶ。文意に合うのは、(C) due。be due to *do* で「〜する予定である」という意味。
(A) (B) (D) いずれも、直後に不定詞 to expire を伴う形容詞として不適切。

137
(A) You may spend it as you see fit.
(B) You should receive it within a week.
(C) However, deliveries have been on schedule.
(D) Please confirm receipt of this letter.

(A) お客さまが適当だと思うだけそれをお使いいただけます。
(B) １週間以内にお手元に届くでしょう。
(C) しかしながら、配達は予定通りに進んでいます。
(D) この手紙の受領をご確認ください。

正解 **B** 空所の前文までに、新しいクレジットカードが発行されたこと、それは現在のクレジットカードと交換されるものであることが述べられている。一方、空所の直後の文では、新しいクレジットカードの到着後に必要な手続きが案内されている。よって空所には、到着時期について知らせている (B) を入れると、流れとして自然。
(A) spend「〜（金・時間）を費やす」、see fit「適当だと思う」。
(C) However「しかしながら」とあるが、前文と対立する内容ではない。delivery「配達」、on schedule「予定通りに」。
(D) confirm「〜を確認する」、receipt「受領」。

138
(A) Suddenly
(B) Specifically
(C) Accordingly
(D) Alternatively

(A) 突然に
(B) 明確に
(C) それに応じて
(D) あるいは

正解 **D** 選択肢は全て副詞。空所の直前では、銀行のオンラインのアカウントを介して、新しいクレジットカードを有効にするように案内されている。一方、空所を含む文では、最寄りの支店へ行き、担当者にクレジットカードを有効化してもらう方法が紹介されている。これらは同じ処理の２通りの方法を案内していると考えられるため、空所には「あるいは」という意味の (D) Alternatively を入れると、意味が通る。
(A) (B) (C) いずれも文意に合わない。

Questions 139-142 refer to the following memo.

To: All Alanaga Corporation Employees
From: Corporate Travel Office
Subject: Travel policy update

❶ Over the past year, the Corporate Travel Office has been working hard to save the company money ------- cost-effective travel arrangements. Yesterday we ------- an agreement with the
　　　　　　　　　　139.　　　　　　　　　　　　　　　　　　　　　140.
Bellaria Taxi Company. From this point forward, when traveling on official Alanaga business, you are required to take a Bellaria taxi. ------- , Alanaga will receive a large discount from
　　　　　　　　　　　　　　　　　　　　　141.
Bellaria for its services. This arrangement will be used primarily for transportation between branch offices. ------- . If you have a suggestion to make your business travel easier, please
　　　　　　　　　142.
call the Corporate Travel Office at extension 523.

問題139-142は次のメモに関するものです。

宛先：Alanaga社従業員各位
差出人：法人旅行課
件名：出張方針の改訂

ここ1年法人旅行課は、費用対効果の高い出張を手配することで、会社の費用の節約に励んできました。当社は昨日、Bellariaタクシー会社との契約を成立させました。これより以降は、Alanaga社の公的な仕事で出張の際は、Bellaria社のタクシーを利用していただく必要があります。これと引き換えに、Alanaga社はBellaria社から、同社のサービスの利用に対し大幅な割引を受けられます。この契約は、主に支店間の移動手段に運用されるものとします。*しかしながら、空港との行き来にも利用して構いません。出張旅行をより簡便にするためのご提案がありましたら、内線523番の法人旅行課までお電話ください。

*問題142の挿入文の訳

┃語　注
corporation　企業、会社　　employee　従業員　　corporate　法人の、会社の　　policy　方針　　update　改訂情報、更新
❶ past　これまでの、過去の　　save　～を節約する　　cost-effective　費用対効果の高い　　arrangement　手配
agreement　契約、契約書　　from this point　この時点から　　forward　今後は　　on business　仕事で
official　公的な　　be required to *do*　～する必要がある　　discount　割引　　primarily　主に
transportation　移動手段、交通　　branch office　支店　　suggestion　提案　　extension　内線、内線番号

139
(A) it made
(B) by making
(C) and makes
(D) the maker of

＊選択肢の訳は省略

> **正解 B** 文頭から空所の直前までですでに文として成立しているので、------- cost-effective travel arrangements は修飾語句の可能性が高い。(B) by making を入れると、空所以降が「費用対効果の高い出張を手配することで」という方法・手段を表すことになり、文意が通る。
> (A) 空所に it made を入れて the company money を後ろから修飾する関係詞節の形を考えたとしても、意味が通らない。
> (C) Over the past year と現在完了進行形の時制から、1年前から現在に至るまでの取り組みを述べた文なので、現在形では意味がつながらない。
> (D) 空所の前の部分とつながらない。maker「作る人」。

140
(A) finalized
(B) canceled
(C) highlighted
(D) considered

(A) ～を成立させた
(B) ～を中止した
(C) ～を強調した
(D) ～を考慮した

> **正解 A** 文意に合う動詞の過去形を選ぶ。直後の文で、「これより以降は、Alanaga 社の公的な仕事で出張の際は、Bellaria 社のタクシーを利用する必要がある」とあるので、空所には動詞 finalize「～を成立させる、～を最終決定する」の過去形の (A) finalized を入れて、「Bellaria タクシー会社との契約を成立させた」とすると文意が通る。
> (B) ❶ 3 ～ 4 行目より、「Bellaria タクシー会社を利用する必要がある」とあるので、不適切。
> (C) (D) いずれも文意に合わない。

141
(A) If not
(B) However
(C) Regardless
(D) In turn

(A) そうでなければ
(B) しかしながら
(C) それにもかかわらず
(D) 引き換えに

> **正解 D** 直前の文では、これより以降の出張の際は、Bellaria 社のタクシーを利用する必要があること、空所を含む文では、Alanaga 社はサービスの利用で Bellaria 社から大幅な割引を受けられることが説明されている。よって、契約の内容とは、出張時に Bellaria 社を大いに利用すると割引を受けられるというものだと考えられる。「引き換えに」という意味の (D) In turn を入れると、両社の契約の説明として文意に合う。
> (A) (B) (C) いずれも文意に合わない。

142
(A) However, it may also be used for travel to and from the airport.
(B) On the other hand, taking a train may be more expensive.
(C) Bellaria Taxi Company has been providing transportation for 25 years.
(D) The Corporate Travel Office has an emergency phone number.

(A) しかしながら、空港との行き来にも利用して構いません。
(B) その一方で、電車を利用すると料金がもっと高くなるかもしれません。
(C) Bellaria タクシー会社は 25 年間、移動手段を提供し続けてきました。
(D) 法人旅行課には緊急用の電話番号があります。

> **正解 A** 直前の文で、Bellaria 社との契約は、主に支店間の移動手段に運用される予定だと書かれている。副詞 However「しかしながら」で始まり、空港との行き来での利用も可能だと言及している (A) を入れると、支店間の移動以外の用途も認められるという流れになり、意味が通る。
> (B) 前後の意味がつながらない。on the other hand「その一方で」、expensive「料金が高い」。
> (C) Bellaria タクシー会社を紹介する文。❶ 2 ～ 3 行目の、会社名が初めて出た直後であれば適切だが、この箇所では文脈的に不自然。
> (D) 直後に通常の内線番号を案内しており、前後の意味がつながらない。emergency「緊急事態」。

Questions 143-146 refer to the following letter.

---

4 February

Liya Lim
1228 Dunlop Street
Singapore 23885

Dear Ms. Lim,

❶ To show appreciation for your continued patronage with the Good Day Cable Company, we

invite you to our annual Good Day at the Park event at Paya Park on 20 March. The evening

------- at 5:00 P.M. with a private reception at the Paya Clubhouse. While beverages and
143.

appetizers are ------- , listen to performances from local musicians. ------- . Afterward, dessert
144.   **145.**

will follow in the form of an ice cream social. ------- the social, clients are also invited to
146.

participate in a raffle and trivia games. Prizes will be awarded!

❷ Kindly RSVP by 28 February. We hope to see you there!

Sincerely,

Jet Khoo
President of Good Day Cable Company

問題 143-146 は次の手紙に関するものです。

2月4日

Liya Lim
Dunlop 通り 1228 番地
シンガポール 23885

Lim様

Good Day ケーブル会社への変わらぬご支援に感謝を込めて、3 月 20 日、Paya 公園にて毎年恒例のイベント「公園での良き 1 日」に皆さまを招待いたします。この夕べは、午後 5 時に Paya クラブハウスでのプライベートレセプションとともに始まります。飲み物やアペタイザーが給仕される中、地元の音楽家による演奏をお聞きください。*午後 6 時にはファイアピットへ向かい、バーベキューディナーをお楽しみください。その後は、アイスクリームパーティー形式でのデザートが続きます。そのパーティーの間、顧客の皆さまはくじ引きや雑学ゲームにもぜひご参加ください。景品をご用意しております！

2月28日までに出欠のお返事を頂きますようお願いします。会場でお会いできるのを楽しみにしております！

敬具

Jet Khoo
Good Dayケーブル会社社長

*問題 145 の挿入文の訳

語 注

❶ appreciation　感謝　　continued　変わらぬ、継続的な　　patronage　支援　　annual　毎年の、年次の
private　プライベートな、内輪の　　reception　レセプション、歓迎会　　clubhouse　クラブハウス　　beverage　飲み物
appetizer　アペタイザー　★食前酒や前菜のこと　　performance　演奏　　local　地元の　　afterward　その後は
dessert　デザート　　follow　後に続く　　in the form of ～　～の形式で　　social　パーティー、懇親会
participate in ～　～に参加する　　raffle　くじ引き　　trivia　雑学的知識　　prize　景品　　award　～を授与する
❷ kindly　どうか（～してください）　　RSVP　お返事ください　★フランス語の répondez s'il vous plaît の略

143 (A) will have commenced
(B) will commence
(C) commenced
(D) has commenced

* 選択肢の訳は省略

正解 **B** 選択肢には動詞 commence「始まる」が変化した形が並ぶ。空所を含む文の主語は The evening「夕べ」で、空所の後には時を表す at 5:00 P.M.「午後 5 時に」が続くので、文意に合う動詞の時制を選べばよい。❶ 1〜2 行目より、手紙の目的は 3 月 20 日の Paya 公園での毎年恒例のイベントに招待することであり、ここではイベントの開始時間が案内されていると考えられるので、空所には未来形の (B) will commence が適切。
(A) 未来完了形。
(C) 過去形。
(D) 現在完了形。

144 (A) seated
(B) dined
(C) served
(D) played

(A) 席に着いて
(B) ごちそうされて
(C) 給仕されて
(D) 演奏されて

正解 **C** 空所の直前に be 動詞 are があるので、受動態を作る過去分詞として文意に合うものを選ぶ。while 節の主語が beverages and appetizers「飲み物やアペタイザー」なので、serve「〜（飲食物など）を給仕する」の過去分詞である (C) served が文意に合う。
(A) seat「〜を着席させる」の過去分詞。
(B) dine「〜（人）にごちそうする」の過去分詞。
(D) play「〜を演奏する」の過去分詞。

145 (A) At 6:00 P.M., head to The Firepit for a barbecue dinner.
(B) The Clubhouse had to be reserved two months ago.
(C) Please make sure your account number is written on your check.
(D) Guests may pay for their tickets at the door.

(A) 午後 6 時にはファイアピットへ向かい、バーベキューディナーをお楽しみください。
(B) クラブハウスは 2 カ月前に予約する必要がありました。
(C) ご自身の預金口座番号が小切手に記載されていることをご確認ください。
(D) 招待客は入り口でチケットの代金をお支払いいただけます。

正解 **A** 空所の前文では飲み物やアペタイザーが給仕されることが、空所の後ろの文ではデザートの時間があることが案内されている。よって、メインディッシュの barbecue dinner の提供場所に言及した (A) を入れると、イベント当日の料理の内容を順に説明する流れになり自然。head to 〜「〜へ向かう」、firepit「ファイアピット、（屋外の）炉」。
(B) クラブハウスの予約については述べられていない。reserve「〜を予約する」。
(C) make sure (that) 〜「〜であることを確認する」、check「小切手」。
(D) pay for 〜「〜の代金を支払う」。

146 (A) During
(B) Including
(C) Inside
(D) Meanwhile

(A) 〜の間
(B) 〜を含めて
(C) 〜の中で
(D) その間に

正解 **A** 空所の直後にある the social「そのパーティー」は、空所の直前で言及されているアイスクリームパーティーのことで、カンマ以降では、also を用いて「顧客の皆はくじ引きや雑学ゲームにも参加してほしい」とあるので、空所に前置詞 (A) During を入れると、同じ時間帯に行われる催しを紹介する流れになり、自然。
(B) 前置詞。意味が通らない。
(C) 主に空間の内側を表す前置詞なので、不適切。
(D) 副詞。後ろに名詞句の the social は続かない。

Questions 147-148 refer to the following instructions.

How to Perform a Global Reset

❶ Resetting your television remote-control device will delete individual settings and restore all functions to the standard manufacturer settings. To perform a global reset, follow the steps below.

❷ **Step 1**
Hold the POWER button down for five seconds and release.

❸ **Step 2**
Press the right ARROW button. You will hear a short beep.

❹ **Step 3**
Press CLEAR. The red light at the top should turn off. If it remains lit, press the button again before proceeding to step 4.

❺ **Step 4**
Enter your user code. A green light will flash, indicating that the standard settings are restored.

❻ If desired, you can now reprogram your remote to customize the settings.

問題 147-148 は次の説明書に関するものです。

全体リセットの操作方法

テレビのリモコン装置のリセットをすると、個々の設定を消去し、全ての機能を工場出荷時の標準の設定に戻します。全体リセットを行うには、下記の手順に従ってください。

手順1
「電源」のボタンを5秒間長押ししてから離します。

手順2
右の「矢印」のボタンを押します。短いピッという音が聞こえます。

手順3
「消去」を押します。一番上の赤色のライトが消えます。もし点灯したままならば、手順4に進む前に再度ボタンを押します。

手順4
ユーザーコードを入力します。緑色のライトが光って、標準の設定に戻ったことを示します。

ご希望の場合は、ここでリモコンを再びプログラムして、設定をカスタマイズすることができます。

147 What do the instructions explain?

    (A) How to turn on lights remotely

    (B) How to remove customized settings

    (C) How to order additional television channels

    (D) How to improve picture quality

説明書は何を説明していますか。

    (A) 遠隔操作でライトを点灯する方法

    (B) カスタマイズされた設定を削除する方法

    (C) 追加のテレビのチャンネルを申し込む方法

    (D) 画質を改善する方法

正解 **B**　説明書の見出しに「全体リセットの操作方法」とあり、❶1～2行目で「テレビのリモコン装置のリセットをすると、個々の設定を消去し、全ての機能を工場出荷時の標準の設定に戻す」と説明されている。さらに、❷以降で全体リセットの手順の説明が続いていることから、(B) の「カスタマイズされた設定を削除する方法」が正解。remove「～を取り除く」。

(A) ❹、❺でライトについての言及はあるが、リモコンの表示部品として述べられているだけである。remotely「遠隔操作で」。

(C) チャンネルについての言及はない。order「～を注文する」、additional「追加の」。

(D) 画質についての言及はない。improve「～を改良する」、picture quality「画質」。

---

148 According to the instructions, what step might need to be repeated?

    (A) Step 1

    (B) Step 2

    (C) Step 3

    (D) Step 4

説明書によると、どの手順が繰り返される必要があるかもしれませんか。

    (A) 手順1

    (B) 手順2

    (C) 手順3

    (D) 手順4

正解 **C**　❹の手順3で、「消去」を押すと一番上の赤色のライトが消えると説明した後、「もし点灯したままならば、手順4に進む前に再度ボタンを押す」と指示されている。よって、ボタンを押しても赤色のライトが消えない場合、手順3は繰り返される必要がある。(C) が正解。

(A) (B) (D) いずれも、説明書内で繰り返すよう指示している箇所はない。

Final Test

語 注

instructions 〈複数形で〉説明書　　perform ～を行う　　global 全体的な　　reset リセット

❶ reset ～をリセットする　　remote-control リモコンの　　device 装置、機器　　delete ～を消去する　　individual 個々の　　setting 設定　　restore ～を元に戻す　　function 機能　　manufacturer setting 工場出荷時の設定　　follow ～に従う

❷ hold down ～ ～を押さえたままにする　　power 電力　　release （～を）離す　　★目的語 (the button) は省略されている

❸ beep ピッという音

❹ turn off 消える　　remain ～のままである　　lit 点灯した　　★動詞 light「～（明かりなど）をつける」の過去分詞　　proceed 進む

❺ enter ～を入力する　　user code ユーザーコード、利用者番号　　flash ぴかっと光る　　indicate ～を示す

❻ reprogram ～を再度プログラムする　　remote 〈remote control の略で〉リモコン　　customize ～をカスタマイズする　　★好みに合わせて設定すること

Questions 149-150 refer to the following notice.

Attention All Manning & Murdoch Employees

❶ The staff kitchen will be closed from August 15 to August 19. During this period, the kitchen will be painted and a new dishwasher and refrigerator will be installed. Please do not enter the kitchen during this time for any reason, including to make tea or coffee. A temporary beverage station will be set up for your use in the office foyer. Thank you for your cooperation.

問題149-150は次のお知らせに関するものです。

Manning & Murdoch社の従業員各位

従業員用の給湯室は、8月15日から8月19日まで閉鎖されます。この期間中、給湯室は塗装され、新しい食器洗い機と冷蔵庫が設置されます。紅茶やコーヒーを入れることを含め、どのような理由でも、この期間内は給湯室に立ち入らないでください。会社のロビーに、皆さんが利用できる臨時の飲み物用の場所が設置されます。皆さんのご協力に感謝します。

149 What is one purpose of the notice?

(A) To advertise the opening of a company café

(B) To ask employees to keep the kitchen clean

(C) To notify employees about upcoming renovations

(D) To announce that a building will be closed temporarily

お知らせの1つの目的は何ですか。

(A) 社内カフェの開店を周知させること。

(B) 従業員に給湯室を清潔に保つようお願いすること。

(C) 従業員に近日中の改装について知らせること。

(D) 建物が一時的に閉鎖される予定であると知らせること。

正解 **C**	見出しに「Manning & Murdoch 社の従業員各位」とあることから、お知らせは会社から従業員に宛てたものである。❶ 1～2行目に「従業員用の給湯室は、8月15日から8月19日まで閉鎖される。この期間中、給湯室は塗装され、新しい食器洗い機と冷蔵庫が設置される」とあるので、お知らせの1つの目的は、従業員に給湯室の改装を知らせることだと分かる。よって、(C) が正解。notify「～に知らせる」、upcoming「近づいている、今度の」、renovation「改装」。

(A) ❶ 4～5行目に「臨時の飲み物用の場所が設置される」とあるだけで、カフェの開店ではない。advertise「～を周知させる」、opening「開店」。

(B) ❶ 3～4行目に「給湯室に立ち入らないでほしい」とある。keep ～ …「～を…に保つ」。

(D) ❶ 1～2行目より、閉鎖されるのは給湯室であり、建物ではない。temporarily「一時的に」。

Final Test

150 What will be available in the office foyer?

(A) A catered lunch
(B) A sign-up sheet
(C) Snacks for purchase
(D) Tea and coffee

会社のロビーでは、何が入手できますか。

(A) ケータリングの昼食
(B) 登録用紙
(C) 購入用の軽食
(D) 紅茶やコーヒー

正解 **D**	❶ 3～4行目に「紅茶やコーヒーを入れることを含め、どのような理由でも、この期間内は給湯室に立ち入らないでほしい」という指示があり、同 4～5行目で「会社のロビーに、皆が利用できる臨時の飲み物用の場所が設置される」との説明がある。よって、ロビーで入手できるのは (D) の「紅茶やコーヒー」である。available「入手できる、利用できる」。

(A) cater「～に仕出し料理を出す」。
(B) sign-up「登録」、sheet「用紙」。
(C) snack「軽食」、purchase「購入」。

語 注

Attention ～　～宛て

❶ dishwasher 食器洗い機　　refrigerator 冷蔵庫　　install ～を設置する、～を取り付ける　　temporary 臨時の
beverage 飲み物　★水以外の飲料を指す　　station 場所、局　　set up ～　～を設置する　　foyer ロビー、ホール
cooperation 協力

Questions 151-152 refer to the following text-message chain.

❶ Frances Murphy (11:25 A.M.)
Hi Debbie. You mentioned you were stopping at the office supply store today. Would you mind picking up some file labels for me?

❷ Debbie Emhof (11:27 A.M.)
No problem. I'm at Office Check now. What exactly do you need?

❸ Frances Murphy (11:28 A.M.)
I need a pack of multicolored labels.

❹ Debbie Emhof (11:35 A.M.)
Well, those seem to be out of stock. Do you want me to get a different style? There are white labels available.

❺ Frances Murphy (11:36 A.M.)
I can wait. Are we still on for lunch?

❻ Debbie Emhof (11:37 A.M.)
Of course. I'll meet you at the cafeteria on the second floor at 12:30 P.M. Ken Mitani from the billing department is going to join us, too.

問題 151-152 は次のテキストメッセージのやり取りに関するものです。

Frances Murphy（午前 11 時 25 分）
こんにちは、Debbie。今日、事務用品店に立ち寄ると言ってましたよね。私にファイル用ラベルを何枚か買ってきてくれませんか。

Debbie Emhof（午前 11 時 27 分）
いいですよ。今、Office Check にいます。あなたは、どんなものが正確には必要なのですか。

Frances Murphy（午前 11 時 28 分）
いろいろな色のラベルが入ったパックが 1 袋必要です。

Debbie Emhof（午前 11 時 35 分）
ええと、それは在庫切れのようです。違う型のを買いましょうか。白のラベルならありますよ。

Frances Murphy（午前 11 時 36 分）
待てますのでいいです。私たちのランチはまだ予定に入っていますか。

Debbie Emhof（午前 11 時 37 分）
もちろんです。2 階のカフェテリアで、午後 12 時半に会いましょう。経理部の Ken Mitani も、私たちに合流する予定です。

151 At 11:36 A.M., what does Ms. Murphy most likely mean when she writes, "I can wait"?

(A) She is not very hungry.
(B) She wants only colored labels.
(C) She needs Ms. Emhof to find an item.
(D) She can meet Mr. Mitani at a later date.

午前 11 時 36 分に、"I can wait"と書くことで、Murphy さんは何を意図していると考えられますか。

(A) あまり空腹ではない。
(B) 色付きのラベルだけが欲しい。
(C) Emhof さんに品物を探してもらいたい。
(D) 後日、Mitani さんに会うことができる。

 正解 B 下線部は、❸でいろいろな色のラベルが入ったパックが必要と述べる Murphy さんに対し、❹で Emhof さんが「それは在庫切れのようだ。違う型のを買おうか。白のラベルならある」と提案した後に、Murphy さんがした発言。つまり、Murphy さんは、いろいろな色のラベルが入ったパックだけが欲しいので、入荷を待つことができると提案を断っている。(B) が正解。
(D) ❺の下線部の発言までに、Mitani さんは話題に上っていない。later date「後日」。

---

152 What is probably true about the writers?

(A) They work in the same building.
(B) They commute to work together.
(C) They manage an office supply store.
(D) They are late for a business lunch.

書き手たちについて正しいと思われることは何ですか。

(A) 同じ建物で働いている。
(B) 一緒に通勤している。
(C) 事務用品店を経営している。
(D) 仕事の昼食会に遅れている。

正解 A ❶より、Murphy さんが Emhof さんの外出先を知っていて買い物を依頼していること、❺、❻より、2 人がランチの約束をしており、待ち合わせ場所を「2 階のカフェテリアで」と Emhof さんが伝えていることから、2 人はおそらく同じ建物で働く職場の同僚であると考えられる。よって、(A) が正解。
(B) 通勤に関する言及はない。commute「通勤する」。
(C) ❶より、Emhof さんは事務用品店へ買い物に行っている客である。manage「〜を経営する」。
(D) ❺、❻より、ランチは予定通りに行われる。また、2 人が約束しているのが仕事の昼食会かどうかは不明。

Final Test

語 注

❶ mention (that)　〜であると述べる　　stop at 〜　〜に立ち寄る　　office supply store　事務用品店
pick up 〜　〜を買う、〜を入手する
❷ exactly　正確には
❸ pack　（数個入りの）パック、包み　　multicolored　多色の
❹ out of stock　在庫切れの　　style　型　　available　入手できる、利用できる
❺ wait　延期する、遅らせる　　on　予定されて
❻ billing department　経理部

Questions 153-155 refer to the following advertisement.

Excelsior Style—Your First Name in Fashion!
For a short time only, receive up to 50 percent off on all purchases!
Offer valid through May 31

❶ Excelsiorstyle.com is your go-to Web fashion hub with thousands of items of women's and children's apparel. Browse our site for the newest styles in coats and jackets, dresses, tops, skirts, swimwear, sleepwear, shoes, and accessories.

❷ Plus, we now offer fashions for your home through our brand-new line of interior decoration products! Visit Excelsiorstyle.com now to find the latest in home décor.

❸ Take advantage of our long-standing policy of free delivery for purchases over $75.00.

問題 153-155 は次の広告に関するものです。

Excelsior Style ―― ファッションの一番手！
期間限定で、全てのご購入品に対し最大50パーセントの割引が受けられます！
提供は5月31日まで有効　　　　.

Excelsiorstyle.com は、数千点の婦人服と子ども服を取りそろえた、大人気のウェブのファッションの拠点です。当社のウェブサイトで、コートやジャケット、ワンピース、トップス、スカート、水着、寝間着、靴、アクセサリー類の最新のスタイルをご覧になってください。

さらに、当社ではただ今、インテリア用品の新商品ラインを通じ、ご家庭のためのファッションインテリアも提供しています！ 今すぐ Excelsiorstyle.com を訪れて、インテリア用品の最新の流行を見つけてください。

当社の従来からの方針である 75 ドル超のご購入での無料配送をご利用ください。

語 注

first トップの　　name 評判の人・物　　up to ～ ～まで　　purchase 購入、購入品　　offer 提供　　valid 有効な
through ～ ～を通じて
❶ go-to 人気の、訪問者が多い　　hub 拠点　　item 品物、品目　　apparel 衣服　　browse ～を閲覧する
　 tops 〈複数形で〉トップス ★上半身に着る衣服
❷ brand-new 真新しい　　line 商品ライン　　interior decoration インテリア、室内装飾
　 the latest 最新の流行、最新のもの　　décor 装飾品
❸ take advantage of ～ ～を利用する　　long-standing 従来からの、長年にわたる　　policy 方針、規定

153 What is being advertised?　　　　　　　　何が宣伝されていますか。

- (A) A department store's new name
- (B) A recently upgraded Web site
- (C) A discount on online purchases
- (D) A change to shipping policy

- (A) デパートの新しい店名
- (B) 最近改良されたウェブサイト
- (C) オンライン購入での割引
- (D) 配送方針の変更

 正解 C　見出しの2行目に、「期間限定で、全ての購入品に対し最大50パーセントの割引が受けられる」とある。また❶、❷より、割引はExcelsiorstyle.comというウェブサイトでの購入品に関することだと分かるので、(C) が正解。
(A) 見出しの Your First Name「一番手」はデパートの店名ではない。
(B) ウェブサイトの宣伝ではあるが、改良されたとは書かれていない。
(D) 無料配送の方針についての言及はあるが、変更があるとは述べられていない。

---

154 Based on the advertisement, what will happen on June 1?　　広告に基づくと、6月1日に何が起こりますか。

- (A) Customers will pay regular prices.
- (B) A children's department will open.
- (C) Purchases will be eligible for a free gift.
- (D) All shipping costs will be discounted.

- (A) 顧客は通常価格を支払う。
- (B) 子ども服の売り場がオープンする。
- (C) 購入すると、無料プレゼントの対象となる。
- (D) 全ての配送料が割引になる。

正解 A　見出しの3行目に、割引の提供は5月31日まで有効とある。従って、翌日の6月1日には、割引の期間が終わって通常価格での販売に戻ると推測できる。よって、(A) が正解。based on ～「～に基づいて」。regular「通常の」。
(B) ❶1～2行目より、子ども服はすでに取り扱いがある。department「(デパートなどの) 売り場」。
(C) eligible for ～「～の資格のある、～の対象となる」。
(D) 全配送料については述べられていない。shipping「配送」。

---

155 What is available for the first time?　　何が初めて入手できますか。

- (A) Footwear
- (B) Home-decorating items
- (C) Outerwear
- (D) Children's clothing

- (A) 履き物
- (B) 家庭用のインテリア用品
- (C) 上着類
- (D) 子ども服

正解 B　❷に「さらに、当社ではただ今、インテリア用品の新商品ラインを通じ、家庭のためのファッションインテリアも提供している」とあるので、Excelsior Style 社は新しく家庭用のインテリア用品を取り扱い始めたことが分かる。よって、初めて入手できるのは (B) の「インテリア用品」。available「入手できる、利用できる」、for the first time「初めて」。
(A) (C) (D) ❶より、いずれもすでに販売されている品目。

Questions 156-158 refer to the following article.

Warm Welcome & Special Thanks

❶ (September 7)—*Karimun Post* readers may have noticed the addition of Mei Chandra to this newspaper's masthead. We are pleased to welcome her as our first-ever intern reporter at the paper.

❷ Ms. Chandra recently moved to Jakarta after studying English and journalism in the United States. For her first assignment, she has researched the challenges currently faced by our country's textile industry from an international perspective. Her initial article on this topic appears in this issue.

❸ The addition of internships is just one more way we fulfill our educational mission. For the past year and a half, the *Karimun Post* has been sustained primarily by funding from local academic institutions. The paper is now focused not only on keeping the local community informed but also on serving career-development purposes.

❹ A bonus of this new direction for the paper is the number of students who now contribute to the publication in multiple ways. The editor would like to take this opportunity to thank the many students who volunteer their time each month—including those who deliver the print version of the newspaper to the doorsteps of our subscribers on time every week.

問題156-158は次の記事に関するものです。

心からの歓迎と深い感謝を表して

(9月7日) ── 『Karimun Post』紙の読者の皆さんは、当紙の奥付に Mei Chandra という名前が加わったことにお気付きかもしれません。当紙初のインターン記者として、彼女を迎えることを喜ばしく思っています。

Chandra さんは、アメリカ合衆国で英語とジャーナリズムを学んだ後、最近ジャカルタに移り住みました。彼女は最初の担当業務として、わが国の織物産業が現在直面している課題について、国際的な視点から調査をしています。このトピックに関する彼女の最初の記事が今号に掲載されています。

インターンシップ制度の付加はまさに、当紙が教育的使命を全うするための、もう1つの手段です。この1年半、『Karimun Post』紙は、主に地元の教育機関からの資金提供によって支えられてきました。当紙は今や、地域社会に情報を伝え続けることだけでなく、キャリア開発という目的に尽力することにも、重点を置いています。

当紙にとってこの新たな方向性による思いがけない贈り物は、今や、さまざまな方法で刊行物に貢献してくれている学生の数です。編集人として、この機会に、毎月自分たちの時間を自発的に提供してくれる多くの学生たち──定期購読者の家の戸口まで、毎週時間通りに紙版の新聞を配達してくれる人々も含めて──お礼を述べたいと思います。

語 注

welcome　歓迎

❶ notice　～に気付く　　addition　追加、付加　　masthead　(新聞・雑誌などの)奥付、発行人欄
be pleased to *do*　喜んで～する　　first-ever　史上初の　　intern　インターン、研修生

❷ assignment　業務　★割り当てられた仕事　　research　～を調査する　　challenge　課題　　face　～に直面する
textile　織物　　perspective　視点　　initial　最初の　　issue　(定期刊行物の)号

❸ internship　インターンシップ、研修期間　　fulfill　～を果たす　　mission　使命、任務　　sustain　～を支える
primarily　主に　　funding　資金提供　　academic institution　教育機関　　serve　～(目的)にかなう
career-development　キャリア開発の　　purpose　目的

❹ bonus　思いがけない贈り物　　direction　方向性、方針　　contribute to ～　～に貢献する　　publication　刊行物
multiple　多数の　　editor　編集人、編集者　　opportunity　機会　　volunteer　～(奉仕・尽力)を自発的に提供する
doorstep　家の戸口　　subscriber　定期購読者

156 What is stated about the intern position?

    (A) It is new to the publication.
    (B) It requires international travel.
    (C) It is based in the United States.
    (D) It requires a degree in journalism.

インターンの職について何と述べられていますか。

    (A) その刊行物にとってこれまでなかったことである。
    (B) 外国への出張が必要である。
    (C) アメリカ合衆国に拠点を置いている。
    (D) ジャーナリズムの学位が必要である。

正解 A 記事では、❶の1～3行目でMei Chandra さんの名前を出した後、続けて同3～5行目で「当紙初のインターン記者として、彼女を迎えることを喜ばしく思う」と述べられている。よって、『Karimun Post』紙がインターンを受け入れたのは、今回が初めてだと分かる。(A) が正解。position「職、地位」。
(B) (C) インターンの職の条件や活動内容については記載がない。
(D) degree「学位」。

---

157 What is suggested about Ms. Chandra?

    (A) She is an experienced translator.
    (B) She is writing a series of articles.
    (C) She will help recruit more interns.
    (D) She used to work in the textile industry.

Chandra さんについて何が示唆されていますか。

    (A) 経験豊かな翻訳者である。
    (B) 連載記事を書いている。
    (C) さらに多くのインターンを採用するのを手伝う。
    (D) 以前は織物産業で働いていた。

正解 B 記事には、Chandra さんの経歴の他、最初の担当業務として彼女が国内の織物産業の課題について調査をしており、❷の6～7行目「このトピックに関する彼女の最初の記事が今号に掲載されている」と書かれている。ここから、次の記事も同じトピックに関するものだと考えられるので、(B) が正解。a series of ～「一連の～」。
(A) ❷1～3行目に英語を学んだとあるが、翻訳者とは述べられていない。experienced「経験を積んだ」、translator「翻訳者」。
(C) Chandra さんがインターン採用に関わるとの言及はない。recruit「～を採用する、～を募集する」。
(D) ❷3～6行目より、Chandra さんは織物産業について調査をしているだけで、働いていたとは書かれていない。

---

158 What is indicated about the *Karimun Post*?

    (A) It is free to local residents.
    (B) It is distributed by volunteers.
    (C) It is printed in multiple languages.
    (D) It is funded by advertising revenue.

『Karimun Post』紙について何が示されていますか。

    (A) 地元の住民には無料である。
    (B) ボランティアによって配達されている。
    (C) 複数の言語で印刷されている。
    (D) 広告収入によって資金を得ている。

正解 B ❹の4～9行目に、「毎月自分たちの時間を自発的に提供してくれる多くの学生たち——定期購読者の家の戸口まで毎週時間通りに紙版の新聞を配達してくれる人々も含めて——礼を述べたい」とある。よって、(B) の「ボランティアによって配達されている」が正解。distribute「～を配達する」。
(A) 購読料については言及がない。free「無料の」、resident「住民」。
(C) 使用言語については記載がない。
(D) ❸3～5行目より、地元の教育機関が主な資金提供元であることが書かれている。revenue「収入」。

Questions 159-160 refer to the following memo.

MEMO

From: Harumi Ohta, Kitchen Manager
To: All Staff

❶ It is essential that all food handlers practice good personal hygiene throughout the year, but it is especially important during the upcoming cold and flu season. Viruses can be carried on hands, linger on work surfaces such as countertops and cutting boards, and find their way onto utensils and plates.

❷ Therefore, all employees who work with food must wash their hands before handling any food or utensils used in the preparation or delivery of food. Instructions on the proper method for washing your hands are posted at the entrance to the kitchen, in the restrooms, and in the meeting room next to the lobby. Please follow them diligently.

Harumi

問題159-160は次のメモに関するものです。

メモ

差出人：Harumi Ohta、調理場主任
宛先：従業員各位

食品取扱業者は全員、年間を通して、個人の衛生状態を良好に保つことが欠かせませんが、来る風邪やインフルエンザの時期には特にそれが重要になります。ウイルスは手に付いて運ばれ、調理台やまな板のような作業台の上に残り、調理用具や皿にたどり着く可能性があります。
ですから、食品を扱う従業員は全員、食品あるいは調理や食品の運搬で使われる調理用具を扱う前には、手洗いをしなければなりません。手洗いの正しい仕方についての指示書が、調理場の入り口、トイレ、ロビーの隣の会議室に掲示されています。どうかそれにしっかりと従ってください。

Harumi

◢ 語 注

❶ essential　必須の　　handler　取り扱う人　　practice　〜を実践する、〜を行う　　hygiene　衛生状態
upcoming　来る　　virus　ウイルス　　linger　残存する　　work surface　作業台　　countertop　調理台、カウンター
cutting board　まな板　　find *one's* way onto 〜　〜の上へたどり着く　　utensil　調理用具、台所用品

❷ handle　〜を取り扱う　　preparation　調理、準備　　delivery　運搬、配達　　instructions　〈複数形で〉指示書、説明書
proper　正しい、適切な　　method　方法　　post　〜を掲示する　　follow　〜に従う　　diligently　しっかりと、入念に

159 What is the memo about?

(A) Treating a common illness
(B) Following a safety practice
(C) Reviewing a sick-leave policy
(D) Using new kitchen equipment

メモは何についてのものですか。

(A) 一般的な疾患を治療すること。
(B) 安全性に関する慣行に従うこと。
(C) 病気休暇の方針を見直すこと。
(D) 新しい台所用品を使うこと。

正解 B メモは調理場の主任が従業員全員宛てに出したもの。❶で、食品取扱業者にとって風邪やインフルエンザの時期は特に個人の衛生状態を良好に保つことが欠かせないと述べた後、❷1〜4行目で、全従業員の手洗いを指示し、同5〜9行目で、職場に掲示される手洗いの正しい仕方についての指示書に従ってほしいと求めている。手洗いの正しい仕方を safety practice「安全性に関する慣行」と表している (B) が正解と判断できる。practice「慣行、やり方」。
(A) cold「風邪」や flu「インフルエンザ」は出てくるが、治療については述べられていない。treat「〜を治療する」、common「一般的な」。
(C) 病気休暇に関する言及はない。review「〜を見直す」、sick-leave「病気休暇の」、policy「方針」。
(D) utensils「調理用具」は出てくるが、感染経路として示されているだけである。

---

160 What items are most likely mentioned in the posted instructions?

(A) Soap and water
(B) Milk and cheese
(C) Forks and plates
(D) Ovens and refrigerators

掲示された指示書には、何の物品が言及されていると考えられますか。

(A) せっけんと水
(B) 牛乳とチーズ
(C) フォークと皿
(D) オーブンと冷蔵庫

正解 A ❷の5〜9行目に「手洗いの正しい仕方についての指示書が、調理場の入り口、トイレ、ロビーの隣の会議室に掲示されている」とあり、掲示された指示書には詳細な手洗いの方法が記載されていると分かる。手洗いに関わりのある物品は (A) の「せっけんと水」。
(B) (C) (D) いずれもウイルスの付着に関わりのある食品、あるいは食器や電化製品だが、手洗いの方法を説明した指示書に直接関係するとは言えない。

Questions 161-163 refer to the following e-mail.

```
╔══════════════════════════════════════════════════════════╗
║                        *E-mail*                          ║
╠══════════════════════════════════════════════════════════╣
║  To:      │ Staff@holmana.co.uk                          ║
║  From:    │ Robin Ruiz, Facilities Manager               ║
║  Date:    │ 12 October                                   ║
║  Subject: │ New Desks                                    ║
╠══════════════════════════════════════════════════════════╣
```

Dear staff,

❶ We will soon be replacing all employee desks with new hybrid ones that will allow you to work while either seated or standing. The new desks are due to arrive on 20 October. — [1] —. I have requested that the delivery occur early in the morning before office hours so it does not interrupt our work. — [2] —. To make the transition go faster, please move the contents of your current desk, including personal items, into a cardboard box on the 19th.

❷ You can read more about the model we've ordered at wilsonofficefurniture.com/hybrid56. — [3] —. My research showed this one to be the most user-friendly option. The height of the desk can be changed by simply flipping a latch and pushing a button.

❸ Many of you have been requesting hybrid desks for some time now, so I am glad we are able to make this happen. This is only one of the changes management plans to implement this year in our efforts to make Holmana a healthier and happier workplace. — [4] —.

Best regards,

Robin Ruiz

問題161-163は次のEメールに関するものです。

受信者：Staff@holmana.co.uk
送信者：Robin Ruiz、施設責任者
日付：　10月12日
件名：　新しい机

スタッフの皆さま

当社では近日中に、全ての従業員の机を、座った状態でも立った状態でも仕事ができる新型のハイブリッドのものと交換します。新型机は、10月20日に入荷する予定です。配達を就業時間前の早朝に行うよう依頼していますので、私たちの業務の妨げにはなりません。入れ替えをより迅速に行うため、19日には、皆さんが現在使用している机の中身を、私物を含め、段ボール箱に移しておいてください。

当社が発注した型については、wilsonofficefurniture.com/hybrid56で詳しく読むことができます。調べたところ、これが最も使い勝手のいい選択肢であることが分かりました。机の高さは、留め金を反転させて外しボタンを押すだけで変更できます。

ここしばらくの間、皆さんの多くから、ハイブリッドの机を望む声が寄せられていたため、当社がこれを実現できることを、うれしく思います。これは、Holmana社を今より健全で楽しい職場にしようとする当社の取り組みにおいて、経営陣が今年実行を計画している変革の1つに過ぎません。*その他にも皆さんが当社のためにお持ちのアイデアがあれば、歓迎します。

敬具

Robin Ruiz

*問題163の挿入文の訳

◢ 語 注
───
facility　施設
❶ replace ～ with …　～を…と取り換える　　hybrid　ハイブリッドの　　seat　～を着席させる
　　due to do　～する予定で　　delivery　配達　　occur　行われる　　interrupt　～を妨げる　　transition　移行、変更
　　contents　〈複数形で〉（具体的な）中身　　current　現在の　　item　品物　　cardboard box　段ボール箱
❷ model　型　　show ～ to be …　～が…であることを示す　　user-friendly　使い勝手のいい　　option　選択肢
　　flip　（指先などで）～をぱちんと裏返しにする　　latch　留め金
❸ management　経営陣　　implement　～を実行する　　effort　取り組み、努力　　workplace　職場

161 How can employees help prepare for a delivery?

(A) By packing their belongings
(B) By collecting cardboard boxes
(C) By completing their work in the morning
(D) By moving furniture out of their offices

従業員はどのようにして、配達の準備を手助けできますか。

(A) 所持品を荷造りすることによって。
(B) 段ボール箱を集めることによって。
(C) 午前中に仕事を終えることによって。
(D) オフィスの外に家具を移動させることによって。

正解 **A** 施設責任者が従業員へ宛てた E メール。❶の 1〜4 行目で、従業員の机を新型のハイブリッドのものに交換すること、それらが 10 月 20 日の早朝に届くことを案内した後、同 4〜6 行目で「入れ替えをより迅速に行うため、19 日には、皆が現在使用している机の中身を、私物を含め、段ボール箱に移しておいてほしい」と指示している。このことを packing their belongings「所持品を荷造りすること」と表した (A) が正解。pack「〜を荷造りする」、belongings「〈複数形で〉所持品」。
(B) ❶の 4〜6 行目より、所持品を段ボールに移すよう指示されているだけである。collect「〜を集める」。
(C) 仕事を終える時間については言及がない。complete「〜を完了する」。
(D) ❶の 4〜6 行目より、移動させるのは机の中身である。

162 Why has the desk been chosen?

(A) It has a large storage area.
(B) It is easy to adjust.
(C) It can be delivered quickly.
(D) It is the cheapest option available.

なぜその机が選ばれたのですか。

(A) 広い収納スペースがあるから。
(B) 調節するのが簡単だから。
(C) すぐに配達してもらえるから。
(D) 手に入る中で最も安い選択肢だから。

正解 **B** ❷の 2 行目に「調べたところ、これが最も使い勝手のいい選択肢であることが分かった」とあり、続けて同 3 行目で、「机の高さは、留め金を反転させて外しボタンを押すだけで変更できる」と説明されている。よって、Ruiz さんは、高さの調節が簡単な点を user-friendly「使い勝手のいい」と考えて購入を決めたと判断できる。adjust「〜を調節する」。
(A) (C) (D) 収納、配達日数、価格についての言及はない。
(A) storage「収納、保管」。

163 In which of the positions marked [1], [2], [3], and [4] does the following sentence best belong?

"Any other ideas you have for us are welcome."

(A) [1]
(B) [2]
(C) [3]
(D) [4]

[1]、[2]、[3]、[4] と記載された箇所のうち、次の文が入るのに最もふさわしいのはどれですか。

「その他にも皆さんが当社のためにお持ちのアイデアがあれば、歓迎します」

正解 **D** ❶、❷では、新型の机に交換する案内と机の特徴が書かれている。一方、❸の 1〜2 行目では、ハイブリッドの机の導入が従業員の要望に応えて実現した施策であること、続く同 2〜3 行目「これは、Holmana 社を今より健全で楽しい職場にしようとする当社の取り組みにおいて、経営陣が今年実行を計画している変革の 1 つに過ぎない」ということが示されている。その後の [4] の箇所に挿入文を続けると、変革を進めるために、その他のアイデアを歓迎するという意味になるため、文脈に合う。よって、(D) が正解。

Questions 164-167 refer to the following online chat discussion.

❶ Ann Novak [1:31 P.M.]
Hello, everyone. Last week when we met, I asked you to come up with strategies to bring attention to the community garden program. Does anyone have progress to report?

❷ Jay Goodwin [1:32 P.M.]
I reached out to Stuart Chan of *City Wide Now*, the local newspaper. You probably know his "City Living" column.

❸ Mike Louden [1:33 P.M.]
The one that runs on Mondays? I never miss it!

❹ Jay Goodwin [1:34 P.M.]
He has a large online following, too. He'd like to interview me for an upcoming issue. So that's happening next week.

❺ Ann Novak [1:34 P.M.]
Wonderful. Will you talk about the community garden in general?

❻ Jay Goodwin [1:35 P.M.]
I explained to Stuart that we are surveying members of the garden about issues regarding access to water. So he wants to focus on that.

❼ Mike Louden [1:36 P.M.]
Lori and I are writing up the survey results. Ann, I'm getting ready to send you a draft. As soon as you have approved it, I can post it on our Web site.

❽ Ann Novak [1:37 P.M.]
OK. I'll look it over this afternoon.

問題 164-167 は次のオンラインチャットの話し合いに関するものです。

Ann Novak [午後 1 時 31 分]
こんにちは、皆さん。先週の会合の際、私はあなた方に、共同庭園プログラムに注目を集めるための施策を提案するようお願いしました。進捗報告がある方はいますか。

Jay Goodwin [午後 1 時 32 分]
私は、地元の新聞『都市部の今』の Stuart Chan さんと連絡を取りました。皆さんは、彼の「都市の暮らし」というコラム記事をおそらくご存じだと思います。

Mike Louden [午後 1 時 33 分]
毎週月曜日に掲載されているものですか。僕は欠かしたことはないです！

Jay Goodwin [午後 1 時 34 分]
彼はインターネット上でも多くのファンがいます。彼が次の号で、私に取材をしたいと言っています。それで、来週それが行

われる予定です。

Ann Novak [午後 1 時 34 分]
素晴らしいです。共同庭園全般について話をしてもらえますか。

Jay Goodwin [午後 1 時 35 分]
Stuart さんには、私たちが今、庭園の会員の方々に水の利用に関する諸問題について調査を行っていることを説明しました。そこで彼は、それに焦点を絞りたがっています。

Mike Louden [午後 1 時 36 分]
Lori と私で調査結果を書き上げています。Ann、今あなたに下書きを送る準備をしているところです。あなたが承認してくれればすぐに、私たちのウェブサイトに投稿できます。

Ann Novak [午後 1 時 37 分]
分かりました。今日の午後に、それに目を通しましょう。

語 注

❶ come up with ～　～を提案する、～を思い付く　　strategy　方策、戦略　　attention　注目
community　共同体、コミュニティー　　garden　庭園　　progress　進捗　　report　～を報告する
❷ reach out to ～　～と連絡を取る　　local　地元の　　probably　おそらく　　column　コラム記事
❸ run　（新聞・雑誌などに）掲載される　　miss　～を見逃す
❹ following　ファン、熱心な支持者　　upcoming　近づいている、今度の　　issue　（定期刊行物の）号、出版物
❺ in general　一般の、一般に
❻ survey　～を調査する　　issue　問題　　regarding ～　～に関して　　focus on ～　～に焦点を合わせる、～に重点を置く
❼ write up ～　～を書き上げる　　draft　下書き、草稿　　approve　～を承認する　　post　～を投稿する
❽ look over ～　～に目を通す

164 What is indicated about Ms. Novak?

(A) She missed last week's meeting.
(B) She has just returned from a trip.
(C) She does not like Mr. Goodwin's idea.
(D) She gave her colleagues an assignment.

Novakさんについて示されていることは何ですか。

(A) 先週の会議を欠席した。
(B) ちょうど旅行から戻ってきたところだ。
(C) Goodwinさんの案を気に入っていない。
(D) 同僚たちに課題を与えた。

正解 D 共同庭園プログラムを運営するスタッフ同士のチャットだと考えられる。❶でNovakさんは、「先週の会合の際、私はあなた方に、共同庭園プログラムに注目を集めるための施策を提案するようお願いした」と述べている。よって、Novakさんは先週の会合で、同僚たちに課題を出したと分かる。assignment「課題」。
(A) ❶より、Novakさんは会議に出席している。miss「～を欠席する」。
(B) Novakさんが旅行に行っていたとは述べられていない。
(C) ❹のGoodwinさんの発言に対して、Novakさんは❺で「素晴らしい」と述べている。

---

165 Who is Mr. Chan?

(A) A city official
(B) A local reporter
(C) A job candidate
(D) An expert gardener

Chanさんとは誰ですか。

(A) 市の職員
(B) 地元の記者
(C) 求職者
(D) 熟練した庭師

正解 B Goodwinさんは❷で、地元の新聞のChanさんと連絡を取ったと述べた後、「都市の暮らし」という彼のコラム記事について言及している。よって、Chanさんは地元の新聞記者だと分かる。reporter「記者」。
(C) candidate「候補者、志願者」。
(D) expert「熟練した、専門的な」、gardener「庭師」。

---

166 At 1:33 P.M., what does Mr. Louden most likely mean when he writes, "I never miss it"?

(A) He enjoys participating in community activities.
(B) He always meets project deadlines.
(C) He subscribes to *City Wide Now.*
(D) He reads a column regularly.

午後1時33分に "I never miss it" と書くことで、Loudenさんは何を意図していると考えられますか。

(A) 地域活動に参加することを楽しんでいる。
(B) プロジェクトの締め切りを常に守っている。
(C) 『都市部の今』を定期購読している。
(D) 定期的にコラム記事を読んでいる。

正解 D ❷でGoodwinさんがChanさんのコラム記事に言及したところ、Loudenさんは❸で毎週月曜日に掲載されているものかと尋ね、直後に下線部の発言をしている。よって、(D)の「定期的にコラム記事を読んでいる」が正解。regularly「定期的に」。
(A) participate in ～「～に参加する」、activity「活動」。
(B) meet「～を満たす、～をかなえる」、deadline「締め切り、最終期限」。
(C) 新聞の定期購読への言及はない。subscribe to ～「～を定期購読する」。

---

167 What does Mr. Louden indicate he will do?

(A) Conduct a survey
(B) Post a document online
(C) Prepare interview questions
(D) Help improve access to water

Loudenさんは何をする予定だと述べていますか。

(A) 調査を行う。
(B) インターネット上に文書を投稿する。
(C) インタビューの質問を準備する。
(D) 水の利用状況を改善する。

正解 B Loudenさんは❼で、調査結果の下書きをNovakさんへ送る準備をしており、彼女が承認すればウェブサイトにそれを投稿できると発言している。それを受けてNovakさんは❽で、今日の午後に、下書きに目を通すと応じている。このことから、Loudenさんはこの後Novakさんの承認を待って、調査結果の文書をインターネット上に投稿する予定だと考えられる。document「文書」、online「インターネット上で」。
(A) ❼より、Loudenさんは調査後の結果を文書にまとめる作業をしている。conduct「～を実施する」、survey「調査」。
(C) ❷、❹、❻より、インタビューをするのはChanさんで、受けるのはGoodwinさんである。prepare「～を準備する」。
(D) ❻より、水の利用についての調査を実施しただけである。improve「～を改善する」。

Questions 168-171 refer to the following notice.

Associate Publicist Wanted
Blackhorse Publishing House

❶ Blackhorse Publishing House produces a variety of contemporary works including fiction, nonfiction, and poetry. Some of our fiction authors include Simon Delacorte, Peter Simkin-Hall, and Katarina Sanchez. — [1] —. Our nonfiction list focuses primarily on the areas of gardening, home design, architecture, and cooking.

❷ We are looking for an associate publicist to join our busy team. — [2] —. The successful candidate will support senior staff as well as lead publicity campaigns for authors. He or she will also organize and oversee event bookings for authors, including national and international speaking tours and other public appearances at festivals and bookstores, among other venues.

❸ Ideal candidates will have 1–2 years of experience in trade publishing, either in a publicity or an editorial role. — [3] —. Job applicants must have wide knowledge of social media use in publishing as well as expertise with word-processing systems, excellent language and verbal skills, and commendable attention to detail. — [4]—.

❹ If this sounds like you, please e-mail a cover letter and your résumé no later than September 21 to efine@blackhorsepublishing.com.

問題168-171は次のお知らせに関するものです。

副広報担当求む
Blackhorse出版社

Blackhorse出版社は、フィクション、ノンフィクション、詩を含め、さまざまな現代作品を制作しています。当社のフィクション作家には、Simon Delacorte、Peter Simkin-Hall、Katarina Sanchezなどがいます。ノンフィクションの作品の目録は主に、ガーデニング、家のインテリア、建築、料理の分野が中心となっています。

当社は、多忙な当チームに加わってくださる副広報担当を募集しています。採用された方には、上級スタッフのサポートや著者の宣伝活動の主導をしていただきます。また、著者のイベント出演契約の手配と監督もしていただきますが、これには国内外の講演ツアーおよび、その他の会場での催しや書店への出演が含まれます。

望ましい候補者は、出版業界において、広報または編集の職務で1〜2年の経験をお持ちの方です。*これらの職での職業上の推薦状が2通必須です。応募者は、出版におけるソーシャルメディアの利用について幅広い知識を持ち、また同様に、文書作成ソフトに関する専門的技能、優れた言語能力、そしてコミュニケーション能力を備え、細部へ素晴らしい目配りができる方である必要があります。

ご自身が該当するという方は、9月21日までにカバーレターと履歴書をefine@blackhorsepublishing.com宛てにEメールでお送りください。

*問題171の挿入文の訳

語 注

associate ～〈名詞を続けて〉副～、準～　publicist 広報担当者　wanted （広告で）求む
publishing 出版　house 会社
❶ a variety of ～ さまざまな～　contemporary 現代の　work 作品　author 著者　list 目録、リスト
　　focus on ～ ～に重点を置く　primarily 主に　architecture 建築
❷ successful 成功した　candidate 候補者　senior 上級の、上役の　lead ～を主導する　publicity 広報
　　organize ～を手配する　oversee ～を監督する　booking 出演契約　appearance 出演
❸ trade 業界　editorial 編集の　role 職務、役職　applicant 応募者　expertise 専門知識　verbal 口頭の
　　skill 能力　commendable 立派な、推奨に値する　attention 注意力　detail 細部
❹ cover letter カバーレター、添え状　★履歴書などに添えて出す手紙　résumé 履歴書　no later than ～ ～までに

168 What is the purpose of the notice?

(A) To promote an upcoming job fair
(B) To notify employees about changes in senior staffing
(C) To encourage recent graduates to gain internship experience
(D) To invite qualified individuals to apply for a job

お知らせの目的は何ですか。

(A) 近日行われる就職説明会を宣伝するため。
(B) 上級スタッフの配置転換について従業員に知らせるため。
(C) 新卒者に、インターンシップの体験をするよう勧めるため。
(D) 適性のある個人に仕事に応募するよう促すため。

正解 **D** 見出しに「副広報担当求む」とあること、❷で職務内容、❸で候補者の条件として必要な経験や技能について言及していることから、求人の募集だと分かる。(D) が正解。invite 〜 to do「〜に…するよう誘う」、qualified「適性のある」、individual「個人」、apply for 〜「〜に応募する」。
(A) promote「〜を宣伝する」、upcoming「近づいている、今度の」、job fair「就職説明会」。
(C) encourage 〜 to do「〜に…するように勧める」、graduate「卒業生」。

---

169 What do Mr. Delacorte and Ms. Sanchez have in common?

(A) They edit architecture books.
(B) They have the same publisher.
(C) They work as event planners.
(D) They have given international speaking tours.

Delacorte さんと Sanchez さんの共通点は何ですか。

(A) 建築の本の編集をしている。
(B) 同じ出版社と仕事をしている。
(C) イベント企画者を務めている。
(D) 国際的な講演ツアーを行ってきている。

正解 **B** ❶の2〜3行目の「当社のフィクション作家には、Simon Delacorte、Peter Simkin-Hall、Katarina Sanchez などがいる」より、2人は Blackhorse 出版社から本を出している作家だと分かる。
(D) give a speaking tour「講演ツアーを行う」。

---

170 What is mentioned as one of the responsibilities of an associate publicist?

(A) Arranging author appearances
(B) Updating word processing systems
(C) Interviewing prospective interns
(D) Attending professional conferences

副広報担当の責務の1つとして述べられているのは何ですか。

(A) 著者の出演の手配をすること。
(B) 文書作成ソフトを更新すること。
(C) 有望なインターン生を面接すること。
(D) 専門家の会議に出席すること。

正解 **A** 副広報担当の責務について、❷の3〜5行目より、「著者のイベント出演契約の手配と監督もしてもらう」とある。arrange「〜を手配する」。
(B) update「〜を更新する」。
(C) prospective「有望な、見込みのある」。

---

171 In which of the positions marked [1], [2], [3], and [4] does the following sentence best belong?

"Two professional references from these positions are essential."

(A) [1]   (C) [3]
(B) [2]   (D) [4]

[1]、[2]、[3]、[4]と記載された箇所のうち、次の文が入るのに最もふさわしいのはどれですか。

「これらの職での、職業上の推薦状が2通必須です」

正解 **C** 文意から応募条件や応募方法を案内している箇所が適切だと考えられ、[3] か [4] に絞られる。[3] に挿入すれば、these positions「これらの職」が直前の「広報または編集の職務」を指すことになり、文脈に合う。professional「職業上の」、reference「推薦状」、position「職」、essential「必須の」。

Questions 172-175 refer to the following e-mail.

To:	Isla Garrick <igarrick@gandgre.co.au>
From:	Owen Clement <oclement@congreveads.co.au>
Subject:	New service
Date:	January 7

Dear Ms. Garrick,

❶ I noticed that you placed an order recently, and before we fill it, I wanted to tell you about an exciting opportunity. Congreve Advertising is now offering another way for you to reach your customers: automated text messages. We're combining our eye-catching lawn advertisements with the latest mobile phone technology to create a quick, easy method of increasing your customer base. We've already helped many property rental agents in your area, and we're giving free trials to new users.

❷ Our automated text-messaging service involves just a few simple steps.

❸ 1. Go to our Web site, congreveads.co.au. Click on the Registration page and select New User. You will be guided through our quick and easy registration process, which will allow you to set up an account.

❹ 2. Once your account is set up, you can start entering the automated responses that you want interested renters to receive. Include the details about each property. You can also add images, audio, and videos, as well as links to Web sites.

❺ 3. Select a unique keyword for each property. This is what prospective renters will text in order to receive more information about a rental. The keyword shouldn't be too long or difficult to spell, and it should be easy for customers to remember.

❻ 4. Then wait. Apartment seekers will pass by the property and see the keyword. When they text it, they will instantly receive the message you programmed!

❼ As part of your free trial, we'll print new rental signs for one of your properties so that your advertisements include the keyword. And, if you contact me by Friday, I'll add two more properties to the order. So, in addition to a month of our text-messaging service, you'll get updated signs for three rental units, all at no cost to you. After the trial period, you can choose from six reasonably priced packages, which include the option of sending daily updates to preferred customers.

I look forward to hearing from you!

Owen Clement

問題172-175は次のEメールに関するものです。

受信者：Isla Garrick <igarrick@gandgre.co.au>
送信者：Owen Clement <oclement@congreveads.co.au>
件名：新サービス
日付：1月7日

Garrick様

先日貴社からご注文を頂いたと存じますが、それに対応させていただく前に、非常に素晴らしい機会についてお知らせさせていただきたく思っておりました。Congreve広告社は現在、顧客の心を動かす新たな手法を提供しています——それは自動テキストメッセージです。当社は、人目を引く芝生の上に立てられた看板広告と最新の携帯電話技術を組み合わせ、手早く簡単に貴社の顧客基盤を拡大する手法を生み出します。すでに貴社の地域にある数多くの不動産賃貸業者のお手伝いをしており、新規のご利用者の方には無料のお試しを提供しています。

当社の自動テキストメッセージサービスは、ほんの幾つかの簡単な手順を伴います。

1. 当社のウェブサイト congreveads.co.au へ行きます。「登録」ページのボタンをクリックし、「新規ユーザー」を選びます。当社の手早く簡単な登録の流れに沿って進んでいただくと、アカウントの設定ができます。

2. アカウントがいったん設定されたらすぐに、物件に興味を持つ賃借人に受信してもらいたい自動返信文を入力し始めることができます。それぞれの物件について詳細情報を盛り込みましょう。画像、音声、ビデオ、そしてウェブサイトへのリンクも追加できます。

3. それぞれの物件に固有のキーワードを選びましょう。これは、借りる見込みのある人々が、物件情報をもっと受け取るために入力して送信するテキストになります。キーワードは、長過ぎたり、つづりが難し過ぎたりせず、顧客が覚えやすいものの方が良いです。

4. その後は、待ちます。アパート探しをしている人たちが物件の横を通り過ぎると、キーワードを目にするでしょう。彼らがそれをテキスト送信したら、彼らは即座に、貴社がプログラムしておいたメッセージを受け取ることになるのです！

当社では無料のお試しの一環として、貴社の物件の1カ所に賃貸用の看板を新しく印刷して、貴社の広告にキーワードが含まれるようにします。そして、金曜日までに私にご連絡いただいた場合、ご注文に対し、さらに2カ所の物件を追加いたします。そうすれば貴社は、一切の費用のご負担なく、1カ月間のテキストメッセージ・サービスに加え、賃貸物件3カ所の新しくなった看板を入手されることになるでしょう。お試し期間の後は、6種の手頃な価格設定の商品パッケージからお選びいただけますが、それらには優待顧客へ毎日最新情報を送るというオプションが含まれます。

ご連絡をお待ちしております！

Owen Clement

172 What is implied about Ms. Garrick?

- (A) She is interested in finding a rental property.
- (B) She works as a property rental agent.
- (C) She recently bought a new mobile telephone.
- (D) She sends text messages frequently.

Garrickさんについて何が示唆されていますか。

- (A) 賃貸物件を見つけることに興味を持っている。
- (B) 不動産賃貸業者として働いている。
- (C) 最近新しい携帯電話を買った。
- (D) 頻繁にテキストメッセージを送信する。

> **正解 B**　Garrick さんは E メールの受信者で、本文内では you で示されている。送信者の Clement さんは❶で、Congreve 広告社の新サービスを紹介し、地域の多くの不動産賃貸業者を手伝っていると述べた後に、❷以降で新サービスの利用の手順を説明している。このことから、Garrick さんは不動産賃貸業者だと考えられる。
> (A) ❹の 2 行目に interested renters「(物件に) 興味を持つ賃借人」とあるが、Garrick さんのことではない。
> (C) ❶ 3 ～ 5 行目に携帯電話に関する言及はあるが、Garrick さんが新しい機器を買ったとは述べられていない。
> (D) ❺、❻にテキストメッセージについての言及はあるが、送信することになるのは、❺ 1 ～ 2 行目より prospective renters「借りる見込みのある人々」であり、Garrick さんのことではない。

173 What is indicated about Congreve Advertising?

- (A) It is a newly created company.
- (B) It fills orders quickly.
- (C) It is providing a new service.
- (D) It recently merged with another company.

Congreve 広告社について何が示されていますか。

- (A) 新しく設立された会社である。
- (B) 注文に素早く対応する。
- (C) 新しいサービスを提供している。
- (D) 最近、他社と合併した。

> **正解 C**　❶ 2 ～ 3 行目で Congreve 広告社が新しいサービスを提供していることが述べられ、❷以降では、サービス利用の具体的な手順が説明されている。(C) が正解。provide「～を提供する」。
> (A) ❶ 2 ～ 3 行目より、新しく提供されたのは自動テキストメッセージのサービス。create「～を生み出す、～を作り出す」。
> (B) 注文に対応するまでの日数について、言及はない。
> (D) 他社との合併について、言及はない。merge with ～「～と合併する」。

語注

❶ notice (that) ～　～であることに気付く　　place an order　注文をする　　fill　～に応じる　　opportunity　機会　offer　～を提供する　　reach　～ (人) の心に達する　　automated　自動化された　text message　(携帯電話の) テキストメッセージ　　combine ～ with …　～を…と組み合わせる　eye-catching　人目を引くような　　lawn advertisement　★物件の芝生や敷地内に設置された広告看板のこと　method　方法　　base　基盤　　property　不動産、物件　　agent　仲介業者　　trial　試み
❷ involve　～を伴う　　step　手順
❸ registration　登録　　guide　～を案内する　　process　手順　　set up　～を設定する　account　(サービス利用のための) アカウント
❹ once　いったん～すれば　　enter　～を入力する　　response　返答　　renter　借り手　　include　～を含む　image　画像　　audio　音声
❺ unique　独自の、唯一無二の　　prospective　見込みのある、有望な　　text　～ (テキストメッセージ) を送信する　rental　賃貸物件
❻ seeker　探している人　　pass by ～　～のそばを通り過ぎる　　instantly　即座に　　program　～を組み込む
❼ sign　看板　　contact　～と連絡を取る　　in addition to ～　～に加えて　　updated　更新された　　period　期間　reasonably　手頃に　　priced　値段を付けられた　　update　最新情報　　preferred　優先の

174 What is mentioned about the automated responses?

(A) They are different for each property.
(B) They can be sent to an e-mail address.
(C) They include pictures taken by Congreve Advertising.
(D) They require apartment seekers to create a password.

自動返信文について何が述べられていますか。

(A) それぞれの物件によって異なる。
(B) Eメールアドレスに送られる。
(C) Congreve広告社によって撮影された写真を含む。
(D) アパートを探している人たちに、パスワードを作成するように求める。

> **正解 A**　❹2行目に、自動返信文の入力について「それぞれの物件について詳細情報を盛り込もう」とある。また、❺と❻より、物件固有のキーワードを不動産業者が選んでおくと、借りる見込みのある人々がそのキーワードをテキストメッセージで送信した際に、物件固有の自動返信のメッセージが彼らへ届くことが分かる。よって、(A)が正解。
> (B) Eメールではなく、携帯電話にテキストメッセージとして送られる。
> (C) ❹2～3行目で「画像を追加できる」とあるが、Congreve広告社が撮影するとは述べられていない。
> (D) キーワードについての説明はあるが、パスワードについては言及がない。

175 According to the e-mail, why should Ms. Garrick contact Mr. Clement by Friday?

(A) To renew a subscription
(B) To talk about fees
(C) To schedule a property viewing
(D) To receive free services

Eメールによると、なぜGarrickさんは、金曜日までにClementさんに連絡を取るべきなのですか。

(A) 定期購読を更新するため。
(B) 料金について話すため。
(C) 物件の見学の予定を決めるため。
(D) 無料のサービスを受けるため。

> **正解 D**　❼1～4行目に、金曜日までにGarrickさんがClementさんに連絡を取った場合に受けられるサービスの全てが書かれている。無料のお試しにもともと含まれる、1カ所の物件に対する1カ月のテキスト送信サービスの利用と広告看板に加え、費用の負担なく「さらに2カ所の物件を追加」することができると説明されている。(D)が正解。
> (A) renew「～を更新する」、subscription「定期購読」。
> (B) fee「料金」。
> (C) schedule「～を(特定の日時に)予定する」、viewing「見学」。

Questions 176-180 refer to the following article and review.

1 記事

New This Week . . . .

❶ After months of editing and several postponed release dates due to production delays, the documentary series *The Hidden Side of Architecture* finally hits television screens this week. The four-part program directed by Michael Moussa and Tina Erskine looks at little-known facts behind the world's most iconic buildings. Fans of actor and comedian Wesley Fleming will be happy to hear that he is the host for the series. The program was produced by Leif Bergen and will appear on the Knowledge Now channel on the dates below.

EPISODE	AIRDATE
❷ 1 **"Against All Odds"**	**April 3**

The first part takes us to Ancient Egypt, where builders managed to solve formidable engineering problems.

❸ 2 **"Building Without Modern Technology"**　**April 10**

How, without modern tools and technology, did medieval builders in Europe construct the great cathedrals that dominated cityscapes for nearly a thousand years?

❹ 3 **"Modern Cities"**　　　　　　　　**April 17**

In this episode, we admire the beauty of modern urban structures, and we learn some gripping stories behind their planning and construction.

❺ 4 **"Road Ahead"**　　　　　　　　　**April 24**

The last part looks at ideas still in the making: new designs of ever-taller skyscrapers, bio-inspired buildings with smaller footprints, and other marvels that will one day grace our cities.

2 批評

❶ **Drena Kraakevik ★ ★ ★ ★ ★**

After the first episode of *The Hidden Side of Architecture*, I can only say that I can't wait to see the remaining three parts! Fleming does a tremendous job narrating the story; he's informative yet funny. Don't miss the free downloadable booklet accompanying the series on Knowledge Now's Web site. It's a must-have if you want to learn more about the buildings featured on the program.

問題176-180は次の記事と批評に関するものです。

今週の新番組
何カ月間もの編集と、制作の遅れによる何回かの放送延期を経て、ドキュメンタリーシリーズ「建築の裏側」がついに今週、テレビ画面に登場する。Michael Moussa と Tina Erskine が監督の、4部から成るこの番組は、世界で最も象徴的な建造物の背後にあるあまり知られていない事実に注目する。俳優でコメディアンの Wesley Fleming のファンの皆さんは、彼が同シリーズの案内役と聞いて喜ぶだろう。番組は Leif Bergen による制作で、Knowledge Now チャンネルで、以下の日付に放送される。

放送回	放送日
1「あらゆる困難を乗り越えて」	4月3日

第1部は古代エジプトへ視聴者を誘う。そこでは建築者たちが、手ごわい土木工事の難題を何とかして解決していた。

2「現代技術のない建築」	4月10日

現代の道具や技術もなく、中世ヨーロッパの建築者たちはいかにして1,000年近くもの間都市景観の中心となった壮大な大聖堂を建設したのか。

3「現代の都市」	4月17日

この放送回では、現代の都市構造の美を称賛するとともに、それらの建築計画と工事の背後にある幾つかの感動のストーリーを知る。

4「前途」	4月24日

最終回では、いまだ発展途中の構想を見ていく。絶えず高さを増す超高層ビルの新設計、生物から着想を得たより狭い敷地面積の建物、いつの日か都市を彩ることになるその他の驚異の数々。

Drena Kraakevik　★★★★★
「建築の裏側」の第1回の放送後は、ただただ、残りの3回を見るのが待ちきれないとしか言えない！ Fleming は物語の語りで素晴らしい仕事をしている。彼の話は有益でありながら、なお愉快である。Knowledge Now のウェブサイトから無料でダウンロードできるシリーズの付録冊子を見逃さないでほしい。この番組で特集された建造物についてもっと知りたければ絶対に手に入れるべき1冊である。

176 What is indicated about the making of the program?

(A) It was very expensive.
(B) It took longer than planned.
(C) It was financed by several sponsors.
(D) It involved a large team of producers.

番組の制作について、何が示されていますか。

(A) 非常にお金がかかった。
(B) 計画よりも長く時間がかかった。
(C) 複数のスポンサーから資金を提供された。
(D) 大規模なプロデューサーたちのチームが関わった。

> **正解 B** 記事の❶❶の1～3行目で、「何カ月間もの編集と、制作の遅れによる何回かの放送延期を経て、ドキュメンタリーシリーズ『建築の裏側』がついに今週、テレビ画面に登場する」と述べられていることから、番組の制作には当初の計画より時間がかかったことが分かる。(B) が正解。
> (A) (C) 制作資金や資金提供に関する言及はない。
> (D) 制作に関わったプロデューサーとして言及があるのはLeif Bergenだけなので、不適切。involve「～を伴う」。

177 Who appears in the program?

(A) Mr. Moussa
(B) Ms. Erskine
(C) Mr. Fleming
(D) Mr. Bergen

誰が番組に出演していますか。

(A) Moussaさん
(B) Erskineさん
(C) Flemingさん
(D) Bergenさん

> **正解 C** ❶❶の4～5行目に「俳優でコメディアンの Wesley Fleming のファンの皆は、彼が同シリーズの案内役と聞いて喜ぶだろう」とある。また、第1回の放送の批評である❷❶の3～4行目には、「Fleming は物語の語りで素晴らしい仕事をしている。彼の話は有益でありながら、なお愉快だ」とあり、彼が第1回の放送で語り役として出演していたことが分かる。appear「出演する」。
> (A) (B) ❶❶3～4行目より、番組を監督した人物の名前。
> (D) ❶❶5～7行目より、Leif Bergen は番組のプロデューサーの名前。

178 What episode focuses on urban planning?

(A) Episode 1
(B) Episode 2
(C) Episode 3
(D) Episode 4

都市計画を重点的に扱っているのはどの放送回ですか。

(A) 第1回
(B) 第2回
(C) 第3回
(D) 第4回

> **正解 C** ❶❹に「この放送回では、現代の都市構造の美を称賛するとともに、それらの建築計画と工事の背後にある幾つかの感動のストーリーを知る」とあることから、第3回は都市の計画や建設について取り上げることが分かる。よって、(C) が正解。

179 When did Ms. Kraakevik most likely watch the program?

(A) On April 3
(B) On April 10
(C) On April 17
(D) On April 24

Kraakevik さんは、いつ番組を見たと考えられますか。

(A) 4月3日
(B) 4月10日
(C) 4月17日
(D) 4月24日

正解 A Kraakevik さんが書いた批評の**2**❶の2～3行目には、「『建築の裏側』の第1回の放送後は、ただただ、残りの3回を見るのが待ちきれないとしか言えない！」とある。ここから、Kraakevik さんは第1回を見たすぐ後に批評を書いており、第2回以降はまだ見ていないことが分かる。記事の**1**の❷を見ると、第1回の放送日は4月3日なので、(A) が正解。

180 What does Ms. Kraakevik recommend doing?

(A) Purchasing movies that feature a particular actor
(B) Visiting the buildings shown in the program
(C) Obtaining additional materials online
(D) Watching other programs by the same director

Kraakevik さんは何をすることを勧めていますか。

(A) 特定の俳優の主演映画を購入すること。
(B) 番組で紹介された建造物を訪れること。
(C) 追加資料をインターネット上で入手すること。
(D) 同じ監督による他の番組を見ること。

正解 C Kraakevik さんは、批評の**2**❶の4～5行目で、「Knowledge Now のウェブサイトから無料でダウンロードできるシリーズの付録冊子を見逃さないでほしい」と述べた後、冊子について、番組の建造物についてもっと知りたいなら絶対に手に入れるべき1冊だと断言している。(C) が正解。booklet を material「資料」と表している。recommend *doing*「～することを勧める」。obtain「～を入手する」、additional「追加の」、online「インターネット上で、オンラインで」。
(A) (B) (D) いずれも**2**の批評で言及がない。
(A) purchase「～を購入する」、particular「特定の」。

Final Test

語 注

1 記事 ❶ editing 編集　postpone ～を延期する　release 公開　due to ～ ～のために　production 制作
series シリーズもの、一続き　hidden 秘密の、隠された　architecture 建築
hit ～に登場する、～に達する　program 番組　direct ～を監督する　little-known ほとんど知られていない
fact 事実　behind ～ ～の背後に　iconic 象徴的な　host 案内役、司会者　produce ～を制作する
episode 1回の放送、1話　airdate 放送日
❷ odds 〈複数形で〉見込み、可能性　ancient 古代の　builder 建築者　manage to *do* 何とか～する
solve ～を解決する　formidable 難しい、手ごわい　engineering 土木工事
❸ technology 技術　medieval 中世の　construct ～を建設する　cathedral 大聖堂
dominate ～の中心となる、～を支配する　cityscape 都市景観
❹ admire ～を称賛する　urban 都市の　structure 構造、構造物　gripping 心を強く捉える
construction 建設
❺ ahead 前へ向かって　in the making 発展途上の、進行中の　ever-taller 絶えず高さを増す
skyscraper 超高層ビル　bio-inspired 生物から着想を得た　footprint （建物の）土地専有面積
marvel 驚異　grace ～を飾る
2 批評 ❶ remaining 残りの　tremendous 素晴らしい　narrate ～の語り手をする
informative 有益な、情報を与える　funny 愉快な　miss ～を見逃す　downloadable ダウンロード可能な
booklet 小冊子　accompany ～に付随する　must-have 手に入れるべきもの　feature ～を特集する

Questions 181-185 refer to the following e-mails.

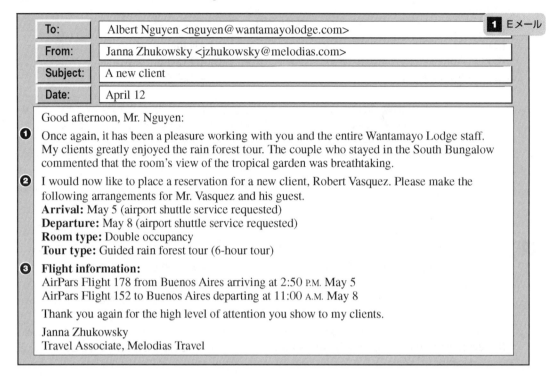

To: Albert Nguyen <nguyen@wantamayolodge.com>
From: Janna Zhukowsky <jzhukowsky@melodias.com>
Subject: A new client
Date: April 12

Good afternoon, Mr. Nguyen:

❶ Once again, it has been a pleasure working with you and the entire Wantamayo Lodge staff. My clients greatly enjoyed the rain forest tour. The couple who stayed in the South Bungalow commented that the room's view of the tropical garden was breathtaking.

❷ I would now like to place a reservation for a new client, Robert Vasquez. Please make the following arrangements for Mr. Vasquez and his guest.
Arrival: May 5 (airport shuttle service requested)
Departure: May 8 (airport shuttle service requested)
Room type: Double occupancy
Tour type: Guided rain forest tour (6-hour tour)

❸ **Flight information:**
AirPars Flight 178 from Buenos Aires arriving at 2:50 P.M. May 5
AirPars Flight 152 to Buenos Aires departing at 11:00 A.M. May 8

Thank you again for the high level of attention you show to my clients.

Janna Zhukowsky
Travel Associate, Melodias Travel

1 Eメール

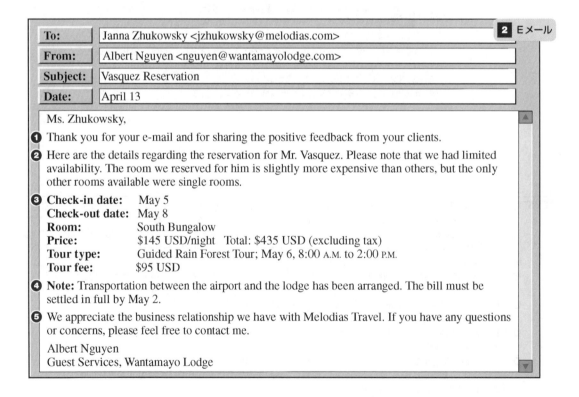

To: Janna Zhukowsky <jzhukowsky@melodias.com>
From: Albert Nguyen <nguyen@wantamayolodge.com>
Subject: Vasquez Reservation
Date: April 13

Ms. Zhukowsky,

❶ Thank you for your e-mail and for sharing the positive feedback from your clients.

❷ Here are the details regarding the reservation for Mr. Vasquez. Please note that we had limited availability. The room we reserved for him is slightly more expensive than others, but the only other rooms available were single rooms.

❸ **Check-in date:**　May 5
Check-out date:　May 8
Room:　South Bungalow
Price:　$145 USD/night　Total: $435 USD (excluding tax)
Tour type:　Guided Rain Forest Tour; May 6, 8:00 A.M. to 2:00 P.M.
Tour fee:　$95 USD

❹ **Note:** Transportation between the airport and the lodge has been arranged. The bill must be settled in full by May 2.

❺ We appreciate the business relationship we have with Melodias Travel. If you have any questions or concerns, please feel free to contact me.

Albert Nguyen
Guest Services, Wantamayo Lodge

2 Eメール

問題181-185は次のEメールに関するものです。

受信者：Albert Nguyen <nguyen@wantamayolodge.com>
送信者：Janna Zhukowsky <jzhukowsky@melodias.com>
件名：　新規顧客
日付：　4月12日

こんにちは、Nguyen さん

あらためて、あなたと Wantamayo ロッジの全スタッフの皆さまと一緒にお仕事ができたことは喜びでした。当社の顧客は、熱帯雨林ツアーを大いに楽しんでおられました。南バンガローに滞在されたご夫婦は、お部屋からの熱帯庭園の眺めに息をのんだと評されていました。

さて、新規顧客の Robert Vasquez 様の予約を取りたく存じます。Vasquez 様と彼のお客さまのために、次の手配をお願いします。
到着：5月5日（空港のシャトルバスを希望）
出発：5月8日（空港のシャトルバスを希望）
部屋のタイプ：ダブルの部屋
ツアーのタイプ：ガイド付き熱帯雨林ツアー（6時間のツアー）

航空便の情報：
AirPars 航空 178便　ブエノスアイレス発、5月5日午後2時50分着
AirPars 航空 152便　ブエノスアイレス行き、5月8日午前11時発

当社の顧客に対する貴社の格別のご配慮に重ねて感謝いたします。

Janna Zhukowsky
旅行取扱担当、Melodias 旅行社

受信者：Janna Zhukowsky <jzhukowsky@melodias.com>
送信者：Albert Nguyen <nguyen@wantamayolodge.com>
件名：　Vasquez 様のご予約
日付：　4月13日

Zhukowsky さん

Eメールを頂戴し、また貴社のお客さまからの好意的なご意見を共有いただき、ありがとうございます。

こちらが、Vasquez 様のご予約についての詳細です。当方がご用意できる部屋に限りがあったことをご了解ください。当方がお客さまのために予約した部屋は、他の部屋より多少料金が高いですが、他にご用意できる部屋は全て1人部屋でした。

チェックイン日：5月5日
チェックアウト日：5月8日
部屋：南バンガロー
料金：1泊145 USドル　合計：435 USドル（税抜き）
ツアーのタイプ：ガイド付き熱帯雨林ツアー；5月6日午前8時から午後2時
ツアー料金：95 USドル

ご注意：空港とロッジの間の移動は手配済みです。請求額は、5月2日までに全額ご精算いただく必要がございます。

Melodias 旅行社様とのお取引関係に感謝いたします。ご質問やご懸念の点がございましたら、どうぞお気軽に私までご連絡ください。

Albert Nguyen
宿泊客サービス部、Wantamayo ロッジ

181 Why did Ms. Zhukowsky write to Mr. Nguyen?

(A) To suggest a new tour destination
(B) To request flight information
(C) To assist a client
(D) To revise an itinerary

ZhukowskyさんはなぜNguyenさんにEメールを書いたのですか。

(A) 新しいツアーの目的地を提案するため。
(B) 航空便の情報の提供を要求するため。
(C) 顧客を手伝うため。
(D) 旅程表を修正するため。

正解 C Zhukowsky さんが書いたのは1つ目のEメール。**1**のEメールの件名は「新規顧客」で、同**2**の1行目で、「新規顧客の Robert Vasquez 様の予約を取りたい」と切り出し、同3行目から手配の依頼事項を箇条書きで伝えている。よって、顧客の予約の代行をすることがEメールを書いた目的だと考えられる。(C) が正解。assist「〜を手伝う」。
(A) destination「目的地」。
(D) revise「〜を修正する」、itinerary「旅程表」。

182 What is suggested about Melodias Travel?

(A) It has done business with Wantamayo Lodge in the past.
(B) It specializes in rain forest destinations.
(C) It is located near Wantamayo Lodge.
(D) It is owned by Ms. Zhukowsky.

Melodias旅行社について何が分かりますか。

(A) 過去にWantamayoロッジと取引をしたことがある。
(B) 熱帯雨林の旅行先を専門にしている。
(C) Wantamayoロッジの近くに位置している。
(D) Zhukowskyさんがオーナーである。

正解 A Melodias 旅行社の Zhukowsky さんは**1** **1**で、Wantamayo ロッジと仕事を一緒にできることに謝意を表し、過去の顧客のロッジに対する評価を伝えている。一方、ロッジの従業員 Nguyen さんも、**2** **5**で Melodias 旅行社との関係に感謝を述べていることから、Melodias 旅行社は以前から、Wantamayo ロッジと取引をしていると分かる。(A) が正解。
(B) specialize in 〜「〜を専門とする」。
(C) Melodias 旅行社の所在地については言及されていない。
(D) Zhukowsky さんの肩書きは旅行取扱担当で、オーナーかどうかの言及はない。own「〜を所有している」。

183 What does Mr. Vasquez request?

(A) A frequent customer discount
(B) A confirmation of his reservation
(C) A meal plan
(D) A transportation service

Vasquezさんは何を希望していますか。

(A) 得意客向けの値引き
(B) 予約の確認
(C) 食事のプラン
(D) 交通サービス

正解 D 旅行社からロッジへ予約の手配を依頼する**1**のEメールの**2**3〜4行目より、Vasquezさんは到着日と出発日の両方に、ロッジと空港間のシャトルバスのサービスを希望していることが分かる。また、予約の手配完了を伝える**2**のEメールの**4**1行目には、移動は手配済みだと書かれている。よって、(D) が正解。
(A) **1**の**2**1行目で新規顧客だと説明されている。frequent「頻繁な」。
(B) (C) いずれも、**1**の**2**の Vasquez さんの手配依頼の内容には記載されていない。

184 What is indicated about Mr. Vasquez?

(A) He has visited Wantamayo Lodge on a previous occasion.
(B) He will stay in a room overlooking a garden.
(C) He has traveled with Mr. Nguyen.
(D) He plans to travel alone.

Vasquezさんについて何が示されていますか。

(A) 以前の機会にWantamayoロッジを訪れたことがある。
(B) 庭園を見渡せる部屋に滞在する予定だ。
(C) Nguyenさんと旅行したことがある。
(D) 1人で旅行する計画である。

> 正解 **B**　予約の手配完了を伝える **2** のEメールの **❸** 3行目より、Vasquezさんが宿泊する予定の部屋は南バンガローだと分かる。一方、予約の手配を依頼する **1** のEメールの **❶** 2～3行目には、「南バンガローに滞在した夫婦は、部屋からの熱帯庭園の眺めに息をのんだと評した」とある。よって、南バンガローは庭園を見渡せる宿泊施設と考えられる。(B)が正解。overlook「～を見渡す」。
> (A) previous「以前の」、occasion「機会」。
> (C) NguyenさんはVasquezさんが宿泊予定のロッジの従業員。
> (D) **1❷** 1～2行目より、Vasquezさんは彼の客1名と一緒に滞在予定だと分かる。

185 By when does Mr. Nguyen expect payment?

(A) April 13
(B) May 2
(C) May 5
(D) May 8

Nguyenさんは、いつまでに支払いがされることを見込んでいますか。

(A) 4月13日
(B) 5月2日
(C) 5月5日
(D) 5月8日

> 正解 **B**　支払いについては、**2** のEメールの **❹** 1～2行目に「請求額は、5月2日までに全額精算する必要がある」と記載されている。(B)が正解。expect「～を見込む」、payment「支払い」。
> (A) 4月13日は、ロッジの従業員のNguyenさんがZhukowskyさんにEメールを送信した日。
> (C) 5月5日は、VasquezさんがWantamayoロッジにチェックインする予定の日。
> (D) 5月8日は、VasquezさんがWantamayoロッジをチェックアウトする予定の日。

語 注

1 Eメール client 顧客
❶ pleasure 喜び、光栄　entire 全体の　lodge ロッジ、ホテル　greatly 大いに　rain forest 熱帯雨林
tour ツアー　couple 夫婦、恋人同士　bungalow バンガロー、棟 ★平屋の小さな宿泊家屋
comment 批評する　view 眺め　tropical 熱帯の　breathtaking 息をのむような
❷ place a reservation 予約をする　arrangement 手配　guest 招待客
request ～を希望する、～を依頼する　double occupancy 2人部屋　guided ガイド付きの
❸ flight 飛行機の便　attention 配慮
2 Eメール **❶** share ～を共有する　positive 好意的な、肯定的な　feedback 意見
❷ details 〈複数形で〉詳細　regarding ～に関して　note ～に注目する　limited 限られた
availability （予約や部屋の）空き、利用の可能性　reserve ～を予約する　slightly わずかに
available 空いている、利用できる
❸ excluding tax 税抜きで　fee 料金
❹ transportation 移動手段、交通　arrange ～を手配する　bill 請求額、請求書　settle ～を精算する
in full 全額で
❺ appreciate ～に感謝する　business 取引　concern 懸念、心配　contact ～に連絡する

Questions 186-190 refer to the following Web page and e-mails.

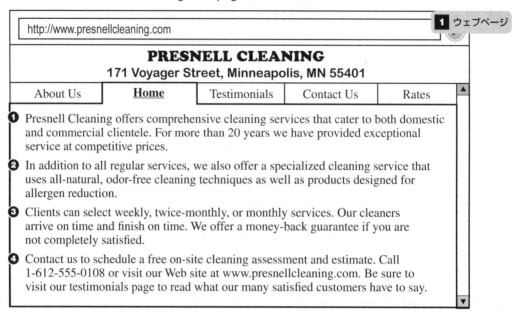

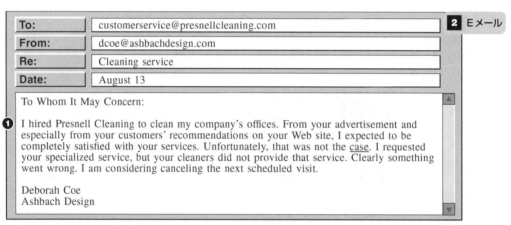

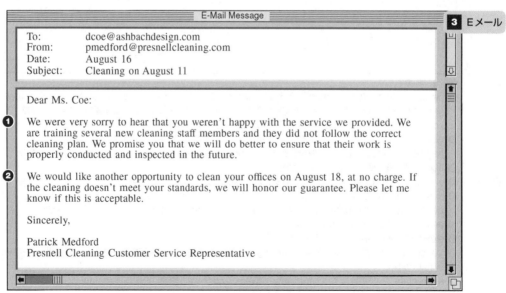

問題 186-190 は次のウェブページと 2 通の E メールに関するものです。

http://www.presnellcleaning.com

PRESNELL 清掃社
Voyager 通り 171 番地、ミネアポリス、MN 55401

当社について　　　　**ホーム**　　　　お客さまの声　　　　お問い合わせ　　　　料金表

Presnell 清掃社は、個人と法人のどちらのお客さまにも対応する総合的な清掃サービスを提供しています。当社は 20 年を超える期間、他社より低価格でひときわ優れたサービスを提供してきました。

あらゆる通常サービスに加え、当社は、全て天然で無臭の清掃技術を使った特殊清掃サービスやアレルゲン削減のために考案された製品も提供しています。

お客さまは、週 1 回、月 2 回、月 1 回のサービスからお選びいただけます。当社の清掃員は時間通りに到着し、時間通りに終了いたします。十分にご満足いただけない場合には、返金保証を致しております。

当社にご連絡の上、現場で無料の清掃の査定と見積もりを受ける日時をご予約ください。1-612-555-0108 までお電話いただくか、当社のウェブサイト www.presnellcleaning.com にアクセスしてください。ぜひお客さまの声のページを訪れて、ご満足いただいた多くのお客さまのご意見をお読みください。

Final
Test

受信者：customerservice@presnellcleaning.com
送信者：dcoe@ashbachdesign.com
件名：　清掃サービス
日付：　8 月 13 日

ご担当者様

当社オフィスの清掃のため、Presnell 清掃社を利用しました。貴社の広告、そして特に貴社のウェブサイトにある顧客の推薦の言葉から、私は貴社のサービスにすっかり満足することを期待しておりました。残念ながら、そのような状況ではありませんでした。私は、貴社の特殊清掃サービスを希望しましたが、貴社の清掃員はそうしたサービスを提供しなかったのです。明らかに手違いがありました。私は次回の予定されている訪問の清掃をキャンセルしようかと考えています。

Deborah Coe
Ashbach デザイン社

受信者：dcoe@ashbachdesign.com
送信者：pmedford@presnellcleaning.com
日付：　8 月 16 日
件名：　8 月 11 日の清掃

Coe 様

当社が提供したサービスにご不快な思いをされたと伺い、誠に申し訳なく存じます。当社では数名の新人清掃スタッフを研修している最中で、彼らは正しい清掃プランに従っていませんでした。今後は、彼らの業務の適切な遂行と点検を徹底できるように、業務を改善することを貴社にお約束いたします。

8 月 18 日にあらためて貴社のオフィスを無料で清掃する機会を頂きたく存じます。もしその清掃が貴社の基準を満たさない場合、当社は保証に応じさせていただきます。これにつきましてお受けいただけますかどうかを、どうぞお知らせくださいますようお願いします。

敬具

Patrick Medford
Presnell 清掃社顧客サービス担当

186 What is indicated about Presnell Cleaning?

(A) It is a new business.
(B) It offers daily cleaning services.
(C) It provides complimentary evaluations.
(D) It recently added home-cleaning services.

Presnell清掃社について、何が示されていますか。

(A) 新しい会社である。
(B) 1日1回清掃サービスを提供している。
(C) 無料の査定を提供している。
(D) 最近、家庭用清掃サービスを追加した。

正解 C　❶❹の1行目で、「当社に連絡の上、現場で無料の清掃の査定と見積もりを受ける日時を予約してほしい」とあるので、Presnell清掃社は無料の査定を提供していることが分かる。a free on-site cleaning assessment を complimentary evaluations「無料の査定」と表した (C) が正解。
(A) ❶の❷2～3行目より、20年を超える期間続いている会社だと分かる。
(B) ❶の❸1行目より、1日1回のサービスは提供されていない。daily「1日に1回の」。
(D) 家庭清掃サービスを最近追加したという記述はない。recently「最近」、add「追加する」。

187 What is suggested about Ms. Coe?

(A) She researched other cleaners before contacting Presnell Cleaning.
(B) She was referred to Presnell Cleaning by a friend.
(C) She is interested in applying for a position with Presnell Cleaning.
(D) She read online testimonials prior to hiring Presnell Cleaning.

Coeさんについて何が分かりますか。

(A) Presnell清掃社に連絡を取る前に、他の清掃業者の調査をした。
(B) 友人からPresnell清掃社を紹介された。
(C) Presnell清掃社の職に応募することに興味を持っている。
(D) Presnell清掃社を雇う前に、インターネット上の顧客の声を読んだ。

正解 D　❶の❹2～3行目には、Presnell清掃社のウェブページにある Testimonials「お客さまの声」というページについて、「満足した多くの客の意見を読んでほしい」と書かれている。一方、CoeさんのEメール❷の❶1～3行目には、「貴社の広告、そして特に貴社のウェブサイトにある顧客の推薦の言葉から、私は貴社のサービスにすっかり満足することを期待していた」と書かれている。ここから、Coeさんはウェブページにある「お客さまの声」を読んだ後に、清掃の仕事を依頼したと考えられる。よって、(D) が正解。prior to ～「～に先立って」。
(A) ❷のEメールには、他の清掃業者を調査したとは述べられていない。research「～を調査する」。
(B) ❷のEメールには、友人に紹介されたとは述べられていない。refer ～ to …「～を…に紹介する」。

188 In the first e-mail, the word "case" in paragraph 1, line 3, is closest in meaning to

(A) project
(B) example
(C) situation
(D) container

1通目のEメールの第1段落・3行目にある "case" に最も意味が近いのは

(A) 企画
(B) 例
(C) 状況
(D) 容器

正解 C　❷の❶1～3行目より、Coeさんは Presnell清掃社のサービスにすっかり満足することを期待していたと述べた後に、that was not the case. と述べ、その理由を後に続けている。つまり、期待したような清掃内容が提供されず、予期していた状況にならなかったと考えられるので、(C) situation がこの case の意味に最も近いと考えられる。

189 Why did Ms. Coe write to complain?　　Coeさんはなぜ苦情を述べるEメールを書いたのですか。

(A) The office floors were not waxed.　　(A) オフィスの床がワックス掛けされていなかった。

(B) The office kitchen was not sterilized.　　(B) オフィスの給湯室が殺菌消毒されていなかった。

(C) The cleaners did not shampoo the carpets.　　(C) 清掃員たちがカーペットを洗剤で洗わなかった。

(D) The cleaners did not use natural products.　　(D) 清掃員たちが天然素材の製品を使用しなかった。

> 正解 **D** ❷の❶ 3～4行目に「私は、貴社の特殊清掃サービスを希望したが、貴社の清掃員はそうしたサービスを提供しなかった」とあり、Coeさんはこれについて苦情を申し立てるためにEメールを書いていると分かる。「特殊清掃サービス」とは、❶の❷より、全て天然で無臭の清掃技術を使ったサービスのことなので、Coeさんのオフィスの清掃で清掃員はこれを行わず、洗剤を用いたと推測できる。よって、(D) が正解。
> (A) floor「床」、wax「～にワックスを掛ける」。
> (B) sterilize「～を消毒する、～を殺菌する」。
> (C) shampoo「～を洗剤で洗う」。

Final Test

190 What does Mr. Medford offer to do if Ms. Coe is not satisfied after August 18?　　Medfordさんは、8月18日の後にCoeさんが満足しなかった場合、何をすることを申し出ていますか。

(A) Refund her money　　(A) 彼女が支払ったお金を返金する。

(B) Create a new cleaning plan　　(B) 新しい清掃プランを作成する。

(C) Send different cleaning staff members　　(C) 別の清掃スタッフを派遣する。

(D) Provide a discount on future cleaning services　　(D) 今後の清掃サービスに割引を提供する。

> 正解 **A** Presnell社から返信されたEメールの❸❷ 1行目には、「8月18日にあらためて貴社のオフィスを無料で清掃する機会をもらいたい。もしその清掃が貴社の基準を満たさない場合、当社は保証に応じる」とある。「保証」とは、❶の❸ 2行目にある a money-back guarantee「返金保証」のことを指すので、(A) が正解。refund「～ (金銭) を払い戻す」。
> (B) create「～を作り出す」。
> (D) discount「割引」。

語注

❶ ウェブページ testimonial お客さまの声、証言　contact ～に連絡を取る　rate 料金

❶ comprehensive 総合的な　cater to ～ ～に対応する　domestic 家庭の　commercial 営利の
clientele 顧客　provide ～を提供する　exceptional ひときわ優れた
competitive （価格が）競争力のある

❷ in addition to ～ ～に加えて　regular 通常の　specialized 特殊な　all-natural 全て天然の
odor-free 無臭の、臭いの出ない　technique 技術　～ as well as … …はもちろん～も、…だけでなく～も
allergen アレルゲン、アレルギーを起こす物質　reduction 減少

❸ client 顧客　weekly 週に1回の　twice-monthly 月に2回の　monthly 月に1回の
cleaner 清掃員　on time 時間通りに　guarantee 保証　completely 完全に　satisfied 満足した

❹ schedule ～を (特定の日時に) 予定する　on-site 現場での　assessment 査定
estimate 見積もり　be sure to do 必ず～する

❷ Eメール ❶ hire ～を (一時的に) 雇う　recommendation 推薦　expect to do ～することを期待する
be satisfied with ～ ～に満足する　unfortunately 残念ながら　case 状況、事態
request ～を依頼する、～を希望する　clearly 明らかに　go wrong 間違える、うまくいかない
consider doing ～することを検討する　cancel ～を中止する、～をキャンセルする

❸ Eメール ❶ be sorry to do ～して申し訳なく思う　train ～ (人) の研修を行う　follow ～に従う
promise ～ that … ～に…であることを約束する　ensure (that) ～ ～であることを確実にする
properly 適切に　conduct ～を行う　inspect ～を検査する

❷ opportunity 機会、チャンス　charge 料金　meet ～を満たす　standard 基準
honor ～ (約束など) を守る　acceptable 受け入れられる　representative 担当者

Questions 191-195 refer to the following postcard, Web page, and article.

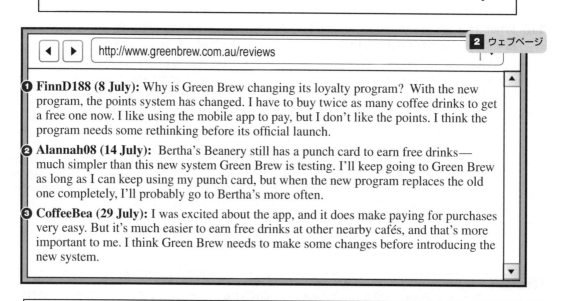

★ ★ ★ ★
Attention Loyal Green Brew Customers!
★ ★ ★ ★

1 はがき

❶ Green Brew Café is redesigning our loyalty program—it's not just for coffee anymore! As a frequent customer, you're invited to participate in testing the new program. Interested? Go to greenbrew.com to read more and download the new Green Brew app. Then start accumulating points by enjoying our sandwiches, smoothies, and salads in addition to your favorite coffee drinks. When you post a review on our Web site, you will receive twenty extra points as a thank-you gift!

Green Brew Café

2 ウェブページ

http://www.greenbrew.com.au/reviews

❶ **FinnD188 (8 July):** Why is Green Brew changing its loyalty program? With the new program, the points system has changed. I have to buy twice as many coffee drinks to get a free one now. I like using the mobile app to pay, but I don't like the points. I think the program needs some rethinking before its official launch.

❷ **Alannah08 (14 July):** Bertha's Beanery still has a punch card to earn free drinks—much simpler than this new system Green Brew is testing. I'll keep going to Green Brew as long as I can keep using my punch card, but when the new program replaces the old one completely, I'll probably go to Bertha's more often.

❸ **CoffeeBea (29 July):** I was excited about the app, and it does make paying for purchases very easy. But it's much easier to earn free drinks at other nearby cafés, and that's more important to me. I think Green Brew needs to make some changes before introducing the new system.

3 記事

A Lesson in Loyalty
By Hudson Aird
27 August

❶ Maintaining customer loyalty can be difficult. Just ask Green Brew Café owner Taylah Carver. She recently began experimenting with a change to the café's loyalty program to reward her regular customers. Instead of the old punch-card system, which rewarded customers for coffee purchases only, the new program allows customers to earn points for buying food items as well. The points are tracked through the Green Brew app, which customers download to their mobile devices. The app can also be used to pay for orders.

❷ The program was originally scheduled to be introduced to the general public in September, but after nearly 60 customers tried out the app for a month, Carver decided to defer the launch. Most users liked the fact that the app allows them to pay using their mobile devices, but there were many complaints about the new points system. It now <u>takes</u> twice as many purchases before customers accumulate enough points to be eligible for a free coffee drink, and that was too much, reviewers said. The lesson, says Ms. Carver: know your customers.

問題191-195は次のはがき、ウェブページと記事に関するものです。

Green Brew のロイヤルカスタマーの皆さんにご案内申し上げます！

Green Brew カフェは、当店のロイヤルティープログラムの内容を再設計する予定です――それはもはや、コーヒーだけではありません！ 頻繁にご来店いただいているお客さまとして、あなたを新しいプログラムのお試しにご招待いたします。ご興味がおありですか。greenbrew.com にアクセスして、さらに詳しい説明をお読みになり、新しい Green Brew アプリをダウンロードしてください。そして、お気に入りのコーヒーに加え、当店のサンドイッチ、スムージーそしてサラダもお楽しみいただき、ポイントを貯め始めてください。当店のウェブサイトにレビューをご投稿いただくと、お礼のギフトとして 20 ポイントを追加でお受け取りいただけます！

http://www.greenbrew.com.au/reviews

FinnD188 (7 月 8 日)：Green Brew はなぜ、ロイヤルティープログラムを変更しようとしているのだろうか。新しいプログラムでは、ポイントの制度が変わってしまった。今では、無料のコーヒー 1 杯をもらうためにはコーヒーを以前の 2 倍も買う必要がある。携帯電話のアプリを使って支払うのはいいが、ポイントは好きではない。正式な運用開始の前にプログラムは何らかの再考が必要だと思う。

Alannah08 (7 月 14 日)：Bertha's Beanery には今でも、無料の飲み物がもらえるパンチカードがある――それは Green Brew が試しているこの新制度よりずっと分かりやすい。私は自分のパンチカードを使い続けられる限り、Green Brew に通い続けるつもりだが、新しいプログラムが古いものに完全に取って代わったら、おそらく Bertha's の方により頻繁に行くだろう。

CoffeeBea (7 月 29 日)：私はそのアプリが楽しみだったし、確かに購入の際の支払いはとても楽になっている。しかし、近隣の他のカフェの方が無料の飲み物をもらうのはずっと簡単であり、私にとってはその方が重要である。Green Brew は、新制度を導入する前に、幾つかの変更をする必要があると思う。

顧客のロイヤルティーに関する教訓
Hudson Aird 記
8 月 27 日

顧客のロイヤルティーを保ち続けることは、難しい場合もある。Green Brew カフェのオーナー、Taylah Carver さんに尋ねてみればいい。彼女は最近、カフェの常連客に報酬ポイントを与えるため、カフェのロイヤルティープログラムの変更を試み始めた。コーヒーの購入に対してのみ顧客に報酬ポイントを与えていたという、従来のパンチカードシステムに代わり、新しいプログラムでは、食品の購入に対しても顧客がポイントを獲得できるようになっている。ポイントは、顧客が自分の携帯端末にダウンロードする Green Brew のアプリで確認できる。アプリは、注文した商品の支払いに使うことも可能だ。

プログラムは、もともと 9 月に一般向けに導入される予定だったが、60 人近い顧客が 1 カ月間アプリを試した結果、Carver さんは運用開始を延期すると決めた。ほとんどの利用者が、アプリによって携帯端末を使って支払いができる点を好んだが、新しいポイントの制度について多くの苦情があったのだ。現在、顧客が無料のコーヒーを 1 杯もらうのに十分なポイントを貯めるには、2 倍の購入数が必要で、それでは多過ぎるとレビュアーたちは述べた。教訓は「汝の顧客を知れ」ということだと Carver さんは語る。

191 Why was the postcard sent?

(A) To encourage customers to place orders online
(B) To announce a change in café hours
(C) To introduce a new price list
(D) To recruit customers to test a rewards system

はがきはなぜ送られたのですか。

(A) 顧客にインターネットで注文をするよう促すため。
(B) カフェの営業時間の変更を知らせるため。
(C) 新しい価格表を紹介するため。
(D) ある報酬制度を試す顧客を募集するため。

正解 D

❶は Green Brew カフェが常連客へ送ったはがきである。❶の1～4行目でロイヤルティープログラムを再設計する予定を伝え、「頻繁に来店するお客として、あなたを新しいプログラムのお試しに招待する」と述べている。ロイヤルティープログラムとは、利用金額に応じてポイントを付与するプログラム。よって、(D) が正解。recruit「～を募集する」。reward system「報酬制度」は、利用金額に応じてポイントを付与する制度。
(A) encourage ～ to *do*「～に…するよう促す」、place an order「注文をする」、online「インターネット上で、オンラインで」。
(B) 営業時間についての言及はない。announce「～を知らせる」。
(C) 価格についての言及はない。price list「価格表」。

192 What is suggested about the people who posted reviews?

(A) They received bonus points for reviewing an app.
(B) They often meet friends at Green Brew Café.
(C) They tried some new lunch items at Green Brew Café.
(D) They are pleased about a reduction in prices.

レビューを投稿した人々について何が分かりますか。

(A) アプリのレビューをすることで、ボーナスポイントを受け取った。
(B) Green Brewカフェでよく友人と会う。
(C) Green Brewカフェで幾つかの新しいランチ商品を試した。
(D) 価格の値下げを喜んでいる。

正解 A

❶のレビュアーを募集するはがきには、❶5～6行目でアプリのダウンロードを促す呼び掛けをした後、同9～11行目に「当店のウェブサイトにレビューを投稿すると、お礼のギフトとして20ポイントを追加で受け取れる」と案内している。このことから、❷のウェブページにレビューを投稿した人々は皆、追加のボーナスポイントを得たと考えられる。
(D) pleased「喜んで」、reduction「減少」。

語 注

❶ はがき　attention　案内、知らせ　　loyal customer　常連客　★商品やサービスを繰り返し購入・利用してくれる顧客
❶ café　カフェ　　redesign　～を再設計する
loyalty　ロイヤルティー　★顧客の企業に対する愛着・忠実さを表す　　not ～ anymore　もはや～ではない
participate in ～　～に参加する　　test　～を試す　　download　～をダウンロードする
app　〈application の略で〉アプリ　　accumulate　～を貯める、～を蓄積する　　smoothie　スムージー
in addition to ～　～に加えて　　post　～を投稿する　　review　レビュー、批評　　extra　追加の
thank-you gift　返礼のギフト
❷ ウェブページ　❶ twice　2倍　　mobile　携帯電話　　rethinking　再考　　official　正式な　　launch　運用開始
❷ as long as ～　～する限り　　punch card　パンチカード　　replace　～に取って代わる
❸ purchase　購入　　earn　～を獲得する　　nearby　近くの　　introduce　～を導入する
❸ 記事　❶ maintain　～を保つ　　experiment with ～　～を試みる　　reward　～に報酬を与える　　regular　常連の
instead of ～　～の代わりに　　item　品物、品目　　as well　～もまた　　track　～を追跡して記録する
device　端末
❷ originally　もともと　　be scheduled to *do*　～する予定である　　general　一般の　　public　一般の人々
nearly　およそ　　try out　～を試す　　defer　～を延期する　　allow ～ to *do*　～に…することを許す
complaint　苦情　　be eligible for ～　～に資格のある　　reviewer　レビュアー、評価をする人

193 What is implied about Ms. Carver?

(A) She runs a business that competes with Bertha's Beanery.
(B) She is not the original owner of Green Brew Café.
(C) She expects sales to increase in September.
(D) She decided to find a new vendor for punch cards.

Carverさんについて、何が示唆されていますか。

(A) Bertha's Beaneryと競合する事業を経営している。
(B) Green Brewカフェの最初のオーナーではない。
(C) 9月に売り上げが増えると期待している。
(D) パンチカードの新しい販売業者を見つけると決めた。

> **正解 A** ③の記事の❶より、Carver さんとは Green Brew カフェのオーナーである。②の❷1行目でレビュアーの1人は、Bertha's Beanery には今でもパンチカードのシステムがあることに言及した後、2〜4行目で「私は自分のパンチカードを使い続けられる限り、Green Brew に通い続けるつもりだが、新しいプログラムが古いものに完全に取って代わったら、おそらく Bertha's の方により頻繁に行くだろう」と述べている。このことから、両者は同じ客層を持つ競合店であることが分かる。run「〜を経営する」、business「事業、会社」、compete with 〜「〜と競合する」。
> (B) Carver さんが最初のオーナーかどうかは不明。
> (C)(D) いずれも言及がない。

194 According to the article, what is a common criticism of a new loyalty program?

(A) It is difficult to download the mobile app.
(B) Customers must spend more money to earn free items.
(C) Food purchases are not included.
(D) Points are not tracked accurately.

記事によると、新しいロイヤルティープログラムに対してよくある批判は何ですか。

(A) 携帯電話用アプリのダウンロードが難しい。
(B) 顧客は無料の品物を獲得するためにより多くのお金を使わなければならない。
(C) 食品の購入が算入されていない。
(D) ポイントが正確に追跡されない。

> **正解 B** 新しいロイヤルティープログラムに対する批判について、③の❷5〜8行目で多くの苦情があったことが述べられ、同8〜11行目に「現在、顧客が無料のコーヒーを1杯もらうのに十分なポイントを貯めるには、2倍の購入数が必要で、それでは多過ぎるとレビュアーたちは述べた」とある。よって、顧客の多くは、無料の飲み物を得るためにより多くのお金を使わなければならなくなったことを批判していると分かる。common「よくある、ありがちな」、criticism「批判」。
> (C) ③❶より、新しいプログラムでは食べ物の購入にもポイントが与えられると述べられている。

195 In the article, the word "takes" in paragraph 2, line 8, is closest in meaning to

(A) removes
(B) provides
(C) requires
(D) delivers

記事の第2段落・8行目にある "takes" に最も意味が近いのは

(A) 〜を取り除く
(B) 〜を提供する
(C) 〜を必要とする
(D) 〜を配達する

> **正解 C** takes を含む文は、新しいロイヤルティープログラムに寄せられた苦情の内容を説明している箇所。無料のコーヒーを1杯もらうのに十分なポイントを貯めるには、It now takes twice as many purchases とあり、「それでは多過ぎるとレビュアーたちは述べた」と続けて説明されている。これと同じ内容が②のウェブページの❶2〜3行目にも書かれており、「今では、無料のコーヒー1杯をもらうためにはコーヒーを以前の2倍も買う必要がある」とある。これらのことから、最も意味が近いのは「〜を必要とする」という意味の (C) requires だと判断できる。

Questions 196-200 refer to the following Web page, letter, and schedule.

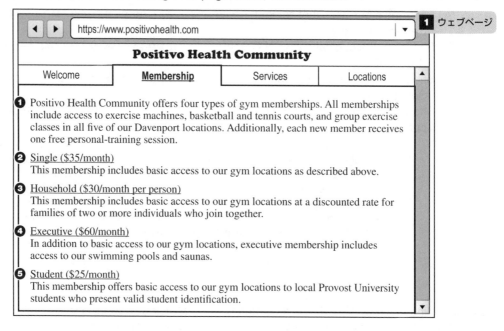

February 28

Dear Ron Mapleton,

❶ Thank you for making Positivo Health Community a part of your total-body health program. It was so nice to meet you and your family when I showed you around our Davenport Central location in December.

❷ We noticed that you have not yet taken advantage of your free hour of personal training. Each person on your account is entitled to one free session, but this perk expires three months after your contract is signed. Next week, the week of March 4, is the last week you will be able to use your free sessions. Please contact us today to schedule your personal-training sessions!

❸ As a reminder, we offer one-on-one training for power yoga, Pilates, weight training, and power lifting. If you should choose to make personal training a regular part of your fitness routine, <u>packages</u> start at only $70 per month in addition to your monthly membership dues.

Your partner in health,

Janie Park

Janie Park, Membership Manager

2 手紙

Personal-Training Schedule for Next Week March 4–8 **Employee:** Kevin Pinto **Location:** Davenport Central					
	Monday	**Tuesday**	**Wednesday**	**Thursday**	**Friday**
8:00 A.M.		Stacey Lin Power Yoga	Ron Mapleton Power Yoga		Kim Dobbs Weight Training
9:00 A.M.	Pilar Hernandez Weight Training				
10:00 A.M.				Jean-Luc Curran Power Lifting	
11:00 A.M.		Jaylon Hill Power Yoga			

3 日程表

問題196-200は次のウェブページ、手紙、日程表に関するものです。

http://www.positivohealth.com

Positivo Health Community

| ようこそ | 会員資格 | サービス | 場所 |

Positivo Health Community では 4 種類のジムの会員資格を提供しています。全ての会員資格には、Davenport の全 5 店舗におけるエクササイズ機器、バスケットボールおよびテニスのコート、グループエクササイズの講習の利用が含まれます。さらに、新規会員はパーソナルトレーニングの無料レッスンを 1 回受けられます。

個人 (35 ドル / 月)
この会員資格は、上記のジム各店舗での基本的な利用を含みます。

家族 (30 ドル / 月・お 1 人様)
この会員資格は、ご一緒に入会いただく家族 2 名様以上について、割引料金にてジム各店舗での基本的な利用を含みます。

上級 (60 ドル / 月)
上級会員資格は、当ジム店舗の基本的な利用に加えて、プールとサウナの利用を含みます。

学生 (25 ドル / 月)
この会員資格は、有効な学生証を提示した地元の Provost 大学の学生に対して、ジム各店舗での基本的な利用を提供します。

Final
Test

2 月 28 日

Ron Mapleton 様

Positivo Health Community をお客さまの全身健康計画の一部としていただき、ありがとうございます。12 月に Davenport 中央店でご案内した際、お客さまとご家族にお会いできて光栄でした。

お客さま方はまだ、無料のパーソナルトレーニングのレッスンを利用されていらっしゃらないと存じます。お客さまの契約アカウントのお一人お一人が、無料レッスンを 1 回利用する権利を有していますが、この特典は契約締結後 3 カ月で期限切れになります。来週、つまり 3 月 4 日の週が、お客さまが無料レッスンを利用できる最後の週になります。ぜひ今日にでもご連絡いただき、パーソナルトレーニングの時間をご予約ください！

あらためてお知らせしますと、当店はパワーヨガ、ピラティス、筋力トレーニング、パワーリフティングのマンツーマンのトレーニングを提供しています。もしお客さまがパーソナルトレーニングを定期的なフィットネス習慣の一部にすることをご選択されるなら、毎月の会費に加え、パックを 1 カ月につきわずか 70 ドルから提供しております。

あなたの健康パートナー、
Janie Park (署名)
Janie Park、会員資格担当マネジャー

次週のパーソナルトレーニングの日程表 3 月 4 日～8 日 スタッフ：Kevin Pinto 店舗：Davenport 中央店				
	月曜日	火曜日	水曜日	木曜日	金曜日
午前 8 時		Stacey Lin パワーヨガ	Ron Mapleton パワーヨガ		Kim Dobbs 筋力トレーニング
午前 9 時	Pilar Hernandez 筋力トレーニング				
午前 10 時				Jean-Luc Curran パワーリフティング	
午前 11 時		Jaylon Hill パワーヨガ			

196 What is indicated about Positivo Health Community?

(A) It offers swimming lessons.
(B) Its members can use multiple facilities.
(C) Most of its members are students.
(D) All new members receive discounts.

Positivo Health Communityについて、何が示されていますか。

(A) 水泳のレッスンを提供している。
(B) 会員は複数の施設を利用できる。
(C) 会員の大半は学生である。
(D) 新規会員は全員、割引を受ける。

正解 **B**　**1**のウェブページの**❶** 1～3行目で、「全ての会員資格には、Davenport の全5店舗におけるエクササイズ機器、バスケットボールおよびテニスのコート、グループエクササイズの講習の利用が含まれる」と述べられているので、会員は複数の施設を利用できると分かる。(B) が正解。multiple「複数の」、facility「施設」。
(A) **1**の**❹**にプールについての言及はあるが、レッスンを提供しているかどうかは不明。
(C) 会員数やその内訳についての言及はない。
(D) **1**の**❸** 3～4行目より、新規会員が受けられるのはパーソナルトレーニングの無料レッスン1回。

197 What type of membership does Mr. Mapleton most likely have?

(A) Single
(B) Household
(C) Executive
(D) Student

Mapletonさんはどの種類の会員資格を持っていると考えられますか。

(A) 個人
(B) 家族
(C) 上級
(D) 学生

正解 **B**　Mapleton さん宛ての手紙の**2**の**❶** 2～3行目に、Park さんが12月に Davenport 中央店で、Mapleton さんと彼の家族を案内したことが述べられている。さらに、同**2**❷ 2～3行目で Park さんは、「契約アカウントの一人一人が、無料レッスンを1回利用する権利を有しているが、この特典は契約締結後3カ月で期限切れになる」と説明しているので、Mapleton さんの契約には家族複数人の会員資格が含まれていると分かる。**1**の**❸**から、家族複数人が利用できる会員資格は、(B) Household である。

198 What is indicated about Ms. Park?

(A) She is a personal trainer.
(B) She started her job in December.
(C) She creates weekly schedules for gym employees.
(D) She gave Mr. Mapleton a tour of the gym.

Parkさんについて何が示されていますか。

(A) 個人トレーナーである。
(B) 12月に仕事を始めた。
(C) ジムの従業員のために毎週のスケジュールを作っている。
(D) Mapletonさんにジムの案内をした。

正解 **D**　**2**の**❶** 2～3行目より、12月に Davenport 中央店で Park さんが Mapleton さんと家族にジムを案内したことが分かる。よって、(D) が正解。tour「案内、見学」。
(A) **2**の署名欄の肩書きから、Park さんは会員資格担当マネジャーである。
(B) Park さんが仕事を始めた時期についての言及はない。
(C) 毎週のスケジュールの作成者に関する情報は示されていない。

199 In the letter, the word "packages" in paragraph 3, line 3, is closest in meaning to

(A) gifts
(B) boxes
(C) products
(D) plans

手紙の中で、第3段落・3行目にある "packages" に最も意味が近いのは

(A) 贈り物
(B) 箱
(C) 製品
(D) プラン

正解 **D** ②の❸1～2行目でParkさんは、パワーヨガやパワーリフティングなどのマンツーマンのトレーニングを提供していると説明した後、2～4行目でpackagesを用いて、「パーソナルトレーニングを定期的なフィットネス習慣の一部にすることを選択するなら、毎月の会費に加え、packagesを1カ月につきわずか70ドルから提供している」と述べている。月額の料金に追加されることから、このpackagesは、各パーソナルトレーニングのサービスを指すと考えられる。最も意味が近いのは、商品サービスとしての「プラン」を表す(D) plans。
(C) product「製品」は製造加工された品物や生産された作物を表す語。

---

200 What is probably true about Mr. Pinto?

(A) He does not work on Fridays.
(B) He primarily teaches power lifting.
(C) He has not trained Mr. Mapleton before.
(D) He has requested a change to his schedule.

Pintoさんについて、何が正しいと思われますか。

(A) 毎週金曜日には勤務していない。
(B) 主にパワーリフティングを教えている。
(C) Mapletonさんを指導したことがない。
(D) 自分の日程表への変更を依頼した。

正解 **C** Pintoさんは❸のパーソナルトレーニングの日程表のスタッフの名前。Pintoさんの日程表を見ると、3月6日に当たる水曜日に、Mapletonさんがパワーヨガのパーソナルトレーニングを受ける予定だと分かる。一方、②の手紙の❷3～4行目に、3月4日の週は無料レッスンを利用できる最後の週だと書かれているので、Mapletonさんは2月28日の時点でパーソナルトレーニングをまだ利用したことがないと分かる。よって、Pintoさんの日程表の3月6日の水曜日は、Pintoさんが初めてMapletonさんを指導する日だと推測できる。(C)が正解。
(A) ❸の日程表から、Pintoさんは金曜日に勤務がある。
(B) ❸の日程表には、パワーリフティング1回の他に筋力トレーニングとパワーヨガが入っており、主にパワーリフティングを教えているとは言えない。
(D) 日程表の変更については言及がない。

Final Test

語注

1 ウェブページ membership 会員資格　location 所在地
　❶ offer ～を提供する　gym ジム　include ～を含む　access 利用する権利
　　additionally さらに　personal パーソナルの、個人の　session 課業、会
　❷ single 1人　describe ～を説明する　above 上記で
　❸ household 世帯　per ～につき　discounted 割引された　rate 料金　individual 個人
　　join 入会する
　❹ executive 幹部、重役　in addition to ～ ～に加えて　sauna サウナ
　❺ local 地元の　present ～を提示する　valid 有効な　identification 身元証明書

2 手紙　❶ total-body 全身の　show ～ around … ～に…を案内する
　❷ notice that ～ ～であることに気付く　take advantage of ～ ～を利用する
　　account （契約の）アカウント、取引　be entitled to ～ ～の権利がある　perk 特典
　　expire 期限が切れる、失効する　contract 契約　sign ～に署名する
　　schedule ～を（特定の日時に）予定する
　❸ reminder 思い出させるもの　one-on-one 1対1の　yoga ヨガ　Pilates ピラティス
　　weight training 筋力トレーニング　power lifting パワーリフティング　regular 定期的な
　　fitness フィットネス　routine 決まってすること　package パック、セット　monthly 毎月の
　　dues 〈複数形で〉会費　partner パートナー、仲間　manager マネジャー、管理者

3 日程表　❶ employee 従業員

Mini Test 1 解答用紙

READING SECTION

PART 5

No.	ANSWER A B C D
1	Ⓐ Ⓑ Ⓒ Ⓓ
2	Ⓐ Ⓑ Ⓒ Ⓓ
3	Ⓐ Ⓑ Ⓒ Ⓓ
4	Ⓐ Ⓑ Ⓒ Ⓓ
5	Ⓐ Ⓑ Ⓒ Ⓓ
6	Ⓐ Ⓑ Ⓒ Ⓓ
7	Ⓐ Ⓑ Ⓒ Ⓓ
8	Ⓐ Ⓑ Ⓒ Ⓓ
9	Ⓐ Ⓑ Ⓒ Ⓓ
10	Ⓐ Ⓑ Ⓒ Ⓓ

No.	ANSWER A B C D
11	Ⓐ Ⓑ Ⓒ Ⓓ

PART 6

No.	ANSWER A B C D
12	Ⓐ Ⓑ Ⓒ Ⓓ
13	Ⓐ Ⓑ Ⓒ Ⓓ
14	Ⓐ Ⓑ Ⓒ Ⓓ
15	Ⓐ Ⓑ Ⓒ Ⓓ

PART 7

No.	ANSWER A B C D
16	Ⓐ Ⓑ Ⓒ Ⓓ
17	Ⓐ Ⓑ Ⓒ Ⓓ
18	Ⓐ Ⓑ Ⓒ Ⓓ
19	Ⓐ Ⓑ Ⓒ Ⓓ
20	Ⓐ Ⓑ Ⓒ Ⓓ
21	Ⓐ Ⓑ Ⓒ Ⓓ
22	Ⓐ Ⓑ Ⓒ Ⓓ
23	Ⓐ Ⓑ Ⓒ Ⓓ
24	Ⓐ Ⓑ Ⓒ Ⓓ
25	Ⓐ Ⓑ Ⓒ Ⓓ

No.	ANSWER A B C D
26	Ⓐ Ⓑ Ⓒ Ⓓ
27	Ⓐ Ⓑ Ⓒ Ⓓ
28	Ⓐ Ⓑ Ⓒ Ⓓ
29	Ⓐ Ⓑ Ⓒ Ⓓ

Mini Test 2 解答用紙

READING SECTION

PART 5

No.	ANSWER A B C D
1	Ⓐ Ⓑ Ⓒ Ⓓ
2	Ⓐ Ⓑ Ⓒ Ⓓ
3	Ⓐ Ⓑ Ⓒ Ⓓ
4	Ⓐ Ⓑ Ⓒ Ⓓ
5	Ⓐ Ⓑ Ⓒ Ⓓ
6	Ⓐ Ⓑ Ⓒ Ⓓ
7	Ⓐ Ⓑ Ⓒ Ⓓ
8	Ⓐ Ⓑ Ⓒ Ⓓ
9	Ⓐ Ⓑ Ⓒ Ⓓ
10	Ⓐ Ⓑ Ⓒ Ⓓ

No.	ANSWER A B C D
11	Ⓐ Ⓑ Ⓒ Ⓓ

PART 6

No.	ANSWER A B C D
12	Ⓐ Ⓑ Ⓒ Ⓓ
13	Ⓐ Ⓑ Ⓒ Ⓓ
14	Ⓐ Ⓑ Ⓒ Ⓓ
15	Ⓐ Ⓑ Ⓒ Ⓓ

PART 7

No.	ANSWER A B C D
16	Ⓐ Ⓑ Ⓒ Ⓓ
17	Ⓐ Ⓑ Ⓒ Ⓓ
18	Ⓐ Ⓑ Ⓒ Ⓓ
19	Ⓐ Ⓑ Ⓒ Ⓓ
20	Ⓐ Ⓑ Ⓒ Ⓓ
21	Ⓐ Ⓑ Ⓒ Ⓓ
22	Ⓐ Ⓑ Ⓒ Ⓓ
23	Ⓐ Ⓑ Ⓒ Ⓓ
24	Ⓐ Ⓑ Ⓒ Ⓓ
25	Ⓐ Ⓑ Ⓒ Ⓓ

No.	ANSWER A B C D
26	Ⓐ Ⓑ Ⓒ Ⓓ
27	Ⓐ Ⓑ Ⓒ Ⓓ
28	Ⓐ Ⓑ Ⓒ Ⓓ
29	Ⓐ Ⓑ Ⓒ Ⓓ

※このマークシートは Mini Test (全29問) に対応したものです。

※このマークシートは Mini Test (全 29 問) に対応したものです。

Mini Test 3 解答用紙

READING SECTION

PART 5

No.	ANSWER A B C D
1	Ⓐ Ⓑ Ⓒ Ⓓ
2	Ⓐ Ⓑ Ⓒ Ⓓ
3	Ⓐ Ⓑ Ⓒ Ⓓ
4	Ⓐ Ⓑ Ⓒ Ⓓ
5	Ⓐ Ⓑ Ⓒ Ⓓ
6	Ⓐ Ⓑ Ⓒ Ⓓ
7	Ⓐ Ⓑ Ⓒ Ⓓ
8	Ⓐ Ⓑ Ⓒ Ⓓ
9	Ⓐ Ⓑ Ⓒ Ⓓ
10	Ⓐ Ⓑ Ⓒ Ⓓ

No.	ANSWER A B C D
11	Ⓐ Ⓑ Ⓒ Ⓓ

PART 6

No.	ANSWER A B C D
12	Ⓐ Ⓑ Ⓒ Ⓓ
13	Ⓐ Ⓑ Ⓒ Ⓓ
14	Ⓐ Ⓑ Ⓒ Ⓓ
15	Ⓐ Ⓑ Ⓒ Ⓓ

PART 7

No.	ANSWER A B C D
16	Ⓐ Ⓑ Ⓒ Ⓓ
17	Ⓐ Ⓑ Ⓒ Ⓓ
18	Ⓐ Ⓑ Ⓒ Ⓓ
19	Ⓐ Ⓑ Ⓒ Ⓓ
20	Ⓐ Ⓑ Ⓒ Ⓓ
21	Ⓐ Ⓑ Ⓒ Ⓓ
22	Ⓐ Ⓑ Ⓒ Ⓓ
23	Ⓐ Ⓑ Ⓒ Ⓓ
24	Ⓐ Ⓑ Ⓒ Ⓓ
25	Ⓐ Ⓑ Ⓒ Ⓓ

No.	ANSWER A B C D
26	Ⓐ Ⓑ Ⓒ Ⓓ
27	Ⓐ Ⓑ Ⓒ Ⓓ
28	Ⓐ Ⓑ Ⓒ Ⓓ
29	Ⓐ Ⓑ Ⓒ Ⓓ

Mini Test 4 解答用紙

READING SECTION

PART 5

No.	ANSWER A B C D
1	Ⓐ Ⓑ Ⓒ Ⓓ
2	Ⓐ Ⓑ Ⓒ Ⓓ
3	Ⓐ Ⓑ Ⓒ Ⓓ
4	Ⓐ Ⓑ Ⓒ Ⓓ
5	Ⓐ Ⓑ Ⓒ Ⓓ
6	Ⓐ Ⓑ Ⓒ Ⓓ
7	Ⓐ Ⓑ Ⓒ Ⓓ
8	Ⓐ Ⓑ Ⓒ Ⓓ
9	Ⓐ Ⓑ Ⓒ Ⓓ
10	Ⓐ Ⓑ Ⓒ Ⓓ

No.	ANSWER A B C D
11	Ⓐ Ⓑ Ⓒ Ⓓ

PART 6

No.	ANSWER A B C D
12	Ⓐ Ⓑ Ⓒ Ⓓ
13	Ⓐ Ⓑ Ⓒ Ⓓ
14	Ⓐ Ⓑ Ⓒ Ⓓ
15	Ⓐ Ⓑ Ⓒ Ⓓ

PART 7

No.	ANSWER A B C D
16	Ⓐ Ⓑ Ⓒ Ⓓ
17	Ⓐ Ⓑ Ⓒ Ⓓ
18	Ⓐ Ⓑ Ⓒ Ⓓ
19	Ⓐ Ⓑ Ⓒ Ⓓ
20	Ⓐ Ⓑ Ⓒ Ⓓ
21	Ⓐ Ⓑ Ⓒ Ⓓ
22	Ⓐ Ⓑ Ⓒ Ⓓ
23	Ⓐ Ⓑ Ⓒ Ⓓ
24	Ⓐ Ⓑ Ⓒ Ⓓ
25	Ⓐ Ⓑ Ⓒ Ⓓ

No.	ANSWER A B C D
26	Ⓐ Ⓑ Ⓒ Ⓓ
27	Ⓐ Ⓑ Ⓒ Ⓓ
28	Ⓐ Ⓑ Ⓒ Ⓓ
29	Ⓐ Ⓑ Ⓒ Ⓓ

Final Test
解答用紙

REGISTRATION No. 受験番号

フリガナ

NAME 氏名

READING SECTION

PART 5

No.	ANSWER
101	Ⓐ Ⓑ Ⓒ Ⓓ
102	Ⓐ Ⓑ Ⓒ Ⓓ
103	Ⓐ Ⓑ Ⓒ Ⓓ
104	Ⓐ Ⓑ Ⓒ Ⓓ
105	Ⓐ Ⓑ Ⓒ Ⓓ
106	Ⓐ Ⓑ Ⓒ Ⓓ
107	Ⓐ Ⓑ Ⓒ Ⓓ
108	Ⓐ Ⓑ Ⓒ Ⓓ
109	Ⓐ Ⓑ Ⓒ Ⓓ
110	Ⓐ Ⓑ Ⓒ Ⓓ

No.	ANSWER
111	Ⓐ Ⓑ Ⓒ Ⓓ
112	Ⓐ Ⓑ Ⓒ Ⓓ
113	Ⓐ Ⓑ Ⓒ Ⓓ
114	Ⓐ Ⓑ Ⓒ Ⓓ
115	Ⓐ Ⓑ Ⓒ Ⓓ
116	Ⓐ Ⓑ Ⓒ Ⓓ
117	Ⓐ Ⓑ Ⓒ Ⓓ
118	Ⓐ Ⓑ Ⓒ Ⓓ
119	Ⓐ Ⓑ Ⓒ Ⓓ
120	Ⓐ Ⓑ Ⓒ Ⓓ

No.	ANSWER
121	Ⓐ Ⓑ Ⓒ Ⓓ
122	Ⓐ Ⓑ Ⓒ Ⓓ
123	Ⓐ Ⓑ Ⓒ Ⓓ
124	Ⓐ Ⓑ Ⓒ Ⓓ
125	Ⓐ Ⓑ Ⓒ Ⓓ
126	Ⓐ Ⓑ Ⓒ Ⓓ
127	Ⓐ Ⓑ Ⓒ Ⓓ
128	Ⓐ Ⓑ Ⓒ Ⓓ
129	Ⓐ Ⓑ Ⓒ Ⓓ
130	Ⓐ Ⓑ Ⓒ Ⓓ

PART 6

No.	ANSWER
131	Ⓐ Ⓑ Ⓒ Ⓓ
132	Ⓐ Ⓑ Ⓒ Ⓓ
133	Ⓐ Ⓑ Ⓒ Ⓓ
134	Ⓐ Ⓑ Ⓒ Ⓓ
135	Ⓐ Ⓑ Ⓒ Ⓓ
136	Ⓐ Ⓑ Ⓒ Ⓓ
137	Ⓐ Ⓑ Ⓒ Ⓓ
138	Ⓐ Ⓑ Ⓒ Ⓓ
139	Ⓐ Ⓑ Ⓒ Ⓓ
140	Ⓐ Ⓑ Ⓒ Ⓓ

No.	ANSWER
141	Ⓐ Ⓑ Ⓒ Ⓓ
142	Ⓐ Ⓑ Ⓒ Ⓓ
143	Ⓐ Ⓑ Ⓒ Ⓓ
144	Ⓐ Ⓑ Ⓒ Ⓓ
145	Ⓐ Ⓑ Ⓒ Ⓓ
146	Ⓐ Ⓑ Ⓒ Ⓓ
147	Ⓐ Ⓑ Ⓒ Ⓓ
148	Ⓐ Ⓑ Ⓒ Ⓓ
149	Ⓐ Ⓑ Ⓒ Ⓓ
150	Ⓐ Ⓑ Ⓒ Ⓓ

PART 7

No.	ANSWER
151	Ⓐ Ⓑ Ⓒ Ⓓ
152	Ⓐ Ⓑ Ⓒ Ⓓ
153	Ⓐ Ⓑ Ⓒ Ⓓ
154	Ⓐ Ⓑ Ⓒ Ⓓ
155	Ⓐ Ⓑ Ⓒ Ⓓ
156	Ⓐ Ⓑ Ⓒ Ⓓ
157	Ⓐ Ⓑ Ⓒ Ⓓ
158	Ⓐ Ⓑ Ⓒ Ⓓ
159	Ⓐ Ⓑ Ⓒ Ⓓ
160	Ⓐ Ⓑ Ⓒ Ⓓ

No.	ANSWER
161	Ⓐ Ⓑ Ⓒ Ⓓ
162	Ⓐ Ⓑ Ⓒ Ⓓ
163	Ⓐ Ⓑ Ⓒ Ⓓ
164	Ⓐ Ⓑ Ⓒ Ⓓ
165	Ⓐ Ⓑ Ⓒ Ⓓ
166	Ⓐ Ⓑ Ⓒ Ⓓ
167	Ⓐ Ⓑ Ⓒ Ⓓ
168	Ⓐ Ⓑ Ⓒ Ⓓ
169	Ⓐ Ⓑ Ⓒ Ⓓ
170	Ⓐ Ⓑ Ⓒ Ⓓ

No.	ANSWER
171	Ⓐ Ⓑ Ⓒ Ⓓ
172	Ⓐ Ⓑ Ⓒ Ⓓ
173	Ⓐ Ⓑ Ⓒ Ⓓ
174	Ⓐ Ⓑ Ⓒ Ⓓ
175	Ⓐ Ⓑ Ⓒ Ⓓ
176	Ⓐ Ⓑ Ⓒ Ⓓ
177	Ⓐ Ⓑ Ⓒ Ⓓ
178	Ⓐ Ⓑ Ⓒ Ⓓ
179	Ⓐ Ⓑ Ⓒ Ⓓ
180	Ⓐ Ⓑ Ⓒ Ⓓ

No.	ANSWER
181	Ⓐ Ⓑ Ⓒ Ⓓ
182	Ⓐ Ⓑ Ⓒ Ⓓ
183	Ⓐ Ⓑ Ⓒ Ⓓ
184	Ⓐ Ⓑ Ⓒ Ⓓ
185	Ⓐ Ⓑ Ⓒ Ⓓ
186	Ⓐ Ⓑ Ⓒ Ⓓ
187	Ⓐ Ⓑ Ⓒ Ⓓ
188	Ⓐ Ⓑ Ⓒ Ⓓ
189	Ⓐ Ⓑ Ⓒ Ⓓ
190	Ⓐ Ⓑ Ⓒ Ⓓ

No.	ANSWER
191	Ⓐ Ⓑ Ⓒ Ⓓ
192	Ⓐ Ⓑ Ⓒ Ⓓ
193	Ⓐ Ⓑ Ⓒ Ⓓ
194	Ⓐ Ⓑ Ⓒ Ⓓ
195	Ⓐ Ⓑ Ⓒ Ⓓ
196	Ⓐ Ⓑ Ⓒ Ⓓ
197	Ⓐ Ⓑ Ⓒ Ⓓ
198	Ⓐ Ⓑ Ⓒ Ⓓ
199	Ⓐ Ⓑ Ⓒ Ⓓ
200	Ⓐ Ⓑ Ⓒ Ⓓ

リーディングセクションの問題形式の訳

PART 5、6、7 サンプル問題の訳（p.209-211）

PART 5

1. 採用担当者と会う前に、応募者の方々は人事部の受付で署名して到着を記録してください。

(A) 動詞 meet「会う」の三人称単数現在形
(B) 動名詞 ★
(C) 不定詞
(D) 受動態の過去形

PART 6

問題 1-4 は次の記事に関するものです。

サンディエゴ（5月5日）—Matino 産業社は、同社の再生不能エネルギーの使用を5年以内に20パーセント未満に削減するという公約のおかげで、環境意識の高い顧客にとっての同社のイメージを強化したところである。*この目標を達成するために同社は、自社のエネルギー効率を改善することから始める予定だ。機器を使用していないときには電源を落として接続を切ることを推奨するために、最良実践ガイドラインがすでに改定されているところである。さらに、早くも来年には、ソーラーパネルの列が構内に設置される予定である。天候条件が晴れのときには、これらのパネルが、増え続ける多くの企業に対してすでにそうしているように、Matino 社の送電網依存を弱めることになる。

*問題2の挿入文の訳

1. (A) 製品
   (B) 公約 ★
   (C) 競争
   (D) 全従業員

2. (A) 全ての自社製品に対する割引が、Matino 社の顧客基盤を拡大してきた。
   (B) 経営陣は、その企業買収は財務上の純利益をもたらすと予測している。
   (C) この目標を達成するために同社は、自社のエネルギー効率を改善することから始める予定だ。 ★
   (D) 第1段階には、会社のロゴとスローガンを作り直すことが含まれる予定だ。

3. (A) 〈be 動詞の過去分詞＋現在分詞〉
   (B) 現在完了形
   (C) 動詞の三人称単数現在形
   (D) to 不定詞 ★

4. (A) 条件 ★
   (B) 指示
   (C) 見解
   (D) 報道

PART 7

問題 1-2 は次のテキストメッセージのやりとりに関するものです。

Jen Bosco [午後1時31分]
調理場の中をのぞいて、私が大きな保温トレーを置き忘れたかどうかを確かめてくれるかしら。

Jim Dumas [午後1時32分]
待ってて。確認するよ。

Jim Dumas [午後1時35分]
見つけた。調理台の上にあるよ。

Jen Bosco [午後1時36分]
それをここに持ってきてくれる？ 結婚式が1時間足らずで始まるの。

Jim Dumas [午後1時37分]
もちろん。でも、新しい冷蔵装置がまだ届いていないことを知っておいた方がいいよ。

Jen Bosco [午後1時38分]
冗談でしょう？ 朝一番には私たちにそれを届けてくれると、彼らは約束したのよ。

Jim Dumas [午後1時39分]
僕はどうしたらいい？

Jen Bosco [午後1時40分]
とにかく、どこにそれを置けばいいか、Francis さんに必ず指示を残しておいて。

Jim Dumas [午後1時41分]
そうするよ。約40分後にトレーを持って君に会うね。

1. 書き手たちはどこに勤めていると考えられますか。
   (A) ケータリング会社 ★
   (B) ホームセンター
   (C) キッチン設計会社
   (D) 電化製品メーカー

2. 午後1時38分に Bosco さんは、"Are you kidding" という発言で、何を意味していると考えられますか。

   (A) Dumas さんが誇張していると思っている。
   (B) 長い間待たなくてはならないことを知っていた。
   (C) 冷蔵装置がもうすぐ届くだろうと見込んでいる。
   (D) 配達が行われていないことに動揺している。 ★

公式TOEIC® Listening & Reading
プラクティス リーディング編

2020 年 8 月 25 日　第 1 版第 1 刷発行
2023 年 6 月 30 日　第 1 版第 4 刷発行

著者　　　ETS

編集協力　株式会社エディット
　　　　　株式会社オレンジバード
　　　　　株式会社ウィットハウス

発行元　　一般財団法人 国際ビジネスコミュニケーション協会
　　　　　〒 100-0014
　　　　　東京都千代田区永田町 2-14-2
　　　　　山王グランドビル
　　　　　電話　(03) 5521-5935
　　　　　FAX　(03) 3581-9801

印刷　　　図書印刷株式会社

乱丁本・落丁本・不良本はお取り換えします。許可なしに転載、複製することを禁じます。

ETS, the ETS logo, PROPELL, TOEIC and TOEIC BRIDGE are registered trademarks of
Educational Testing Service, Princeton, New Jersey, U.S.A., and used in Japan under license.
Copyright ©2020 Portions are copyrighted by Educational Testing Service and used with permission.
Printed in Japan
ISBN 978-4-906033-60-7

公式 *TOEIC*® Listening & Reading
プラクティス
リーディング編

別冊付録
単語集＋
速読用英文
Key Words &
Quick Reading

別冊付録の使い方

単語集（p.4 ～ 23）

本誌「Step 1：ユニット学習」の *TOEIC*® L&R の問題英文から、覚えておくとよい語句を 300 語ピックアップしました。*TOEIC*® L&R でよく目にする関連語も併せて紹介していますので、繰り返し参照して記憶に定着させましょう。p.47 の「単語学習法のヒント」も参考にしてください。

●リストの見方

各ユニットの「チャレンジ」の英文から、15 語をピックアップしています。

※掲載スペースの関係で、初出ではないユニットに掲載されている場合もあります。

① → Unit 1　文の要素と品詞

➡ 本誌 p.16-18

001 **② ③** during **④**	前 ～の間	
002 offer	動 ～（言葉）を述べる、～を申し出る	offer to *do*「～することを申し出る」 名 offer「申し出、提案」 名 offering「申し出、提供（品）」 **⑤**
003 result	名 成績、結果	動 result「結果として生じる」 result in ～「～という結果になる」
004 quarter	名 四半期	形 quarterly「四半期の、年 4 回の」
005 congratulations	名〈複数形で〉お祝いの言葉	動 congratulate「～（祝辞）を述べる」

❶ 本誌のユニット番号

❷ 通し番号

❸ 見出し語

❹ 品詞・語義

　　……本文中の語義を中心に紹介

❺ 関連情報

　　……見出し語の語法、別の語義、派生語、関連語など

品詞・その他略語の説明

名 名詞（複合名詞なども含む）

代 代名詞

動 動詞（句動詞なども含む）

形 形容詞

副 副詞

前 前置詞

同 同義語

対 対義語

米 アメリカ英語

英 イギリス英語

★ 文法や語法についての説明

速読用英文（p.24 〜 45）

本誌「Step 1：ユニット学習」の *TOEIC*® L&R の問題英文を使った速読練習用のページを用意しました。以下の「音声ダウンロードの手順」に従って特典音声をダウンロードした後、「速読練習の進め方」を参考に取り組んでみましょう。

●音声ダウンロードの手順

1. パソコンまたはスマートフォンで音声ダウンロード用のサイトにアクセスします。右のQRコードまたはブラウザから下記にアクセスしてください。
   https://app.abceed.com/audio/iibc-officialprep

2. 表示されたページから、abceedの新規会員登録を行います。既に会員の場合は、ログイン情報を入力して上記1.のサイトへアクセスします。

3. 上記1.のサイトにアクセス後、本書の表紙画像をクリックします。クリックすると、教材詳細画面へ移動します。

4. スマートフォンの場合は、アプリ「abceed」の案内が出ますので、アプリからご利用ください。
   パソコンの場合は、教材詳細画面の「音声」からご利用ください。
   ※ 音声は何度でもダウンロード・再生ができます。

   ダウンロードについてのお問い合わせは下記にご連絡ください。
   Eメール：support@globeejphelp.zendesk.com
   （お問い合わせ窓口の営業日：祝日を除く、月〜金曜日）

●速読練習の進め方

[PART 5、6]

1. ⬇のファイル番号の音声を再生し、音声と同じスピードで、英語の語順のまま英文を読み進める。
2. 英文を読み終わった直後に、意味がきちんと取れたかどうかを本誌の参照ページに戻って確認する。理解があやふやだと感じた箇所は、単語集で語句の意味を調べたり、本誌の訳を確認したりする。

[PART 7]

1. ⬇のファイル番号の音声を再生し、音声と同じスピードで、英語の語順のまま英文を読み進める。
2. 文書を読み終わった直後に、下の 5 つの問題に挑戦し、解答を見て、正解数をページ上部の表に記入する。
3. 間違えた箇所や理解があやふやだと感じた箇所は、単語集で語句の意味を調べたり、本誌の参照ページで訳を確認したりする。
4. 全問正解できるようになるまで 1 〜 3 の手順を繰り返す。

Unit 1　文の要素と品詞

➡ 本誌 p.16-18

001 ☐☐	**during**	前 〜の間	
002 ☐☐	**offer**	動 〜（言葉）を述べる、 〜を申し出る	offer to *do*「〜することを申し出る」 名 offer「申し出、提案」 名 offering「申し出、提供（品）」
003 ☐☐	**result**	名 成績、結果	動 result「結果として生じる」 result in 〜「〜という結果になる」
004 ☐☐	**quarter**	名 四半期	形 quarterly「四半期の、年4回の」
005 ☐☐	**congratulations**	名〈複数形で〉 お祝いの言葉	動 congratulate「〜（祝辞）を述べる」
006 ☐☐	**diet**	名 食事	形 dietary「食事の」
007 ☐☐	**consumer**	名 消費者	名 consumption「消費」 動 consume「〜を消費する」
008 ☐☐	**increasingly**	副 ますます	名 increase「増加」 動 increase「増す」「〜を増大させる」
009 ☐☐	**significant**	形 かなりの	「重要な」の意味もある 副 significantly「かなり」
010 ☐☐	**expansion**	名 拡張、拡大	名 expanse「（広大な）広がり」 動 expand「〜を拡張する、〜を発展させる」
011 ☐☐	**precisely**	副 正確に	形 precise「正確な」
012 ☐☐	**achievement**	名 業績	動 achieve「〜を成し遂げる」
013 ☐☐	**remarkable**	形 素晴らしい、注目に値する	副 remarkably「著しく、際立って」
014 ☐☐	**vision**	名 構想、ビジョン	「視力、視野、光景」の意味もある
015 ☐☐	**success**	名 成功	動 succeed「成功する」 形 successful「成功した」

4

Unit 2　動詞

➡ 本誌 p.24-26

016	product development	名 商品開発	名 product「商品、製品」 名 development「開 発、進展」
017	consider	動 〜を検討する、 〜を考慮する	consider *doing*「〜すること を検討する」 名 consideration「検討、考慮」
018	compelling	形 説得力のある	「強制的な」の意味もある
019	management	名〈集合的に〉 経営陣、管理者	「経営、管理」の意味もある 動 manage「何とかする」「〜 を経営する、〜を管理する」
020	convince 〜 to *do*	動 〜に…するよう説得する、 〜を納得させて…させる	convince 〜 (that) …「〜に …であると納得させる」
021	retail store	名 小売店	形 retail「小売りの」
022	employee	名 従業員	名 employment「雇用」 名 employer「雇い主」 動 employ「〜を雇用する」
023	rehire	動 〜を再雇用する	動 hire「〜を雇用する」
024	application	名 申込書、申請書	「申し込み、申請」の意味もある 名 applicant「申込者、応募者」 動 apply (for 〜)「(〜を)申し込む」
025	observe	動 〜を観察する、 〜をよく見る	「〜(規則)を順守する」、「〜(祝祭日)を祝う」の意味もある
026	submit	動 〜を提出する	名 submission「提出」
027	familiarize	動 〜を習熟させる	familiarize 〜 with … 「〜(人)を…に習熟させる」 形 familiar「なじみの」
028	inform	動 〜に知らせる	inform 〜 of …「〜に…を知らせる」 名 information「情報」 形 informative「有益な」
029	aim to *do*	動 〜することを目指す	aim 〜 at …「〜(言葉・行為)を…に向ける」
030	business owner	名 事業主	名 business「事業、会社」 名 owner「所有者」

031	recommend	動 〜を推薦する、〜を勧める	名 recommendation「推薦、推薦状」
032	reference	名 照会先、推薦状	for your reference「ご参考までに」 in reference to 〜「〜に関連して」 動 refer (to 〜)「(〜を)参照する」
033	be scheduled for 〜	動 〜(日時)に予定されている	be scheduled to do「〜する予定である」
034	postpone	動 〜を延期する	
035	formerly	副 以前は、かつては	形 former「前の、先の」
036	tentatively	副 暫定的に、仮に	形 tentative「暫定的な、仮の」
037	construction	名 建設、建築	名 constructor「建設者、建設会社」 動 construct「〜を建設する、〜を組み立てる」
038	demand	名 需要	動 demand「〜を要求する」 形 demanding「骨の折れる、多くを要求する」
039	skilled	形 熟練した	skilled at 〜「〜に長けて」 形 skillful「熟練した」 副 skillfully「巧みに」
040	sizable	形 かなり大きな	
041	permanent	形 恒久的な	「常設の、常置の」の意味もある 対 temporary「一時的な、臨時の」
042	process	動 〜を処理する、〜を加工する	名 process「処理、手順、工程、過程」
043	order	名 注文、注文品	place an order「注文をする」 動 order「〜を注文する」
044	typically	副 典型的に、通常は	形 typical「典型的な、よくある」
045	be likely to do	〜しそうである	形 likely「ありそうな」

046 ☐☐	**grant**	名 助成金、寄付金	「許可、認可」の意味もある 動 grant「～を認める、～(権利)を授与する」
047 ☐☐	**electricity usage**	名 電気使用量	名 electricity「電気、電力」 名 usage「使用量、使用(法)」
048 ☐☐	**log on to ～**	動 ～にログインする	log out of ～「～からログアウトする」
049 ☐☐	**account**	名 (コンピューターなどの) アカウント	「預金口座、取引」の意味もある 動 account for ～「～の主な要因である」
050 ☐☐	**promote**	動 ～を昇進させる、 ～の販売を促進する	名 promotion「昇進、販売促進」 形 promotional「昇進の、(販売)促進の」
051 ☐☐	**factor**	名 要因、要素	
052 ☐☐	**determine**	動 ～を決定する、 ～を決心する	名 determination「決定、決意」 形 determinative「決定力のある、限定的な」
053 ☐☐	**alongside**	前 ～と並んで	
054 ☐☐	**primarily**	副 主として	形 primary「主たる、最上位の」
055 ☐☐	**be located**	動 位置する	動 locate「～を置く、～の場所を定める」 名 location「場所、所在地」
056 ☐☐	**slightly**	副 少し、やや	形 slight「わずかな」
057 ☐☐	**among**	前 ～の間に、～の中の1つで	
058 ☐☐	**past**	前 ～を過ぎた所に	「～時過ぎに」の意味もある
059 ☐☐	**search for ～**	動 ～を探し求める	search into ～「～を調査する」 search through ～「～をくまなく探す」 名 search「捜索、追求」
060 ☐☐	**job opportunity**	名 就業機会	名 job「職、仕事」 名 opportunity「(良い)機会、チャンス」

7

Unit 5　動名詞・不定詞・分詞

➡ 本誌 p.48-50

061	growth	名 成長	動 grow「成長する」「〜を育てる」
062	inspector	名 検査官	名 inspection「検査」 動 inspect「〜を検査する」
063	ensure	動 〜を保証する、 〜を確実にする	
064	commercial	形 商業の、商用の	名 commercial「コマーシャル、CM」
065	comply with 〜	動 〜を順守する	名 compliance「順守」
066	regulation	名 規則	動 regulate「〜を規制する」
067	potential	形 潜在的な、可能性のある	名 potential、potentiality「潜在力、可能性」
068	upcoming	形 近づいている、今度の	
069	diversity	名 多様性	動 diversify「〜を多様化する」 形 diverse「多様な」
070	win	動 〜(賞など)を獲得する	「(〜に)勝つ」という意味もある 名 winner「受賞者、勝利者」 形 winning「勝利を収めた」
071	prize	名 賞、賞金	★コンペや競技などで勝ち取る賞を指す top prize「最高賞、最優秀賞」
072	depict	動 〜を描く、 〜を描写する	名 depiction「描写、表現」 同 describe
073	allow 〜 to *do*	動 〜が…することを可能にする	名 allowance「許容、許可量、手当て」
074	suspicious	形 疑わしい、 疑惑を起こさせる	名 suspicion「疑い、疑惑」 動 suspect「〜を疑う」
075	monitor	動 〜を監視する	名 monitor「監視装置、(コンピューターなどの)モニター」

No.	見出し	意味	補足
076	**provide**	動 〜を提供する、 〜を支給する	provide 〜 with … 「〜に…を提供する」 provide for 〜 「〜に提供する」
077	**details**	名〈複数形で〉 詳細、詳細な情報	名 detail 「細部」 形 detailed 「詳細な」
078	**public awareness**	名 市民の意識、社会の認識	名 awareness 「気付いていること、自覚していること」
079	**environmental**	形 環境の、環境保護の	名 environment 「環境」 副 environmentally 「環境(保護)上」
080	**issue**	名 問題、論点	「(出版物の)号」という意味もある 動 issue 「〜を発行する」
081	**mission**	名 使命	
082	**arrangement**	名 手配、お膳立て	「配置、配列」の意味もある 動 arrange 「〜を手配する、〜を並べる」
083	**coordinate**	動 〜を取りまとめる、 〜を調整する	「連携する」の意味もある coordinate with 〜 「〜と連携する」
084	**focus group**	名 フォーカスグループ	★市場調査のために抽出された集団(マーケティング用語)
085	**responsibility**	名 責務、職務、責任	形 responsible 「責任のある」 responsible for 〜 「〜に責任のある」
086	**in place of 〜**	〜の代わりに	名 place 「立場」
087	**earn**	動 〜(評判)を博する、 〜を得る	earn 〜 … 「〜に…をもたらす」 名 earnings〈複数形で〉「収益」
088	**virtually**	副 ほとんど、事実上	副 nearly 「ほとんど」
089	**be intended for 〜**	〜を対象としている、 〜に向けられている	動 intend 「〜を意図する」 形 intended 「意図された」
090	**medical**	形 医療の、医学の	medical checkup 「健康診断」 medical clinic 「診療所」 名 medicine 「薬、医術」

9

Unit 7 つなぐ言葉（接続詞・前置詞）

➡ 本誌 p.64-66

091	attend	動 〜に参加する、 〜に出席する	「〜に付き添う」の意味もある 名 attendance「出席(者数)」 名 attendee「出席者」
092	marketing	名 マーケティング、 販売促進活動	名 market「市場」
093	nomination	名 指名、推薦	動 nominate「〜を指名する、 〜を推薦する」
094	board	名 役員会、委員会	「掲示板」の意味もある
095	post	動 〜を掲示する	名 post「(ネット掲示板など への)投稿メッセージ」
096	find out 〜	動 〜を明らかにする、 〜を発見する	
097	meet	動 〜に応える	「(〜と)会う」の意味もある 名 meeting「会合、会議」
098	expectation	名 期待、予期	meet one's expectation「〜 の期待に応える」 動 expect「〜を期待する」
099	merger	名 合併、統合	動 merge「合併する」「〜を 合併させる」 merge with 〜「〜と合併する」
100	conclude	動 〜を締結する、 〜と結論を下す	名 conclusion「締結、結論」
101	last-minute	形 土壇場の、直前の	
102	negotiation	名 交渉	動 negotiate「交渉する」 negotiate with 〜「〜と交渉 する」
103	proposed	形 提案された	名 proposal「提案」 動 propose「〜を提案する」
104	branch	名 支店	「本社、本店」は headquarters、head office
105	cost effective	形 費用対効果の高い	名 cost「費用、経費」 形 effective「効果的な」

Unit 8 広告・お知らせを読む

➡ 本誌 p.74-76

#	見出し語	意味	備考
106	**reward**	名 報酬、見返り	動 reward「〜に報酬を与える」 形 rewarding「価値のある」
107	**double**	形 2倍の	名 double「2倍(のもの)」 動 double「〜を2倍にする」
108	**purchase**	名 買い物、購買	make a purchase「買い物をする」 動 purchase「〜を購入する」
109	**redeem**	動 〜を景品に換える、 〜を現金に換える	「〜(名誉など)を回復する」の意味もある
110	**reserve**	動 〜を予約する	「〜を取っておく」の意味もある 名 reservation「予約」 形 reserved「予約された」
111	**priority boarding**	名 優先搭乗	名 priority「優先すること、優先事項」 名 boarding「搭乗、乗車、乗船」
112	**annual**	形 年間の、年1回の	副 annually「年に1回」 形 biannual「年2回の」 形 biennial「隔年の」
113	**fee**	名 料金、手数料	
114	**comprehensive**	形 包括的な、総合的な	名 comprehension「包括性、理解(力)」
115	**approve**	動 〜を承認する、 〜を認可する	名 approval「承認、認可」
116	**selected**	形 選ばれた、えり抜きの	名 selection「選ぶこと、選択」 動 select「〜を選ぶ」 形 select「えり抜きの」
117	**therefore**	副 従って、それゆえ	
118	**regardless**	副 それにもかかわらず、 ともかく	形 regardless「無頓着な、気にかけない」
119	**in addition**	さらに、加えて	名 addition「追加、増加分」
120	**for instance**	例えば	名 instance「例、実例」 同 for example

11

Unit 9　記事を読む

121	extend	動 〜（期間など）を延ばす	「〜（祝辞など）を述べる」の意味もある 名 extension「延長、内線電話」
122	occur	動 起こる、生じる	名 occurrence「発生、出来事」
123	given 〜	形〈前置詞的に〉 〜を考慮すると	★〜には名詞（句）が続く。節を続けて、接続詞的に「〜であると仮定すると」の意味もある
124	review	名 評論、レビュー	「再検討、見直し」の意味もある 動 review「〜を批評する、〜を見直す」
125	critic	名 批評家	動 criticize「〜を批判する」 形 critical「批評の、批判的な、危機的な」
126	following	前 〜に続いて	動 follow「〜の後に続く」
127	popular	形 人気のある	popular with 〜「〜に人気のある」
128	online sources	名 オンラインの情報源	名 sources〈複数形で〉「情報源」
129	exploration	名 探求	動 explore「〜を探求する、〜を詳しく調べる」
130	economic	形 経済の、経済学の	名 economy「経済」 名 economics「経済学」 形 economical「安価な」
131	career	名 職業、職歴	
132	brilliant	形 素晴らしい、立派な	名 brilliance「光輝、優れた才気」
133	harsh	形 厳しい、過酷な	
134	prompt	形 即座の、敏速な	名 prompt「きっかけ」 副 promptly「即座に」
135	initial	形 当初の、初期の	動 initiate「〜を始める」 副 initially「当初は」

12

Unit 10　Eメール・手紙を読む

➡ 本誌 p.90-92

136 ☐☐	**apply for ～**	動 ～を申請する、 ～を申し込む	apply to ～「～に適用される」
137 ☐☐	**loan**	名 融資、ローン	動 loan ～ …「～に…を融資する」
138 ☐☐	**demonstrate**	動 ～を証明する、 ～を実演する	名 demonstration「証明、実演」 形 demonstrative「例証的な」
139 ☐☐	**eligibility**	名 適格性、適任性	形 eligible「適格な、適任の」 be eligible for ～「～にふさわしい」
140 ☐☐	**assistance**	名 支援、手助け	名 assistant「助手、補佐」 動 assist「(～を)手助けする」 形 assistant「助けとなる」
141 ☐☐	**in one's favor**	～の有利に	名 favor「好都合、利益」
142 ☐☐	**report**	動 ～を報告する、 ～を報道する	report to ～「～に出向く、～に直属する」 名 report「報告書、報道」
143 ☐☐	**be pleased to do**	喜んで～する	形 pleased「喜んで、うれしい」
144 ☐☐	**terms and conditions**	名 契約条件	名 terms〈複数形で〉「(契約の)条項」 名 condition「条件」
145 ☐☐	**enclosure**	名 同封物	動 enclose「～を同封する」 形 enclosed「同封された」
146 ☐☐	**accept**	動 ～を受け入れる、 ～を承諾する	名 acceptance「承諾、受容」 形 acceptable「容認できる」
147 ☐☐	**examine**	動 ～を審査する、 ～を検査する	名 examination「検査、試験」 名 examinee「被験者、受験者」
148 ☐☐	**rate**	名 金利	「料金、値段」の意味もある 動 rate「～を評価する」
149 ☐☐	**competitive**	形 競争力のある、 他に負けない	名 competitor「競合他社」 動 compete (with ～)「(～と)競争する」
150 ☐☐	**guarantee**	動 ～を保証する、 ～を確約する	名 guarantee「保証、保証書」

Unit 11　文書の概要をつかむ

➡ 本誌 p.102-105

151 ☐☐	request	名 依頼、要請	request form「申請書、依頼書」 動 request「～を依頼する、 ～を要請する」
152 ☐☐	contact	動 ～に連絡する	名 contact「連絡、接触、接点」
153 ☐☐	shortly	副 間もなく、じきに	
154 ☐☐	venue	名 会場、開催地	
155 ☐☐	preference	名 好み、優先	動 prefer「～の方を好む」 prefer to do「～する方を好む」
156 ☐☐	require	動 ～を必要とする、 (条件として)～を要求する	名 requirement「必要条件」 名 requirements〈複数形で〉 「必需品」
157 ☐☐	lodging	名 宿	動 lodge「泊まる」「～を泊める」
158 ☐☐	brochure	名 パンフレット、カタログ	同 pamphlet
159 ☐☐	customer service	名 顧客サービス部、 顧客サービス	名 customer「顧客、得意先」 名 customer satisfaction「顧客満足」
160 ☐☐	payment	名 支払い	make a payment「支払いをする」 動 pay「～を支払う」
161 ☐☐	charge to ～	動 ～に代金を請求する	charge for ～「～の代金を請求する」 名 charge「請求額、料金」
162 ☐☐	description	名 明細、記載事項	動 describe「～を言い表す、 ～を説明する」
163 ☐☐	mail	動 ～を郵送する	名 mail、mailing「郵便物」
164 ☐☐	be sure to do	必ず～する	形 sure「確信して、確かな」
165 ☐☐	nonrefundable	形 払い戻し不可能な	名 refund「払い戻し、返金」 対 refundable「払い戻し可能な」

Unit 12　詳細情報をつかむ

➡ 本誌 p.112-115

No.	見出し語	品詞・意味	補足
166	**work**	名 作品、著作、成果物	「研究、作業、職、職場」など の意味もある
167	**series**	名 シリーズもの、一続き	a series of ～「一連の～」
168	**gain**	動 ～を得る	名 gain「獲得、利益」
169	**recognition**	名 注目、 （力量などを）認めること	動 米 recognize 英 recognise 「～を認める、～を表彰する」
170	**exhibit**	動 ～を展示する、 ～を公開する	名 exhibit「展示品、展示」 名 exhibition「展示会」 名 exhibitor「出展者」
171	**including**	前 ～を含めて	名 inclusion「包含」 動 include「～を含める」 形 inclusive「包括的な」
172	**feature**	動 ～を特集する、 ～を大々的に扱う	名 feature「特徴、呼び物、目玉」
173	**invoice**	名 送り状、請求書	
174	**item**	名 商品、品目	
175	**due**	形 当然支払われるべき、 期限が来て	due to ～「～が原因で」
176	**upon receipt of ～**	～を受領して、 ～を受け取り次第	名 receipt「受領、領収書」
177	**goods**	名〈複数形で〉 商品	
178	**ship**	動 ～を発送する、 ～を出荷する	名 shipment「積み荷、発送、出荷」 名 shipping「発送、出荷」
179	**currently**	副 現在は、目下	形 current「現在の」
180	**warehouse**	名 倉庫	

181	effective ~	形 ~以降有効で、 ~以降効力のある	★~には日時が入る 「実行力のある、効果的な」の 意味もある
182	revise	動 ~を改定する、 ~を修正する	名 revision「改定、改訂、修正」
183	need to *do*	動 ~する必要がある	名 need「必要、必要性」
184	alternate	形 代わりの	「交互に起こる、互い違いの」 の意味もある 形 alternative「別の、代替の」
185	appreciate	動 ~を感謝する	名 appreciation「感謝の表明、 真価を認めること、鑑賞眼」
186	feedback	名 意見、感想	
187	fill out ~	動 ~に記入する	★ fill ~ out の語順でも使わ れる
188	survey	名 調査票、調査、アンケート	動 survey「~を調査する」
189	appearance	名 外観、見掛け、外見	動 appear「現れる、姿を見 せる、出演する」 appear to *do*「~するようだ」
190	add	動 ~を追加する	add to ~「~を増す」 名 addition「追加、増加分」 形 additional「追加の」
191	comment	名 意見、見解	動 comment「意見を述べる」 「~に注釈を付ける」
192	suggestion	名 提案、示唆	動 suggest「~を提案する、 ~を示唆する」
193	well-equipped	形 設備が整った	名 equipment「設備、機器」 動 equip「~に備え付ける」 形 equipped「装備された」
194	regarding	前 ~に関して	同 in regard to ~
195	award	名 賞	動 award「~を(賞など)を授与 する」

16

Unit 14　複数人のやりとりを読む

➡ 本誌 p.132-136

196	be meant for ～	動 ～に宛てられている、～に向けられている	動 mean「～を意味する、～のつもりで言う」
197	accounting	名 経理部、経理、会計	名 accountant「会計士」
198	administration	名 管理部、管理、運営	名 administrator「管理者」 形 administrative「管理の」
199	head to ～	動 ～へ向かう	動 head「進む、前進する」
200	Legal Department	名 法務部	★部署名は語頭大文字もあり 形 legal「法律の、法律上の」 名 department「部署、部局」
201	drop off ～	動 ～(荷物)を届ける、～(人)を(車から)降ろす	★drop ～ off の語順でも使われる
202	information technology	名 情報技術部、情報技術	名 information「情報(伝達)」 名 technology「技術」
203	update	動 ～を更新する、～を最新のものにする	名 update「最新情報、更新」
204	take a look at ～	～を見る	名 look「見ること、一見」 圏 have a look at ～
205	complaint	名 苦情、不満	動 complain「苦情を申し立てる、不平を言う」
206	look into ～	動 ～を調べる	
207	remove	動 ～を削除する、～を取り除く	「～を片付ける、～を脱ぐ」の意味もある 名 removal「削除、除去」
208	just in case	念のため、万一の場合に備えて	名 case「場合、事例」
209	apology	名 謝罪、おわび	動 apologize「謝る」
210	fix	動 ～を解決する	「～を確定する、～を直す、～を治す」の意味もある

17

211 ☐☐	**subject**	名 テーマ、題目、件名	形 subject「受けやすい」 be subject to *do*「〜する可能性がある」
212 ☐☐	**conduct**	動 〜を実施する、 〜を行う	名 conduct「行為、指揮」 名 conductor「(バスなどの)車掌、指揮者」
213 ☐☐	**public opinion**	名 世論	
214 ☐☐	**poll**	名 世論調査	「投票」の意味もある 名 polling「世論調査(すること)、投票(すること)」
215 ☐☐	**decade**	名 10 年	
216 ☐☐	**be based on 〜**	動 〜に基づいている	動 base「〜の基礎を置く」
217 ☐☐	**interview**	名 インタビュー、取材調査、面接	名 interviewee「面接を受ける人」 名 interviewer「面接する人」 動 interview「(〜を)面接する」
218 ☐☐	**specific**	形 特定の	副 specifically「特に」
219 ☐☐	**randomly**	副 無作為に	形 random「無作為の」
220 ☐☐	**generate**	動 〜を生み出す	名 generation「発生、生成、世代」
221 ☐☐	**weekly**	副 週に 1 回	形 weekly「毎週の、1 週間の」 形副 monthly「毎月の」「月に1回」 形副 yearly「毎年の」「年に1回」
222 ☐☐	**store**	動 〜を保管する、 〜(データ)を記憶する	名 storage「貯蔵、保管、物置」
223 ☐☐	**accessible**	形 利用できる、近づける	名 access「利用できる機会、出入り、アクセス」 動 access「〜を入手する」
224 ☐☐	**permission**	名 許諾、許可	名 permit「許可、許可証」 動 permit「〜を許可する」 形 permissible「許容できる」
225 ☐☐	**response**	名 回答、返事	動 respond「返答する」 形 responsive「反応する、反応が良い」

226	traffic	名 交通量、交通	
227	complex	名 複合施設	形 complex「複雑な」
228	problematic	形 問題のある	名 problem「問題、課題、障害」
229	official	名 役人、当局者	形 official「当局の、公式の」
230	widen	動 ～を広げる	名 width「広さ、幅」 形 wide「幅の広い、広範な」
231	accommodate	動 ～を収容できる、 ～を入れる場所がある	「～を適応させる」の意味もある 名 accommodation「収容設備、宿泊施設」
232	finalize	動 ～を最終決定する、 ～を成立させる	★「最終的な形に仕上げる」ことを示す
233	infrastructure	名 インフラ、基幹設備	
234	congestion	名 混雑、密集	
235	commit to ～	動 ～を約束する、 ～を決意する	commit ～ to …「～を…に委ねる」
236	solid	形 確かな、確固たる	
237	commute	名 通勤、通学	名 commuter「通勤者、通学者」 動 commute「通勤する、通学する」
238	in the meantime	そうする間に	名 meantime「合間」
239	encourage ～ to *do*	動 ～に…するよう勧める、 ～が…することを促す	名 encouragement「奨励、励まし」
240	incentive	名 奨励金、 励みになるもの	

Unit 17　複数文書を関連付けて読む ①

No.	見出し語	意味	補足
241	**locally**	副 現地で、地元で	名 local「土地の人、地元民」 形 local「地元の、土地の、各駅停車の」
242	**vehicle**	名 車、車両	
243	**match**	動 〜に釣り合わせる	「〜に匹敵する」の意味もある match 〜 with …「〜を…と釣り合わせる」
244	**available**	形 利用できる、応じられる	名 availability「利用の可能性、(人の)都合、空き状況」
245	**suitable**	形 適切な、ふさわしい	suitable for 〜「〜に適した」 動 suit「〜に合う、〜に似合う」
246	**passenger**	名 乗客	
247	**in person**	直接に、 (代理ではなく)本人が	
248	**discounted**	形 割引された	名 discount「割引」 動 discount「〜を割引する」
249	**saving**	名 節約	名 savings〈複数形で〉「貯金」 動 save「節約する、貯金する」「〜を救い出す」
250	**inquiry**	名 問い合わせ	動 inquire (about 〜)「(〜について)問い合わせる」
251	**the second half**	名 後半	the second half of 〜「〜の後半」 対 the first half「前半」
252	**colleague**	名 同僚	同 coworker
253	**mindful**	形 気を配って、注意して	mindful of 〜「〜に気を配って、〜に注意して」
254	**book**	動 〜を予約する	名 booking「予約」
255	**pick up 〜**	動 〜を受け取る、 〜を拾い上げる	「〜を車に乗せる、〜を買う」の意味もある ★ pick 〜 up でも使われる

20

Unit 18　複数文書を関連付けて読む ②

256 ☐☐	**retired**	形 退職した、引退した	名 retirement「退職」 動 retire「退職する」「〜を退職させる」
257 ☐☐	**executive**	名 役員、重役	形 executive「重役の、幹部の」
258 ☐☐	**guest speaker**	名 ゲスト講演者、 招待講演者	
259 ☐☐	**be engaged in 〜**	〜に従事している	名 engagement「関与、契約」 動 engage「〜を従事させる」 形 engaged「参加して、関与して」
260 ☐☐	**share 〜 with …**	動 〜を…と共有する	名 share「共有、割り当て、株式」 動 share「〜を共有する、〜を伝える」
261 ☐☐	**enroll**	動 〜を(受講生として)登録する、入会する	enroll in 〜「〜に登録する」 名 enrollment「登録、入会」
262 ☐☐	**objective**	名 目標、目的	形 objective「客観的な」
263 ☐☐	**grasp**	動 〜を理解する、 〜を把握する	「〜を握る」の意味もある 名 grasp「理解、把握、握ること」
264 ☐☐	**practical**	形 実用的な	名 practice「実践、実施」 動 practice「練習する」「〜を実践する、〜を練習する」
265 ☐☐	**approach**	動 〜に話を持ち掛ける、 〜に近づく	名 approach「申し入れ、提案、接近」
266 ☐☐	**associated with 〜**	〜と結び付いた、 〜と関係を持っている	動 associate「〜を関係させる、〜を連想する」
267 ☐☐	**perspective**	名 視点、見方	
268 ☐☐	**mentor**	動 〜を指導する	名 mentor「指導者、教育係」
269 ☐☐	**internship**	名 インターンシップ、 職業訓練	名 intern「インターン、研修生、実習生」
270 ☐☐	**be willing to *do***	〜する意思がある、 進んで〜する	形 willing「いとわない」

271 ☐☐	**vendor**	图 販売業者	图 vending machine「自動販売機」 動 vend「〜を行商する、（自動販売機で）〜を販売する」
272 ☐☐	**eatery**	图 飲食店	★簡易で安価な店を指すことが多い
273 ☐☐	**supplies**	图〈複数形で〉 備品、補給品	office supplies「事務用品」 動 supply「〜を供給する」
274 ☐☐	**incorrect**	形 誤った	副 incorrectly「誤って」 対 correct「正しい」
275 ☐☐	**standard**	形 普通の、標準の	图 standard「標準、基準」
276 ☐☐	**shipping rate**	图 送料	图 shipping「発送、出荷、輸送」 gift wrapping rate「ギフト包装料」
277 ☐☐	**reflect**	動 〜を反映する	reflect 〜 on …「〜を…に反映する」 图 reflection「反映」
278 ☐☐	**overcharge**	图 過剰請求	動 overcharge「〜に過剰請求する」 対 undercharge「過少請求」
279 ☐☐	**according to 〜**	〜によれば	
280 ☐☐	**misunderstanding**	图 誤解	動 misunderstand「誤解する」「〜を間違った意味に取る」
281 ☐☐	**representative**	图 担当者、代表	sales representative「販売担当者」 動 represent「〜を代表する」
282 ☐☐	**credit**	图 控除、還付金	「履修単位」の意味もある 動 credit 〜 for …「…を〜の功績だとする」
283 ☐☐	**minimum**	形 最低限の、最小限の	图 minimum「最低値、最低限、最小限」 対 maximum「最大限(の)」
284 ☐☐	**right away**	直ちに、すぐさま	同 immediately、at once
285 ☐☐	**compensation**	图 補償	動 compensate「補償する」 compensate for 〜「〜を埋め合わせる」

286 ☐☐	**tour**	名 施設の見学、ツアー	guided tour「ガイド付きツアー」 動 tour「小旅行をする」「〜を見学する」
287 ☐☐	**shipyard**	名 造船所	
288 ☐☐	**renowned**	形 有名な、名高い	
289 ☐☐	**best-selling**	形 ベストセラーの	名 bestseller「ベストセラー」
290 ☐☐	**author**	名 著者、作家	
291 ☐☐	**article**	名 記事	
292 ☐☐	**unfortunately**	副 残念なことに	形 unfortunate「不運な」 対 fortunately「幸運なことに」
293 ☐☐	**figure**	動 〜と判断する、 〜と理解する	figure out 〜「〜を解き明かす、〜を見つけ出す」 名 figure「形、図」
294 ☐☐	**spend 〜 doing**	動 〜（時間）を…することに費やす	
295 ☐☐	**fascinating**	形 魅力的な、素晴らしい	動 fascinate「〜を魅了する」 形 fascinated「魅せられた、うっとりした」
296 ☐☐	**definitely**	副 きっと、絶対に	形 definite「確定的な、明白な」
297 ☐☐	**draft**	名 草稿、下書き	
298 ☐☐	**briefly**	副 簡潔に、手短に	名 briefing「状況説明」 形 brief「簡潔な、短い」
299 ☐☐	**depart**	動 〜を出発する、 〜を発つ	自動詞で「出発する、発つ」の意味もある 名 departure「出発」
300 ☐☐	**go with 〜**	動 〜と調和する、 〜によく合う	

速読用英文

PART 5　問題の英文

Unit 1　⬇ 02-07　➡ 本誌 p.16-18

1　During yesterday's meeting, Ms. Milne offered her congratulations to the sales team for their excellent results this quarter.

2　At Reyo Foods, we know that a healthy diet is increasingly important to consumers.

3　The expansion of the Kawagoe factory has had a significant impact on Inagi Technology employees' productivity.

4　Ms. Lai's draft of Sientech Industries' new mission statement expresses the company's goals precisely.

5　Among her many remarkable achievements, Dr. Ahn wrote sixteen books and served as editor for three major journals.

6　The university's vision is to increase graduates' success in the global workplace.

Unit 2　⬇ 08-13　➡ 本誌 p.24-26

1　The product development team for Herbeve Cosmetics is considering a package redesign to try to increase sales.

2　Karl Byquist's compelling presentation convinced the management of Parkland Press to hire his company.

3　Lundquist Electronics will have twelve retail stores in Japan by March of next year.

4　Former seasonal employees seeking to be rehired must submit a new application.

5　Ding's Café in Hong Kong aims to serve the freshest possible seafood.

6　Smooth Tek's newest software makes it much easier for business owners to create newsletters.

Unit 3　⬇ 14-19　➡ 本誌 p.32-34

1　Mr. Ashburton has been highly recommended by all three of his references.

2　The switch to the specialized database is tentatively scheduled for May 18, but it may need to be postponed.

3　The planned construction of several new office buildings in Newbury has created a sizable demand for skilled workers.

4　While the closure of Park Street's southbound lane is not permanent, it will not reopen this year.

5　This month, Mr. Choi has excelled at quickly processing incoming orders.

6　The employee satisfaction survey results are likely to differ among departments.

Unit 4　⬇ 20-25　➡ 本誌 p.40-42

1　Our staff will accept grant proposals from March 3 to April 3.

2　You can look at your electricity usage by logging on to your online service account.

3　Ms. Chang was promoted to section chief after only six months on the job.

4　Research shows that, alongside eating healthily, exercise is the most important factor in determining adult health.

5　The Sook-Joo Gyo Library is located slightly past the Green Treat Market on Jacob Avenue.

6　The open access database can be used to search for job opportunities at Steinach Publishing.

Unit 5 ⬇ 26-31 → 本誌 p.48-50

1. By opening offices in London, Paris, and Madrid, Sedgehill Ltd. has continued its growth into markets overseas.

2. The inspector will ensure that all newly constructed commercial buildings comply with applicable codes and regulations.

3. When speaking with potential clients, remember to tell them about Gansen Capital's upcoming promotional event.

4. *Trees Across the World*, a documentary film depicting forest diversity, won a top prize at the arts festival.

5. The new computer security program allows users to monitor any suspicious activity on their account.

6. Poland Cell Tel is beginning a multibillion-euro process to expand its network.

Unit 6 ⬇ 32-37 → 本誌 p.56-58

1. Please provide as many details as possible when leaving a message for the technical-support team.

2. Building public awareness of environmental issues is the primary mission of the Florida Conservancy Group.

3. Responsibilities of the marketing assistant include coordinating focus groups and writing detailed reports.

4. Today, in place of spokesperson Hiro Ueda, President Akiko Nomura herself will speak with reporters.

5. Joanna Nugent, CEO of Freshest Face, Inc., has earned the respect of virtually everyone in the cosmetics industry.

6. The course taught by Prof. Brennink is intended for those interested in medical or health-related careers.

Unit 7 ⬇ 38-43 → 本誌 p.64-66

1. If the kiln's heat is set too high, the ceramic objects inside may be ruined.

2. Ms. Drew was able to attend the popular summer marketing seminar in Lisbon because she bought her tickets early.

3. Once all the nominations for board members have been received, a complete list will be posted.

4. The purpose of this survey is to find out whether the performance of Evonee Cosmetics meets customers' expectations.

5. The lawyers report that the merger was successfully concluded thanks to last-minute negotiations.

6. The proposed location for the bank branch is not only the most convenient for our customers, but also the most cost effective.

PART 6　問題の英文

Web page

Violet Sky Rewards

The Violet Sky Rewards card has the most comprehensive travel rewards program of any card available. Rewards card members earn one point for every dollar spent. During special events, members can earn double points for purchases made at specially selected locations. Points can be redeemed to purchase airline tickets, reserve hotel rooms, or rent cars anywhere in the world. In addition, the card offers special perks, including free checked bags and priority boarding when members book travel with Tilles Airlines. To get all this for no annual fee, apply at www.vsrewards.com.

Article

The Crimson Bay Regional Theater will be extending its run of *Winter in Monterrey*, a play by Edna Riley. Because of a sudden surge in demand for tickets, the last performance will now occur on April 19. The move comes as something of a surprise, given the harsh reviews written by critics following the show's opening on March 2. The initial box office sales had also been weak. The show, however, has suddenly become popular with younger people, many of whom get their news from online sources. They are apparently interested in the play's exploration of economic issues and career choices.

Letter

17 July

Hanna Morrison
12 Hecuba Road
St. John's
Antigua and Barbuda

Dear Ms. Morrison,

Thank you for applying for a business loan with MUN Bank of Antigua & Barbuda. You were able to demonstrate your eligibility for MUN Bank's loan-assistance program. This was greatly in your favor as your application was being considered. We can now report our decision to approve your loan application.

MUN Bank is pleased to offer you a loan of $50,000 under the terms and conditions set forth in the enclosure. Please let me know by 1 August whether you intend to accept the offer. We cannot guarantee the same loan terms after that date.

Feel free to contact me with any questions. I look forward to speaking with you soon.

Sincerely,

Joanne Yearwood
Loan Officer, MUN Bank of Antigua & Barbuda
Enclosure

1 **Form**

Crossroads New Melbourne: Conference Space for a New Age

Thank you for your interest in Crossroads New Melbourne. Please complete the request form below. We will contact you shortly with the plan and pricing that will suit the needs of your group.

Organization Name: _____　**Contact Name:** _____

E-mail: _____　**Phone:** _____　**Date(s):** _____

Venue preference:
[ ] 33 Brightwood Square　[ ] 608 Westway Street　[ ] 1057 Portside Highway

Basic room layout:
[ ] Lecture (rows of chairs)　　　　　　　　[ ] Classroom (rows of tables and chairs)
[ ] Boardroom (chairs around one long table)　[ ] Other: _____

Number of attendees: [ ] 10–34　[ ] 35–100　[ ] 100+

Computer rental required: [ ] Yes　[ ] No

Nearby lodging required for some guests: [ ] Yes　[ ] No

Crossroads New Melbourne

---

1. A customer can rent a computer from Crossroads New Melbourne.　(T / F)

2. Crossroads New Melbourne allows customers to choose from five venues.　(T / F)

3. A phone number is required for completing the registration.　(T / F)

4. What will Crossroads New Melbourne staff do after receiving the form?

_____

5. What extra arrangements is Crossroads New Melbourne able to make?

_____

解答（例）　1. T　2. F　3. T
4. They will contact the client with a plan and a price.
5. Computer rental and lodging.

回数	01	02	03	04	05
正解数	/ 5	/ 5	/ 5	/ 5	/ 5

2 **Receipt**

Receipt # 84502-11516
(Keep this receipt number handy. You will need it if you have to contact customer service.)

April 17, 6:43 P.M.
Received from Jasmine Shalib:
$54 payment to Pilgrim Theater
Charged to credit card ending in xxxx-1394
Description: Tickets for Philip Dadian in concert
Friday, May 1, 7:30 P.M.
Unit price: $27 / Quantity: 2 / Amount: $54

IMPORTANT: Please print this receipt and bring it with you to the venue. No paper tickets will be mailed. Be sure to arrive early to check your name on the preorder list at the ticket counter. Tickets are nonrefundable.

8 84502 11516 1

1. A paper ticket will be mailed shortly to Ms. Shalib.   (T / F)

2. Ms. Shalib paid by credit card.   (T / F)

3. Ms. Shalib has paid for two people to attend the event.   (T / F)

4. When is Ms. Shalib going to Pilgrim Theater?

_____

5. Where should Ms. Shalib go when she arrives at Pilgrim Theater?

_____

解答（例）　　1. F　2. T　3. T
　　　　　　　4. Friday, May 1.
　　　　　　　5. To the ticket counter.

回数	01	02	03	04	05
正解数	/ 5	/ 5	/ 5	/ 5	/ 5

1 | **Information**

> **Takashi Fujioka**
> *Kyoto at Twilight*
> Oil on canvas
> 114.3 cm x 99.06 cm
>
> This work is the first in Takashi Fujioka's *Kyoto Nightfall* series, which gained international recognition. Works from this series of paintings have been exhibited in museums and galleries around the world, including the Moto Contemporary Art Museum in Tokyo, the Fontaine-Shields Gallery in New York City, and the Starlit Art Gallery in London. *Kyoto at Twilight* was featured on the cover of *Modern Painting* magazine the year it was painted. It was bought four years ago by Thomas Chester Gaines for his private collection and was sold to the Clarkson-Walker Museum for our permanent collection two years ago. It has remained here with us since. Mr. Fujioka famously called this painting "my finest hour."

1. Mr. Fujioka works for the museum. (T / F)

2. The painting described is one of a famous series. (T / F)

3. The painting is currently part of a private collection. (T / F)

4. Where is the painting now?

_____

5. According to the information, who is Mr. Gaines?

_____

解答(例)   1. F 2. T 3. F
4. In the Clarkson-Walker Museum.
5. The owner of a private collection.

2 **Invoice**

Omicron Premier Services Ltd.
83 Malet Street
London
WC1E 7HU

Invoice: 1Z67HN2
Arrival Date: 3 April

Bill to:
Dr. John Kwang
Overbrook Hospital

Ship to:
Overbrook Hospital
27 St. Stephens Green
Dublin, Ireland

Item Number	Description	Item Price
12B	5 Boxes Small Bandages	£12
12C	10 Boxes Large Bandages	£30
431Z*	2 Boxes Large Sterile Gloves	£5
10CD	5 Large Knee Braces	£25
	TOTAL	£72

Payment due upon receipt of goods.

*Item 431Z will be shipped at a later date as it is
currently not in the warehouse.*

1. Omicron Premier Services Ltd. is a pharmacy in Dublin. (T / F)

2. Dr. Kwang works at Overbrook Hospital. (T / F)

3. Some goods will be delayed. (T / F)

4. Where is Omicron located?

_____

5. How much does Overbrook Hospital have to pay for the entire order?

_____

解答(例)   1. F 2. T 3. T
4. In London.
5. £72 (Seventy-two pounds).

31

1 **Letter**

Patel Dental Clinic
Block V, Rajouri Garden
New Delhi 110027

12 June

Radhika Hathi
Flat Number 1155
Navya Apartments
Tilak Nagar
New Delhi 110018

Dear Ms. Hathi:

At Patel Dental Clinic, ensuring that you have current information about your account with us is a priority. Effective 1 July, all invoices not paid at the time of service must be paid within 30 days. Please find enclosed a complete and detailed explanation of our revised billing schedule.

This necessary revision will allow us to continue to provide dental care to you and your family without increasing the cost of services this year. Should you need to make alternate payment arrangements, please contact our office manager, Jigna Gupta, at 11-2616 0002.

Sincerely,

Dr. Satish Patel
Dr. Satish Patel
Enclosure

1. Ms. Hathi is most likely a patient of the clinic. (T / F)

2. Dr. Patel is applying for a doctor position at the clinic. (T / F)

3. A payment policy is attached to the letter. (T / F)

4. How long after a treatment do patients have to pay?

_____

5. Who should patients contact when they want to make alternate payment arrangements?

_____

解答(例)　1. T　2. F　3. T
4. 30 days.
5. Ms. Gupta.

回数	01	02	03	04	05
正解数	/ 5	/ 5	/ 5	/ 5	/ 5

2 Survey

THE BROAD LAKE INN

Thank you for staying at the Broad Lake Inn! Customer satisfaction is very important to us, and we would appreciate your feedback. Please fill out the survey below and leave it with the receptionist at the front desk when you check out.

How satisfied were you with the Broad Lake Inn?
Please circle one selection for each category:

Service	Not satisfied	Satisfied	(Very satisfied)
Cleanliness	Not satisfied	Satisfied	(Very satisfied)
Appearance	Not satisfied	(Satisfied)	Very satisfied
Restaurant	(Not satisfied)	Satisfied	Very satisfied

Would you recommend the Broad Lake Inn to others?
　　　No　　　　　Maybe　　　(Yes)

Please add any comments or suggestions you may have in the space below.

Overall, I had a wonderful experience at the inn. The employees were extremely friendly, and the inn was very clean and comfortable. Thanks to the well-equipped computer center, I was able to get a lot of work done. The restaurant, however, was quite expensive, and the food was not particularly tasty.

If you wish to be contacted regarding your feedback, please provide your name and phone number or e-mail address below:

Minna Haataja
mhaataja@feridia.fi

1. Ms. Haataja is in charge of quality control at the Broad Lake Inn. 　　(T / F)

2. Ms. Haataja's feedback is largely positive. 　　(T / F)

3. This survey was most likely handed directly to a manager. 　　(T / F)

4. What is Ms. Haataja's opinion of the employees?

_____

5. What did Ms. Haataja feel about the restaurant?

_____

解答(例)　　1. F　2. T　3. F
4. They were very friendly.
5. She was not satisfied.

33

1 **Instant-message discussion**

Laura Kalama (9:34 A.M.)
We received another package that's meant for you.

Taro Murase (9:35 A.M.)
Not again! I don't understand why this keeps happening.

Laura Kalama (9:36 A.M.)
I think it's the company Web site. The department addresses are listed in a chart, and accounting is right above administration.

Taro Murase (9:37 A.M.)
So that could explain why my mail has my name on it but the Accounting Department's address.

Laura Kalama (9:38 A.M.)
Exactly. I'm heading to your building for a meeting with the Legal Department. I'll drop your package off then.

Taro Murase (9:39 A.M.)
Thanks! I'll e-mail information technology and ask if they can update the Web site to make the chart clearer.

1. Ms. Kalama received a package that was not meant for her department.　　(T / F)

2. The mix-up is probably caused by the layout of a Web page.　　(T / F)

3. Ms. Kalama most likely works in the Legal Department.　　(T / F)

4. How will Mr. Murase get his package?

5. What will Mr. Murase do to fix the problem?

解答(例)　1. T　2. T　3. F
4. Ms. Kalama will bring it to him.
5. He will ask the IT department to improve the Web site.

回数	01	02	03	04	05
正解数	/ 5	/ 5	/ 5	/ 5	/ 5

2 | Online chat discussion

Lisa Howland [11:08 A.M.]:	David, can you take a look at our Web site? I can't see the pictures of our products on my computer. Do they display on yours?
David Tanner [11:13 A.M.]:	No, same here. How long has this been going on?
Lisa Howland [11:14 A.M.]:	Probably not long. I was just contacted by someone who wanted to review an item she'd purchased but couldn't see now. No complaints earlier today or yesterday. Can you tell our IT team?
David Tanner [11:15 A.M.]:	Tim, something happened to the image files in the online store section of our Web site. Can you look into it?
Timothy Warner [11:18 A.M.]:	That's strange… Looks like they've been removed.
David Tanner [11:19 A.M.]:	I hope we've kept backup files.
Timothy Warner [11:20 A.M.]:	We always do, just in case. I'll upload them again now.
David Tanner [11:21 A.M.]:	Good. And we'll need to write a brief apology online saying that the problem has been fixed.
Lisa Howland [11:22 A.M.]:	I'll take care of that.

1. Mr. Tanner first discovered the problem.   (T / F)

2. Mr. Warner most likely works for the IT department.   (T / F)

3. The problem will be fixed by uploading backup files.   (T / F)

4. Who will upload the missing images?

_____

5. Who will write the apology for the Web site?

_____

解答(例)   1. F   2. T   3. T
                4. Mr. Warner.
                5. Ms. Howland.

Web site

Home	Subject Guide	Latest Polls	Contact Us

Pondress
Because Your Opinion Matters

The Pondress Corporation has been conducting public opinion polls on current issues for more than three decades. All our polls are based on telephone interviews with adults 18 years of age or older who live in specific polling areas. To ensure that every adult living within a polling area has an equal chance of being contacted, potential interviewees are selected by a computer that randomly generates phone numbers from all working exchanges.

To find out what people think about what is happening in the world these days, visit our Latest Polls page. New polls are published weekly, and all polls are stored and accessible online. If you prefer to search for polls by subject, go to our Subject Guide page. If you would like to reproduce tables, charts, or any other graphics created by Pondress, go to the Contact Us page and click the link for our Permissions Department. There you will find an easy-to-use online form to fill out with details about how and where you intend to use the information. In most cases, a response is provided within 24 hours of submission.

1. Pondress Corporation conducts polls on product brand awareness.   (T / F)

2. All polls are conducted online.   (T / F)

3. People who are polled are at least 18 years of age.   (T / F)

4. Where can people access and view the results of the polls?

_____

5. How can people receive permission to reproduce graphics?

_____

解答(例)   1. F   2. F   3. T
                 4. On the Web site of the Pondress Corporation.
                 5. By contacting Pondress' Permissions Department through an online form.

回数	01	02	03	04	05
正解数	/ 5	/ 5	/ 5	/ 5	/ 5

Article

Construction to Add to Traffic

GREYHAVEN (12 May)—With the construction of several new office complexes under way in the downtown business district, the city's already problematic traffic is only expected to get worse. City officials are discussing a number of solutions, such as creating a new underground motorway or widening Highway 92 to accommodate more lanes of traffic. No decisions have been finalized, however.

"We simply don't have the infrastructure to support all these cars, and it is clear that something needs to be done," said Carla Radwanski, spokesperson for the highway commission.

"Any major construction project will take years to complete, so whatever we decide will just add to road congestion in the short term," Ms. Radwanski added. "That's the main reason we haven't committed to anything yet. The more time we spend developing a solid plan, the better managed the project will hopefully be once we begin."

While the city is considering its options, office workers are becoming increasingly agitated.

"My commute to work is becoming unbearable," said Paul Hodgkin, a lawyer who works downtown. "The distance from my house to the office is only about 11 kilometers, but it takes me over an hour."

To help alleviate traffic issues in the meantime, office managers are starting to take matters into their own hands. Some are encouraging employees to ride together or are offering incentives to employees who ride bicycles to work. Others are letting their employees work from home on certain days.

---

1. Several new office complexes are being constructed. (T / F)

2. City officials believe that building a new subway line is the best solution to the traffic problem. (T / F)

3. Some employers have encouraged employees to commute by bicycle. (T / F)

4. For what organization does Ms. Radwanski speak as a representative?

---

5. What is Mr. Hodgkin's opinion of his commute to work?

解答(例)　1. T　2. F　3. T
4. The highway commission.
5. It is unbearable.

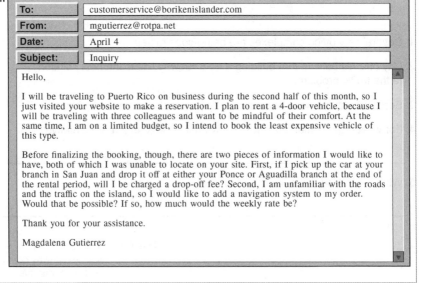
1 **Advertisement**

Boriken Islander

Boriken Islander is Puerto Rico's largest locally owned car rental company. We offer a range of vehicles at the lowest possible prices. If you can get a lower rate with any of our local competitors, we will match that rate and pay for a full tank of fuel! The following vehicles are available for rent:

Car Class	Description	Weekly rate
Economy	2-door vehicle suitable for 4 passengers and 2 large bags	$199.00
Compact	4-door vehicle suitable for 4 passengers and 3 large bags	$229.00
Standard	4-door vehicle suitable for 5 passengers and 4 large bags	$259.00
Premium	4-door vehicle suitable for 5 passengers and 5 large bags	$309.00

Rates listed refer to payments made in person at our customer service counter. Discounted rates and details about the features of each car type are available on our website, www.borikenislander.com. Looking for even more savings? Use our services during April and May and receive an additional 10% off the weekly rate.

2 **E-mail**

To:	customerservice@borikenislander.com
From:	mgutierrez@rotpa.net
Date:	April 4
Subject:	Inquiry

Hello,

I will be traveling to Puerto Rico on business during the second half of this month, so I just visited your website to make a reservation. I plan to rent a 4-door vehicle, because I will be traveling with three colleagues and want to be mindful of their comfort. At the same time, I am on a limited budget, so I intend to book the least expensive vehicle of this type.

Before finalizing the booking, though, there are two pieces of information I would like to have, both of which I was unable to locate on your site. First, if I pick up the car at your branch in San Juan and drop it off at either your Ponce or Aguadilla branch at the end of the rental period, will I be charged a drop-off fee? Second, I am unfamiliar with the roads and the traffic on the island, so I would like to add a navigation system to my order. Would that be possible? If so, how much would the weekly rate be?

Thank you for your assistance.

Magdalena Gutierrez

1. Boriken Islander offers an extra 10% discount for rentals during April.　(T / F)

2. Ms. Gutierrez is going to Puerto Rico on vacation.　(T / F)

3. Ms. Gutierrez will be accompanied on her trip by two coworkers.　(T / F)

4. What equipment does Ms. Gutierrez want to add?

_____

5. What kind of limitation does Ms. Gutierrez mention in her e-mail?

_____

解答(例)　1. T　2. F　3. F
4. A car navigation system.
5. She has a limited budget.

39

1 Article

Spotlight on Real-World Business

September 15—Since retired marketing executive Warren Cralley began teaching at Ormandy Technical Institute a few years ago, he has invited guest speakers who are engaged in real-world business activities to address his classes. The speakers share their experiences with the students enrolled in introductory marketing and economics courses at Ormandy Tech.

The professor's objective is to help students to grasp how the theories they study in the classroom have practical applications in their future careers. The visitors show them that the lessons they learn in everyday life can be just as important as anything they read in a textbook.

Cralley lets students propose and invite their own classroom guests, including relatives, friends, and acquaintances. They are encouraged to approach people associated with businesses they are curious about.

Cralley's students all agree that the speakers are interesting. Although the class includes a few weeks in which students work as interns in various local companies, the guest speakers provide a very different perspective of the world of business.

2 E-mail

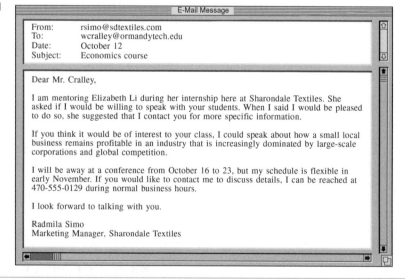

E-Mail Message

From: rsimo@sdtextiles.com
To: wcralley@ormandytech.edu
Date: October 12
Subject: Economics course

Dear Mr. Cralley,

I am mentoring Elizabeth Li during her internship here at Sharondale Textiles. She asked if I would be willing to speak with your students. When I said I would be pleased to do so, she suggested that I contact you for more specific information.

If you think it would be of interest to your class, I could speak about how a small local business remains profitable in an industry that is increasingly dominated by large-scale corporations and global competition.

I will be away at a conference from October 16 to 23, but my schedule is flexible in early November. If you would like to contact me to discuss details, I can be reached at 470-555-0129 during normal business hours.

I look forward to talking with you.

Radmila Simo
Marketing Manager, Sharondale Textiles

40

1. Mr. Cralley is teaching economics. (T / F)

2. Ms. Li is Mr. Cralley's former student. (T / F)

3. Ms. Simo will attend a conference in October. (T / F)

4. Where does Mr. Cralley teach?

---

5. When will Ms. Simo be available?

解答(例)　　1. T　2. F　3. T
4. At Ormandy Technical Institute.
5. In early November.

PART 7　文書の英文

回数	01	02	03	04	05
正解数	/ 5	/ 5	/ 5	/ 5	/ 5

1 | **Credit-card statement**

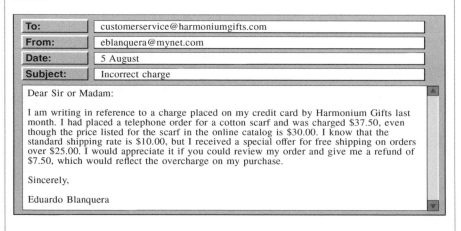

Eduardo Blanquera	Page 2
Account Number: XXXX XXXX XXXX 8191	3 July–2 August

Purchases

Date	Vendor	Amount
5 July	Le Petit Bateau Café	40.05
8 July	Meyers Men's Shop	48.25
11 July	Midtown City Diner	24.11
17 July	Theta Restaurant	33.88
21 July	Harmonium Gifts	37.50
30 July	Ithaca Eatery	56.60
2 August	New Wave Office Supplies	99.87

2 | **E-mail**

To:	customerservice@harmoniumgifts.com
From:	eblanquera@mynet.com
Date:	5 August
Subject:	Incorrect charge

Dear Sir or Madam:

I am writing in reference to a charge placed on my credit card by Harmonium Gifts last month. I had placed a telephone order for a cotton scarf and was charged $37.50, even though the price listed for the scarf in the online catalog is $30.00. I know that the standard shipping rate is $10.00, but I received a special offer for free shipping on orders over $25.00. I would appreciate it if you could review my order and give me a refund of $7.50, which would reflect the overcharge on my purchase.

Sincerely,

Eduardo Blanquera

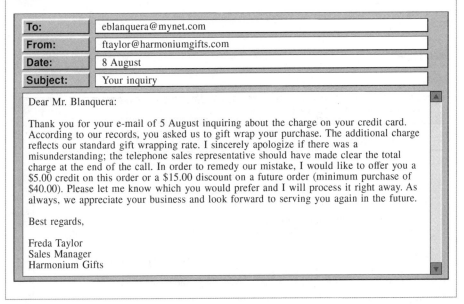

To:	eblanquera@mynet.com
From:	ftaylor@harmoniumgifts.com
Date:	8 August
Subject:	Your inquiry

Dear Mr. Blanquera:

Thank you for your e-mail of 5 August inquiring about the charge on your credit card. According to our records, you asked us to gift wrap your purchase. The additional charge reflects our standard gift wrapping rate. I sincerely apologize if there was a misunderstanding; the telephone sales representative should have made clear the total charge at the end of the call. In order to remedy our mistake, I would like to offer you a $5.00 credit on this order or a $15.00 discount on a future order (minimum purchase of $40.00). Please let me know which you would prefer and I will process it right away. As always, we appreciate your business and look forward to serving you again in the future.

Best regards,

Freda Taylor
Sales Manager
Harmonium Gifts

1. Mr. Blanquera shopped in person at a gift shop in July. (T / F)

2. Ms. Taylor explained that the amount charged to Mr. Blanquera's card was in fact correct. (T / F)

3. Harmonium Gifts offered Mr. Blanquera a discount of $15 on a future purchase. (T / F)

4. What did Mr. Blanquera buy at Harmonium Gifts?

_____

5. Who is Ms. Taylor?

_____

解答(例)　1. F　2. T　3. T
4. A cotton scarf.
5. The Sales Manager of Harmonium Gifts.

43

1 | Web page

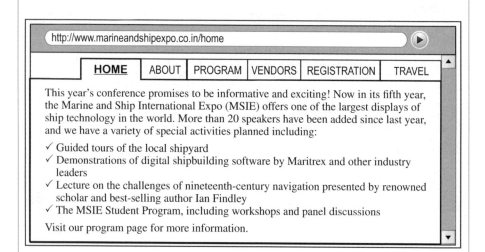

http://www.marineandshipexpo.co.in/home

HOME | ABOUT | PROGRAM | VENDORS | REGISTRATION | TRAVEL

This year's conference promises to be informative and exciting! Now in its fifth year, the Marine and Ship International Expo (MSIE) offers one of the largest displays of ship technology in the world. More than 20 speakers have been added since last year, and we have a variety of special activities planned including:

✓ Guided tours of the local shipyard
✓ Demonstrations of digital shipbuilding software by Maritrex and other industry leaders
✓ Lecture on the challenges of nineteenth-century navigation presented by renowned scholar and best-selling author Ian Findley
✓ The MSIE Student Program, including workshops and panel discussions

Visit our program page for more information.

2 | E-mail

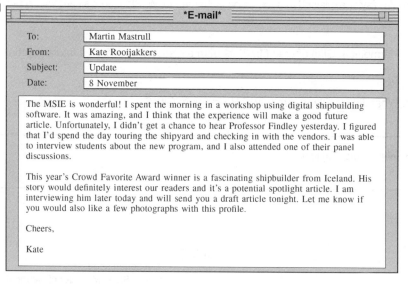

E-mail

To:	Martin Mastrull
From:	Kate Rooijakkers
Subject:	Update
Date:	8 November

The MSIE is wonderful! I spent the morning in a workshop using digital shipbuilding software. It was amazing, and I think that the experience will make a good future article. Unfortunately, I didn't get a chance to hear Professor Findley yesterday. I figured that I'd spend the day touring the shipyard and checking in with the vendors. I was able to interview students about the new program, and I also attended one of their panel discussions.

This year's Crowd Favorite Award winner is a fascinating shipbuilder from Iceland. His story would definitely interest our readers and it's a potential spotlight article. I am interviewing him later today and will send you a draft article tonight. Let me know if you would also like a few photographs with this profile.

Cheers,

Kate

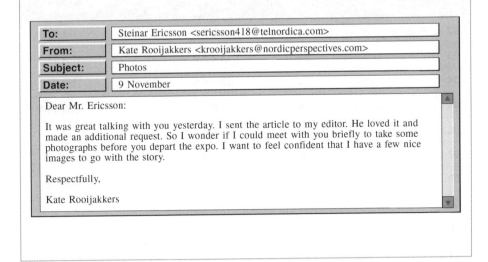

3 **E-mail**

To:	Steinar Ericsson <sericsson418@telnordica.com>
From:	Kate Rooijakkers <krooijakkers@nordicperspectives.com>
Subject:	Photos
Date:	9 November

Dear Mr. Ericsson:

It was great talking with you yesterday. I sent the article to my editor. He loved it and made an additional request. So I wonder if I could meet with you briefly to take some photographs before you depart the expo. I want to feel confident that I have a few nice images to go with the story.

Respectfully,

Kate Rooijakkers

1. The MSIE conference has been held five times now. (T / F)

2. Ms. Rooijakkers is most likely a journalist or a writer. (T / F)

3. Mr. Ericsson is a student who participated in the panel. (T / F)

4. What is the connection between Ms. Rooijakkers and Mr. Ericsson?

_____

5. Where is Mr. Ericsson from?

_____

解答(例)　1. T　2. T　3. F
4. She interviewed him.
5. Iceland.

45

特典音声ファイル一覧

→ 「音声ダウンロードの手順」は p.3 参照

File No.	Contents	File No.	Contents	File No.	Contents
02	PART 5　Unit 1-1	26	Unit 5-1	50	Unit 12-2
03	Unit 1-2	27	Unit 5-2	51	Unit 13-1
04	Unit 1-3	28	Unit 5-3	52	Unit 13-2
05	Unit 1-4	29	Unit 5-4	53	Unit 14-1
06	Unit 1-5	30	Unit 5-5	54	Unit 14-2
07	Unit 1-6	31	Unit 5-6	55	Unit 15
08	Unit 2-1	32	Unit 6-1	56	Unit 16
09	Unit 2-2	33	Unit 6-2	57	Unit 17-1
10	Unit 2-3	34	Unit 6-3	58	Unit 17-2
11	Unit 2-4	35	Unit 6-4	59	Unit 18-1
12	Unit 2-5	36	Unit 6-5	60	Unit 18-2
13	Unit 2-6	37	Unit 6-6	61	Unit 19-1
14	Unit 3-1	38	Unit 7-1	62	Unit 19-2
15	Unit 3-2	39	Unit 7-2	63	Unit 19-3
16	Unit 3-3	40	Unit 7-3	64	Unit 20-1
17	Unit 3-4	41	Unit 7-4	65	Unit 20-2
18	Unit 3-5	42	Unit 7-5	66	Unit 20-3
19	Unit 3-6	43	Unit 7-6		
20	Unit 4-1	44	PART 6　Unit 8		
21	Unit 4-2	45	Unit 9		
22	Unit 4-3	46	Unit 10		
23	Unit 4-4	47	PART 7　Unit 11-1		
24	Unit 4-5	48	Unit 11-2		
25	Unit 4-6	49	Unit 12-1		

　※ 01はタイトルコールです。読み上げ音声は日本で収録したもので、標準的な北米発音を採用しています。

単語学習法のヒント

1. 見出し語を見て、語義がすぐに分からなかった語句のチェックボックスに✓を入れる。
2. 品詞・語義や、関連情報を確認する。
3. 本誌の参照ページへ行き、訳文を参考に、その語句が英文中でどのように使われているかを確認し、用法やコロケーションを頭に入れる。
4. 一定の期間を置いて再度見出し語を見て、□に✓の入った語を覚えたかどうかを確認する。自信がなければ、2つ目の□に✓を入れ、2～4を繰り返す。
5. □に✓が入ったものは「覚えたい語句」として自分で別にまとめてもよい。

また、予習として、本誌「Step1：ユニット学習」をする前に、該当ユニットの単語を頭に入れてから取り組むと、問題にスムーズに解答できるようになります。

ボキャブラリー学習は、見出し語の語義だけではなく、用例とともに覚えることが重要です。本誌の英文を参考に、その語句が使われているシチュエーションや文脈も同時に頭に入れ、自分でも使えるようにして、発信力も含めた英語の実践的な力を高めていきましょう。

公式TOEIC® Listening & Reading
プラクティス リーディング編　別冊付録

2020 年 8 月 25 日　第 1 版第 1 刷発行
2023 年 6 月 30 日　第 1 版第 4 刷発行

著者　　　ETS

編集協力　株式会社エディット
　　　　　株式会社オレンジバード
　　　　　株式会社ウィットハウス

発行元　　一般財団法人 国際ビジネスコミュニケーション協会
　　　　　〒 100-0014
　　　　　東京都千代田区永田町 2-14-2
　　　　　山王グランドビル
　　　　　電話　(03) 5521-5935
　　　　　FAX　(03) 3581-9801

印刷　　　図書印刷株式会社

乱丁本・落丁本・不良本はお取り換えします。許可なしに転載、複製することを禁じます。

ETS, the ETS logo, PROPELL, TOEIC and TOEIC BRIDGE are registered trademarks of
Educational Testing Service, Princeton, New Jersey, U.S.A., and used in Japan under license.
Copyright ©2020 Portions are copyrighted by Educational Testing Service and used with permission.
Printed in Japan
ISBN 978-4-906033-60-7